sundance
LITTLE GREEN READERS

Tigers

Set 3

ACKNOWLEDGMENTS

Developed by Macmillan Education Australia in consultation
with the Gould League, Australia.

The author and publishers are grateful to the following for permission to reproduce
copyright photographs:

Cover: Bio-Images/Jason Edwards

ANT Photo Library, pp. 11 © Frithfoto, 12 © Martin Harvey, 5 © Gerard Lacz, 10 ©
Fredy Mercay, 7 © Natfoto, 9 © C & S Pollitt, 3, 13 © Silvestris ; Bio-Images/Jason
Edwards, pp. 8, 15; Gary Lewis Photography, pp. 1, 2, 4, 6, 14.

While every care has been taken to trace and acknowledge copyright, the publishers
tender their apologies for any accidental infringement where copyright has proved
untraceable.

Color separation by Tenon & Polert Colour Scanning Ltd

Printed in Hong Kong

Item 15220
ISBN 0-7608-4152-7

Tigers

Focus: Endangered Animals

Meredith Costain

Tigers are the largest cats.
Tigers are larger than lions.
Some tigers are as long
as a minivan!

Tigers can live in many places. They live in hot rainforests, dry woods, and in cold, snowy places.

Tigers are good hunters.
Tigers hide until they see,
smell, or hear an animal
they want to eat.
Their stripes help them hide
in tall grass and shadows.

Tigers are fast and strong.
When they see an animal
they want to eat, they
sneak up and pounce on it!
Tigers like to eat deer,
wild pigs, and other
large animals.

Tigers are strong swimmers.
They can swim across
a river to hunt for food.
On hot days, they might rest
in the water to keep cool.

Tigers live and hunt alone.
Sometimes they share food
with other tigers.
Sometimes they will roar
or fight to keep other
tigers away.

Tigers are animals at risk.
Tigers do not hunt people,
but some people hunt tigers.

Some people hunt tigers for their skins. They make tiger skins into coats or rugs.

Some people hunt tigers for their bones. They crush the bones into powder. Some people think the powder makes magic pills.

Some people hunt tigers for their teeth and their claws. They make tiger teeth and claws into jewelry.

Some people cut down forests where tigers live. They use the trees for wood. They use the land for farming. But the tigers lose their place to hunt.

Some people are trying
to help tigers.
People are doing things
to keep tigers safe.

People have made
safe places for tigers.
These places are called
tiger reserves.
Tigers cannot be hunted
in a reserve.

People no longer trap tigers
to put in zoos.
Almost all zoo tigers
were born in the zoo.
But tigers in the wild
are still at risk.

Index

Third Edition

Executive Decisions

Organization Development • Management Control • Executive Responsibility

Rossall J. Johnson

Professor, Graduate School of Management
Northwestern University

Published by

 G38 **SOUTH-WESTERN PUBLISHING CO.**

CINCINNATI   WEST CHICAGO, ILL.   DALLAS   PELHAM MANOR, N.Y.
PALO ALTO, CALIF.   BRIGHTON, ENGLAND

1 2 3 4 5 Ki 0 9 8 7 6

Printed in the United States of America

60,692

Preface

This book of cases is structured to meet the needs of those who are studying administration.

As in the previous editions, the cases, which fall into broad categories of administrative concerns, emphasize the decision-making process at the top level of management. The selection and integration of cases are based on the assumption that the executive is continually confronted with a wide spectrum of decision-making situations: some that inspect interpersonal relationships, others that are primarily concerned with the financial, production, or marketing functions, and still others that involve the interface with the external environment.

Today top executives have the opportunity to make greater use of quantitative analysis and to use the computer to assemble facts and digest information. Several cases, therefore, are included which will give emphasis to these tools of analysis and data processing.

The most important change in the business environment in the last few years has been the increased concern for the social responsibility and morality of business. The sediment left over from the Watergate incident and the United Brands exposé has caused great concern for those who are interested in maintaining an orderly environment without excessive controls. But controls, which some feel excessive and others necessary, have come. High on the list of the controversial controls is the legislation concerned with the equal employment opportunity for minority group members and women. For these administrative concerns there are cases which emphasize these decision areas.

Because of the importance of foreign trade, a number of cases are included which focus upon the decision situations in international business. The student, through these cases, is exposed to the practices of global corporations and the business environment in Asia, Latin America, Africa and Europe.

ACKNOWLEDGMENTS

Thanks and recognition are due to those who have contributed cases or have reviewed and commented on the materials. Foremost, of course, are those executives who have contributed the basic information for the cases. At the Graduate School of Management, Northwestern University, the author is indebted to Professors Richard Barseness, Frank Hartzfeld, Charles Hofer, and Ram Charan. Also aiding in this edition have been Professor Harold Stevenson of Arizona State University and Professor Robert Wasley of the University of Colorado. A special note of recognition is due to Professor Frank L. Kaufman of California State University, Sacramento, for his thorough review and suggestions.

CONTENTS

Part Four—Decisions Involving Public Responsibility

Part Five—Decisions Involving Organized Labor

Part Six—Decisions Involving Planning, Strategy, and Policy Formulation

INDEX OF CASES

Introduction

Decisions made at the upper levels of management are not disconnected incidents; they are decisions concerned with more than a single function. Indeed, top-level decisions are very much a series of interrelated and continuing activities. In this book are descriptions of business situations that require the careful review of top management and which call for an analysis leading to policy formulation, planning, strategy, and decisions.

All the cases are descriptions of real events in business, but some have been disguised to maintain anonymity. A cross section of management functions is covered—including sales, advertising, production, finance, industrial relations, purchasing, and public relations. The industries represented vary from large multiplant or branch management operations to relatively small businesses. Regardless of the function or the industry, the administrative process and the environment of the executive are presented for study in depth and for critical analysis.

THE INTERNAL ENVIRONMENT AND THE EXECUTIVE

Within the administrative hierarchy, there are functional identifications that may stand in the way of a smooth operation of the decision-making process. Thus, in situations where an executive identifies strongly with a department, the tendency is for the manager to make decisions that consider the interest of a particular department first and the total organization second.

It is the broader approach to management problems that results in greater rewards to the company. That is, all management must make decisions on the basis of overall organization objectives as well as departmental goals. It is the broader environmental outlook that is considered in this book. Yet it is recognized that one must at times also have a parochial frame of reference.

In such an amorphous environment, the members of top management must make decisions, maintain control, and at the same time carry out their responsibilities to society. Not all people are capable of performing well under these conditions; but the executive, given

1

these boundaries, can be taught to operate more effectively and to meet company objectives with greater efficiency. Having a complex environment within the company, the top executive officer of the company must be a specialist, and, at the same time, a generalist. It is one where the job specifications are very broad, where overlap of responsibilities is common practice, and where communication on important matters is frequently carried out on an informal basis.

The cases presented are designed to aid in the education of the executive or student whether in a formal university course, a seminar, or an advanced management program.

THE CASES

Included in this book is a series of case situations that give consideration to the various functions of management. They are not limited to the gross decisions that the executive would make in deciding such things as the marketing niche or the drawing up of basic policy. Rather, while some cases are concerned with these broad policy areas, others are less encompassing and present some of the narrower problems that cross the executive desk.

Arranged in a useful and logical sequence, these cases give stress to each of the critical areas such as policy, control, and organization. However, the fact that a case appears under one heading does not necessarily indicate that discussion should be limited to that area. Indeed, the student may disagree with the classification; and this fact should give emphasis to the point that each case raises complex issues. Nor do the cases have to be studied in the sequence as listed. Their order is a function of the course objective, and may vary from one instructor to another.

Whether a case is long or short should not be indicative of the time allotted for analysis or the depth of diagnosis. Some cases are presented in considerable detail, while others represent a single incident with relatively little specific information. These, of course, are typical of the types of actual situations encountered by the executive. Sometimes there is more than enough information that must be sifted through, but more often there is not enough information, and yet a decision must be made. Frequently, there is not time to get additional information; consequently, the executive must make the best use of the available facts.

In spite of what may seem a paucity of information, the student should make recommendations for the future gathering and processing of the facts. At the same time the cost, in dollars, for having the information available should be weighed against the penalties for its not being available. In the cases in this book, there is enough information given on which to base judgments and to render decisions.

THE TEAM—HIGH, MIDDLE, OR LOW VIEW

The decisions, the rationale, and the points of view that result from the analyses of these cases are just as important for the middle and lower rungs of management as for the highest executive. In this era of team effort, it is essential for each member to understand the frames of reference, attitudes, and points of view of the others.

The tendency for the echelon at the top of the management pyramid to view objectives, policies, and strategies, differently from those on the lower levels is a probable indication of organization weakness. If the lower levels of management do not fully comprehend the significance of the decisions made by top management, as related to objectives, policies, etc., then inefficiencies may occur at all levels. This lack of understanding is not just a result of miscommunication, in the general sense of the word. It is a result in part of not knowing of the need for having the same points of view and in part not knowing that different points of view exist. The implication is that there is considerably less team activity under such conditions.

Frequently, each executive, because of individual duties and level in the company, sees the problem from a different point of view; and like the blind men describing the elephant, each recognizes only a part of the problem—that which falls within one area of operation. Viewing the problem from its many sides will give the executive a greater understanding of the situation. Such an examination will also give the executive some opportunities to explore and develop alternative solutions.

CASE ANALYSIS

In making an analysis, the student will find it useful to look upon a case as a multisided problem, which, when considered from each view, presents different facets of the management problem. If a student makes an error in judgment, the company described in the case will not be affected. But when the student is a business executive in a similar situation, mistakes can be costly. Therefore, case analysis should be viewed as an opportunity to learn without the accompanying penalties of dollar losses. To take full advantage of this learning situation, the student should approach the case analysis as if a job hung in the balance.

The cases are not simple—there are complex relationships and implications that must be dug out. Case analysis requires time—a single reading is not sufficient, it is just the beginning. A step-by-step evaluation of the facts and ideas presented is necessary before a statement of the problem can be formulated or before plans or strategy may be developed. The shortest case requires considerable analysis.

The uninitiated student will read the case through once and then write an analysis. A quick once-through reading is a good way to begin an analysis, but additional readings are essential for an adequate analysis. As the student rereads the case, it is frequently helpful to take notes on relationships, to raise questions, and to write down observations about tables and charts. It is only after such preliminary analysis that the student is ready to make a complete diagnosis.

It is difficult to set up a standard procedure of analysis that would be suitable for every case problem. A checklist of things to look for can be helpful, and a series of questions can also be used as reminders of areas to investigate. However, since the cases cover a cross section of the many problems of top management, it is advisable that an additional technique be used.

Several centers may be critical in the diagnosis of a case. All but one of these diagnostic centers pertain to internal factors, which are illustrated in Exhibit 1. The external environment of the firm is an important additional diagnostic center.

In a very complex problem all of the critical factors would be involved so that it would be necessary to include them when making the diagnosis. Thus, as shown in Exhibit 1, the analysis starts with sizing up and continues on to objectives, policy, and so forth. Whether a center is critical or not depends upon the scope of the problem and its relationship to the other diagnostic centers. Such relationships will be indicated by the connections or paths between them. The following discussion is intended to indicate an approach to case analysis which has some flexibility. It should be considered as an analytical framework, a way of thinking about the relationships between the various factors that bear upon the success and stability of an organization.

Sizing Up

In setting out on the diagnostic cycle, it is best to size up the situation first by deciding what areas are to be analyzed and in what order. Analysis centers that seem to be critical should be identified at the beginning. This ought to be viewed as a preliminary determination of diagnostic procedure that may be altered as the analysis proceeds. The purpose of selecting diagnostic centers is to aid in getting an overview of the total situation, and to decide what approach to take so that problems may be pinpointed and resolved efficiently.

Some of the cases require a complete examination of every factor, going through the complete diagnostic cycle; but other cases are concerned with only part of the diagnostic scheme. For instance, as

Exhibit 1

Critical Diagnostic Centers and Paths

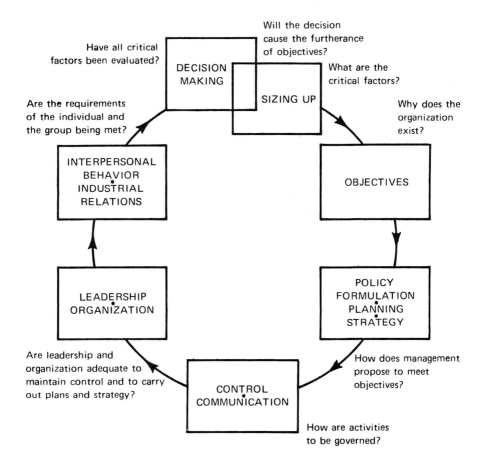

illustrated in Exhibit 2(A), it may be found that a case requires an analysis of leadership, organization, and interpersonal behavior, and that policies, planning, and strategy are not critical to the decisions. Thus the diagnostic paths would bypass the less critical centers. But on the other hand, if an examination of a case on controls is being made, it may be found that this factor has important implications in the areas of objectives, policy, planning, and strategy. This means the diagnostic paths would not include leadership, organization, interpersonal behavior, and industrial relations, as is indicated in Exhibit 2(B).

Sizing up also means an examination of the evidence, determining the relationship of facts, making some prejudgments on possible cause and effect situations, and deciding what additional information

Exhibit 2

Sample Diagnostic Paths

A

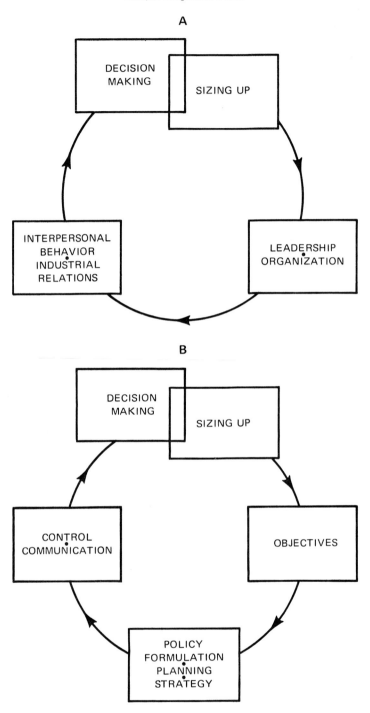

EXECUTIVE DECISIONS

or facts would facilitate the decision-making process. Sizing up is the initial move that determines which one of the diagnostic centers to consider first.

Objectives

Why does the organization exist? What are the objectives of the organization? Is there a general recognition of or agreement on the company objectives? Should the objectives be adjusted or changed? Is the company now on a course of action that will meet the company's objectives?

The objectives of a company must be defined in workable or useful terms so that they can be related to the executive decisions. "Maximizing profits," for instance, is a broad definition of objectives, which can be a useful backdrop when making an analysis. More helpful, though, is to define objectives in such specific terms as product, quality, market, and services.

Repeating the original question—why does the organization exist? To produce a certain quality of product? To offer a specific type of service? To sell the product or service in a specific market? These objectives in the business world are set up so that a profit can be obtained. Thus, in seeking operational objectives, it may be useful to ask: By what means or techniques does the company seek a profit?

Keeping an eye on the profits is, of course, a very suitable activity for an executive, but just as important is the continuous reevaluation of the product or service objectives. The number of automobile companies that have failed because they did not reevaluate their niche in the market is legion. And it does no good, for instance, for the owner of the chain of dry-cleaning stores to watch the profits if the next year the owner will be out of business because of coin-operated, self-service dry-cleaning machines or because of the increased use of drip-dry clothing. The dry cleaner must be aware of these realities and weigh personal service objectives against the potential inroads of these two developments. The owner must decide what changes need to be made in the personal objectives. The executive may decide to liquidate or to buy coin-operated dry-cleaning equipment; or the executive may come to the conclusion that these new innovations will not drastically affect this particular business and therefore, no changes need be made. Objectives should be considered for the future profits as well as the present, and therefore, the executive must not consider them as being sacred and unchangeable but rather as being flexible to meet the dynamics of the business environment.

In the analysis of a case, the student should first determine if the objectives seem to play a critical role in the immediate situation. Even if objectives are not critical in the resolving of the case, any decision must be realistic in terms of profits and losses.

Policy Formulation, Planning and Strategy

Not all cases are primarily concerned with policy, planning, and strategy. But part of the diagnostic technique is to determine whether fundamental policies are involved. This means that a determination must be made as to whether the present policy of the firm is adequate or appropriate, or whether a formal policy exists at all.

The interrelationships between objectives and policy are direct and critical. Policy establishes the general ground rules for meeting the objectives, and it is imperative that policies be related to objectives. This is another way of saying that policies are not formulated in a vacuum; and they are not altered without determining the effects upon the objectives. In other words, if objectives are changed, policies should be reviewed.

As an example, if a clothing manufacturer decides to sell its products through high quality retail outlets, then its policies must be consistent with this objective. In this situation, if the manufacturing company established a policy that no suits would be made that retailed for more than $85, then the policy would probably be at odds with the objectives. Thus, it would be necessary to decide whether the statement of the objective or the policy represents the true desires of the company.

Once objectives are confirmed and compatible policies established, the company is in a position to examine the planning and strategy used to carry out the policies. Strategy is dependent on the resources available and controlled by the executive. Planning is the determination of how best to carry out the strategy. The dry-cleaning executive may decide that financial resources are not adequate to discard present equipment, and may convert to a self-service operation. But after some investigation, the dry cleaner finds that funds and space are available to install rented coin-operated equipment. The dry cleaner's strategy may become to operate both types of equipment in the present location. Planning involves subsequent decisions concerning such matters as placement of the equipment and informing customers of the dual operation. The dry cleaner does not, however, make this decision before checking on the other critical decision centers.

Communication and Control

As necessary as nerves to the human body are the control and communication networks of an organization. At this stage of the analysis, several obvious questions need to be answered. How are the activities of the company to be governed? What techniques and devices have been established so that the executive will know what is going on in the company? In some situations, it will be apparent that management is oblivious to the need for control or communication. In other instances, management may assume that controls or communications are operating when actually they are not. On the other hand, the controls may be so confining that the plans and strategies cannot be effected.

More elusive and more difficult to evaluate are the communications aspects; yet they are an integral part of the control system within an organization. Reports, written memoranda, and official notices are part of communications; but there are other types of communication that are more subtle, yet just as important. Informal conversations, for instance, are frequently more effective in the control system than the written word. Wordless actions, feedback, and lack of communications are also part of the communications network. Thus, if a new system or procedure is introduced without explanation, employees are likely to interpret the action according to their own frames of reference or points of view. The executive also is subject to these lack of communication conditions and may base decisions on misinterpreted communications.

In diagnosing a case, the student should examine the controls and communications involved to determine their adequacy and, indeed, to see if the appropriate controls exist. Appropriateness is determined by whether the controls aid in carrying out the plans and strategy, and also whether they are suitable for the existing organization and leadership.

Leadership and Organization

The analysis of leadership and organization is related very closely to the control and communication factors. Actually, because there is such a close integration, it is not always clear which center should be diagnosed first; it may be that an investigation of the communications or controls is meaningless without relating them to the organization.

Are the leadership and organization adequate to maintain control and to carry out the plans and strategy? Is the organization structure as established the best for the types of control desired? Are communications facilitated or restricted by the structure? Are the controls established mainly in the chief executive officer's hands, or are there regulatory devices all through the organization?

Under consideration here are not only the line and staff relationships, but also informal organizational arrangements, spans of control, centralization versus decentralization, delegation of responsibility, authority, democratic leadership versus autocratic, and other aspects of organization and leadership.

Interpersonal Behavior and Industrial Relations

Touching the other analysis factors is the one where a diagnosis of the human element or interpersonal relationships is carried on. The organization is established by people and is operated by people. This factor involving people can be the least predictable and is the one that most frequently spells the difference between the success or failure of an enterprise. It is the human element that is affecting the decisions.

It is in the area of human behavior where one finds that the "logical" decision may not be the "correct" decision. This is frequently the situation when one makes decisions that involve the human factor. There is an increasing number of instances where a management decision to become more efficient by reducing labor costs has caused not only a disruption of production or service but in some cases has brought the company to a complete standstill.

It is difficult to relate profits to human activity. In these cases, there are some opportunities to observe relationships between dollars and people. Even in those cases where the connection between profits and people is not immediately obvious, it is well to keep the ultimate company objectives in mind. Since the company is a profit-making organization, human-element decisions should be oriented in that direction. Profits are necessary for the continuation of the company and the livelihoods provided to the employees. In each of the cases, the student should examine the human factors or anticipate a change in human behavior.

Social and Economic Setting

The social and economic setting, the external environment, constitutes an eighth critical diagnostic center. An integral and important part of case analysis, this external environment surrounds the organization, and there is a continual series of deviations from the internal diagnostic cycle to the external critical center. Since the company is dependent entirely on society, it must continuously refer to this "outside world" which may include legal requirements, social mores, and economic conditions. (As shown in Exhibit 3, the social and economic setting affects all other critical centers.)

Thus, as the size-up of the situation progresses, it is necessary and critical to check on the outside forces. Are the objectives compatible with the social setting and economic conditions? Is there a market for the product? As the analysis continues, it is necessary to direct attention from each specific diagnostic center and look outside for conditions and situations in the environment that affect the ultimate decision. For instance, when the organization is examined, the

Exhibit 3

Effect of External Environment on Diagnostic Centers

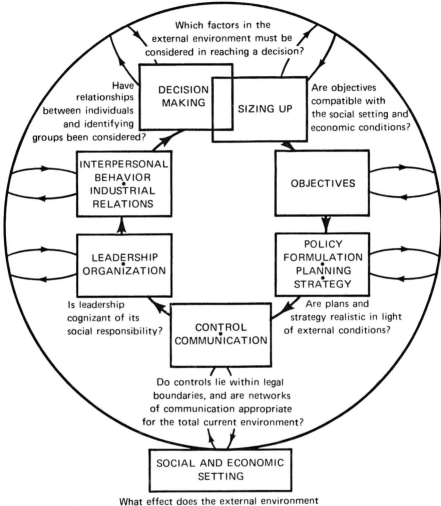

student may find that a vertically integrated company conflicts with antitrust laws. Or the hiring policies of industrial relations may be "out of step" with a local fair employment practices act. Or it may be that public indignation may prevent a company from carrying out plans which are quite legal and within the "rights" of the company.

Executives have come to recognize that the community is looking to them for leadership in the area of business ethics. For this reason, cases have been included that give some emphasis to the social responsibilities and ethical behavior of the executive. Managers are called upon to make decisions concerned with the welfare of employees, the community, and even the nation. These executives are also hard pressed to weigh their responsibilities to the community against their responsibilities to stockholders. At times the laws governing business are so ambiguous that the executive does not know what is a legitimate decision and what is not. The executive may also be faced with the situation where the competitors are not accepting their social responsibilities and, therefore, seem to have a competitive advantage.

Society has set up certain guides for the acceptable conduct of business. These expectancies of society are becoming more stringent and less tolerant of deviation. The executive also finds it difficult to adhere to legal requirements that may vary in interpretation from year to year. Most difficult, it seems, is the executive's task of balancing responsibilities to the individual employees and to the company. But if management does not take the initiative in attempting to discover its responsibilities, society will impose the responsibilities upon the company and executive through legal channels.

Decision Making

When making an analysis, it is well to keep in mind that the end result should be a recommendation for action. A decision is to be reached and implemented. It is necessary, therefore, to pause at each critical center to see if there are facts that will aid in making the decision.

The process of analysis includes asking the appropriate questions indicated on the diagnostic diagram. However, an examination should be made of related factors, such as (1) assessing the risks involved in one course of action as compared with another; (2) predicting the obstacles of making the various plans of action operational; (3) evaluating the financial resources and cost; (4) considering the human factor when recommending changes.

The student will certainly find other areas for consideration. Each area must be related to the others, with a continual assessment of the best combination. As in the world of business, the student must finally make a decision which is based on the various possibilities developed during analysis.

The decision-making process is sometimes described in terms of models that contain *inputs, variables,* and *outputs.* (See Exhibit 4.) The results or outputs of a decision are not always as predicted, but may vary from the anticipated results due to variables. The executive works with probabilities. What is the probability that the desired

Exhibit 4

Sample Variables

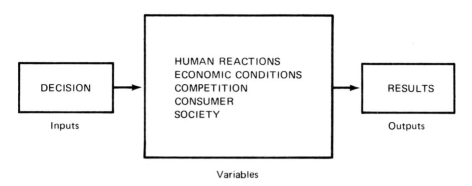

Variables

results will take place for a given decision? By reducing the number of variables, the probability factor can be improved. This points to the information available for decision making. If all facts were available so that all variables were eliminated, the executive could make a decision knowing that the expected results would take place. However, all facts are never available, so that there is some element of risk in every decision.

The dry-cleaning executive expected that the decision to have coin-operated machines as well as the "old" type would result in at least maintaining profits by reducing labor requirements and decreasing the overhead cost per unit cleaned. However, when employees slowed down, the dry cleaner was forced to maintain the previous work force; the consumer was suspicious of a combination type of dry-cleaning shop, and so it was necessary for the dry cleaner to increase advertising expenditures to overcome the customer reluctance. Competitors moved in nearby with only coin-operated machines, and as a result, total sales declined. Did the dry-cleaning executive make the wrong decision? After all, these facts were not available to the dry cleaner at the time.

Part of the job of the executive is to decide what information is to be available for decision making. Sales, cash, inventory, accounts payable, and receivables are the obvious facts that most companies maintain. Other information such as customer preference, employee morale, competitors' positions, market trends, changing labor needs, evaluation of employee performance, certain nondirect costs, and changing social mores, are examples of information frequently not available when needed for decision making. In deciding what information should be continuously available, management must determine the probable cost of the information, and weigh this cost against the contribution of the facts to the decision.

As indicated earlier, the amount of information varies from case to case. The student must recognize the risks involved when making decisions. If some vital fact is missing, the calculated risks are greater. It is appropriate for the student to indicate what additional information would reduce the risk, but at the same time the lack of information should not be used as a rationalization for inaction. Once the decision has been made, it is well to size up the situation again to be sure that vital information has not been overlooked. The potential effect on the organization, the output, should be reexamined, and the implementation of the decision should be drawn up.

This last step completes the diagnostic cycle. However, changing variables may have caused the problem to be returned for another decision—starting the diagnostic procedure again.

ARE THERE "RIGHT" ANSWERS?

At the end of the case discussion, the student will find that there is an urge to ask: "Okay, we have gone over this case in great detail, but there has been no agreement as to the problem or the decision— what *is* the right answer?"

To such a query, one can reply that, although a single decision may not have been agreed upon, some general problem areas have been outlined. Establishing the problem depends upon interpretation, assumptions, and evaluation of the risks made by the student. This does not mean that wide degrees of latitude are allowed in determining the problem, but rather that the class discussion offers the opportunity for different points of view to be examined. As in the business world, decisions are not always unanimous, nor does the executive always make the correct decision. Instead, management attempts to raise the percentage of decisions that are correct. In these cases, the instructor does not have *the* right answer.

CONCLUSION

The case-discussion method has been developed so that you as a student can increase your skills in the analysis of business problems by being able to distinguish between symptoms and causes, by recognizing the importance of certain factors and the irrelevance of others, and by establishing relationships between relevant factors. Your decision must be based on your evaluation of the facts and your judgment concerning the probability of the success of the decision in light of your analysis of the critical areas. As you progress with the practice of thinking through management problems, your assessment of the situations in succeeding cases will become more astute. The result should be greater ability in making decisions when you become part of management.

Part One

Decisions—Introduction

Radford Corporation

The Radford Corporation was involved primarily in making wooden handles—broom handles, mop handles, and the like. The company had 60 employees. It had been highly successful over the years, building up its equity to $250,000. There were seven directors on the board, including John Caldwell, Caldwell's mother, his brother-in-law, and his uncle.

FORMULATION OF THE BOWLING ALLEY IDEA

The president of the company, the secretary, and the engineer developed the idea of investing in a bowling alley. They did the preliminary research on such an investment and were strongly in favor of it. Only Caldwell was hesitant about the idea. Caldwell felt two other alternatives were preferable:

1. Invest more money in the advertising business.
2. Build a new handle factory in another part of the country.

He believed that these were the areas in which the company officials had experience and special skills. He felt that almost anyone was qualified to establish a bowling alley and that competition would be more severe in that field. He doubted that the rate of return would be as high in the bowling alley alternative.

Originally it was planned to set up the bowling alley, if it were established, as a subsidiary corporation. The possibility of creating two corporations, one to own the land and buildings, the other to run the bowling alley itself, was considered. This might have had the advantage of keeping both corporations in lower corporate income tax brackets. On the other hand, if the bowling alley were not successful, all the earnings would be in the land and building, so this would no longer be an advantage. The idea of two subsidiary corporations was dropped.

Two alternative types of equipment for the bowling alley were considered. The first involved equipment by AMF. Later the Brunswick Company took an interest, and offered to deduct the $5,000 that

Reproduced with permission of Dean Warren W. Haynes, New York University at Albany.

had been deposited with the other company from its charges. Thus the decision involved an analysis of the proposals of these two possible suppliers. In this case the figures are all based on the AMF alternative.

Several members of the board of directors committed themselves to the bowling alley idea early in the game before the full analysis had been made.

First Version Considered

The first estimates of cost and revenue based on the AMF alternative, including an analysis of fixed and variable costs, are shown in Exhibit 1.[1] The fixed costs were estimated to total $81,800. The variable costs were estimated at $.116 per customer. The revenue was estimated at $.56 per customer (of which $.42 was the average charge per line and the remainder the revenue from shoe rentals and the sale of food). This gave a break-even point of 184,000 customers, which would be at about two thirds of the estimated level of business. The profit would be about $22,000 at the expected level of 250,000 customers (lines). Exhibit 2 is a break-even chart based on some early revisions of the estimates in Exhibit 1. This exhibit reflects higher fixed costs and thus a higher break-even point. But it also indicates greater optimism about sales, with revenues of $140,000 instead of $132,500.

Refinements on the First Version

Exhibits 3, 4, 5, 6, and 7 show various refinements of the analysis. Considerable thought went into the financing. The Radford Corporation would purchase $50,000 of stock in the subsidiary corporation. Even this $50,000 would be borrowed. These exhibits show a higher net income than in the original estimates in Exhibit 1. A slightly higher volume is estimated—252,000 customers instead of 250,000 customers. The restaurant is eliminated, but some revenue from a snack bar is included. The total effect of these changes is to decrease the revenue figures. On the expense side, the salaries, rental, and service costs remain the same. The depreciation expenses are lower, being spread over 40 years and 10 years rather than 20 years and 5 years. The advertising promotion expenses are cut in half. The insurance estimates are $700 lower. The tax estimates are over $1,000 lower. The social security taxes are also estimated at a considerably lower figure. No interest expense is deducted in arriving at net income, so that this exhibit is not directly comparable with the first. On

1. The minor discrepancies in the figures are a result of rounding and the roughness of certain company computations. These discrepancies are insignificant.

the other hand, $10,000 of parent company overhead expenses are shown in Exhibit 4.

Further Revisions

Exhibits 8, 9, 10, and 11 show further consideration of the AMF alternative. One important difference at this stage was that estimated operations for only 300 days were considered, on the assumption that the business would be closed on Sundays. Two of the directors, Caldwell's mother and his uncle, insisted on Sunday closing on religious grounds. Thus the number of customers was reduced by about 25,000. This reduced revenue in proportion and reduced the rental charges and service costs. Another difference in this later estimate was a complete revision of the estimates of fixed and variable costs.

OUTSIDE INVESTIGATIONS

As part of the analysis for this decision, Caldwell and other members of the firm tried to learn about the profitability of bowling alleys elsewhere. They were able to obtain copies of a confidential national report covering 370 bowling alleys, which gave information on form of ownership, number of lanes, charge per lane, proportion of business in various categories (open, league, tournament, junior), the volume of automatic pinsetters, extent to which these are leased, ownership of building, size of investment, etc. This report also gave a breakdown of receipts and expenses as percentages. The report included a special collection of statistics on 16-lane establishments.

Caldwell spent considerable time interviewing the owners of two bowling alleys in a nearby location. He also telephoned an alley in a small town in Illinois, where the situation was more like the situation the new alley would face. For example, he found that the company in Illinois charged 45 cents per line (30 cents for children). This company did $300 to $400 business per day, which would be slightly more than the estimates for the Radford Corporation. The company used Brunswick pinsetters. The total investment was $650,000, which was more than the Radford Corporation had in mind. It operated on Sundays. The company also provided information on nearby bowling lanes within 35 to 40 miles.

Similar information was obtained from other bowling alleys. One of these companies expressed a preference for Brunswick equipment because of better maintenance and greater experience. This company suggested that it might be possible to get a franchise from the town to keep other establishments from coming in. One company official suggested that there must be a thousand population per lane within the trade area. It suggested that the break-even point was at 42 to 43 lines per lane per day. Another company put the break-even point at 30 lines a day. Officials of this company believed that there was no difference between AMF and Brunswick equipment. One of these companies charged 40 cents (children 35 cents) while the other stated that it could not do business below 45 cents. All of these companies gave considerable detailed information on operations.

Exhibit 12 is illustrative of the kinds of correspondence that took place among members of the board as the plan was being formulated.

DEMAND AND POTENTIAL COMPETITION

The location of the alley was to be Pikeville, Missouri, a town of 10,000 people where the broom handle plant was located. Caldwell believed that the town could support only one alley, making it unlikely that a competitor would move in. Nevertheless, he continued to worry about what would happen if a second alley were to locate in the town or if the bowling "fad" were to diminish. No towns within a radius of 50 miles were large enough to support a bowling alley, so that the Pikeville location should draw customers from other towns.

The estimates of revenue were based on the experience of other bowling alleys in similar locations and the advice of the equipment producers. Caldwell believed that if the bowling alley were to prove unprofitable, the building would be useful as a grocery store. The possibility of renting the building to the grocery business would reduce the risk somewhat.

OTHER ALTERNATIVES

None of the directors had made an analysis of the probable results of expansion of broom handle manufacturing. Caldwell did give considerable attention to the possibility of expanding the advertising activities in which he and his brother-in-law were engaged as partners. He believed that the Radford Corporation might do better by purchasing some advertising companies which were located in towns with a population of 15,000 or less. Caldwell knew that some such companies were available for purchase. He and his brother-in-law had operated similar companies with great success over the past 15 years.

Exhibits 13 and 14 show Caldwell's estimates if the Radford Corporation were to invest $206,000 (an amount comparable with the proposed investment in the bowling alley) in the advertising business. Exhibit 14 differs from Exhibit 13 only in that it is more optimistic about potential revenues for the advertising alternative.

Exhibit 1

Radford Corporation
First Version
of Cost and Revenue

16 Alleys
350-Day Operation

		Fixed	Variable
Income ($.56/customer)			
Gross bowling income @ 42¢ ..	$105,000		
Restaurant, soft drinks, candy (Net)	12,800		
Shoe rental	7,800		
Net sales—Balls, bags, shoes ..	1,900		
Amusements, cigarettes, ball cleaning	5,000		
	$132,500		
Expenses			
Salaries	$ 20,000	$20,000	
Pinspotter rental	23,000		.092
Service cost	7,200	7,200	
Replacement reserve	1,800	800	.004
Utilities	4,500	4,500	
Advertising and promotion	2,400	2,400	
Insurance	2,200	2,200	
Federal and state taxes	4,900		.02
Federal and state licenses	1,100	1,100	
FICA and payroll taxes	1,500	1,500	
AMF payments	14,300	14,300	
Interest on alleys	2,000	2,000	
Interest on building	2,200	2,200	
Depreciation on building (20 Years)	5,000	5,000	
Depreciation on alleys (5 Years)	18,600	18,600	
	$110,700	$81,800	.116

Paid-in capital $50,000 from Radford 6%
Loan $80,000 to $100,000 @ 6% from Insurance Company

Exhibit 2

Radford Corporation
Break-Even Chart

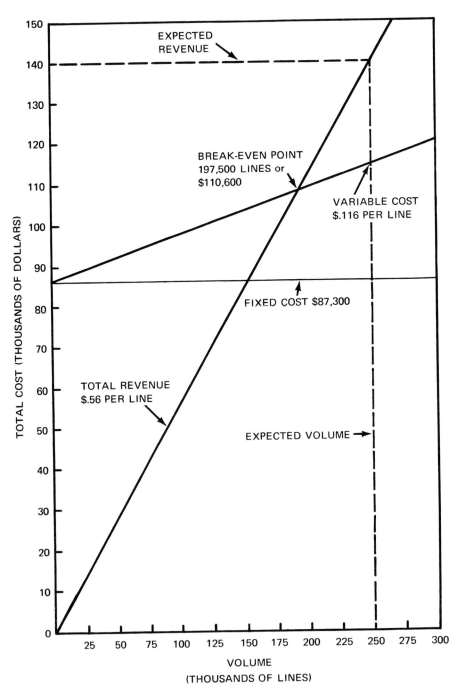

DECISIONS—INTRODUCTION

Exhibit 3

Radford Corporation
Proposed Financing

1. Set up new corporation—"Radford Bowling Lanes, Inc."
   Radford Corporation to hold all stock.
2. (a) Radford Bowling Lanes to negotiate loan with an insurance company
      such as Prudential for the purchase of the building at an estimated
      $85,000, this amount to be underwritten by the Radford Corporation.
   (b) Interest on above loan presumed to be 6 percent.
   (c) Radford Corporation to purchase stock in bowling corporation for
      estimated $50,000. Funds for purchase of this stock which constitutes
      the "paid-in capital" of new corporation would be made available
      by loan from First National Bank on possibly a five-year basis. This
      loan to be repaid principally by means of approximately $10,000 per
      year in salary overhead being transferred from present corporation
      to new corporation. See expense section of Exhibit 4.

   The paid-in capital would probably be used as follows:

Down Payment to AMF Equipment	$22,000
Purchase of Land	15,000
Operating Capital	13,000
	$50,000

Exhibit 4

Radford Corporation
Projected Income and Expense

Lines per day—720   350 Days   Per Year 252,000

Income

16 lanes × 45 lines per day 350 per lane @ 42¢	$105,840.00
Shoe rental per day (300)—239 customers × 60% = 143 @ 15¢	7,507.50
Sales—Balls, bags, shoes	2,000.00
Cigarettes, ball cleaning, snack bar—Net	3,000.00
	$118,347.50

Expenses

Salaries—Schedule	$ 20,000.00
AMF rental 160,000 @ 10¢ = 16,000.00	
80,000 @ 8¢ = 6,400.00	
12,000 @ 6¢ = 720.00	23,120.00
Service costs, pins, supplies ½ AMF estimate	7,200.00
Depreciation 40 years on 100,000 = 2,500.00	
10 years on 88,000 = 8,800.00	11,300.00
Utilities	4,700.00
Advertising and promotion	1,400.00
Insurance (fire) on $188,000	1,600.00
Taxes—Ad valorem	3,300.00
Federal, state, and local licenses	1,000.00
Social security tax	600.00
Overhead absorbed from Radford	10,000.00
	$ 84,220.00
NET INCOME	$ 34,127.50*

* Interest expense not included above. Included with principal payments on another schedule (Schedule A). Also see Schedule D for amount.

Exhibit 5

Radford Corporation
Schedule A

(1) AMF Equipment Loan—Approximately $88,000.00

16 lanes @ $5,500.00 each	$88,000.00
Less 25% down payment	22,000.00
Balance to be paid in 5 years	$66,000.00 Principal

Interest/Year

Total $66,000.00 × 6%	$3,960.00
— 23,760.00 (36%) Principal—1st Year	
42,240.00 × 6%	2,534.00
— 15,840.00 (24%) Principal—2nd Year	
26,400.00 × 6%	1,584.00
— 10,560.00 (16%) Principal—3rd Year	
15,840.00 × 6%	950.00
— 7,920.00 (12%) Principal—4th Year	
7,920.00 × 6%	475.00
TOTAL INTEREST 5 YEARS	$9,503.00

(2) Loan for Building—Insurance Company—Approximately $85,000

On 15-Year Term—
Payments $844 Month per $1,000.00 (Inc. Interest) Year $8,608.80
(1st Year—Each $1,000.00 of Principal Only Reduced to $957.50)

(3) Total Cash Payments—Principal and Interest

1st Year	Insurance Company	$ 8,608.80
	AMF	27,720.00
		$36,328.80
2nd Year	Insurance Company	$ 8,608.80
	AMF	18,374.00
		$26,982.80
3rd Year	Insurance Company	$ 8,608.80
	AMF	12,144.00
		$20,752.80

Exhibit 6

Radford Corporation
Schedule B
Source and Disposition of Funds

Estimated profit per statement $34,127.50
Add: Expense charges which do not require cash
    outlay 11,300.00

Total funds available annually $45,427.50

	1st Year	2nd Year	3rd Year
Available cash	$45,427.50	$45,427.50	$45,427.50
Repayment schedule	36,328.80	26,982.80	20,752.80
To surplus	$ 9,098.70	$18,444.70	$24,674.70
Less estimated income taxes (Schedule D)	8,676.00	8,676.00	8,676.00
Unappropriated surplus	$ 422.70	$ 9,768.70	$15,998.70

Exhibit 7

Radford Corporation
Schedule C
Estimated Ad Valorem Taxes

City Taxes

Real: Property at $15,000 × 30% = 4,500.00 @ .4612*	$ 207.45
Personal: Max. $188,000 × 30% = 56,400 @ .4612	2,600.00

County Taxes $2,807.45

Real: Same valuation $4,500.00 @ .3	$ 135.00
Personal: Estimated ½ of city assessed $28,000 @ .3	840.00

$ 975.00

Total ad valorem tax $3,782.45

* Tax factor for ten dollars of assessed evaluation.

Schedule D
Estimated Income Tax

Earnings per operating statement	$34,127.50	
Interest payments not included on statement .	* 7,100.00	(Average/Year)

$27,027.50

Estimated federal tax	$7,605.00
Estimated state tax	1,071.00
Total	$8,676.00

* This is an average amount of interest per year over the life of the notes. Total interest paid first few years would be somewhat higher than the average of $7,100.00 per year.

1st Year Interest	AMF	$3,960.00
	Insurance Company	5,003.00
		$8,963.00

Exhibit 8

Radford Corporation
Break-Even Chart

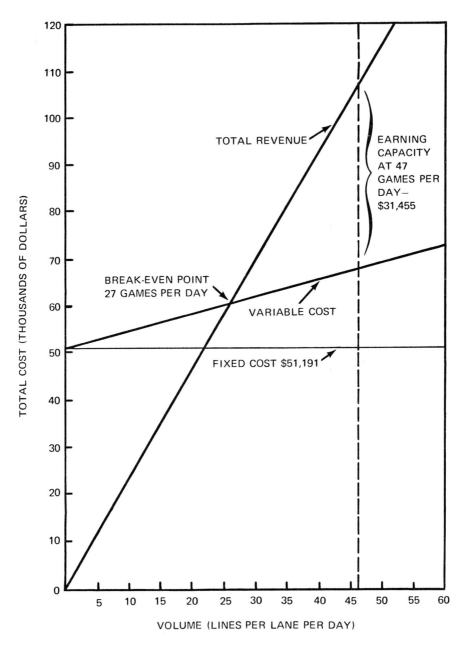

Exhibit 9

Radford Corporation
Projected Income and Expense

Lines per day—752   300 Days   Per Year 225,600

Income

16 lanes × 47 lines per day (300) per lane @ 42¢	$ 94,752.00
Shoe rental per day (300)—250 customers × 60% = 150 @ 15¢	6,750.00
Sales—Balls, bags, shoes	2,000.00
Cigarettes, ball cleaning, snack bar—Net	3,000.00
Gross Income	$106,502.00

Expense

Salaries—Schedule	$ 20,000.00
AMF rental 160,000 @ 10¢ = $16,000.00	
65,600 @ 8¢ = 5,248.00	
—— @ 6¢ =	
	21,248.00
Service costs, pins, supplies	
Total 5.5% Gross Income	5,857.00
Depreciation 40 years on $100,000 = $2,500.00	
10 years on 80,000 = 8,000.00	10,500.00
Utilities	4,500.00
Advertising and promotion	1,200.00
Insurance (fire) on $188,000	1,500.00
Taxes—Add valorem	3,800.00
Federal, state, local licenses	1,000.00
Social security tax	600.00
Overhead absorbed from Radford	10,000.00
	$ 80,205.00
NET INCOME	$ 26,297.00*

* Interest expense not included above. Included with principal payments on another schedule (Schedule A).

Actual earning capacity 5-year average:

Above	$26,297.00	
Add overhead absorbed	+ 10,000.00	$1,800 Net Expense Line
Less interest average	− 4,842.00	
	$31,455.00	

Exhibit 10
Radford Corporation
Source and Disposition of Funds

Estimated profit per statement $26,297.00
Add: Expense charges which do not require cash
    outlay—Depreciation 10,500.00

    Total funds available annually $36,797.00

	1st Year	2nd Year	3rd Year
Available cash	$36,797.00	$36,797.00	$36,797.00
Repayment schedule	36,328.80	26,982.80	20,752.80
To surplus	$ 468.20	$ 9,814.20	$16,044.20
Less estimated income taxes			
(Schedule D)	——	5,770.00	6,237.67
Unappropriated surplus	$ 468.20	$ 4,044.20	$ 9,806.53

Exhibit 11
Radford Corporation
Schedule C
Estimated Ad Valorem Taxes

City Taxes
Real: Property at $15,000 × 30% = 4,500.00 @ .4612* . . . . $ 208.00
Personal: Max. $188,000 × 30% = 56,400.00 @ .4612 . . . .   2,600.00
    $2,808.00

County Taxes
Real: Some valuation $4,500.00 @ .3 . . . . $ 135.00
Personal: Estimated ½ of city assessed $28,000 @ .3 . . . .   840.00
    $ 975.00

    Total ad valorem tax $3,783.00

    * Tax factor for $10 of assessed evaluation.

Schedule D
Estimated Income Tax—First Year Only

Earnings per operating statement $26,297.00
Interest payments not included on statement . . .   * 8,963.00 (Aver. 5 years

    Taxable income $17,334.00 $4,842.00)
Estimated federal tax $5,203.00
Estimated state tax 567.00

    $5,770.00

    * This is the actual amount of interest the first year (average first five years is $4,842.00). Total interest paid first few years would be somewhat higher than the average of $4,842.00 per year.

1st Year Interest	AMF	$3,960.00
	Insurance Company	5,003.00
		$8,963.00

Exhibit 12

Radford Corporation

Springfield, Illinois

Mr. J. C. Frederick, President
Radford Corporation
Pikeville, Missouri

Dear John:

I am enclosing the results of my investigation on the bowling situation. I visited three establishments and called another.

Most everything I heard would encourage one to go into the business. However, I learned that many, many mistakes were made by people not being able to see into the future. The most common was, "Parking Lot Too Small." As an example, one alley has a 6:30 p.m. league and a 9:00 p.m. league (sixty bowlers in each league plus spectators and substitutes, etc.) All the nine o'clock crowd comes before the six-thirty crowd leaves, so he needs at least 120 spaces at this time. The lot looks awfully big, but he says it is much too small.

Another mistake he made—he can call his pin jumper over the speaker system, but the pin jumper has no mike with which to reply, and many trips to the back of the alleys are necessary.

I believe our estimated costs are too low. One owner said it would take $15,000 to cut 3 feet from a plot of land 150 × 200 and put a good base and blacktop the area. Then I believe we left out entirely the lights for the parking lot, and tall towers or poles and big lights are necessary for this.

The same owner also told me that his cash register, desk, chairs, and necessary equipment of this kind cost him $5,000.

He put in tile (under the spectators' and bowlers' seats) and wishes he didn't have it, and put in carpet in the lobby and is glad he did.

One thing I picked up should bear investigating—one man rents his pins and finds that more satisfactory than owning them.

One man told me Brunswick will also lease the pinspotters now.

However, I am about convinced that AMF is better. Evansville, Indiana, has 4 or 5 big places, all with AMF. I looked at the Brunswick and AMF in operation, and could see or find out nothing wrong with either one. One man said AMF was extremely nice to do business with. They all said both Brunswick and AMF would treat you right.

My recommendation is:

Go slow and be very careful about Sunday, as this is decidedly the second best day in the week for the people with whom I talked. I cannot say I am against the plan, but I believe we will be at a very definite disadvantage without the Sunday income, possibly enough to make the difference between a highly successful operation and a mediocre one. Looking ahead a little, I believe the pressure for Sunday operation would mount after the opening, and a situation might develop between those who want to run on Sunday and those who do not.

If, however, you and the rest of the board think it is all right to do so, I will be in favor of it.

Exhibit 12 (cont'd)

Radford Corporation

One more thing I think of: I'd suggest a review of the cost estimates to arrive at good figures for the parking lot, lights, signs, cash register, furniture, etc., and that a safety factor be put in to take care of unforeseen contingencies (a rather liberal one).

I'm enclosing an expense sheet on the traveling and phone calls I made. The phone is an estimate, but I believe it is close.

Sincerely,

(signed)   John Caldwell

John Caldwell

Exhibit 13

Radford Corporation
Estimate for Advertising Operations—Company A

$206,000	INVESTMENT
12,360.00	Per month
12	Months
$148,320.00	Potential
.80	
$118,656.00	Estimated annual revenue
.20	
$ 23,731.20	Profit
20,600.00	Depreciation
$ 44,331.20	Available to pay off (gross)
12,331.20	Tax
$ 32,000.00	Available to pay debt and interest
6,000.00	Interest
$ 26,000.00	Apply to debt

7.9 Years

Exhibit 14

Radford Corporation
Estimate for Advertising Operations—Company B

	$206,000	INVESTMENT
	16,524.00	Per month
	12	Months
	$198,288.00	Potential
	.80	
	$158,630.40	Estimated annual revenue
	.20	
	$ 31,726.08	Profit
	20,600.00	Depreciation
	$ 52,326.08	Available to pay off (gross)
	16,000.00	Tax
	$ 36,326.08	Available to pay debt and interest
	6,000.00	Interest
	$ 30,326.08	Apply to debt
6.8 Years		

Hawaii Best Company

Gradually rising from his chair in his third-floor plush office overlooking Waikiki Beach in Honolulu, James Lind, President of Hawaii Best Company (HBC), greeted Charles Carson, Vice-President and General Manager of the company's Islands Division, and invited him to take the seat across from his desk.

"Charlie, I am sure that something has gone wrong," he said as Carson remained standing. "You have many fine qualities—I was the one who recognized them when I promoted you to vice-president—but I have been reviewing your progress these past few months and . . . and the results have not met our expectations."

Carson fidgeted at the window, watching the October morning across the harbor. His face reddened, his pulse quickened, and he waited for Lind to continue.

"The costs in your division are higher than budgeted, the morale is low, and your branch managers are unhappy with your steward-ship," Lind said. "And your cooperation with Gil Harris has fallen short of satisfactory."

Carson grew angrier at the mention of Harris, a young aggressive man with a master's degree from a well-known eastern business school. Harris was a latecomer to HBC, but Carson knew that every-one was pleased with his performance.

"Charles, at the country club last week, I was speaking to one of our vendors. He intimated that your dealings with him had not been entirely clean. This is what hurts me the most.

"I know you are 49, that your son is only eight, that this is a difficult time for you and your family," Lind concluded as Carson stared out the window. "You have spent almost all your life in Hawaii; . . . it would be difficult for you to move to the mainland. It will be even harder for you to find a similar position in the Honolulu com-munity. But I must ask for your resignation, and I will do my best to help you find a more suitable opportunity."

This case was made possible by a corporation which prefers to remain anonymous. All names, figures, and locations have been disguised. It was pre-pared by Ram Charan, Associate Professor of Policy & Environment.

"Jim, I can't believe it," Carson finally replied. "It's just all wrong." He turned slowly from the window, his face blood-red.

"I have been with this company for ten years. I built this division. Sure, this year's results are not quite what you expect but my division is still the largest contributor to corporate profits. I'll bet your friend Gil has been telling you about the vendor deals. Well, it's a damned lie, and I won't stand for it! That boy will stop at nothing to grab power."

There was a long silence as Lind and Carson stared at opposite corners of the large office. "I will not resign," Carson suddenly declared, and he left the president's office coughing, his face flushed and his heart pounding.

Lind stood motionless as he watched the door close. He was uncertain about what to do; it never had occurred to him that Carson might refuse to resign. He decided to proceed as he had planned, but with one modification.

"Janice, please take a memo," he said to his secretary, and he dictated a note to Charles Carson informing him that his employment with HBC was terminated as of that afternoon, October 10, 1972.

After sending out a general release memo informing all division heads that Carson had resigned and that Joseph Ward, a promising young executive, presently employed as the manager of planning in the operations division, would assume the position of acting general manager of the Islands division, Lind hurriedly left the office. He had less than an hour to catch the 12:30 plane, intending to visit each of the seven branch heads on the outer islands, to tell them about the change and their new Acting General Manager.

While Lind was having his memos sent out, Carson was trying to contact his previous boss and old friend, Roy North, past president of HBC and presently an influential member of the company's board of directors and its powerful executive committee. Carson intended to have the matter taken to the board for deliberation.

BACKGROUND

North was one of five members of the board's executive committee, which customarily approved the appointments, promotions, stock options and salary adjustments of personnel earning over $10,000. This included department heads, division managers, and vice-presidents. The committee held at least one meeting a month, and these, like the regular monthly meetings of all 12 board members, were well-attended. (Exhibit 1 shows selected data about the directors).

Several of the directors were descendants or close friends of the founders of the Hawaii Best Company, but only James Lind and

Exhibit 1

Hawaii Best Company
Board of Directors—1972

Name	Age, Place Most of Life Spent	Background	Current Activity	Previous Association in Years		No. of Shares Represented
				Industry	Company	
Choy, Eduardo	65, Hawaii	No academic degree Financial	Entrepreneur, corporate chairman, banker	0	15 as Director	3,000
Donahue, John	70, Hawaii	Engineer Retired	Retired corporate exec. of the company VP of a property management company	40 with co.	8 as Director	500
Eichi, Ishi	40, Hawaii	Legal, Attorney	Practicing attorney	0	2 as Director	0
Fields, J. B. *	54, Hawaii	M.B.A. (Harvard) Finance	Exec. VP of a large multinational company headquartered in Honolulu	0	15 as Director	2,500 + 4% owned by his company
Fong, Charles	40, Hawaii	M.B.A. (Harvard) Finance	Exec. VP of a real estate development & investment firm	0	2 as Director	500
Hanley, Don *	70, Hawaii	Secretary	Retired	19	19 as Director	10,000

Name	Age, Origin	Background	Position		Tenure	Shares
Johnson, T.	48, Hawaii	Accounting	Corporate Treasurer	15	2 as Director	1,000
Lind, James *+	53, Mainland	Engineer, Alumnus of Columbia Business School	Corporate President	28	2 as President & Director	4,000
North, Roy *	56, Mainland & 16 years in Hawaii	Engineer, Financial Analyst	Exec. VP of a conglomerate, headquartered in Honolulu	16	10 as Director	1,500
Rusk, Dean *	52, Hawaii	Accounting & Finance Insurance, An Alumnus of Harvard Business School	Exec. VP of a local large company operating in insurance, sugar, real estate and merchandising business	0	5 as Director	0
Simon, A. F.*	65, Hawaii	Contractor, Entrepreneur	Corporate Chairman & President, Entrepreneur	0	20 as Director	30,000
Vogel, Lawrence	63, Hawaii	Finance, Fiduciary	Corporate President, Fiduciary Agent, Represents a large local trust	0	10 as Director	0

* member of the board's executive committee
+ HBC employee

Thomas Johnson were HBC employees. Board members held 5 percent of outstanding stock; the rest was widely owned by the people and business concerns in Hawaii. No one outside the board represented more than 1 percent of the HBC stock.

In 1971, with $30 million in sales and an e.p.s. of $1, the Hawaii Best Company was a manufacturer and marketer of a special formula. The company was listed on the Pacific Coast Stock Exchange with 1 million shares outstanding which yielded a stable dividend of $1 per share over the last five years. It sold its line of special formula X to industrial, commercial and residential customers in the state of Hawaii. Its manufacturing facilities and three sales branches were strategically located in Honolulu, and seven other sales branches were spread over the outer islands. The company usually negotiated hard for its basic raw material K, used in the manufacture of special formula X, from its only locally available long-term supplier. Imports of the raw material were deemed uneconomical for HBC and a second source of local supply did not appear on the horizon.

The company also sold special formula Y but only in the outer island branches and not in Honolulu. It was purchased in finished packaged form from several vendors within and outside the state of Hawaii, but the company was in no way involved in its manufacture.

Over the past five years the company's sales grew at an average annual rate of 4 percent, but its market share remained constant. Relative to the competition, HBC's profit performance had declined and, according to one competitor, "it was only through some 'creative' accounting that the company barely made its dividend in 1971."

HBC had two rivals in its industry: the larger company had annual sales of $60 million, the smaller sales of $15 million a year. It was a fiercely competitive industry, and special favors or discounts, although illegal, were sometimes granted to woo customers from another company. And customers were precious; just 10 clients accounted for one quarter of HBC sales.

HBC'S ORGANIZATION STRUCTURE

Exhibit 2 shows HBC's skeletal organizational structure. The president, James Lind, was responsible to the board of directors. Thomas Johnson, vice-president finance and secretary, and president James Lind regularly attended the monthly board meetings, and other vice-presidents were also invited frequently to keep the board informed on matters of importance in the area of their specialty. According to Andrew Simon, chairman of the board of directors, "This practice gives us an opportunity to know what we have underneath the first layer."

Exhibit 2

Hawaii Best Company (A)
Organization Structure 1972

BOARD OF DIRECTORS
CHAIRMAN • A. SIMON

PRESIDENT
J. LIND

VP OPERATIONS
OFFICE
VACANT

- MANAGER RESEARCH
- MANAGER MANUFACTURING
- MANAGER PLANNING JOSEPH • WARD

VP & GENERAL MANAGER
ISLANDS DIVISION
C. • CARSON

- PURCHASING & WAREHOUSING SPECIAL FORMULA Y
- BRANCH A SPECIAL FORMULA X & Y
- BRANCH B X & Y
- BRANCH G X & Y

VP INDUSTRIAL RELATIONS
J. • WYLE

- PERSONNEL MANAGER

VP MARKETING & GENERAL MANAGER
HONOLULU DIVISION
G. • HARRIS

- HONOLULU DIVISION
  - BRANCH A SPECIAL FORMULA X
  - BRANCH B X
  - BRANCH C X
- MARKET RESEARCH
- MARKET PLANNING
- ADVERTISING

VP FINANCE & SECRETARY
T. • JOHNSON

- PURCHASING
- ACCOUNTING
- TREASURY
- COMPUTER
- COLLECTIONS
- CONTROLLER

In addition to managing five divisions and attending to the normal duties of the president, Lind took a special interest in the negotiations involving labor contracts and purchasing of raw material K and special formula Y. The specific responsibility for negotiating labor contracts rested with the Vice-President of Industrial Relations, John Wyle. Control of the purchase of raw material K lay with the senior vice president of operations. The vice president and general manager, Islands division, was responsible for buying special formula Y.

In all these negotiations, however, it was not uncommon for Johnson to get involved as well.

Among the corporate vice-presidents in 1971, John Wyle, 51, had been the longest with the company. However, he had suffered two serious heart attacks since joining the company in 1945—one in 1959 and the other in 1968. According to former HBC president North, "Wyle is the best industrial relations man we can find and he is a good personal friend of ours (their wives played cards together) but, frankly, his health concerns me and several of the directors."

Since joining the company in 1947 as a clerk, Thomas Johnson had risen to the position of vice president finance by 1968. In 1970 at the age of 46, he was elected to the company's board of directors at the suggestion of President Lind. Johnson had been actively under consideration for the presidency when Roy North vacated the position in December, 1969. One member of the selection committee put it this way: "Johnson is quite happy in his present position. He is a little lazy. He never wanted the top job."

Gil Harris, 33, joined the company in March, 1970 as vice president for marketing and general manager of the Honolulu division, responsible for the conduct and performance of the three Honolulu branches and for the company-wide market research, market planning and advertising campaigns.

As vice president and general manager of the Islands division, Charles Carson had controlled the conduct and profit performance of all the branches in the state outside Honolulu. Carson also participated in the marketing decisions such as advertising and promotions, and his division was charged a pro-rata share of expenses on the basis of divisional sales.

The Islands division and the Honolulu division were created by Lind in February, 1970, after the sudden death of Vice President Sales Robert Gellerman, 46. Gellerman had been responsible for the company-wide sales and advertising throughout the state. Prior to the establishment of the two divisions, Lind consulted Chairman Simon, former HBC president North, and other members of the executive committee, and received their unanimous support. Also included in the restructuring were the functions of market planning and market research, which were consolidated under the new vice president for marketing and general manager, Honolulu division.

The position of senior vice president operations had been vacant since May, 1970, when Lind asked for the resignation of the man who had held that office. The three managers within the division—manufacturing, planning, and research—had since been reporting directly to Lind. They constantly vied for the attentions of the president and the corporate vice-presidents in the hope that one of them could assume the vice-presidency. Three key members of the board were acquainted with Donald May, the research manager, but the other two were virtually unknown to the board.

ARRIVAL OF JAMES LIND

On January 1, 1970, James Lind replaced Roy North as president of Hawaii Best Company when the latter left the company to become an executive vice-president of a multinational conglomerate headquartered in Honolulu. North, under whose control HBC had prospered for seven years, recommended Lind for the presidency after an unfruitful search for a candidate within the company and the Hawaiian community. The board of directors accepted Lind, then a top executive in a trade association in New York, and he soon proved to be a man of integrity, dedication, and charm.

Although the business community in Hawaii, according to some observers, was tight-knit and nearly impervious to outsiders, Lind was readily admitted and liked. The morale at HBC soared during the early months of his presidency, because he was a man who was both extraordinarily hardworking—he put in up to 70 hours a week —and "human." He was one of the best fund raisers for community projects in Hawaii.

Financially, however, the company was not performing well under Lind's leadership. Rising labor and material costs, and the combination of the inflationary spiral and fierce competition put pressure on the profit margins. Lind began to make changes in key personnel in an effort to offset the problem. In February, he promoted Charles Carson, a man who had been with the company for over eight years, to vice president and general manager of the newly created Islands division. Three months later he asked for the resignation of Frank Adams, senior vice-president of operations. Lind felt that Adams, after 27 years at HBC was "utterly lacking in an ability to negotiate for key raw materials," and brought his grievance to the board of directors. Before Adams was asked to resign, a severance package was worked out and approved by the board. Adams, then 53, was utterly shaken. He became an estimator for a local construction firm at one-quarter of his former salary. This was the first such severance in the history of the company and as one director put it: "The event was extremely painful; it left deep scars on us and our families."

Lind's final major organizational change was to bring in an old friend of his whom he hoped could develop new marketing strategies for the entire company. Gil Harris, from the Global Chemical Company of New York, was made vice-president for marketing and general manager of the newly formed Honolulu division.

LUNCH AT THE CLUB

"Jason, thank you for meeting me here, and for cancelling your other engagement to see me. I'm sorry, but I had to talk to you; something has happened that I think you should know about."

Charles Carson leaned heavily on the table in the restaurant of Honolulu's only country club. The man across from him curiously fingered the stem of his martini glass. Jason Fields, the executive vice-president of the third largest international company based in Hawaii, was a busy and important man. An illustrious graduate of the Harvard Business School, Fields was one of the three most influential members of the company's board and its executive committee. Field's employer controlled 4 percent of the HBC's outstanding stock. He did not have too much time to spend with Carson, his golf buddy and a VP of one of the two companies of which Fields was a director. (The other company was a major buyer from Carson's division at HBC).

"I'll try to be brief," Carson said. "Jim called me to his office this morning and asked me to submit my resignation. I refused. But before he left for his bloodsucking trip, he terminated my association with the company as of this afternoon."

Fields raised his eyes briefly.

"I control the company's three largest customers, you know," Carson continued. "I can easily take them to the competition. But he still has the gall to accuse me of taking a kickback, with absolutely no proof! I think Harris has put him up to it. He's been charging a substantial proportion of his division's expenses to my division. I have been arguing with him about these expenses during the last several weeks, and he finally told me he'd have my head if I went to Lind about it.

"Not even a note of thanks. Not even a mention of it to the board," Carson murmured. "I wonder how long the board will allow Lind to destroy the very people who built this company. I don't know what to do."

"Neither do I, Charlie," Fields answered. "I'm truly sorry to hear about this. This is strange. I had no idea this was even being considered. The executive committee met this morning and Jim, of course, was there, but this was never mentioned. I'd like to help in any way I can, Charlie. . . . All I can say is wait and see what happens at the next board meeting. It's scheduled for October 17."

"Well," said Carson, "I just hope the board takes this chance to finally straighten up the organization. Its relationship to the company, the delegation of responsibility, the criteria for employee evaluation—there are a lot of things that have remained garbled and unclear ever since Frank Adams was asked to resign. The morale of the executive staff is low. Earnings are not improving. Everyone is concerned about his own skin. Who will be axed next?"

LIND'S TURBULENT RIDE

Lind was deeply shaken over Carson's refusal to resign, and on the plane to Maui he tried to analyze the situation. He realized that he had made a mistake in promoting Carson a year and a half ago, although the psychological tests that he had had administered to all executives at the time pointed strongly to Carson as the man for the job. Lind remembered too the annual physical checkup the company executives were required to undergo, and recalled sadly the high blood pressure and excessive cholesterol level that Carson's exams revealed.

"I must stick to my guns," Lind mused. "I refuse to be blackmailed by the three powerful customers Charlie has in his pocket. I cannot let my authority be challenged, especially by a man I believe has taken kickbacks."

After a sleepless night, Lind telephoned Andrew Simon to inform him of Carson's resignation.

"Yes, Jim, Jason Fields called me yesterday to tell me," Simon relayed. "He was quite upset. And I saw Roy North at a cocktail party last night. He, too, knew about the event, and he appeared visibly disturbed. This is a sad situation. I am a little more than concerned, but you are the boss. We'll try to handle the matter appropriately at the board meeting next week."

Simon returned the receiver to the cradle thoughtfully. For the first time in his 20 years as chairman of the board, he felt that there was a conflict between the management of company affairs and the way he thought they ought to be managed.

Approaching 65, Simon was still active and healthy, and never missed a board meeting. He was once the caretaker president of HBC for one year in 1956. His deep concern for the company was reflected in the way he usually helped in its decision-making process—carefully—after long consideration and debate. He had discussed the matter of Adams' resignation privately first with Lind, then with the executive committee, and then with the entire board before Simon had been fully convinced that Adams should go. Similarly, he had spent long hours deciding on Lind's appointment, consulted extensively with several members of the board individually. Both Mr. and Mrs. Lind were interviewed thoroughly before the board selected him for the presidency.

MEETING OF THE BOARD

The board of directors of the Hawaii Best Company met at 7:30 a.m. on October 17 and, as usual, the meeting promptly came to order. The items on the agenda were: the company's performance for the third quarter; the long-term lease on the HBC building; the anticipated state of the nation's economy for the upcoming year; the contributions that HBC made annually to three local charities.

Lind's announcement was the last item.

"Mr. Chairman, members of the board," he said, "I regret to inform you that as of October 10, 1972, Charles Carson resigned from our company. . . ."

St. John's Hospital

"You can go on making short-range moves here and there, but the time comes when you have to consider the long-range direction of the hospital. You need to determine where you are, what the community needs, and where you *should* be going." This was the thinking of Sister Macrina Ryan as she reflected on her decision to hire an outside consultant to assist in long-range planning for St. John's Hospital in October, 1972.

Sister Macrina had been the administrator at St. John's for the previous seven years. She received her undergraduate training in personnel after which she worked for two years in a Cheyenne hospital and 11 years at St. Joseph's Hospital in Denver. While at St. Joseph's she gained experience in both the business office and the personnel department. Before coming to St. John's, she had completed the Hospital Executive Development program offered by St. Louis University. After six years at St. John's, she was offered an opportunity for advancement to a larger hospital operated by the Sisters of Charity. She declined to apply for the position, though, because she felt she needed more time to complete her work at St. John's.

Sister Macrina's administration at St. John's had been marked by several significant changes in both the physical plant and the medical services of the hospital. A number of important issues faced St. John's which required resolution by the end of 1972, however. In attempting to deal with them she felt the need for some independent, outside counsel. Therefore, after gaining the approval of the Board of Trustees in Leavenworth, Kansas, and discussing the matter with the president of the lay advisory board in Helena, she hired the Medical Planning Associates (henceforth referred to as MPA), a consulting firm based in Malibu, California, to make a comprehensive study of the hospital's capabilities and the health needs of the Helena community. MPA's contract also called for the development of a long-range plan for St. John's based on the results of these studies.

This case was prepared by John Bringhurst under the preceptorial guidance of Gerald Leavitt and the casewriting supervision of Professor Charles W. Hofer.

ST. JOHN'S HISTORY

St. John's, which was organized in 1870 by the Sisters of Charity of Leavenworth, Kansas, was the first private hospital in the territory of Montana. It had its beginnings in a small frame building located in a tiny mining settlement which eventually became the capitol of the state. In the early years of its existence, the hospital's patients were mostly miners, prospectors, and lumbermen. Soon charity patients from Lewis and Clark, Meagher, and Jefferson Counties were added to its patient load. In 1873, a small building behind the hospital became the first mental hospital in Montana. It offered care for psychiatric patients until its abandonment when the state established its own mental health institution in 1877. After the coming of the Northern Pacific Railroad in 1883, the original frame building became inadequate and was replaced by a larger brick and stone structure. This building was damaged beyond repair in the earthquakes of 1935. While a new building was being erected, St. John's utilized the facilities of the Montana Children's Home—now Shodair Hospital. The new unit, which was still the core of the hospital in 1972, was completed in 1939. Since then St. John's has expanded its facilities twice. Specifically, a new cafeteria and kitchen were added in 1958, and in 1965 the hospital's north and south wings were completed. The north wing contained ten medical-surgical private rooms, a labor and delivery unit, an X-ray department, and a general storeroom. The south wing consisted of a laundry, the boiler room, physical therapy, the dental room, and the chaplain's quarters. In addition, the south wing had rooms for 25 patients and also housed facilities for extended care patients. (See Exhibit 1 for a layout of St. John's facilities in October, 1972.)

In 1968, St. John's maternity department was closed temporarily to provide space for medical-surgical patients while the latter area was being refurbished. This renovation also involved conversion of the Sisters' living quarters into a medical records department and a modern coronary intensive care unit. After a little more than a year without maternity facilities, during which time St. Peter's Community Hospital handled the maternity patient load in Helena, St. John's Board of Trustees decided not to reopen the department. The trustees believed that this action would eliminate "one of the most expensive examples of duplication and underutilization of services in Helena." [1] More specifically, they felt their decision would reduce losses for both St. John's, which would be freed of a perennial deficit operation, and St. Peter's, which would gain maternity patients with little or no increase in overhead costs. Additional benefits to St. John's were

1. From a memorandum of November 26, 1969, from Sister Macrina to the medical staff.

Exhibit 1

Layout of
St. John's
Hospital

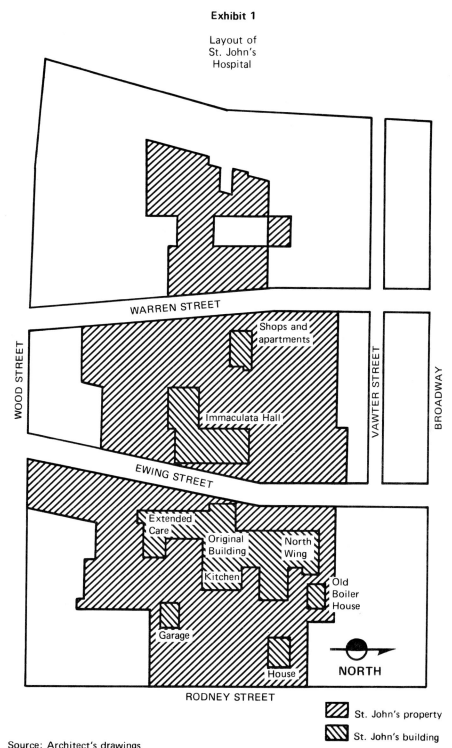

WARREN STREET

WOOD STREET

Shops and apartments

Immaculata Hall

VAWTER STREET

BROADWAY

EWING STREET

Extended Care

Original Building

North Wing

Kitchen

Old Boiler House

Garage

House

NORTH

RODNEY STREET

St. John's property

St. John's building

Source: Architect's drawings

expected to result from the use of the newly-available rooms for additional medical and surgical bedspace.

St. John's also established the first school of nursing in Montana. When the earthquakes of 1935 destroyed the school building, the hospital's nursing students were transferred to other schools to complete their training. The nursing school was reopened in 1940 and continued full scale operations until 1965. At that time, because of financial losses incurred by the school and changing requirements in the field of nursing, the board of trustees decided to close the school. Nursing training at St. John's ceased in 1968 with the graduation of the class which had entered in 1965.

HOSPITALS AND HEALTH SERVICES IN HELENA

The city of Helena, which had a population of approximately 26,000, was served by three hospitals in 1972. St. John's and the Shodair Crippled Children's Hospital were located in the downtown area, with St. Peter's Community Hospital situated on the extreme east side of town. In addition, a Veteran's Administration Hospital was located at Fort Harrison, a military post about six miles west of Helena. However, it served only armed forces veterans, most of whom were not from the Helena area. (See Exhibit 2 for a map indicating the locations of the three Helena hospitals.)

St. Peter's Community Hospital was established in 1887. It expanded to a new location in 1924, and in 1968 moved into a modern new facility at its present location. This facility had space for 111 beds, most of which were used for medical-surgical, pediatric, and maternity services. The completion of St. Peter's new building had reduced the utilization of St. John's, in the opinion of many St. John's administrators. Specifically, they pointed out that the average occupancy rate and the total number of ancillary services demanded at St. John's began to decline following the completion of St. Peter's new facility—a trend which continued through 1972. (See Exhibits 3, 4, and 5 for utilization statistics for St. John's.)

Shodair Crippled Children's Hospital was originally established as a residence for homeless children. The hospital, which was built as an addition to the home in 1937, was a focal point in the community during the polio epidemic of the 50s. With the widespread adoption of Salk and Sabin vaccines, however, Shodair's census declined to the point where its 45-bed capacity averaged less than 40 percent occupancy in the 1970s.

Although the 160 beds of the Veterans' Administration Hospital were filled largely with patients from outside the community,[2] it

2. During the 1970s, approximately 20 percent of the V.A. Hospital's patients were from the Helena area.

Exhibit 2

Locations of
Helena Hospitals

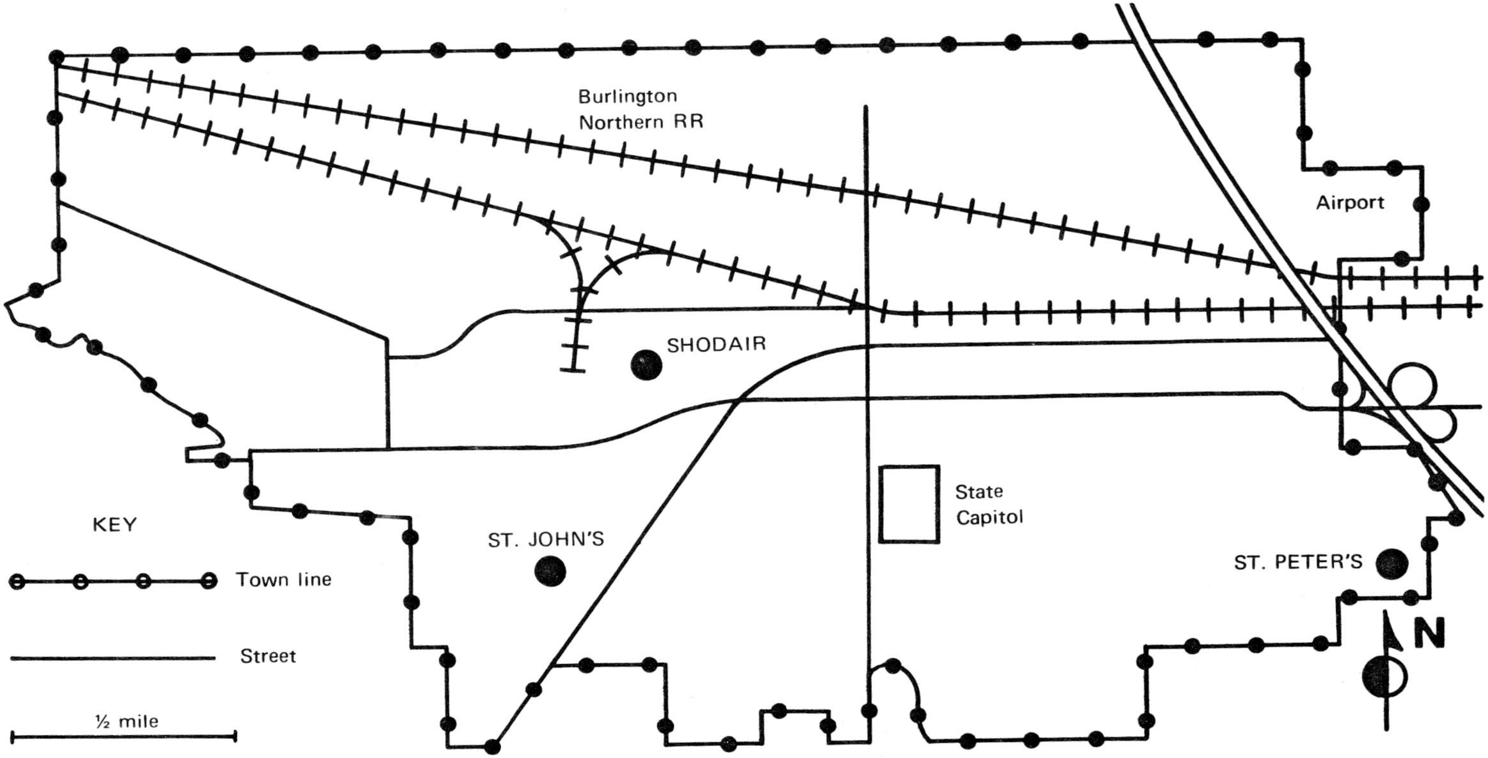

Airport

ST. PETER'S

State
Capitol

Burlington
Northern RR

SHODAIR

ST. JOHN'S

KEY

● Town line

—— Street

|—| ½ mile

ST. JOHN'S HOSPITAL

Exhibit 3

St. John's Hospital
Patient Days, 1966-72

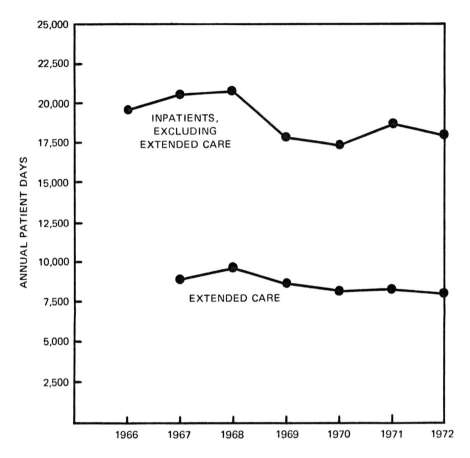

Source: St. John's Hospital records, by fiscal year.

nevertheless offered some competition to the other three Helena area hospitals and thus added to the surplus bedspace problem which these hospitals faced in the 1970s. Specifically, with the exception of the V.A. Hospital, which often had an admissions waiting list, all the hospitals in the Helena area operated at dangerously low occupancy levels in the early 1970s. For instance, in 1971, St. John's average occupancy was 72 percent, St. Peter's average was 64 percent, and Shodair's was only 37 percent. Moreover, in 1972, St. John's average occupancy dropped to just under 58 percent while St. Peter's and Shodair's averages remained close to their 1971 levels. (See Exhibit 6 for various operating statistics on all four hospitals in the greater Helena area.)

DECISIONS—INTRODUCTION

Exhibit 4

Surgeries Performed
at St. John's Hospital

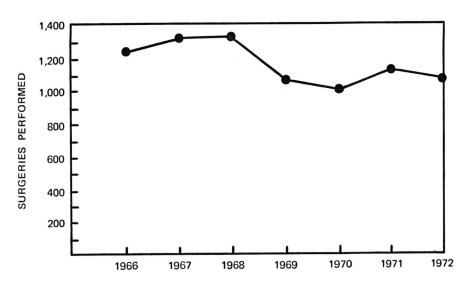

Source: St. John's Hospital records, by fiscal year.

Exhibit 5

Occupancy Rates
at St. John's Hospital

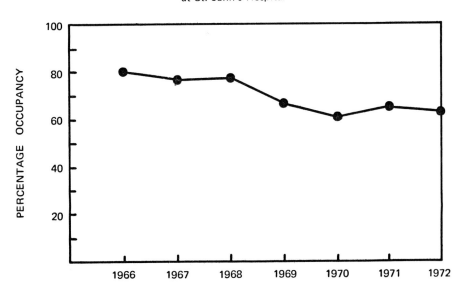

Source: St. John's Hospital records, by fiscal year.

Exhibit 6

Utilization, Employment, and Payroll Data
of Helena Area Hospitals in 1971 and 1972

	St. John's		St. Peter's		Shodair		Vet. Admin.	
	1971	1972	1971	1972	1971	1972	1971	1972
Number of Beds [1]	114	112	111	111	45	32	160	160
Admissions [2]	3064	2950	4147	4278	1119	1115	2240	2315
Average Daily Census [3]	82	65	71	72	15	13	139	139
Percentage Occupancy [4]	71.9	57.5	64.0	64.9	36.6	40.6	86.9	86.9
Personnel [5]	219	218	224	246	77	80	242	250
Payroll Expense (000) [6]	$1273	$1322	$1452	$1485	$ 331	$ 336	$2366	$2624
Total Expense (000) [7]	$2010	$2259	$2684	$2822	$ 517	$ 773	$3501	$3956

[1] As of September 30. Does not include bassinets for newborn infants.

[2] Number of patients accepted for inpatient service during 12-month period ending September 30. Does not include newborn.

[3] Average number of inpatients each day during 12-month period ending September 30. Does not include newborn.

[4] Ratio of census to average number of beds maintained during 12-month period ending September 30.

[5] Excludes trainees, private nurses, and volunteers. Statistic stated as full-time equivalents. According to Sister Macrina, a possible explanation for St. John's having a lower ratio of personnel to patients than St. Peter's lay in the difference between the two hospitals' plants: St. John's had a compact, four-story building while St. Peter's had a rambling, two-level structure with larger distances between departments.

[6] For the fiscal year ending September 30. St. John's paid the Motherhouse a sum equal to the salaries that lay workers would receive if they filled the Sister's positions. These sums are included in the payroll expense totals for St. John's.

[7] For the fiscal year ending September 30.

Note: September 30 does not coincide with the end of St. John's fiscal year.

Source: The AHA Guide to the Health Care Field, 1972 and 1973 editions. Published by the American Hospital Association.

On a national basis, an occupancy rate of 80 to 90 percent was usually considered desirable in the early 1970s although most hospitals also tried to hold some beds open for emergency patients. Thus, by comparison with this standard, there were on an average about 60 excess hospital beds in the greater Helena area in mid-1972. Because of this overbedding, considerable competition existed among the city's three private hospitals. The competition was keenest, however, between St. John's and St. Peter's because of the similar types of services offered by the two institutions. For instance, Sister Macrina observed that: "If one hospital purchased a new piece of equipment, there was often pressure from physicians, patients, and personnel of the other hospital to purchase the same kind of equipment or something better." Helena's physicians were in a particularly strong position vis-a-vis the city's hospitals because they could strongly affect a hospital's financial stability by referring their patients elsewhere. Such gambits enabled these physicians to exert considerable leverage on the policies of all three hospitals in the early 1970s.

ST. JOHN'S PRESENT SITUATION

Competition from other hospitals was only one of the issues confronting Sister Macrina, however. In the spring of 1972, St. John's received the results of a fire and safety survey by the State Department of Health and Environmental Sciences. Among the deficiencies noted in the survey were some requiring extensive renovations of the main building to comply with new fire standards. For example, one of the required renovations was the installation of a fire warning and sprinkler system in the older portion of the building.[3] Although no exact estimates of the cost of all the required renovations had been made by the end of June, it appeared that these costs might well be greater than the value of the hospital sections which were affected.[4] Since the portion of the hospital which required renovation was 35 years old, Sister Macrina questioned the wisdom of making such extensive and expensive renovations. On the other hand, it was difficult to entertain any thoughts of building a separate new facility when about 40 percent of the existing building was less than five years old.

Another issue facing Sister Macrina was the question of whether to renovate St. John's emergency room, which was somewhat outdated and inconveniently located. Like most other hospitals across the country, St. John's had experienced a dramatic increase in demand for outpatient services in recent years. With industry forecasts predicting a continuation of this trend, Sister Macrina was considering the modification of the emergency room and the surgery department to facilitate an increased outpatient workload. To serve as both an outpatient clinic and an emergency room, the existing emergency room would have to be extensively remodeled.[5] On the other hand,

3. The portion affected comprised one third of the total floor space in St. John's main building. See Exhibit 1 for a layout of St. John's physical plant.
4. One of the major reasons for the anticipated high cost of renovations was the fact that St. John's facility had been designed to be earthquake proof when it was constructed in 1935.
5. No estimates of the costs of a new emergency room had been made by October, 1972.

only minor alterations would be required to develop the capability for outpatient surgery within the present surgery department.[6] The new requirement for fire protection safety complicated this type of expansionary planning, however, since both surgery and the emergency room were located in the older portion of the hospital.

Another decision facing Sister Macrina involved the sale of certain buildings and properties owned by the hospital. Specifically, the model cities and urban renewal programs of Helena had been negotiating with the hospital over the purchase of St. John's property west of Warren Street. While the city had appraised the property at $20,000, St. John's lay advisory board believed that it was worth twice that amount and was in the process of obtaining their own appraisal.

In addition, the hospital was considering the sale of Immaculata Hall, which was adjacent to the hospital. In recent years, this building had been used as a residence for the Sisters who served at St. John's, as a meeting hall for the hospital, and for storage. It had also been used to house student nurses up to 1968. Over the last decade, however, its occupancy had decreased to the point where the lay advisory board no longer felt it was economical for the hospital to keep the building.[7] The board considered $85,000 a fair price for the structure together with the former school of nursing [8] and the land immediately adjacent to both buildings. The board also believed that the price would rise to $125,000 if the rest of the block were included in the offer. By the end of October, they had been approached by two interested parties. Nonetheless, even though St. John's could use the cash generated by the sale of these assets, Sister Macrina felt consideration also had to be given to possible future expansion needs of St. John's before a final decision was reached.

Another issue which Sister Macrina discussed with the MPA consultant was the question of the services which should be offered at St. John's. This issue was especially important since one possible answer to the problem of competition in an overbedded community such as Helena would be for the different hospitals to specialize in one or more services. For instance, since there had never been enough demand for maternity services in the greater Helena community for two hospitals to efficiently operate obstetric departments, St. John's had closed its maternity service in 1968 and conceded the entire volume to St. Peter's. Similarly, St. John's elected to close its special pediatric department in order to eliminate the duplication of services

6. No cost estimates for any of these options had been obtained by October, 1972.

7. Including Sister Macrina, only seven Sisters were serving at St. John's in October, 1972.

8. The former School of Nursing building was being used as apartments and shops in 1972, as indicated in Exhibit 1.

when Shodair Children's Hospital's expansion in 1969 enabled it to meet the community's needs for pediatric care. Furthermore, even though St. Peter's continued to operate its pediatric department, its 12-bed ward was generally less than 50 percent occupied and was reportedly operating at a small deficit. Sister Macrina felt that this was a good indication that St. John's should remain out of pediatric services.

The more important question in her opinion, though, was whether St. John's should eliminate other services in areas of duplication or expand their services in areas not adequately covered at present in Helena. For instance, in addition to its general medical-surgical services, St. John's Hospital operated a high quality extended care unit for long-term patients.[9] Althoug the price to the public for these extended care services was almost double that of most nursing homes in the area, many residents of Helena apparently felt that the extra cost was justified by the quality of nursing care available. Moreover, Sister Macrina felt that the fact that the unit was always nearly full and had a sizeable waiting list was further evidence that there was sufficient demand for such a unit.

The possibility of offering some completely new specialty beyond those presently offered by St. John's and the other hospitals in Helena was particularly appealing to Sister Macrina since such services might increase the draw of patients from areas outside Helena. For example, a specialized burn center might attract a large number of patients from the greater Northwest since the nearest existing burn center was in Austin, Texas, and that unit drew patients from the entire western half of the United States. Another possibility was the establishment of a special stroke ward, as there were no other specialty units for stroke patients in Helena at the time. Although the demand for such a facility was difficult to estimate, there were enough stroke victims in the area that local hospital administrators occasionally discussed the possibility of such a unit among themselves. Still another alternative would be to combine a stroke ward with the present extended care facility at St. John's to create a geriatric specialty hospital.[10] Supporting this option was the degree to which St. John's was already involved in service to Medicare patients. Although no statistics had been gathered, it was believed by some of St. John's administrators that the older people of the community generally preferred St. John's Hospital to St. Peter's.

9. Extended care was an intermediate stage for patients who could get along with less extensive nursing care than usually required in a hospital but were not yet independent enough for a nursing home. Consequently the cost for such a unit was below what hospitals would normally charge and greater than what nursing homes typically charged. A majority of St. John's extended care cases came from Helena itself.

10. A hospital for the aged.

There were, of course, other ways in which St. John's might specialize such as becoming a rehabilitation hospital [11] or a self-care nursing facility,[12] both of which had been mentioned by Helena health officials as areas requiring consideration. No studies of the demand for such facilities in Helena had ever been made, though. Moreover, any such alternative would have to be considered in light of the potential difficulty of bringing a specialty medical staff to this remote community in west-central Montana. Thus, while some doctors in the Helena area believed that remoteness would not be a factor as long as the patient demand was there, others felt that the long, hard winters would be a deterrent to an influx of specialized physicians. In summary, one of the big questions for St. John's involved the kinds of services it should offer in order to best meet the needs of the community. (See Exhibit 7 for a listing of the services offered by Helena's three private hospitals in 1972).

The most drastic response to the problem of competition would be for St. John's to close its doors. Even though such an idea was unpalatable to a large number of the hospital employees and also to many people in the area, it was generally conceded that a 50-bed addition to St. Peter's Hospital could handle the present patient-load at St. John's with the exception of the extended-care patients.[13] Furthermore, such a move might provide a significant reduction in cost to the community since ancillary services, such as the X-ray units, the laboratory, and surgery, were not being fully utilized at either hospital.[14] Thus, while the purpose of the MPA study was to assist in long-range planning for St. John's, Sister Macrina felt that the needs of the Helena community were probably the most important factor to be considered in the study. Consequently, she believed the possibility of closing operations altogether had to be considered as a realistic alternative.

FINANCIAL AND OTHER CONSIDERATIONS

In 1972, St. John's Hospital was considered to be financially sound. Like most not-for-profit hospitals, the cost-revenue picture

11. A hospital that provides coordinated multidisciplinary physical and restorative services rather than treatment of acute illnesses.

12. A facility for ambulatory patients who need minimal nursing care but must remain hospitalized.

13. Construction costs per bed for new hospitals averaged between $20,000 and $30,000 in 1972.

14. Both St. John's and St. Peter's were self-sufficient in laboratory services. Shodair, although smaller, was also adequate for all of the hospital's normal tests. The VA hospital contracted with St. John's for some lab services, but these were also available and underutilized at St. Peters.

Exhibit 7

Hospital Services Available
in Helena (September, 1972)

Service [1]	St. John's	St. Peter's	Shodair	V.A.
Postoperative Recovery Room	X	X	X	X
Intensive Care Unit	X	X		
Pharmacy	X	X	X	X
X-Ray Therapy		X		
Cobalt Therapy		X		
Radium Therapy		X		
Diagnostic Radioisotope		X		
Therapeutic Radioisotope		X		
Histopathology Laboratory	X	X		X
Blood Bank	X	X		X
Inhalation Therapy	X	X	X	
Extended Care Unit	X			
Inpatient Renal Dialysis		X		
Outpatient Renal Dialysis		X		
Physical Therapy	X	X	X	X
Clinical Psychologist			X	
Outpatient Department				X
Emergency Department	X	X	X	X
Social Work Department	X		X	X
Genetic Counselling		X		
Inpatient Abortions		X		
Dental Department	X			X
Speech Therapy	X		X	
Hospital Auxiliary	X		X	
Volunteer Services	X			X

[1] Services are defined in the American Hospital Association's *Uniform Hospital Definition*.
Source: The 1973 AHA Guide to the Health Care Field.

showed the hospital to be operating close to its break-even point. Since charitable contributions for St. John's, as well as for most other area hospitals, had declined to an insignificant level in recent years, operating losses in any particular year had to be balanced by gains in other years. During the past three years, St. John's had averaged an annual net loss of 0.18 percent on annual revenues which averaged $2.1 million.[15] (See Exhibits 8 and 9 for St. John's income statements and balance sheets.)

Many of the other factors which needed to be considered in any long-range plan were social, political, and economic in origin. One of

15. According to figures compiled for the Internal Revenue Service.

Exhibit 8

St. John's Hospital
Income Statements
(1967–1972)

	1967	1968	1969	1970	1971	1972
REVENUES:						
Revenues from patients						
Daily patient care	$ 785,299	$ 879,177	$1,019,526	$1,090,527	$1,260,093	$1,290,043
Departmental services	598,258	691,037	759,408	797,573	938,959	1,077,428
Gross patient revenues	$1,383,557	$1,570,214	$1,778,934	$1,888,100	$2,199,052	$2,367,471
Deductions from gross revenues						
Provision for uncollectibles	$ 84,125	$ 63,461	$ 79,937	$ 87,984	$ 85,627	$ 57,314
Contractual discounts and other adjustments[1]	67,640	32,078	16,479	23,835	89,857	79,400
Total deductions from gross revenues	173,571	106,073	101,053	114,117	175,484	$ 136,714
Revenues from patients	$1,209,986	$1,464,141	$1,677,881	$1,773,983	$2,023,568	$2,230,757
Cafeteria and recovery of expenses	59,938	53,985	52,615	51,840	52,091	50,813
Grants	8,713	24,930	13,162	9,853		
Total operating revenues	$1,278,637	$1,543,056	$1,743,658	$1,835,676	$2,075,659	$2,281,570

ST. JOHN'S HOSPITAL

EXPENSES:

Salaries and wages	$ 749,176	$ 966,192	$1,085,109	$1,197,130	$1,321,761
Supplies and expenses	430,455	532,951	575,741	636,745	829,607
Depreciation	59,945	107,975	113,870	83,466	107,464
Total operating expenses	$1,239,576	$1,607,118	$1,774,720	$2,061,896	$2,258,832
Net revenue from operations	$ 39,061	$ (64,062)	$ (30,062)	$ (81,665)	$ 22,738
NONOPERATING REVENUE:					
Interest income	$ 0	$ 4,679	$ 4,970	$ 18,552	$ 6,871
Net revenues	$ 39,061	$ (59,383)	$ (25,092)	$ (63,113)	$ 30,665

[1] Discounts from St. John's standard rates resulted from contractual agreements with commercial insurers and nonprofit third-party payers and from differences between full costs and allowable costs for Medicare reimbursements. The treatment of such deductions was consistent with accepted hospital accounting procedures.
Source: St. John's Hospital annual audits, 1968–1972.

the most important of these was the national health insurance legislation which was pending in Congress. Because of the many and varied packages which Congress was considering, it was extremely difficult to anticipate the scope, form or type of national health insurance that might ultimately be adopted. Yet, because of the tremendous impact which any resulting legislation might have on the health care system, it was difficult to ignore the issue. For instance, an increase in the government's involvement in health care seemed sure to entail more control over how federal funds were to be spent. Regardless of the form of any legislation adopted, one likely target for such government control would be the area of hospital planning. Thus, it was quite possible that the future directions open to St. John's after the enactment of such legislation might be determined by some regional public planning agency rather than by the hospital. On the other hand, Sister Macrina felt she would have to make a decision about St. John's scope of operations within the next six months. Even if this were done before any legislation was passed, however, an unwise choice might restrict the amount of federal revenues the hospital could receive in the future.

Further complications were created by the federal government's wage-price freeze and subsequent Phase II requirements. St. John's had been in need of a small price increase to cover operating losses when price controls had been imposed in August, 1972. Phase II, however, negated practically any plans for an increase in prices. This was particularly critical since extensive renovations of any buildings or expansion of any services would require far greater financial reserves than St. John's had available in October, 1972.

Other variables which the MPA consultants would have to take into consideration in developing their recommendations were the demographic trends of the greater Helena area, possible changes in the region's ratio of population to hospital beds, and the availability of medical personnel in the community.

Overall, the population of Helena was projected to grow by 13 percent [1973] [16] to 32 percent [1970] between 1970 and 1980, depending on the assumptions made with respect to birth and death rates and migration trends.[17] Under the same assumptions, the population of Lewis and Clark county as a whole was forecast to grow by 19 percent [1973] to 27 percent [1970] during the same period. (See Exhibits 10 and 11 for more detailed demographic data for the

16. The numbers within the bracket refer to the date of the forecast.
17. Both birth and death rates were, in turn, influenced by several other variables. Birth rates, for example, were dependent on the age distribution of the population, and net rate of family formation, the average family size, and the percentage of out-of-wedlock births. Death rates were primarily influenced by the age distribution of the population and the age conditional mortality rates for the area in question.

Exhibit 10

Population Records and Projections
Lewis and Clark County, Montana

	Actual				Projected	
	1960	1964	1968	1970	1975	1980
City of Helena	20,227	23,000	24,395	25,850	29,750	34,200
Rest of County	7,779	not available		8,014	none made	8,900
Total County	28,006	not available		33,864	none made	43,100

Sources: 1960 and 1970 actual: U.S. Census
1964 and 1968 actual: Lewis & Clark County records
1975 and 1980 projections: 1970 Lewis & Clark County forecasts

Exhibit 11

Population Age Distribution
for Lewis and Clark County, Montana

	Actual				Projected	
	1960		1970		1980	
Age	Male	Female	Male	Female	Male	Female
0–9	3099	2959	3203	3049	3940	3776
10–19	2321	2574	3392	3574	3494	3689
20–29	1428	1592	1976	2294	2905	3184
30–39	1754	1794	1802	1848	2502	2664
40–49	1761	1874	1858	1933	1913	1994
50–59	1481	1379	1762	1919	1853	1981
60–69	1077	1100	1182	1284	1407	1786
70–79	620	723	657	835	731	982
80+	184	276	260	453	350	515
Total	13,725	14,271	16,092	17,189	19,095	20,571

Assumptions: Continued 1960–1970 migration trends

Source: Information Systems Bureau, Department of Intergovernmental Relations, U.S. Government, 1973

greater Helena area). The factor primarily responsible for the differences between the 1970 and 1973 forecasts was the rapid drop that occurred in average family size in the early 1970s. During this same interval, there were also some changes in national migration trends. Most demographers felt that Helena was not likely to benefit from the latter trends, however, because the poor rail and road transportation through the area did not encourage a buildup of industry in that part of the state, especially since other nearby cities such as Great Falls and Bozeman had excellent transportation networks.

Under almost all sets of assumptions, though, the number of persons over 60 was forecast to increase at a rate more than 20 percent higher than that for the area's population as a whole. Thus, if past illness ratios and the medical procedures associated with them remained unchanged, the demand for geriatric services in the area would increase by 23 percent or more by 1980.

At the same time, the population-to-hospital-bed ratio for Helena in 1972 was substantially higher than the nationwide median of 3.5 beds per 1,000 persons. The latter statistic could only be regarded as a ball-park figure, however, since it varied widely among different communities according to their locations. For instance, Alabama had a ratio of 2.5/1,000 in 1970, while North Dakota had a ratio of 4.6/1,000 the same year. (See Exhibit 12 for a listing of hospital-bed ratios by state for 1950 and 1960.) Among the factors which could influence this ratio were the age and wealth of the area's population, the degree to which outpatient facilities were used, and the geographic characteristics of the area. In the latter regard, St. John's received some of its patients from the outlying areas of Lewis and Clark County, as well as approximately 13 percent of its caseload from outside the county.[18]

In terms of availability of medical personnel, there was only a moderate increase in the number of physicians in the greater Helena area between 1964 and 1972, as indicated in Exhibit 13. There was, however, a noticeable trend away from general practice and general surgery toward more specialized fields of medicine. In addition, there was a general shortage of nursing personnel in the area—a condition which had been aggravated by the closing of St. John's nursing school in 1968.

A final, but important set of considerations in any decision on St. John's future were the goals of the Mother House of the Sisters of Charity. In the past, the policy of the Sisterhood had been to concentrate on providing general acute care through community-based hospitals in any community they entered. Once in a community, though, they adapted their facilities to the overall medical needs of the community insofar as those needs were unmet by other organizations and were within the financial resources of the Sisterhood. Given the range of services offered by St. Peter's and Shodair, Sister Macrina felt that the Mother House might not approve a plan for a major modification in St. John's mission unless she could demonstrate that such modifications were required to meet some aspects of the community's medical needs that St. Peter's or Shodair would not be able to provide, or that the costs of such modifications would be

18. In 1972, St. John's admissions were distributed among three geographic sources: 86.9% from Lewis and Clark county, 11.4% from adjoining counties and 1.7% from other areas.

low, or that the necessary capital could be raised in the community or repaid relatively quickly.

As she described St. John's situation to the MPA consultants, Sister Macrina reflected on the fact that the factors influencing long-range planning at St. John's were numerous and difficult to assess. Nonetheless, long-range objectives and policies would have to be made in order to give some direction to the hospital's future operations. Thus, the major question facing Sister Macrina and the MPA consultants was: "What should these objectives and policies be?"

Exhibit 12

Bed-Population Ratios, By State
1950 and 1960

Beds per 1000 Population

State Area	1950	1960	State Area	1950	1960
Alabama	1.9	2.5	Nebraska	4.0	3.9
Arizona	3.3	2.5	Nevada	4.1	3.3
Arkansas	1.8	2.7	New Hampshire	3.9	3.7
California	3.6	3.0	New Jersey	2.9	2.9
Colorado	3.7	3.8	New Mexico	2.7	2.6
Connecticut	3.3	3.4	New York	3.5	3.6
Delaware	3.1	2.9	North Carolina	2.5	2.8
D.C.–Md.–Va.	3.5	3.3	North Dakota	3.9	4.6
Florida	2.5	2.7	Ohio	3.1	3.3
Georgia	2.2	3.0	Oklahoma	3.0	3.6
Idaho	3.0	2.8	Oregon	3.5	3.1
Illinois	3.7	3.8	Pennsylvania	3.2	3.7
Indiana	3.2	3.3	Rhode Island	3.1	3.6
Iowa	3.9	3.7	South Carolina	2.7	3.2
Kansas	3.7	3.7	South Dakota	3.9	3.8
Kentucky	2.1	3.1	Tennessee	2.1	2.8
Louisiana	2.5	2.8	Texas	2.8	3.1
Maine	3.1	3.8	Utah	2.5	2.8
Massachusetts	3.9	3.7	Vermont	4.0	4.1
Michigan	2.7	3.1	Washington	3.4	3.2
Minnesota	3.9	4.0	West Virginia	2.7	4.0
Mississippi	1.7	2.6	Wisconsin	3.6	4.1
Missouri	3.1	3.6	Wyoming	3.4	4.1
Montana	4.0	4.3			

Source: American Hospital Association

Exhibit 13
Physicians and Dentists Serving
on Staffs of Helena Hospitals

	1964	1968	1971	1972
Physicians				
Age category				
30–39		10	9	11
40–49		19	20	20
50–59		10	9	9
60 & over		4	5	6
Classification				
Active	32	40	36	41
Courtesy	10	3	7	4
Inactive	0	0	3	0
Privileges				
Anesthesiology		2	2	2
Dermatology		0	1	1
Eye, Ear, Nose, & Throat		1	2	2
General Practice		19	15	12
General Surgery		9	7	4
Internal Medicine		5	4	5
Neurology		0	0	1
OB Gynecology		2	2	2
Opthamology		1	3	4
Orthopedics		2	2	3
Pathology		1	1	3
Pediatrics		4	4	4
Radiology		2	3	4
Urology		0	1	1
Total Physicians on Hospital Staffs	42	43	43	46
Dentists				
Age Category				
30–39		6	6	2
40–49		4	4	3
50–59		1	0	3
60 & over		3	4	1
Classification				
Active	0	0	0	0
Courtesy	2	14	14	9
Inactive	0	0	0	0
Total Dentists on Hospital Staffs	2	14	14	9
Total Physicians & Dentists on	44	57	57	55
Hospital Staffs				

Source: St. John's Hospital records

Mileage Contract Tires

The Heavy Tread Tire and Rubber Company of Dayton, Ohio, has made a practice for some years of leasing tires to large trucking companies on a mileage-contract basis. For a certain rental charge per tire per mile, the Heavy Tread Tire and Rubber Company guarantees to keep good tires on as many trucks of the client as desired. At the present rate charged per mile, however, the company finds that it is consistently losing money.

When top management became aware of the magnitude of this problem, as will be noted in Exhibit 2, they directed an urgent question to the controller of the company as follows: "What will we have to do for the Mileage Contract Program to return 6.9 percent on our investment?"

The controller turned this question over to his Economic Analysis Section which prepared the following four exhibits as a means of analyzing the problem, as well as suggesting a solution. The alternatives available seemed to be to increase the rate charged per mile, improve the quality of the tire, or a combination of these two factors.

As the first step in finding a solution to this problem, the classification of the fixed and variable expenses in this operation were studied. (See Exhibit 1.) It was determined that $28,444 worth of service salaries were in reality fixed and would be present whether the company was in the business of leasing tires or not. These salaries were therefore transferred to "office salaries" and recognized as fixed expenses.

Exhibit 2 analyzes the effect of proposed changes in the rate per mile without any variation in the quality of the tire. From this, it would appear that if the rate were increased 34.9 percent to $.02172, without changing the cost, the rate of return on investment would be approximately 6.9 percent. Cash and accounts receivable would go up slightly, but fixed investments and inventory value remain the same.

Reproduced with permission of Professor Robert S. Wesley, University of Colorado.

Exhibit 3 assumes different percentage amounts of improvement in the wearing quality of the tire with no increases in cost. It is recommended that the wearing quality or performance of the tires would have to be improved by 76 percent. This means that the mileage received from the tires would be 176 percent of the present mileage which, in turn, would mean that the cost of goods sold in relation to the sales would decrease. Cost of goods sold in 1964 was 95.8 percent of sales, while with the proposed 76 percent improvement in performance of the tires, the percentage is 64.39 percent. The net result of this improvement would be a 7.0 percent return on investment. The total dollar investment would remain approximately the same, with the exception of the inventory which would increase slightly due to its having a greater value at any point in time because of the improvement in wearing quality of the tire.

Exhibit 4 was prepared by utilizing linear computer programming. The objective to be optimized was the return on investment of 6.9 percent which was required by top management. The available alternatives were: (1) increases in the rate per mile; and (2) improvement in the wearing quality of the tire. Various possible combinations of product improvement and increases in the rate per mile are explored, all of which produce the objective of a 6.9 percent return on the investment. The controller recommended a 5 percent rate increase, along with a 64 percent improvement in the quality of the tire, but it is top management that must determine the most feasible alternative.

DISCUSSION QUESTIONS

1. Why did the controller make the recommendation which he did?
2. Explain fully the figures in Exhibits 1, 2, 3, and 4. What are the numerical relationships between changes in price and the items which appear in Exhibit 2? What are the numerical relationships in Exhibit 3 regarding quality improvement? In Exhibit 3, derive the figures that would result in a 6.9 percent to 7.0 percent return on investment after taxes.
3. Construct a computer program which will reproduce Exhibit 4. Assume that price is inflexible downward from $.01609. Compute the combinations which fall between 6.8 percent and 7.0 percent by varying price and quality one percent at a time up through 100 percent.
4. When the decision maker receives the computer output listing of all of the combinations possible under the stated constraints, what questions are relevant to the ultimate selection of a combination?

Exhibit 1

Heavy Tread Tire and Rubber Company
Revised Variable and Fixed Expenses

	Fiscal 1964 Present Books	Revised
Variable Expense:		
Commissions	$ 7,384	$ 7,384
Service salaries	89,695	61,251
Sales tax	10,861	10,861
FICA tax	2,607	2,607
Total	$110,547	$ 82,103
Fixed Expense:		
Office salaries	1,053	29,497
Depreciation—Equipment	1,621	1,621
Freight charges	7,120	7,120
Equipment (new and repair)	2,818	2,818
Truck and car rental	15,008	15,008
Travel expense	1,890	1,890
Repairs—Discount tires	2,697	2,697
Insurance	568	568
Miscellaneous expenses	1,480	1,480
Total	$ 34,255	$ 62,699
Total Operating Costs	$144,802	$144,802

Exhibit 2

Heavy Tread Tire and Rubber Company

Analysis Using Various Degrees of Rate Increase

Without Product Improvement

	1964 Fiscal	$.0170	$.0180	$.0190	$.0200	$.0210	$.0217	$.0220
Rate/mile	$.01609	$.0170	$.0180	$.0190	$.0200	$.0210	$.0217	$.0220
Sales	700,618	740,243	783,787	827,330	870,874	914,418	945,760	957,961
Cost of goods	670,582	670,582	670,582	670,582	670,582	670,582	670,582	670,582
Gross profit	30,036	69,661	113,205	156,748	200,292	243,836	275,178	287,379
Variable expenses ...	82,103	84,388	89,352	94,316	99,280	104,244	107,816	109,208
Gross contribution ..	(52,067)	(14,727)	23,853	62,432	101,012	139,592	167,362	178,171
Fixed expenses	62,699	62,699	62,699	62,699	62,699	62,699	62,699	62,699
Net profit B. T.	(114,766)	(77,426)	(38,846)	(267)	38,313	76,893	104,663	115,472
Taxes					19,156	38,446	52,331	57,736
Net profit A. T.					19,157	38,447	52,332	57,736
Percent to sales ...					2.20	4.20	5.53	6.03
Return on investment A. T.	(15.49%)	(10.42%)	(5.20%)	(00.03%)	2.55%	5.09%	6.91	7.61%
Total mileage	43,543,695	43,543,695	43,543,695	43,543,695	43,543,695	43,543,695	43,543,695	43,543,695
Investment								
Current								
Cash	$ 9,646	$ 10,196	$ 10,797	$ 11,396	$ 11,996	$ 12,595	$ 13,027	$ 13,196
Accounts receivable .	38,950	41,139	43,559	45,979	48,399	50,819	52,561	53,239
Inventory	679,104	679,104	679,104	679,104	679,104	679,104	679,104	679,104
Total	$727,700	$730,439	$733,460	$736,479	$739,499	$742,518	$744,692	$745,539
Fixed								
Equipment	12,914	12,914	12,914	12,914	12,914	12,914	12,914	12,914
Total all investment	$740,614	$743,353	$746,374	$749,393	$752,413	$755,432	$757,606	$758,453

Exhibit 3

Heavy Tread Tire and Rubber Company

Analysis Using Various Degrees of Product Improvement

Percent Improvement	1964 Fiscal	10%	25%	50%	70%	72%	75%	100%
Sales	$700,618	$700,618	$700,618	$700,618	$700,618	$700,618	$700,618	$700,618
Cost of goods	670,582	641,747	598,427	526,206	468,469	462,702	454,051	381,896
Gross profit	30,036	58,871	102,191	174,412	232,149	237,916	246,567	318,722
Variable expenses	82,103	82,103	82,103	82,103	82,103	82,103	82,103	82,103
Gross contribution	(52,067)	(23,232)	20,088	92,309	150,046	155,813	164,464	236,619
Fixed expenses	62,699	62,699	62,699	62,699	62,699	62,699	62,699	62,699
Net profit B. T.	(114,766)	(85,931)	(42,611)	29,610	87,347	93,114	101,765	173,920
Taxes 50%				14,805	43,673	46,557	50,882	86,960
Net profit A. T.	—	—	—	14,805	43,674	46,557	50,883	86,960
Percent to sales	—	—	—	2.1%	6.23%	6.65%	7.26%	12.4%
Breakdown sales	—	—	—					
Return on investment A. T.	(15.49%)	(11.6%)	(5.74%)	1.99%	5.85%	6.24%	6.81%	11.6%
Total mileage	43,543,695	43,543,695	43,543,695	43,543,695	43,543,695	43,543,695	43,543,695	43,543,695
Investment								
Current								
Cash	$ 9,646	$ 9,646	$ 9,646	$ 9,646	$ 9,646	$ 9,646	$ 9,646	$ 9,646
Accounts receivable	38,950	38,950	38,950	38,950	38,950	38,950	38,950	38,950
Inventory	679,104	679,931	681,171	683,238	684,891	685,056	685,304	687,371
Total	$727,700	$728,527	$729,767	$731,834	$733,487	$733,652	$733,900	$735,967
Fixed equipment	12,914	12,914	12,914	12,914	12,914	12,914	12,914	12,914
Total all investment	$740,614	$741,441	$742,681	$744,748	$746,401	$746,566	$746,814	$748,881

Exhibit 4
Heavy Tread Tire and Rubber Company
Analysis Showing Both Rate Increase and Product Improvement

Product Improvement Rate Increase	Fiscal 1964	17% 27%	23% 24%	32% 20%	41% 16%	49% 12%	64% 5%	73% 1%
Rate/Mile	$ .01609	$ .02043	$ .01995	$ .01931	$ .01866	$ .01802	$ .01689	$ .01625
Sales	700,618	889,784	868,766	840,741	812,716	784,692	735,648	707,624
Cost of goods	670,582	621,505	604,184	578,202	552,220	529,126	485,823	459,841
Gross profit	30,036	268,279	264,582	262,539	260,496	255,566	249,825	247,783
Variable expense	82,103	101,435	99,039	95,844	92,649	89,454	83,863	80,669
Gross contribution	(52,067)	166,844	165,543	166,695	167,847	166,112	165,962	167,114
Fixed expenses	62,699	62,699	62,699	62,699	62,699	62,699	62,699	62,699
Net profit B. T.	(114,766)	104,145	102,844	103,996	105,148	103,413	103,263	104,415
Taxes 50%		52,072	51,422	51,998	52,574	51,706	51,631	52,207
Net profit A. T.	—	52,073	51,422	51,998	52,574	51,707	51,632	52,208
Percent to sales	—	5.852%	5.919%	6.185%	6.469%	6.589%	7.018%	7.378%
Breakdown sales	—							
Return on investment A. T.	(15.49%)	6.896%	6.818%	6.906%	6.993%	6.890%	6.900%	6.988%
Total mileage	43,543,695	43,543,695	43,543,696	43,543,695	43,543,695	43,543,695	43,543,695	43,543,695

Investment

Current								
Cash	$ 9,646	$ 12,254	$ 11,965	$ 11,579	$ 11,193	$ 10,807	$ 10,132	$ 9,746
Accounts receivable	38,950	49,449	48,281	46,724	45,166	43,609	40,883	39,326
Inventory	679,104	680,509	681,005	681,749	682,493	683,154	684,394	685,138
Total	$727,700	$742,212	$741,251	$740,052	$738,852	$737,570	$735,409	$734,210
Fixed equipment	12,914	12,914	12,914	12,914	12,914	12,914	12,914	12,914
Total all investment	$740,614	$755,126	$754,165	$752,966	$751,766	$750,484	$748,323	$747,124

Part Two

Decisions Involving Control

Modern Steel, Incorporated

At 8:05 a.m., Greg Garth, superintendent, and Donna Harp, assistant superintendent, made a surprise tour through the offices of the process control section for a quick inspection of the two main offices and the adjoining office trailer. Only Milt Sharp, Stan Frame, and the two secretaries were present from the full complement of 21 employees.

PROBLEM OF EMPLOYEE TARDINESS

Earlier that morning, Greg Garth, Donna Harp, and four other assistant superintendents were gathered for their usual morning meeting. It was standard procedure for Greg and his assistants to review the previous night's electrical delays the first thing in the morning. However, this sunny Friday morning in July was different.

Greg Garth: Donna, how are your troopers today?
Donna Harp: Fine, I guess. All set for a day with their electronic wonders.
Greg Garth: Sure, I'll bet you a cup of coffee that there isn't a half dozen of your computer buffs ready for work.
Donna Harp: You're on, Greg!
Greg Garth: Let's go, Donna. This is one cup of coffee you're not going to forget.

The situation had been building for some months, and Greg had been aware of the tardiness problem for some time. Now he finally had reached the boiling point. This morning at 7:55, he saw only one car in the process control parking lot and he was determined to do something about it.

On the way back to his office, Greg said to Donna, "I want to see you, Larry Cart, and Jean Lark in my office at nine, sharp! Now we have to look at the delays."

Background

The electrical department is a service department of a large eastern steel company. The department supervises the electrical maintenance and service for the entire plant. There are five assistant superintendents who are responsible for five different areas of production (see Exhibit 1).

Any delay in production that is related to an electrical failure is charged to the electrical department. The primary function of the department is to keep electrical delays to a minimum by proper maintenance and repair. Secondary functions include overseeing the electrical aspects of new installations and updating obsolete or defective equipment.

Each morning the electrical sections located in the production mills must report the electrical delays and breakdowns, if any, to the electrical department. The superintendent and assistants review the delays and report production critical data to higher management.

The process control section is a relatively new group in the electrical department. It was created in 1968 when management decided that a specialized group was required to maintain the computers installed in the plant. The new section consisted of eight personnel, two supervising engineers and six engineers. Their responsibility was four process computers operating in different production areas.

By July the section had expanded to three supervising engineers and sixteen engineers (see Exhibit 2). Donna Harp was the assistant superintendent in charge of the section from the beginning. The work load increased, and by this time there was a total of 20 process computers scattered throughout the plant. The section was involved with updating the computer programs and maintaining as well as specifying computers for new facilities.

The engineers in the process control section were all college graduates of various fields. They were on full salary and subject to call when the computers developed problems. It was not uncommon to have 10-to-12-hour-days and 50-to-60-hour weeks (see Exhibit 3). As a result, the employees did not feel obligated to be at their desk at 8:00 sharp. This was a constant sore spot with the superintendent and assistant superintendent. Every few months, a crackdown on starting at 8:00 would ensue.

Meeting

However, this July morning was different. It was the first time the superintendent called the process control supervisors in for an explanation. Before this, the control was exercised through Donna Harp, the assistant superintendent in charge of the section.

9:00 a.m.—Superintendent's office

Greg Garth: Larry, what do you have to say about your people this morning? No rain, snow, or accidents on the expressway?

Larry Cart (supervising engineer, process control): My people work hard. In this type of work, you can't turn them on at eight and shut them off at five like a switch. Sure, they might not be here at eight, but they do put

Exhibit 1

Electrical Department

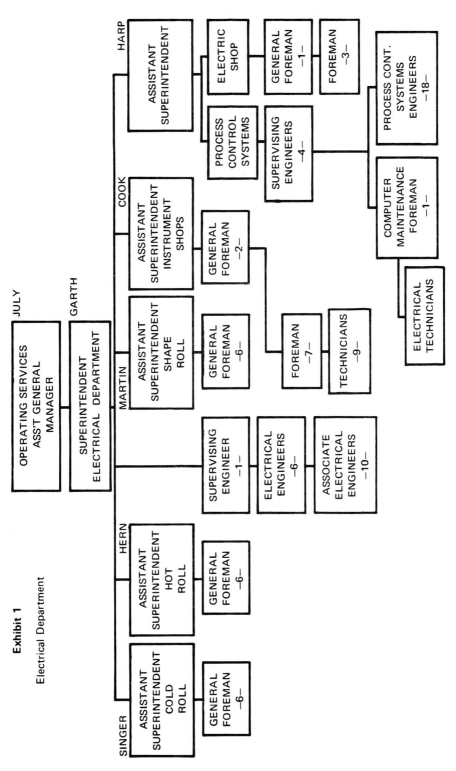

Exhibit 2

Process Control Section

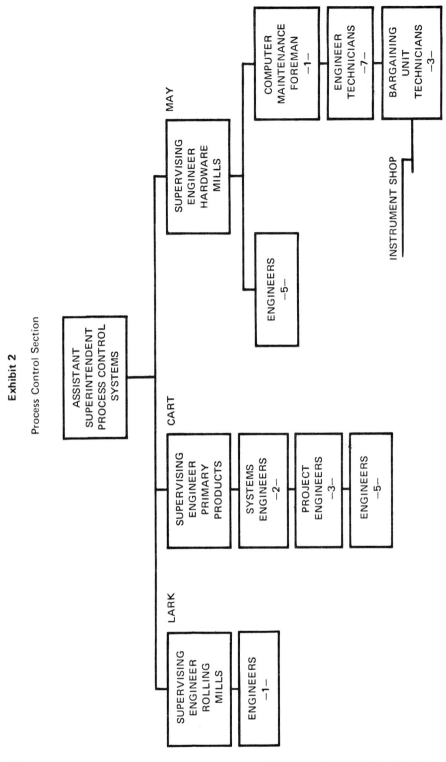

Exhibit 3
Process Control Actual Hours
Week Starting

NAME	5/27	6/3	6/10	6/17	6/24	7/1	7/8	7/15	7/22	7/29	8/5	8/12	8/19	8/26	9/2	9/9	Actual Hours Worked	Vacation Hours	Sick Hours	Personal Hours	Total Hours	Time Coming Claimed Hours	±Norm
L. Cart	37	48	58	43	40	32	47	40	40	46	53	40	47	38	37	37	683	8	—	—	691	4	+43
J. Lark	S	S	S	S	S	S	S	20	20	40	40	40	40	16	32	40	288	—	288	—	576	—	−74
J. May	32	38	V	52	32	26	42	40	32	40	37	48	42	40	32	52	595	40	—	20	655	24	+7
S. Arthur	32	32	40	40	40	32	16	V	24	40	38	40	40	40	40	40	534	80	—	8	622	—	−26
S. Frame	40	40	41	32	42	33	40	40	49	44	42	36	V	V	40	32	551	80	—	—	631	16	−17
A. Fortune	32	40	V	40	49	24	40	40	52	40	51	32	40	38	40	42	600	40	8	—	648	16	0
T. Flavin	32	40	37	48	44	38	53	44	V	45	40	48	38	32	V	48	587	80	—	2	669	16	+21
R. Gold	32	40	24	40	29	55	40	52	46	40	42	V	V	40	32	48	560	80	16	11	667	4	+19
A. Hurst	32	40	40	40	32	V	40	40	40	48	40	48	40	40	32	48	600	40	—	—	640	8	+8
G. Jankowitz	32	49	54	40	40	40	40	28	48	41	41	38	40	51	28	47	617	48	—	—	665	8	+17
R. Porter	V	32	40	47	40	V	V	48	38	44	16	40	35	V	24	40	444	160	32	—	632	8	−16
E. Swan	32	48	40	8	40	32	V	V	40	40	41	48	V	V	32	40	481	160	32	—	633	—	−15
C. Todd	40	40	45	40	40	40	40	40	40	40	40	40	40	40	40	40	549	80	—	—	629	—	−19
G. Verdi	41	28	V	40	48	V	40	53	53	40	40	32	48	44	32	40	587	88	—	—	675	8	+27
S. Noble	35	32	40	38	40	48	48	40	40	40	40	48	40	37	32	40	616	8	8	4	636	—	−12
T. Eliot	32	40	40	40	40	V	V	V	V	V	32	V	40	40	37	48	395	240	—	—	635	8	−13
D. Packer	32	40	40	40	40	32	35	—	—	—	—	—	—	—	—	—	259	0	—	—	259	—	+11
M. Sharp	—	—	—	—	—	40	48	40	40	40	40	40	40	40	V	32	400	40	—	—	440	—	−80
J. Caster	32	40	40	48	48	32	48	48	44	36	37	V	V	48	32	44	577	80	—	8	665	4	+17
Norm (42 Hr/Wk less Holidays)	32	40	40	48	40	32	40	48	40	40	40	48	40	40	32	48							+34

Holiday Week

→160 → 160 → 168 → 160

Norm Total
Hours 42 Hr/Wk
Less Holidays

S = Sick
V = Vacation

Total Hrs = (Act.hrs) + (Vac.hrs) + (Sick) + (Personal)

±Norm = (Tot.hrs) − 648

648

their time in plus more. It is not uncommon for them to be here until six or seven at night, not to mention being called to work at all hours of the night.

Greg Garth: I've been through that same argument with Donna before. This department works from eight to five. If there is a computer delay to explain to the general manager, I need facts that only you or your people can give me, and that is at 8:00, not 8:30 or 9:00.

Jean Lark: Sure, all the employees don't get here at eight, but you don't see a mass exodus at five either. These are dedicated people; they do not need to be regimented. They consider themselves to be professionals.

Reaction

After the 9:00 meeting, Larry Cart and Jean Lark returned to the process control offices. The engineers were gathered in groups waiting for some word of what was happening. As they arrived at work that morning, each person was clued of the 8:00 "bed check," as some called it.

Tex Flavin (engineer): If he wants us here at eight, fine. Then I'm leaving at five, and not one minute after.

Stu Noble (engineer): Let him make us punch a clock if he wants. He'll get his eight to five, 40 hours of time, but not work.

Larry Cart was talking to several employees, Robb Gold, Ernestine Swan, and Clarice Todd. "Greg is really mad, and this time he means business. In fact, I don't think he will hesitate about firing somebody just to set an example."

At 5:15 that afternoon, Glenna, Ernestine, Stu, and Jake were talking about the day's events at the coffee machine when Greg Garth and Donna Harp made another visit to the offices.

Ernestine and Stu: Hi Greg, Donna!
Greg: Hi!
Donna: Hi, Stu, Ernestine, Jake . . . Glenna.
Ernestine: Greg, you just missed me this morning. You should have been here five minutes later.
Greg: Yeah.
Noble (stepping out of his office): You should have been here yesterday at 7:30 in the morning. I was here then.
Greg and Donna left immediately.
Ernestine: Do you believe that they actually came down to see if anybody was here after five?

RESULTS

The following week all but one or two arrived after 8:00. But the same was true at 5:00. All were gone except Larry Cart and one engineer. Don Packer made one of the many remarks about time, "It's boring watching the clock for those last few minutes before five."

On August 1, Greg reorganized the area responsibilities of the assistant superintendents (see Exhibit 4). Ralph Hern was now in charge of the process control section. No new policies or rules ensued from the eight o'clock roll call in mid July. After several more weeks, the engineers in the group returned to their old hours of work.

Exhibit 4

Electrical Dept. Areas of Responsibility

Prior to August	After August
Greg Garth—Superintendent	Greg Garth—Superintendent
Roy Singer—Cold Roll Products	Roy Singer—Cold Roll Products
Jeff Martin—Shape Roll +	Donna Harp—Shape Roll +
Primary Products	Primary Products
Motor Shop	Ralph Hern—Process Control
Donna Harp—Process Control	Motor Shop
Jim Cook—Service Shops	Jim Cook—Service Shops
Ralph Hern—Hot Roll +	Jeff Martin—Hot Roll +
Steel Production	Steel Production

Crown Manufacturing Company

March 3 marked the end of an era for Crown Manufacturing Company. On that day a new board of directors was elected, thus culminating the acquisition proceedings started by Able and Beth Corporation five months earlier to gain control of the midwest appliance manufacturer.

BACKGROUND

Crown Manufacturing Company had been founded 85 years ago by Henry Crown and had remained under his family's control until the March 3 election. From 1922 to 1946, Crown's son-in-law, Frank Jordan, served as president of the firm, and when he assumed chairmanship of the board in 1946, George Westerberg, treasurer, succeeded him as president. In the March 3 election, Westerberg was retained as president by the new board of directors as were his officers: Roberta Simpson, vice-president of sales; Sidney Bilby, vice-president; Raymond Morris, treasurer; and Alfred Kingston, vice-president of manufacturing (Exhibit 1).

Following the end of World War II, Crown Manufacturing Company had enjoyed only a modicum of success. The postwar boom in the appliance business was never fully capitalized upon. The reasons for failure to make more than modest gains were stated by Morris (treasurer since 1947) as:

Morris: Due to the company's inability to obtain steel from its prewar supplier, American and Northern Steel, during the crucial expansion period of the economy in the years 1947–1949 with steel being sold on priority basis, suppliers took care of their prewar customers and Crown was unable to obtain another source when American failed to meet their requirements.

About the time steel was becoming available to allow Crown more production, the Korean War erupted and forced curtailment of steel.

To meet the situation of limited production, we adopted the policy of "limited distribution." An analysis of our prewar sales was made, and it was determined that sales to utility companies accounted for 50 percent of sales but only 20 percent of the customers. The other 50 percent of sales came from the 80 percent of the customers represented by department stores, furniture stores, and appliance dealers.

Exhibit 1

Crown Manufacturing Company
Partial Organization Chart

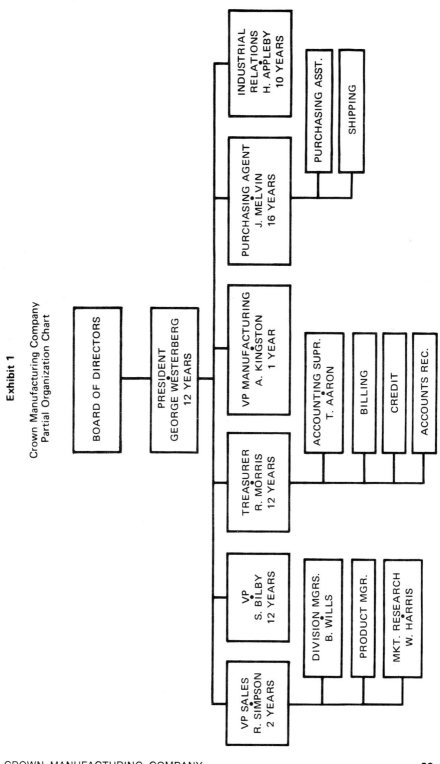

With the "limited distribution" policy, the company could concentrate its sales personnel on selling what could be produced to utility companies. Westerberg believed this policy to be best in that the company could sell its major prewar customers with the minimum number of salespeople.

The end of hostilities in Korea saw a new surge in the appliance industry (see Exhibit 2) for the years 1953 through 1955. After 1955, the industry began to decline from its previous heights. Crown Manufacturing, however, showed more marked declines, losing 26 percent of its market position in the period 1955 through 1958.

To offset the decline, Westerberg believed that the company should follow a policy of product diversification that would end the reliance on a one-product line that was subject to moderate seasonal fluctuations. It was in this period, 1953–1955, that Westerberg recommended five product lines be added. Only two of the five products, however, had the same channels of distribution as Crown's line. The other three products each had their own distribution channels: one product was sold through wholesalers, one through plumbing and heating dealers, and one direct to builders. However, Bilby, then vice-president of sales, indicated to Westerberg the disadvantages of these three products. They did not conform to their present sales channels, and they would put an excessive burden on his sales force in that his people had no experience selling the particular outlets. Disregarding Bilby's caution, Westerberg recommended to the board the addition of all five products to Crown's line, and the board approved his recommendations.

Utility business represented 12 percent of the industry sales of the appliances manufactured by Crown in 1955. In 1958, utility sales were down to 8.5 percent of industry sales, but Crown's sales to utilities were still running approximately 50 percent of total sales.

Many discussions were had about the problem of getting increased distribution of the company's appliances through dealers and department stores. Industry records of sales by outlet type indicated the trend of manufacturers to merchandise through these appliance store dealers. As a result, a campaign using direct-mail promotions was inaugurated in 1955 to expand the number of dealers selling the company's products. Morris, the treasurer, was in charge of records regarding the follow-up on and scheduling of the mailings. The plan worked well for approximately one and a half years, but then it was abandoned by Westerberg as being "too expensive for the results." The many years of Crown's policy in selling only to utilities had affected the dealers' attitude toward the company. Many felt "And now you want me to buy from you after all the years you wouldn't sell to me."

The increased burden on the sales force of the new products Westerberg had thought vital to the company's growth was diluting

Exhibit 2

Relationship Between Crown Manufacturing Company and Industry Sales
Postwar Period — 1946 – 58

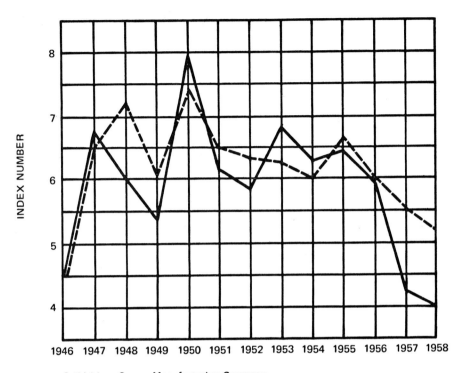

Solid Line: Crown Manufacturing Company
Broken Line: Industry

effectiveness of the sales force, and the products did not show the volume anticipated by Westerberg. The tightfisted approach Westerberg took with regard to the cost of the dealer program was also exemplified in his policy of not increasing the number of salespeople to handle the new lines. In addition, the original Crown line sales continued to decrease.

In March, 1957, Westerberg called in a management consulting agency to investigate the company's lack of progress, and Bilby was relieved of his responsibilities for the sales organization. However, because of his many friends in the industry and long service record with the Crown Manufacturing Company, Bilby was retained as a titular vice-president. To fill Bilby's former position Westerberg selected Roberta Simpson, an outsider. Simpson, who was in her late forties, came from a manufacturer of appliances dissimilar to those manufactured by Crown and whose distribution was, for the most part, through wholesale distributors. Simpson expressed her dislike for utility customers by often saying, "Those damn utilities are noth-ing but a bunch of leeches who'll just bleed you to death."

In the two years with Crown (1957–1959), Simpson made sev-eral attempts to obtain more appliance dealer business. The attempts were in the form of incentives to the salespeople to open new dealers. While the plans were supposed to have merit, they had very little re-sult in obtaining new dealers. Sales continued to decline, even those made to utilities, since Simpson would not carry on the usual ameni-ties that the utilities had received from the personable Bilby.

The decline in sales resulted in a decline in profits. According to Morris, the profit for the year 1957 "would not have been enough salary for a medium-priced executive." In 1958, the profit was less than in 1957. No dividend had been paid on common stock since the fall of 1956, but the company had met its 4 percent obligation on preferred shares of stock.

POST ELECTION

The company's dilemma did not end on March 3, however, with the election of the new board of directors. The first week of January, still before actual control of Crown was taken, Able and Beth Manu-facturing Corporation requested that all Crown executives present expense forecasts for their particular divisions. The sales forecasts were to be used, according to Able and Beth Corporation, for financial budgeting of all departments. For example, based on the forecast sales, the manufacturing division would set its labor requirements, tooling, etc., to maintain desired inventory. Likewise, the purchasing department purchased raw materials in accordance with the sales forecast requirements prepared by Simpson. These reports were made monthly up to six months in the future, and they included estimates for selling and advertising expenditures for the periods included in the sales forecast. The sales forecast format was by model, and an average unit selling price was used to express the forecast in dollars. It was Simpson's duty to provide this information.

In previous years, the Crown Manufacturing Company's Sales Department had made similar forecasts, but no officer of the com-pany except Morris seemed concerned about the actual result or the realistic approach to what the actual sales would be. When presented with a low sales forecast, Simpson would say to her marketing man, William Harris, "Bill, you have to be more optimistic. Let's raise this model another 1,000 units for April." When the results were obtained, Bill was usually correct in the original estimate. Morris often said to Bill, "Roberta is skywriting if she thinks she'll sell all these that she's forecasting."

During the first week of February, the actual results of the month of January were compared with that month's forecast sales. As expected, the forecast was much higher than actual sales. Simpson was questioned about the "whys" of the variations by Peter Nichols, Able and Beth Corporation's Controller.

Simpson: This forecasting business, at least the way you want us to do it, is something new to us. We don't really get the kind of data from our Accounting Department that we need to do a good job. The information we do get from them usually comes three to four weeks after the end of the month.

Nichols: What information are you talking about?

Simpson: That's a good question; I don't know. It's been so long since I've had anything from them I can't remember.

(Laughter)

Later, Nichols approached Morris and artfully asked to see what type of information his accounting department was supplying the sales department. Morris showed him the computer reports, which showed sales by model, sales by outlet type, sales by sales territory, and sales by customer.

Morris: The Sales Department gets all this information from us in units and dollars every month. I've often wondered if it's worth the cost. Nobody over there (pointing at Simpson's office) seems to know it exists. We've been giving Sales this type of information for years. It's really good stuff if someone would make use of it.

Nichols: You don't feel anybody uses it?

Morris: No! Except I do believe Bill Harris uses it for some of his work.

The new demands by the management of Able and Beth Corporation kept the Crown management busy for several weeks after the conversation between Simpson and Nichols about the data supplied Simpson by Morris' accounting department.

The usual 9 a.m. Monday meetings Westerberg had had with his management staff prior to the merger were now being called not only on Monday but on the average of four out of five days in the week. The meetings averaged two hours in length. No formal agenda was used nor were minutes of the meetings kept.

At the Monday morning meeting on March 22 the subject of production scheduling was being discussed.

Kingston (vice-president of manufacturing): We're having a terrible time with our production. Able and Beth Corporation is trying to get us to reduce our inventory of finished goods and work in progress. Right now, we've got 8,400 units in finished goods inventory and from last week's shipment record, we're only selling at a rate of 2,500 units for this month. With a 45-day inventory, which we all feel is adequate, we only should have approximately 4,000 units in stock. I'm running out of space. According to the March sales forecast Roberta gave us, which estimated sales at 4,500, we're going to be increasing our inventory by 2,000 units.

Westerberg: How did this happen?

Morris: I don't understand. The sales estimate we got from Roberta for the financial budget showed a forecast of 3,000 units.

Westerberg: Let's get the two forecasts in here.

The two forecasts for March were brought in and the statements that Morris and Kingston made were verified.

Westerberg: Raymond, isn't it necessary that the sales forecast for financial budgeting purposes be identical to the one used by manufacturing for production scheduling? If they're not the same, I would imagine our budget expenses would be out of line either at the sales end or in manufacturing. Am I right?

Morris: You're correct.

Simpson: I think that before this goes any further I should say a few words. I've been handicapped for a long time now by lack of information and lack of merchandise. Manufacturing hasn't given me the items I needed when I could sell them. Take the new line we brought out in December. Manufacturing was to make 100 units per day and we had actual production of only 50 units. I could have sold twice as many as I did. The reason I set the forecast for manufacturing at 4,500 was because I didn't believe I'd get enough of our spring promotion model if I didn't. Another thing, I've not had the information required for forecasting. Take this report I have here, sales by models. It comes out quarterly. I need this information every month.

Westerberg: I can understand your point of view, Roberta.

The meeting went on to other subjects.

Later that day, Morris approached William Harris.

Morris: Say, Bill, doesn't your boss know about our monthly sales by model report we get from our computer equipment?

Harris: I'm sure she does. We discussed it some time ago and I showed her the sheet I use for keeping my personal record when I forecast by model. I also made up a booklet for her and one she could give to Able and Beth Corporation that showed all the computer reports the accounting department furnished and their frequency. Here's the booklet, and see, here's sales by model by month.

Morris: That's what I thought. O.K., thanks.

The following conversation between Bill and Morris' assistant, Tom Aaron, occurred shortly after Bill Harris had talked with Morris.

Harris: What's up? Raymond is asking me if Roberta knows about the computer sales by model report.

Aaron: I understand Simpson claims she didn't know about the report coming out monthly. Raymond showed her the report and told her how it had been coming out monthly for the last three years. All Roberta said was, "Bill Harris never told me about it." I guess everybody's on edge. You know 5 out of 40 of her salespeople have quit in the past month.

Sullivan Paper Bag Company (A)

In March, 1960, the executive committee of the Sullivan Paper Bag Company was considering shutting down the company's Bellows Falls, Vermont, bag manufacturing plant and increasing the capacity of their Anniston, Alabama, plant to produce those bags currently made at Bellows Falls. To assist them, the comptroller had recently had his assistant, Mr. Frederick King, prepare, for his signature, a report on the matter with particular emphasis on the costs involved. This report has been reproduced as Exhibit I.

COMPANY HISTORY

The Sullivan Paper Bag Company had been founded in 1892 by two brothers, Thomas J. and Robert P. Sullivan. It had originally been in the business of reclaiming and then selling cloth sacks. In 1900 it added paper bags to its product line and by 1912 it was manufacturing its own paper bags. Later, in the twenties, it acquired the assets of a small paper mill in Bellows Falls, Vermont.

By 1959, the company had two paper mills, the one in Vermont and one in Talladega, Alabama, in its Paper Division, and four bag manufacturing plants in Bellows Falls, Vermont, in Anniston, Alabama, in St. Louis, Missouri, and in Portland, Oregon. In addition, six sales offices and distribution points were maintained in Boston, New York, Atlanta, Houston, Chicago, and San Francisco, to assure prompt delivery to the customer.

The company's major product was now multiwall shipping sacks. It no longer handled cloth sacks, as these could not be competitively priced with comparable multiwall bags. The company, for similar reasons, no longer sold as many single-wall paper bags as it once did.

CHARACTERISTICS OF MULTIWALL PAPER SACKS

Multiwall paper sacks were paper bags with three to six walls. The factors determining the number of walls and types of material for these walls were as follows: composition and flow qualities of the bag contents; the desired moisture contents within the bag and the resultant need to protect against the loss or gain of moisture; chemical properties of the contents; the filling, closing, and weighing methods to be used; and the desired methods of shipping, handling, and storage.

A multiwall paper sack was essentially a combination of bags, one within another, each carrying its proportional share of the weight of the contents. The combination was, however, both stronger and more flexible than a single bag made of heavyweight paper.

Furthermore, various moistureproof and waterproof barriers could be included among the walls. The walls could be held together by a variety of adhesives which would make the bag resistant to grease, acid, and scuffs, and would prevent the paper from sticking to such contents as synthetic rubber, asphalt, waxes, and resins.

Multiwall sacks could withstand complete immersion in water, were capable of being stored outdoors for over a year, and could resist gas, heat, fire, flame, cold, acids, alkalis, oil, grease, sunlight, insects, mildew, mold, caustic, and creasing.

There were five general types of multiwall sacks in general use in early 1960:

1. Sewn valve sack
2. Pasted valve sack
3. Sewn bottom, open mouth sack
4. Pasted bottom, open mouth sack
5. Open corner sack

The valve sacks were closed at both top and bottom at the bag manufacturing plant either by sewing or pasting except for a small triangular opening in the upper corner called the "valve." These bags were filled by special machines and were self-closing due to the internal pressure of the contents against a flap of paper in the "valve." Valve bags were used for the bulk packaging of foods, chemicals, rock products, and fertilizer. They were particularly adaptable to high-speed mechanical filling methods. In fact, in some applications it was possible to get as many as 24 one-hundred-pound bags filled per minute with only one operator.

The open-mouth sacks were closed by the filler on a special pasting or sewing machine or by hand stapling, wire-tying, or rope-tying. These bags were less adaptable to high-speed filling but did not require special filling machines. Their use was as widespread as that of the valve bags.

The open-corner sack was a combination of the open-mouth and valve bags; that is, only part of the top was closed by the bag manufacturer. The remainder of the top was usually stapled shut by the filler. This kind of bag was typically filled with a hot liquid which hardened when cool into a cake of the shape and size of the bag.

A variant of the valve sack was the bag with a special sleeve valve which provided a more positive check against leakage and sifting than the regular valve bag. This kind of sack was used mainly for fertilizers and other finely powdered and pulverized products.

In 1959, about 40% of the multiwall sacks sold in the United States were of the sewn valve type (including open corner and sleeve valve sacks); 35% of the sewn open mouth type; 15% of the pasted valve type (including open corner and sleeve valve sacks); and 10% of the pasted open mouth type.

SULLIVAN'S POSITION IN THE MULTIWALL PAPER SACK MARKET

In 1959, there were about 45 manufacturers of multiwall paper sacks. Of these, only four companies offered a complete line of bags, filling machines, and repair and consulting services. Five companies sold both textile and paper bags; eight were integrated paper shipping sack firms. Ten simply converted kraft wrapping papers to bags but had more than one plant; the rest did the same in only one plant.

In late 1959, some 34% of the bag manufacturing plants in the country were located in the Southeast, 28% in the Middle West, 15% in the Northeast, 14% in the Far West, and 9% in the Southwest.

Total industry sales amounted to about 800,000 tons or 2,400,000,000 multiwall sacks in 1959. About 30% of these were for cement; 25% for fertilizers; 20% for animal feed; 10% for flour; 10% for sugar; and 5% for lime. These sales were geographically distributed as follows: 30% in the Middle West; 25% in the Southeast; 20% in the Northeast; 15% in the Southwest; and 10% in the Far West.

Usage of multiwall sacks had grown at a rate of about 3% per year over the previous ten years. This growth was not uniformly distributed over the different geographical areas nor over the different end uses of the bags. In the more recent years, the animal feed market in the Middle West had grown the fastest.

By 1960 multiwall paper sacks were replacing steel drums, wooden barrels and boxes, fiberboard and corrugated cartons and drums, and fabric or fabricized bags. The paper sacks had proven to be less expensive to purchase, more adaptable to high-speed filling, and easier to ship and store.

The Sullivan Company was about the fifth largest producer of multiwall sacks in the country. Its major competition came from Union Bag-Camp Paper Company, International Paper Company, St. Regis Paper Company, and the Bemis Brothers Bag Company.

In 1959, Sullivan's sales amounted to about 48,000 tons of multi-wall sacks, or about 6% of the total industry sales. These were distributed as follows:

By industry served:

Cement	39%
Fertilizer	33%
Animal feed	4%
Flour	5%
Sugar	7%
Lime	12%

Geographically:

Northeast sales out of Boston office	2,500 T	5%
Northeast sales out of New York office	9,600 T	20%
Southeast sales out of Atlanta office	15,200 T	32%
Southwest sales out of Houston office	5,100 T	11%
Midwest sales out of Chicago office	8,400 T	17%
Far West sales out of San Francisco office ..	7,300 T	15%
	48,100 T	100%

The average delivered price of the bags sold by the entire industry throughout the country was about $250 per ton in 1959; five years earlier this price had been $200 per ton. Sullivan's average delivered price in 1959 was also about $250 per ton.

Several members of Sullivan Bag's executive committee believed that 1959 had been a typical year. They added that the paper bag business in general was now typified by two characteristics:

1. Very close tie-in with the fluctuations of the general business conditions in the country, particularly the construction business.

2. A productive capacity in excess of the average year's requirements. In fact, the Sullivan sales manager said he thought the industry did not need any further facilities for at least another five years.

Buying Habits of Multiwall Paper Sack Purchasers

As was noted earlier, the nature of the multiwall sack was such that innumerable combinations of materials were possible. This meant that the multiwall sack was essentially tailor-made to meet the individual customer's requirements. The ability to produce the paper sack to satisfy the customer's needs was of primary importance in the multiwall bag market.

On the other hand, once an adequate bag had been found, almost any company in the industry was capable of producing it. It was the opinion of the Sullivan sales manager that speedy delivery then became the most important sales consideration. It was for this reason that the Sullivan Company had added regional distribution points in Boston, New York, Atlanta, New Orleans, Chicago, and San Francisco to stock fast-moving customer items.

Close personal relationships with customers were also thought to be significant sales considerations. The Sullivan Company maintained a staff of 20 salesmen throughout the country calling on its major customers. In addition, agents and manufacturing representatives were used in areas where there were few major customers.

Neither price nor quality seemed to be of great importance in the sales picture. The prices charged and the product quality were essentially the same to a customer no matter what his source of supply was. The prices were normally quoted delivered to the customer's plant, with the bag manufacturer absorbing the freight costs. To keep their transportation costs at a minimum, most of the bag manufacturers, including Sullivan, tried to place their plants near their markets.

Multiwall Paper Sack Production Process

The multiwall sacks began as rolls of kraft paper weighing anywhere from 400 to 1,000 pounds each, depending on the type and weight of the paper and the diameter and width of the roll. The roll width depended on the bag width desired. For example, a bag 19" (face width) $\times$ 3½" (bottom depth) $\times$ 37¾" (length) required a 46" roll width, as calculated below:

Perimeter of bag when open = $2 \times (19 + 3½) = 45"$
Overlap needed to longitudinal seam = $1"$

Because of its strength and low cost, unbleached kraft bag stock was the most frequently used material. However, unbleached kraft did not print up very well; and, in more recent years, bleached kraft had become popular for the outer wall of the multiwall sack. Glassine and asphalt-coated kraft were frequently used as inner walls. There were, moreover, at least ten other different kinds of inner wall materials.

Prior to any use, the paper rolls were sample-tested for weight, tear, sizing (finish), and grease resistance.

As the first step in the manufacturing process, the outer wall paper was printed in much the same way as a newspaper. A variety of colors was possible, depending on the printing press used. What was printed on the outer wall was the choice of the customer.

The printed outer wall roll was then set up for feeding into a tuber alongside the inner wall rolls. These were simultaneously drawn into the tuber around a formed plate of the width and configuration (side pleats or not) desired. The longitudinal bag seam was being pasted together and small wheels were indenting the tube for the side pleats (if any) at the same time. When the tube had traveled the desired length, a striker bar cut it off. This might be actuated by hand or by electric eye guided by impressions made in printing at the desirable cutoff point.

Most tubers were adjustable to handle a variety of bag widths and types; the better pieces could even accommodate the majority of the sizes desired commercially. Depending on the number of plies, the paper weight, and the inclusion of special sheets, a well-regulated tuber was capable of producing 5,000 to 12,000 bags per hour.

If the bags were of the valve type, a special tuck was placed in the bag during the tubing operation. If they were of the sleeve type, a sleeving machine added a piece of kraft paper to form a tube coming out of one end of the bag.

All bags then either went to a bottomer for gluing or to a sewing machine for stitching one or both ends of the tube.

The bags were inspected after each operation for good glue bond, valve formation, color impression and clarity, and proper dimensions. The finished bags themselves were sometimes sample tested by filling them with the material they would be used for and subjecting them to various types of rough handling, such as a 48-inch drop test on each corner.

The completed bags were finally bundled and wrapped or palletized for shipment.

Sullivan's Paper Production Facilities

The Sullivan company had two paper mills, one in Bellows Falls, Vermont, and one in Talladega, Alabama. Both produced unbleached and bleached kraft bag stock of the type used in the manufacture of bags. Only the Bellows Falls mill made asphalted kraft, an inner wall material used in over 80% of the multiwall sacks made.

The Bellows Falls mill operated at 83% of its one-shift capacity in 1959, producing 20,000 tons of regular and asphalted kraft. Of this amount, 4,000 tons were sold locally in New England by one salesman to smaller bag manufacturers without their own paper production facilities. Competition in this market was very keen, since there were several kraft mills in the area with considerable excess capacity. The remainder of the Bellows Falls mill production was used by the Bellows Falls bag plant, the Anniston bag plant, and the St. Louis bag plant. The latter two plants received all of their asphalted kraft from the Bellows Falls mill; the Bellows Falls bag plant had all of its paper requirements supplied by the Bellows Falls mill.

The Talladega mill, on the other hand, was operating a two-shift capacity in 1959, producing 15,000 tons of regular kraft. There was no asphalting facility at Talladega. All of the Talladega output was used by the Anniston bag plant.

Both of the paper mills operated with old equipment with an efficiency which the company officials believed was extremely low. Both mills were maintained for essentially two reasons:

1. The company was not enthusiastic about closing facilities unless there were strong financial reasons to do so. There were 65 employees in the Bellows Falls mill and 50 in the Talladega mill in 1959 who would be affected by any mill shutdown.
2. The mill served as an assured source of paper during those periods when paper became scarce. Scarcity had occurred during both World War II and the Korean conflict.

In recent years, the cost of manufacturing the bag paper had run from 97% to 107% of the market value of that paper. In 1959, for example, the cost of a ton of regular kraft made at either location was about $131 compared to the going-market price of $130. This cost was broken down by the company as follows (rounded to the nearest dollar):

Pulp and other materials	$95
Direct labor	15
Indirect labor & supervision	10
Vacation and holiday pay, unemployment compensation, social security taxes	3
Heat, light, power, insurance	4
Depreciation	1
Freight absorbed	3

Sullivan's Bag Manufacturing Facilities

In 1959, the one-shift capacity and actual production of each of the bag manufacturing plants was as follows:

	One-Shift Capacity in 1959	Actual Production in 1959	% Production of One-Shift Capacity in 1959
Bellows Falls	14,000 T.	12,300 T.	80%
Anniston	12,000 T.	15,500 T.	129%
St. Louis	16,000 T.	13,400 T.	84%
Portland	12,000 T.	7,500 T.	63%
Total	54,000 T.	48,700 T.	

Because the age of the plants and equipment varied considerably from location to location, there was a large range in productivity of the plants. In part this was counterbalanced by the differing wage scales, paid as follows:

	Age of Plant in 1959	Average Age of Equipment in 1959	Direct Labor Man-hrs. per ton in 1959	Average Direct Labor Rate
Bellows Falls	60	15	33.5	$1.55
Anniston	12	10	26.2	$1.48
St. Louis	33	8	23.2	$1.61
Portland	3	3	19.2	$1.60

The direct labor payrolls of the bag manufacturing plants were as follows in 1959:

	No. of Direct Labor Employees	Total 1959 Dollars
Bellows Falls ..	207	$ 638,800
Anniston	203	601,000
St. Louis	155	500,500
Portland	72	230,300
Total	637	$1,970,600

Overhead charges for each of the bag plants were the following in 1959:

	Indirect Labor & Supervision	Vacation & Holiday Pay, Unempl. Comp., Social Security Taxes	Heat, Light & Power Insurance	Plant & Equipment Deprecia-tion	Total
Bellows Falls .	$ 50,200	$ 76,900	$25,000	$ 15,000	$167,100
Anniston	30,500	69,500	13,000	25,000	138,000
St. Louis	23,000	57,600	10,000	40,000	130,600
Portland	18,600	27,400	8,000	30,000	84,000
Total	$122,300	$231,400	$56,000	$110,000	$519,700

To keep their freight costs low, the company had established a policy in 1950 of supplying each distribution point from the plant nearest it. As a result, the Bellows Falls plant produced to match the needs of the Northeast area (Boston and New York distribution points). The Anniston plant supplied the Southeast through the Atlanta office. The St. Louis plant supplied both the Middle West and Southwest through the Chicago and Houston offices. The Far West's requirements were taken care of by the Portland plant through the San Francisco office.

Production was scheduled for each plant based on a general three-month forecast of demand, a more detailed one-month forecast by bag type and size, and specific customer orders. Generally about three weeks to a month elapsed between the customer order and delivery of the finished product to the customer. This might take a week longer if new printing plates had to be prepared.

About 15–20% of the plant's work involved so-called "priority orders," in which about one week was cut out of the order processing and manufacturing cycle. Part of this time saving also resulted from direct shipments from the factory to the customer instead of the normal car- or truck-load shipments to the distribution point where they were split into smaller customer shipments.

Sullivan's Bag Cost Structure

In 1959 the largest single element in the cost of a multiwall sack was that of the paper used. This represented about 68% of the cost of a bag. Other materials accounted for another 7%. Direct labor averaged about 20% of cost of sales, and overhead about another 5%. For reasons noted earlier, there were individual plant variations within this structure as follows:

Cost per ton of goods output

	Paper *	Other Mat'ls	Direct Labor	Other Overhead	Total
Bellows Falls	$136.00	$13.60	$52.00	$13.60	$215.20
Anniston.	139.00	13.60	38.80	8.90	200.30
St. Louis	137.00	13.50	37.30	9.70	197.60
Portland	136.00	13.60	30.70	11.20	191.50

* About 10% of paper used was asphalted kraft.

The cost of sales itself in 1959 amounted to about 80% of the sales value throughout the company. Selling and administrative expenses were an additional 8% of sales and freight absorbed another 4%. The company broke these expenses down by sales office as follows:

	Selling Price	Per Ton Cost of Sales	Selling & Admin.	Freight Absorbed	Net Profit Before Taxes
Boston	$250.00	$215.20	$19.00	$ 8.60	$ 7.20
New York	250.00	215.20	21.50	11.20	2.10
Atlanta	250.00	200.30	18.50	12.50	18.70
Chicago	250.00	197.60	20.00	13.90	18.50
Houston	250.00	197.60	20.50	18.80	13.10
San Francisco ...	250.00	191.50	21.00	20.50	17.00

SULLIVAN PAPER BAG COMPANY (A)

Included in the selling and administrative expense was a 4% commission paid to the company's salesmen. Freight absorbed included the cost of shipment from the plants to the sales distribution points and the subsequent shipment on to the customers.

An investigation of the cost data for the period 1949–1959 revealed the following:

1. Cost of paper gradually increasing with time (3% per year), but subject to severe cyclical and random fluctuations.
2. Gradually increasing unit cost of other materials (2% per year).
3. Direct labor cost gradually increasing per unit over time (4% per year), but unusually high unit cost in periods of low volume and vice versa.
4. Indirect labor, other overhead, and selling and administrative expense increasing in total cost over time (4% per year). Tendency to be higher than expected in high volume periods and vice versa.
5. Freight absorbed increasing in unit cost over time (2% per year).

The bag plants were charged with the market price of paper, even when their paper was produced by the company's own paper mills. In addition, the Anniston and St. Louis plants, which received their asphalted paper from Bellows Falls, were charged with the freight cost of shipping the paper. Since they could purchase asphalted paper without any freight charges locally, these two plants were paying a premium of about 1½ cents and 2 cents per pound of asphalted paper used. The company treasurer justified this practice as follows:

1. If the asphalted paper were purchased locally, this would leave unused capacity at the asphalting facility in the Bellows Falls paper mill.
2. It would be unfair to make the mill absorb the freight for shipment to such distant points as Anniston and St. Louis.
3. The Anniston and St. Louis facilities could afford to absorb the freight, whereas the Bellows Falls paper mill was a very marginal activity.

COMPANY INVESTMENT POLICY

To strengthen its financial position, the company had embarked on a cost reduction program in 1952. As the first step, it had modernized and expanded its St. Louis plant to match the increased sales effort it was expending to capture a larger amount of the animal feed business in the Middle West.

The next step was to build a plant in Portland, Oregon, near several paper mills to supply the growing West Coast market, which had been previously supplied by the St. Louis plant. A major savings in freight costs was achieved as a result of the new plant.

Several new pieces of equipment had been installed in 1957 at the Anniston plant to keep pace with the expanding southern market. The plant now had adequate printing, valving, and bottoming equipment to handle twice the 1959 production volume. The tubing operation was a bottleneck and ran two shifts a day during 1959.

The big production problem facing the company was the Bellows Falls plant. It was the opinion of the company engineering department that no amount of modern equipment could make the plant as efficient as the company's other plants, due primarily to materials handling problems inherent in a multistory building. Furthermore, there was doubt expressed whether the building's floors were strong enough to handle the newer, heavier equipment.

An engineering proposal for a new plant in Bellows Falls had been turned down in 1954, because the company did not feel that the $700,000 investment required would provide an adequate return on the company's investment. The company tried to avoid investments with an expected after-tax return of less than 8%.

A suggestion was then made to expand the company's Anniston plant in order to close down the Bellows Falls plant. This had not been acted upon at the time because the management was preoccupied with building the Portland plant.

Finally, in June of 1959, Mr. King had been given the assignment of looking into this project. Excerpts from his report are attached in Exhibit I.

Exhibit I

Excerpts from Report Concerning Transfer of Production
from Bellows Falls to Anniston

Memorandum to: Executive Committee
From: Comptroller
Subject: Closing Down Bellows Falls Bag Plant & Expanding An-
                 niston Plant to Compensate for Loss in Capacity.

1. It is recommended that our Bellows Falls bag plant be closed down and our Anniston plant capacity be increased to supply the Northeast area as well as the Southeast. This recommendation is based on an expected rate of return of 23.4% after taxes on the investment needed and a payback of 4.3 years.

2. It is anticipated that an average of 14,000 tons of extra production per year will be required at Anniston to meet the sales needs of the Northeast area (3,000 tons out of the Boston office, 11,000 tons out of the New York office). This analysis is based on this assumption, although large fluctuations from this average value can be expected in any one year.

3. Since the Anniston plant has excess capacity in some areas, it is estimated that only the following equipment will be required for the Anniston plant to achieve the desired increase in production:

3 Johnson tubers at	$55,000 each	$165,000
25 Stitching machines at $10,000 each		250,000
1 Coty double-ended pasted valve bottomer		65,000
		$480,000

This equipment will be depreciated on a straight-line basis over a ten-year period.

4. One hundred eighty-four additional direct-labor employees will be needed in Anniston:

    3 press operators at $2.01 per hr. each
    3 press helpers at $1.57 per hr. each
    6 tuber operators at $2.01 per hr. each
    6 roll shafters at $1.57 per hr. each
    12 stockers at $1.37 per hr. each
    24 inspectors at $1.48 per hr. each
    12 reclaim girls at $1.33 per hr. each
    18 balers at $1.40 per hr. each
    10 sewing machine adjusters at $2.01 per hr. each
    82 sewing machine operators at $1.41 per hr. each
    4 towmotor operators at $1.37 per hr. each
    2 clean-up men at $1.37 per hr. each
    2 truckers at $1.37 per hr. each

These rates represent the present prevailing wages paid at our Anniston plant and will cause an increase in the direct labor payroll of about $544,000 per year. These people will work within the present two-shift operation at Anniston.

5. It is recommended that all asphalted kraft and regular kraft in excess of the Talladega mill's capacity be purchased locally to avoid the freight charges on shipments of paper from Bellows Falls. Since the capacity of the Talladega mill is about 15,000 T. per year at present, this will amount to 12,000 T. of regular kraft and 2,500 T. of asphalted kraft per year. An average price of $155 per ton for regular kraft and $160 per ton for asphalted kraft is projected from present cost trends. There will, of course, be substantial variations from this average in any one year.

6. It is estimated that the cost of other direct materials will average around 10% of that of paper.

7. Material wastage of 2% is anticipated.

8. An average selling price of $300 per ton is expected, based on projections of present price trends. In years of low demand, our actual selling price will probably be below this and vice versa.

9. There will be additional freight costs incurred in shipments from Anniston to New York or Boston in place of Bellows Falls to New York or Boston as follows:

From	To	Rate per cwt.	Estimated No. of T.	Estimated Cost	
Anniston	New York	$1.20	11,000	$264,000	
Anniston	Boston	1.30	3,000	78,000	
					$342,000
Additional cost:					
Bellows Falls	New York	.50	11,000	$110,000	
Bellows Falls	Boston	.40	3,000	24,000	
					134,000
Net additional cost					$208,000

10. Because present volume at the Bellows Falls bag plant is, on the average, below that expected, the savings anticipated in the future from closing down the plant could not be determined on the basis of present costs. The Bellows Falls cost statement for 1955, when the volume was 14,138 tons, was used as a guide in estimating the future savings. The 1955 cost of sales percentage at Bellows Falls was 84%. Therefore, on expected annual sales volume of $4,200,000 (14,000 tons × $300 per ton), a saving of $3,528,000 can be anticipated.

11. The highest quotation received for the Bellows Falls plant and all of the equipment within it amounted to $20,000 despite its present net book value of $120,000.

12. It is not anticipated there will be any change in our inventory levels as a result of the proposed change in production facilities.

13. The following increases in the Anniston overhead are expected:

Supervision	$ 6,000
Indirect labor	5,000
Vacation & holiday pay, unemployment compensation, social security taxes (11% of additional total payroll)	61,000
Heat, light, power, insurance	2,000
Depreciation	48,000
Total	$122,000

14. Therefore the total additional costs resulting from the Anniston expansion are as follows:

Paper	$2,300,000
Other material	230,000
Direct Labor	544,000
Overhead	122,000
Freight	208,000
Total Additional Cost	$3,404,000

15. With a $3,528,000 saving from closing down the Bellows Falls plant, there will be a net annual saving of $124,000 before taxes or $59,500 after taxes. However, since the depreciation charge of $48,000 per year is a noncash expense, a net cash inflow of $107,500 per year can be anticipated.

16. The net investment required is as follows:

Additional equipment needed at Anniston	$480,000
Less: Salvage value of Bellows Falls plant	20,000
Total Investment	$460,000

17. This provides an after-tax return of 23.4% over the expected equipment life of 10 years. There is a 4.3 year payback of the original investment.

18. It is estimated that the cost of moving the key personnel from Bellows Falls to Anniston will not exceed $10,000.

19. The expansion of the Anniston facility will take at least six months. It is recommended that the Bellows Falls plant be gradually phased out over the same period.

Joseph T. Henry
Comptroller

Sullivan Paper Bag Company (B)

One day in the middle of July, 1960, Joseph Henry, the Sullivan comptroller, received a memorandum from the company president, Mr. Robert Chase, which read as follows:

> While reading a recent issue of the *Paper Trade News*, I came across an article on the use of linear programming at the Bemis Bag Company to allocate their production at different plants to their various sales distribution points. I wonder if you could make up a report for me by July 31 answering the following questions:
>
> 1. Would linear programming be of any value to us?
> 2. How much can we afford to pay a consultant to apply linear programming to our problems?
> 3. Will linear programming have any effect on the desirability of closing down the Bellows Falls plant and expanding the Anniston plant?

Mr. Henry was not sure where to begin, but he did remember reading an article several years earlier in the *Harvard Business Review* on linear programming. After a careful examination of his old *Reviews*, he found what he was looking for: "Mathematical Programming, Better Information for Better Decision Making," by Henderson and Schlaifer.

As a result of reading the article, he obtained from the company traffic manager a table of freight rates (see Exhibit I).

In talking to the manufacturing vice-president, Mr. Charles Hall, he learned that 150% of one-shift capacity was the normal rule-of-thumb used by the company as the production ceiling possible before facilities had to be expanded. (See Exhibit II for the 1959 one-shift capacities of the company's bag plants.) Mr. Hall warned, however, that all of the company's machines were not capable of producing all sizes and types of bags. For example, he said that the St. Louis production of large chemical bags with special liners could be expanded only 20% without a new ending machine.

Mr. Henry also checked with the purchasing agent to see how far he had gone in placing contracts for the new equipment for the Anniston plant. He learned that a firm order had been placed for the Coty double-ended pasted valve bottomer in the amount of $65,000. This contract could be canceled but involved a penalty of $10,000. None of the other equipment had as yet been ordered.

Mr. Henry knew that the closing of the Bellows Falls plant had been announced two weeks earlier and had caused great community distress. In addition, the closing of the Bellows Falls paper mill was under investigation by the State Legislature at that very moment.

He determined from the Anniston personnel manager that efforts had already been started for hiring new people there. The Sullivan Company had received a large amount of favorable local publicity for expanding the plant there.

Assignment: If you were Mr. Henry, how would you answer the president's memorandum?

Exhibit I

Sullivan Paper Bag Company (B)
Sullivan Transportation Rates in 1960 per cwt

	Bellows Falls	Anniston	St. Louis	Portland, Oregon
Boston	.40	1.30	1.40	2.80
New York	.50	1.20	1.30	2.80
Atlanta	1.60	.50	1.40	2.60
Chicago	1.40	1.40	.50	1.70
Houston	1.80	1.40	.80	1.70
San Francisco	2.60	2.20	1.60	.50

Sullivan Transportation Rates in 1960 per Ton

	Bellows Falls	Anniston	St. Louis	Portland, Oregon
Boston	8.00	26.00	28.00	56.00
New York	10.00	24.00	26.00	56.00
Atlanta	32.00	10.00	28.00	52.00
Chicago	28.00	28.00	10.00	34.00
Houston	36.00	28.00	16.00	34.00
San Francisco	52.00	44.00	32.00	18.00

Exhibit II

Sullivan Paper Bag Company (B)
1959 One-Shift Capacities of the Sullivan Bag Plants

Bellows Falls	14,000 T.
Anniston	12,000 T.
St. Louis	16,000 T.
Portland, Oregon	12,000 T.
Total	54,000 T.

Sullivan Paper Bag
Company (C)

After receiving the memorandum from Mr. Chase quoted in the (B) case, Mr. Henry called in Mr. James Frank, senior partner in Clumby Associates, Inc., a large business consulting firm held on retainer by Sullivan. Mr. Henry described Sullivan's situation to Mr. Frank, and requested that Clumby prepare a report designed primarily to indicate whether or not Sullivan should close the Bellows Falls bag plant and expand the Anniston plant, but designed to also shed some light upon the use of linear programming in optimizing company operations. The report prepared by Clumby is given in Appendix A.

After carefully reading Clumby's report, Mr. Henry felt that the Bellows Falls plant probably should not be closed, and believed he knew a little more about one way in which linear programming could be used by Sullivan. But before reaching any definite conclusions regarding either the Bellows Falls decision or the usefulness of linear programming, Mr. Henry felt he had to answer for himself the following questions which had arisen in his mind while he was reading and studying the report:

    1. Are the two alternatives considered (a. the status quo; b. closing Bellows Falls and expanding Anniston) the only ones which should be studied? Or are there other feasible alternatives? Might one of these other alternatives be preferable to both of those studied?

    2. Are the producing and shipping choices called for by the "Transportation Problem" linear programming solution really the optimal ones for the alternatives studied? Or do the "indirect" costs impinge upon the problem in such a way that optimization is not always provided by the approach used by Clumby?

    3. How valid is Clumby's procedure of estimating savings (resulting from the alternative of expanding Anniston) in years other than 1961, 1965, and 1970? If the detailed calculations were

made for the intermediate years, would the results yield a curve similar to the one of Exhibit XIII?

4. Would the use of linear programming actually create the savings shown in Exhibit XV of the report? Or are the savings so small compared to the total costs that figures calculated in this way really have no valid statistical significance?

APPENDIX A

Clumby Associates, Inc.

July 29, 1960

Mr. Joseph Henry
Comptroller
Sullivan Paper Bag Company

Dear Mr. Henry:

We have completed our analysis of Sullivan's problem of whether or not to close the Bellows Falls bag plant and expand the plant in Anniston. Our conclusion is that such a venture would be expected to yield a very low rate of return on the investment required, and cannot therefore be justified on purely financial grounds.

We have also studied the potential usefulness to Sullivan of linear programming. The results of our calculations indicate that operating savings of $7,000 to $60,000 per year could be realized through the use of linear programming in scheduling production and shipping. The way in which these figures were obtained will be brought out further along in this letter, the remainder of which will describe the approach we used for your problem. The description will include an explanation of how linear programming fits into the analysis and will illustrate how it could be useful for Sullivan.

In our investigation, we assume that under each alternative the object would be to minimize the cost of producing and shipping for the company as a whole, while meeting the demand for paper bags at each of the company's six main distribution points. Cash flows resulting from shipping and producing had to be estimated, then, for the company with the Bellows Falls plant in operation and with Bellows Falls closed but Anniston expanded. We were able to do so from the cost and demand data which you gave us. We chose to divide the cost data into variable and non-variable production costs, and transportation costs. This we did first for the year 1959 as shown in Exhibits I, II, and III.

We assumed in all cases that overtime could be used in any plant up to 50% of the single shift capacity, as you suggested, but with 50% higher direct labor costs.

In order to determine the anticipated rate of return for the proposed investment in Anniston, we needed to figure cash savings for the next 10 years, the anticipated economic life of the investment. (We assumed, as you suggested, that we view the situation as a "now-or-never" one.)[1] Your data indicates that your costs have been rising irregularly but steadily for the past 10 years, with paper costs climbing at a rate of 3% per year, labor at 4% per year, and other costs at about 2% per year. Since the paper industry has recently seen paper prices become rather soft due to excess productive capacity and since unemployment has been slowly increasing over the past business cycle, we anticipate that cost increases will be less severe in the future. Also, since we do not feel the information justifies estimates of different rates of increase for different items, we assume that all of Sullivans costs would rise at a rate of 2% per year for the next decade. The variable costs thus predicted for 1961, 1965, and 1970 have accordingly been tabulated in Exhibit IV.

The selection of these three years for study calls for a brief explanation. In our study of the cash flows relevant to the investment decision, we assume the only items that change from year to year are the producing, shipping, and indirect costs, and the demands at the six main distribution points. (The demands were assumed to increase 3% per year as we discussed and agreed in our conversation.) All of the factors relevant to the investment calculation, then, we have assumed will be varying smoothly over time. Accordingly we deduced that the relevant cost differential between the alternatives studied would also vary smoothly over time, and decided to make the optimization calculations necessary for a definitive investment analysis only for the first, last, and one intermediate year.

This slight shortcut was felt desirable because of the extreme time pressure under which the study was made, and also because of our constant desire to provide our clients with the best possible analyses at the lowest possible price, that is, without any unnecessary work being performed.

The reason that making calculations for each separate year would have involved more time becomes clear when one introduces the factor which leads to use of the linear programming, namely the operation in each year under the lowest cost production and shipping plan possible with the physical facilities provided under the alternative being considered.

1. Sullivan officials had reached the conclusion that they should make the decision regarding the closing of Bellows Falls very quickly and then stick with it. They felt this would be the only responsible and practical way to deal with the Bellows Falls workers. They knew a large company in another industry was planning to construct a plant only about 10 miles from Bellows Falls, and that many of the workers could obtain jobs there if laid off by Sullivan. If Sullivan decided to keep the Bellows Falls plant open, however, the workers would probably stay with the company, because they would be forced to accept lower skilled (and lower paying) jobs if they changed to the other industry. Then the other company would get workers elsewhere, and if Sullivan decided to close the plant in four years, for example, the workers would have very poor chances of locating work without moving.

Or to state our approach more directly: to evaluate the proposed plan of closing Bellows Falls and expanding Anniston, one should base the calculations on operating conditions that are optimal for each alternative. Obviously if your existing mode of operation were optimal given your existing plants, but the mode assumed for the alternative with Anniston expanded was not the best for those facilities, then the calculations would yield results which would be biased against the investment, and vice versa.

So we used linear programming to optimize the production and shipping schedules for each alternative for each of the years studied. Since our conversation showed that you have a firm basic understanding of linear programming, I will not need to explain here why we found it useful in optimizing these operations. But I will point out explicitly that, because linear programming handles only costs that are directly variable with the activity in question, we split the production costs into variable and nonvariable as described earlier and combined the variable costs with the costs of shipping to find the best *combined* production and shipping schedule for each case.

As you have probably realized by this time, the special case of linear programming known as "the transportation problem" fits this situation very easily, and for the transportation problem virtually all of the information regarding the optimization calculation can be presented on three tableaus. In order to give you as much data as we felt would be of use to you, we have included Exhibits IV through X. Exhibit IV gives the cost coefficients for each of the production and shipping possibilities for each of the three years, as discussed before. Exhibits V through X show, for each case, the optimum shipping schedules and the tableaus of imputed rates which resulted with the optimum schedule. The imputed rates (z_{ij}'s) show for each route the cost imputed by the overall shipping schedule. If a particular route is being used, the cost is not merely imputed but is the actual cost for that route. But many routes are not used; the overall shipping pattern satisfies demands in the cheapest way and removes any need for using many routes. An imputed rate (or a "substitution route rate") represents the cost per unit of satisfying or removing any need to use the route in question.

The optimality of a schedule can be checked by comparing all z_{ij}'s with actual route costs. If any z_{ij} is greater than its corresponding cost, then the total cost could be lowered by using this route.

After finding the optimal production and shipping schedules for each alternative, we calculated the variable costs, the nonvariable costs (see Exhibit XI), and the total costs for each alternative for each year, as shown in Exhibit XII. The savings which would result from making the proposed investment at Anniston were then plotted against time in Exhibit XIII in order to enable us to estimate savings in intermediate years without having to make the time-consuming LP calculations for these years. Finally, these savings were used to calculate the rate of return which the proposed investment would be expected to yield. The results, given in Exhibit XIV, show an expected return of about 7.6%. Since your usual cutoff rate is around 8%, we concluded that the proposed plan of closing Bellows Falls and expanding Anniston did not represent an attractive investment possibility for Sullivan.

Our other main conclusion, that linear programming can be used by Sullivan to effect significant cost savings, results from the comparison shown in Exhibit XV. Column A gives the variable costs for the optimal production and shipping schedules as determined by the "transportation problem" solution. Column B gives the variable costs which would result if the schedules were made according to the simple decision rule "supply each distribution point from the plant nearest it." Column C gives the difference, which represents the savings the use of linear programming could generate in each case.

We believe this analysis of Sullivan's situation will be of use to you. If you have any questions regarding our analysis or any other data you would like examined, please be sure to let me know.

Sincerely,
J. Frank
Senior Partner
Clumby Associates, Inc.

Exhibit I

Sullivan Paper Bag Company (C)
Variable Production Costs Per Ton, 1959

	Paper	Other Materials	Direct Labor	Vacations & Holidays *	Total Variable Production Costs
Bellows Falls	$136.00	$13.60	$52.00	$5.70	$207.30
Anniston	139.00	13.60	38.80	4.30	195.70
St. Louis	137.00	13.50	37.30	4.10	191.90
Portland	136.00	13.60	30.70	4.00	184.30

Overtime Costs **

	Paper	Other Materials	Direct Labor	Vacations & Holidays *	Total Variable Production Costs
Bellows Falls	$136.00	$13.60	$78.00	$5.70	$233.30
Anniston	139.00	13.60	58.20	4.30	215.10
St. Louis	137.00	13.50	55.95	4.10	210.55
Portland	136.00	13.60	46.05	4.00	199.65

* Vacation and holiday pay, unemployment compensation, social security taxes, etc., are estimated at 11% of direct labor.
** Only change in variable production costs assumed to be 50% extra direct labor cost.
Note: See case (A), page 89.

Exhibit II

Sullivan Paper Bag Company (C)
Nonvariable Production Costs, 1959

	Indirect Labor & Supervision	Vacation & Holiday Pay, etc.*	Heat, Light, Power, & Insurance	Plant & Equipment Depreciation	Total
Bellows Falls ..	$ 50,200	$	$25,000	$ 15,000	
Anniston	30,500		13,000	25,000	
St. Louis	23,000		10,000	40,000	
Portland	18,600		8,000	30,000	
Total	$122,300	$14,634	$56,000	$110,000	

* Does not include vacation and holiday pay, etc., for direct labor workers. See Exhibit I.

Note: See case (A), page 89.

Exhibit III

Sullivan Paper Bag Company (C)
Shipping Costs and Total Variable Costs, 1959

Sullivan Shipping Rates in 1959, $/Ton

From	Boston	New York	Atlanta	Chicago	Houston	San Francisco
Bellows Falls	$ 7.84	$ 9.80	$31.36	$27.44	$35.28	$50.96
Anniston ...	25.48	23.52	9.80	27.44	27.44	43.12
St. Louis ...	27.44	25.48	27.44	9.80	15.68	31.36
Portland ...	54.88	54.88	50.96	33.32	33.32	17.64

Total Variable Costs * in 1959, $/Ton
Distributed through:

	Boston	New York	Atlanta	Chicago	Houston	San Francisco
Bellows Falls	$215.14	$217.20	$238.66	$234.74	$242.58	$258.26
Anniston ...	221.18	219.22	205.50	223.14	223.14	238.82
St. Louis ...	219.34	217.38	219.34	201.70	207.58	223.26
Portland ...	239.18	239.18	235.26	217.62	217.62	201.94

Overtime production:

	Boston	New York	Atlanta	Chicago	Houston	San Francisco
Bellows Falls	$241.14	$243.20	$264.66	$260.74	$268.58	$284.26
Anniston ...	240.58	238.62	224.90	242.54	242.54	258.22
St. Louis ...	237.99	236.03	237.99	220.35	226.23	241.91
Portland ...	254.53	254.53	250.61	232.97	232.97	217.29

* Variable production costs plus shipping costs.

Exhibit IV

Sullivan Paper Bag Company (C)
Variable Production and Shipping Costs,
Rounded to Nearest Dollar per Ton

	Boston	New York	Atlanta	Chicago	Houston	San Francisco
1961						
Bellows Falls	224	226	248	244	252	269
Anniston ...	230	228	214	232	232	248
St. Louis ...	228	226	228	210	216	232
Portland ...	249	249	245	226	226	210
Overtime						
Bellows Falls	251	253	275	272	279	296
Anniston ...	250	248	234	252	252	269
St. Louis ...	248	246	248	229	235	252
Portland ...	271	271	267	249	249	233
1965						
Bellows Falls	242	245	269	264	273	291
Anniston ...	249	247	231	251	251	269
St. Louis ...	247	245	247	227	234	251
Portland ...	269	269	265	245	245	227
Overtime						
Bellows Falls	272	274	296	294	302	320
Anniston ...	271	269	253	273	273	291
St. Louis ...	268	266	268	248	255	272
Portland ...	287	287	282	262	262	245
1970						
Bellows Falls	267	270	297	292	302	321
Anniston ...	275	273	255	277	277	297
St. Louis ...	273	270	273	251	258	278
Portland ...	297	297	292	271	271	251
Overtime						
Bellows Falls	300	302	329	324	334	353
Anniston ...	299	297	280	301	302	321
St. Louis ...	296	293	296	274	281	301
Portland ...	316	316	312	290	290	270

Exhibit V

Sullivan Paper Bag Company (C)
Status Quo, 1961

Optimal Schedule

	Boston	New York	Atlanta	Chicago	Houston	San Francisco	Slack	Total Productive Capacity
Bellows Falls	2,650	10,180					1,170	14,000
Anniston			12,000					12,000
St. Louis			1,680	8,910	5,410			16,000
Portland						7,740	4,260	12,000
Overtime								
Bellows Falls							7,000	7,000
Anniston			2,450				3,550	6,000
St. Louis							8,000	8,000
Portland							6,000	6,000
Total Demand	2,650	10,180	16,130	8,910	5,410	7,740	29,980	81,000

Z_{ij}'s, Substitution Route Rates

	D_1	D_2	D_3	D_4	D_5	D_6	D_7	U_i
S_1	224*	226*	234	216	222	210	0*	0
S_2	204	206	214*	196	202	290	−20	−20
S_3	218	220	228*	210*	216*	204	− 6	− 6
S_4	224	226	234	216	222	210*	0*	0
S_5	224	226	234	216	222	210	0*	0
S_6	224	226	234*	216	222	210	0*	0
S_7	224	226	234	216	222	210	0*	0
S_8	224	226	234	216	222	210	0*	0
V_j	224	226	234	216	222	210	0	

* Significant costs per unit factors associated with output figures in Optimal Schedule above.

Exhibit VI

Sullivan Paper Bag Company (C)
Close Bellows Falls, Expand Anniston, 1961

Optimal Schedule

	Boston	New York	Atlanta	Chicago	Houston	San Francisco	Slack	Total Productive Capacity
Bellows Falls							—	—
Anniston	2,650	7,220	16,130					26,000
St Louis		2,960		8,910	4,130			16,000
Portland					1,280	7,740	2,980	12,000
Overtime								
Bellows Falls							13,000	13,000
Anniston							8,000	8,000
St. Louis							6,000	6,000
Portland								
Total Demand ...	2,650	10,180	16,130	8,910	5,410	7,740	29,980	81,000

Z_{ij}'s, Substitution Route Rates

	D_1	D_2	D_3	D_4	D_5	D_6	D_7	U_i
S_1	230*	228*	214*	212	218	202	—8	0
S_2	228	226*	212	210*	216*	200	—10	—2
S_3	238	246	222	220	226*	210*	0*	8
S_4	—	—	—	—	—	—	—	—
S_5	238	246	222	220	226	210	0*	8
S_6	238	246	222	220	226	210	0*	8
S_7	238	246	222	220	226	210	0*	8
S_8	238	246	222	220	226	210	0*	8
V_j	230	228	214	212	218	202	—8	

* Significant costs per unit factors associated with output figures in Optimal Schedule above.

Exhibit VII

Sullivan Paper Bag Company (C)
Status Quo, 1965

Optimal Schedule

	Boston	New York	Atlanta	Chicago	Houston	San Francisco	Slack	Total Productive Capacity
Bellows Falls	2,990	11,010						14,000
Anniston			12,000					12,000
St. Louis		450	150	10,030	5,370			16,000
Portland					720	8,720	2,560	12,000
Overtime								
Bellows Falls							7,000	7,000
Anniston			6,000					6,000
St. Louis							8,000	8,000
Portland							6,000	6,000
Total Demand	2,990	11,460	18,150	10,030	6,090	8,720	23,560	81,000

Z_{ij}'s, Substitution Route Rates

	D_1	D_2	D_3	D_4	D_5	D_6	D_7	U_i
S_1	242*	245*	247	227	234	216	−11	0
S_2	226	229	231*	209	218	200	−27	−16
S_3	242	245*	247*	227*	234*	216	−11	0
S_4	253	256	258	238	245*	227*	0*	11
S_5	253	256	258	238	245	227	0*	11
S_6	248	251	253*	233	240	222	−5	6
S_7	253	256	258	238	245	227	0*	11
S_8	253	256	258	238	245	227	0*	11
V_j	242	245	247	227	234	216	−11	

* Significant costs per unit factors associated with output figures in Optimal Schedule above.

Exhibit VIII

Sullivan Paper Bag Company (C)
Close Bellows Falls, Expand Anniston, 1965

Optimal Schedule

	Boston	New York	Atlanta	Chicago	Houston	San Francisco	Slack	Total Productive Capacity
Bellows Falls	—	—	—	—	—	—	—	—
Anniston	2,990	4,860	18,150					26,000
St. Louis		3,160		10,030	2,810			16,000
Portland					3,280	8,720		12,000
Overtime								
Bellows Falls	—	—	—	—	—	—	13,000	13,000
Anniston		3,440					4,560	8,000
St. Louis							6,000	6,000
Total Demand	2,990	11,460	18,150	10,030	6,090	8,720	23,560	81,000

Z_{ij}'s, Substitution Route Rates

	D_1	D_2	D_3	D_4	D_5	D_6	D_7	U_i
S_1	—	—	—	—	—	—	—	—
S_2	249*	247*	231*	229	236	218	−19	0
S_3	247	245*	229	227*	234*	216	−21	−2
S_4	258	256	240	238	245*	227*	−10	9
S_5	—	—	—	—	—	—	—	—
S_6	268	266	250	248	255	237	0*	19
S_7	268	266*	250	248	255	237	0*	19
S_8	268	266	250	248	255	237	0*	19
V_j	249	247	231	229	236	218	−19	

* Significant costs per unit factors associated with output figures in Optimal Schedule above.

116

DECISIONS INVOLVING CONTROL

Exhibit IX

Sullivan Paper Bag Company (C)
Status Quo, 1970

Optimal Schedule

	Boston	New York	Atlanta	Chicago	Houston	San Francisco	Slack	Total Productive Capacity
Bellows Falls	3,460	10,540						14,000
Anniston			12,000					12,000
St. Louis				11,630	4,370			16,000
Portland					1,900	10,100		12,000
Overtime								
Bellows Falls							7,000	7,000
Anniston			6,000					6,000
St. Louis		2,750	3,040		790		1,420	8,000
Portland							6,000	6,000
Total Demand ...	3,460	13,290	21,040	11,630	7,060	10,100	14,420	81,000

Z_{ij}'s, Substitution Route Rates

	D_1	D_2	D_3	D_4	D_5	D_6	D_7	U_i
S_1	267*	270*	273	251	258	238	−23	0
S_2	249	252	255*	233	240	220	−41	−18
S_3	267	270	273	251*	258*	238	−23	0
S_4	280	283	286	264	271*	251*	−10	13
S_5	290	293	296	274	281	261	0*	23
S_6	273	293	280*	258	265	245	−16	7
S_7	290	293*	296*	274	281*	261	0*	23
S_8	290	293	296	274	281	261	0*	23
V_j	267	270	273	251	258	238	−23	

* Significant costs per unit factors associated with output figures in Optimal Schedule above.

Exhibit X

Sullivan Paper Bag Company (C)
Close Bellows Falls, Expand Anniston, 1970

Optimal Schedule

	Boston	New York	Atlanta	Chicago	Houston	San Francisco	Slack	Total Productive Capacity
Bellows Falls	—	—	—	—		—	—	
Anniston	3,460	1,500	21,040					26,000
St. Louis				11,630	4,370			16,000
Portland					1,900	10,100		12,000
Overtime								
Bellows Falls								
Anniston		4,580					8,420	13,000
St. Louis		7,210			790			8,000
Portland							6,000	6,000
Total Demand ...	3,460	13,290	21,040	11,630	7,060	10,100	14,420	81,000

Z_{ij}'s, Substitution Route Rates

	D_1	D_2	D_3	D_4	D_5	D_6	D_7	U_i
S_1	—	—	—	—	—	—	—	—
S_2	275*	273*	255*	254	261	241	-24	0
S_3	272	270	252	251*	258*	238	-27	-3
S_4	285	283	265	264	271*	251*	-14	10
S_5	—	—	—	—	—	—	—	—
S_6	299	297*	279	278	285	265	0*	24
S_7	295	293*	275	274	281*	261	-4	20
S_8	299	297	279	278	285	265	0*	24
V_j	275	273	255	254	261	241	-24	

* Significant costs per unit factors associated with output figures in Optimal Schedule above.

DECISIONS INVOLVING CONTROL

Exhibit XI

Sullivan Paper Bag Company (C)
Nonvariable Costs

Bases for Calculations:

1959 Costs	Base case all 4 plants, no expansion and no overtime	Add for each plant on overtime	Add for expansion of Anniston	Subtract if close Bellows Falls
Indirect labor and supervision	$122,300	$15,000	$11,000	$50,200
Vacation and holiday pay, etc. ...	14,634*	1,600	1,200	5,500
Heat, light, etc.	56,000	2,000	2,000	25,000
	$192,934	$18,600	$14,200	$80,700

All costs increase 2% per year.

Case		
Status Quo, 1961: $(1.02)^2$	$(192,934 + 18,600) =$	220,082
Close and expand, 1961: $(1.02)^2$	$(192,934 + 14,200 - 80,700) =$	131,542
Status Quo, 1965: $(1.02)^6$	$(192,934 + 18,600) =$	238,208
Close and expand, 1965: $(1.02)^6$	$(192,934 + 14,200 - 80,700 + 18,600) =$	163,323
Status Quo, 1970: $(1.02)^{11}$	$(192,934 + 2 \times 18,600) =$	286,126
Close and expand, 1970: $(1.02)^{11}$	$(192,934 + 14,200 - 80,700 + 2 \times 18,600) =$ 203,446	

* $14,634 = 231,400 - (.11) (1,970,600)$. See page 96, case (A).

Exhibit XII

Sullivan Paper Bag Company (C)
Costs for Two Alternatives

Alternative	Year	Variable Cost	Nonvariable Cost	Total	Savings
Status Quo	1961	$11,083,680	$220,080	$11,303,760	—
Close Bellows Falls, Expand Anniston	1961	11,054,300	131,542	11,185,842	$117,918
Status Quo	1965	13,547,560	238,208	13,785,768	—
Close Bellows Falls, Expand Anniston	1965	13,544,210	163,323	13,707,533	78,235
Status Quo	1970	17,533,790	286,126	17,819,916	—
Close Bellows Falls, Expand Anniston	1970	17,517,570	203,446	17,721,016	98,900

DECISIONS INVOLVING CONTROL

Exhibit XIII

Sullivan Paper Bag Company (C)
Estimated Savings from Proposed Anniston Investment

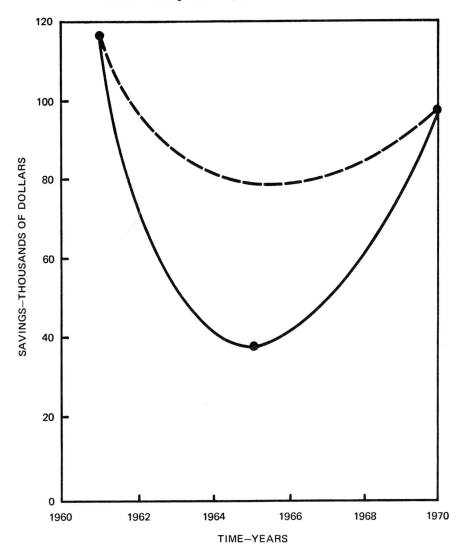

Exhibit XIV

Sullivan Paper Bag Company (C)
Rate of Return on Investment

Year	Operating Saving	Cash Flow	P.V. Factor @ 8%	Discounted Cash Flow	P.V. Factor @ 7%	Discounted Cash Flow
1960	—	$-480,000*	1.0000	$-480,000	1.0000	$-480,000
1961	$117,900	145,750**	.9259	134,950	.9346	136,218
1962	93,000	61,800****	.8573	52,981	.8734	53,976
1963	85,000	57,960	.7938	46,008	.8163	47,313
1964	80,000	55,560	.7350	40,836	.7629	42,387
1965	78,200	54,700	.6806	37,228	.7130	39,001
1966	80,000	55,560	.6302	35,014	.6663	37,020
1967	83,000	57,000	.5835	33,260	.6228	35,500
1968	87,000	58,920	.5403	31,834	.5820	34,291
1969	92,000	61,320	.5003	30,678	.5439	33,352
1970	98,900	64,630	.4632	29,937	.5084	32,858
				$- 7,274		$ 11,916

* Investment, see case (A).

** (.48) (117,900) operating savings + $20,000 from sale of equipment + $52,000 tax shield from loss on sale + (.52) (33,000) due to increased depreciation.

*** 0.48 times operating savings plus (.52) (33,000) due to increased depreciation (same for years 1963 through 1970).

$$\text{R.O.R.} = 7\% + \frac{11,916}{11,916 + 7,274} = 7.6\%.$$

DECISIONS INVOLVING CONTROL

Exhibit XV

Sullivan Paper Bag Company (C)
Savings in Variable Costs Possible from
Use of Linear Programming

	A Variable Costs Optimal Schedule	B Variable Costs with Policy Rule *	C Savings from Use of L.P.
Status Quo, 1961	$11,083,680	$11,093,760	$10,080
Close and Expand, 1961	11,054,300	11,106,620	52,320
Status Quo, 1965	13,547,560	13,555,210	7,650
Close and Expand, 1965	13,544,210	13,587,810	43,600
Status Quo, 1970	17,533,790	17,577,540	43,750
Close and Expand, 1970	17,517,570	17,577,200	59,630

* Rule is "supply each distribution point from the plant nearest it."

Electric Sign Company

In terms of sales volume, number of manufacturing plants and sales offices, and number of leases and maintenance contracts in effect, Electric Sign Company is one of the leaders in the custom electrical outdoor advertising industry in the United States. In contrast to the typical company in the sign industry which has fewer than 100 employees, Electric Sign Company provides a full range of services—including sign design, manufacturing, installation, and maintenance through more than 40 branch offices in cities from coast to coast.

While most of the branch offices handle work in their respective cities, one branch of the company is called the National Marketing Group. This branch, located in the Midwest, is comprised of four salespeople, three sales coordinators, and three secretaries. Its specific goal is to secure sign identification for national accounts—in other words, nationwide companies with standard identification and logos and numerous offices throughout the country such as large insurance agencies, car rental agencies, fast-food franchises, and retail stores. When the National Marketing Group salesperson secures an account, the upper level management of Electric Sign Company has one or two of its branches manufacture the required signs in large quantities to maximize the benefits of lower cost per unit output. The sales coordinators handle the order writing and coordinate the manufacture and installation of the signs for the national accounts through Electric Sign Company, various branches, and also through subcontractors in cities and small towns where a company branch does not exist.

The manufacturing branch provides National Marketing with an estimate of the cost of fabricating a sign or group of signs, and this estimate is the basis of the customer selling price. The manufacturing branch in turn bills the National Marketing Group the estimated cost upon completion of the job.

One of the sales coordinators, Terry Smith, is having difficulty with the Cleveland branch plant manager, Bill Clark, who is not following standard company procedures in billing National Marketing for completed sign work.

Smith is on the phone from her office in Chicago and Clark is in Cleveland:

Smith: Hello, Bill. This is Terry Smith from the National Marketing Group.

Clark: Hi, Terry. What can I do for you?

Smith: Bill, I just received your invoice in the mail today for the prototype sign you built for us for Economy Rent-A-Car. As you know, we are trying to secure the entire sign program for the Economy Company. That's why Jim Davis, the salesperson handling the account, had a prototype sign built. Economy agreed to pay $2,000 for this prototype sign.

Clark: And what's your problem?

Smith: Bill, your invoice to us is for $1,400, but your original estimate for the sign was only $800. This, plus the installation price for the sign which was given to us by our subcontractor, is what we based our selling price on.

Clark: We had some unforseen problems with the prototype, and besides that, we improved on the design which you gave us.

Smith: I know you recommended and built the sign with lexan faces—an unbreakable material—but if you'll recall, you increased your estimate $100 for the use of the lexan. I can't accept these extra costs which you have billed us.

Clark: Go back to the customer for more money.

Smith: Come on, Bill, I can't do that. We're trying to get their entire program. How can the salesperson ask for more money on the first sign we build for them? We'll lose the account for sure.

Clark: We improved that sign for you, and if you get the account, it will be because of our design.

Smith: I appreciate the work you did for us, Bill, and the Economy Rent-A-Car people were impressed with the sign; but I've already accepted the extra $100 you requested for the improvement of the sign. If I accept the $1,400 invoice now, the cost of the sign will be more than the selling price.

Clark: That's not my problem. My job is manufacturing—to get the sign built and built properly.

Smith: Bill, it is your problem. I can't help it if your estimator blew this job and didn't take into account all of the variables in fabricating the prototype sign. I'm not going to eat the extra cost because of your error.

Clark: If you're going to be so concerned about extra costs incurred in the job, then don't bother to give us any more of that kind of work.

Smith: Come on, Bill. You know as well as I do that this account will mean $300,000 worth of business to our company, not to mention that your plant will get the majority of the work. I can't pass along any more cost to the customer and jeopardize the account.

Clark: All right. Send the invoice back to me, and I'll see if I can lower it a little, but I'm not promising you anything.

Smith hangs up the phone just as John Drake, another coordinator, walks by her desk.

Drake: What was that all about? I could hear you across the office.

Smith: I was talking to Bill Clark in Cleveland. He's trying to make us absorb his cost for a job. Take a look at this invoice from Cleveland—$1,400 for a job that was estimated at and should have been billed to us for $800. Sometimes I wonder if we're one company or not.

Drake: I know what you mean, Terry. I feel like I'm always fighting the other branches, especially Cleveland, for fair pricing. They treat us like we're a regular customer rather than a branch of the same company. I would think that the branches would want the work from our national accounts. Take the Nickels Department Store—that brought in $2,000,000 worth of business for the company last year, and half of that work was done by the Cleveland branch.

Smith: I know I've only been working here for six months, but I can see that things should be different between branches.

Drake: The problem is that plant managers are trying to make their branches number one. At the end of each year the company comes out with a ranking of each branch's performance, and naturally, each plant manager wants to be at the top. They try to cut corners and avoid extra costs no matter what.

Smith: But what about the company—is a branch more important than the entire company?

Drake: Sometimes, I think that's the way these plant managers think. They haven't been exposed to the national scope of the company. There seems to exist an attitude of "every man for himself."

Smith: Have you had other problems with Bill Clark?

Drake: You bet I have. Take the State Life Insurance account, for instance. Cleveland built the prototype signs for the program and the original quantity order of signs once the account was secured. When we needed a second quantity order of signs, Clark tried to increase his estimate. I told him there was no way we could pass the increase in cost on to the customer. We secured the account because we could fabricate the signs for the least possible cost.

Smith: What was Clark's answer to that?

Drake: He told me that State Life was a lousy seven percent of his plant's business and that he didn't need it. He wanted the extra cost to insure more profit for his branch. Of course, he didn't come right out and say it, but that was the inference I drew.

Smith: Doesn't he realize you can't keep asking the customer for more money? We wouldn't have any national accounts if we continually kept raising prices as Clark wants us to do. We have all the facilities to service these national accounts—that's the strong point of Electric Sign Company. We can coordinate the manufacture and installation of large quantities of signs in many locations.

Drake: We can't if we don't get cooperation from our branches. Cleveland is the perfect example of noncooperation. After Clark told me he didn't need the State Life account, I went to some other branches with engineering drawings to obtain estimates for the sign program.

Smith: That seems a logical thing to do.

Drake: You should have heard Clark when he found out I was looking for another plant to fabricate the State Life signs. He got right on the phone and told me he wouldn't allow me to have them built elsewhere. Of course, Clark doesn't have the authority to tell me that, but he was really shook up.

Smith: I can appreciate the difficulties in running a plant, but I don't feel a manager can be insensitive to the needs of a customer—especially a large account customer—merely to make his branch look good. These large accounts give so much business to our company that it's ridiculous to jeopardize the programs to satisfy one plant manager.

Drake: It's easy enough to talk about what's right, but it's another thing to convince Clark our ideas will benefit everyone.

Smith: I suppose you're right, and I hope our upper level management will get things turned around.

Drake: I hope so, too. If things don't change soon, we're going to have to ask management for a ruling on situations like these.

Smith: I suppose we will. I hate to do that, though, because it makes it look like we're incapable of handling our problems without running to our bosses for help. We can't let Clark keep overcharging us for work either, and the guy just won't seem to listen to our argument.

Terry Smith begins sifting through some papers on her desk and runs across another invoice from Bill Clark.

Smith: Here's another bill from Cleveland asking us to go back to one of our other national accounts for more money. Cleveland blew the estimate again, and Clark is trying to pass the cost along to us.

Drake: Clark should shake up his estimating department and get some better people in there. We have to base our customer selling price on the estimates we receive from the branches, and bad estimating hurts the whole company.

Smith: Well, I guess I'd better get on the phone and talk to Clark again— maybe I'll convince him this time.

Drake: I doubt it, but you've got to give it a try anyway.

Smith dials Clark's number on the phone.

Smith: Hello, may I speak to Bill Clark, please?

Clark: This is Bill.

Smith: Bill, this is Terry Smith, again. I have another one of your invoices here, and you've billed us a figure which is way over your estimated cost.

Clark: Let me guess. You don't want to accept the charges, right?

Smith: Of course I don't, Bill. What if you agreed to buy a TV at a store and then when the TV was delivered to your house, the store wanted $300 more for the set? Would you accept the extra cost?

Clark: The analogy doesn't fit here, Terry. Whenever we exceed our estimated cost, it's for a justifiable reason. Either we improve upon the design of the sign or we run into some unforeseen difficulties which raise our cost.

Smith: What can I do about that?

Clark: Let me give you my side of the story. I'm trying to run a factory and produce so much output per day at the best possible profit. Obviously, you are not aware of the difficulties of running a plant day-to-day.

Smith: And you aren't aware of the problems of the sales force.

Clark: Let me finish. I have to deal with machines, materials, people, and scheduling. I have to please both my boss with a good profit and the salespeople with low cost so they can sell a sign. It's difficult to do both, besides handling day-to-day problems. Therefore, when justifiable costs are incurred in a job over and above the estimated figure, I feel that the sales force should absorb the costs. We try to anticipate all problems, but we can't be perfect. I'm trying to turn out the best product possible at a decent profit; my boss wants our branch at the top, and if I continually absorb costs which rightfully belong to you or the customer, we won't be number one for long. I'll admit it when we make a mistake, but when a sign is made right and when the customer is happy with it, then the customer can pay for it.

Smith: It's obvious neither one of us is going to give ground on this issue, so I guess we'd better drop it for now. I'll talk to you on this tomorrow. Goodbye, Bill.

Clark: Goodbye.

Part Three

Decisions Involving Organization Management

Conflict
Change
Motivation
Leadership

Albert Steamship Company

Specializing in short-run, small-tonnage service, the Albert Steamship Company's ships operated along the coast and on international routes. While some ships operated on scheduled runs, others operated on a tramp basis—picking up cargo where it could be found. Since the tramp ships did not restrict their ports of call, they were in a position to bid on many cargoes. Over a nine-year period, the Albert Steamship Company had increased its fleet by either purchase or charter. Mainly, the company chartered vessels to have flexibility over the long run as well as rechartered these ships if it was found they would be idle. By the ninth year, the company was operating a fleet of 86 ships which, although of the low-tonnage variety, required direction from the central office. (See Exhibit 1.)

Exhibit 1

Vessels and Tonnages
Operated by Albert Steamship Company

Year	Number of Vessels	Total Gross Weight (Tons)
1	21	20,450
2	45	36,750
3	51	51,100
4	44	36,400
5	46	46,300
6	50	58,020
7	61	117,487 deadweight
8	84	172,127 deadweight
9	86	182,127 deadweight

INTERNAL ORGANIZATION

To control the movement of these ships, the company established offices in the main ports of call and staffed them with traffic personnel. These people reported to the local agent, who, in turn, reported to the general manager in the head office. (See Exhibit 2.) Through radio, telephone, cable, and in certain instances, telex communications, the main office directed the operation of the entire system.

In the main office and reporting to the general manager was the manager of the operation department, Eliot. The task of this department was to utilize the vessels to serve all routes—considering the types of the vessels, the varieties of the cargoes, and the terminal facilities—and to dispatch and control the over-the-route vessels to insure regular sailing over the scheduled routes. To handle this broad range of tasks, the department was divided into three divisions—course of the vessels, terminal, and chartered division. The assistant department manager, Wellington, had full authority over the course of vessel division, while Eliot assumed authority over the other two.

Wellington's Responsibilities

Wellington, age 27, had taken a two-year course at a maritime school and then had continued to study in this area in a night school. As the assistant department head, his job was to receive the communications concerning the current situation of the vessels, both those in operation and those undergoing repairs. He also sent orders and information about the time of departure or estimated time of departure as well as estimated time of arrival to or from successive ports of call. This was done by making such computations as the speed of the vessel, the distance to the next terminal, the weather, and the other conditions that would affect the time. This information was then sent directly to the agent in the port of destination.

Another decision for which Wellington was responsible concerned whether certain ships should wait for cargoes or whether they should call at scheduled ports of destination. The captains of the ships were required to keep in contact with him and to inform him as a central dispatcher of their movements. Also responsible for maximizing the utilization of cargo capacity and passenger space of the vessels, Wellington sent his estimates of available cargo and passenger space to the traffic department. This department then lined up the cargo and passengers to fill the available space.

McKinley's Responsibilities

McKinley, head of the traffic department, had held this position for the past 15 years. This department's tasks were to determine which port had available cargo as well as passengers, the kinds of cargo, destination of the cargo, and allotment for each port. On the basis of these allocations, the operation department was to move the ships as efficiently as possible. The traffic department also

Exhibit 2

Albert Steamship Company
Partial Organization Chart

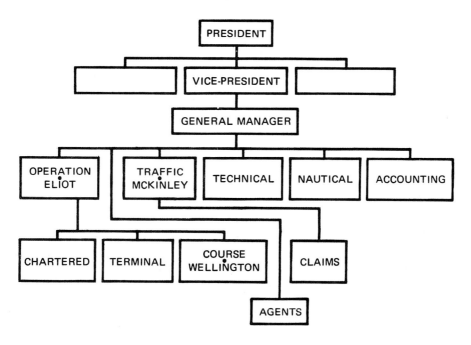

was responsible for the security of the cargo. To perform these tasks, the traffic department was divided into scheduled line, tramp line, passenger, and claim divisions.

In the early days of its operation, McKinley almost always met difficulties in getting enough cargo for the ships, but when Albert Steamship Company became better known, there was no longer such a serious difficulty. Even so, underutilization had persisted over the years as indicated in Exhibit 3.

McKinley was called into the office of the president shortly after the underutilization figures were available. The following conversation took place:

President: Mac, I don't understand these underutilization figures. We have more demand for space than we can possibly sell, and yet, we are running around with a third of our capacity lying idle. How do you explain that?

McKinley: Well, sir, this is not my responsibility alone. We line up enough cargo at a port, but if the dispatcher decides that the ship will not stop to pick up the cargo, then the ship may travel empty.

President: What do you mean—decides not to stop and pick up the cargo? Give me an example of how this could happen.

Exhibit 3

Utilization of the Vessels' Cargo Capacities

Year	Number of Vessels Used	Cargo Capacity (Total)	Transported Goods	Unused Capacity	Percent of Unused Capacity
			in 1,000 ton/days *		
2	45	280	na	–	–
3	51	604	437	167	27.6%
4	44	985	720	265	26.9
5	46	1,333	968	365	27.3
6	50	1,489	1,006	483	32.6
7	61	1,763	1,193	570	32.3
8	84	2,147	1,435	712	33.2
9	86	2,203	1,478	725	32.9

* Note: ton/days = total cargo carried in tons multiplied by the days of operation to carry it.

McKinley: Well, for instance, the *S.S. Alton* was supposed to stop at a port to pick up 600 tons of cargo that we had lined up, and then it was to go on from there. Wellington decided to skip the port because of the uncertainty of the labor conditions. It appeared that some sort of work stoppage might break out and tie up the ship, so Wellington routed it to some other port. You can see that the underutilization is outside of my responsibility.

Not satisfied, the president approached Eliot with a question about underutilization. Eliot replied by describing the difficulties faced by the department in its daily operation of dispatching the ships to run over the scheduled routes and on scheduled times.

Eliot: Difficulties arose because of the lack of means of communications as well as insufficient terminal facilities and technical assistance. Thus, emergencies arose, upsetting schedules and causing delays. It meant that the sailing schedules had to be revised as soon as information was received as to the difficulties. Revisions might take place in the time schedule as well as in the route.[1] Difficulties required delays of between 5 and 25 days. So, revision in the schedule meant that the ship would arrive from 5 to 25 days late. This might result in losing the cargo because of shifts to other shipping lines. Often, after revising the schedule, there was no return cargo available in the next port of call. So, the undercapacity utilization is outside of our competence. (See Exhibit 4.)

1. Revision in *time* means the ship would arrive late in terms of the scheduled time, while revision in the *route* means the ship or ships would not call at the scheduled port of call after the schedule was revised.

Exhibit 4

The Cause and Number of Delays

	Total Delays	1st Quarter	2d Quarter	3d Quarter	4th Quarter
	Operating days *				
Operating Days					
Planned	11,500	2,490	2,582	3,146	3,282
Realized	12,535	2,680	2,825	3,404	3,626
Delays	1,035	190	243	258	344
Causes of Delays:					
Technical reasons [1]	276	59	89	83	45
Insufficiency of terminal facilities [2]	360	48	72	115	125
Forced by regulation [3]	106	28	7	14	57
Waiting for cargo	58	9	28	10	11
Holidays	48	11	22	3	12
Natural causes [4]	102	25	7	9	61
Other company's account	8	—	1	—	7
Personal causes [5]	30	9	13	2	6
Financial causes	4	1	2	1	—
Reasons unknown	43	—	2	21	20

* The number of days needed to serve a round-trip route multiplied by the number of vessels operating that route.

1. Including technical breakdowns in equipment, lack of spare parts, other emergency breakdowns within the vessel itself; including insufficient technical assistance to make prompt repairs.

2. Including shortages of loading and unloading equipment and shortage of warehousing; shortage of labor supplied by the agent for loading and unloading the vessel at the time of arrival; delays caused by waiting for letter or certificate permitting entrance or departure at the harbors (these permits are obtained by the agent from the local Maritime Administrator, a government official).

3. Includes delays required by local maritime to accommodate use of the harbor for government or military or ceremonial purposes.

4. Natural causes include heavy rains or heavy seas that make it impossible to sail or to load and unload the vessels.

5. The absence of the captain, officers, or other key personnel of the vessel at the time of departure, or their objections to sailing until routes and sailing schedule disagreements have been resolved.

INTERNAL PROBLEMS

As time went on, the capacity continued to be underutilized. A few months later, Wellington tried to make an arrangement to increase utilization by signing a contract with a shipper to carry several hundred tons of cargo. He had succeeded in such arrangements only after the schedule of the route had been revised in the previous months. When rain caused a considerable amount of damage to the special cargo, the shipper placed a $5,000 claim for the damage. After checking the goods, the head of the claim division proposed to his superior, McKinley, a settlement of the claim for $3,500. The occasion was vague to McKinley; he did not remember when the contract was signed. McKinley was reminded by the claims manager that Wellington had lined up and signed the cargo contract. "This, then, is the responsibility of the operation department," he said. He objected to payment of the claim and sent it to the operation department. But the latter sent it back to McKinley because they said it was the responsibility of the traffic department.

The operation department head, Eliot, tried to determine why McKinley had sent him that claim which actually was under McKinley's jurisdiction. He asked Wellington about this: "I think this is connected with what we proposed in the last manager's session."

REORGANIZATION PLANS

Wellington, on behalf of his department, had proposed the reorganization of the operation and traffic departments, because he had been to several branches where it was impractical to separate these two departments. Since there was much functional relationship between them and if one lacked information from the other, then losses in efficiency resulted. Similarities in the nature of these two departments made it possible to unify them under one head with the title of manager, business section. (See Exhibit 5.) Advantages of the reorganization had been explained at the session. These included, among others, the fact that as contact between departments became closer, the efficient utilization of space became the common objective and responsibility. Definite responsibility for utilization lay with the manager of the business section. Conflicting plans of the two departments could be avoided as could any shortcomings in communication. If an emergency upset the schedule, the manager of the business section would be able to make prompt decisions, based on maximum efficiency of the utilization of resources. With fewer sources of functional orders to the agent, the advantages of the principle of unity of command could be more nearly attained.

Wellington had met considerable opposition to his proposal. One of the serious opponents to the plan was McKinley, who said the existing structure of organization was sound because the authority might be delegated to several managers. He explained at the session:

McKinley: The dispersion of the tasks and authority to several persons is far better than if concentrated in one hand—that is, the manager of the business section. We expect from the existing structure that one department

Exhibit 5

Albert Steamship Company
Proposed Reorganization Chart

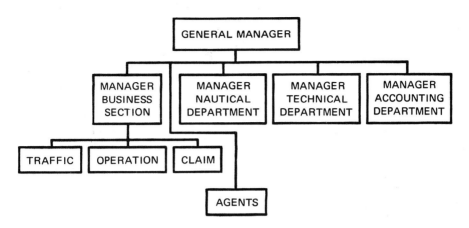

will control the others. So, the one who dislikes the decentralization of authority is the one who is unwilling to be controlled. Centralization of the tasks and authority in one hand would bring inefficiency because of personal limitations. The defect is not in the organization structure, but in the lack of the right person behind the right structure and in the unsound cooperation between departments. And finally, to add a manager of a business section in the chain of command violates the principle of management that communication is improved by holding the vertical levels of command at a minimum.

Henderson Specialties, Inc.

A manufacturer and distributor of food products, Henderson Specialties, Inc. was located in a metropolitan area of approximately 300,000. Limiting its sales to relatively small local bakeries, restaurants, and hotels, Henderson's products were sold in small quantities. The main product line included food colors, artificial flavors, cake icings, baking chocolate, ice cream, spices, and pudding powders. In order to carry a full line of these products, the company bought approximately 40 percent of them in a finished or semi-finished state from other manufacturers.

Although the Henderson Specialties line had a good reputation, the company encountered strong competition from two other manufacturers of similar products located in the same city. In recent years these competitors had succeeded in increasing their market share—a fact attributed to more aggressive marketing methods and faster delivery service. This latter service was particularly important since most of the customers were small businesses which bought food products on a small quantity basis.

The customers seemed to be interested mainly in price and service. Quality and price of the various products were about the same among the competitors. Even ice cream was of almost uniform quality from one company to another. Since there was little evidence of customer loyalty to a company or a brand, the salespeople knew the first of them to enter a customer's office would get an order.

Henderson Specialties, Inc. was formerly owned and operated by two partners, William Henderson and his brother, Alvin Henderson. The two brothers founded the company in the '30s and succeeded in selling their products nationally in the '40s. After suffering a substantial gambling debt which seriously impaired the company's financial condition, William Henderson left the company. Five years later, 54-year-old Alvin became seriously ill and was no longer able to participate actively in management. During a seven-year period, sales declined from $2 million to $300,000. When Jane Shanks (28 years of age) purchased the company, the year-end financial position was as indicated in Exhibits 1 and 2.

Shanks held approximately 80 percent of the company's stock, and a few relatives held the remainder. Shanks, who had recently

Exhibit 1

Henderson Specialties, Incorporated
Income Statement

Net sales		$303,000
Cost of Goods Sold:		
Inventory, January 1	$ 39,000	
Purchases	192,000	
Cost of Merchandise Available	$231,000	
Less Inventory, December 31	51,000	
Cost of Goods Sold		180,000
Gross Profit on Sales		$123,000
Selling Expenses	$ 78,000	
Gen. and Adm. Expenses	39,000	117,000
Net Profit before Taxes		$ 6,000

Exhibit 2

Henderson Specialties, Incorporated
Balance Sheet—Year End

ASSETS			LIABILITIES AND CAPITAL		
Current Assets:			Current Liabilities:		
Cash		$ 5,000	Accounts Payable ...		$ 57,000
Accounts Re-			Notes Payable		21,000
ceivable ..		39,000	Total Current		
Inventory ...		51,000	Liabilities		$ 78,000
Total Current					
Assets ...		$ 95,000			
Fixed Assets:			Net Worth:		
Delivery			Henderson, Capital ..		$120,000
Equip	$ 9,000				
Furniture &					
Fixt	5,000				
Machinery ..	89,000				
Total Fixed					
Assets ...		103,000	Total Liabilities and		
Total Assets .		$198,000	Net Worth		$198,000

received a Ph.D. in economics, had approximately two years of practical business experience. She was elected the president after the incorporation. When asked by a friend, Bob Rogers, why she had invested money in the company, the following conversation took place:

Shanks: I think the company is almost on the rocks, Bob, but it has great potential. After all, a few years ago it was the leading company in the field. I think I can shape it up and make it profitable again. If not, I can sell it in a few years. It certainly is worth the risk. I like this challenge, Bob. I believe I can build this company into the largest of its kind in the area.

Rogers: But you have very little business experience and practically none in the food line, Jane.

Shanks: That's true. But I think I'm not exactly stupid. Besides, there are a few good people in the company. Take Andy Green, the production manager, for example. He has served an apprenticeship as a baker and has been with the company for over 10 years. I think he is a very competent man and a nice guy besides. (See Exhibit 3.)

Rogers: How about the other people?

Shanks: There is Florence Dillen the controller and office manager. She has been with the company for almost 20 years. Although she seems to know her business, I think she is a little narrow-minded. I bet she watches every penny in the company. Well, I suppose she has to. The financial position of the company is not exactly rosy. She is about 50 and pretty well set in her ways. I hope I can get along with her. You know, Bob, it is not exactly easy for her to take orders from a woman so much younger than herself.

Rogers: And how about the sales manager, Jane?

Shanks: To tell you the truth, there is none. Old Mr. Henderson used to handle that, and I think I'm going to shape up the sales force myself. You know, I have always been interested in the marketing end of business. I will be plenty busy in these areas: The company's sales force is too small. Packaging is old-fashioned. And as far as merchandising and advertising are concerned, I think these people have never even heard the words.

During the first week of January, Shanks had a conference with Green and Dillen.

Shanks: Florence, can you give me your candid thoughts on our financial position?

Dillen: Rather strained. For one thing, we are very short on cash. All our money is tied up in receivables and inventory. (See Exhibit 2.) We almost never take advantage of cash discounts because we have trouble meeting our obligations on time. For another thing, I think we should concentrate more on the profitable items in our line.

Shanks: If I understand you correctly, we have to reduce the amount of money tied up in inventory and push some profitable items that we can produce ourselves. I don't think we can do too much about our money tied up in receivables because of the terms of the industry.

Dillen: That is correct.

Shanks: Andy, which items in our line are relatively cheap to produce and permit a good markup?

Green: I would say ice cream and cake icing. I have also been thinking that, with our equipment, we could manufacture artificial honey which would be ideally suited for baking.

Exhibit 3

Henderson Specialties, Incorporated
Organization Chart

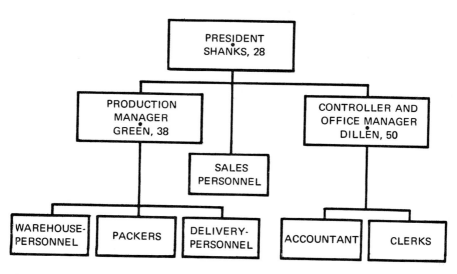

Shanks: An excellent idea, Andy. We will look into that more thoroughly after I've talked with our sales personnel. In conclusion, I would like to say that I am convinced we can compete successfully and regain a large part of the market share which the company has lost under the previous management. It will take a lot of hard work on the part of all of us. But as we grow, you'll grow with the company. I will appreciate your help and cooperation. Thank you.

In the spring, Henderson Specialties introduced its honey which, after initial sales resistance, became a full success. Green, the production manager, also experimented with new ice cream flavors, and in the summer the company entered the market with a complete line of ice cream. Shanks spent much of her time in the field working with the sales force as she hired several new salespeople and developed new accounts. Together with the office manager, Dillen, the president designed new packages and containers in order to give the products a modern, high-quality image. Shanks and Dillen spent many evenings together in order to determine how the company's cash position could be improved. On several occasions Shanks visited the office after hours to find the production manager, Green, working on new recipes, whistling while he was experimenting.

As a result of increased ice cream production, the income statement as of the end of the first year under Shanks indicated the company had increased substantially both sales and profits. (See Exhibits 4 and 5.)

Exhibit 4

Henderson Specialties, Inc.
Income Statement
First Year

Net Sales		$541,000
Cost of Goods Sold:		
Inventory, January 1	$ 51,000	
Purchases	258,000	
Cost of Merchandise Available	$309,000	
Less Inventory, December 31	38,000	
Cost of Goods Sold		271,000
Gross Profit on Sales		$270,000
Selling Expenses	$162,000	
Gen. and Adm. Expenses	56,000	218,000
Net Profit before Taxes		$ 52,000

Exhibit 5

Henderson Specialties, Inc.
Balance Sheet
First Year

ASSETS			LIABILITIES AND NET WORTH		
Current Assets:			Current Liabilities:		
Cash		$ 11,000	Accounts Payable		$103,000
Accounts Re-			Notes Payable		29,000
ceivable		152,000	Total Current Liabilities ..		$132,000
Inventory		38,000			
Total Current					
Assets		$201,000			
Fixed Assets:			Net Worth:		
Delivery			Capital Stock		170,000
Equip	$ 9,000				
Furniture &					
Fixt	5,000				
Machinery	87,000				
Total Fixed					
Assets		101,000	Total Liabilities and		
Total Assets		$302,000	Net Worth		$302,000

Shanks sought additional capital for expansion purposes, but she found that the banks had little interest in negotiating a loan. Loans based on the highly perishable food inventory were difficult to obtain. Even when successful, a loan of about one tenth of the value of the inventory was possible.

In the fall of the first year Shanks investigated the possibility of expanding by merging with the Sidney Food Flavoring Company. Before making overtures to the Sidney Company, Shanks sounded out Dillen and Green. Dillen was apprehensive and cautious about the financial position of the Sidney Company, and she felt a merger at this time should be given a great deal of thought. She stated that Henderson Specialties was still in shaky financial condition.

Green was more concerned about Paul Sidney, the owner. Henderson Specialties purchased large amounts from Sidney Food Flavoring, and through this contact Green had become acquainted with Sidney. Green felt that Sidney was hardheaded and gave the following as an example: "I have occasionally asked him to modify this or that product for us, but, although I'm sure that it would have increased his sales to other customers as well, he never did." Green did go on to say that he felt that Sidney knew his food chemistry and that the Sidney Food Flavoring products were of good quality.

Both Dillen and Green queried Shanks as to the advantages of such a merger. Shanks stated her reasons:

Shanks: We need additional production facilities, additional management know-how, and an expanded sales force. To build these characteristics into our business will take time and more capital than we now have or can get. But we can obtain all of these things if we merge. There are several other advantages to this merger. We can reduce our production and administrative costs, broaden our product line, and increase sales. In addition, we can be sure of our source of supply. You must remember that a company which stands still is a dying company. We have to grow if we expect to survive.

THE SIDNEY FOOD FLAVORING COMPANY

The Sidney Company was a manufacturer of a few specialty items in the food industry. Food flavors and colors accounted for the majority of the company's sales which amounted to approximately $112,000. (See Exhibits 6 and 7.) The Sidney Company sold direct to bakeries, restaurants, hotels, and also to several manufacturers of food products, including Henderson Specialties, Inc.

Customer contacts were made by either the one salesperson, John Reiner, or Sidney personally. Sidney was also in charge of the company's production, employing one or several employees on a part-time basis when business conditions required it. Sidney delivered most orders personally in his station wagon. In the evenings Sidney did some paper work, although he employed a full-time bookkeeper-secretary, Ms. Miller. The company was located in an old, ill-laid-out building, and storage was often a problem. But the main problem seemed to center around the machinery, which needed either to be replaced or to be completely overhauled.

In October, Sidney discussed the possibility of a merger with his salesperson, John Reiner.

Exhibit 6

Sidney Food Flavoring Company
Income Statement

Net Sales		$112,000
Cost of Goods Sold:		
Inventory, January 1	$11,000	
Purchases	78,000	
Cost of Merchandise Available	$89,000	
Less Inventory, December 31	10,000	
Cost of Goods Sold		79,000
Gross Profit on Sales		$ 33,000
Selling Expenses	$21,000	
Gen. and Adm. Expenses	8,000	29,000
Net Profit before Taxes		$ 4,000

Exhibit 7

Sidney Food Flavoring Company
Balance Sheet

ASSETS			LIABILITIES AND CAPITAL		
Current Assets:			Current Liabilities:		
Cash		$ 3,000	Accounts Payable		$25,000
Accounts Re-			Notes Payable		6,000
ceivable		31,000	Total Current Liabilities...		$31,000
Inventory		10,000			
Total Current					
Assets		$44,000			
Fixed Assets:			Net Worth:		
Delivery			Sidney, Capital		40,000
Equip	$ 6,000				
Furniture &					
Fixt	2,000				
Machinery	19,000				
Total Fixed					
Assets		27,000	Total Liabilities and Net		
Total Assets		$71,000	Worth		$71,000

Sidney: You know, John, Jane Shanks of Henderson Specialties was over the other day sounding me out about merging with them. I think a merger at this time would not be a bad idea.

Reiner: They have a pretty good name, but haven't they been going down-hill?

Sidney: Not since Shanks took over as president. She's young and relatively inexperienced, but she has a lot of drive and initiative. I think they did pretty well this year, especially as far as their ice cream sales are concerned.

Reiner: I guess you're right at that. They did sell quite a bit of that stuff. But where do we fit in?

Sidney: Well, our products are definitely related, John. We may do quite well together. Besides, this place is too small for us and our machinery is old. I hate to admit it, but their production facilities are better than ours.

Reiner: If you say so, boss. But we have been doing all right so far.

Sidney: Sure. But I'm getting too old to handle everything alone. I would like to concentrate on production and let other people do the paperwork and the selling.

Reiner: So you want to make an ice cream seller out of me. I thought I would never see the day when I would be peddling that stuff. It's like putting a new ball-point pen on the market!

Sidney: Come on now, John. We have been together for a long time. I'm going to see that you handle most of our old customers.

Reiner: Well, if you put it that way, boss, I think it's all right.

THE MERGER

On January 1, the two companies merged, retaining the name Henderson Specialties, Inc. Shanks, the major stockholder, remained president, and Sidney, now a stockholder in the merger, became production manager. Green remained in charge of production of some of the company's products.

In March, the following exchange took place between Sidney and Green:

Sidney: Andy, would you give me a hand mixing these dyes?

Green: Sorry, but I'm pretty busy getting the ice cream production on the way. Easter is just around the corner, and the orders will be pouring in within the next few days.

Sidney: If we don't get these dyes mixed, you won't have any coloring for your ice cream.

Green: I have enough in stock to carry us through Easter.

Sidney: You must think the whole company centers around your ice cream, don't you?

Green: It did last year. This is our profit-making product. If we don't sell this, we're out of business.

In the spring, after the Easter rush, Shanks called a sales meeting to discuss "common problems."

Shanks: I have asked you to come here today in order to discuss our plans for the months ahead. As you know, we're going all out this year to promote our ice cream and our cake icings. These two items are of excellent quality and are very profitable. This does not mean, of course, that you should neglect our other products. But before I go on, I would like to hear your opinions. You are, of course, best qualified to tell just what our customers think of us and our products. Please feel free to speak your mind.

Salesperson: Some of my customers complain about our long delivery periods. Our competitors are willing and able to deliver their orders within 24 hours.

Shanks: Yes, I know. I am planning to purchase two additional delivery trucks in the very near future in order to make us more competitive in this respect.

Salesperson: I don't think that we get enough sales promotion support. I find it difficult to introduce some of our newer items.

Shanks: I certainly appreciate this handicap. As you know, our funds are rather limited at this time. However, I'll see if we cannot start a mail advertising campaign in order to entrench our product image more thoroughly and to make selling easier for you.

Salesperson: I think that our take-home pay should be increased. Although I consider myself a pretty good sales rep, I find it difficult to support a family on a straight commission basis alone. Competition is tough enough, and we have to do a lot of missionary work before we can sell some of the newer items.

Shanks: I'll take this matter up with the controller and see what we can do. As I said before, we're more or less starting from scratch and our funds are rather limited at this time. But I'll do what I can. Are there any other comments? Well, then, let us discuss our plans for this summer . . .

Several weeks after this meeting, the company purchased the two delivery trucks and also started a mail advertising campaign. Halfway through the second year, the president went over the interim financial statements submitted to her by the controller. When she noticed that sales were behind forecasts and that production costs were out of line, she called Sidney into her office.

Shanks: Paul, our production costs seem to be way out of line. What, in your opinion, is the reason for it?

Sidney: I don't think that our production costs are too high at all. But we could possibly lower them, if I could get a little more cooperation from Green.

Shanks: I don't quite understand. I have always thought that Andy was a very competent man. What is the trouble?

Sidney: Well, for one thing, I don't think Andy cares very much how we are doing. He puts in his eight hours a day all right, but that's about all. When I ask him to give me a hand on a job, he usually replies that he is busy with other production work. All he cares about is his ice cream and his recipes. For another thing, he never consults me when he orders any supplies. He goes directly to the controller. How can I exercise cost control if I don't know what's going on in the department?

Shanks: I'll talk to him about it. Thanks for coming in.

On the same day Shanks talked to Green:

Shanks: Andy, I just talked to Paul about our production costs and, frankly, I think they are too high. Do you know what's wrong?

Green: I'm not sure I know what's going on any more.

Shanks: Come on now, Andy, there is something on your mind. We have always trusted each other, haven't we?

Green: There are several things on my mind, but I was not so sure that anybody was interested in my opinion.

Shanks: I have always valued your opinion.

Green: Well, first of all, I don't quite like the way in which Paul runs things. If I give an instruction to one of the packers or boys in the warehouse, I often find that he changes my instructions. I don't know any more whether or not I'm boss in my own house.

Shanks: I see. Go on.

Green: For another thing, he often changes the instructions I give to our delivery people. Yesterday, for example, Paul told one of our drivers to deliver an order immediately to one of his old customers. The driver had to drop everything and run off just with this one order. No wonder our costs are going up!

Shanks: I'll take up the matter with him. Thank you for your frankness.

In January Dillen presented the company's second year financial statements to the president. (See Exhibits 8 and 9.) After studying the statements, Shanks called a conference with Sidney and Dillen.

Shanks: Florence, would you be kind enough to interpret these statements for us?

Dillen: Well, our financial position is not very good. Our cash position is very strained, despite the fact that we managed to turn over our inventory ten times this year. Sales are below budget. Selling expenses have increased several percent during the last six months, and production costs are far too high.

Sidney: Maybe we are spending too much money on all that fancy stuff: containers, packages, and advertising. I suspect that some of these containers cost almost as much as the products we put into them. And I can't see any sense in advertising. I bet our customers don't even read the literature we send them.

Shanks: These promotional expenditures are necessary, Paul. We are facing a highly competitive market, and many items in our line just aren't competitively priced because of their high production cost.

Sidney: In other words, it's my fault that sales are below budget.

Shanks: I did not say that. All I said is that many items in our line cost too much to produce when compared with the production costs of previous years. Can you explain that, Paul?

Sidney: As I've told you before, I don't get the cooperation I need in the

Exhibit 8

Henderson Specialties, Inc.
Income Statement
Second Year

Net Sales		$752,000
Cost of Goods Sold:		
Inventory, January 1	$ 48,000	
Purchases	442,000	
Cost of Merchandise Available	$490,000	
Less Inventory, December 31	41,000	
Cost of Goods Sold		449,000
Gross Profit on Sales		303,000
Selling Expenses	$226,000	
Gen. and Adm. Expenses	70,000	296,000
Net Profit before Taxes		$ 7,000

Exhibit 9

Henderson Specialties, Inc.
Balance Sheet
Second Year

ASSETS		LIABILITIES AND NET WORTH	
Current Assets:		Current Liabilities:	
Cash	$ 8,000	Accounts Payable	$145,000
Accounts Re-		Notes Payable	37,000
ceivable ...	198,000	Total Current Liabilities	$182,000
Inventory	41,000		
Total Current			
Assets	$247,000		
Fixed Assets		Net Worth:	
Delivery		Capital Stock	$210,000
Equip ..... $ 24,000			
Furniture &			
Fixt 7,000			
Machinery ... 114,000			
Total Fixed			
Assets	145,000	Total Liabilities and Net	
Total Assets ...	$392,000	Worth	$392,000

production department, neither from Andy nor from some of the other people. And I'm just about sick and tired of it. For another thing, our machinery is old and inefficient.

Shanks: But we used the same machinery last year. And this year we added a new automatic mixing unit for $6,000.

Dillen: Plus a heating unit for $4,000.

Shanks: What heating unit?

Sidney: I ordered it. It was absolutely necessary.

Shanks: But you should have cleared this purchase with me first. You know that . . .

Sidney: Just a minute, now. I'm a major stockholder in this company and just as interested in profitable operations as you are. Don't forget that. The machine was necessary, as I explained to Florence at the time of its purchase. You were in the field when I ordered the unit, so I could not check with you. Besides, you did not consult me either when you purchased your delivery trucks.

Shanks: In the future, I must insist that you clear matters of this importance with me first, Paul.

Sidney: Let me ask you something, Jane: John Reiner told me that he lost most of his old customers because of a reshuffling of sales territories. What's going on in the field? You know, I wouldn't mind being told about these things occasionally!

Shanks: Well, it was necessary to change the boundaries of some sales territories and to reallocate some of the accounts. Before the merger, Reiner sold only your products. Now he is selling our entire line and his territory is, necessarily, somewhat smaller.

Sidney: Well, Reiner doesn't like it. And I cannot blame him. After all, he lost some of his best accounts.

Shanks: The very same thing happened to a lot of our old sales reps. They don't particularly like it either, I'm sure, but I hope they understand why it was necessary and that they will be better off in the future: broader line, less traveling, more selling time, and—most important—more frequent calls. As you all know, most of our customers are small and are buying on a hand-to-mouth basis from any sales rep that just happens to be calling on them. In other words, we have to call on all small bakeries, restaurants, and hotels at least every 14 days. In a sense our salespeople are merely order-takers for the standard products (food colors, artificial flavors, cake icings, baking chocolate, pudding powders, etc.). But, at the same time, they can be missionary sellers for our newer products (new ice cream flavors, baking honey, etc.). Our marketing strategy, then, should be somewhat as follows: First, frequent personal calls to pick up all the orders for our standard products we can possibly get—it is, in my opinion, better to take several small orders that the average customer can pay for within 30 days or so, rather than to load up a lot of stuff which might spoil if not needed right away and which cannot be paid for within a reasonable period of time. Second, because our clients have usually very little time to listen to long sales presentations and because of the greater impact on the client, our sales reps should present only one new product at each call, thus functioning as missionary sellers. This technique, together with reenforcing mail advertising, smart packaging, fast delivery, and reasonable prices should, in my opinion, result in success.

At the beginning of the third year, Shanks hired Julia Young, 48, for the position of assistant to the president. (See Exhibit 10.) Young was a college graduate and had over 20 years of experience in the

Exhibit 10

Henderson Specialties, Incorporated
Organization Chart

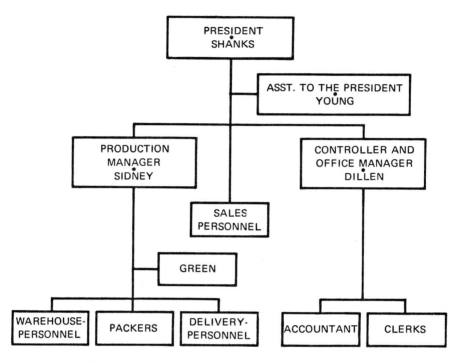

marketing of food products. Her job assignment was to coordinate the production, financial, and marketing activities of the company and to report directly to the president.

Shortly after she had joined the company, Young talked to Sidney.

Young: Hello, Mr. Sidney. How are things in production these days?

Sidney: Not so good. I just don't get any cooperation from Andy. We are doing a lot of unnecessary work. The best thing would be to get rid of him. Then I could get things done around here.

Young: Well, Andy has been with the company for a long time. Jane Shanks thinks highly of him. I'll talk to him and see what I can do.

Sidney: You do that, but don't forget that I'm part owner of this company.

Young talked to both Green and Dillen. Green admitted to having differences with Sidney, but he didn't know what could be done. Young pointed out that the whole team had to pull together and suggested that Green attempt to work with Sidney.

When Young asked Dillen about obtaining purchase approvals, she replied that her job was to pay the bills that were approved by Green, Sidney, or Shanks. Dillen also pointed out that she was not in a position to question the decisions of these people.

Young later requested Dillen to submit semimonthly statements and budget reports. Dillen questioned the necessity of these, but Young insisted that these statements and reports were essential.

In April, Jim Miller, a Henderson salesperson, and Paula Olson, a recently resigned rep., met by chance on the street.

Miller: Hi, Paula! It's good to see you. I heard you quit!

Olson: That's right, Jim. I quit last week. I was pretty fed up with the money I was making during the last few months.

Miller: I don't blame you, Paula. Our products are overpriced and competition is tough. It's almost impossible to make a living on a straight commission basis.

Olson: That wasn't the only reason I quit, Jim. I didn't like the reallocation of sales territories. Here I was, trying to build up a good bunch of customers and before you know it, they change the territories around. You know what I mean.

Miller: I sure do. One never knows what's going on. I wish Shanks would tell us occasionally about their plans, before they make all these changes, I mean.

Olson: I bet Young has a lot to do with all this reshuffling of territories. Shanks is nice, but I don't think she really knows too much about selling.

Miller: May be. You can't learn that in college. Where are you working now, Paula?

Olson: I got a pretty good job lined up with the Top Brand Company: guaranteed minimum salary plus ½ percent commission on sales.

Miller: Sounds good. Maybe I should start looking around for another job myself.

In September of the third year, Florence Dillen met Green on his way home.

Dillen: How about a cup of coffee, Andy?

Green: I could stand one after this day, Florence!

Dillen: What's the matter? Young getting you down?

Green: She's all right, although I can't figure her out. In my opinion she is a "middle-of-the-roader." She came down to see me a few times trying to iron things out between Paul and myself. But, as you know, it's almost impossible to get along with him.

Dillen: I guess you're right. I think that's one reason why the boss hired Young. This way she doesn't have to talk to Paul too often. I know one thing, though: Young is sure causing me a lot of extra work with all the reports she wants.

Green: Are they really worth all the trouble?

Dillen: I'm not so sure. Analyzing reports is one thing, making the appropriate decision is another.

Green: How are things, financially?

Dillen: Not very good, Andy. Not very good at all. I think we are heading for serious trouble in the very near future. (See Exhibits 11 and 12).

Green: I didn't know that things were that bad. What does the boss say?

Dillen: Not very much. She's out in the field most of the time and lets Young pretty well run the house. Things sure have changed.

Green: You can say that again! It isn't like it was a couple of years ago. Sure we had to work like mad, but it was fun then.
Dillen: I feel the same way.
Green: Keep me posted, will you?
Dillen: You bet.

Exhibit 11

Henderson Specialties, Inc.
Income Statement
Third Year

Net Sales		$729,000
Cost of Goods Sold:		
Inventory, January 1	$ 41,000	
Purchases	473,000	
Cost of Merchandise Available	$514,000	
Less Inventory, December 31	39,000	
Cost of Goods Sold		475,000
Gross Profit on Sales		$254,000
Selling Expenses	$234,000	
Gen. and Adm. Expenses	77,000	311,000
Net Loss		($ 57,000)

Exhibit 12

Henderson Specialties, Inc.
Balance Sheet
Third Year

ASSETS			LIABILITIES AND NET WORTH		
Current Assets:			Current Liabilities:		
Cash		$ 4,000	Accounts Payable		$203,000
Accounts Re-			Notes Payable		55,000
ceivable ...		213,000	Total Current Liabilities ..		$258,000
Inventory		39,000			
Total Current					
Assets		$256,000			
Fixed Assets:			Net Worth:		
Delivery			Capital		
Equip	$ 24,000		Stock	$210,000	
Furniture &			Earned		
Fixt	7,000		Surplus ...		
Machinery ...	124,000		(Deficit)	57,000	
Total Fixed			Total Net Worth		153,000
Assets		155,000	Total Liabilities and Net		
Total Assets ...		$411,000	Worth		$411,000

St. Luke's Hospital (A)

Two days after she assumed her duties as director of nurses and of the nursing school of St. Luke's Hospital, Jenny Stewart started on the first of her "get acquainted" rounds. As she turned the knob of the door to the operating room, she heard her name called. The supervisor of the Pediatrics Department approached.

"Won't you let me show you around my department?" Miss Robbins asked. "An operation is in progress, and I think they would prefer that you wouldn't go into the operating room now."

"I know there's an operation going on," the director answered. "That's why I'm going in. You see, I want to observe the methods being used."

Miss Robbins looked uncomfortable to Miss Stewart. "I know that's a very natural desire on your part, but I do hope you will put it off until you are better acquainted. *Please* come with me today and see my department."

Miss Stewart thought the nurse's request rather strange; nevertheless, she looked over the Pediatrics Department and did not return to the operating room. The same afternoon Lois Richards, supervisor of nurses in general surgery, appeared in the doorway of the director's office.

"I understand that you intended to call on us in the operating room this morning," she said.

Miss Stewart looked up from her desk and saw a trim, wide-awake looking woman. "Ah, then you're Miss Richards," Miss Stewart said. "Won't you come in. As a matter of fact, I should like to have dropped in on you this morning but I was sidetracked; so I had to postpone my first visit."

Miss Richards remained in the doorway. "Well, I thought I'd better tell you that you will not need to call on us. When any discussion comes up between the operating room and the nursing office, I come here to settle it."

Miss Stewart was surprised by the flatness of Miss Richards' remark, but she said, "I'm glad to hear that. This is certainly the place for any discussions between department heads to take place. But I shall want to visit you to acquaint myself with the technique used in surgery and with the students in your department."

"Well, I suppose you can come if you want to, but our surgeons won't like it very much. You see, we feel that our technique isn't open to question; so we hardly need any advice. *I* see that the students do their work well. You needn't have any worries about work in my department."

Miss Stewart smiled. "I can assure you that I'm not worried about the work or the technique used in your department. I just want to get acquainted."

"All right, come ahead, but remember that I told you it would be better if you didn't," Miss Richards said over her shoulder as she disappeared from the doorway.

Miss Stewart felt bewildered. She could not recall anything in her long experience as a nursing instructor and as a director of nursing schools which would have prepared her for what she believed was an antagonistic attitude on the part of the operating room supervisor.

Jenny Stewart's career included graduation from a large midwestern college, graduation from a school of nursing, ten years as teacher in schools of nursing, and seven years as director of schools of nursing. In addition she had spent one summer at the University of Wisconsin, taking courses in anatomy and bacteriology. Before accepting her first position as director of a nursing school, she had taken a course in nursing school administration at the University of Chicago.

As director of nurses and the nursing school at St. Luke's, Miss Stewart was directly responsible to the board of directors, although the superintendent of the hospital was nominally her superior.[1] She planned to carry her serious problems to the superintendent, however, because she believed that her work would be easier and more pleasant. The superintendent of the hospital was Carleton B. Fischer, ex-city editor of the local *Centreville Press.* He had no training in hospital administration, but Miss Stewart considered him cooperative and intelligent. He was 50 years of age, a college graduate, and had been appointed to his position the previous July.

As director of nurses, Miss Stewart was responsible for the proper care and treatment of all patients in the 250-bed hospital.

Her responsibilities as nursing school director included the education of student nurses, the selection and employment of graduate assistants, and the overseeing of nurse instructors. A Nursing School Committee helped her formulate educational policies and advised her on disciplinary matters concerning student nurses.

1. See Exhibit 1 on page 159.

The director of nurses, Miss Stewart had learned, was expected to take the advice of the Nursing School Committee on vitally important policies. When the committee was of the opinion that any drastic action needed to be taken in the nursing school, it notified the board of directors of its decision. Miss Stewart was an ex officio member of both the Nursing School Committee and the board of directors.

As she sat in her office contemplating what the operating room supervisor had said, Miss Stewart wondered if she had said anything to make Miss Richards angry. She concluded that she had not.

Three days later Miss Stewart visited the operating room while surgery was being performed. She observed carefully the work of the surgeons and was satisfied that what Miss Richards had said about their technique was correct. The surgeons appeared to Miss Stewart not to notice that she was present. She remembered that in former positions the doctors had seemed pleased when she watched them work.

About two weeks later two student nurses from the operating room, Clarice Maltz and June Bader, appeared in Miss Stewart's office. Miss Bader was in tears. Between sobs she blurted out, "Miss Richards kicked me. I used a forceps to take a soiled sponge off the table, but before I reached the sponge rack to hang it up, she kicked me so hard I dropped it. Then she struck my arm with an instrument and screamed in my ear. She said I was a little fool and if I knew anything I would have had the sponge on the rack. When I bent over to pick it up, she kicked me so hard I fell over. Oh, I hurt all over!"

"That's right, Miss Stewart," said Miss Maltz. "I was there when she did it. She kicked her and she hit her."

Miss Stewart, believing that both girls were immature and emotionally upset, thought that imagination and exaggeration must have played a great part in their account of the incident. She thought Miss Maltz's, "That's right, Miss Stewart," rather childish.

She asked both girls to sit down. They talked over the importance of operating room work. She told them that tensions in the operating room developed easily and that the life-and-death responsibility of persons in the room often led them to be irritable at times.

"We understand that," Miss Bader said. "Dr. Tompkins can be very snappy during surgery, but I think he forgets it afterwards."

"We don't like to have our clothing torn by the supervisor, though," Miss Maltz added.

After a 15-minute talk the student nurses left the nursing director's office. Miss Stewart decided to check on the condition of the operating room gowns to ascertain if they would tear easily. Her investigation showed that enough gowns were in good condition. A few which might have torn easily Miss Stewart ordered put to another use.

Miss Martin, a graduate assistant teacher, accosted Miss Stewart in the hall some ten days later. "I hate to confront you with a problem so soon," she said. "You undoubtedly know that for the past four years our directors of nursing have stayed only about one year each. But what you probably don't know is that each one has tried to do something about the way Miss Richards mistreats student nurses. What happens is that the director leaves in a few months and Miss Richards stays on. I think the situation is getting worse. One of the students—Bernice Smith—came to my room last night and showed me bruises on her legs. Miss Richards had kicked her while they were in the operating room. Bernice said that she was going to tell her parents but the other girls talked her out of it. They're afraid to let any outsiders know about the situation for fear that Miss Richards will find out about it and have her "gentleman friend," Dr. Schwartz, make life miserable for them for the rest of their training period. Bernice told me about Virginia Smeck who has scratches from her shoulders to her wrists—the result of Miss Richards' fingernails when something went wrong in the operating room. Bernice asked me not to take her word for it but to see for myself, but I told her that the best thing for me to do, since I knew about all this already, was to tell you about it. You are, after all, the only one whose position gives you the right to do anything about it."

"Yes, you're quite right," Miss Stewart answered.

"I heard that Clarice Maltz and June Bader tried to tell you but that you didn't quite believe them. I realize that you haven't been here long enough to know everything that's going on, so I thought I'd tell you about this myself," said Miss Martin.

"Miss Bader and Miss Maltz did come to see me," Miss Stewart admitted. "But, you see, they were so emotional at the time. . . . Besides, the story they told me just didn't fit into our way of life today —not the American way of life, anyway. I thought that the girls might not understand the intensity of the operating room situation. . . . I still think their story is most unusual, to say the least. How about you? Are you convinced that all you've told me is true?"

"You don't live in the nurses' home, Miss Stewart; so you don't know how thin the walls are. For years I've heard that sort of thing discussed. Since Miss Richards hasn't lived in the nurses' home for years, the students discuss her rather freely. I don't know whether or not they realize that anyone else can hear them. You know, your predecessors knew about this situation, but they found themselves in pretty hot water when they inquired into it. I want to tell you how badly I feel about it, though, because I know if you attempt to do anything about it, you will have to leave, too. And you've been here such a short time."

"You can stop worrying about my leaving," said Miss Stewart. "I'm asking you now to tell me anything that you know to be true and are willing to declare to the board of directors."

Miss Martin said, "Oh, I don't want to get mixed up in it at all. But for your own information I'll tell you this: the doctors are back of Miss Richards one hundred percent. They will probably like you in direct proportion to the completeness with which you let Miss Richards alone." She hurried away.

The next day Miss Stewart made it a point to look up Virginia Smeck. The director noticed the scratches. "Why, Miss Smeck, what happened to your arm?" she asked.

"Oh nothing—just a little accident. Excuse me. I've got to hurry to the laundry. Miss Richards sent me for some linen."

Miss Stewart asked Miss Richards to come to her office later that day. The operating room supervisor arrived two hours after the director's request. Miss Richards sat down near Miss Stewart's desk.

"I'm wondering, Miss Richards, if it is difficult here to get students to carry out procedures as taught or if, on the whole, they are quite sincere in their efforts," she began.

"The modern girl is just plain dumb, very careless, and often insubordinate. But don't worry. I don't let them get the best of me."

Said Miss Stewart, "Those are rather harsh words, Miss Richards. What do you mean—insubordinate?"

"Oh, you know very well what it means," Miss Richards replied.

"If there's a question of insubordination, don't you think I should know about it?" asked Miss Stewart.

"I haven't come up against anything yet that I couldn't handle. The students all act the same, but I take care of them."

"But, Miss Richards, if I am to cooperate with you in the handling of students, it seems to me I ought to know a little more about their foibles. What do you mean they all act the same way?"

"Is this kind of talk all you called me down here for?" Miss Richards asked abruptly.

"Something like that," Miss Stewart answered. "You said that you don't let the students get the best of you. Just what do you mean?"

"You take care of the nursing office business and I'll take care of operating room business. See!" Miss Richards replied.

"Are you implying that I should not be interested in what goes on in the operating room?"

"I'm telling you frankly to keep out of what goes on there. Otherwise you'll be sorry. Now I'm busy, and I think I'll go." Miss Richards rose to leave.

Miss Stewart quickly walked to the door and held her hand on the knob. "It's not time for you to go just yet," she said. "I insist upon answers to my questions. As two grown women we should be able to lay our cards on the table and keep levelheaded while we do it."

"Well, just what do you want?" asked the operating room supervisor.

Miss Stewart said, "I'll come directly to the point then. Some very unpleasant stories concerning your treatment of students have been told to me. They are very hard to believe, yet at the present time there is no one but you who can prove whether or not they are true. Did you ever shake, scratch, or kick nurses in the operating room?"

"Certainly not. I'm warning you to keep out of my business. If you don't, you'll be sorry I can promise you."

Miss Stewart continued, "If I ever attended to my own business, I'm doing it now. I still hope that you can prove that you do not do that sort of thing."

Miss Richards pushed the director aside and left the office.

Other matters of importance came to the attention of Miss Stewart in the next few days, and she did not have time to think about the affair with Miss Richards.

A week later the nursing director asked Miss Richards to step into a room where they could be alone to talk for a few minutes.

Miss Richards answered, "Our schedule has been heavy today, and our cleaning will take all afternoon. I cannot talk to you today."

Although Miss Stewart tried to find opportunity for another interview, she was never able to find the operating supervisor alone. One of her two graduate assistants was invariably nearby. The nursing director asked her secretary, Miss Patton, about the assistants. Miss Patton, who was also assistant director of the nursing school, told Miss Stewart that Miss Short, the first assistant, was the best graduate assistant on the staff in the school of nursing. Miss Reed, the other assistant, Miss Stewart learned, was also an efficient nurse. Both nurses got along well with Miss Richards.

When the nursing director finally found Miss Richards alone, she asked the supervisor to come into her office. Miss Richards replied "I do not intend to have time to talk to you "

Exhibit 1

St. Luke's Hospital Organization Chart

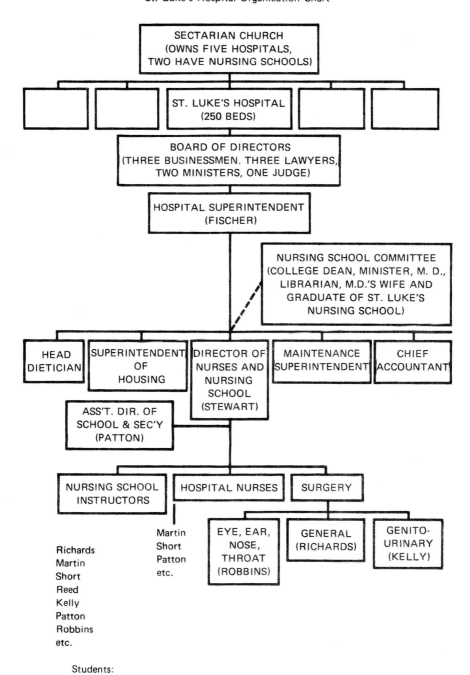

SECTARIAN CHURCH
(OWNS FIVE HOSPITALS,
TWO HAVE NURSING SCHOOLS)

ST. LUKE'S HOSPITAL
(250 BEDS)

BOARD OF DIRECTORS
(THREE BUSINESSMEN, THREE LAWYERS,
TWO MINISTERS, ONE JUDGE)

HOSPITAL SUPERINTENDENT
(FISCHER)

NURSING SCHOOL COMMITTEE
(COLLEGE DEAN, MINISTER, M. D.,
LIBRARIAN, M.D.'S WIFE AND
GRADUATE OF ST. LUKE'S
NURSING SCHOOL)

HEAD DIETICIAN

SUPERINTENDENT OF HOUSING

DIRECTOR OF NURSES AND NURSING SCHOOL (STEWART)

MAINTENANCE SUPERINTENDENT

CHIEF ACCOUNTANT

ASS'T. DIR. OF SCHOOL & SEC'Y (PATTON)

NURSING SCHOOL INSTRUCTORS

HOSPITAL NURSES

SURGERY

Martin
Short
Patton
etc.

EYE, EAR, NOSE, THROAT (ROBBINS)

GENERAL (RICHARDS)

GENITO-URINARY (KELLY)

Richards
Martin
Short
Reed
Kelly
Patton
Robbins
etc.

Students:
Smith, Bader
Smeck, Maltz, etc

St. Luke's Hospital (B)

Two days after Miss Richards, the supervisor of nurses in general surgery, had told Miss Stewart that she did not intend to find time to talk with her, Helen Sommers, an alumna of St. Luke's, visited the nursing director at her apartment. In the course of their evening's conversation together, Miss Sommers confirmed what Miss Stewart had learned about Miss Richards.

"I still have some scratch marks on my arm, thanks to Miss Richards," she told Miss Stewart.

The nursing director went to see the superintendent of the hospital the following day. She told him of her concern about the mistreatment of student nurses and waited for his reply.

"I don't doubt that what you say is true, Miss Stewart," he said. "As a matter of fact, I've heard something about this myself from two or three members of the community. I don't mind telling you that the situation has me worried, but frankly I don't know what to do about it. What would you suggest?"

"Well, first of all, I feel directly responsible for all the nurses in the entire Nursing Department. Miss Richards' treatment of student nurses reflects as much on me as it does on the school of nursing. I was thinking that it might be best to take the matter to the Nursing School Committee first. Then . . . well, then perhaps I'll have a better idea of what to do about it."

"I think that would be the thing to do," Mr. Fischer said. "Please keep me posted on what the outcome is. I'm deeply concerned."

Miss Stewart promised to do so and left. That evening she wrote a list of grievances against Miss Richards. In it she included statements made by nursing students, Maltz, Bader, Smith (to Miss Martin), Miss Martin, Miss Sommers, and Superintendent Fischer. Three days later she took the statements, signed by herself, to the bimonthly meeting of the Nursing School Committee which was composed of a retired doctor, a minister, a college dean, a librarian, a graduate of St. Luke's nursing school, and a doctor's wife who was also a registered nurse.

At the meeting Miss Stewart laid before the committee the statements which she had prepared. Although some members of the committee expressed surprise at the disclosure of maltreatment of nursing students by Miss Richards, some committee members, it seemed to Miss Stewart, seemed to know about the state of affairs.

The college dean asked why the situation had not been reported before.

Said Miss Stewart, "I think my short tenure of office and the fact that the last four directors of nursing have occupied the position for a relatively short period of time make the answer to that question rather obvious."

"Something certainly ought to be done if this is true," said the minister, "and from the evidence Miss Stewart has cited, it certainly appears to be true. I think Miss Richards should be made to resign."

The doctor said, "Let's not be hasty in our judgment, ladies and gentlemen. Our surgeons are very proud of their record of no infections. It seems to me that they would be extremely averse to anything which might lead to Miss Richards' resignation and the possibility of incompetent nursing in general surgery."

"Are our nurses of no consequence as young women, sir?" the minister asked.

"Certainly no one wants to see them mistreated," the doctor rejoined, "but it seems to me that we must not lose sight of the fact that Miss Richards has a reputation as an efficient nurse in surgery."

"Or the fact that nurses are not easily hired these days," rejoined the college dean. "It seems to me. . . ."

The nursing school graduate interrupted him. "I wonder if the fact that one of our surgeons, Dr. Schwartz, dates Miss Richards could explain her being allowed to mistreat students without reprimand. I know of certain instances in which nursing students have been mistreated, and I think—in reply to Dean Harmon's question before—that each student has been somewhat hesitant about reporting Miss Richards for fear that certain surgeons might make their lives miserable during the rest of their training."

"But that's foolish," said the doctor.

"Foolish, but possible. I worked in operating rooms, and I've seen that sort of thing; so I know it can happen," she answered.

The doctor's wife finally moved that the Nursing School Committee recommend to the board of directors that the director of nurses be given complete support in any measure to stop physical violence in the operating room. The motion was carried unanimously.

Miss Stewart, as an ex officio member of the board of directors, decided to take the recommendation to the next board meeting, the following Monday, but she first talked to Mr. Fischer. He advised her to consult the board. In the meantime Miss Stewart again attempted to talk to Miss Richards. The operating room supervisor told her that she was far too busy to be bothered with trivialities. Miss Stewart waited another day before she tried to interview Miss Richards again. They met in the hall outside the operating room. Miss Stewart said, "I'd like you to drop into my office this afternoon."

Miss Richards' reply was: "Stop bothering me."

On Monday evening Miss Stewart arrived at the directors' conference room early. She watched the various directors as they entered and made mental notes of what she remembered about them from their previous meetings. She nodded to the Reverend William Blakesly when he entered. (He had been chiefly responsible for informing the board of Miss Stewart's qualifications for the position of supervisor.) He had introduced her to Dr. Stephen R. Rauch, an elderly, retired minister, and James B. Davison, a lawyer, two more members of the board. Miss Stewart knew well the chairman of the board, Judge Selwyn C. Roberts of the State Supreme Court, and Thomas L. Alberts, a businessman, whom she had met because of his daily visits to the hospital to see his daughter who was recovering from an operation. Miss Stewart knew the other members were either lawyers or businessmen who were prominent in the community.

After the usual order of business, Miss Stewart asked for and was granted the floor.

"Gentlemen," she began, "I'm sorry that so soon after our first meeting together I must place a problem before you; nevertheless, a situation has come up with which I am unable to cope, so I've come for some advice. First, I would like to read to you a resolution of recommendation from the Nursing School Committee." She read from a paper: "The Nursing School Committee of St. Luke's Hospital hereby recommends to the board of directors that Miss Jenny Stewart, director of nurses of the hospital, be given complete, unwavering support in any measure to prevent physical violence under the guise of teaching in the operating room."

Miss Stewart awaited comments; when none were forthcoming, she continued:

"I had intended to seek the board's permission to ask Miss Lois Richards, supervisor of nurses in general surgery, to resign her position, but just before I came to this meeting I received her resignation sent through the mail—special delivery. So now you see that Miss Richards has perhaps solved the problem which I am posing for you. Of course, there is one possibility of difficulty: Miss Richards states that her two assistants will leave with her, but I do not accept her statement as final for them."

The members of the board expressed surprise.

"What's this all about?" asked one of the businessmen. "What prompted this resignation?"

In answer Miss Stewart read the report which she had presented to the Nursing School Committee.

"And now you'd like permission to accept Miss Richards' resignation?" Davison, the lawyer, asked.

"That's correct," Miss Stewart answered. "There is no other course open in view of the evidence, is there?" she asked in surprise.

Davison looked at Judge Roberts, who recognized Alberts.

"Now, Miss Stewart, don't you think that you're being a little hasty? I believe we can easily have one of the doctors explain to Miss Richards that she must not continue to mistreat student nurses," said Alberts.

"I'd like to ask you a question, Mr. Alberts," Miss Stewart said. "Do you think that she will listen to a doctor and suddenly mend the ways in which she has been conducting herself for so long? And suppose she decided not to change her attitude, what then?"

The judge answered for Alberts. "It seems to me that we would then know that we had the wrong doctor speak to her. We could easily arrange to have the right man speak to her."

"And in the meantime the students would continue to be kicked and scratched?"

"That is your responsibility," one of the businessmen interjected.

"No, it isn't. For my part I won't be responsible for what goes on in the operating room—I can't be—if Miss Richards is not responsible to me, and right now she's not."

"But you can't avoid your responsibility to the entire hospital. After all, you haven't yet found a way to influence Miss Richards," said elderly Dr. Rauch. "You wouldn't want to remember that you failed in your job because you were unable to make Miss Richards responsible to you."

"Believe me, Dr. Rauch, I would much rather that Miss Richards and I could have settled this. I had not given up really trying until last Friday. I attempted to see Miss Richards twice to talk the matter out—even after my meeting with the Nursing School Committee, but she rebuffed me on both occasions. As a matter of fact, since I began to show interest in the matter of physical violence in the operating room, it seems to have increased. I have no reason to believe that a truce will be called while we wait for doctors to find time to talk this matter over with her. I want to accept her resignation. Of course, I realize that I must have the sanction of this board before I can."

"Have you talked to Mr. Fischer about this?" Davison asked.

"Yes, I have, and he recommended that I bring the problem before the board."

The judge said, "Miss Stewart, you know that Dr. Tompkins, our leading surgeon, is out of town for a few days. Would you not rather we just hold Miss Richards' resignation until you have a chance to talk this situation over with him?"

"No, I wouldn't. Dr. Tompkins does not share any of the responsibility over student nurses with me," Miss Stewart answered.

"But, Miss Stewart, you must remember that Miss Richards has been with us for four years. During that time we have never had any complaints about her techniques in the operating room," one of the lawyers said.

"And after all, the primary purpose of a school of nursing is to teach students to do accurate work," Alberts added. "The results have been excellent for four years; so Miss Richards must have carried out the responsibility of teaching the students an accurate technique. I would hate to think what might have happened to my daughter while she was in the operating room if the nurses, as well as the surgeons, were not doing competent work. Miss Richards must be teaching them something of a very definite value in the operating room."

"I have to agree with Mr. Alberts," said the Reverend Mr. Blakesley. "Miss Stewart, you certainly realize that the lives of patients who go into the operating room must be safeguarded at all costs."

"And I agree with you that every patient must be safeguarded at all costs," said Miss Stewart. "But it seems to me that the real question is: 'Is physical violence to nursing students a necessary cost?'"

A brief silence ensued, then the judge spoke:

"You must realize, Miss Stewart, that you are not only asking the board to decide whether the hospital can get along without a trusted employee or not but that—well, you see—you are so new in your position. . . . It is hard for the board to decide by such an action as you now ask us to take—that you have already proved yourself er— equal to the situation which confronts us. I say that with no sense of recrimination. As far as I know, the board is completely satisfied with your work . . . and your interest in the hospital is undoubtedly founded upon a sincere desire to do your job well."

Davison said: "No one has mentioned yet the scarcity of nurses today. It might be some time before we can get a capable successor for Miss Richards. In the meantime, Miss Stewart, can we expect that the lives of patients will be safeguarded in the operating room? There is such a shortage of nurses that it might be dangerous to lose Miss Richards at this time."

"I'd like to remind the board that there are two capable nurses who are Miss Richards' assistants in the operating room: Miss Short and Miss Reed. Although both of them are only graduate assistants, I believe that at least one of them should be able of taking over the responsibilities of operating room supervisor in general surgery. From what I've seen of Miss Short and from what I've heard of her previous record, it seems to me that we would not be inviting trouble if the board would appoint her to the position of supervisor."

"But you said yourself that Miss Richards promised that the two assistants would leave with her," said one of the lawyers.

"And I added that I didn't accept her statement as final for them. . . ."

"But both those girls are *only graduate assistants*," said Alberts.

"From the tenor of the conversation which I've been hearing around the table," the judge said, "I would surmise that the board is not yet ready to approve the resignation of Miss Richards. . . ."

"I move that we lay on the table this matter of accepting Miss Richards' resignation," said Alberts.

Davison seconded the motion, and it was carried unanimously.

The judge said, "Suppose, Miss Stewart, that you attempt to interview Miss Richards again between now and the next time the board meets. I'd like you to come into the next meeting and report any progress that you've been able to make toward securing her co-operation in this matter. I think I am expressing the feelings of the entire board when I say that we are assured of your deep-rooted interest in the case, and I also want to assure you that the board is completely in sympathy with your attitude toward the—the conduct —in the operating room. You can count on the board to cooperate with you in any further decisions that are made."

The meeting was adjourned, and Miss Stewart left. She walked slowly back to her office, repeating to herself: "And now what can I do?"

Cargo Agents

Bill Smith had developed an interest in the transportation field and had in previous years worked during the summers as a bus driver or travel agent in order to gain experience in the industry. Having recently received his Bachelor of Science degree and having enrolled in graduate school for the following fall, he again looked for a summer job in the transportation field. Since both the rail and airline businesses were slack, his search proved difficult.

On a lead from the transportation professor, however, he did learn that World Airlines of Chicago was interested in starting a new program using undergraduate students. Bill contacted the personnel department of World Airlines, and he learned more about the program through the employment officer. The student would work for two summers, each summer in a different capacity, and at the end of the program if both airline and employee were satisfied the student would be hired as a management trainee. Neither the other employees nor the supervisory personnel, however, would be told of the program so as to assure that no favoritism would be shown toward the trainees.

The employment officer with whom Bill talked thought there would be difficulty in hiring him since he was a graduate and theoretically would not be available for another summer's work if the company wanted him. Bill argued that if a second summer was needed, he was available, and that his knowledge of the industry would make him more desirable. After some discussion, the head of the program hired Bill, and he was assigned as a cargo agent at O'Hare Airport in Chicago.

During the summer, the training program was scrapped due to the poor financial showing of the airline within the first six months of the year. Bill chose to remain with the job after he heard this because it still provided good experience in transportation.

CARGO AGENT JOB

The cargo agent job included loading the airplanes for departure and unloading them upon arrival. Cargo agents handled luggage, mail, and freight and were responsible for transporting these items between the ramp (where the planes are loaded) and the post office, express office, or freight house. They provided the muscle power primarily, although they were required to keep track of reports on how the outgoing planes were to be loaded, releases for mail and express for which the airline assumed responsibility, and freight waybills. They did not come into contact with passengers and had only limited interaction with other airline employees.

The cargo agent job was the least skilled within the ranks of airline employees. Operated under a union shop where all employees joined the union after ninety days, the position was characterized often by a high rate of turnover of personnel. No schooling was required, and usually young men were preferred in hiring. The work was often hard, usually consisting of lifting heavy articles either on the ground or within the cramped belly of an airplane. Such work, however, was not continuous and usually lasted no longer than 45 minutes without relief. During periods of light activity when few planes arrived or departed or during inclement weather, periods of up to three hours without work were not unusual. In addition, some of the jobs done by cargo agents were those of jeep or tractor drivers. These jobs were continuous but were not usually difficult.

Promotion was available if the employee merited it, but the only road was from cargo to passenger agent, which required working directly with passengers and wearing a uniform including a coat and tie.

THE GROUP

The makeup of the permanent group of cargo agents (in relation to Bill who had a fixed period, slightly over three months, in which he could work before school started) seemed to emphasize a few similarities. First, most were young, ages ranging from 17 to 25, and most were generally poorly educated. A few had been working while they were in high school, and even fewer were working to earn money to start or to continue with college. Most, though, had finished high school, but there were some who had dropped out of high school for some reason or other. Two had never finished grammar school.

Secondly, the group was predominantly white, although there were increasing numbers of black cargo agents being transferred from Midway Airport as operations were shut down there. The blacks had generally been with the company longer and had accumulated greater seniority. They had stuck with the job, although the pay at World was less than other lines, because of the security (there were very few layoffs due to the normal turnover rate being quite high) and because of the ease of attaining seniority as others quit to go back to school or to get better jobs.

The third characteristic of the group of agents centered around their lack of security, and many passed up the promotion to passenger agent for a number of reasons. First, they did not trust themselves with the passengers. Many felt that they did not have enough education and would look bad if they tried to be agents. Some felt that they would not have the patience to be nice to stubborn or difficult passengers. A number simply didn't want to leave their friends in cargo. Others didn't want to lose the freedom they had to smoke, dress sloppily (frowned on, but generally not disciplined), and hide from supervisors from time to time. One, for reasons known only to himself, accepted a promotion and then simply never showed up again.

Not only was there a lack of security, but the group also evidenced a lack of competition. Naturally, World Airlines was in constant competition with other airlines to set the best overall on-time record, and there was competition between departments and between cities. (Chicago and St. Louis competed in total for a trophy given for the best performance each month.) For instance, delays were charged against maintenance, cargo, passenger agents, etc., so that each function and each supervisor tried to have the best record. However, this competition did not filter down to the cargo agents. There was a feeling among this group that luggage handled did not belong to a passenger and that if a piece was roughly handled or missed its flight no one cared. To the cargo agent, the passenger who would no longer fly World Airlines because of his anger simply did not exist.

Yet, they shared an interesting image of the airline. They felt that the line was very big and very wealthy because of all the new jet planes they saw arriving and that were on order. When Bill told them about the poor financial showing of the line, they simply refused to believe that such a big, rich company could ever lose money. They felt that the company was much too opulent to be harmed by the ducking of assignments or shirking of work by the employees.

This was the group in which Bill found himself. He did not make an attempt to get very close to them, which he could have done by joining them after work each night for a beer session. During working hours, however, he got along very well, partially because he offered to do the hard work and partially because they felt protective since he didn't know the shortcuts. They seemed somewhat awed by the amount of education that Bill had completed but approved of his future plans to work for the line since they knew he would be at a high level; they complained that management couldn't make good decisions concerning them since none had ever done that kind of work.

WORK HABITS

Bill's attitude, which was one of enthusiasm and participation, as well as his identification with the airline, came sharply in conflict with that of the group as a whole. Bill first was aware of the conflict when he was working on a flight that had arrived late, and in order to depart on time, would have to be loaded and serviced in 20 minutes of ground time rather than the normal 30. Maintenance had finished their check and ground service had completed fueling with about five minutes to spare, a very commendable performance. The luggage, however, for one reason or another had not been brought out to the flight until ten minutes before departure. The procedure to load both luggage and freight usually took about 15 minutes at normal pace.

Bill stepped up his efforts, and one of the "regulars" drove up in a tractor.

Regular: What's the hurry?
Bill: Well, I thought we could get this out on time if I stepped up a bit.
Regular: Take it easy. It wasn't our fault this time; it wasn't in on time.
Bill: But we can get it out.
Regular: Yeah, but it's not worth the sweat. Hell, save yourself; you've got a lot more flights to work today.

Bill was surprised, but he acquiesced. Another time, he and another college student were struggling with an above-average amount of air freight.

Another regular: Don't touch that stuff; that's too much for two of you.
Bill: No one else was assigned. . . .
Regular: But, if you do that, they'll expect you to handle that much stuff all the time, and they won't assign three men like they're supposed to do.

In times of agent shortage, due to extra flights on the ground at one time or due to sickness, Bill was told to send the flights out late because "they're damned well supposed to call overtime when this happens." As the airline's financial results grew worse, the company gave out orders to cut expenses. Some of the cost reduction methods used rankled the regulars. For instance, it had been standard procedure for the cargo agents to either work or duck during the regular lunch hours. When that time was over, late or paid lunches were taken, for which extra money was paid. No one had complained about this before and agents were not told when to go to lunch.

When the cost cutting began, supervisors searched out agents to get them to lunch within the proper times. If agents were working, they were usually relieved by agents who had eaten. Previously, if agents were working, they finished the job and then took lunch so that planes loaded during the regular lunch times were considered good assignments because the cargo agents received overtime.

Prior to the cost cutting emphasis, the drivers (of jeeps and tractors) had not been called until a natural break occurred, always during late lunch. When the cost cutting drive was on, they were relieved for lunch at the appropriate time and often did not get the easy driving job afterwards. This brought on another conflict into which Bill was drawn. The regulars decided that they would teach management a lesson. Bill was told to "hold a flight as long as possible during lunch time." Another regular advised Bill, "The rules say that you get a ten-minute washup period before lunch; so take it in order to get a late lunch." Bill was concerned and wondered, "What if I'm relieved? He (the supervisor) will know that I should have punched out on time." "Relax," said the regular, "tell him about the washup time." As it happened, Bill did get caught for just that offense. The supervisor let him off with a warning, "since you didn't know the rules." The supervisor stated that an agent gets a ten-minute break morning and afternoon, but that any no-work times, such as between flights, were considered breaks. After that, Bill went to lunch when told but gained considerable respect for having courage to break the rules; the regulars began to consider him as one of the gang.

Another conflict took place when scheduling changes gave the agents free time from 10:30 p.m. to the end of the shift at midnight. One of the supervisors decided that the cargo agents should wash equipment during that time. The regulars were furious and hit upon a scheme for revenge. They included Bill in the plans since he personally found the job distasteful and shared with them some of the ways he found to duck it. He did not think this was treasonous because cleaning equipment had been the job of the cabin cleaners. The cabin cleaners were supposed to clean all terminating planes and passenger loading equipment; but since the jets operated through Chicago, the cabin cleaners had only two planes to clean in eight hours.

The scheme the cargo agents came upon was to be carried out on the motorized stairs that were used between the plane and the ground. The stairs were to be washed each evening by the agents on their free time. "What we do," one regular explained, "is to wash it nicely, but when the supervisor leaves, we put the hose in the motor and drown it." "Isn't that risky?" Bill wondered. "No, they won't know who did it," he answered, "and we can say it just didn't start." Again Bill acquiesced, and in this instance, the gambit worked. The idea of cargo agents washing equipment was quietly given up.

Bill's conflict lessened as time went on. He learned the ground rules of how the regulars wanted the game played. There was wonder but no hard feelings about Bill's enthusiasm for his work, and they tolerated his sitting out on the ramp waiting until the last possible minute to show up at the plane. Nor did they mind his curiosity about the job duties. They taught him the shortcuts that they knew to make the job easier, though not particularly better done. What they desired in return was that Bill do his work without making them look bad.

Bill found that they had pretty potent ways of punishing a person who made the group "look bad." They could punish in a number of ways. First, they could see that when the work list was made up, you were put with a regular who dodged most of the work, leaving it for you to do. When you began to get irked, he just disappeared and you had no choice but to finish alone. Another method was to simply give you either the hardest or most undesirable job or the most work. This was usually the bagroom, a dingy, dusty cavern under the main airport building with no sun and no chance to take breaks. A more subtle way was for someone close to the supervisor to "suggest" to him that you get the worst assignments so that he could keep a closer eye on you than on others. As you "learned," your assignments got better.

Fortunately, Bill did not incur much enmity, both by dint of personality and because he learned fast. He even helped arrange a system that would speed baggage handling and which was accepted because, while doing so, it actually lessened the amount of work that had to be done.

Bill's personal sense of moral obligations bothered him at first; but under the cold light of reasoning, he was able to make some pertinent generalizations. First, these cargo agents stayed with the airline, even though they were paid less than other similar lines. Second, the management did try to cut some corners during the economy measures and often worked shorthanded, trying to save on costly overtime. While the principle is sound, there were many days when even without the slowdowns, the number of cargo agents on hand could not satisfactorily service the normal number of flights. Third, working cargo was these agents' job and there were other employees who were supposed to wash equipment. What was missing and what troubled Bill most was the lack of positive identification of the cargo agents with World Airlines and its goals.

McIntyre Products Company

In July the McIntyre Products Company placed an order for an IBM electronic data processing machine for its general office located in Chicago, Illinois. The electronic data processing machine was one of the larger electronic computers—or, as popularly called by many, electronic brains—which were available to business concerns. In a span of a few minutes, this machine performed many types of book-keeping and clerical operations that would have required months of human labor. It could also perform more sophisticated calculation work, as ordinarily performed by skilled scientists and engineers, in a fraction of the time required by these people. According to the company report, the computer should lead to great increases in operating efficiency of business enterprises, since it quickly analyzed detailed operations. As a result of such efficiency and speed, the computers could perform record keeping and computation work, jobs which would be eliminated for people. Such people would be required to acquire new skills to maintain their white-collar jobs. The computers would also cause many dislocations and shifts within offices, but it was predicted the computers would lead to substantial benefits for all in terms of higher wages and more challenging work.

McIntyre Products prepared for the delivery of the computer. The company recruited a group of above-average, relatively young employees from various general office departments in which the computer would find the greatest immediate application. These employees were given a training course in the new field of electronic computer programming. The computer group was placed in the controller's department, since most of the early computer applications would deal with certain large-volume accounting procedures. It was also hoped that the accounting personnel affected would be less inclined to look upon the computer group as outsiders.

Six months after the order for the computer was placed, two employees of the computer group were given the assignment of converting the sales accounting department procedure for handling the sales department fixed asset (plant investment) records to an electronic computer procedure. One of these employees was June Pestal, formerly of the general auditing section of the controller's department.

She was an accountant, 30 years old, who had eight years of accounting experience with the company. The other was Peter Murchinson,
also an accountant, 35 years old, who had 13 years of service, chiefly
in the manufacturing accounting section of the controller's department. (See Exhibit 1.)

To develop the computer procedure, it was necessary that these
employees closely work with the personnel in the plant investment
section of the sales accounting department. A thorough understanding
of the procedure used in that section and its objectives had to be
gained as a first step in developing the computer application.

To initiate the work, Sidney Simpson, supervisor of the computer
group, met with John Terrance, supervisor of reports and procedures,
and Curtis Swanson, assistant controller. Simpson requested proper
arrangements be made so that June Pestal and Peter Murchinson
could work closely with Steven Barn, supervisor of plant investment
in the sales accounting department to develop the computer procedure. Swanson, the assistant controller in charge of general auditing
and procedures, passed this request on to William Everglade, the controller of McIntyre.

Everglade called Michelle Finebar, the assistant controller in
charge of the accounting departments, into his office to explain the
situation. Everglade pointed out the great possibilities of electronic
computers, their popularity, and their increases in office work efficiency. Everglade also pointed out that it was good business to make
the maximum possible use of this machine when it was delivered to
the company. He told Finebar that the board of directors was firmly
in agreement with these statements, and he also pointed out that
many of McIntyre's major competitors were becoming actively interested in this new field. He then requested Finebar to make the necessary arrangements within her department and to permit the beginning
of the work as quickly as possible. Finebar was an older employee who
had many years of service with the company. She was somewhat over-
whelmed by the discussion, but since she had more than usual respect
for the authority of the controller, she consented to make the arrangements.

Finebar then called Keith Rockford, the auditor of sales, and
Steven Barn, the supervisor of plant investment, into her office. When
Rockford and Barn heard Finebar describe her discussion with the
controller, they were plainly upset, especially Barn. Like Finebar, both
Rockford and Barn were older employees of many years service with
the company. Rockford was due for retirement at 65 within a year,
while Barn had five years before his retirement. All three employees
had spent their entire careers as accountants and had strong aptitudes
for detail; and the existing organizational relationship between the
three had prevailed for many years. Steven Barn had developed the

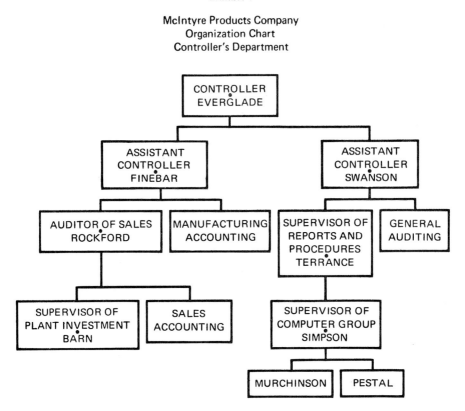

Exhibit 1

McIntyre Products Company
Organization Chart
Controller's Department

manual system for recording sales department plant investment 20 years ago, and he had been in charge of its operation since that date. It was recognized to be a good manual system, having been operated successfully by Barn and the six employees under him for the entire 20 years. The information available from the system was referred to as "the Barn Data" by many others in the company.

In discussing the situation with Simpson, Pestal and Murchinson made the following comments:

Murchinson: Every time we meet with Barn, he tells us the computer won't work on his material.

Simpson: Why won't it work? Does he say?

Murchinson: Oh, he comes up with some piddling, insignificant point. He will show you how one item cannot be processed by the machine in the same manner he now does it with his system.

Pestal: Or he will relate for the tenth time how the company had once tried to introduce electric accounting machines and how it had failed. He's the voice of doom.

Simpson: Well, just keep at it. I'm sure you can convince him of the merits of the computer.

Murchinson: I wish we were as optimistic as you. Right now, I don't see how we are going to be ready by the deadline.

Pestal: Another thing, how can you convince someone when you can't meet with him? Everytime we call a meeting, he has something more important to do. Sometimes, he shows up at the meeting, and ten minutes later his secretary calls and he leaves for some reason or another.

Finally, after six months, Simpson complained to Terrance. The controller then put more pressure on Finebar, Rockford, and Barn to make progress. They replied that their study of the possibilities of the computer procedure, thus far, indicated to them that the whole idea was impractical.

Upon suggestion of Rockford, Steve Barn wrote a memorandum entitled "Plant Investment Computer Study." He started the report by stating that he knew little about electronic computers, but he had seen one operate once and the machine broke down during the test. He pointed out that no other company, to his knowledge, had ever used a computer for plant investment work. In 11 pages he itemized reasons why the computer would not work. He ended by taking a strong stand against the entire idea. This memorandum was approved by Rockford and Finebar and was submitted to the controller.

In spite of the stand taken by these employees, the controller was convinced by those familiar with the computer in Swanson's department and from IBM company representatives that the computer would do the job with a great increase in efficiency, accuracy, and speed, and with a substantial saving of clerical expense. In addition, Everglade was subjected to pressure from the board of directors to put an end to the delay and to get the job done as quickly as possible.

Nervona Manufacturing Company

A large multiplant company with subsidiaries and sales offices all over the United States and Canada, the Nervona Manufacturing Company manufactured a large variety of products, many of which were not related in any way. Due to the large, unrelated product line, the company was organized according to products. Each product division was headed by a vice-president who directly reported to the executive vice-president and president of Nervona. A general manager and a national sales manager reported directly to the vice-president of each division. Under the sales manager were various regional sales managers who were responsible for the sales of their products in the region assigned to them. At the lower rung of hierarchy were the branch sales officers who were located in the principal cities in a region. (See Exhibit 1.) For example, in Chicago, the regional sales managers were responsible for the midwestern area, extending from Cleveland, Ohio, to Denver, Colorado, and from the Canadian border to Texas. Handling the entire line of Nervona products, the Chicago sales office serviced Wisconsin, Illinois, part of Michigan, and part of Indiana. Each division had a branch office sales manager located at that office who was responsible for sales in the branch office area and who reported directly to the regional sales manager.

Originally located on the southwest side of Chicago about 15 blocks southwest of the Loop, the Chicago branch office utilized the second floor and part of the third floor of a warehouse building. The branch warehouse had been located in the same building, but in 1960 it was moved into more spacious quarters in one of the southwest suburbs. The sales office remained in the same quarters until late in 1962.

Nelson, the branch office manager, had no direct organizational relationship with the branch sales managers and had no authority over the sales representatives. He only supplied the sales reps with cars, promotional materials, etc., and he supervised the office force of 150 employees who performed the clerical work for the branch. However, he was responsible for all the plans involved in the moving

Exhibit 1

Nervona Manufacturing Company
Partial Organization Chart

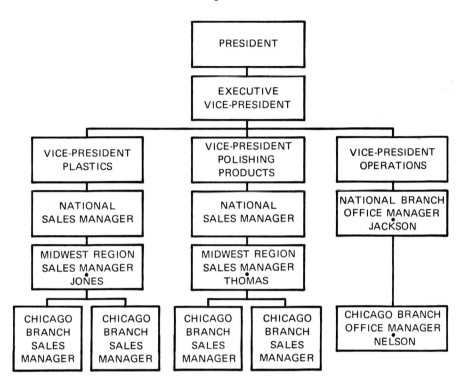

of the office to the suburbs. Nelson had been responsible for the entire relocation, subject to instructions from the home office. He planned the office arrangement at the new location and also arranged for new equipment, new help, car pools, etc. Although he was given aid by the same office, the bulk of the detail work fell on his shoulders.

Nelson's work included the assignment of offices for the personnel, and as a result, conflict arose.

At the old location, each sales manager had had a small office along one side of a large room. For the most part, the midwest regional sales managers were located at the home office of the company in St. Louis. In the case of the Polishing Products Division, however, the regional sales manager, Thomas, was located in the Chicago branch office, mainly because of the large demand for polishing products in the Chicago area. Because of her high rank, Thomas had been given the corner office, which was not only larger but also contained two sets of windows instead of the usual one or none. In accordance with Thomas' rank, Nelson decided that she would again have the corner office at the new location. The new corner office was considerably larger than the rest of the private offices, and again it would have two sets of windows.

Offices had been assigned, new furnishings moved in, and the final details of the move completed when the home office announced that Jones, regional sales manager for the Plastic Products Division, would be moved to the Chicago sales office. Nelson was immediately notified that he was to provide suitable office space for Jones. Since all of the offices had been assigned and were occupied, it was necessary for Nelson to ask several of the sales managers to move so that the office next to Thomas could be vacated for Jones. The sales manager who finally lost a private office and had to take a desk in the main office was a subsidiary firms' sales manager. The sales managers who had to move one office down the line expressed some resentment toward Nelson, the company, and Jones. The office vacated for Jones was smaller than the corner office occupied by Thomas and it had only one window. However, Nelson saw to it that the furnishings in Jones' office were identical in size and quality with those in Thomas' office.

When Jones arrived in January, 1963, he was greeted by Nelson and then shown to his office. Since his new office was right next to Thomas' large office, he immediately noticed the difference in size. He complained about his small office and said that he was entitled to one as large as Thomas'. Nelson explained that Thomas' office, being a corner office, was the only one of its size in the building. Jones demanded that his office be enlarged so that it would be the same size as Thomas' office, and he further stated that he wanted to have another window added. Nelson said that this was impossible since the planning and development section at the home office had allocated only a specific amount of money for construction and furnishing of the branch office. Furthermore, Nelson said that he did not have the authority to reconstruct the office. Jones then said that he would call the home office and talk to the president if necessary to have his office enlarged.

Jones carried through with his threat and did call the home office. When the problem was referred to the national branch office manager, Jackson, Jackson instructed Nelson to "handle the problem to the satisfaction of all concerned." These instructions, however, did not allow authorization to enlarge Jones' office.

The discussion over the size of the room and the number of windows had been overheard by the office force. As time went on, it was evident that the incident was viewed as being extremely humorous. Much idle gossip and many remarks in the following weeks centered around "Two Window Jones," as he was referred to by the office clerical staff.

Jones was an extremely competent sales manager and had an excellent record with the company. A vigorous, energetic man, he was also known to have a quick temper. His objections to the size of his office were frequent and vocal so that the two branch sales managers under him and all of the plastics salespeople knew of his complaint. During this time, Thomas remained friendly to Jones but remained aloof from the situation involving the office. Jones, however, showed no signs of forgetting his complaint, nor did he stop talking and complaining about it. His remarks were directed at both the home office and Nelson.

After some thought on the matter, Nelson approached Jones with a solution, which was to put another door into Jones' office. "This," Nelson explained, "would, in effect, give Jones the additional room he needs in his office. Even though no other office has two doors," Nelson said, "I think I can get authorization for the expenditure." (He had previously cleared the expenditure with Jackson.) Jones accepted this suggestion, and a second door was placed ten feet from the original one.

Parker City Transportation Company (A)

When the Central Transportation Company merged with the Great Lakes Bus Company to form the Parker City Transportation Company, all employees of the new company received credit for past service with their former companies. Richard Hawk, Freda Fitzgerald, and Al Birch were employees of the Great Lakes Bus Company before the merger. The present manager of the Sales Accounting Department, Richard Hawk, was due to retire on December 31 of next year. Mr. Hawk's predecessor, Freda Fitzgerald, 61 years old, had held the position for 4 years and was now the general accounting manager and assistant controller. Freda's predecessor, Al Birch, held the position for 3 years and during this period had installed all of the procedures in the department when the Parker City Transportation Company was formed. He had 35 years of service with the company, about 5 years less than Freda. At 55 years of age (less than 2 years ago), Al had had a serious heart attack and was still under a doctor's care.

Paula Mason was the financial vice-president. She was employed as controller in 1952 after having spent 20 years with a local public accounting firm. Paula had helped in the organization of the Parker City Transportation Company while a member of the public accounting firm.

Pete Potter was almost certain he would be appointed as the next manager of the Sales Accounting Department. With a little over 21 months remaining before Mr. Hawk's retirement, Pete had been appointed as his assistant, and he had assumed many of Hawk's management duties. Even though Pete had 28 years of service (actually, Pete had spent 18 years as an employee of the Central Transportation Company before the merger to form Parker City), he was only 46 years old. Although he lacked a college education, he had earned a reputation as an excellent worker and a very good supervisor. His superiors rated him highly on his job, and he mixed well socially. Also, he was a good family man, another rumored requirement for advancement in the company.

The position of manager of the Sales Accounting Department was one of the better jobs in the accounting group. The minimum salary for the position was almost 50 percent greater than Pete's present salary. There were over 60 people in the Sales Accounting Department, and historically former managers of the department had almost always been advanced to higher positions in the company.

This department consisted of two sections. Section A consisted of about 35 clerks performing high-volume repetitive-type work. Section B consisted of about 20 clerks who performed miscellaneous accounting and clerical jobs. The Section A clerks were divided into 3 groups as follows:

Group 1: 10 clerks performing manual audit work. This work involved comparing the starting and ending register readings on Operators' Reports and noting all differences in register readings.

Group 2: 15 bookkeeping machine operators. Their work involved processing the Operators' Reports to calculate the amount of revenue collected.

Group 3: 10 final audit clerks. Their work involved reconciling the calculations made by the bookkeeping machine operators with the cash receipts turned in by the vehicle operators. Any differences were reported to the general accountant who would then settle with the individual operators.

The bookkeeping machines used in Section A had been in use for 5 to 10 years. Many of these machines were in need of an overhaul. Newer bookkeeping machines were much more efficient than the present bookkeeping machines.

Pete had made a study of the feasibility of overhauling existing equipment as compared to purchasing the newer equipment and had summarized the economics as follows:

Feasibility of Overhauling Present Machines

Cost of Overhauling 15 machines	$30,000
Maintenance Charges (for 5 years)	15,000
Total Outlay	$45,000
Reduction in Present Number of Bookkeeping Clerks (1 Clerk @ $5,000/Year Including Fringe Benefits) . .	$ 5,000

Feasibility of Purchasing New Machines

Cost of 12 New Machines	$60,000
Maintenance Charges (for 5 years)	6,000
Total Outlay	$66,000
Reduction in Present Number of Clerks (4 Clerks @ $5,000/Year Including Fringe Benefits)	$20,000

A meeting was held in Mason's office to discuss the new versus the overhaul report. Al Birch, Freda Fitzgerald, Richard Hawk, and Pete Potter attended this meeting. In addition, Paula Mason invited Wesley Craig, a partner in the accounting firm with whom Paula was formerly employed, to sit in on this meeting. Craig was a consultant and had been engaged by Mason to review the systems of the company in connection with the annual audit.

Birch: Freda, Dick, Pete, and I have seen a demonstration of the newer machines, and we all agree that we would be able to save four clerks by installing them in the department. The decision to be made is obvious. An additional investment of $21,000 in new equipment will enable us to save $15,000 per year, compared to the economics of overhauling the present machines. Could anyone justify any other decision?

Mason: Well, Al, there is no question about it. Of the two alternatives presented, I think we'd all agree that the best course of action is to buy new equipment. The real question is: Do we have any other alternatives? What do you think, Wes?

Craig: I think there is at least one other good alternative that needs investigation. As part of our survey, we've reviewed the procedures in the department and we think it should be possible to convert the system to use your data processing equipment. Furthermore, you're only using this equipment on a one-shift basis at present, and the processing could be done on the second shift at very little additional machine rental costs to the company.

Birch: (Smiling) I think we should forget that alternative right now. That'll only get us into trouble. (Turning to Paula) You know, Paula, at least six different companies in our industry have tried to install their sales audit procedures on data processing equipment and every one has failed. I talked to the people at the Eastern Transportation Company last year at our convention, and they told me their company spent $15,000 trying to install the procedures on their computer. They went back to the bookkeeping machines $15,000 poorer but a lot smarter. At the convention, representatives of four of the six companies held a group discussion on the subject and their unanimous conclusion was that it will be feasible to install the sales audit procedures on a computer when the moon turns to blue cheese.

Craig: I wouldn't argue with those facts at all, Al. And I wouldn't even claim that it is feasible to use the computer. But on the other hand, Al, most of the data processing people working in your industry are just unsophisticated. I wonder what would happen if you gave a real "pro" about two months to study your system. I suspect there is at least a one to two chance that your company could then save about $100,000 a year in clerical costs. Would you spend that for a chance to save $100,000 a year?

Mason: I certainly would, Wes. Also, it would be a credit to our company if we could make a breakthrough on this system. Why, if we could find a method of performing this work on our data processing machines, Al and I would be the featured speakers at our industry conventions for the next five years. Our counterparts in the other companies in our industry who think our company is a bit backward would change their minds about us in a hurry.

Birch: You can't be serious, Paula. You'd be better off donating the $10,000 to charity. All that $10,000 will buy is a chance to join the round table discussion with other companies who've tried this and add our voice to the opinion that this can be done when the moon turns to blue cheese.

Mason: (Turning to Freda, Dick, and Pete) Do any of you have an opinion?

Potter: I think Al is right. Our Data Processing Department can't even do the easy jobs properly. Our Sales Audit Department is the best in the organization right now, and I'd hate to see the data processing department get involved in our work. Even if you could save money on paper, we'd lose money for sure if any part of our work was turned over to them.

Craig: I'm convinced someone will work out a method to put your system on a computer, Pete. With the number of people and the volume of repetitive work, it just has to happen. (Turning to Paula) Paula, I think you'd look bad if you invested $60,000 without studying this further. At least, you should be on record with the board of directors that you have made a thorough study of this before making a decision.

Mason: I think you're right, Wes. I'm going to ask the board for approval to spend $10,000 for the study. I'll present the facts as they've been presented here. I know they'll approve. How should we proceed?

Craig: Pete knows your present system better than anyone. So, I think he should be assigned full time to the study. Your systems manager, Howard O'Brien, also should be assigned to work on the study. I'll have Warren Reed, one of our data processing specialists, assigned full time to the project. We'll start as soon as you give the word.

Mason: (Turning to Pete, Freda, Al, and Dick) I know you do not all agree with my decision, but I hope you understand why I've made it. I want everyone here to be objective about this and to reach a conclusion based on the facts. And, Pete, I want you to cooperate with Reed and see that he gets the information he requires. (Turning to Wes) Let's set June 30 as the deadline for your report. You can start as soon as you're ready.

THE FEASIBILITY STUDY

Shortly after the above meeting took place, work on the study of the feasibility of using data processing equipment for sales audit procedures was started. Howard O'Brien, Warren Reed, and Pete Potter prepared a work schedule for the study. The schedule provided for six weeks of research work and two to three weeks on developing conclusions and writing the report. Warren Reed and Pete Potter were assigned to do the research work together. Howard O'Brien was not assigned to participate in the research phase due to other commitments. However, he was assigned to participate with Potter and Reed in the work of developing conclusions for the report.

Pete Potter and Warren Reed worked together on a full-time basis during the first month of the study. In this time, they reviewed procedures of the Sales Audit Department in detail, studied the procedure which the operators used to prepare their sales audit reports, and contacted other companies in the industry to determine the systems which were being used by them.

On the Monday of each workweek, Warren Reed would give a verbal progress report to O'Brien. Their conversation on the Monday morning of the fifth workweek of the study was as follows:

O'Brien: Say, Warren, Pete came in early this morning and told me that he has been taken off the project for this week. Apparently Hawk's mother is seriously ill and he flew out to Phoenix Sunday afternoon to be with her. Hawk called Pete Sunday morning and asked him to run the department while he's gone. Hawk said he planned to stay in Phoenix for the entire week, at least.

Reed: Well I'm sorry to hear about Hawk's mother, and I certainly agree that Pete should spend his time in the department while Dick is away. Actually, it will work out OK because I have some ideas that I want to think through and develop on my own. I'll go back to the office and call you later in the week.

O'Brien: Is Pete giving you all of the cooperation you need?

Reed: We're doing fine, Howard. I've really enjoyed working with Pete. The people in the company know him, like him, and respect him, and this has helped a great deal. Pete knows where to go to get the information I need, and he gets it without any lost motions. It's apparent to me that Pete wants to do what is best for the company, and he has been very objective in his work. He doesn't know very much about data processing equipment, but he's making a good effort to learn. We've talked a lot about different ways in which we might use EDP equipment for the procedures in his department, and he's been very interested. In fact, I'd say he's been enthusiastic. He's a pleasant person to work with, and that helps too.

O'Brien: Do you think your conclusion will be that data processing equipment is feasible?

Reed: At this point, I'd have to say no! But let's wait a while. We've still got two more weeks before we complete our work.

On that same day, Al Birch and Freda Fitzgerald invited Pete to have lunch with them.

Birch: It's been a few weeks since we had lunch together, Pete. That fellow Reed seems to be taking over all of your time.

Potter: There's no doubt about that, Al. Reed comes to work to work. He's really done a thorough job of studying and analyzing these procedures. He's come up with some good suggestions, too, on how we could improve our present procedures. It wouldn't surprise me if he did develop a system for the department that would be an improvement over our bookkeeping machine system.

Fitzgerald: It sounds like you've been brainwashed, Pete. You'd better keep on your toes.

Birch: I've been in this business for thirty years, Pete, and I put that bookkeeping machine in operation. We've got one of the best sales audit systems in our industry, and I don't want anyone tampering with it.

On Thursday of that same week, Warren Reed called O'Brien and arranged for a meeting with him. The two men met in O'Brien's office on Friday morning. At their meeting, Warren discussed an idea that he had for installing an EDP system for sales auditing.

O'Brien: I think you've got it, Warren. The idea sounds tremendous. You've developed a simple system when everyone else was trying to make this system complicated. In fact, it seems almost too simple to be true. Have you thought through the details of the system?

Reed: Howard, I said the same thing to myself. The solution is so simple that it seems almost impossible that no one had thought of it before. I've flowcharted the system in detail, designed all of the reports, and I've even had one of our programmers check it out. It's got to work.

At this point, O'Brien made arrangements to meet with Paula Mason, Wesley Craig, and Warren Reed. The meeting was held on Monday morning. Reed presented his ideas at this meeting.

Mason: It looks like Warren may have found the answer to our problems in the Sales Audit Department, Wes. I can't get over how simple the answer is.

Craig: I think so, Paula. We might just as well stop our work now and write our report.

Mason: Why don't you do that, Wes. Let's set a week from this Friday as the deadline for your rough draft of the report.

Craig: That'll give us enough time. You set the time of the meeting and we'll be here.

THE FEASIBILITY REPORT

Copies of the consultant's report were given to Mason for distribution about two days before the scheduled meeting. The report contained the following summary of the feasibility of using EDP equipment for sales audit procedures.

SUMMARY OF FEASIBILITY—USING EDP EQUIPMENT

Expected Savings (Annual)	Clerical Personnel Net Change
1. Changes in Clerical Personnel	
a) Discontinue	−10
b) Discontinue Bookkeeping Machine Operations	−15
c) Reduction in Balance Clerks (from 10 to 8)	− 2
d) Add Keypunch Operators	+ 6
Estimated Savings	$5,000 × − 21 = $105,000
2. Depreciation of Bookkeeping Machines and Maintenance Costs	10,000

3. Reduction in Forms Costs from $50.00 to
   $35.00/m × 500,000/Year   7,500

      Gross Savings $122,500

Additional Costs (Annual)
   1. Key punch Machine Rentals   4,000
   2. Use of EDP Equipment—Night Shift   3,600
   3. Machine Operators (1½)—Night Shift ..   7,500

      Total Additional Costs .... $ 15,100

        Net Minimum Annual Savings $107,400

Parker City Transportation Company (B)

After the consultant's report was distributed, the findings seemed in favor of changing to the electronic data processing equipment. However, several matters were introduced in the next meeting.

FEASIBILITY REPORT MEETING

The meeting to discuss the feasibility report was held in Mason's office. Birch, Fitzgerald, Hawk, Potter, Craig, and O'Brien were present at this meeting. The discussion was as follows:

Mason: I've reviewed this report and the proposed procedures for the EDP system, and it sounds workable to me. The projected savings are significant, but they seem realistic. I'll have to rely on you, Howard, to tell us if our EDP equipment is capable of performing the required work.

O'Brien: I've reviewed the proposed procedures very carefully, Paula. The system seems workable to me, and I think the projected savings are on the conservative side.

Birch: I think there are some pretty flagrant errors in this report.

Mason: Hold it a second, Al. Let Howard finish what he started to say.

O'Brien: As I was saying, the estimated savings are conservative. For one thing, forms costs have been estimated at $35.00 per thousand. We can easily get the proposed form for $20.00 per thousand. Also, there is no provision for savings in office space rental. The proposed system will save us at least 3,000 square feet of floor space. Consequently, I think it is more realistic to estimate that our savings will be in the range of $125,000 to $135,000.

Mason: What about that, Wes?

Craig: Well, our estimate was conservative. The $107,400 estimate is a minimum amount. I agree, Howard's estimate is certainly achievable. In fact, there is another savings that hasn't even been included in our estimated savings. The proposed system provides a 100 percent audit, whereas the present manual audit is only as good as your manual audit clerks. As our survey indicated, these clerks fail to detect about 25 percent of all of the operator errors that are made.

Mason: That's a good point, Wes. But now, Al, let's hear your views.

Birch: If we take a critical look at this proposal, we'll find that the proposed system won't save anything. All it will do will be to cause us all a lot of grief. For one thing, the report claims we will need only six keypunch operators. The proposal does not provide for verifying the cards. Now, there isn't any data processing job we've got now that doesn't require 100 percent verification.

Also, the estimate of six keypunch operators is based on each operator punching 49,000 key strokes per day, or 7,000 strokes per hour for seven hours. I have records here that show that our present operators punch about 30,000 to 35,000 strokes per day.

Consequently, my revised estimate is that we need at least 14 keypunch operators instead of six, and that isn't my only criticism.

Second, the report indicates that we need only eight balance clerks. In actuality, the proposed system will increase the work of our balance clerks by 20 to 30 percent. So, we will need five more balance clerks.

Third, no one works on the night shift now. Consequently, if we start a night shift, we'll need a night watchman, and we'll have to heat, light, and air-condition our offices at night. If we do the job on the day shift, we'll add at least $30,000 more of EDP equipment.

Finally, our Sales Audit Department is always the source of extra people to help out in other departments. At least three or four people included in the savings would have to be added back to the payroll in other departments to compensate for the discontinuance of this service. When you adjust the estimate to reflect the above facts, you'll find that the proposed system will actually increase our costs by about $10,000 per year.

Mason: Do you agree with Al, Howard?

O'Brien: No! I don't. However, I will agree that we could have problems with the system if the cards are not verified. We'll have to have good keypunch operators. The worse that could happen, though, is that we might have to add an extra keypunch operator or two to slow them down and increase their accuracy.

Mason: Then you have some doubts?

O'Brien: I suppose you could say that. But on the high side, the number of keypunch operators we will need is about 50 percent of Al's estimate of 14. We don't have to verify the cards.

Mason: How do you feel about this Freda?

Fitzgerald: I agree with Al.

Mason: What about you, Dick?

Hawk: Our present system is a good one. I don't like the system that is proposed. I can't understand it. I don't see how the operators would understand it.

Mason: Pete, how do you feel?

Potter: I don't think I can express a good opinion, Paula. Frankly, I am in agreement with Al that we would have to verify the cards. On the other hand, the only way we'll ever know is to try it and see. We could try it on a test basis for one of our smaller lines.

Mason: It seems we're hopelessly divided. I like Pete's idea of trying the system on a test basis for one line. If that works, OK, we'll add another line and so on until the system is installed. If it doesn't work, well then we'll stay with our present system. Is that fair?

Craig: Who will you make responsible for installing the system?

Mason: I think Pete and Howard should work on this together.

O'Brien: I think Warren Reed should be assigned to help us whenever we run into trouble.

Birch: We don't need outside help.

Mason: I'll leave that matter up to you, Howard. But I do think we should do as much of the work ourselves as we possibly can. At any rate, let's get started on this work right away.

THE TEST INSTALLATION

Before work on the test installation started Al Birch called Pete Potter into his office.

Birch: You disappointed me a lot at the meeting, Pete. You should have taken a strong position against that ridiculous proposal.

Potter: Well, Al, I felt I had to give a little and show good faith with Paula and Howard. Anyway, I'm going to use our south line for the test installation, and that's the toughest audit we've got. If there are any flaws at all in the proposed system, it will never work for the south line, as you know.

Birch: That makes some sense, Pete, but you'd better keep me posted on your progress.

Potter: OK, Al, anything else?

Birch: Yes there is. As I told you before—we're not going to make any radical change in our sales audit system. Do you understand?

Potter: I certainly do.

Birch: Well, then, I'll see you at lunch tomorrow.

For the next six weeks, O'Brien, Potter, and two of O'Brien's systems people worked on the new system. O'Brien's two people programmed the data processing equipment. O'Brien developed written procedures for the system and Pete Potter selected and trained the people in his department. During this period, Warren Reed spent two mornings each week working with O'Brien and Potter to answer their questions. The typical dialogue at one of these meetings was as follows:

Potter: Our operators aren't the brightest in the world, you know. Sometimes they write the wrong register number or badge number on their report. We catch this in our system because our operators are alert for these errors. But the new system won't catch these errors.

Reed: I went over that last Friday, Pete. The new system will catch all of these errors and a lot more that your people don't catch now. They will all appear on the printed report that the EDP Department prepares for the balance clerks.

Potter: Then the balance clerks will have to do the work that the manual audit clerks now do!

Reed: I went over that, too. We will add a little more work for the balance clerks. But we save on the report with the new system. In the present system, they work from at least three different documents. This alone will cut their time by 30 to 40 percent.

Potter: I still say we should verify the cards after they are punched in order to reduce the work of the balance clerks.

O'Brien: Come on now, Pete. We showed you why the keypunch operators' work is easier than the work your bookkeeping machine operators now do. You don't verify the bookkeeping machine operators' work. Their errors are caught by the balance clerk.

Potter: You're going to have to prove to me that this new system is as good as you say it is. Remember, I'm the guy that's going to have to live with it.

After each meeting with Potter, Reed and O'Brien would discuss the meeting.

Reed: Pete sure acts strange at times.

O'Brien: Al Birch is putting a lot of pressure on him. But I'm not worried about Pete. He will try to make the system work, despite Al.

Reed: Now what's the story with Birch?

O'Brien: He's always been against using EDP equipment.

Reed: If that's the case, Howard, why does the EDP Department manager report to Birch? No wonder that department is operated inefficiently.

O'Brien: I've already talked to Paula about that. Birch instructed the department manager to have the most inexperienced person assigned to do the work on the new audit system. When Pete told me that, I went directly to Paula and objected. I think she is very much aware of the problem.

African Production Company

African Production Company was a subsidiary of a large international corporation. The top four executives were from the parent company, and the heads of the technical and engineering staff were also expatriates. The company manufactured various types of metal products for sale in Tanzania. The factory consisted of three large buildings where the metal products moved from one operation to another on conveyor lines. The equipment was the usual general-purpose metal-working equipment with some specialized machines. The products moved from shearing operations to the punch presses or forming machines, then on to seam or spot welding machines with additional forming operations. The final stages were inspection, painting, and storing or shipping.

Working conditions were good. The heavy lifting was done by machinery, but the plant was hot, dusty, and noisy due to the nature of the operations. Because of the large amount of mechanical equipment, African Production Company depended on the technical and maintenance staff to keep the plant operating. When a critical machine broke down, it was necessary for all technical personnel to combine as a team and to set immediately about repairing it so that a minimum of production time was lost. The technical staff also aided in making innovations in the equipment that would reduce the physical handling of products or would eliminate bottlenecks in the production processes. According to Jackson, the General Manager, the technical staff was considered to be highly important in plant operations and the staff members were respected by the plant personnel.

In April a vacancy occurred in the technical staff, and in order to fill it, Jackson visited a technical school and interviewed students who would be graduating in June. Five of these students were invited to visit the plant (with expenses paid by the company) to view the operations and to be interviewed by the management personnel.

The five applicants agreed to meet with the plant manager on a Friday morning at 9. On the morning of the appointment, only one of the five arrived at 9; the other four came between 10 and 10:30 a.m. When Jackson commented on their being late, they explained that the heavy city traffic had delayed them.

When interviewing the candidates later, Jackson posed the question: "If you were in charge of relieving the traffic congestion, what would you do?" One responded that his degree was a technical one and had nothing to do with traffic control. A second one responded that this was up to the government, and two other applicants did not offer any suggestions. The fifth one said that the person who had cleared up the cargo mess in the harbor should be hired to clear up the traffic congestion. Later, when reviewing the candidates with others in management, Jackson expressed disappointment that four of the applicants were unwilling to consider the problem and that the fifth one quickly handed it to someone else—the person who cleared the harbor.

During the day, the candidates talked to the Plant Manager, they had lunch with Jackson and others on the staff, and they also had an opportunity to closely inspect the plant. Jackson pointed out to these people that the company was following an indigenization [1] program and that advancement opportunities were very good. It was up to the employee as to how high advancement in the organization would be. Although they did not say so, Jackson felt the candidates would prefer a job where most of the work could be done in an air-conditioned office.

The Plant Manager and Jackson were in agreement that one of the students should be made an offer of the position. This candidate was the same one who had arrived on time and had suggested hiring of the harbor attendant to clear up the traffic congestion. The applicant accepted the position and came to work for the company. After two and a half weeks he turned in his resignation. He explained to Jackson that there was too much work.

EDUCATION FOR SELF-RELIANCE [2]

Our present system encourages school pupils in the idea that all knowledge which is worthwhile is acquired from books or from 'educated people'—meaning those who have been through a formal education. The knowledge and wisdom of other old people is despised, and they themselves regarded as being ignorant and of no account. Indeed it is not only the education system which at present has this effect. Government and Party themselves tend to judge people according to whether they have 'passed school certificate,' 'have a degree,' etc. If a man has these qualifications we assume he can fill a post; we do not

1. *Indigenization* meant replacing foreign managers with local people.
2. Excerpt from policy directive on education: Education for Self-Reliance, President Nyerere, Tanzania, 1967.

wait to find out about his attitudes, his character, or any other ability except the ability to pass examinations. If a man does not have these qualifications we assume he cannot do a job; we ignore his knowledge and experience. For example, I recently visited a very good tobacco-producing peasant. But if I tried to take him into Government as a Tobacco Extension Officer, I would run up against the system because he has no formal education. Everything we do stresses book learning, and underestimates the value to our society of traditional knowledge and the wisdom which is often acquired by intelligent men and women as they experience life, even without their being able to read at all.

This does not mean that any person can do any job simply because they are old and wise, nor that educational qualifications are not necessary. This is a mistake our people sometimes fall into as a reaction against the arrogance of the book-learned.

A man is not necessarily wise because he is old; a man cannot necessarily run a factory because he has been working in it as a laborer or store-keeper for 20 years. But equally he may not be able to do so if he has a Doctorate in Commerce. The former may have honesty and ability to weigh up men; the latter may have the ability to initiate a transaction and work out the economics of it. But both qualifications are necessary in one man if the factory is to be a successful and modern enterprise serving our nation. It is as much a mistake to over-value book learning as it is to under-value it.

The same thing applies in relation to agricultural knowledge. Our farmers have been on the land for a long time. The methods they use are the result of long experience in the struggle with nature; even the rules and taboos they honor have a basis in reason. It is not enough to abuse a traditional farmer as old-fashioned; we must try to understand why he is doing certain things, and not just assume he is stupid. But this does not mean that his methods are sufficient for the future. The traditional systems may have been appropriate for the economy which existed when they were worked out for the technical knowledge then available. But different tools and different land tenure systems are being used now; land should no longer be used for a year or two and then abandoned for up to 20 years to give time for natural regeneration to take place. The introduction of an ox-plough instead of a hoe— and, even more, the introduction of a tractor—means more than just a different way of turning over the land. It requires a change in the organization of work, both to see that the maximum advantage is taken of the new tool, and also to see that the new method does not simply lead to the rapid destruction of our land and the egalitarian basis of our society. Again, therefore, our young people have to learn both a practical respect for the knowledge of the old 'uneducated' farmer and an understanding of new methods and the reason for them.

Yet at present our pupils learn to despise even their own parents because they are old-fashioned and ignorant; there is nothing in our existing educational system which suggests to the pupil that he can learn important things about farming from his elders. The result is that he absorbs beliefs about witchcraft before he goes to school, but does not learn the properties of local grasses; he absorbs the taboos from his family but does not learn the methods of making nutritious traditional foods. And from school he acquires knowledge unrelated to agricultural life. He gets the worst of both systems!

Finally, and in some ways most importantly, our young and poor nation is taking out of productive work some of its healthiest and strongest young men and women. Not only do they fail to contribute to that increase in output which is so urgent for our nation; they themselves consume the output of the older and often weaker people. There are almost 25,000 students in secondary schools now; they do not learn as they work, they simply learn. What is more, they take it for granted that this should be so. Whereas in a wealthy country like the United States of America it is common for young people to work their way through high school and college, in Tanzania the structure of our education makes it impossible for them to do so. Even during the holidays we assume that these young men and women should be protected from rough work; neither they nor the community expect them to spend their time on hard physical labor or on jobs which are uncomfortable and unpleasant. This is not simply a reflection of the fact that there are many people looking for unskilled paid employment—pay is not the question at issue. It is a reflection of the attitude we have all adopted.

How many of our students spend their vacations doing a job which could improve people's lives but for which there is no money—jobs like digging an irrigation channel or a drainage ditch for a village, or demonstrating the construction and explaining the benefits of deep-pit latrines, and so on? A small number have done such work in the National Youth Camps or through school-organized, nation-building schemes, but they are the exception rather than the rule. The vast majority do not think of their knowledge or their strength as being related to the needs of the village community.

Martin Food Products Company

In June Ralph Christensen, vice-president in charge of sales of the Martin Food Products Company, visited the company's Milwaukee sales branch to handle the problem arising from the actions of Harvey Abbott, a sales representative, and Sandra Gallberg, an office clerk.

Harvey Abbott, 43 years old, had just completed 28 years of service with the company. After two years of high school, he had started with Martin as an office boy in the company's main office in Chicago. He advanced through a series of office positions until he was the supervisor of a group of seven employees. His superiors considered him an extremely able and conscientious employee and an able supervisor of those working for him. Several times Abbott had applied for a transfer to the sales force, but was turned down each time as being of more value to the company in his present job. Again in his 24th year with Martin he applied for a transfer to the sales force; he felt that the promotional and earning prospects were greater in the Sales Department than in the office. This time his application was approved. After a short sales training period, he was transferred to the Milwaukee sales branch.

At the time of his transfer, Abbott was 39 years old, married, and had five small children. In his new job he was to call on the retail grocery stores in a territory in Milwaukee's south side. His job was to promote the company's canned food line by building displays of Martin's products, aiding the store managers in promoting sales, putting up advertising posters, and holding demonstrations on Fridays and Saturdays in the stores. He would prepare suggested orders of Martin's products for the store managers to order from their wholesale suppliers or central warehouses.

Harvey Abbott was an immediate success in his sales position. This success was ascribed by his sales manager, Joe Fuller, to his basic familiarity with the company and its products built up over his previous 24 years in the office and to hard work. It was not unusual for him to work two or three nights a week in aiding store managers in getting their stores ready for sales. He was not regarded as being the aggressive type or a smooth talker; rather, Abbott seemed to get his results by sheer hard work and honesty in dealing with the individual store managers.

Financially, Abbott was having trouble making ends meet. Although he had received several increases in salary since his transfer, he found his living expenses much higher than in Chicago, and his family seemed to incur almost continuous medical expenses. In spite of this, he kept up his social connections and was very active in his church affairs and in various civic and fraternal clubs.

Sandra Gallberg was 53 years of age and had been in Martin's employ for 35 years. She started after graduation from high school and had been employed in various clerical positions in the Milwaukee office ever since. She was regarded as a very able worker and conscientious, but somewhat hard to get along with. Barbara Lee, the office manager, found she was best when she could be assigned jobs where she worked independently and did not have much contact with the other employees. While being regarded as somewhat irritable by her coworkers, everyone admitted she had a "heart of gold" and would always go out of her way to help anyone in trouble—financially or otherwise.

It was not necessary for her to work for a living, as her family had considerable means. Usually when she asked for a raise, it was not because she actually needed it to live on, but it was more as a sign of recognition for her work and to keep up to other employees with whom she worked.

Salespeople in the Milwaukee branch were paid a fixed salary on a weekly basis, plus their expenses. Included in their expenses was a reimbursement for funds paid out by the salespeople for spoiled or dented cans picked up in the various retail stores and for which they paid the grocer the cost price. Salespeople were allowed to redeem up to $5 worth of such spoiled merchandise at one time without prior authorization and to pay cash to the grocer. If the value of the merchandise ran greater than this amount, the salesperson would instruct the store owner to return the spoiled items to the central warehouse where the product would be destroyed, and a credit memorandum would be issued by Martin's office for the value of the spoilage.

When a salesperson reimbursed the grocer for spoiled cans, a receipt listing the number of cans of each product picked up, cost per unit, and total cost was given the grocer who signed the receipt form. Then the salesperson would destroy the spoiled product or bring it into the office for inspection. The salesperson attached the receipt form to the weekly expense report and obtained reimbursement for the funds spent. Since it was the company's policy to keep all damaged or otherwise unsightly appearing merchandise off the grocer's shelves, expenditures by salespeople for this purpose varied from $5 to $25 per week. So that they were not in position of taking this money out of their own funds until reimbursed, each salesperson had a standing advance of $25 to cover such expenditures.

Sandra Gallberg usually spent about two days of each week in checking these expense reports, verifying additions, checking receipts, etc. When this part of her work was finished, she would turn them over to Joe Fuller for final review and approval, advising him of any irregularities. After being approved by the sales manager, the reports were returned to Gallberg who entered the total amounts on the payroll for reimbursement to the salespeople. Lee, the office manager, would occasionally spot-check her work, and in the absence of Fuller, hers would be the final approval on the expense reports. She expressed complete satisfaction with the way in which Gallberg was handling her work.

In June the company's internal auditor, Williams, visited the Milwaukee office for a review of the office setup and an audit check of the sales and expense records. Included in his review was a testing of payments made to salespeople for expenses, samples, and spoils.

In his spot-check of payments for spoils, he noted some slight irregularities in the receipts turned in by Abbott. On some receipts there were extension errors; in other cases it appeared as if the original receipts had been altered. When asked about it, Gallberg denied any knowledge of any alterations but admitted a possibility of errors in extension and addition that she may have passed through in the haste of trying to meet the payroll deadlines.

Williams, not entirely satisfied, decided to review all Abbott's spoilage receipts for the last four years. Here he noted an almost consistent pattern of what appeared to be receipt alterations or errors of extension or addition—all in favor of Abbott amounting to an average of $1.50 to $2 per week. At this point Williams strongly suspected connivance between Abbott and Gallberg in raising the receipts. When apprised of this, Gallberg appeared visibly shaken but still denied any knowledge of any errors. At this point Fuller called in Abbott and told him what was suspected and asked for an explanation. Abbott also disavowed all knowledge of any errors, and stated that he often had items added or deducted from his expense reports which he could not explain so that he never really knew in exact dollars and cents what he was going to get in his check each week, and that if the check came within a few dollars over or below what he thought it should be, he never questioned it. To prove he had no knowledge of any so-called alterations, he offered to bring in his copies of spoils receipts for comparison with the office copies. When this was done, the alterations suspected were confirmed.

Gallberg was confronted with Abbott's copies. She again denied any knowledge of any wrongdoing and appeared in a condition of great emotional upset. When advised that the alterations made were apparently all in her own handwriting, she broke down crying and hurried out of the office. Later in the day she telephoned Fuller and asked for a private conference with him and Lee. When she came in, she admitted having made alterations in Abbott's receipts almost every week for the last two and one-half years. She stated that she was on very friendly terms with Abbott and his family and knew of their close financial circumstances. She also felt that Abbott was being underpaid in comparison with some of the other salespeople, and she also felt that the other salespeople were deliberately padding their spoils receipts while Abbott was not. By padding Abbott's account, she was only trying to equalize the situation, and she denied emphatically getting anything out of the situation herself. She also mentioned that Abbott had asked several times if he was being paid too much, but she advised him that everything was all right.

Abbott was again brought in and admitted he had on several occasions questioned his payments. He admitted a suspicion that something was wrong, but did not want to say anything to get Gallberg in trouble. He further stated that if the auditor could compute the amount of false payments, he would gladly make restitution to the company.

In the meantime, despite efforts to maintain secrecy in the investigation, word had gotten out in the office and sales force that there was something wrong with Abbott's expense reports and that Gallberg was included. At this same time the company also had several other cases of mishandling of expense reports in its other sales branches.

It was at this point that Ralph Christensen, the vice-president, visited Milwaukee to make whatever disposition should be made of the case, considering the admitted defrauding of the company by two employees, the length of service of the employees, and the other attendant circumstances.

Fosdick Engineering
Service Corporation

The Fosdick Engineering Service Corporation provided engineering services to manufacturing companies throughout the country. Approximately 1,000 people were employed, 20 percent of whom were graduate engineers. Services were performed by five Engineering Departments and one Field Service Department. The Engineering Departments conducted original engineering investigations, and the Field Service Department conducted subsequent inspections on the products selected in the field as a means of judging performance under actual operating conditions. The organization of the various departments and the executive personnel were as shown in Exhibit 1.

For many years it had been company policy to fill supervisory, administrative, and executive positions from personnel who had worked up through the ranks. With rare exceptions, such as positions related to accounting and legal phases of the work, these positions had been filled by personnel having degrees in engineering.

The normal course of events had produced a situation where all officers and department heads and a majority of section heads were at least 55 years of age. Plans had to be made to fill the vacancies as they would occur (due to retirements and deaths) over a five- to ten-year period.

One spring the president initiated the Administrative Training Program. Ten engineers, ranging from the ages of 30 to 40, were given the title of administrative engineer. Three of the ten administrative engineers selected had served for relatively short periods as section heads, and the others had performed various duties in one or more of the departments. They were told to take courses in selected fields at the evening school of the local university. A program was also initiated whereby they would be rotated through various departments of the company, as directed by the president, to obtain a broad concept of the company's operations.

During the five years that the program had been in effect, all new executive, administrative, or supervisory positions created or old positions vacated had been filled from this pool of administrative engineers. No department heads or section heads (with the exception

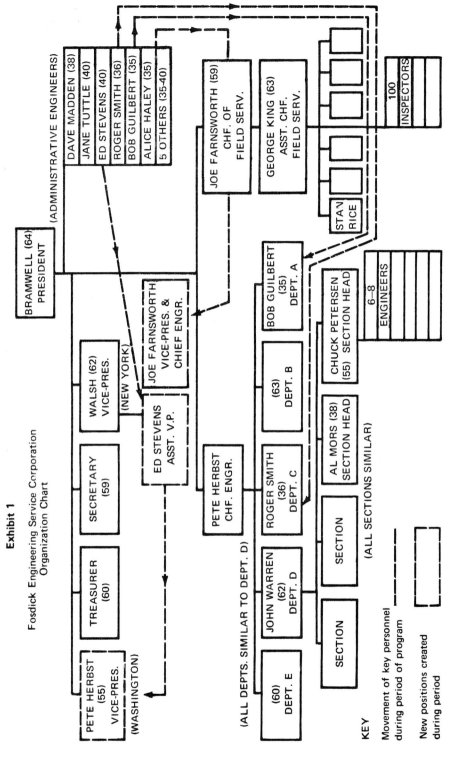

Exhibit 1

Fosdick Engineering Service Corporation
Organization Chart

BRAMWELL (64)
PRESIDENT

(ADMINISTRATIVE ENGINEERS)

DAVE MADDEN (38)
JANE TUTTLE (40)
ED STEVENS (40)
ROGER SMITH (36)
BOB GUILBERT (35)
ALICE HALEY (35)
5 OTHERS (35-40)

JOE FARNSWORTH (59)
CHF. OF FIELD SERV.

GEORGE KING (63)
ASST. CHF. FIELD SERV.

100 INSPECTORS

STAN RICE

PETE HERBST (55)
VICE-PRES.
(WASHINGTON)

TREASURER (60)

SECRETARY (59)

WALSH (62)
VICE-PRES.
(NEW YORK)

JOE FARNSWORTH
VICE-PRES. & CHIEF ENGR.

ED STEVENS
ASST. V.P.

PETE HERBST
CHF. ENGR.

BOB GUILBERT (35)
DEPT. A

ROGER SMITH (36)
DEPT. C

(63)
DEPT. B

CHUCK PETERSEN (55)
SECTION HEAD

6–8 ENGINEERS

(60)
DEPT. E

JOHN WARREN (62)
DEPT. D

SECTION

AL MORS (38)
SECTION HEAD

SECTION

(ALL SECTIONS SIMILAR)

(ALL DEPTS. SIMILAR TO DEPT. D)

KEY

Movement of key personnel
during period of program

New positions created
during period

of those appointed administrative engineers) had been promoted to higher positions.

One morning, Dave Madden, administrative engineer at the Fosdick Engineering Service Corporation, returned to his office in Chicago after an out-of-town business trip. He was greeted by Stan Rice, a field engineer and fellow worker in the department·

Rice: Say, Dave, have you heard the latest news?

Madden: No. Who's had a baby now?

Rice: It's more than that. We have a new chief of field service.

Madden: (Surprised) Oh, is that right? Who's the lucky person?

Rice: Your friend, Alice Haley, the wonder girl.

Madden: When did this happen?

Rice: At the board of trustees meeting on Thursday.

Madden: What happened to Farnsworth?

Rice: Farnsworth was made vice-president and chief engineer.

Madden: Well, I'm certainly glad to see he finally made the grade. What happened to Pete Herbst?

Rice: Oh, they kicked him upstairs to get him out of the way. He's been shanghaied to Washington.

Madden: Well, at least he's out of our hair.

Rice: Yeah, I guess nobody's shedding any tears over that move, unless it's Washington. I sure feel sorry for the people out there.

Madden: Did . . . anyone else get promoted?

Rice: Sure. Ed Stevens is going out to New York to be assistant to the vice-president out there.

Madden: Looks like the good jobs are about taken, doesn't it?

Rice: You said it.

Madden: I guess that means Stevens will be made vice-president when Walsh is promoted to president.

Rice: You never know what's going to happen around here, the way they run things.

Madden: I think Stevens will get it, and I don't feel so bad about *him*— because I think he's qualified for the job.

Rice: He's a good man all right, and he's been here a long time.

Madden: How long has Haley been in field service? About two years, isn't it?

Rice: She was transferred here when you went to Department A.

Madden: Looks like she was making time while I was working on that special project.

Rice: Oh, she's a smooth talker, all right.

Madden: How does George feel about everything?

Rice: He certainly isn't shouting with joy. He's been with this department for 30 years, and assistant chief for 8 years.

Madden: I guess he feels like he's been passed over again.

Rice: Even if he had only two more years to retirement, it would have been nice for him to have had it.

Madden: He's been hoping for it for a long time.

Rice: Well, he's in the same boat as the older people all through the company. They aren't going any place because the administrative engineers will get the jobs as they open up.

Madden: Administrative engineers! Doesn't look like there's anything left for me.

Rice: Something will turn up. After all, you're one of the chosen ten.

Madden: I don't know. Doesn't seem that I'm making much progress.

Rice: Something's bound to break for you.

Madden: I spent three years in Department D and four years in field service before they started this so-called Administrative Training Program. Since then I have spent one year in Department D, two years in Department A, and two years in Department B. I had to work like hell to learn the business in each of those departments so I'd have a better understanding of the company as a whole. Now, I'm right back where I was five years ago.

Rice: If it'll make you feel any better, I think you're better for the job than Haley. You should have had the job, in my opinion, but . . . well, that's the way it goes. Guess I'd better go see the new boss.

Madden: Give her my congratulations.

At noon that same day, as Madden was leaving for lunch, he ran into George King, assistant chief of field service, in the hall. King looked discouraged, and Madden asked him to go to lunch with him. A few minutes later the two men were seated at a table in a restaurant across the street, where the following conversation took place.

Madden: What'll it be today, George?

King: I'm not very hungry.

Madden: The ox-tail joints sound good.

King: I'll just settle for a cup of coffee today, Dave. Don't feel so good.

Madden: Oh, come on, George. Things aren't that bad. You'd better eat something.

King: I'm through, Dave! This was my last chance, and I didn't make the grade.

Madden: I know how you feel. I wish there were something I could say.

King: There's nothing to say. I'm a failure and everybody knows it.

Madden: Oh, now, George, you know that's not . . .

King: (Interrupts) It's not the first time it's happened. Remember Harold Richert?

Madden: Yes, I remember.

King: He was younger than I was and had less experience. And he hadn't been with the company as long as I had. But they made him assistant chief right over my head. If he hadn't died of a heart attack, I wouldn't be where I am.

Madden: A lot of us thought you should have had the job in the first place, George.

King: Now to have a young woman like Alice Haley . . . not dry behind the ears . . . Why, she's thirty years younger than I am. It's pretty hard to take.

Madden: I'm not exactly happy about this situation either, you know.

King: What do you mean?

Madden: Well, I always hoped that someday I'd be chief of field service. Of course, I naturally assumed that if the job opened up before you retired, you'd get it.

King: Maybe I'm crazy, but I thought that's what they had assistant chiefs for—so they could learn the business and then be promoted when the time came.

Madden: Now that Haley's head of field service it'll be a hell of a long time before she retires. It looks like I'm out in the cold.

King: Oh, I'm sure they've got something in mind for you.

Madden: I'd sure like to know what the devil it is. I'm sick of going to night school all the time. And my wife's getting fed up with it, too.

King: Is night school required of all the president's ten administrative engineers?

Madden: It's supposed to be required, but Haley hasn't taken anything for the last four years. She was supposed to be taking this extension course at the University of Chicago, but she hasn't done much with it.

King: How about the others?

Madden: As far as I know they aren't taking anything either. I'm the only one who's plugging along, and I think I'm about ready to throw in the sponge.

King: Oh, I think you ought to keep working, Dave. I'm sure they've got something in mind for you. You're young. It's different with me. I'm old. You've got a lot of time ahead of you.

Madden: I don't want to spend it sitting around playing second fiddle to Alice Haley.

King: Maybe they have you slated for another department.

Madden: All I've done for the last five years is shift around from department to department. I've never been anywhere long enough to really do anything. I feel like I'm neither fish nor fowl.

King: It does sort of leave you with one foot up.

Madden: I spent two years in Department A, but I knew I wasn't getting anywhere there because Guilbert obviously had that job sewed up.

King: What about Department D?

Madden: Oh, Jane Tuttle will get that. She's an electrical engineer.

King: So are you.

Madden: Well, Jane as much as told me she expects to get that job. She seemed pretty sure of it.

King: There are going to be a lot of angry section heads down there if she does. Those people have been waiting a long time for Warren to retire.

Madden: Well, you can see the pattern. They just aren't promoting from within departments. Look at your case, George.

King: Yes, look at it.

Madden: I'm sorry, but hell, that's the situation.

King: It seems like most of the ten A.E.'s are pretty well set except for you, Dave.

Madden: I didn't mind floating around so much in the various departments because I thought it would be good background when I got to be chief of field service.

King: Looks like you called that one all wrong.

Madden: You're damned right I did! Looks like I've called the shots wrong all along. Unless I want to stay here and rot for the next 25 years, I'd better get out and fast.

King: You're a good man, Dave. It would be too bad for the company to lose you. But if I'm any example, maybe you ought to get out and look around a little. A man of your age and ability shouldn't have too much trouble finding a good job somewhere.

Several days later, two of the company's best section heads, Al Mors and Chuck Petersen, were working together on a project in Department D. Naturally, their conversation turned to what everyone in the company was talking about.

Mors: What do you think about the latest promotion, Chuck?

Petersen: You mean Haley?

Mors: Yes. I can't understand it. Everybody thought George King was in line for that job. Look how long he's been here.

Petersen: Length of service and hard work aren't what count around here. Haley's been with the company only ten years, and she's already up in the top bracket.

Mors: If you ask me, it helps to have a nice family. Looks like the president's more impressed by the families than he is by the engineers.

Petersen: Well, that lets me out.

Mors: Oh, I was just kidding. After all, you're in line for Warren's job when he retires. You're the senior section head in Department D.

Petersen: Get wise. You don't really think any section head will get that job, do you?

Mors: You've been in the department for 25 years, Chuck. That should carry some weight.

Petersen: It didn't carry much weight where George King was concerned. No, we might as well face it. The president has his chosen few, and as fast as the old managers retire he's going to shove his young war-horses in their places. The rest of us can grin and bear it or get out.

Mors: Do you really think that's the way things are shaping up?

Petersen: Looks that way to me. I've been doing some serious thinking on this, Al. There's a definite pattern developing. Haley was put in field service, Guilbert in Department A, Roger Smith in Department C, and Stevens, assistant to the vice-president.

Mors: Well, who do you think will get the job here when Warren retires?

Petersen: I think Madden will get it.

Mors: Hell, he's in field service!

Petersen: That doesn't mean anything. He's had four years in Department D. You remember he worked for me for two years.

Mors: But he's never even been a section head.

Petersen: You think that will make any difference? Stop kidding yourself.

Mors: Boy, a fat chance I have to get anyplace. I'm the youngest section head in the department, and I've had this job for eight years. If one of the administrative engineers is made the department head, I don't stand a chance of ever being promoted.

Petersen: It's affecting our project engineers, too. They know that if the section heads don't have anyplace to go, they won't have a chance for promotion either.

Mors: I guess it's pretty general all through the company. I've heard of several other project engineers who are quietly lining up jobs elsewhere.

Petersen: Can you blame them?

Mors: No, I can't. But it's knocking the devil out of production. I'm spending all my time just training new people.

Petersen: Morale has been bad since they first announced this administrative training program. These people aren't dumb. They knew what that meant.

Mors: Where does that leave us?

Petersen: I don't know about you, but it's too late for me to leave now. All I can do is float along until I retire.

Mors: I don't know. Maybe I should look around. If you stay here after you're forty, you're pretty well stuck.

Around the first of February, or approximately one month after Haley had been made head of field service, Dave Madden decided to beard the lion in his den, and using as his pretext a memorandum which Bramwell, president of Fosdick, had issued to his administrative engineers the previous day, went to the president's office to find out what he could about his standing in the company. This conversation took place in the president's private office.

Bramwell: Good morning, Dave. How are Norma and the children?

Madden: They're fine, except you know how kids are in the winter. One after the other gets sick. Right now we're going through chicken pox. How's Mrs. Bramwell?

Bramwell: Same as always, just fine. (Pause) What can I do for you, Dave?

Madden: Well, I received this copy of that memo you sent out yesterday and . . . well, to tell you the truth, I came in here to find out where I stand.

Bramwell: What do you mean?

Madden: I've been in this training program for five years now, but I don't feel like I'm getting anywhere.

Bramwell: Now, you know we can't expect things to happen overnight. This is a long-range program.

Madden: But I've been shifted between departments so much, I never really get familiar with any of them.

Bramwell: How's your educational program coming? Are you taking Spanish?

Madden: I've taken one semester.

Bramwell: Well, I'd like to see you take some more. Some day we're going to have a lot of business south of the border, and . . .

Madden: But, Mr. Bramwell, I really can't see how Spanish is helping me in this administrative training program. What I'd really like to know is where I'm going to eventually end up.

Bramwell: Now, Dave, I can't reveal everything I know. Just rest assured that there will be a very good place for you in this company. After all, we're expanding. Our overseas market is increasing every day. That's why I like to see my engineers increasing their linguistic abilities. We must be able to communicate with these people.

Madden: This whole training program is so nebulous I just don't know where I stand. It seems to me if I knew which department I was heading for, I could better prepare myself for it.

Bramwell: That's my worry. The important thing now is for you to get a broad picture of all of our operations. That's why I want you to take these night school courses. Get something besides engineering under your belt.

Madden: I'm confused about that, too. There doesn't seem to be any definite pattern to these courses. I've had a hard time selecting subjects that I felt would help me in my work in the company.

Bramwell: Well, now, you really ought to take some more Spanish. But, on the other hand, maybe some business courses would be a good idea. An engineer who has some business sense will have a great opportunity in this company.

Madden: I'm willing to work hard to get ahead. I think I've proved that. But I could do a better job if I knew what spot I was heading for.

Bramwell: I'd be foolish to tell all my subordinates what I thought the future held for them. After all, I'll be retiring soon. I can't tell you what my successor will do.

Madden: That's why I want to find out now what my job is supposed to . . .

Bramwell: (Interrupts) I've done my best to train a group of young engineers to fill our administrative posts. I know you have an excellent engineering background because we both went to the same school. But that's not enough. I never had the chance to learn systematically. I got my training the hard way. That's why I want you to take these courses.

Madden: I appreciate the confidence you have in me, Mr. Bramwell, but I've got to have something more concrete to go on.

Bramwell: Keep working, Dave, you won't regret it. Tell Norma "hello" for me.

Madden: Goodbye, Mr. Bramwell.

After considerable thought and a long talk with his wife, Madden submitted his resignation to the president on February 15. On February 27, Warren, head of Department D, died suddenly. Chuck Petersen succeeded him as department head. A week after this unexpected turn of affairs, the following conversation took place between the president and the new vice-president and chief engineer.

Farnsworth: I'd like to talk to you about several problems which have come up, Fred.

Bramwell: I suppose you refer to Department D.

Farnsworth: Well, that's one of them; Petersen's sure got his hands full.

Bramwell: Chuck Petersen's a good engineer, but he'll never make a good administrator, I'm afraid.

Farnsworth: As you know, our project engineers have been dissatisfied for some time. There have been two more resignations in Department D this week, and Al Mors told me this morning he's planning to quit.

Bramwell: How's this affecting our service to clients?

Farnsworth: Our output has slowed down about 25 percent.

Bramwell: We've got to stop this immediately! I sure wish I had Dave Madden back here. He could have stepped right into Department D and taken over. I had him tagged for that job.

Farnsworth: (Surprised) You did?

Bramwell: Of course. He was a natural for it. I wonder if there's any chance of getting hold of him and asking him to reconsider. We need someone with his training mighty bad right now.

Farnsworth: I understand he took a job with the Yonkers Company. From what I've heard, he's very happy there.

Bramwell: I can't understand why he resigned so suddenly. He had every chance for advancement here.

Farnsworth: The company spent a lot of time and money training him. It's too bad to lose a person like that.

Bramwell: How's your old department coming?

Farnsworth: Well, Haley's doing the best she can, but she can't seem to cope with it all.

Bramwell: What do you mean?

Farnsworth: Personnel problems, for one thing. There's been a lot of hard feelings because such a young woman was put in as head of the department.

Bramwell: Oh, well, that's bound to happen.

Farnsworth: Then, too, Alice hadn't been in field service very long. She just doesn't understand a lot of things about the department. She's made some very foolish mistakes.

Bramwell: I can't understand that, with all the training she's had. . . .

Coastal Bell
Telephone Company

Coastal Bell Telephone Company, one of three operating sub sidiaries which was wholly owned by Telecommunications, Incorporated, provided telephone service to the residents of nearly 100 communities in a 75-mile continuous ring around a major East Coast city.

The area served by Coastal Bell still employed nearly as many operators as was needed immediately following World War II when less than half of the phones were dial operated. Ernest Michaels, traffic department personnel manager, had said, "As far as the number of operators we require is concerned, it has been a battle of attrition. The effects of our mechanization programs such as dial conversions, direct distance dialing, etc., have been offset by two factors. The first is the population explosion in the suburbs, and the second is an increased calling rate per telephone."

Graham Walters, Coastal Bell's president, was responsible to the operations vice-president of the parent firm. Each of the five major departments at Coastal Bell was headed by a general manager reporting to Walters. Personnel services were provided by staff units in each department; however, there was considerable guidance in this field from the Telecommunications personnel staff. (See Exhibit 1.)

Coastal Bell maintained 29 operator offices in its territory. Twenty were strictly "toll centers," handling long-distance calls and calls outside the local dialing area. Five were information centers; operators in these offices provided only information service. The remaining offices provided both toll and information service. Generally the combination offices were harder to manage for a number of reasons. First, the managers had to be familiar with both types of business and the equipment required for each. Second, it was often necessary to cross-train operators to enable them to run both toll and information, and some degree of specialized efficiency was thought lost when this occurred. Third, often smaller team sizes, particularly on information, made it more difficult to schedule operators economically.

The Traffic Department was essentially the Operator Department: instead of moving physical goods, they moved telephone calls.

Exhibit 1

Organization Chart
Costal Bell Telephone Company

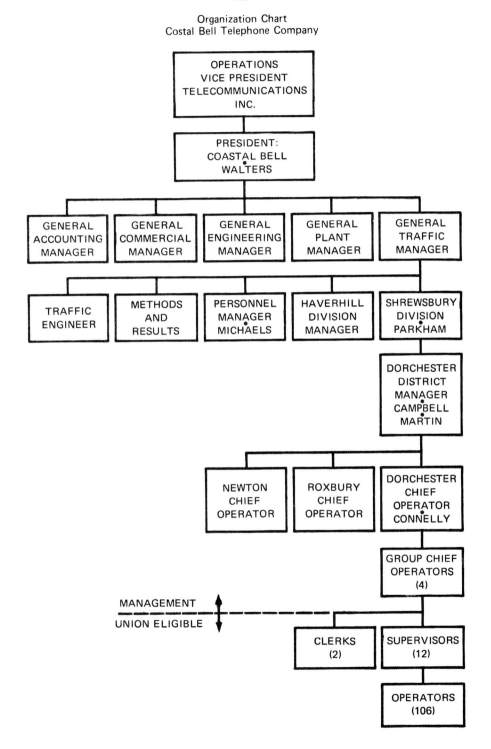

Coastal Bell's Traffic Department used standards of measurement that were virtually universal throughout the telephone industry. In fact many regulatory commissions insisted upon uniform systems of measure. The service index was designed to measure the caliber of service being given to subscribers. The index was a composite of several items such as wrong numbers, speed of answer, correctness of billing information, etc. Separate indexes were compiled for both information and toll service. Another measure was the "load." In computing the load, various types of calls with varying work time requirements were converted into a common measure—units. Employee hours were then divided into the units and the resultant figure was the load. The "efficiency of operation" was essentially a standard cost system based upon 1,000 units. Theoretically, since units were comparable, the higher the cost per thousand units, the less efficient the office. Other more conventional measures were also used by the Coastal Bell Telephone Company. These would include absence rates and overtime hours measurements.

The Coastal Bell Traffic Department employees were represented by the Amalgamated Telephone Workers of America, AFL-CIO. Amalgamated was the largest union in the telephone industry, representing several hundred thousand workers from coast to coast. While the Coastal Bell-Amalgamated contract did not provide for compulsory union membership, approximately 80 percent of the eligible employees had joined the union. Since Amalgamated replaced an independent union some 12 years ago, relationships between the company and the union had been "businesslike but friendly," according to Michaels. (See Exhibit 2.)

The Dorchester office, which employed 125 operators, handled both information and toll traffic. Dora Connelly had been the chief operator at the Dorchester Exchange for nearly five years. A very attractive woman in her early forties, Connelly had begun her career as an operator in a nearby office. She progressed rapidly and was promoted to chief operator in Roxbury. After four years as chief in Roxbury, she was transferred to Dorchester, a somewhat larger office.

Four group chief operators assisted Connelly in managing the office. The remainder of the employees were operators (106), supervisors (12), and clerks (2). Group chief operators (G.C.O.'s) were the lowest level of management. They were responsible for supervising the office during evenings and week-ends. Three supervisors and approximately 30 operators reported to each G.C.O. Specializing in functions such as training, service, analysis, etc., the group chief operator was responsible for the individual performance of each subordinate. Supervisors were bargaining unit personnel; their primary duties consisted of training operators and providing necessary assistance when operators encountered difficulties in handling calls.

Exhibit 2

Organization Chart
Amalgamated Telephone Workers, AFL-CIO

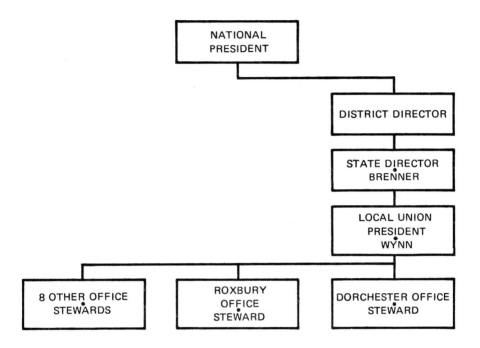

The clerks performed routine duties such as maintaining records, caring for payroll changes, etc.

John Martin was the Dorchester district traffic manager until he was laterally transferred to a staff position in the general office. As district manager, Martin was responsible for operator offices in Dorchester, Roxbury, and Newton. During his administration the service results and loads for the district were often lower than those for the combined 29 offices comprising Coastal Bell. Usually the results from the Dorchester office were the poorest in the district. It was generally conceded, however, that the Dorchester district was a tough one; consequently, pressure was exerted only sporadically when the results dropped well below the average.

Martin, a college graduate in his midforties, was characterized by Parkham of the Shrewsbury Division as "slow but relatively thorough." Michaels remarked after Martin's transfer, "It's interesting to note that in the 3½ years Martin had been out there, we didn't have a single union grievance at the top level from that Dorchester office. Before that we had plenty."

An aggressive young man, Jim Campbell, was promoted into the Dorchester district traffic manager's job. "Everybody knows that's a hard district," noted Parkham, "but maybe with some new blood and fresh ideas we'll be able to bring those measurements up a bit. Besides, Martin was due for a change; you get stagnant when you're on one job too long."

Shortly after the change in district managers, Michaels telephoned Connelly to ask if she would serve as hostess at an open house to be held for Telecommunications stockholders. After having secured her agreement, the conversation continued:

Michaels: Well, I'm glad that's settled and you will be a hostess. You know that often the shareholders have many questions to ask, and I wanted to make sure that we had someone who knows this business. With you in charge, Dora, I know they'll be in good hands.

Connelly: Thank you for asking me, Mr. Michaels. I'm sure that I'll enjoy myself, and I just hope you haven't overestimated my knowledge of the company.

Michaels: Well, I'm sure I haven't. Say, by the way, you've had a new boss for over a month now. How does Campbell like the Dorchester district?

Connelly: Fine, I guess.

Michaels: Fine, you guess?

Connelly: Well, it's hard to tell. He's quite different from Mr. Martin. But it takes a while to get used to the way a new boss operates.

Michaels: Oh? Campbell operates differently from Martin?

Connelly: I should say! Mr. Martin was so understanding. Why last year during the Christmas season, I remember the chief operator in one of the offices in the district scheduled ten more operators than Martin's estimate called for. It was on a Sunday, too; so most of the operators were getting double time and the remainder time and a half.[1] As it developed, the original estimate was quite accurate. Do you know what Mr. Martin told the chief operator? "You should really check with me before you do something like that again. It cost us quite a bit of money you know, and our estimates have been very good." He was quite understanding and never made you feel as though you really goofed—even when you did.

Michaels: I see. And Campbell is not like that?

Connelly: I don't think so; he's more direct; he lets you know exactly where you stand. One morning he came into the office and asked one of the group chiefs what the load was for the preceding day. When she replied she didn't know, he really let her have it. Then later he lectured me and said he expected each of my G.C.O.'s to know how the office is performing and why. I can't say we didn't have it coming, because we did. Maybe sometimes that direct approach is the best method, but it sure is hard to get used to after having Mr. Martin for 3½ years.

Michaels: That's interesting. Have you noticed any other differences?

Connelly: Oh yes, several. Mr. Martin always tried to understand both sides of any problem—particularly when the union was involved. As you know,

1. The Coastal Bell-Amalgamated contract provided for time and a half for the first Sunday worked in a given calendar month and double time for any subsequent Sunday worked.

the company policy has been to work every operator at least one Sunday per month, thereby reducing the number of double-time payments. When we put this into effect, the union really raised a fuss, so Mr. Martin discussed the problem with our local union officials. He told them he supported the Sunday work policy, but under extenuating circumstances we could make some adjustments. He said we could be flexible in certain cases, for instance, where there were transportation difficulties or vacation time during the month. As a result, we've probably paid some extra premium pay, but I think this pleased many of the employees who don't like to work on Sunday.

Michaels: Um hum.

Connelly: I recall another incident that also involved the union. We were planning to use stopwatches for a special study, but Mrs. Wynn, the union president, complained they made the operators too nervous. Mr. Martin examined the situation and determined that we could get the necessary information by another method.

Michaels: And Campbell doesn't see the other side of these problems?

Connelly: Oh, I didn't mean to imply that. I'm sure Mr. Campbell sees both sides. It's just that he is much more forceful. Why he mentioned just today that he thought it might be necessary to begin some stopwatch studies in my office. I informed him that Mr. Martin had previously agreed not to use the stopwatches in this office. Mr. Campbell said we would use them anyway—'a management prerogative,' he called it.

Michaels: That should prove interesting. Say, I have another call waiting. Been nice talking to you, Dora, and I'll see you at the open house on the 19th.

Connelly: Thank you for asking me. Bye.

Shortly after Campbell assumed the district manager's job, a number of grievances emanated from the Dorchester office. Few, if any, were resolved at the local level despite frequent meetings between Campbell and Wynn, the local union president and a supervisor in the Dorchester office. Usually the grievances were set for eventual settlement at a higher level.

Recently a staff man was explaining a new policy to the three chief operators in the Dorchester district. At the conclusion of the presentation, the staff man asked the chief operators for comments and suggestions. "I think it's a real good idea. We need something like that out here!" Campbell interjected. Then having glanced over to the chief operators, he added, "Don't you?" Dutifully they all nodded in agreement, and the subject was closed.

Wynn: Stopwatches went out of style a long time ago. Why, they haven't been used for observing in the Dorchester office since before Mr. Martin was assigned here. It's out of the question to time work operations; this is a throwback to the Dark Ages.

Campbell: We're having lots of problems with our scheduling and, in order to do a better job, it's imperative that we know how long it takes an operator to perform certain tasks. For instance, we must know how long it takes an operator to check ticket work on one call before answering another signal. Now that we are using computer cards to record the details of the call, the operators must be very careful to enter the correct information or we will have billing errors. I suspect they are taking a little longer to check over their ticket work now. It is quite important that we ascertain how much longer, and the only way we can do this is by using a stopwatch.

Wynn: Then you mean you'll continue taking stopwatch observations?

Campbell: Definitely! At least until we accrue a sample large enough to be meaningful.

Wynn: I'm not satisfied with your decision; we'll have to appeal this case to the next level. (See Exhibit 3.)

The stopwatch grievance was not settled at the intermediate level, and consequently the state director of Amalgamated, Brenner, presented the grievance to Michaels.

Brenner: As you know, they are taking stopwatch observations in the Dorchester office.

Michaels: Yes, I know about it. It seems to be a rather minor incident for the first top-level grievance from that office in four years.

Brenner: I guess this is our first in a long time, but I don't know how minor it is. Stopwatches upset our operators. I can't understand why the company must resort to this type of action.

Michaels: Stopwatches are an integral part of our business; we are using them in most of our operator offices right now. Why, we're even using them in the Roxbury office in the same district; we've had no complaints there. Besides, we notified your assistant steward before beginning the observations, and we were told there was nothing wrong with the plan.

Brenner: Stopwatches aren't the only problem in Dorchester. We had a union meeting there last week, and the complaints I heard were astonishing. Our people are very unhappy with the administration of that office. One employee who brought into the operating room a book for a coworker was chastized. Yet at the same time it was okay for the chief operator to show off a new pair of shoes in the operating room. This, like many of the other complaints we heard, is really petty, but they all add up when an office is mishandled.

Michaels: Mishandled?

Brenner: Yes, the chief operator and the group chief operators are quite sarcastic to the employees. When an employee calls in sick, the operator gets a smart comment like "What's wrong with you now?" Another problem is the fact that there are too many programs running in that office. Everybody gets all upset when the service index is down just a little, and they start going in all directions at once. For instance, during the planned training time, the supervisor and the operator who is being instructed sit at the end of the switchboard and overlap by answering calls. They probably average about twenty minutes actual training per hour. However, their time shows as an hour on the training records; I suppose this makes top management happy because the operators are getting lots of training. There's just too much tension in that office. The new district manager often looks over the shoulders of operators to observe their work; this makes them nervous. Several of the employees attending our meeting had transferred to Dorchester from other offices. They reported never having worked under tension like that at Dorchester.

Michaels: I'm surprised about your comments regarding the chief operator. I had the impression the union employees thought quite highly of Miss Connelly. Why just a few months ago, I was in the office on Miss Connelly's birthday, and Mrs. Wynn surprised her with a big cake she had baked.

Brenner: I could go on with several more stories that were related during our meeting, but I doubt if it would serve any purpose. Many of these items when considered individually seem rather minute, but when they upset an entire office, I become quite concerned.

Michaels: I, too, am quite concerned about the state of affairs in Dorchester. You know their service and loads haven't been very good. I'm glad that you had your meeting and called these problems to my attention. I think I'd like to discuss some of these problems a little further with our local management. (See Exhibit 4.)

Exhibit 3

Grievance Procedure Steps

Steps	Company	Union
1	Chief operator or Group chief operator	Steward or assistant steward
2	District traffic manager	Local union president
3	Division traffic manager	Local union president
4	General traffic manager (Represented by personnel manager)	State director
5	Arbitration	

Exhibit 4

Measurements:
Coastal Bell Telephone Company
Dorchester Office

	2 Years Ago	Last Year	Current Year									
			Jan.	Feb.	Mar.	Apr.	May	June	July	Aug.	Sept.	Oct.
Service Index ¹—Toll												
Dorchester	96	97	95	97	95	95	96	97	95	96	95	95
Coastal Bell	98	98	98	98	98	97	97	96	96	96	97	97
Service Index—Information												
Dorchester	77	78	89	93	86	86	87	88	91	93	88	83
Coastal Bell	98	97	97	98	97	97	95	97	98	98	96	94
Overall Load ²												
Dorchester	141	147	157	153	154	158	155	152	149	156	154	157
Coastal Bell	154	160	162	162	163	167	168	165	160	161	161	162
% Total Absence ³												
Dorchester	4.4	3.7	7.9	8.4	7.1	6.6	6.4	5.7	6.2	5.2	5.9	7.4
Coastal Bell	4.9	3.9	4.8	5.5	4.9	4.4	4.5	3.7	3.2	3.1	3.2	4.0
Workweek Actual ⁴												
Dorchester	5.08	5.14	5.31	5.23	5.11	5.08	5.21	5.25	5.11	5.12	5.27	5.22
Coastal Bell	5.11	5.07	5.08	5.06	5.05	5.07	5.34	5.21	5.11	5.13	5.20	5.23
Efficiency of Operation ⁵												
Dorchester	NA	$18.62	18.31	18.89	18.63	18.17	18.56	19.18	19.00	18.51	18.95	18.25
Coastal Bell	NA	$17.57	17.42	17.58	17.37	16.98	17.16	17.36	17.65	17.56	17.72	17.62

1. Service Index
   99 .... Outstanding
   96–98 .... Satisfactory
   90–95 .... Poor
   Below 90 ..... Unsatisfactory
2. The overall load is compiled by translating telephone calls into work-time units. The units are then divided by employee hours to determine the overall load. The load therefore is the number of units of work per employee hour.
3. Absence is expressed as a percentage of employees scheduled.
4. The workweek is the number of days worked per week per employee (i.e., 5.00 means no overtime; 5.20 means 20% of the employees in the office worked six days per week).
5. Standard costs divided by 1000 units.

Falcon Grocery Company

One morning John Moran, vice-president of the St. Louis branch of the Falcon Grocery Company, received the following letter:

Gentlemen:

I have been a customer of our Washington Woods Shopping Center store since it opened. I use the term "our" because we also own stock in Falcon. This has been a wonderful store to shop in up to a few months ago. Many of my neighbors who were steady shoppers have quit, and if I didn't own stock, I would quit too without writing this letter.

This used to be such a friendly store to shop in, but lately everyone in the store is so crabby and hostile that I can see why my neighbors don't go there any more.

This morning I wanted some frozen okra. There was none in the case, so I asked the boy in the aisle if there was any in the back. He told me (very curtly) that there was none. I went to the office and asked for the manager. The girl told me that he was busy unloading a truck and couldn't be bothered unless it was important. I told her it was very important. She paged him, and after quite a wait, he came to the office. Rather impatiently he asked me what I wanted. I told him I needed some frozen okra. He told me there was none available and went back into the back room. I went to the River Street store and they had a full row, and the boy stocking the case told me that they get it in twice a week.

I wish you would get Mr. Weeks back. This man Reel is ruining our business. Everything was so nice at this store when Mr. Weeks was here.

Very truly yours,
Jane McAdams

All complaint letters came across the desk of the vice-president. This was the second letter that day and about the tenth in a week about the Washington store. He decided to call a meeting with the operations manager and the zone manager of this store for the next day.

Jim Hudson, the operations manager, was familiar with the store because he had been the store manager who opened for business six years ago. Every manager who had been assigned to that store—with the exception of Sam Weeks—had been promoted out of the store to jobs of more responsibility.

Joe Reel had been at this store now six periods.[1] He had been with the company ever since he had graduated from college. Considered a good trainee, a good comanager, and a very good store manager, he was sent by the company to Michigan State where he received his MBA in food distribution. Afterwards, he did a very good job managing a medium-sized store. When Sam Weeks quit, the company decided to assign Reel the Washington Woods store. Reel was told that the sooner he got the store back in shape, the sooner he would be promoted.

Hudson went through the folder for the Washington Woods store to get a recent picture of it. There were copies of letters from customers who were unhappy with the recent change in the store atmosphere, people who wanted Sam Weeks back, people who complained about the surliness of employees who were there when Hudson was the manager six years ago and who he knew were good employees. One section of a letter caught his eye:

> Your Delicatessen Department in this store was the best I have ever seen. The variety and freshness made it a place where I could always get what I wanted. I could take things home and receive compliments for them as being homemade.
>
> Lately, they are always out of so many things, and the things I bring home are stale. The coleslaw I bought yesterday finished me as far as that department is concerned. It smelled so bad that I had to open the windows in my kitchen.

Hudson read this again because he knew Charlie Swanson, the delicatessen manager, very well. Charlie had been his manager of the Delicatessen Department when the store opened. Charlie was not only a good sales rep but also an excellent craftsman who too great pride in his work.

Hudson read parts of some of the other customer complaint letters:

> The check-out lines in your store lately have been terrible. Why don't you have baggers now as you did when Mr. Weeks was there?
>
> You put big ads in the paper telling us to come to your store to buy Hills Brothers Coffee at $1.09; then, when we get there, you have a sign on the display saying, "One Limit." Why didn't you tell us in those big ads that there was a one only limit? My sister told me that there was no limit at your Central Street store.
>
> I think it's very misleading to put ads in the paper and then be out of the advertised items.
>
> Thursday, I bought two chickens. I asked the clerk to put them in a double bag, but she told me that they couldn't do that any more.

1. One period is four weeks, making thirteen periods per year

Well, the chickens soaked through and ruined my slacks.

Your Washington Woods store was so nice, but now it is one of the dirtiest stores I know.

Hudson also came across a letter from every department manager of the store asking for a transfer to another store. He read the one from Charlie Swanson carefully.

Dear Mr. White:

I would appreciate it if you would consider me for *any* new store that you have opening up. You know that I can do a very good job in the Delicatessen Department of any store where I receive co-operation. I believe it would be to the best interests of the company if I could leave this store as soon as possible.

I have worked in this store since it opened and always have run a good department, but lately I have been receiving so much inter-ference from the store manager that I can't do the job as it should be done. I have had to let some of my experienced help go and re-place them with part-time people. They are new to the business and know little about waiting on trade.

You know the Delicatessen Department, Mr. White; it's one where you have to spend time in preparing foods right and then you have to spend time waiting on the trade. You can speed things up, but there is no way that you can take any drastic shortcuts.

This department has never had as few people in it as we have now, and Mr. Reel told me today that he wants me to cut another 30 hours off my schedule.

If you don't have a new store opening soon, I would consider going to another store as a journeyman until something new opens up.

Sincerely yours,
Charles Swanson

Hudson read Sam Weeks' letter of resignation. (He left to go to a competing chain.) He read some copies of memos that were sent to Weeks by Frank White, the zone manager.

To: Sam Weeks, Store #457
Subject: Wage Control
Your wages last week were 260 hours over plan. I will be in your store Thursday to discuss this with you. Have your schedules on hand.

Frank White 12/10/61

To: Sam Weeks, Store #457
Subject: Period Operating Statement
At our meeting next week, Thursday, be prepared to explain why your grocery markup dropped 1 percent while division was up 5 percent; also, why your wrapping supplies cost is consistently the highest in the division.

Frank White 1/12/62

FALCON GROCERY COMPANY

To: Sam Weeks, Store #457
Subject: Wage Control
I will be in your store Thursday afternoon to discuss your wage costs with you. Your store was 272 over plan.

Frank White 2/21/62

Reading these memos recalled to Hudson that Sam Weeks was a manager that people liked, but he did not have control of his store. Washington Woods was a large store. It had over sixty employees. The lack of close attention to any phase showed up in the operating statements. The main office was insisting on better operating figures from the divisions. These divisions, in turn, were insisting on better operations from the stores. Sam Weeks found another job because of the pressure that was being put on him to bring the operating statement back into line.

Hudson scanned through the operating statements for some key figures and for some comparison of Weeks' and Reel's managements. (See Exhibits 1, 2, and 3.)

Exhibit 1

Profit Margins of Top Ten Food Retailers *

	Percent Profit Margin	
Company **	1960	1961
A and P	1.12	1.10
Safeway	1.41	1.44
Kroger	1.26	.92
American Stores	1.25	1.29
National Tea Co.	1.01	1.05
Grand Union	1.17	1.12
Jewel Tea	1.91	1.82
Colonial	.67	.81
Red Owl	.82	.85
Mayfair	.94	.79

* From *Food Topics*, June 1962, Vol. 17, No. 6.
** Listed in order of sales volume.

Exhibit 2

Store #457 (Sam Weeks, Manager)
1960

Period	3	4	5	6	7	8
Sales	$253,000	$251,000	$248,000	$252,000	$249,000	$251,000
Markup % *	17.8%	17.7%	17.9%	18.2%	17.9%	17.7%
Company Average	18.1%	17.9%	17.8%	18.2%	18.0%	17.9%
Wages % of Sales	9.2%	8.9%	9.0%	9.2%	9.3%	9.4%
Company Average	7.3%	7.2%	7.2%	7.4%	7.5%	7.6%
Variable Expenses % of Sales	3.3%	3.8%	3.7%	3.6%	3.5%	3.8%
Company Average	3.0%	3.2%	3.1%	3.2%	3.0%	3.2%
Net Profit % of Sales	.8%	.9%	.5%	.6%	.7%	.7%

* Based on cost delivered to store.

Exhibit 3

Store #457 (Joseph Reel, Manager)
1961

Period	3	4	5	6	7	8
Sales	$246,000	$231,000	$225,000	$201,000	$192,000	$187,000
Markup % *	18.1%	19.0%	19.6%	20.1%	20.1%	20.2%
Company Average	18.2%	18.4%	18.9%	19.2%	19.3%	19.6%
Wages % of Sales	8.9%	7.2%	7.1%	7.0%	6.9%	6.8%
Company Average	7.8%	7.8%	7.9%	7.9%	7.9%	7.9%
Variable Expenses % of Sales	3.7%	3.6%	3.4%	3.2%	2.9%	2.9%
Company Average	3.4%	3.5%	3.6%	3.6%	3.7%	3.6%
Net Profit % of Sales	.9%	1.3%	1.3%	.6%	.3%	−.1%

* Based on cost delivered to store.

Central Georgia
Telephone Company

Carl Campbell was a sales representative in the Sales Department of the Central Georgia Telephone Company. He worked in Metropolis, the headquarters location of the company. The Central Georgia Company served Metropolis, a city of about 250,000, and the surrounding towns within a fifty-mile radius.

The period between the end of World War II and the mid-fifties was characterized by rapid expansion for the company. The policy of the Sales Department during these years was simply to handle business customers' requests for new and additional telephone service. The primary reason for this type of policy was the shortage of supplies due to the war years and the resulting pent-up demand for telephone service. This situation existed until about 1955. As a result, the job of a sales representative was mostly order-taking as opposed to actual selling in the usual sense of the word.

During 1955, the upper management of the company changed their thoughts concerning the sales policy. Since there was no longer a shortage of supplies and telephone facilities and since the rapid expansion following the war was coming to an end, it felt that the company must begin some aggressive selling to maintain a satisfactory earnings level and growth rate. In addition, there were indications of competitive communications services being offered in the business market. In effect, the management changed its sales policy from one of order-taking and improving customer relations to one of aggressive selling, improving customer relations, and promoting new services and equipment.

From Atlanta, Georgia, Carl had grown up in a closely knit family led by a strict disciplinarian father. Attending public elementary school and high school, he graduated from high school in 1942. After graduation, Carl enlisted in the Army, and after his release from active duty and subsequent to his employment by Central Georgia, he married and had two sons. When employed by Central Georgia, Carl and his family made their home in Metropolis.

When first employed, Carl requested the job of a truck driver in the supplies division. However, there was no job opening of this type at the time. Instead, he accepted a job of collecting the coins from public pay telephones. This job involved driving a truck on a scheduled route, removing a coin receptacle from the telephone, and replacing it with an empty one. The coins were counted later by a separate group of workers at a coin counting center. Carl performed these duties quite satisfactorily. He was characterized as a good worker with an excellent attendance record, but he tended to be a loud talker and somewhat critical of the top management of the company. As a result of his satisfactory performance, however, he was promoted to a commercial representative.

Promotion among nonmanagement employees of Central Georgia, who were unionized, was based primarily upon seniority. If two people had the same seniority exactly, job performance and other factors were then considered. Seniority was not a factor in the promotion from nonmanagement to management. Central Georgia, therefore, had no merit-rating system for nonmanagement employees until an employee was considered for promotion to management ranks based upon job performance, initiative, attitudes, supervisory characteristics, and the proper job knowledge.

Carl's duties as a commercial representative were to call upon customers to collect overdue accounts and to settle complaints when the customer could not be reached by telephone. Although Carl indicated from time to time that he preferred his previous job to this one, he performed his duties satisfactorily. Thus, when he was eligible for promotion on a seniority basis, he was advanced to a sales representative and given sales training. At first, he called upon customers in answer to their requests for service. Later, his duties became strictly promotional in nature for the purpose of selling additional telephone equipment and usage. These sales contacts were strictly company initiated, and a cold call was made upon the customer.

After graduating from Vanderbilt University with a degree in business administration and following two years of active duty in the military service, Don Wells was employed by Central Georgia. He was in the company's management training program for a year and a half and was then assigned as an assistant manager. In July, he was assigned as a trainer in the sales department's training staff. During October of that year, Wells was transferred to sales manager of the Central City Group and in May was transferred to sales manager of the North City Group, and thereby became the supervisor of Carl Campbell and 5 other sales representatives.

Don Wells was enthusiastic about his job, was a good sales rep himself, and enjoyed working for Central Georgia. He believed that the sales policy formulated by the top management of Central Georgia was the right one and was quite willing to carry it out. His job as a sales manager was to select the customers to be called upon, to assign them to a sales representative for a contact, and through field visits with the representatives to supervise and coach them in their work. Don Wells was adept in analyzing the sales job done by each of his sales representatives but was hesitant in criticizing them about the things they did poorly. He appeared to be fearful of offending them and causing them to dislike him.

One day in October, Don Wells made a field visit with Carl Campbell. They called upon three customers in the morning and then stopped for lunch. After they had eaten, Don began discussing the three sales contacts with Carl.

Don: Carl, what did you think of these three contacts this morning?

Carl: Oh, I don't know. I don't think they were very good prospects to call on. Maybe I should have done a better job preparing for them.

Don: Then you feel that you could have done a better job if you had called on better prospects.

Carl: Yeah, I think so. You know, I don't agree with this latest push about trying to force our customers into buying something.

Don: Our sales efforts are too forceful, huh?

Carl: Yes, I think so. I think we should call on customers only when they have called us and requested that we come out and talk with them about their complaints and problems. I was much happier when I was doing that. But now that we are calling on them cold, it is much harder for me.

Don: In what way is it harder for you?

Carl: Well, Don, you know I haven't had all of the schooling you have had. I only went through high school. When I came to work here, I wanted to be a truck driver. I still would like that type of job. I am fascinated by trucks. I find it hard to call on customers like this. I always have.

Don: It was much easier when the customer called you first.

Carl: You bet. He told me what he wanted and I wrote the order for it. No fuss. No muss. That's all there was to it.

Don: I see. (Pause.)

Carl: But this isn't what the managers at the top want. They want us to go out and push the customer into buying something just to get rid of us. I think this is downright rotten service to the customers—making them buy something they don't want or need. I don't see how we get away with it. I'm just not a salesperson. Sometimes, I wish I were back collecting pay telephones.

Don: Pay cut and all.

Carl: You're darned right! What's a job if you don't like what you're doing. There's not that much difference in the pay between the two jobs anyway.

Don: How did you feel about being promoted to a sales representative?

Carl: I thought all I was going to be doing was taking orders—not forcing a customer to buy something unwanted.

Don: The customer knows best, huh?

Carl: That's right. But not always, I guess.
(Pause.)

Carl: Take this last customer. I think he could use another line and three more telephones. He has those six salespeople sharing three telephones.

CENTRAL GEORGIA TELEPHONE COMPANY

You know that one salesperson says that job is like the Army. All you do is hurry up and wait. You rush out to see a customer and then sit in the reception room waiting to get in. Then you make a sale. You rush back to the office and then wait for someone else to get off the telephone so that you can call the order over to the plant. Seems like a lot of wasted time to me. Maybe some more telephones could solve their problems.

Don: You didn't think of this at the time.

Carl: I sure didn't. That's my problem. I'm too darned dumb and slow. I guess I'm not capable of being a seller.

Don: But you came up with an answer just now.

Carl: Yeah, but after the door is closed. Too darned late. How would you have handled this?

Don: Well, let's start from the beginning. I think that before I went out I would have found out all I could about this customer—rate for present service, present equipment, number of local and long-distance calls made, quantity of yellow-page advertising, and the date of a rep's last visit. You know the clerk can provide you with all this information. Then, I would try to recall other customers I might have called upon who are in the same line of business, what their problems were, and what we sold them. With this background, I think I would try to foresee what communications problems this customer might have and formulate my recommendation to solve them. Then . . .

Carl: But these might not be the customer's problems at all.

Don: Quite true. But, we shouldn't be so rigid as to be thrown off by this. Of course, I would telephone in advance for an appointment to see the customer. Then with my preapproach, this recommendation gives me a vantage point—a place to start. Then, by asking a few key questions —you remember those in the training course—I can get myself back on course. By analyzing the customer's answers to my questions, I would change my recommendation accordingly, and then present it. All that remains is answering the customer's questions and closing the sale.

Carl: Just like out of the training course. You make it sound easy. It probably is for you. It's not for me. I am just not cut out for this job. Apparently you don't think so either. A lot of the time when we are out on a contact, you jump in and finish it for me.

Don: Well, I don't want to see you go astray.

Carl: Sometimes, I wish you would let me go on my own. You could correct me later if you wanted to.

Don: I supose you are right. I just hate to see you lose the sale.

Carl: I probably would. It's easier for you young college people. It's tougher for us old fogies. The brass think we are stupid anyway. They are watching out for you. You start in as our supervisors before you're even dry behind the ears. Oh well, I am too dumb to be a sales rep anyway. I don't like to push customers around.

Don: Carl, I think that you are a lot more capable than you think you are. Well, I think that we had better get out of here. I see the waiter giving us the eye. I think he wants the table for someone else. I'll take the checks. Say, let me handle this next contact, and you watch how I do it. Maybe you can criticize some of the things I do and we'll both learn.

The Association of Insurance Dealers

The Association of Insurance Dealers (AID), a nonprofit corporation, employs approximately 500 people. It functions as a trade association for its 70 members and is also a contractor with the Department of Health, Education and Welfare. Under its contract with the federal government, the association is responsible for the operation of a significant portion of the federal National Insurance Program. In order to accomplish this task, the association subcontracts with its member companies nationally. Although the member companies perform the actual claim processing and related functions, it is the association's responsibility to assure compliance with the National Insurance Program's requirements via the efficient and economical processing of insurance claims and payment for only those services covered under the program.

While approximately half of the association's employees work with the National Insurance Program, only a portion of these employees work in the federal program area. The preponderance of the employees working with National Insurance work in an "under arrangement" capacity to the federal program area. As a result of this organization, employees report to different vice-presidents. The vice-presidents are comparable in status in the organizational hierarchy; however, the vice-president of the federal program area has prime accountability for the contractual responsibilities pertaining to the National Insurance Program. Thus, while all of the employees work with the same program, the involvement of two vice-presidents results in different and constantly changing approaches to fulfilling responsibilities, priorities, and accountabilities. Additionally, the two vice-presidents frequently become involved with the same issues.

While none of the association's employees were federal employees, the association's contract with the federal government necessitated ongoing contact and communication with federal employees through the Federal National Insurance Bureau. As a result of this ongoing contact, it was common practice of the association's employees to make comments about the federal government and its employees.

227

Comments regarding "bureaucrats," "paper shufflers," and "paper factories" were frequently made while discussing any subject.

As a result of a reorganization of one of the departments working under arrangement with the National Insurance Program, the position of manager of claims processing was created. The responsibility of the position of manager included all aspects of the claims processing function in the subcontracting member companies. A staff of seven professionals and two secretaries were to report to the manager once the position was filled. The manager was to report to the senior manager of the department who in turn reported to the vice-president of insurance services.

Although several of the professional staff in the claims processing department were eligible for the job, the manager's position was filled with an applicant outside of the association. Pamela Mason, the individual selected for the job, had insurance experience and came to the position highly recommended. Pamela was also a former employee with the National Insurance Bureau.

During the first few days on the job, Pamela was oriented to the association by her boss, Tom Fleming. The orientation included meeting the association staff, including her staff, and briefings on the scope of her responsibilities and accountabilities. Based on her past experience with the National Insurance Bureau, Pamela had previously met and worked with one of her new staff, Mark Haney.

At the end of her first week at work, Pamela and Mark ate lunch together:

Pamela: I've heard that I'm viewed as a bureaucrat in the midst. Have you heard any reaction to my being hired by the association?

Mark: There have been a few comments about working for a bureaucrat. Don't pay any attention though. Your staff just doesn't know what to expect. I guess they think you're going to turn them into "paper pushers" and do everything by the book. Really, we could use a little more order around here. It seems that every time a project, goal, or objective is established around here, it's changed the next day. And everyone gets into the act. You think you're responsible for a project, and the next thing you know one of the VPs gets involved. You never have a chance to follow a project through to completion without one of the VPs or Tom putting their fingers in the pie. They end up doing more staff work than the staff does.

Pamela: It's really too soon for me to see that. I guess time will tell though. Since I know the program, I think the hardest part of the job will be learning how they do things around here. The organization is really quite a bit different, and it's hard to figure out why they have two vice-presidents working with the same program. Doesn't that cause problems?

Mark: It sure does! As I said, everybody seems to get involved with projects for which your staff is supposed to be responsible. That includes both vice-presidents, and they don't always have the same approach to the same thing. The staff really gets frustrated and discouraged.

Pamela: Well, I guess I'll just have to wait and see. As I said, I don't think I'll have any problems with the program areas. I don't think I'll have any staff problems, either, since I always got along with the people I supervised. I'm responsible for hiring and firing now—which I never had to do before—but I don't think I'll ever have to fire anyone. I also have to approve time, travel, and expense requests; but I've done that before and never had any problems. I really think my biggest challenge will be to get to know how the company operates. Well, back to work!

During lunch about three weeks after their initial conversation, Pamela commented to Mark on her initial observations:

Pamela: You know, Mark, you were right! I spend more time reacting to vice-presidents and Tom getting involved with projects my staff and I are supposed to be responsible for than I spend actually working with the staff on the projects. It's driving me crazy. I can see why the staff is frustrated. It's not necessary for them to even think; they can just wait until someone higher up gets involved and then react to commands.

Mark: I wasn't kidding when I said everyone gets involved. If management would just stay out of staff work and manage, everyone would be a lot happier.

As time on the job progressed, Pamela began to notice other behavior which initially didn't seem to present a problem. Staff behavior began to reflect patterns, which, as they became more evident, concerned Pamela. Staff personnel would frequently call in the morning to advise they wouldn't be at work that day, and they would also arrive at work 30 to 45 minutes after the official starting time and leave early without telling her. Lunch hours lasted an hour and a half. The practices were not relegated to one or two staff members but seemed to be manifested by everyone, including the secretaries. Based on her concern, Pamela began commenting to the staff as she saw such instances occur:

Pamela: John, I was looking for you, but no one seemed to know where you were yesterday afternoon.
John: I went home early. Bad day.
Pamela: Please let me know from now on, OK?
John: Right.

Pamela: Jim, I was reviewing your time and expense sheet, and you didn't reflect the three hours you took off last week. Also, drinks aren't covered as a travel expense. I'll give it back to you for your changes before I sign it.
Jim: I'll change the time if you want me to, but I always have a couple of drinks before dinner when I travel. If you don't allow the expense, I'll just hide it somewhere and you'll never find it.

Pamela: Karen, I was looking for you this morning about 9:00, but couldn't find you. I guess you didn't get here until after that. Could you please try to get here on time?
Karen: I'll try, but I just never can seem to get going in the morning.

After multiple occurrences relating to time, attendance, and expenses and continual comments with no appreciable modification in behavior, Pamela approached her boss, Tom Fleming:

Pamela: Tom, could I talk to you? I'm really having some problems, and I don't seem to be getting anywhere in resolving them. Most of the staff show up at work about 9:00 or after, and they leave early too. When they do get here, almost every morning they get coffee and shoot the breeze about 15 minutes before they get to work. Nobody seems to follow the rules. They never could have done this if they worked for the government. I don't want to sound like a bureaucrat, but at my old job everyone had to be there on time and lunch was only for 45 minutes! I've been mentioning it every time I see something happen, but it doesn't seem to have any effect! They're supposed to be professionals, but they sure don't act like it. I don't know what to expect next! I've gone looking for the staff and can't find them. I can't go following them around. The next day, I'll find that they've gone home early. I just found out this morning that one of the staff flew home a day early from a business trip and never bothered to come into work the next day. I only found out by accident. I certainly never thought this kind of thing would be a problem. The way everyone is taking advantage of the rules, I'm about ready to boil! To compound the problem, I don't know how we're expected to do our job when everyone keeps getting involved with projects that are supposed to be our responsibility. Tom, I need your help.

Tom: I know what you mean. When I first came here, the fact that we couldn't do our work without someone else higher up getting involved with the staff work drove me up a tree, but that's just the way the organization is. What you've said about the staff really bothers me because you know how much work we have to do. We can't afford to waste time getting things done. Listen, I've got to go. We'll have to discuss this again. I'll see you when you get back from your trip.

After her trip, Pamela returned to work and met Tom.

Tom: I was so mad yesterday, I couldn't see straight! I was working on one of the projects and needed some help, but no one was around. It was only 3:30 and I couldn't find anyone but Mark who was on his way out the door. I rarely get mad, but I was really steaming!

Pamela: That's it! I've mentioned following the rules time and again, but I'm just going to have to be a bureaucrat and crack down!

Five minutes later, Pamela had all of her staff in her office:

Pamela: I just want you to know that I just heard what happened yesterday while I was gone and that's it! I don't care if it's bureaucratic or not, but from now on everyone is to be here at 8:30 a.m.—no later! No one is to leave before 4:30 p.m.! Lunches are to be one hour—no more! If anyone wants to take time off, then you must request it in advance! All expenses are to be according to the book and substantiated by receipts! Anyone who can't follow the office rules can consider if they still want to work here! I've tried to give you the lattitude that professionals deserve, but it's merely been abused. We've got too much work to do!

Part Four

Decisions Involving Public Responsibility

Affirmative Action and Minority Employment
Antitrust
The Legal Aspects

Mary Worthington

In June, Mary Worthington, a black, graduated from college with a BA degree in history. Her undergraduate career was marked by above-average grades and a variety of extracurricular activities, the most notable of which were theatricals and volunteer work in political campaigns.

Upon graduation, Mary accepted a position as a management trainee with the Midwest Telephone Company and was assigned to the Plaintown area. Her job assignment was in the traffic department, which primarily provided for operator-handled services for long-distance or information.

The first step in the company's management training program was to acquaint the newly hired personnel with the service at the craft level. Mary was to spend two months training and functioning as an operator, which was to be followed by two months as a craft-level supervisor where she would both train and give assistance to an assigned number of operators. She was to spend the last eight months of the year's program as an acting, first-level manager with a number of supervisors and operators reporting to her. In this capacity she would also share administrative responsibilities with the offices' first-level managers and would report to the office manager (or chief operator). At the end of one year, Mary would be promoted to first-level manager if her ability and development were rated satisfactory. If her performance was unsatisfactory, she was told she would promptly be separated from the company. Every three months her field superiors were to submit an evaluation of her performance to the department's training staff. The evaluation was to be brief and to include a list of her responsibilities during the three-month period. This evaluation was intended to serve more as a means of determining whether or not the field management was adhering to the program than as a formal appraisal of Mary's performance.

Mary began her operator's training at the North Town Office, which was located in the company's North End District. (See Exhibit 1.) Marsha Smith, the office manager (chief operator), was on vacation when Mary arrived at the office; and it was Gail Green, a first-level manager, who assigned Mary's training to a newly promoted supervisor.

Exhibit 1

North End District

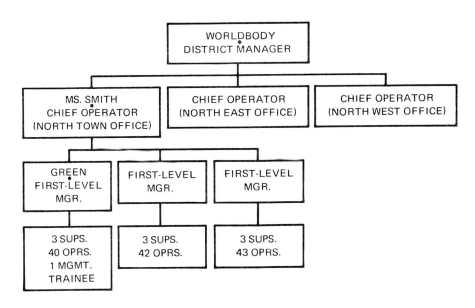

From the very first day of training, it seemed that Mary was not learning enough about the operator's job. This situation was not immediately evident to Green because of an undercurrent of friction between Mary and her immediate supervisor. The trouble had developed, according to the supervisor, because of Mary's "superior attitude" and "the waving about of her college diploma."

When Smith returned from her vacation the following week, she learned that the friction had developed into quarreling which had spread throughout the office. Most of the craft employees had chosen sides—Mary's supporters being the minority in number. When Mary's supervisor was questioned by Smith about what had caused the trouble, her reply was that Mary had refused to accept training and acted as if she "knew everything there was to know about everything." When this matter was discussed with Mary, she explained that she was simply trying to help her supervisor do a more effective job.

When all attempts by Smith—changing Mary's supervisor, admonishing some employees who added to the discord, etc.—failed to end the office feud, Smith sought help from her district manager, Noel Worldbody. After discussing the matter, Worldbody decided that the only way to regain employee serenity in the North Town Office was to have Mary transferred to another office and another district.

(It should be noted that the Midwest Telephone Company was, at this time, publicizing its role in the community as an Equal Opportunity Employer and was actively seeking to add more blacks to its payroll, including management, especially in the Plaintown area. It justified its present policy, construed as "inverse discrimination," by pointing out that one of the company's stated objectives was to actively help the community in which it operated.)

There was very little difficulty encountered by Worldbody in obtaining Mary's transfer to a new district and office. It was looked upon as a fresh start for her after an unfortunate incident in beginning her career at the company. Thus after two weeks at North Town, Mary was transferred to the Clearview Office in the South Line District. (Clearview was an all white office.) Neither Carol Henderson, her office manager, nor Jules Willing, her district manager, were fully informed as to the reason for the transfer after such a brief period at North Town.

During the next month and a half at Clearview, Mary learned and performed the job of a long-distance operator. She demonstrated an exceptional ability to retain and apply her training. She made few errors in handing calls and rarely needed to seek the help of her supervisor in completing calls. The quality of her work was well above the average of the office, and the quantity of calls which she handled was increasing satisfactorily with time. She had good rapport with the office management, but Mary was quiet and did not mix with the other employees. Henderson spent some time trying, as she put it, to get Mary out of her shell, but no amount of talking or gentle pushing could get Mary to socialize with the other employees.

During the next two months Mary completed her training as a craft-level supervisor and was assigned the responsibility of training and giving assistance to a group of approximately ten operators. Her ability to retain the details of her own operator training proved valuable in helping her assist operators with difficult customer calls.

It was during these two months that Mary exhibited a willingness to accept greater responsibility normally reserved for the first-line and/or office manager. She began to suggest to the management the need for reducing the number of operators on duty at certain times and increasing the number at other times due to changes in customer daily calling patterns and offered her judgment as to what the correction in the force should be. This task was usually cared for by the office manager, who, by virtue of overall knowledge of office conditions and experience in the particular office, was in the best position for analyzing the situation and making the necessary decisions. However, Henderson also valued the opinions of the first-level managers in this matter.

She was pleased that Mary had taken an active interest in the management of the office. Even though Mary's decisions concerning the force corrections were usually off by quite a bit, Henderson realized this was due to a lack of experience and training in the "nuts-and-bolts" aspect of the traffic office management job, which Mary was to acquire on her next phase of the training program. At the end of three months, Henderson forwarded Mary's performance report to the training staff, via Willing. It was a favorable evaluation which included all of the aforementioned items concerning Mary at Clearview.

After five months of service with the company, Mary began the management phase of her training program and became an acting, first-level manager. She was given the responsibility for supervising the activities of two supervisors and 20 operators and caring for any personnel problems which might arise in her group. She also shared the responsibilities of general administration of the office—which included force adjustment, safety programs, development of office training programs.

It was during this phase that Henderson became ill and was off the job for several weeks. Mary's training as a first-level manager was assigned by Willing to Dora Knox, a first-level manager who temporarily replaced Henderson and was to acquaint Mary with the nuts-and-bolts portion of the job.

Knox was busy with her own responsibilities and found the additional responsibility of training Mary a burden. Instead of covering each facet of the job in detail, she had Mary follow her around, letting her observe how the duties were performed—adjustment of the force, establishment of office and group service and training programs, organization of paper work, and preparation of reports being among such duties.

This might have been effective had it not been for the fact that this detailed training was scheduled to last only two weeks, and in this time span there was little likelihood that all, or even a majority, of the nuts-and-bolts items associated with the first-level manager's job would occur. Therefore, after the two weeks, incidents would appear which had not even been discussed. To complicate matters, Knox had her own way of doing certain things—such as the adjustment of the operating force. Her methods worked well for her, but she could not explain them to anyone else.

When Henderson returned, Mary had completed the allotted two weeks of training and was on her own. Knox informed Henderson that "Mary had done well and had a good insight into the technical aspect of the job."

During the ensuing months Mary's attitude became more and more hostile to the company and its management. She complained to her supervisors and operators that some of the company and office practices were stupid. She voiced to them her dissatisfaction with the amount of pay they and, in particular, she received for doing the work. Her job performance had not improved with time and even began to deteriorate. However, Henderson and Willing were unaware of this because Mary had sought and obtained evening hours where she would be the only management employee on duty. It became obvious to several employees and supervisors that Mary was not performing.

On evenings, Mary became quite friendly with the union representative at the Clearview Office. This representative liked Mary and considered her lack of job knowledge as inexperience which would be eliminated when Mary had more time with the company. She took Mary under her wing and stifled grievances which were directed at Mary. On occasion, Mary did not observe the union contract which called for certain minimum and maximum intervals between an operator's lunch periods and reliefs and the starting and ending times of her tour of duty. She would violate this by holding an operator at the switchboard for an excessive period to handle surges of customer calls. In this and other instances, the union representative would speak to the operator involved and convince her that reporting or grieving this would not help anyone.

Mary began to depend heavily on the experienced evening supervisors to aid in managing the office. She let them decide how to manipulate the number of operators at the board, what service programs were necessary, etc. Because of this, the office's evening results continued at a high level. The service and training programs developed by the supervisors kept customer service at a high level. They managed to place the evening force so as to keep the number of calls handled per operator at a respectable level. Besides, the evening hours were considered a "choice" time to work, and senior, experienced operators selected this as their tour of duty.

Because of the work done by the evening supervisors and the unusual cooperation of the union representative, Mary's results, as seen by Henderson and Willing, indicated that she was coming along well as a manager. This they cited in the appraisal sent to the training section after Mary had completed six months with the company.

However, in May, one month before Mary was to complete her year as a trainee, the Bridgeview Office in the South East District of the company put in a plea to upper management for a first-line manager. Bridgeview had been operating with three, instead of its required four, first-line managers for two months, and the backlog of the work plus day-to-day routine was too much for its management to handle. Since the Clearview Office had surplus of first-line managers (including Mary), Willing was asked to select one for transfer to Bridgeview.

Willing and Henderson were aware that Bridgeview was located in a black area of the city and its force was approximately 50 percent black; they seized upon the idea that perhaps a transfer to this environment might bring Mary out of her shell and allow her to feel more at ease and mix with the employees. They both thought highly of her capabilities as a manager and recommended her as Bridgeview's first black management employee—acting or otherwise.

Mary was immediately transferred to Bridgeview and a glowing report of her performance at Clearview was sent to her new district manager, Bill Budd, and to her office manager, Peggy Case. However, after several hours of interviewing and discussing the job assignment with Mary that day, Case realized Mary's deficiencies in regard to her knowledge of the first-level manager's job.

Case immediately set up a schedule of training for Mary and supervised the administering of it. While Mary was learning all aspects of the job, Case assigned her no operators or supervisors but gave her the job of coordinating all aspects of training in the office: scheduling of classes, appraising of students, submitting of performance reports, and the like. This was an important task because of the high force turnover and high summer influx of new employees. It also removed a burden which was shared by all three of the first-line managers.

In June, Budd received a call from the division manager, Arnold Wright, reminding him that Mary would complete her year as a management trainee in one week and that it was normally the practice to promote the employee at that time. After discussing this matter with Case, Budd submitted a recommendation for Mary's promotion to first-line manager. Both agreed it would not be fair to penalize Mary for the lack of job knowledge due to incomplete training at Clearview. Also, during her first month at Bridgeview Mary indicated an eagerness to learn and showed management potential by her ability to reason well and grasp her training. Mary was promoted on time.

Two months following her promotion Mary was assigned a group of 15 long-distance operators and two supervisors—one black, one white. Case felt that she had received sufficient training and that it was time that she began practicing what she had learned in a capacity equivalent to her position.

Mary came out of her shell rapidly and began socializing (during and after hours) with a number of black operators and supervisors in the office, some of whom had attended high school with her. Once again she sought evening hours where the force was more experienced and where she would be the only management employee on duty.

Shortly after Mary had transferred to the night shift, Case started receiving complaints that Mary was taking extended breaks and was leaving early. The union representative also filed grievances concerning the scheduling of operators in such a way that they were unable to have the 15-minute relief period as guaranteed in the union contract. In addition, there were complaints that Mary used inappropriate language in correcting job performance and that some of the girls were left in tears after these reprimands. Case discounted most of these complaints, since she felt that Mary was still in a learning process and that they might be tied to a resentment of Mary's position in the company. However, she did confront Mary with the report of abuses of her position and her attitude toward other employees. After Mary made several attempts to justify her actions, claiming that these incidents were amplified because she was a black, she broke down and cried. She told Case she would change her ways and exclaimed that Case "didn't know what it was like to be black."

For nine months Case attempted to help Mary use her ability to become an effective manager. Budd, discouraged with the results of these attempts, held an appraisal of Mary with Case to record the facts of Mary Worthington's job performance. It was agreed that Mary's assignments were carelessly done and often incomplete. It was found that even the training records and reports which Mary compiled prior to her promotion contained many errors and were often submitted to the company's Training Department late. It was apparent that any assignment Case gave Mary frequently had to be not only rechecked but often redone. It did not matter whether Mary was assigned the task of setting up training and implementing a new operator practice or simply of assisting an operator fill out a company group insurance form (with Mary's having written instructions and examples); it was equally likely that she would make the same mistakes repeatedly. It was reaching the point where Case's time was being spent wholly in correcting her mistakes.

The Bridgeview Office's service results declined and costs increased because of Mary's faulty-decisions. Mary would schedule either too many or too few operators to handle the customers' calls, which resulted in increased costs or poor service. When Mary scheduled too few operators, it was necessary for Case to schedule an excess of operators (exceeding the number Mary had failed to schedule) in order to keep the service results from being the lowest in the Plaintown area. Also, when operators were overly busy, they were prone to errors in completing calls and/or billing the customer. Budd estimated Mary's mistakes cost the company two operators' weekly salaries.

Often Mary did not do a number of tasks which eventually had to be done by the other first-line managers or Case, which increased their burdens. One of these tasks was acquainting the newly hired personnel with the company's list of benefits and when and how they might avail themselves of the benefits—an item looked upon as necessary during this period of high turnover. Another was the follow-up on an operator's initial training instruction. The first-line managers were to check how a supervisor was progressing in training a new operator. It was their job to spot deficiencies in the training and to take corrective action (it was understood that the same method of training did not achieve the same results with every individual). This was particularly important since a poorly trained operator was a potential loss.

Mary let it be known to her friends that it was the money and not the job that kept her at Midwest Telephone. In fact, she stated that she "would work for the highest bidder." Yet she declined to work an extra day when it was occasionally required because of a heavy work load. She claimed that the company did not pay her enough to give up one of her days off. These remarks led Case to believe Mary did not identify with management. On one occasion Mary prompted an employee who encountered difficulty into placing a call from her home and writing a letter to the president of the Midwest Telephone Company when the matter could have been handled through normal channels.

The conclusions drawn from Mary's appraisal discouraged Budd. Obviously, unless she did a complete and immediate turnabout, it would be necessary to dismiss her. On the other hand, the only bright spot was that a black supervisor was under consideration for promotion to the management ranks.

When the appraisal had been compiled, Budd discussed it with Wright who agreed that the company could not put up with Mary much longer. Budd asked him to check into a rumor that Mary had been hired with a recommendation from a prominent black politician in Plaintown, an item which could prove to be a stumbling block to dismissing Mary.

Budd then reviewed the entire appraisal with Mary. Her only defense was to deny virtually everything and to ask such questions as, "When?" or "How would you know?" Fortunately, Case was present with her records on Mary and supplied the minute details to refresh Mary's memory. When confronted with these, Mary became silent, whereupon Budd told her that she had 60 days to correct, or begin correcting, all of her deficiencies.

During the two months after her discussion with Budd and Case, Mary ceased to take privileges. She even kept a list of all calls she made while at the office, supposedly as proof that her time spent on the telephone was in the line of duty. However, her incompetent decisions continued to cost the company money, and her work remained riddled with careless errors and incompleteness. Case felt that Mary's personnel decisions were proving very erratic. In one instance she recommended that an operator be suspended without pay for two weeks because she failed to report for work one Friday and Mary learned she had gone on a weekend trip. It was not until after the union had been notified by Case of management's intended action that a note in Mary's handwriting to the office clerks was discovered. Mary had previously excused the operator for that day.

As the 60-day period drew to an end, a rumor persistently recurred that if Mary were fired management would be petitioned to reinstate her or the office would be picketed. This was particularly distressing to the management because at that time (August) race relations in Plaintown were strained, and incidents of small riots were becoming more frequent—riots which ignited because of incidents which were less significant than picketing would be.

The Koner Company

The Koner Company is a manufacturer of plastic cups and containers. Recently an opening for a forklift driver had occurred on the third shift. The job included the following responsibilities:

—loading cartons of finished products from a conveyor line onto pallets,
—using a forklift truck to move filled pallets to storage area in warehouse,
—supplying packaging room with bundles of empty cartons,
—supplying printing department with pallets of unprinted product for production, and
—operating one automatic carton taping machine.

A few days after the opening had occurred, warehouse manager Carl Faber bumped into Ken Frank, personnel manager, as he walked into his office.

Frank: Carl, could you step into my office for a minute? There is something I'd like to talk to you about.

Faber: Sure, Ken, what is it?

Frank: It's about this forklift driver you need on third shift. I think . . .

Faber: You know I need a good man for that job, Ken.

Frank: Yes, well, have you ever heard of Affirmative Action, Carl?

Faber: Sure I have. Doesn't that require you to hire people from minority groups?

Frank: Right. It has far-reaching implications. Frankly, Carl, the government people have been on us for discriminating against women in certain job classifications.

Faber: I don't see how this pertains to me.

Frank: It's your forklift driver opening on third shift. I think you should seriously consider a woman for the job.

Faber: Are you kidding? Some of those boxes weigh over 40 pounds and you really have to hustle to keep up. A woman couldn't do the job.

Frank: Carl, all I'm suggesting is you give a woman a chance. If she can't handle the work, then you can let her go; but at least we can say we tried. Besides, that's all the government is concerned about.

Faber: Okay, Ken, I'll give it some thought, but I still don't think it's a good idea.

Exhibit 1

Names and Titles

Ken Frank	Personnel Manager
Bob Jacob	Manufacturing Manager
Joe Stukes	3d Shift Superintendent
Roger Schwartz	Production Control Manager
Carl Faber	Warehouse Manager
Charles Ceber	1st Shift Forklift Driver
John O'Connel	1st Shift Forklift Driver
Peggy Hillard	3d Shift Forklift Driver
Diane Snyker	Shipping Clerk

Later that afternoon Bob Jacob, manufacturing manager, walked into Carl Faber's office.

Faber: What can I do for you, Bob?

Jacob: I was just talking to Ken, and he tells me you are considering hiring a woman to fill that opening for a forklift driver.

Faber: Well, I . . .

Jacob: I think that's just great. This idea of all men in the warehouse is not only old-fashioned but ridiculous. Let me know how you make out.

Faber: Sure, Bob.

Within a few minutes, Carl Faber was in his boss' office.

Faber: Roger, Ken suggested to me this morning that I hire a woman for that forklift opening, and then Bob was just in my office and thinks the idea is great. I'm not sure a woman could handle the job.

Schwartz: I have some doubts, also. She'll have to meet all the job requirements, just as if she were a man.

Faber: I suppose we have to at least give it a try. I'll tell Ken to open the job to women applicants.

Two days later Carl Faber received a phone call from Ken Frank.

Frank: Carl, I have a young woman in my office who is applying for that forklift driver opening we have. She has two years experience driving forklifts and seems interested in this type of work. Could you come up here and talk to her?

Faber: Sure, I'll be right there.

Frank: Ms. Hillard, our warehouse manager, Carl Faber, will be here shortly to interview you. Please have a seat.

A short interview of Peggy Hillard by Faber was followed by a plant tour showing Peggy the job duties for which she was applying.

Faber: Well, Peggy, do you think you can handle it?

Hillard: It doesn't look too bad. I'd like to give it a try.

Faber: Okay, then, Peggy, you can start Monday. I'd like you to spend a couple of weeks on the first shift with Charlie Ceber who will train you.

Hillard: Thank you, Mr. Faber. I'll be in on Monday.

The next day Carl Faber was sitting in his office with the shipping clerk, Diane Snyker, and one of his first shift forklift drivers, John O'Connel.

Faber: Well, I hired someone for third shift yesterday.
Snyker: Oh yea! That's good.
Faber: Her name is Peggy Hillard.
O'Connel: What! You hired a woman! You gotta be crazy!
Faber: Now hold on John . . .
O'Connel: Wait till Charlie hears this. (O'Connel leaves the office.)
Snyker: Do you really think that was a good idea, Carl? I mean all that lifting and everything. That's no job for a woman.
Faber: You may be right, Diane, but the point is we should at least give her a chance.
Snyker: You're the boss, but you would never catch me doing a job like that.

Friday afternoon, Carl Faber talked with Charlie Ceber.

Faber: As you already know, Charlie, Peggy Hillard will be starting work Monday, and I want you to spend a couple of weeks training her.
Ceber: Why me?
Faber: You're the best forklift driver I have and besides, you've trained both new men we hired this year. I'm sure you'll do a good job.
Ceber: Okay, Carl, I'll train her, but what do I do if she can't do the job?
Faber: Don't worry about that. That's my responsibility.

Peggy reported to work Monday morning and began training with Charlie Ceber. When Carl Faber approached Charlie Ceber Wednesday morning for a progress report, the following conversation took place.

Faber: Well, Charlie, how is Peggy coming along?
Ceber: I don't know, Carl. She seems kind of slow. She's not getting the products on the right size pallets. She's mixing different cartons on the same pallets, and yesterday I let her put some full pallets in stock and I found one in the wrong place and had to move it.
Faber: Don't get discouraged, Charlie, we have to give her time to learn. How is she doing with the taping machine?
Ceber: I haven't shown her how to operate it yet, but she shies away from it pretty much. I think she's afraid of machines.
Faber: Make sure you show her how to operate that machine and everything else, Charlie.
Ceber: I will, Carl.

Late Thursday afternoon, Carl Faber spotted Charlie Ceber taking a pallet of product to the printing department.

Faber: Hey, Charlie, got a minute?
Ceber: Sure, Carl, what is it?
Faber: Charlie, why is it I always see you driving the truck and Peggy unloading that conveyor line? She needs practice on that truck.
Ceber: You've got to move on this truck. Printing is screaming for product,

the packaging room needs cartons, and I've got to put finished stock away. I let Peggy drive the truck a little this morning. It took her five minutes to put a pallet away. Within a half hour I was so far behind it took me the rest of the morning to catch up. You really have to move out here, Carl. She's just too slow.

Faber: Well, I guess I better have a talk with her. Could you ask her to stop in my office at quitting time tonight?

Ceber: I sure will, Carl.

Faber: Thank you, Charlie.

Peggy arrived at Faber's office at 4:00 p.m., where he sat alone at his desk.

Faber: Come in, Peggy. Have a seat.

Hillard: You wanted to see me, Mr. Faber?

Faber: Yes I did, Peggy. I wanted to talk to you about the job.

Hillard: Oh, everything's going fine. I got the products mixed up a couple of times, but I think I got that part down now. As for that taping machine, its been jamming up a lot lately. Charlie fixes most of the jams, but this morning he let me try and fix one. I've never worked on machinery before, and I guess I'm not too good yet because it took me a long time, and finally Charlie said he would unjam it himself. I'm not sure where all the products go yet. I think I need more time on the forklift truck. Sometimes it takes me a couple of minutes just to find the right location. I like the work, though. It keeps me busy and the time goes fast.

Faber: Well, Peggy, I'm glad to hear that. I'll see you tomorrow morning.

Hillard: Goodnight, Mr. Faber.

Early Friday morning Roger Schwartz called Faber into his office.

Schwartz: How's our new girl working out, Carl?

Faber: Just fine. She seems to like the work. She may just surprise us all.

Schwartz: I hope so. I was just talking to Bob, and he told me we can no longer afford to cover the third shift forklift driver with overtime people. He wants to move Peggy to third shift this Monday. I suggest that you make sure she knows everything about that job before she leaves today.

Faber: Okay, Roger, but I think we may be acting too quickly. One week is not enough training time.

Immediately Faber rushed out to talk to Charlie Ceber.

Faber: Charlie, Peggy is going to have to start by herself on the third shift Monday. I want you to make sure she knows everything about this job.

Ceber: I'll do my best, Carl.

(Peggy arrives on the scene.)

Faber: Peggy we are going to need you on third shift beginning Monday. I've asked Charlie to go over everything with you today. Do you think you can handle it?

Hillard: If you need me Monday, I'll give it a try.

During the week that followed, Carl Faber received the following complaints from Joe Stukes, third shift superintendent:

On two separate occasions the printing department had to shut off a machine because product was not delivered on time.

The packaging supervisor had to frequently obtain his own bundles of cartons using a spare lift truck because Peggy could not keep up with his requests.

The maintenance department was called numerous times to unjam the taping machine.

Occasionally full pallets were found to have been put in the wrong location.

John O'Connel found one pallet of mixed product in stock.

Early Friday morning Carl Faber stopped at Joe Stuke's office (third shift superintendent).

Stukes: Morning, Faber. You're just the person I want to see. This gal you put on third shift is bad news. She's got my maintenance department tied up all night fixing that taping machine. I don't know what she does all night, but it sure can't be work. I'm on the phone all night with printing; they were low on product, or packaging, or out of cartons. I can't spend all night chasing her around, trying to get her to do her job. Last night she had that tape machine so jammed up, I had to send two people back there for over an hour to clean up the mess. If you ask me, Carl, I think you should look for someone else.

Faber: We've had this trouble before with new employees, Joe. I think we have to give her some time.

Stukes: All our other new guys at least tried to do the job. If they got into trouble, I was glad to lend a hand. I think Peggy figures just because she's a woman she can sit around all night and someone else will do the job for her. Well, she's got another guess coming. I need someone who can handle that job, and you better find someone soon!

Faber: Settle down, Joe, I'll take care of it.

Later that morning Bob Jacob called Roger Schwartz and Carl Faber into his office.

Jacob: I've been talking with Joe, and he tells me this girl you hired on third shift is not working out at all.

Faber: She is having some trouble, but it's only her first week on the job.

Jacob: Second week. I'm beginning to think we may have made a mistake here, Carl. Perhaps this forklift driver work is too difficult for a woman. What do you think, Roger?

Schwartz: Based on her performance so far, I have to agree, Bob. Even though I hate to admit it, this forklift job requires a man.

Jacob: I'm leaving the decision of what to do up to you, Carl, but remember, we need someone on third shift who can handle that job.

Faber: I'll take care of it, Bob.

Jacob: I'm sure you will.

Ron Williams

Ron Williams, a black, had been born and raised in Chicago's South Side ghetto and had lived in numerous foster homes and disciplinary schools before joining the military at the age of 17. Ron had been a very poor student; and if he had not left high school voluntarily his second semester, he probably would have been expelled. His four years of military duty were noteworthy for two reasons: (1) Ron had on numerous occasions barely avoided military discipline because of his disrespectful attitude towards superiors, and (2) Ron's positive accomplishment was to become a very competent radar technician and to improve himself academically by attending night school. After military duty, Ron worked overseas as a technical representative for military contractors and advised in the use of electronic equipment.

CHICAGO SERVICE COMPANY

At age 29 Ron returned to the U. S. and was hired as a supervisor by Chicago Service Company through its college level employment office. Though two years credit short of a college degree (a CSC requirement for "outside" managerial employment), he was hired for a position in the assembly department.

Soon assigned to a rotational training program, Ron reported directly to the Division Manager, Thomas Derrick. In the next few months Ron was assigned to numerous departments on a short-term basis to give him a rapid familiarity with all aspects of the business and to have him become acquainted with the department managers with whom he would be working. Remembering his commitment to get a degree in business administration as soon as possible, Ron enrolled at a local university and attended night classes three times a week.

During his preemployment visits, Ron had noticed there were very few blacks in the assembly areas, and the few there were mainly of lowest pay grade. However, Ron was assured that things were rapidly changing within the company and that his hiring was one of the many steps the company was taking in an effort to bring representative numbers of minorities into responsible positions. Ron was further told that once he had proven himself this fact would help his career advancement.

Ron met another black supervisor, Joseph Bass, who had recently been transferred from assembly to the training department. In private Joe told how happy he was to be out of assembly. Joe had a particularly rough time getting the assemblers' cooperation; the hostility, however subtle, had been a very difficult barrier to overcome. In the end it was Joe himself who requested the change, although he had given other reasons. Joe advised Ron to be "super-cautious" in all his actions within the company. "There are old-liners who will be examining your every move in an effort to find fault. Don't express opinions on politics, race relations, or talk of your personal, private life. The fact that you are black is but one of many problems you will have to deal with. Another is the resentment and hostility that is almost sure to follow when anyone in the department imagines promotional opportunity has been denied by an outside minority managerial hiree. Be careful, and don't let your guard down. Ron agreed that he should be very cautious.

In the next few weeks Ron was kept very busy. He followed Joe's advice as best he could, and he was doing well in night school. Ron also found time to do soliciting work for an African Village Mission. He assembled and mailed magazines and canned food items badly needed by the social assistance group he had encountered during a trip on which he visited his father who taught college English in Liberia. Ron had made a vow never to be too busy to help the Mission.

Later, in the midst of the annual Crusade of Mercy drive by the Chicago Service Company, Ron was called into the division manager's office and was shown a letter from the company president asking all employees to donate a "fair share" to "this worthy cause." The company defined a fair share for management as being one percent of yearly earnings and had already prepared a payroll deduction card in each employee's name. As he read further, Ron noted that the last paragraph of the letter stated in no uncertain terms that contributions were "strictly voluntary" and that "no pressure would be brought against those who chose not to contribute."

Ron sat bewildered as Derrick read aloud to him the contents of the letter word-for-word, just as though Ron did not have a copy in front of him or could not read it for himself. Ron was then instructed to fill in the payroll deduction card with appropriate information no matter what his decision and to turn the card in to Derrick's secretary. After considering it for a few minutes, Ron decided that in view of his recent relocation expenses, his expenses in furnishing a new apartment, and his contributions to the African Mission, he would donate several dollars cash but would not give a fair share. He filled out the card and turned it in as he was instructed to do.

When Ron returned to work the next day, there was a letter marked "personal" on his desk. The letter was in a company envelope with no indication as to who sent it. The letter read as follows:

> Your failure to contribute is keeping the department from achieving 100 percent fair share. For your own good, it would be wise to reconsider your donation. A word to the wise.

Determined that he would not be swayed by threats from an anonymous source, Ron filed away the letter and tried to forget the entire episode.

PERFORMANCE EVALUATION

As part of his continuing rotational training, Ron reported back to the division manager the first Monday of each week to describe his experience and to get feedback on the impressions he made on those in that particular section. From the beginning there were apparent problems. The feedback Derrick received described Ron as intelligent and well-spoken but seemingly "smug and aloof," "unconcerned," "cold and detached," and "acting as though he were above it all." Derrick refused to identify who had what opinion. The following conversation then ensued:

Ron: I, too, was surprised when you told me of the bad impressions from earlier assignments, but I am even more surprised that I came across poorly in the last assignment. I thought I had fit in rather well; and in fact, I even made it a point to ask the engineering department head what he thought of me in private. I was complimented.

Derrick: That was not a wise thing to do. You wouldn't expect a direct criticism when you are expected to report your opinions of that department to me.

Ron: What are the specifics of the criticism of me?

Derrick: That you continue to remain aloof and uninvolved in whatever group activities are in that particular department. The specific examples were that you did not seem to want to join in any of the small talk that allows people to get to know each other and that you read newspapers during the coffee break. On more than one occasion you even sat apart from the group to spread out your paper. Frankly, some expressed offense that their efforts to be friendly to you resulted in what they interpreted to be a rebuff. Once attitudes of that sort are formed, Ron, about any supervisor, the word spreads quickly, and the resentment will be a barrier hard to overcome.

Ron: I can only say in my defense that I read newspapers rather than participate in the bull sessions due to the subject matter discussed which, for the most part, involves the trials and tribulations of suburban living. As an inner-city apartment dweller, I cannot relate to discussions of cutting grass, painting a house, or the latest tax assessments. Nor am I a member of a village volunteer fire department, or of the local PTA. In short, I feel left out. On those few occasions when politics, sex, or religion pop up for discussion, I, of course, choose not to offer any comments; my viewpoints doubtlessly would be diametrically opposite theirs. I did sometimes manage to steer the conversation to sports or movies or even the job itself. But to be truthful, I just didn't have a lot to say. I must add that I feel as though I stand out like a sore thumb. I have confidence in my ability, and I have had no problems getting along before. So, hopefully, when they get to know me, and I them, there will be no problem.

Derrick: I can understand your problem and your situation, Ron, but we must deal with reality. You cannot expect everyone you meet in every department to adjust to your particular problem. It is you who must adjust and adapt; it is you who must gain the confidence of those you encounter. Keep in mind that you will not be doing the craft work yourself; you can only get the job done through the people who work for you. You, therefore, must gain their confidence and let them know you are not above it all.

Ron: I will try to do better.

Derrick: You must if you are going to succeed. It would help immeasurably if you smiled a little more and quit acting as though you have a chip on your shoulder. And for your own sake don't ever discuss that Crusade of Mercy incident. The assemblers make far less than you do and might not understand why they achieved 100 percent and you couldn't give your fair share.

Ron: (angry pause) OK.

SERVICE DEPARTMENT

Two weeks later Ron completed his rotational training and was assigned as a supervisor of a service department that was responsible for obtaining new service for customers and discontinuing service for those who changed locations or cancelled service. The work was performed by young (18 to 22 years of age), entry-level workers, most of whom were white. Service department performance was measured by a monthly performance rating based on numbers of service orders handled, labor expenditures, and number of errors that result in customer complaints. This particular office had established an above average performance rating for several consecutive months.

Soon after Ron arrived and familiarized himself with the job and personnel, he noted two disconcerting items. First, the most senior and best repair worker seemed to operate on a different set of rules than everyone else. The worker, Reginald Martin, would consistently arrive five or ten minutes late, would overstay breaks and lunch periods, and would make several personal telephone calls each day. In spite of this, Martin was able to complete almost twice as many service orders as the next best person and to do so with very few errors. The second disquieting item was that since his arrival, Ron noted numerous racial slurs written on the wall of the main floor corridor with an indelible marker. Ron's only actions were to remind Martin of the department rules and to have the janitor remove the graffiti.

Several days later, toward the end of a very hectic day in which an extraordinary service order workload was delayed in arriving to the office, Williams went looking for Martin to question him as to his availability for overtime. (Martin had not responded to paging over the public address system.) Ron finally found Martin asleep in a basement storage room with the lights out and his overcoat rolled beneath his head as a pillow. Ron fired Martin on the spot and collected his I.D. card. He then informed his supervisor and the union steward. The union immediately appealed the decision, citing the fact that in spite of the seriousness of Martin's action in sleeping on the job, he had in fact completed the work that was available (which was limited owing to the delayed orders) and that his record to date contained nothing but complimentary remarks that lauded him as the best repair worker in the office. After a meeting between Ron's supervisor, Ron himself, and the union steward, it was agreed that Ron had overreacted and that a warning should have been issued since neither he nor the previous supervisor had put into writing any malfeasance by Martin. From that point on the relations between Ron and Martin grew increasingly strained. The next monthly performance rating dropped. Shortly thereafter, Ron received a phone call from Joe Bass who had recently been promoted to second level manager.

Joe: I hear the people out there are giving you a hard time.

Ron: You're not kidding! I guess I overreacted and blew my top. I feel that the entire world has its eyes on me, and I really wanted to do good. Now I have alienated my best worker. So now he is only doing what he calls his fair share of the service order workload. I'm not sure that his definition of fair share isn't a double entendre. Anyway, the index has plummeted since my arrival, and I know who will get credit for that.

Joe: I know what you mean. The grapevine has it that you are trying to appease the blacks in your department by coming down on the whites. Also, it seems that everyone knows about your Crusade of Mercy problem. You haven't discussed that with anyone have you?

Ron: Not at all. I may be dumb, but I'm not stupid! I've got enough problems.

Joe: Well, don't let them get you down. Hang in there.

Ron: Will do!

Less than two weeks following the incident with Martin a snowstorm warning was issued, and Chicago Service Company responded by informing all workers that, in the event they could not reach their normal work office, they were to report to the nearest Chicago Service Company location. Each employee then signed a sheet to acknowledge this directive. At the end of that work day Ron was still at his desk finishing up his paperwork when he glanced at the sheet containing the signatures of the employees acknowledging the emergency weather procedure. Right away Ron noticed that the signature of one employee (Harold Ripley) exactly matched the graffiti scrawled on the corridor walls. The next day Ron confronted Ripley in private. Ripley admitted the markings. For the rest of that day Ron had Ripley wash down the walls to remove the graffiti. The janitor and Ripley later filed a grievance and won.

The performance rating for the next few months remained low. It was not until a year or so later that the rating returned to its former high. By this time the service crew had a 100 percent turnover, and Ron had established a good rapport with the workers.[1]

Shortly thereafter, thinking he had proven himself, Ron asked for and received a transfer to the training department. Although he did not realize it at the time, Ron's experience to a great extent paralleled Joe Bass'. Three years later, however, there was an increasingly noticeable difference between Joe Bass and Ron Williams. Joe became a district level manager, and Ron remained a supervisor

1. Due to growth and union contract most workers were promoted out of service within one year.

Jack Kordel

A year after completing high school Jack Kordel, a black, joined the United States Navy. Based on his academic acheivements and a very high score on his enlistment tests, Kordel was selected for formal machinist training in "A" school. Automatic advancement in rate was a reward for people finishing in the top half of the class, and Kordel was advanced to E-4 upon graduation.

Although he indicated a desire for sea duty on his duty assignment questionnaire, Kordel was assigned upon graduation to a tour of shore duty at the training center. He spent a year at the center before he was finally ordered to sea duty aboard a destroyer in the Pacific.

Almost every ship in the Navy has some form of a check-in procedure for new people when they first report aboard. The orientation interview serves as a device to evaluate a new person's interests and helps to place the person in the right work group within the organization. Kordel was interviewed by his department head shortly after his arrival on board. Kordel indicated no preference to belong to any particular work group during the interview, and he was assigned to the after engine room since several petty officers from that space had been recently discharged.

The after engine room was supervised by Salen, MM-1, a ten-year veteran from Alabama. Salen's immediate supervisor was the departmental leading petty officer, Chief Wright, a black with 24 years of experience. Salen, MM-1, had worked his way up to first-class petty officer without the benefit of formal training and was evaluated by his superiors as an excellent practical machinist but a poor administrator. Salen was a bit apprehensive of assigning responsible tasks to people in his work gang unless he had personally taught them the procedures to be followed in the task. Therefore, most of the repairs were concentrated in the hands of a select few members of the engine room gang. Not much was said about this practice as long as the work was accomplished on time.

Lt. (jg) Brown overheard the following conversation during a routine inspection of the after engine room:

Salen: Keep your eyes on the gland pressure gauge, Kordel. You're letting steam escape into the space. Since you're in charge of the throttle, you have to watch every gauge on your board.

Exhibit 1

Organization Aboard Ship

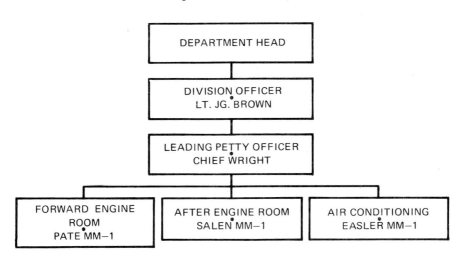

Kordel: Why do we have such a problem controlling the pressure on the gland sealing system to the turbines? In school they told us it was almost automatic.

Salen: I don't have time now to tell you what's wrong with it. Go take one of the books out of the locker and study it.

Brown later related this incident to the engineer officer and the chief machinist when he encountered them in the engineering office. Brown, the department head, and Wright discussed the problem that they had been having with excessive steam leak-off from the sealing system and decided to have the shipyard technicians repair the system at the first opportunity. Chief Wright theorized that Salen might have been curt in his response to Kordel's question because he did not like the fact that most school graduates tended to think that everything was supposed to be "automatic."

During his assignment to the engine room, Kordel not only felt ignored by Salen, but he also began to receive some flak from his shipmates. Kordel's use of spare time was unusual in a group of machinist mates. He spent many of his off hours reading machinery reference books and often played the violin on the fantail of the ship. When asked one day by Chief Wright how he had acquired his violin playing ability, Kordel stated that his parents, who had strong musical backgrounds, had encouraged all their children to play at least one musical instrument. He had chosen the violin because as he stated, "the music from it relaxes me whenever I'm tense." However, some of Jack's shipmates began making uncomplimentary remarks about his violin playing, and they tagged him with the nickname of "Blackjack." Kordel sensed a certain resentment from some of the members of the division and asked Salen to investigate the matter.

Several weeks later Kordel submitted a special request chit to talk with the executive officer. When called up by the engineer officer and the chief to explain his chit, Kordel complained bitterly that "Salen doesn't give a damn about assigning important jobs to anyone but his pets, and I'm sick and tired of being discriminated against because I'm black. My name isn't Blackjack." Wright, Salen's supervisor, said this was the first he had heard of the problem. He told Kordel he would investigate the matter and talk to him later that afternoon.

Salen was called and asked to report to the office.

Wright: How are the new people working out in the after engine room, Mike?

Salen: Things are working out fine in the space. The two new firemen are working very hard and should probably be eligible for promotion during the next exams. Kordel doesn't seem to want to advance because he's got a bad attitude. He wants everything handed to him on a platter.

Engineer: I understand that some of the crew have started a nickname going around—Blackjack. Have you noticed any racial troubles developing?

Salen: I've heard a couple of the firemen refer to Kordel using that nickname, but I think it's a reference to the hard manner in which he assigns the work to the cleaning detail. He kind of goes out of his way to make them know that he's in charge of the detail. I don't think there is any prejudice involved. We never had any problems before, and the Chief can tell you how well we've always gotten along.

Engineer: I appreciate your comments, Salen, but I take a dim view of ethnic jokes and name calling that can possibly offend people within the division. Some people are much more easily offended than others, and it's up to us in our supervisory capacity to make sure these things don't get out of hand. Get your second-class petty officers together after working hours today and make sure that these practices get stopped. I want them to set an example.

Salen: Aye, aye. I didn't realize Kordel was offended by this.

Chief Wright talked with Kordel that afternoon and discussed some of the points that had come up in the earlier conversation. Kordel requested that his chit be withdrawn for the time being to see if the situation improved.

The situation did seem to improve during the ensuing seven-month cruise to Southeast Asia. Maintenance problems were minor and the cleanliness of the space improved considerably. The operations of the ship were linked to objectives which were demanding and a part of national policy versus West Coast exercises. Each person in the division seemed to ignore minor distractions and concentrate on respective duties to accomplish the ship's objectives. Most of the crew seemed to gain a new awareness of how important each job was. Each work group participated in friendly competition with other groups in trying to have the most reliable operation, and attitude and morale changes were evident in the pride with which each person regarded the work space. The atmosphere was further enhanced towards the end of the cruise because each person was scheduled for holiday leave.

Advancements in rate nominations were due shortly after the leave period in order to accomplish the necessary paper work prior to the March examinations. The usual flow of recommendations was from work supervisor to leading chief to department head to executive officer. People to be recommended for advancement were required to have completed certain training courses for their rate, have the required amount of time in their present rate, and have demonstrated certain technical proficiencies for the technical level to which they were trying to advance.

In presenting his list to Chief Wright, Salen stated that "although Kordel has the necessary time in grade and course completed, he hasn't had enough shipboard experience for advancement at this time."

Wright called Kordel aside at quarters the next morning to talk about the recommendations he was making to the engineer officer.

Wright: Your work and technical knowledge have shown great improvement, but I don't feel that you have had the necessary experience in certain areas that you should have for advancement to E-5. I can see no reason why you won't be eligible in October if your present progress continues.

Kordel: I'm ready now. Salen will never recommend me because he doesn't like me. I've been discriminated against since I came abroad. I can't get the necessary experience because Salen will never assign me jobs in different areas.

Kordel was not recommended for advancement, but was transferred to the air-conditioning maintenance group under Easler, since this was one area where he lacked experience. Kordel had been working with this group for about one month when he approached the chief with photostatic copies of an original and duplicate money order.

Kordel stated that he thought he had lost the original money order when he could not find it in his work clothes and had ordered and cashed a duplicate after the allotted waiting period. The original had been signed and cashed by another person in the division even though the records of the ship's postal clerk showed the serial number to have been assigned to Kordel. The Post Office Department had also sent a bill to Kordel for $10 since both money orders had been cashed. Kordel demanded that the other person be placed on report for theft. Chief Wright was assigned to investigate the circumstances surrounding the two money orders. (See Note 1.)

Wright: Jones, what can you tell me about this money order that you cashed last January?

Jones: I found a blank money order on the main deck while I was walking back to the compartment. I cashed it when I didn't hear about anybody looking for a lost money order. I needed the money at the time, and I thought I had just been lucky to find it.

Wright: That money order belonged to another person who cashed a duplicate when he couldn't find the original. He now has a bill from the Postal Department for the $10 since a $10 money order was cashed twice.

Jones: I'm sorry if I've caused any trouble to anyone, Chief, and I will be more than willing to give back the $10 so the person can square away the account with the government.

Wright then dismissed Jones and called for Kordel to come up to his quarters.

Wright: I talked to Jones about the money order and he claims that he found it. He says he is willing to give you the money to pay your bill.

Kordel: The $10 isn't that important, Chief. Jones stole my money order and cashed it. He should be punished and I want him placed on report.

Wright: Did you sign the money order or stub when you first bought it, or was it completely blank?

Kordel: I bought it just before I went on watch and didn't have time to sign it.

Wright: I'll take these documents up to the engineer officer for inspection, Kordel, but I don't think that we have any evidence to prosecute Jones for theft. If you had come to me when you first noticed it missing, we could have put the word out at quarters that the money order was yours. If you had signed it promptly, there would have been no doubt as to whose it was. I don't think we have the necessary evidence to prosecute Jones under the Uniform Code of Military Justice.

The engineer officer concurred that the lack of evidence precluded any chance of proving deliberate theft on the part of Jones. (See Note 2.)

Both Chief Wright and the engineer agreed that Jones was guilty of being imprudent in not seeking to find out whose money order it was, but neither felt that Jones should be recommended for a court-martial due to his excellent service record to date and lack of evidence. Jones, who was considered a cheerful worker, was scheduled to be discharged at the end of his enlisted period in six months.

Kordel had the following to say when he heard of the decision: "I don't understand it. I don't get recommended for advancement, and now anybody can steal my money and personal belongings and get away with it if he's white."

NOTES

1. A major problem aboard ships on extended cruises occurs whenever individuals have a month's or more pay on their person at time without a chance to get to a banking facility or to turn it over to their spouses. Large amounts of money often prove a temptation to thieves, and there are many cases on record where individuals have lost as much as one quarter of their annual salary because someone pilfered their locker during the night. Large sums of money also spawn heavy gambling in card and dice games that are oftentimes run by professionals against the

individual novice player. There are a number of methods advocated to attempt to remedy this situation. Every ship carries at least one postal clerk who is authorized to sell postal money orders. Money orders can be purchased at a nominal fee and mailed to spouses, families, etc., after every payday when the ship is at sea. They cannot be cashed by someone other than the designated payee unless the purchaser has failed to fill in the form. A money order that is lost can be redeemed by requesting a duplicate from the postal clerk. There is a specific waiting period before a duplicate can be issued to minimize the chances of an original and a duplicate being cashed. A person who buys a money order is cautioned to fill it in completely immediately since it is the equivalent of a blank endorsed check and can be cashed very easily by anyone finding it.

2. Naval policy concerning persons convicted of theft is strict and demanding. No person is considered more damaging or unwanted on a ship with people living at close quarters than a thief. The Office of Naval Operations has stressed that maximum punishments should be awarded in all cases where persons are found guilty of theft by a court-martial board. Maximum punishment includes a punitive discharge, a Bad Conduct Discharge, and consequently, few cases are ever recommended for trial unless all the elements necessary to prove theft are clearly supported by physical evidence and/or testimony. One element that must be proved is that the accused *intended* to deprive the person of his property permanently. Intent is usually the hardest element of proof in any court-martial, and unless it can be clearly shown to the board, the preponderance of doubt theory demands acquittal. Court-martial proceedings are long and tedious and not often recommended by investigating officers if one or more elements is lacking.

Mulligan Corporation (A)

Mulligan Corporation, a privately owned company, was started in 1910. In the beginning it produced a general line of hardware equipment and later specialized in electrical hardware supplics. In 1939, the company again shifted to the even more specialized area of electronic equipment. This change came about when the company was able to obtain government contracts to produce military electronic components. The experience gained in the following war years was adequate to give them confidence in their ability to compete in the home appliance field.

From the very beginning of their entry into this field, management deemed it advisable to market directly their own electronic units, which included high quality tape recorders, phonographs, radios, televisions, speakers, and amplifiers. Retail outlets were established and business was highly successful in the postwar boom, so much so that Mulligan Corporation was the leading company of the high quality specialized electronic equipment.

In 1945, the Justice Department of the United States government filed antitrust proceedings against Mulligan Corporation claiming that Mulligan was competing unfairly and that, among other things, by owning the retail outlets the company was violating the provisions of the Sherman Antitrust Act. Although the management of Mulligan did not agree with the charges, they did negotiate a consent decree. The decree stipulated that the company would divest itself of all retail outlets for 15 years.

Raymond Jackson, the vice-president in charge of industrial and public relations of Mulligan Corporation, was disturbed about public and customer reaction to the company as a result of the Justice Department's complaint, but he felt that it would be better at that time to let things ride rather than to attempt to tell the public Mulligan's side of the story. This decision was based on a general feeling on the part of public relations personnel that the public's memory was short and that an announcement by the company a week later would only draw negative attention to the company. It raised the question of telling the public the company had been cited by the Justice Department.

In the summer of 1960, however, the Justice Department again made a public statement. This time it was to the effect that the company had violated the terms of the consent decree. Although the officers felt the charges were unwarranted, they agreed to accept additions to the original decree rather than to seek recourse through the expensive and lengthy litigation procedures.[1]

Jackson at that time decided that a statement of company policy concerning compliance with the law of the land would be in the best interests of the company, and his suggestion seemed agreeable to the moderator of the board of directors and the president. However, they did not feel any great urgency until other companies were indicted.

During the time of Jackson's proposal, the president of an automobile manufacturing company resigned as did the president of an insurance company. In both instances, questions were raised as to whether their personal business was in conflict with interests of the company they headed. The following winter, 29 electrical manufacturing companies were indicted on charges of conspiring to fix prices and to divide the market. The companies involved were fined, and some of the executives were cited for criminal charges and were sent to jail. Public reaction to these acts by respectable business concerns was such that many companies including those involved drew up codes of ethics to insure that such a thing could never happen again. (See Exhibit 1.)

1. By the summer of 1960, Mulligan had acquired several independent distributorships and was operating them as branches or subsidiary sales of the parent company. Some of these operations had been acquired upon the resignation of the franchise by the independent distributor. Some had been acquired through the death of the independent distributor, and some by cancellation of the franchise by the parent company. Where the distributorship was canceled and taken over by the Mulligan Corporation, it was because the company felt that it was not effectively represented in the territory.

Twelve independent distributorships had been so reacquired. Of this number, four had been cancellations. Two of the canceled distributors had complained to the federal government. As a result, the federal government caused an investigation to be made and charged the Mulligan Corporation with violation of the original consent decree. In the main, the specific violations alleged were that (1) the company was using a product sales quota system which had the effect of keeping its distributors from selling products made by other manufacturers, and that (2) Mulligan in purchasing the assets of the reacquired distributors had violated the terms of the original consent decree. (Note: Mulligan officers interpreted the original consent decree as prohibiting the company from purchasing the assets of competitive *manufacturers*—they did not believe this restriction applied to the company franchised distributors where it would, in effect, be buying back its own goods.)

These two matters were settled with the government by excluding certain product lines from the sales quota system, by lengthening the Notice of Termination by either party from 60 to 90 days, and by Mulligan's consenting to purchase of the assets of an independent distributor, only when the independent distributor requested the company to do so.

With these events, the officers of the Mulligan Corporation took renewed interest in Jackson's proposal. It was agreed that all of the executive officers should be consulted on the matter, but that a committee of three should do the initial work. Jackson, Walter Henry, the general counsel, and Jacqueline Phillips, the financial vice-president, composed the committee. (See Exhibit 2.) Almost immediately the committee agreed that, in addition to a statement concerning compliance with the legal requirements, a conflict of interest statement should also be made. These two areas were to be incorporated into a code of ethics.

The committee met to discuss the general tenor of the statement. It soon became evident that Phillips wanted to have a detailed statement that would require affidavits signed by the employees.

Jackson: Jackie, I don't think we need the detail you're talking about. After all, this is not a financial statement that is subject to an audit.

Phillips: I don't know about that, Ray. We may be hauled into court and we should be protected. I've been looking over some of the things other companies are doing. Here, look for yourself—at these reports. (See Exhibit 3.)

Henry: I agree with Ray. You can't have employees answering questionnaires in detail—they just won't do it. On the other hand, we don't want a wishy-washy token statement.

Phillips: What do you mean you can't make employees give details? The Argyle Company was able to get detailed information on the financial interests its employees had in other companies and so was Dupont. Here, let me read some of the questions Chrysler asks:

At any time from January 1, 1950, to date, have you or has your spouse, or any child of yours . . . owned directly or indirectly any stock, bond, option, or right to purchase stock, share in profits, investments, partnership interest, or any other interest of any nature whatsoever in any supplier or in any supplier's representative? (If so, give complete details.)

It goes on to ask about vacations, loans, gifts, etc., and here, the last one should be of interest:

Please prepare and attach a statement of the combined net worth of yourself and your spouse as of March 31, 1960, and also as of July 31, 1960.

Then to top it off they say:

Please execute and swear under oath . . . before a notary public.

Jackson: Oh, come on now, Jackie. You're not thinking of that kind of questionnaire for our employees?

Henry: You use that here and you won't have any employees. Chrysler has a different situation. They've been through the wringer and need to take drastic steps to be sure that they don't have more conflict of interest allegations placed against them.

Phillips: No, I don't think we need to be so detailed, but to protect ourselves, I do think we need to do something. In addition, our outside auditors who certify our financial statements say that if this was a publicly held company, the auditors would want to send questionnaires to all employees. What's good for the public companies is good for us. I'm more concerned about the possibilities of a price conspiracy charge. Conflict of interest is within the company and we can handle that; but when the Justice Department gets into the act, they want concrete evidence.

Jackson: You evidently have something in mind, Jackie. What is it?

Phillips: Well, it seems to me that we need to keep our people constantly aware of the dangers of being accused of price fixing by association. That is, if one of our salespeople meets a representative of one of our competitors on the street and says "hello," who knows how that may be interpreted, especially if our rep keeps bumping into the same person at conventions and so on. Well, to protect the company, I have some forms for our employees to sign, stating there was no connivance to fix prices.

Jackson: What kind of forms?

Phillips: Here, I made up a couple of samples along with the instructions. No need to swear before a notary, just the signature. (See Exhibit 4.)

Henry: I fail to see how this will help, Jackie. It looks like more paper work to me.

Phillips: It will do two things: first, it will show the Justice Department that the company is constantly aware of its obligation to uphold the law of the land and, at the same time, it will remind all concerned not to talk about prices with a competitor.

Jackson: Well, District Attorney, I don't agree with you. If a representative is going to connive with a competitor, this paper isn't going to help. Besides, we haven't had that problem.

Henry: Just because we haven't had a problem doesn't mean we won't. Look, Ray, why don't you draw up what you think we should have and then let's meet again. What do you think, Jackie?

Phillips: It's O.K. with me, but let's get some teeth in it.

Several weeks later, Ray Jackson came up with a draft that he thought was suitable. The committee met and were not in agreement, but they decided to see what the reactions of the other officers were. Jackson sent a copy to the president and the other officers with the exception of the moderator of the board.

Approval was quickly received from Herbert Williamson. Michelle Aronson said she wasn't sure about it and wanted a few days to think it over. Nothing was heard from Robert Baker, so Jackson followed it up with a personal visit.

Jackson: Just stopped by to get your reaction to the legal and ethical statement, Bob. I am guessing that you have a question or two.

Baker: No, I think it's fine. I suppose that purchasing is the department concerned.

Jackson: Yes, the gifts and entertainment statement would apply to them more than anyone else.

MULLIGAN CORPORATION (A)   **261**

Baker: Well, yes and no. Sometimes our buyers are acting more as a rubber stamp. When some of Williamson's reps come over with a purchase order for some of their equipment, we figure we don't know enough about it to make a judgment one way or another. Salespeople from the scientific instrument companies are always taking them out to lunch. There are other exceptions also, especially in the maintenance department where the chief engineer orders things like those mobile floor washers. Sure we bring in samples of the machines so they can be tested, but the engineer makes the final decision, and we put our okay stamp on it.

Jackson: You have a point there, but from a dollar angle, your department still makes decisions on most of the dollars spent. What do you recommend in the way of a change in the statement?

Baker: It seems to me, Ray, that maybe ethical practices for purchasing should be spelled out in more detail.

Jackson: I believe you're right, Bob; but it's your department, and I think you are in the best position to make up your own detailed statement. As a matter of fact, Bob, Jackie and I think you have your own peculiar problems in purchasing just as Michelle had hers in product pricing. It seemed to us that you and Michelle can handle that without us.

Baker: Some guidance from the whole group I think is in order.

Jackson: I don't see how we can help. Why don't you draw up your statement and we'll throw in our comments?

Baker: I'm puzzled as to what to say about Christmas gifts. As you know, each November we send out a letter to our suppliers restating that no Mulligan employee may accept Christmas gifts (see Exhibit 5), yet some trickle through. If not here at the office, they're sent to the buyer's home.

Jackson: What do you think the statement should be on that?

Baker: That's hard to say, Ray, but that's not the only problem. We have the annual fishing trips, too. As you know, these lumber companies that supply the veneer for our cabinets have quite elaborate lodges in their forests. Each year our buyers are invited to spend three or four days there just loafing and fishing with representatives of the lumber company. And then, there is the Ice Follies. Each spring, the Specialty Electronics Company takes the whole purchasing department—secretaries and all—to dinner and to the Ice Follies. They look forward to it. Now what shall I tell the gang?

Jackson: There's a simple answer to that, Bob—you treat the gang.

Baker: You're some help.

Jackson: Bob, you're making me cry, so I guess I'd better get back to my office where my tears will be for my own problems. When you get your statement written up, I'll be glad to check out the loopholes.

Baker: (As Jackson was going out the door). How about Bermuda?

The parting remark was aimed at Samuel Pinkerton, president of the Mulligan Corporation. Pinkerton and his wife had been invited each year for the past ten years to go yachting with the Andersons. Anderson was the president of Anderson Tube and Parts Company. The Pinkertons and the Andersons were close friends, and they belonged to the same country club and played bridge together as well as engaged in other social activities. The yachting trip each January usually was to the Florida Keys and then to Bermuda for golfing, sunbathing, and shopping.

The Anderson Tube and Parts Company manufactured vacuum tubes, resistors, capacitors, transistors, and other components for electronic equipment. The Mulligan Corporation was its largest customer. The Anderson Company was the only source of supply used by the Mulligan Corporation for various parts, including the vacuum tubes and transistors.

The Andersons maintained a yacht in Florida for both personal and business purposes. To differentiate the uses and to allocate expenses, a log was maintained on the yacht. Passengers were logged in, and a notation was made if the outing was considered business or pleasure. If the trip was for business, the practice had been to have a representative from the Anderson Company who was the "opposite number" of the passenger. Thus, for instance, the chief engineer of the Anderson Company would be on board when the chief engineer of Company X was a passenger.

The following week Jackson sent a memo to Pinkerton stating that he thought the executives had given the statement their consideration and, although they had some reservations, they wanted to get Mulligan's reactions. Pinkerton sent a copy of the proposed statement to Mulligan (see Exhibit 6) with a note asking for his remarks and, at the same time, raised the question as to whether there should be a code of ethics for the board of directors. There was no reply from either Pinkerton or Mulligan. After two months another note was sent asking to release the statement to the management personnel.

In response Mulligan called a meeting with Pinkerton and Jackson. In this meeting, Mulligan stated: "In the 50-year history of this company, there has never been any scandal or breach of etiquette so that I really don't see any need for this. When we issue a policy such as this under the present conditions, people will think there is some underhanded business going on in the Mulligan Corporation, and there isn't."

Jackson pointed out that the Mulligan Corporation had taken a beating on the publicity when the consent decrees had been signed and that this statement would tend to counteract it. In addition, the management people should know where the company stood on these issues. By taking this stand, the message would be conveyed to all employees that the company operates on a high ethical plane. This statement, in effect, would reaffirm past practices.

Mulligan referred briefly to the question concerning the board of directors and the code of ethics by stating, "All of our directors are mature. When you reach the position of being on the board, you have already demonstrated your integrity." But, towards the end of the meeting, Mulligan gave a tentative approval:

Mulligan: What about Henry, Phillips, and the rest? What are their feelings? If they approve it, I'll buy it.

Jackson: Phillips, of course, wants to tighten it up with legal terms and signed statements from employees, but will go along if everyone else does. Baker is concerned with the gifts to the buyers in the purchasing department and would like that spelled out. He thinks he should terminate the annual outing sponsored by the Specialty Electronics Company, but he is trying to figure out how to do it since it has been going on for over 15 years.

Pinkerton: Well, I don't know that that's a problem. Have any of the buyers been throwing business to Specialty? I suppose the question of my going to Florida with Andy could be raised. There is room for misinterpretation, I suppose. What do you think, Ray?

Jackson: I don't think we can cover each situation in a statement such as this; some individual judgment is involved.

Pinkerton: I think you're right on that score, and I doubt that my being a guest of Andy's has any influence on our contracts with him.

Mulligan: These are individual problems. What's more important is to have a clear understanding and a willingness to comply. I think we should have all of our management team behind this, Ray, so why don't you fix up a statement so that it has that kind of backing?

Jackson: I'll get to work on Aronson and Baker. They are about ready to submit their statements as they pertain to their own departments.

Exhibit 1

Corporate Ethics *
More Companies Bare Officials' Self Dealing:
Others Press Probes

DuPont to Use Questionnaire Annually
Fruehauf Tells of Selling $15 Worth of Sod

Arvida's Brokerage Fees

"Conflict of interest is currently the hottest topic in our office," declares an executive of a Chicago accounting firm. "Since the Chrysler scandal, practically every corporation we audit has asked us to make a special effort to see that they're clean."

The accountant's comments point up the wide attention companies, stockholders, and government agencies are giving the issue of executives who do business on the side with their own concerns. The issue has been a burning one ever since last summer when Chrysler Corp. forced out its president, William C. Newberg, because of his interest in two companies that were selling hinges, arm rests, and door trim panels to Chrysler. Mr. Newberg has since accused the company of making him a "scapegoat" to hide "incompetence, maladministration, neglect, breaches of duty, and self dealing" by other top Chrysler officials.

* Reproduced with permission, *The Wall Street Journal, April 28, 1961.*

(Conflict of interest within the federal government is a matter of concern, too. Yesterday President Kennedy urged overhauling of laws aimed at preventing government workers from getting outside profits from their government jobs.)

With the season for annual meetings now at its height, many corporate executives are being quizzed hard from the floor by stockholders who want to make sure their companies are free of such conflicts. The brothers Lewis and John Gilbert, who make a specialty of attending stockholder meetings, are personally raising the question at some 150 meetings. In a few cases, shareholders have gone further, instigating proxy fights or court suits where they believe these are justified.

Companies Take Lead

More companies are taking the lead themselves by asking their own employees, from top executives on down, to disclose any actual or potential conflicts, or by asking outsiders, such as law or accounting firms, to come in and conduct impartial investigations. Besides looking for any instances in which an executive holds an interest in a supplier or customer concern, companies were worried about possible conflicts of interests and also are watching for cases in which other employees, especially in purchasing capacities, may be accepting gratuities from suppliers or other outside firms.

There is nothing new, of course, about companies dealing with other concerns in which their officials hold an interest either as stockholders or officers. Regulations of the U. S. Securities and Exchange Commission long have required that any such substantial business be reported in corporate proxy statements. But with the current concern about conflicts of interest, some companies seem to be taking great pains to "tell all."

In its proxy statement for next month's annual meeting, for instance, Fruehauf Trailer Co. has gone so far as to explain in detail how it sold $15 worth of sod to a company headed by a Fruehauf director, James Robbins. The proxy statement also discloses that William Grace, president of Fruehauf, owns an interest in five Fort Worth, Texas, companies which on occasion lend money to finance purchases of Fruehauf trailers, accepting the trailers as security on the loans. Mr. Grace has an interest in still another concern which has bought from Fruehauf an unspecified number of "trailers, parts, and accessories . . . at established distributor prices," the proxy statement adds.

In all, Fruehauf used 108 lines covering two and one-half pages to spell out dealings with its president and six outside directors. Last year only eight lines were devoted to such disclosures.

"Recognition of Fad"

"What we did was in recognition of a fad," says Robert D. Hill, Fruehauf's vice-president of finance. "I think you see many companies giving in their proxy statements absolutely full detail on all kinds of dealings." Maintains Mr. Hill: "We do not think there is any conflict of interest anywhere in the company."

Fad or not, some companies are so upset over possible conflicts of interest that they are quietly investigating dealings of their own key people.

Some months ago Arvida Corp., a Florida real estate development company, named for its majority stockholder, Arthur Vining Davis, hired a Wall Street law firm to look into possible conflicts of interest by officers of the company. One area of investigation: the dealings between Arvida and Mr. M. N. Weir & Sons, a real estate firm in which Milton N. Weir, and his son, John, president and vice-president respectively of Arvida, owned a 60% interest.

In its 1959 and 1960 fiscal years, M. N. Weir received $504,000 in brokerage fees from Arvida. The two Arvida officers also had an interest in an insurance firm which received $209,000 in fiscal 1960 from Arvida. This information had been disclosed in proxy statements issued in 1959 (well before the investigation was launched), and in 1960.

At the end of February of this year, the Weirs resigned from Arvida. The announced reason: They wanted more time to devote to personal affairs.

Directors to Get Report

Arvida officials are slated to get a report on the investigation in a week or so, although the departure of the Weirs reduced the "interest" in the probe, according to one source. However, the investigation also dealt with transactions Arvida has had with other Davis-controlled companies. Example: A previous Arvida proxy statement made note of $2.7 million in construction contracts awarded "as a result of competitive bidding" to a company controlled by Mr. Davis.

Other companies are reporting transactions of some size with concerns controlled by their directors. National Tea Co.'s proxy statement for this year's annual meeting discloses 1960 purchases of $14.7 million from American Processing and Sales Company. John P. Cuneo, a director and also a member of National Tea's executive committee, "owns or controls directly or indirectly," more than 50% of American Processing, according to the statement.

National Tea's president, Harley McNamara, maintains there's no conflict of interest here because the purchases were "competitive." He adds: "If a competitor will bid lower, he'll get the business."

Socony Mobil Oil Co. has fired an engineer for running afoul of the company's conflict-of-interest policy. The man was accused of tipping off "favored contractors" on bids submitted by competitors. This allowed the favored company to submit the lowest bids, or in some cases to raise its intended bid and still win the contract, Mobil contends.

Another company has yet to act on a bribery situation which is common knowledge in the Chicago produce market. Market sources there say that in order to sell fruit and vegetables to a well-known grocery chain it is necessary to pay the buyer at least $100 a month. One source claims to have seen bookkeeping entries which reflect these payoffs.

Westinghouse's Action

One of the more vigorous pursuers of possible conflicts has been Westinghouse Electric Corp. About six months ago Westinghouse had Main & Co., its independent public accountants, investigate some 3,600 management men. Main went over the income tax returns filed for the last three years by an unspecified number of top executives. No examples of conflicts of interest were revealed, Main reported.

Virginia Electric and Power Co.'s investigation of its key employees included a scrutiny of Christmas gifts they had received in 1960; the aim was to determine whether such gifts were of sufficient size to suggest an attempt to influence the recipients.

Across the continent, Lockheed Aircraft Corporation says it has intensified its efforts to prevent conflicts of interest. The company's financial department is now carefully determining the ownership of its suppliers to be sure its no-conflict rules are being faithfully followed.

Lukens Steel, at last month's meeting of directors, considered three instances of outside interests of management personnel. The interests had turned up in an inquiry launched the month before. A Lukens executive says the board decided the interests were minor and no divestments were necessary.

An imposing number of companies are having their management men fill out questionnaires on their outside interests. In most cases these companies also are dusting off old policy statements, framing new ones, and circulating them among key employees. Taking one or more of these steps are such corporations as Socony Mobil Oil, Dress Industries, International Harvester, Philco, DuPont, Lukens Steel, Corn Products, Standard Oil of New Jersey, United Fruit, Liggett & Myers, Textron, Foremost Dairies, Standard Oil of California, Packard-Bell Electronics, and Caterpillar Tractor.

Signed Statements

A month or so ago, United Fruit had some 600 management men sign a statement that they were free of any conflict of interest. DuPont has initiated an annual questionnaire, asking employees to list any interest in excess of 1% in any company with which DuPont has annual transactions amounting to $10,000 or more.

But some companies doubt the value of questionnaires. "The guy who's going to cheat will, and he won't feel honor bound to tell you about it on any questionnaire or affidavit he signs," says Samuel Downer, secretary of Continental Can Co.

Jim Haley, secretary of Cluett, Peabody & Co., maker of Arrow brand shirts, indicates his company shares this opinion: "So we conducted our own examination to make sure we had no Chrysler-type cases."

Dissatisfied stockholders are apt to be suspicious too; they are on the conflict-of-interest issue in attacks on management. Two dissident stockholders at National Theatres & Television, Inc., for example, fought their way onto the board of directors last week, precipitating the resignation of B. Gerald Cantor, board chairman. The dissidents had accused officers and directors of "self-dealing." In a letter to stockholders they said that one director controls companies which received $918,000 in commissions on insurance premiums paid by N.T. & T. The dissidents said that nine directors in all had had some business relations with the company, including one who "sold television sets to the company."

"Sadly we are forced to the opinion that this company apparently is run as a private club for the benefit of certain directors," the dissidents declared in their literature. "And we, as stockholders, are unwilling to sit docilely in our place watching the plum being plucked."

Embarrassing Charges

Regardless of the merit of such charges, they are particularly embarrassing at this time. The same holds true of several other cases pending.

Edward O. Lamb, a director of Seiberling Rubber Co., has brought suit against 11 other directors, charging conflicts of interest. Mr. Lamb contends that Paul A. Frank, a Seiberling director and also president of National Rubber Machinery Co., sold Seiberling $400,000 worth of truck tire machinery in 1960 without competitive bidding. Seiberling has replied, in statements to shareholders, that Mr. Frank did not vote on the purchase, that Mr. Lamb's nominee had voted for it, and that more than one engineering study was made prior to awarding the business to Mr. Frank's firm.

Next month in Portland, Ore., Georgia Pacific Corp. is slated to go to court to defend itself in a suit alleging conflict of interest by John S. Brandis, senior vice-president. Among other things, the suit charges that when Georgia-Pacific purchased Plywood Products Corp. from Mr. Brandis and others last summer it paid a price that was excessive "by at least $2 million."

In Hawaii, Matson Navigation Co. is running afoul of the state legislature over an alleged conflict of interest. Matson, which carries 90% or more of the general cargo between the U. S. mainland and Hawaii, plays a big role in the archipelago's economy. Four companies, which control most of Hawaii's sugar and pineapple production, own 73% of Matson's common stock and have nine men on Matson's board of 18 directors. They are also the main customers for Matson freighters on the run from Hawaii to the mainland.

Rates on Sugar

A Hawaiian House of Representatives report shows that freight rates on sugar have risen only one third of 1% since December, 1958. During the same period, Matson's general freight rates have risen 12.5%. The report charges the "special rate" on sugar throws upon Hawaiian consumers of mainland products "the burden of providing revenue desired by Matson."

Randolph Sevier, president of Matson, maintains that control of the company by its largest customers has had "nothing whatsoever to do" with the number of type of its rate increases. Matson says that part of the reason for the small rise in sugar shipping charges is that the sugar companies now bear the cost of loading and discharging cargo—a cost formerly paid by Matson. Mr. Sevier also declares that in 1957 the sugar companies threatened to acquire their own ships to handle their cargo and that Matson decided to reduce rates to keep the business.

Hawaii is not the only state concerned about conflicts of interests in business. In New York, state insurance superintendent Thomas Thacher is proposing that more searching questions on possible conflicts of interest be put into the uniform annual statement which insurance companies must file with state authorities.

Monopoly Case Damages Faith in Free Enterprise *

The Commonwealth Edison Co., to take only one example of a big utility, buys heavy electrical equipment running into many millions of dollars. The

* Reproduced with permission, *Chicago Daily News,* Wednesday, February 8, 1961.

cost goes into its rate base. If the price it has to pay is inflated by conspiracy or rigged bidding, every consumer in Chicago is nicked for tribute to the suppliers.

This is the material side of the antitrust case against 48 individuals and 32 corporations, including nearly every large manufacturer in the electrical industry. On the moral side and on the ideological side, the offense is even worse. It was well stated by U. S. Judge Ganey of Philadelphia in passing sentences.

This is a shocking indictment of a vast section of our economy, for what is really at stake here is the survival of the kind of economy under which America has grown to greatness.

Judge Ganey backed his indignation by sending seven corporation executives to jail and imposing fines totaling $1,924,000. The punishment was unusually severe for antitrust cases, but so was the offense.

An appalling aspect of the case was the flagrant mockery of the competitive system, which every man involved undoubtedly liked to defend heatedly when discussing labor unions or the Soviet system of state control.

Judge Ganey took note that the executives who took the active roles in the conspiracy may very well have been privately conscience-stricken by their acts. But they were "organization men" whose jobs depended upon conformity. It would be naive to suppose that such a widespread plot was not known somewhere in top management.

The only thing to be said for the defendants is that they faced up to the situation and either freely admitted guilt or pleaded "no contest," thereby saving the government years of expensive trials.

The affair is a black eye from which American industry will suffer for years, if not for generations. Every antibusiness demagogue who rises in Congress to denounce "administered prices" will have a club ready fashioned for his hand, a case with which to document his assault.

Every time Jimmy Hoffa proposes a new combine of transportation unions to write their own ticket on wages and working conditions, he will seek justification in the claim that it is the practice of industry.

Business organizations must not yield to the temptation to excuse or minimize this case. It has done them more harm than a dozen Communist orators. Anybody who felt righteously contemptuous at Hoffa's reported advice to a confederate, "I don't care if you steal, but don't get caught," has no reason to apply any different judgment in this matter.

The electrical equipment industry cannot hope that the affair will be quickly forgotten. The sales involved ran to nearly $2 billion a year, and lawsuits for recovery are inevitable.

Having purged itself by confession, the industry had best set promptly about a reform so thorough and so public that in time people may again believe that it believes what it has been preaching.

Business Ethics II *

Americans live in a mixed economic system which is neither capitalist nor socialist, but which is on balance a sensible accommodation to the

* Reproduced with permission, *The Washington Post*, January 5, 1961.

needs of free men. We have chosen as a people to leave a large part of the responsibility for industrial affairs in private hands. But the responsibility is unmistakable. And responsibility equals accountability.

Within the last year two private industrialists have had to leave their jobs because of this accountability. William C. Newberg was the president of Chrysler, our third largest automobile corporation. Carroll Shanks was the head of Prudential, our second largest insurance company. Both have resigned their offices because personal activity, quite probably well intentioned, led them into conflict with the public responsibilities from which a great corporation cannot escape. In private corporations, the ultimate safeguard of the public interest is the board of directors. But only if directors are vigilant to reflect the public interest is it probable that our so-called free enterprise will continue to present freedom from public regulation.

There is a timely problem before several major American companies which deserves general attention. This is the recent plea of guilty to the criminal act of conspiratorial price-fixing by the country's leading electrical manufacturers.

The gist of the case is simple, obvious, shocking. For years various major corporations met secretly, divided the market for certain equipment needed by governmental agencies and privately owned public utilities, and then set prices free of any domestic competition. In one typical instance, 1956, the market for circuit breakers to governmental agencies was divided among General Electric (45 percent), Westinghouse (35 percent), Allis-Chalmers (10 percent), and Federal Pacific (10 percent).

The companies also fought foreign competition in the name of "national security." In 1959, for example, pleas were made to the White House to revoke the purchase of a British turbine generator by the Tennessee Valley Authority. On the generator General Electric had bid $17,560,000 and Westinghouse $17,630,000, whereas the British bid was $12,100,000. A General Electric vice-president complained that foreign manufacturers could underbid because of "substantially lower wage rates and competitive facilities."

There should be particular public interest in the actions of the board of directors of General Electric. This company is America's fourth largest corporation in annual sales. Its chief executive officer, Ralph Cordiner, is important by reason of his corporate position alone. In addition, he has been chairman of the Business Advisory Council under the Eisenhower Administration.

Mr. Cordiner proclaims his innocence of any personal knowledge of the criminal conspiracy to which his company has pleaded guilty. He also announced his lack of knowledge when two men who at the time were officials of the General Electric Supply Co. of Newark, an organization controlled by General Electric, were shown to have supplied prostitutes to customers at a sales convention in 1956.

Any head of a great enterprise can understandably be unaware of the aberrant conduct of daily affairs. But there can come a time for private business to remember its responsibilities and its limitations. The criminal price-fixing by General Electric can have a considerable effect on the private interests of the stockholders. (The company is subject to suits for millions of dollars by customers.) The act of corporate pimping, we suspect, may also have private effect and certainly it does not enhance the public stature of business.

It is ironical that a man like Mr. Cordiner, so unaware of criminal actions in his own business, could have such a lively omniscience about affairs in general. For example:

Between a businessman and a politician, he would "take my chance on a businessman every time. I'd say that only 20 percent of politicians are really dedicated." *Time,* cover story, January 12, 1959.

"Business might subsidize a 'brain trust' of competent writers (novelists, playwrights, etc.) to begin an active campaign of turning public attention away from the left through the sources of popular attitude formation (television, movies, stage, radio, novels, magazine articles, etc.).

"It is important to pick out opinion molders in each community and 'work on them.' However, as a rule a specific story should not be given to them directly by just anyone at random. For example, if the opinion molder to be influenced is a newspaper publisher, it might be best to have him approached by one of his biggest advertisers."—Recommendations quoted in the Report of the General Electric Task Force to Study Organizing Government Relations Work, November, 1956.

Antitrusters' Breakthrough *

What the Government Found in the Electrical Price-Fix Case:

Among the items of equipment in a big electrical power distributing installation are circuit breakers, power switchgear, power transformers and isolated phase buses. Some run to gigantic size and are priced in the hundreds of thousands of dollars. For example, some circuit breakers, which are not basically much different from similar controls for the flow of electricity in a home, stands as high as 26 feet, are 40 feet long, 12 feet wide, and weigh 85 tons. They are dramatic-appearing objects, looking as much as anything like huge basketballs with two great rabbit ears sprouting from the top. They function to help regulate the flow of large voltages of electricity; they literally keep the power station from blowing up.

In that job they are quite successful. But these gigantic circuit breakers, along with a dozen or so similar items, are at the heart of as big a blowup as has hit the world of industry in some years. The industry that makes them has been shaken from one end to the other, and repercussions are yet to come. For this equipment is sold, manufactured, and distributed by men, and numbers of them, from over a score of companies engaged in wide-ranging hanky-panky in the course of their work.

Secret Meetings

A government indictment charged them with conspiring to fix and maintain prices, with getting together in secret meetings and dividing up markets, and with submitting collusive and rigged bids to customers including the federal government. Of the 29 companies indicted, 19 pleaded guilty on some charges and no contest on others while 10 pleaded no contest. Most of the

* Reproduced with permission, *The Wall Street Journal,* January 9, 1961.

46 individuals named in the indictments variously pleaded guilty or "no contest," while the indictment of one was dropped. Some of these defendants have complained they were pressured into these pleas by the cost of fighting a court case and by indications that the court would deal more rigorously with defendants found guilty by a jury. Says the attorney for one: "It is my opinion that at least one defendant in the industrial control equipment industry has, to my knowledge, actually perpetrated a falsehood in pleading guilty."

Be that as it may, the mass guilty and no contest pleas represent a milestone for the antitrusters. For many of the men involved, though, the cases are a personal tragedy. They could mean a jail sentence of up to a year and a $50,000 fine on each count. In some instances careers have been shattered. There is a bitterness at exile to corporate Siberias for, as some of the men see it, conforming to the corporate way of life in their industry.

Judge J. Cullen Ganey, hearing the 20 allied cases in the United States District Court for the Eastern Division in Pennsylvania, raised a key question in the whole picture when he said: "I have been struck . . . that if they (the General Electric individuals involved) were doing this meeting, making these arrangements, rigging prices, and having these allotments made, certainly I am not naive enough to believe that General Electric didn't know about it and it didn't meet with their hearty approbation."

Disciplined Executives

Some companies have denied their top officials knew; General Electric is one. It has dealt discipline to men involved including loss of $30,000 in pay by one individual. Such meetings with competitors violate a written company policy. But generally the conspiratorial way of doing business was so widespread and so brazen as to raise the question why managements did not know. As Antitrust Chief Robert A. Bicks, who personally handled parts of the government's case, put it: The conspiracies involved "a pattern of violations which can fairly be said to range among the most serious, the most flagrant, the most pervasive" in the history of the Sherman Antitrust Act.

The long list of defendants are engaged in these activities in varying degrees, of course; indeed some are bitter toward the government for painting them with much the same brush as the more flagrant violators. The government's cases were largely built on grand jury testimony of people who had been involved and who won immunity from prosecution for their testimony, another source of bitterness. Jail sentences have seldom been the outcome of criminal antitrust cases, but when an Ohio judge in another case handed some out (and one defendant shot himself) there was a sudden flood of willing witnesses in the electrical case. "We could scarcely believe it ourselves," says one government attorney. "For years we had felt something illegal was going on but couldn't nail it down enough. Then all of a sudden we hit the jackpot."

The government's attorneys have put many details on the court record which allege how the various and differing conspiracies operated.

Consider the circuit breaker case filed against General Electric and others. "The testimony," said Mr. Bicks, "is that it (the conspiracy) was in effect for a quarter of a century. However, the clear evidence of the conspiracy begins in 1951. . . ." Now just how did it work?

Intercompany Memo

"In the early years there was a practice, a practice known as the inter-company memo. Once each week with quite regular precision the top executives responsible for the carrying out of this conspiracy would communicate with each other via memo, which each executive initiated. At this stage bear in mind back in 1951 there were four companies . . . in this conspiracy, G.E., Westinghouse (Electric), Allis-Chalmers, and Federal Pacific. . . .

"There would be communications back and forth among the top people responsible for the conspiracy once a week. The initiator of the communication would change month to month, company to company: the communication known as the intercompany memo would deal generally with jobs that each would bid, and any comments that were to be offered on the general price level. Those communications, in short, dealt generally with the so-called private market, the $55 million to $60 million of nonsealed-bid business each year.

"The sealed-bid business—$15 million or so—was dealt with at local-level, working-level meetings where the sealed-bid business was rotated among the four companies on a fixed percentage: G.E. 45, Westinghouse 35, Allis-Chalmers 10, Federal Pacific 10. That was roughly the percentage that was agreed upon."

In another case involving power switchgear assemblies, a system was worked out apportioning the sealed-bid business without the need for meetings. At some undetermined time there came into being the so-called "phase of the moon" or "light of the moon" formula—so-called because it permitted the bid "winner" to be rotated on a regular basis. "This formula was so calculated," the indictment charged, "that in submitting prices to these customers, the price spread would be sufficiently narrow so as to eliminate actual price competition among them, but sufficiently wide so as to give an appearance of competition. This formula was designed to permit each defendant corporation to know the exact price it and every other defendant corporation would quote on each prospective sale. . . ."

In one instance, the low-bid position was agreed on by drawing lots. "Names were put into a hat and slips of paper were drawn by a company representative from each company. Company X drew the lowest number and thereby acquired the low-bid position. The other companies drew their slips of paper which told them what position they would have above Company X."

This was part of the conspiracy charged by the government in the condenser case. Here Baddia Rashid, chief of the trial section of the Antitrust Division, drew a detailed picture.

"This conspiracy can be divided into three aspects," he said. "One is an alleged agreement to maintain market price levels on the product. The second are agreements to actually fix prices on condenser products. And the third is an agreement in a sense to allocate business among the companies."

"These three types of agreements were carried on by two levels of personnel. We have the high-level group and we have the working-level group. . . . The high-level group was concerned not so much with the fixing of actual prices or the allocation of specific condenser jobs. The high-level group rather was interested in maintaining a certain position, market-level position, so that the companies would always operate within a certain sphere of price-level.

"An example of the type of high-level meetings that were conducted is one in 1955 where the defendants in attendance . . . agreed that they would sell condensers at a price no lower than 5% below published book prices. In other words, they left the actual establishment of the book prices to the working-level group, but they decided at the high-level group that in any sales there would be no pricecutting."

This then is the type of charge the government was prepared to take to trial in what it has called the largest group of criminal cases in antitrust law history. The no contest plea by 10 of the 29 companies involved, while not contesting the government's case nor affecting the possible sentence, cannot be used as evidence in a civil suit. Treble damages are possible for guilt under antitrust law and a plea of guilty can be used as conclusive proof, though the plaintiff must prove his damages. Sentencing in all the cases is expected later this month.

T.V.A.'s Role

It was an argument between the industry and a leading customer, the Tennessee Valley Authority, that kicked off the case at least by one authoritative account. For some time T.V.A. had been noticing that bids from various companies were nearly identical. Partly because of this and rising prices for equipment, T.V.A. issued invitations to foreign manufacturers to make bids. Enraged, the domestic industry called a press conference blasting T.V.A. for looking overseas. Piqued, T.V.A. put out a news release, noting among other things, the similarity of bids. This was printed by a Knoxville, Tenn., newspaper and came to the attention of the Kefauver investigating committee which turned findings over to the Justice Department. This led to the impaneling of four grand juries in Philadelphia and they made the indictments. William L. Maher, chief of the Antitrust Division's Philadelphia office, directed much of the investigation.

Such charges of price-fixing and market allocation have frequently been made both by Congress and the Justice Department but far more often than not have gotten nowhere. Antitrust lawyers consider these cases a tremendous government victory and some note that Robert Kennedy, the new attorney general, is believed to favor price-fixing prosecution as the kind of antitrust action with the most impact on consumers.

But that aside, the question remains: How did these companies and individuals get into such a mess?

Are Big Businessmen Crooks? *

by Leland Hazard

Early in 1961 big business drew down on itself some scathing headlines. Some corporate officials of high rank, close to the top, spent thirty days (less good-behavior time) in jail for conspiring to fix prices and allocate orders among their companies. Honored names were involved, among them West-

Excerpts. Reproduced by permission, *Atlantic Monthly,* November, 1961.

inghouse and General Electric. This was the first time in seventy years that any American big businessman had been incarcerated for violation of the 1890 Sherman Antitrust Act. . . .

That the crimes were committed, there is not a scintilla of doubt. Under the law there were no extenuating circumstances. The guilt was stark. According to most of the editorial writers, the sentences said to businessmen: Compete or go to jail. Judge J. Cullen Ganey, in the Philadelphia federal court, said, "What is really at stake here is the survival of the kind of economy under which this country has grown great, the free enterprise system." That was it—our system had been betrayed. . . .

The GE conspirators, some of them with six-figure incomes, have resigned under pressure from GE; the Westinghouse conspirators are back in their jobs having been punished "enough," according to Westinghouse President Mark A. Cresap, Jr. But a paradox haunts the scene. The crimes seem horrendous. Yet the Attorneys General of the United States and the American courts waited almost three quarters of a century to impose on big businessmen the criminal sanctions which have been in the Sherman Antitrust Act since 1890. This fact must give us some pause.

We have been abandoning competition bit by bit in America for a long time. In two world wars and in the Korean War, our government fixed prices and allocated materials—an obvious necessity, an interference with the marketplace which even Adam Smith might approve. But he would not approve minimum wage and hour laws, farm price supports, tariffs, or subsidies —even health and safety laws for factories, or child labor laws, or laws establishing minimum working conditions for women. In Smith's philosophy these would impede the marketplace in its benign work.

Adam Smith did not foresee powerful labor unions or social welfare or heavy technology. He marveled at the productivity attained by division of labor in the making of pins. He knew nothing about single electric-current circuit breakers big as a house. Although accumulation of capital from profit and its reinvestment in productive equipment were cornerstones of his philosophy, the scale of investment required for the subsequent technological advances was beyond his ken. Amusingly, he saw no future for the corporation, because, in his opinion, such an artificial body could not marshal the selfish, driving search for profit so fundamental to his system. Adam Smith taught Americans a faith in competition which persists despite heavy impingements by government, by big technology, and by social welfare upon the freewheeling, bazaar-like marketplace, in which Smith, two centuries past, saw competition as the benign hidden hand.

But the faith is compromised. On the domestic scene the federal antitrust laws are modified to forbid different prices among buyers of commodities of like grade and quality. Manufacturers of branded products are permitted, by amendment of the antitrust laws, to fix resale prices under state fair-trade laws. These and other amendments of the antitrust laws are said to establish "soft competition." The more rigorous antitrusters deplore these compromises, but Congress does not agree.

Antitrust doctrine forbids certain forms of "hard competition." For example, General Motors would hesitate to price its cars as low as its efficiency might permit, for fear of driving Chrysler, American Motors, even Ford to the wall. As critics put it, businessmen must compete, but no one may win the competition. It is this aspect of antitrust which creates two standards, one for big business, another for small business. No matter how vicious the competition of the little fellow, the big fellow must not countercompete too hard. . . .

We have never faced up to a frank and exhaustive examination of our system. In 1953, Attorney General Herbert Brownell, Jr., appointed a distinguished committee of antitrust lawyers, law teachers, economists, and government officials to make "a thoughtful and comprehensive study of our antitrust laws." There was not one practicing businessman on the committee of sixty. The committee produced a scholarly compendium of comment on the antitrust laws but made no significant recommendations. The report makes no reference to the problem of profits versus competition.

The economist may regard profit as only a transitory agent for producing equilibrium. In his book, profit serves not as a reward but as an inducement to competitors to enter the market and take the profit away from enterpriser after enterpriser. But to the businessman, this is just so much academic nonsense. To him, the profit is the reward for good management, and the loss is the unpardonable business sin.

Practicing antitrust lawyers and government antitrust lawyers are a kind of priesthood spinning ever more gossamer refinements of the antitrust commandments. Businessmen are excluded from the councils in the legal temple. Between the government and businessmen there is a cops-and-robbers atmosphere. This is bad. It is doubtful whether America can long afford such immature attitudes. When Roosevelt moved in the courts against Northern Securities Company, Morgan asked why the President could not have come to him as one gentleman to another and made known the government's wishes. I think Morgan had a point. For some reason, gentlemanly relations were never established. Businessmen move at their peril while the law waits in ambush.

In the electrical cases the record shows that the guilty individuals and companies alternated between fierce, quarterless competition and unabashed price-fixing. There were times when the price-cutting reached as high as 60 percent of the going price. Suppose a study was made to determine the reasonableness of the average prices over the whole period in which the conspiracies were on and off. The antitrust doctrine is that reasonableness does not matter. Very well. But are we afraid even to look? Are we, like medieval doctors, unwilling to test the dogma; like them, unwilling for Galileo to drop the balls?

Suppose Congress should provide an amnesty, forgiving all companies and individuals who would make full disclosures of past infractions of antitrust law. The investigators, turned scientists from prosecutors, would develop a kind of economic Kinsey Report. Then economists, psychologists, sociologists, and people from other relevant professions, having access to all the facts, might evaluate the doctrine and measure the harm, if any, which has ensued from the deviations.

When police methods fail, for example, in curbing juvenile delinquency, we apply investigatory and analytical techniques. Often the detection of the causes of antisocial activity results in social change. If doctrine and dogma on the one hand and business and businessmen on the other will submit to exhaustive fact finding and an uninhibited critique, we may discover the common ground for competition and profit, the way to a more stable economy, and an end to internecine distrust. Our hard-pressed country can no longer afford sadism in government and paranoia in business.

A less ambitious program, but one quite worthwhile, would be an amendment of the Sherman Act which would require the government to employ the noncriminal remedies of the Act before invoking the criminal penalties. In the civil proceedings, the courts' equity powers to order cessation of practices and to require new practices are almost without limit. After having heard a given case, the court might then decide whether civil remedies were enough or whether to authorize the Attorney General to proceed for recriminatory criminal penalties. Such an amendment would take some of the gaming out of antitrust enforcement. It would give a partial answer to Mr. Morgan's reasonable question, Why couldn't the government make known its wishes rather than suing as if he were a "common crook"?

There are those who will say that the men of the electrical conspiracy are common crooks. But the case is not that simple. It is necessary to differentiate. The men whose jail terms must make us think are more like those who violated Prohibition than those who burgle a house. A society which has not resolved the periodic incompatibility between competition and profits, has not cured its business cycles, is not able to explain fully its economics—such a society does not have the right to cast first stones at those who must work its imperfect system. The men were guilty, but guilty in a system which is itself not without blame.

Exhibit 2

Mulligan Corporation
Partial Organization Chart

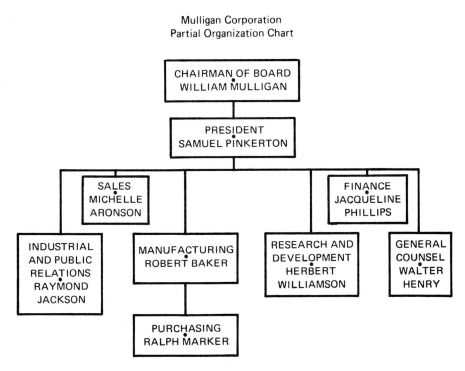

Exhibit 3

Chrysler Will Police Employees' Relations with Outside Concerns *

Management Committee to Report Quarterly to
Board on Operation of Detailed New Regulations

By a *Wall Street Journal* Staff Reporter

Detroit—Chrysler Corp. directors have set up a management committee to police detailed new regulations governing relations between employees and outside concerns.

The committee will report quarterly to the board's finance committee. Details of the new regulations were given in a five-page statement sent to all Chrysler employees having contacts with outside companies.

The new regulations generally follow principles used by two outside firms in clearing Chrysler executives of wrongdoing last fall. Failure to comply with the regulations, the board warned, could result in discharge and, if warranted, legal action.

The new policy states in part:

"No officer or employee shall have or permit his wife or minor children to have any interest, direct or indirect, in any outside concern or competing concern, unless the committee determines in writing, after full disclosure of all the facts, that such interest does not conflict with the interests of the corporation and that there is no reasonable likelihood that such interest will influence his judgment or actions in performing his duties, except that he may acquire or retain securities of an outside concern or competing concern if they fall in one of two categories."

The exceptions are securities of a bank, a public utility, or a transportation company, other than a motor carrier, subject to government authority, and a mutual fund or investment company.

Securities listed on a national exchange or traded in the over-the-counter market also may be owned under certain limitations:

The cost of the securities held by the employee, his wife, and minor children may not exceed $10,000, nor be more than a tenth of one percent of the issue outstanding.

The new rules also say employees may not render services to outside concerns, whether for pay or not, without clearance from the committee.

Employees also are required to report gifts beyond "normal business courtesies" from outside companies.

A company spokesman said the new policies replace those set in 1958, and spell out an employee's responsibility in greater detail.

The statement apparently stems from the forced resignations of two Chrysler officials, William C. Newberg as president, and Jack Minor as director of marketing for a Chrysler division, because of their outside financial interests. Mr. Newberg and Mr. Minor both are suing Chrysler, and the company in turn is suing Mr. Newberg and a former business partner of his, Ben Stone, over the outside interests question. Other suits on the subject also are pending.

* Reproduced with permission, *The Wall Street Journal,* February 2, 1961.

The Matter of Ethics *

We see where the President's new Committee on Ethics is going to study ways to "strengthen" the conflict-of-interest laws for public officials. It probably marks us as antediluvian, but it strikes us that if they strengthen them much more nobody will be able to hold public office but a pauper.

We have already got to the ridiculous point where a Secretary of Defense is not only supposed to yield all control over his investments, but a Congressional committee insists that even his trustees shall not be allowed to hold any securities in "defense industries." Some other officials, hoping to show that they are hororable men, are transferring all their assets to government bonds. Even the President is making elaborate formal arrangements to prove that he is not using his political philosophy to line his private pocket.

All this may sound fine. But what form of investment, these days, isn't affected by public policy? Clothes, bricks, plows, fertilizer, insurance, pencils, banking, or bread—you name it and you will find that somewhere a government policy touches it.

As for putting the money in government bonds, where the essential thing is the whole faith, credit, and monetary policy of the government, will somebody please tell us what investment would give a public official a more direct private interest? A little dash of "easy money," by raising the price of outstanding bonds, could make a nice profit for the holders of them.

Come to think of it, even paupery isn't much protection. A man who has never saved a nickel and depends on the government for his shelter and bread is not exactly disinterested in policies to redistribute the national wealth.

We aren't suggesting that there's anything amiss in a few simple rules by which a man who sells asphalt paving isn't put in charge of awarding highway contracts. But something is seriously amiss if we have to consider that every public official is so lacking in honor that he must be ringed around with laws, so lacking in ethics that a government commission must draw up a code for him.

Once upon a time we considered our public servants honorable until they proved themselves otherwise, and then we flung them out. It's a principle that served us well. And if we can no longer rely on that principle, then things are too amiss for curing by any Presidential committee.

Exhibit 4

To: All Management Personnel

All of us who have any pricing responsibility should have a complete and an accurate view of the way in which the company prices are established. It is absolutely essential that we adhere to proper pricing principles.

Whenever we establish a price to be quoted, bid, or charged for any product, that price is to be determined by sales personnel independently, without any understanding, agreement, or conspiracy with any competitor, exclusively on the basis of their judgment as to what is in the best interest of the company in the light of prevailing economic conditions and taking into account, where applicable, backlogs, capacities, market projections,

* Reproduced with permission, *The Wall Street Journal,* January 24, 1961.

costs, margins, attitude of buyers, and prevailing price levels and other competitive conditions, all to insure fair pricing of products.

You are all familiar with the president's restatement and reemphasis of the company policy of adhering strictly to the antitrust and trade regulation laws and of avoiding any possibility of joint activity with representatives of competitors regarding sales, prices, or market shares or any other action inconsistent with a position of complete commercial independence.

Michelle Aronson
Vice-President

Certificate No. 1

I have caused an investigation to be made of all prices currently being quoted, bid, or charged in my division, and I have satisfied myself that all prices quoted, bid, or charged since _____ (or since date of previous report) on the sale of products for which I have responsibility have been determined exclusively in accordance with the instructions set forth in the pricing policy.

_____
(Signature)

_____
(Title)

_____
(Location)

_____
(Date)

Certificate No. 2

On _____ I attended a meeting at _____ _____ at which representatives of competing companies were present.

I certify that while I was in attendance at that meeting, there was no discussion relating to fixing prices, terms, or conditions of sale to be quoted, bid, or charged in connection with the sale of products to any third party or relating to fixing the market shares for any product or products or relating to any other matter inconsistent with the complete independence of the company in its commercial activities.

I further certify that in connection with the meeting referred to I did not participate in any incidental, collateral, or other discussions of any of the matters set out above, in any informal gathering, "side bar discussion," "rump session," social or unofficial meeting, conversation, or conference.

_____
(Signature)

_____
(Title)

_____
(Location)

_____
(Date)

Certificate No. 3

On _____ I had a phone conversation with _____ of _____ _____, a competing company.

I certify that during this conversation there was no discussion relating to fixing prices, terms, or conditions of sale to be quoted, bid, or charged in connection with the sale of products to any third party or relating to fixing the market shares for any product or products or relating to any other matter inconsistent with the complete independence of the company in its commercial activities.

_____
(Signature)

_____
(Title)

_____
(Location)

_____
(Date)

Exhibit 5

The Mulligan Corporation

Employees:

Subject: Christmas Presents

In connection with the forthcoming holiday season, we would like to call your attention to our company policy which prohibits all employees from accepting gifts from individuals or firms with whom we have business contact. We feel that strict adherence to this policy is the best means of avoiding any possible embarrassment to our friends or ourselves, and we will appreciate your cooperation in our efforts to maintain it.

We wish to express our sincere appreciation for the services which your organization has rendered during the year just closing, and may we express our best wishes for a Merry Christmas and successful New Year.

Yours very truly,
Ralph Marker
Manager of Purchases

P.S. Please do not schedule any deliveries after 11:00 a.m. on Friday, December 22, since our plant is closing at this time for the holiday.

R.M.

Exhibit 6

Reference: Business Ethics

To All Employees

The attached statement is the position that your company has taken on ethical business questions concerning the individual employee. You will recognize that these are the standards which we have maintained in the past, but at this time we feel that it is desirable to emphasize them.

Over the past year the public confidence in business has been shaken by a series of events. These events in no way reflect upon your company, but expressing them now underlines our determination to maintain our reputation in this vital area of individual responsibilities.

Samuel Pinkerton
President

Ethical Standards

It is company policy that all employees obey the laws of the land and maintain a high ethical standard of conduct in all situations which involve the company or its name.

We can expect to succeed over the long term only if we maintain, and deserve, a reputation as a responsible corporate citizen of the highest integrity.

The company relies on every officer and employee who in any way may affect the company's reputation for ethical conduct to assist in carrying out this policy.

While accepted standards of business conduct must apply to all our activities, the following subjects are discussed for your guidance.

1. Legal Aspects

   It is the policy of the company to comply with all federal, state, and local laws governing our operations.

   a. Among the more important of these legal requirements is observance of antitrust laws and trade regulations. These laws and regulations, of course, forbid agreements in any form with competitors to determine bids or fix prices, or to allocate business among customers, competitors, or territories. They forbid discrimination among customers or unreasonable influence upon independent distributors with the intent or effect of restraining trade or practicing unfair competition. The company, as you know, operates under consent decrees with the federal government which set forth certain practices that are permissible and not permissible.

   b. It is recognized that there are numerous and changing antitrust and trade regulation decisions. To facilitate compliance, the company will maintain a continuing program of education, under the overall guidance of the general counsel, so that employees with significant responsibilities under these regulations will be kept informed of activities which are and are not permissible. Questions as to proper interpretation should be referred to the employee's supervisor.

   c. It is expected that managers and supervisors in affected activities will obtain, under this educational program, a working knowledge and understanding of legal requirements pertaining to their duties and will consider it an important part of their responsibilities to cooperate diligently in the company's policy compliance.

   d. No officer or employee of the company is authorized to direct or to approve any violation of this policy; no employee should assume that any violation serves the best interests of the company. Violations of the law, or of accepted standards of ethical business conduct, can only hurt the company, and the individual involved, in the long term.

2. Conflict of Interest
   a. Employees should avoid any action, position, or situation that could be considered, in fact or by implication, to involve a conflict between their personal interests and the company's interests. Employees should not use their position of trust and confidence within the company to further their private interests.
   b. Employees shall be especially mindful of this policy if their position with the company is such that they may influence decisions concerning firms or individuals with whom the company may have business relationships. For example, Mulligan Corporation employees or members of their families should not own a significant interest in a supplier or any other business entity if the employee is in a position to influence orders placed or other decisions involving Mulligan Corporation's interests.
   c. For purposes of this policy a business relationship will be interpreted in its broadest sense as a transaction involving the sale, purchase, or exchange of goods, resources, or services.

3. Supplier and Customer Relationships
   a. Employees must not accept for themselves or their families gifts, favors, expense payments, or entertainment in any form, other than those of the most nominal or token nature, from those with whom the company has, or might have, a business relationship. While this policy applies to all company activities, it should be applied with particular emphasis in the case of suppliers.
   Nominal or token gifts or entertainment are those that are generally recognized as of insignificant value. In case of any doubt, the best policy is not to accept.
   b. Similarly, employees should not extend any but token gifts or entertainment to those with whom they have business relationships. Again, in case of any doubt, the best policy is not to extend.

Mulligan Corporation (B)

Michelle Aronson and Robert Baker submitted their requested reports (see part A) two weeks after Jackson's meeting with Pinkerton and Mulligan. Exhibit 1 is Baker's statement submitted over the signature of Ralph Marker. Exhibit 2 is Aronson's Policy Guide concerning distributors. This statement was drawn up and approved in the hope that the Mulligan Company would not be cited again by the Justice Department for violation of the consent decree.

Exhibit 1

DATE: August 7, 1962
SUBJECT: Ethical and Legal Conduct
REFERENCE: Mulligan Corporation's Policy Statement, Dated June 12, 1962, Section F, Page 22A, Supervisors' Policy Manual
TO: All Purchasing Department Personnel

In addition to the company-wide statement in the Supervisors' Policy Manual, the following supplemental policies have been approved by the president of the Mulligan Corporation:

In order to insure that all purchasing decisions be made in the company's best interest, and entirely on an impersonal basis, it is necessary to comply with the following policies in respect to gifts and entertainment:

Gifts
Acceptance of all gifts are forbidden except those of nominal value bearing the donor's name that could be classed as advertising matter.

Entertainment
In many cases it is desirable to establish an informal relationship between company and vendor personnel, but all entertainment that could conceivably create an obligation must be avoided. Nominal entertainment is permissible if such entertainment does not create an obligation, but even nominal entertainment should not be accepted from companies with whom we have no serious intention of doing business. In no instances should entertainment be accepted that involves more than a nominal expenditure.

Company personnel should pay the cost of such entertainment in appropriate instances so that we bear our fair share of entertainment costs.

If you have any questions regarding the company's policy on ethical and legal conduct or the particular purchasing policies concerning gifts and entertainment, please discuss them with me.

Ralph Marker

Exhibit 2

MEMORANDUM
DATE: August 15, 1962
SUBJECT: Mulligan Corporation Sales
      Policy Guide—Compliance with
      Laws, Regulations, and Decrees
REFERENCE:
TO: Regional Sales Managers
      District Sales Managers
      Sales Office Managers
      Sales Managers—Products
      Sales Division Department Heads

I am attaching for your careful review and consideration our company's policy guide regarding our desire to comply with all laws, regulations, and decrees affecting the operations of our company in the area of sales and distribution.

The preparation of this particular policy guide has been reviewed very carefully by our general counsel and top management because of the extreme importance attached to the need for having a guide of this type for the proper conduct of our business.

You are urgently requested to comply fully with this policy. If, at any time, you are not too sure about any of your actions, consult with your immediate supervisor.

Michelle Aronson: bc

Mulligan Corporation Sales Policy Guide—
Compliance with Laws, Regulations, and Decrees

In the past several months, the president of our company, in his talks to our distributors, stated, among other things, that
  A. The Mulligan Corporation is ethical, considerate, and friendly in all its relations—as an employer, purchaser manufacturer, seller, servicer, and neighbor.
  B. The Mulligan Corporation is a good corporate citizen, responsive to the public interest in the local, national, and international community in which it serves.

Historically, this image of our company has been true, despite our difficulties with the Department of Justice in the late 1940s and, more recently, in 1960. In this connection, it is important to state that the interpretation of our laws by the courts has undergone many changes from year to year.

Actions that formerly were considered perfectly legal and businesslike may later on be considered illegal and unethical in accordance with changes in public and judicial attitudes.

Several federal acts have been enacted for the regulation of business, such as the Sherman Act, the Clayton Act, the Robinson-Patman Act, and the Federal Trade Commission Act. They are primarily designed to prohibit monopolies and maintain free competition. It has been our company's policy to live within the intent and framework of these laws and also to abide by the judgments entered by the Department of Justice under the consent decree issued on March 25, 1948, and later amended September 13, 1960.

The cardinal business policy of our company is to manufacture and sell in a free competitive market products that have specific benefits to our users and for which we expect to obtain a fair return. We are dedicated to the proposition that we must serve the ultimate users in order to earn their business.

Accordingly, in order to make certain that all members of our organization, particularly those engaged in selling and servicing our products, live up to these basic principles, the following statements of policy are detailed for your guidance:

1. Relationship with Distributors

Distributors are independent contractors. They purchase our products at our prices and are free to establish their own business policies.

No one in our organization is to use the threat of cancellation of the distributor franchise to intimidate or coerce distributors to adopt policies recommended by the company.

If distributors do not take the steps necessary to adequately develop the sales potential of their assigned territories or fail to adequately serve customers for Mulligan products, we should call the matter to their attention. We will state and continue to state what are, in our opinion, good business practices that would be beneficial both to distributors and to us if adopted.

2. Markets

Franchised distributors with whom we have an agreement have assigned territories or geographic areas of primary responsibility in which the company agrees, with certain exceptions, not to sell to other purchasers for resale. The reason for this is simply that, in our judgment, the needs of the market and of the users are best served by having, for a particular process or processes, effective and fully qualified distributors in each market who are in a position to carry adequate stocks of our products to meet market needs.

While distributors thus have assigned territories for which they are the only appointed distributors for a particular process or particular processes, they are free to sell our products anywhere inside or outside the United States. We cannot and do not agree with the distributors that no other distributors can or will sell Mulligan products in their territories.

The company, under no circumstances, can enter into an agreement with distributors to divide markets or customers. By divide, we mean, for example, restricting distributors to a particular market area, or to particular types of customers or specific customers.

DECISIONS INVOLVING PUBLIC RESPONSIBILITY

3. Interterritorial Sales

If distributors make a sale of equipment in other distributors' assigned territories and do not choose to make the necessary installation and perform the instructional and warranty service and request Mulligan to perform these services or to arrange for distributors in whose territories the sales have been made to perform these services, they are then obligated to pay for the services in accordance with the conditions of the Distributor Sales and Customer Service Agreement. If the selling distributors elect to make the installation and provide the necessary services, even though sales are made in other distributors' assigned territories, they are under no obligation to compensate the other distributors.

4. Prices

The company has established retail price lists for its own sales offices. These price lists can, of course, be made available to any customer or potential customer who requests them, and the prices at which company sales offices sell at retail may also be set forth in our publication and direct-mail advertising to the public.

a. Distributors

Distributors, on their own volition, can adopt or use the company's established retail price lists. However, they are free to establish their own resale prices, and under no circumstances are we to agree or consult with them as to the prices to be charged by them or by us to users.

b. Sales Offices

Company sales offices are required to adhere, without deviation except under certain conditions, to our published retail prices. More particularly, they are required to adhere to established quantity bracket prices to avoid price discriminations. Jumping price brackets without justification is specifically illegal and is prohibited.

Our sales offices can sell at lower prices than those published retail prices in specific cases to meet competition, provided, however, they can provide evidence of such competitive pricing and provided that the prices offered are no lower than necessary to meet—not beat —competition.

The company is prohibited from selling or leasing at unreasonably low prices for the purpose of destroying competition.

5. Sales of Competitive Products

It is unlawful for us to prohibit or prevent distributors from selling competitive products or to threaten them with cancellation if they do so. Our measure of whether distributors are doing satisfactory jobs depends upon their success in selling and servicing Mulligan products, not upon whether they may be selling other products as well.

6. Quotas

Sales quotas are designed to be used as a measurement of company and distributor sales performance. They are not established as a means for excluding the purchase of other products by distributors.

As a result of the 1960 consent decree, sales quotas for custom tapes are not a part of our total quota for electronic products. Selection of winners of distributor Supersales Awards will be based exclusively on quota performance on electronic products only.

7. Termination of Distributor Sales and
Customer Service Agreement

These agreements between our company and distributors can be terminated either at the election of the company or the distributor, provided a 90-day written notice is given.

If, at any time, the company elects to change distributors, or to establish its own sales office in any market, it has the right under its contracts to do so by giving this notice.

a. Resignation

If a distributor resigns and the company elects to establish its own sales office rather than to appoint another distributor, it can, after receipt of the signed letter of resignation from the distributor, buy the assets of the distributor if the distributor requests it.

b. Cancellation

If the distributor agreement is canceled by the company, the company
1. is forbidden by the consent decree to buy the distributor's assets, even if requested to do so. This prohibition remains in effect until March 25, 1968.
2. is obligated to appoint the distributor as a dealer if so requested on special products only, on the same terms and conditions as other dealers operating through sales offices. This dealer agreement, like the distributor agreement, is subject to cancellation upon 90 days' notice. This particular provision compelling the company to appoint a canceled distributor as a dealer will remain in force until March 25, 1965.

If the cancellation of a distributor is carried out in accordance with the provisions of the distributor agreement, the company incurs no liability to the distributor nor risk of government interference as a result of the cancellation.

A distributor agreement *must* be canceled if a distributor tampers or interferes with the proper operation of equipment to prevent the use of competitive products on Mulligan equipment, or refuses to sell repair or replacement parts on a nondiscriminatory basis to anyone who wants to buy them, or refuses to provide service on Mulligan equipment on the ground that competitive products are used in connection therewith, and repeats the offense after a warning by the company.

It is also unlawful for any company personnel to engage in or encourage any of these practices.

8. Use of Competitive Products with Company Equipment

Both in our advertising and product literature pertaining to equipment, we are required to state that our equipment is not designed primarily for use with Mulligan products, and that other suitable products can be used thereon. We can tell users, to the extent that we believe it to be true, that, in our opinion, best results can be obtained through the use of Mulligan supplies; but we cannot countenance or permit a distributor or sales office to deny mechanical service when competitive products are used.

Similarly, we must not sell or lease equipment on condition that the user use our supplies exclusively.

9. Price Fixing

We cannot, and will not, condone any Mulligan personnel entering into price-fixing agreements with anyone.

10. Acquiring Details of Other Manufacturers of Similar Products

The judgment against our company prevents us from acquiring business details from or information about other manufacturers of similar products other than through the regular course of business.

11. Repair Parts Sales

Repair parts can be purchased by independent technicians directly from the company or from our sales offices at the same prices as independent distributors.

In the case of purchases made from our sales offices, our sales offices are permitted to charge to independent technicians the net distributor price plus the cost of transportation from the home office to the sales office location, inasmuch as these parts, when purchased directly, are f.o.b. the home office.

12. National Accounts

Although National Accounts are qualified as direct customers of the Mulligan Corporation, distributors are free to offer to sell to and service them at their own prices.

13. Federal Government Purchases of Equipment

Under Mulligan Corporation's contract with the General Services Administration, the General Services Administration requires that government purchases of Mulligan equipment be made directly from and billed directly through the Mulligan Corporation.

a. Federal Government Service Agreement

Mulligan Corporation has contracted with the General Services Administration to provide maintenance and repair services through its own sales offices and distributors on definite terms. If the work to be done is on behalf of Mulligan, sales offices and distributors must not deviate from the terms of the contract. If distributors elect to offer to render such service on their own behalf, however, they are free to do so on whatever terms they wish.

14. Bids and Commodity Contracts

There should never be an agreement or discussion between the company, distributors, or competitors that one would bid and the other would refrain from doing so or all would bid same prices or different agreed prices.

15. Separate Franchises

The company's Distributor Sales and Customer Service Contract can be made available to one distributor in a market for all the company's products or it can be confined to one or more processes, thus enabling the company to have two or more distributors in the same market, each one for the particular product handled.

The above statements of policy will provide a basis for the conduct of the affairs of our business in an ethical and legal manner. We plan to review, from time to time, these conditions to make certain that we abide by the accepted principles of good and legal business conduct.

Any question you have regarding these policies should be discussed with your supervisor. If you have doubts, ask before you act.

It is our hope that these guidelines will be useful in the development of our business in conformity with established laws, regulations, and decrees. Our position is that we can and must compete vigorously and effectively in the marketplaces

Mulligan Corporation (C)

Three weeks following the issuance of the Sales Policy Guide (see Exhibit 2 of part B), a customer phoned the general sales manager and stated that he no longer would do business with Mulligan's Lexington distributor. The customer stated that over the past two years the relationship with the distributor had deteriorated to the point where it was impossible to do business. The general sales manager informed the customer that the matter would be checked. The customer then said that if nothing was done, the business which had been given to Mulligan would be given to a competitor. Afterwards, the manager contacted a distributor in a nearby town and asked if the customer could be serviced there.

Later, the general sales manager related the incident to Walter Henry, the general counsel, who took issue with the decision.

Henry: What you have done is clear-cut violation of the law. You are guilty of allocating customers, and that is *prima facie* violation of the law.

General Sales Manager: My gosh, Walt! What should I have done? Just let the customer go over to a competitor?

One month to the day after the release of the policy concerning distributors (see Exhibit 2 in part B), Henry was again disturbed by the actions of the sales department.

A distributor had appealed to the Mulligan Corporation because another had invaded the assigned territory. Christen, the distributor in Whelan (population 89,000), was quite angry that the Brinker Electronics Company had opened a branch outlet in Whelan. Brinker's territory was in neighboring Grand Junction, which was 25 miles from Whelan. Christen had appealed to Mulligan's district sales manager who was unable to settle the problem to Christen's satisfaction.

Michelle Aronson was finally drawn into the dispute when Christen threatened legal action against Brinker and Mulligan. Christen stated that Whelan was her exclusive territory for Mulligan products and that, as long as she met the minimum quota established by Mulligan, she had an exclusive right to that territory. Brinker stated that Christen did not have exclusive rights and that the Brinker Company had signed a lease on the space in Whelan and was not going to move out.

Aronson arranged a meeting with the two in her hotel room in Whelan, and she put the position of the Mulligan Corporation before the two. First, she pointed out that the Mulligan Corporation was prohibited by law from maintaining exclusive territories and, second, that it could not legally put pressure on independent executives to maintain territorial boundaries. Aronson went on to point out that there were advantages to distributors to respect territorial assignments and that in the long run all distributors would be ahead. She called Brinker's attention to his outlay of capital in the branch and wondered if that investment in his own territory might bring a greater return. Aronson also pointed out that Christen was in a position to reduce prices in Whelan and in doing so perhaps make Brinker's venture less profitable than anticipated. In addition, Christen could probably offer better service. Aronson then left the room while Brinker and Christen continued the discussion. The outcome of the whole meeting was that Brinker said he would voluntarily withdraw from Whelan. He stated that he had a lease problem but probably could handle that.

Later when Aronson returned from Whelan, she filled Henry in on the outcome. Henry was quite vocal in his objections.

Henry: Here we are with the Justice Department breathing down our neck, and you are out assigning territories! Our original consent decree stipulated that we are prohibited from doing just that. We have just gotten through straightening out an alleged violation of the consent decree. Michelle, I sure wish you would check with me before you make these moves and not after.

Look, Michelle, point number two of your own policy statement: "We cannot and do not agree with the distributors that no other distributors can or will sell Mulligan products in their territories."

Aronson: Hold on a minute, Walt; I didn't assign or allocate territories. Your legal mind is overlooking one important detail. I didn't pressure those two into an agreement; there were no threats on my part. In fact, I explained that we were quite helpless in settling territorial disputes. Walt, I told them quite frankly that we were prohibited by law and by the consent decree from giving exclusive territories. I just explained the mutual advantages of maintaining territories. And another thing, you must remember that these two people are independent distributors—they own and operate their own businesses and have their own legal and accounting counsels. They also distribute products of other companies. They tell me that these other companies protect the distributor's territory vigorously. Walt, they were simply amazed at what they call Mulligan's naive attitude toward the real facts of business life. Hell, is it getting to the point where I can't even talk to the distributors?

Henry: Michelle, let me ask you one question: If you were an investigator for the Justice Department, how would you interpret what went on in that hotel room in Whelan?

Clorox Chemical Company

The owners of Clorox Chemical Company, nearing retirement age and wanting to sell the company, approached Procter and Gamble with the idea of a merger.[1] At the time, Clorox was the nation's largest producer of household liquid bleach, and P & G, the leading U. S. manufacturer of soap, detergent, and cleanser products. Liquid bleach, like Procter's product lines, was a low-priced, rapid turnover household item sold mainly through grocery stores and supermarkets and presold through mass advertising and sales promotions. After studying the liquid bleach market for two years, Procter's Promotion Department recommended that the company buy Clorox rather than bring out a bleach of its own. Since a very heavy investment would be required to obtain a satisfactory market share for a new bleach, "taking over the Clorox business . . . could be a way of achieving a dominant position in the liquid bleach market quickly, which would pay out reasonably well." The Promotion Department's report predicted that P & G's sales, distributing, and manufacturing setup could increase Clorox's market share in low areas and could induce savings which would increase considerably the profit of the business. Additionally, the department pointed out that P & G could make more effective use of Clorox's advertising budget and achieve substantial advertising economies.

Procter decided to go ahead with the merger, and on August 1, 1957, acquired the assets of Clorox in exchange for Procter stock which had a market value of approximately $30,300,000. Two months later on October 7, 1957, the Federal Trade Commission filed a complaint charging that Procter's purchase of Clorox might substantially

1. In argument before the United States Supreme Court, P & G's attorneys said that initiative for the merger rested solely with Clorox owners, who wanted to dispose of their business for estate purposes "in exchange for the marketable securities of a big company." See *Advertising Age* (February 20, 1967), p. 194.

lessen competition or tend to create a monopoly in the production and sale of household liquid bleaches. This would be in violation of Section 7 of the Clayton Act.[2]

At the time of the acquisition P & G had assets in excess of half a billion dollars and annual sales of $1.15 billion. More than half ($514,000,000) of its total domestic sales were in the soap-detergent-cleanser field; and in packaged detergents alone, its sales were $414,000,000. Procter held 54.4 percent of the packaged detergent market, and together with Colgate-Palmolive and Lever Brothers, accounted for more than 80 percent of this market. In 1957, P & G's percentages of national sales lined up as follows: 54.4 percent packaged detergents; 31 percent toilet soap; 30 percent lard and shortening; and 19 percent shampoo. In addition, the company was a major producer of food and paper products. The giant soap company was also the nation's largest advertiser, and in 1957 spent more than $80,000,000 on advertising and an additional $47,000,000 on sales promotion.

In the liquid bleach industry Clorox, with almost 50 percent of the market, was by far the leader. The company (which in the five years prior to the merger had experienced a steady and continuing growth in sales, profits, and net worth) had assets of over $12,000,000, and annual sales of slightly less than $40,000,000. In 1957, Clorox spent nearly $3,700,000 on advertising and $1,700,000 for promotional activities. The company had no sales representatives but sold its product through brokers and distributors.

Household liquid bleach (5¼ percent sodium hypochlorite and 94¾ percent water) was a relatively inexpensive item to manufacture, but because of high shipping costs and a low sales price, it was not profitable to sell the bleach more than 300 miles from the point of manufacture. And Clorox, with 13 plants scattered throughout the United States, was the only company in the industry distributing its product nationally. Purex, its closest rival had as many plants, but its bleach was available on less than half the national market.[3] Most other manufacturers, having but one plant, were limited to a regional market. In 1957, the six leading producers of household liquid bleach held the following market shares:

2. "No corporation engaged in commerce shall acquire, directly or indirectly, the whole or any part of the stock or other share capital and no corporation subject to the jurisdiction of the Federal Trade Commission shall acquire the whole or any part of the assets of another corporation engaged also in commerce, where in any line of commerce in any section of the country, the effect of such acquisition may be substantially to lessen competition, or to tend to create a monopoly."

3. While Clorox produced only liquid bleach, Purex manufactured other products including abrasive cleansers, toilet soap, and detergents. Total sales of all Purex products were approximately $50,000,000 in 1957.

Brand	Percent of Total U. S. Sales
Clorox	48.8%
Purex	15.7
Roman Cleanser	5.9
Fleecy White	4.0
Hilex	3.3
Linco	2.1
	79.8
All other brands (about 200 producers)	20.2

Only eight bleach manufacturers had assets in excess of $1,000,000; very few had assets of more than $75,000; and total industry sales were less than $100,000,000 annually (less than 10 percent of Procter's annual sales).

PROCEEDINGS BEFORE THE FEDERAL TRADE COMMISSION

The Procter-Clorox case became something of a football before the Federal Trade Commission.

June 7, 1960. Following a series of hearings which extended over a 14-month period, the hearing examiner issued the initial decision, finding the acquisition violative of Section 7 and ordering divestiture.[4]

June 15, 1961. On appeal the Commission set aside the initial decision and remanded the matter to the hearing examiner for the purpose of taking additional evidence on the postmerger situation in the liquid bleach industry.[5]

As the hearing examiner has pointed out, this case involves a conglomerate acquisition and is therefore one of first impression. . . . [S]ince a conglomerate acquisition does not have the . . . 'automatic' effects of a vertical or horizontal merger, . . . a consideration of postacquisition factors is appropriate.

The record as presently constituted, the Commission held, did not provide "an adequate basis for determining the legality" of the acquisition and a remand would provide "a more complete and detailed postacquisition picture . . . allowing the Commission an informed hindsight upon which it can act rather than placing too strong a reliance upon the treacherous conjecture."

4. A brief description of the procedural steps involved in a Federal Trade Commission case is found in Appendix A.
5. 58 *F. T. C.* 1203.

February 28, 1962. The remand hearing took only two days, and the hearing examiner then rendered a second decision, again finding against P & G and ordering divestiture.

December 15, 1963. On a second appeal, the Commission affirmed the hearing examiner's decision and ordered divestiture.[6] In this second decision, the Commission held the postmerger evidence irrelevant. (In the interim between the two decisions, the personnel on the Commission had changed so that only one Commissioner participated in both decisions.) The admission of postacquisition data, the Commission wrote,

> is proper only in the unusual case in which the structure of the market has changed radically since the merger . . . or in the perhaps still more unusual case in which the adverse effects of the merger on competition have already become manifest in the behavior of the firms in the market. If postacquisition data are to be allowed any broader role in Section 7 proceedings, a [company], so long as the merger is the subject of an investigation or proceeding, may deliberately refrain from anticompetitive conduct—may sheathe, as it were, the market power conferred by the merger—and build, instead a record of good behavior to be used in rebuttal in the proceeding.

But more important, said the Commission,

> if a market structure conducive to noncompetitive practices or adverse competitive effects is shown to have been created or aggravated by a merger, it is surely immaterial that specific behavioral manifestations have not yet appeared.

FINAL DECISION OF THE FEDERAL TRADE COMMISSION [7]

Keenly aware that the legality of Procter's purchase of Clorox was a question largely of first impression ("The absence of authoritative, specific precedents in this area compels us to look to basic principles in the interpretation and application of Section 7"), the Commission

---

6. In ordering the divestiture, the Commission said that Procter might spin off the acquired assets to a new corporation owned by P & G stockholders but under separate management.

7. *1963 Trade Cases* 16, 673.

described the acquisition as a "product-extension" merger.[8] Packaged detergents and household liquid bleach are used complementarily, the Commission pointed out, and from the housekeeper's point of view are closely related products. Moreover, since detergents and bleach are low-cost, high-turnover consumer products, sold to the same customers, at the same stores, and by the same merchandising methods, the merger offered possibilities for significant integration at both the marketing and distribution levels.

> By this acquisition, then, Procter has not diversified its interests in the sense of expanding into a substantially different, unfamiliar market or industry. Rather, it has entered a market which adjoins, as it were, those markets in which it is already established, and which is virtually indistinguishable from them insofar as the problems and techniques of marketing the product to the ultimate consumer are concerned.

Taking a look at the premerger liquid bleach industry, the Commission called it highly concentrated, oligopolistic, strongly characterized by product differentiation through advertising, and barricaded to new entry, to a degree inconsistent with effectively competitive conditions. Between them, Clorox and Purex accounted for almost 65 percent of liquid bleach sales, and together with four other firms, for almost 80 percent—and of these six companies, a single one, Clorox, was dominant.[9] Only Purex could be considered to have been a significant competitor of Clorox, and its bleach was not sold in half of the country; in fact, in several areas, Clorox faced no competition whatever from the leading firms in the industry.

8. Here, the Commission wrote: "Another variant of the conventional horizontal merger is the merger of sellers of functionally closely related products which are not, however, close substitutes. This may be called a product-extension merger. The expression 'functionally closely related,' as used here, is not meant to carry any very precise connotation, but only to suggest the kind of merger that may enable significant integration in the production, distribution, or marketing activities of the merging firms. . . . Only when the various subcategories of horizontal and vertical mergers have been exhausted do we reach the true diversification or conglomerate merger, involving firms which deal in unrelated products." But all mergers, said the Commission "whether they be classified as horizontal, vertical, or conglomerate, are within the reach of Section 7, and all are to be tested by the same standard." Definitional distinctions, the Commission continued, "import no legal distinctions under Section 7. The legal test of every merger, of whatever kind, is whether its effect may be substantially to lessen competition, or tend to create a monopoly, in any line of commerce in any section of the country."

9. According to the Commission, Clorox's dominant position was "dramatically" shown by the fact that Procter "preferred to pay a very large premium for the goodwill of Clorox (the $17,700,000 difference between the purchase price of Clorox, $30,300,000, and the valuation of Clorox's assets, $12,600,000, suggests the size of this premium) rather than enter the industry on its own."

Since all liquid bleaches were chemically identical, the success of premium brand Clorox was obviously due to the company's "long-continued mass advertising," whereby its name had become widely known to and preferred by the consumer "notwithstanding its high price and lack of superior quality." Most bleach manufacturers, the Commission observed, could not afford to advertise extensively, and although Purex was a large advertiser, its advertising was very possibly less effective than Clorox's because of its geographically limited market. Thus, the chief effect of Clorox's intensive advertising had been to gain a large share of the market at a higher price to the consumer. Given the importance of product differentiation in the bleach industry, advertising outlays were a formidable barrier to entry even before the merger, for any outsider who hoped to capture a satisfactory share of the market would have to incur a very heavy initial investment to promote its brand.

Having described the liquid bleach industry in these terms, the Commission went on to find that the substitution of multiproduct P & G, with its huge assets and enormous advertising power, for the dominant, but relatively small, single-product Clorox would lend further rigidity to an already oligopolistic industry by scaring off potential competitors and inhibiting active competition from those firms already in the industry.

First, the Commission tried to ferret out the consequences for competition if P & G replaced Clorox in the bleach industry. Pinning much of its argument against the merger on P & G's advertising and promotional power and the cost savings and other advantages resulting therefrom, the Commission found that postmerger Clorox could obtain 33⅓ percent more network TV advertising for the same amount of money it had spent prior to the acquisition. This was due to the discounts which Procter received on its tremendous volume of TV advertising, and, the Commission noted, similar advertising discounts were available to P & G in the other media. But the advertising advantages of the merger were not limited to volume discounts. For example, P & G could afford to buy entire network TV programs on behalf of several of its products—something which premerger Clorox could not have done unless it were willing to put a disproportionate amount of its advertising budget into a single project. Also, if Procter felt Clorox faced stiff competition in a particular locality, it could run a TV commercial in that area alone, while the rest of the country watched an ad for other Procter products. Thus Clorox, the Commission pointed out, could gain the advantage of association with network TV while limiting its advertising outlays to selected regional markets. Additional competitive advantages could be gained by including Clorox in P & G's sales promotion campaigns, cutting down greatly on Clorox's processing and mailing costs. And joint advertising in newspapers and magazines offered further possibilities for considerable cost savings.

The Commission went on to speculate that P & G's sales force might be able to induce retailers to give Clorox more and better shelf space, and that, as a multiproduct firm operating in a market of single-product firms, Procter might engage in systematic underpricing, subsidizing such action with profits from its other markets. And the Commission continued,

> The conditions which retard competition in an industry are to an important degree psychological. They stem from competitors' appraisal of each other's intentions, rather than from the intentions— or the actions taken upon them—themselves. The appropriate standpoint for appraising the impact of this merger is, then, that of Clorox's rivals and of the firms which might contemplate entering the liquid bleach industry. To such firms, it is probably a matter of relative indifference, in setting business policy, how actively a Procter-owned Clorox pursues its opportunities for aggressive, market-dominating conduct. The firm confined by the high costs of shipping liquid bleach, and the high costs of national or regional advertising, within a geographically small area, cannot ignore the ability of a firm of Procter's size and experience to drive it out of business (not necessarily deliberately) by a sustained local campaign of advertising, sales promotions, and other efforts. . . . A small or medium-size firm contemplating entry cannot ignore the fact that Procter is a billion-dollar corporation whose marketing experience extends far beyond the limited horizons of the liquid bleach industry and whose aggregate operations are several times greater than those of all the firms in the industry combined. Even a large firm contemplating entry into such an industry must find itself loath to challenge a brand as well established as Clorox bleach, when that brand is backed by the powerful marketing capacities of a firm such as Procter. If we consider, in other words, not what Procter will in fact do to exploit the power conferred on it by the merger, or has done, but what it can and is reasonably likely to do in the event of a challenge to its dominant market position in the liquid bleach industry, we are constrained to conclude that the merger has increased the power of Clorox, by dominating its competitors and discouraging new entry, to foreclose effective competition in the industry.

Turning next to the substantiality of the merger's anticompetitive effects, the Commission said that five factors taken together persuaded it that Procter's purchase of Clorox violated Section 7:

1. the relative disparity in size and strength as between Procter and the largest firms of the bleach industry;
2. the excessive concentration in the industry at the time of the merger, and Clorox's dominant position in the industry;

3. the elimination, brought about by the merger of Procter as a potential competitor of Clorox;
4. the position of Procter in other markets; and
5. the nature of the 'economies' enabled by the merger.[10]

Procter's financial resources and scale of operations, the decision pointed out, overshadowed the entire liquid bleach industry and the cost advantages enabled by the merger would substantially affect competitive conditions in the market. And the barriers to entry, "already formidable, become virtually insurmountable when the prospective entrant must reckon not with Clorox, but with Procter."

By the merger P & G obtained a protected market position. Clorox's substantial market power might enable Procter to strengthen its position in other industries. And since Clorox and Procter manufacture closely related products, P & G might use Clorox bleach as a tying product, loss leader, or cross-coupon offering, to promote other Procter products.

Still another important factor to consider about the merger was that it eliminated the salutary effect of Procter as a potential competitor of Clorox. In the past, the Commission reasoned, P & G had frequently extended its product lines by going into industries in which it had not been active before; it was one of the very few manufacturers of household cleaning products powerful enough to successfully challenge Clorox's position; and it had actually thought about the possibility of going into the liquid bleach business on its own. Therefore, Procter "must have figured as a tangible influence on Clorox's policies," and was, though in absentia, "by reason of its proximity, size, and probable line of growth, a substantial competitive factor" in the bleach industry. Before the acquisition, Proctor "was not only a likely prospect for new entry into the bleach market, it was virtually the only such prospect." Thus, the merger by eliminating Procter as a potential entrant removed "one of the last factors tending to preserve a modicum of competitive pricing and business policies" in the bleach industry.[11]

Moving on to P & G's strong market position in other product areas, the Commission asserted that Proctor's strength rebutted

10. Here, the Commission noted: "We need not, and do not, consider whether one or more of these factors, taken separately, would be dispositive of the case."

11. Here, the decision noted: "We have no occasion to speculate on such questions as whether or not Procter, had its acquisition of Clorox been blocked, would in fact have entered the bleach industry on its own, or whether or not had it done so, the result would have been to increase competition in the industry—although, with reference to the second question, we note the Supreme Court's recent observation that 'one premise of an antimerger statute such as § 7 is that corporate growth by internal expansion is socially preferable to growth by acquisition.'"

any inference that it could not bring its enormous financial resources to bear on the liquid bleach industry. If P & G were spread thin over its other markets, it might be a different story; but such was not the case. Procter was a highly profitable company with demonstrated ability to mobilize and use its financial strength.

> . . . Just as ownership of Clorox may enable Procter to enhance its competitive edge in other markets, so Procter's position in other markets may enhance its dominance, through its acquisition of Clorox, of the liquid bleach industry. . . . The short of it is that a conglomerate merger involving firms which have dominant power in their respective markets tends to reinforce and augment such power.

Finally in answer to Procter's arguments that the merger should be upheld on grounds of efficiencies (cost savings in advertising and sales promotions), the Commission found that in the instant case this type of "efficiency . . . hurts, not helps, a competitive economy and burdens, not benefits, the consuming public." For while "marketing economies, including those of advertising and sales promotion, are as desirable as economies in production and physical distribution," the point had been reached in the liquid bleach industry where advertising had lost its informative aspect and merely entrenched the market leader.

> . . . The undue emphasis on advertising which characterizes the liquid bleach industry is itself a symptom of and a contributing cause to the sickness of competition in the industry. Price competition, beneficial to the consumer, has given way to brand competition in a form beneficial only to the seller. In such an industry, cost advantages that enable still more extensive advertising only impair price competition further; they do not benefit the consumer.

Though the Commission rejected the postmerger evidence, it noted that Clorox's market share in 1961 was 51.5 percent, compared to its 48.8 percent share in 1957. And it concluded:

> Had Procter in fact fully integrated the marketing and other activities of Clorox in its overall organization, perhaps dramatic postacquisition changes, directly traceable to the merger, would have occurred. But, save for taking advantage of certain advertising cost advantages and introducing sales promotions, Procter in the period covered by the postacquisition evidence has carefully refrained from changing the nature of the operation; even the network of independent brokers has been retained. Such restraint appears to be motivated by a general Procter policy of moving slowly and cautiously in a new field until the Procter management feels totally acclimated to it. It is possible, as well, that the pendency of the instant proceeding has had a deterrent effect upon expansionist activities by Procter in the liquid bleach industry.

U. S. COURT OF APPEALS, SIXTH CIRCUIT [12]

Procter appealed the Commission's order, and the Circuit Court unanimously upheld the acquisition and directed dismissal of the complaint.

> The Commission recognized that complete guidelines for this type of merger have not yet been developed and that the case presented a challenge to it and to the courts "to devise tests more precisely adjusted to the special dangers to a competitive economy posed by the conglomerate merger." We do not believe these tests should involve application of a per se rule.

> The Supreme Court has not ruled that bigness is unlawful, or that a large company may not merge with a smaller one in a different market field. Yet the size of Procter and its legitimate, successful operations in related fields pervades the entire opinion of the Commission, and seems to be the motivating factor which influenced the Commission to rule that the acquisition was illegal.

Findings of illegality, the Appellate Court observed, "may not be based upon 'treacherous conjecture,' possibility, or suspicion. And yet this is exactly what the second Commission indulged in. . . ."

Noting the Commission's opinion that the liquid bleach industry was highly concentrated, with virtually insurmountable barriers to entry on a national scale, the three-judge panel said that, while it probably would be difficult to break into the market on a national basis without expending a large sum of money, there was no evidence that anyone had ever tried to do so. And, the court continued, the fact that in addition to the six leading bleach manufacturers there were 200 smaller companies, both before and after the merger, "would not seem to indicate anything unhealthy about the market conditions."

The justices gave short shrift to the Commission's lengthy discourse on P & G's advertising might:

> Doubtless Procter could advertise more extensively than Clorox, but there is such a thing as saturating the market. We find it difficult to base a finding of illegality on discounts in advertising . . . the fact that a merger may result in some economies is no reason to condemn it.

Nor did the Appellate Court find any merit to the Commission's claim that multiproduct Procter might be able to obtain more shelf space for Clorox. The evidence was clear, the Court wrote, that premerger Clorox obtained very adequate shelf space.

Turning to the Commission's findings that the merger eliminated P & G as a potential competitor, the judges held that there was no evidence tending to prove that Procter ever intended to enter the

12. *Procter & Gamble Company* v. *F.T.C.*, 358 F. 2d 74 (1966).

bleach business on its own; in fact, its Promotion Department had recommended against such a move. Therefore, the Commission's finding, the Court held, was based on "mere possibility and conjecture." [13]

> Household liquid bleach is an old product; Procter is an old company. If Procter were on the brink [of entering the market on its own], it is surprising that it never lost its balance and fell in during the many years in which such bleach was on the market. It had never threatened to enter the market.

The reviewing court did not engage in any discussion as to the type of merger involved but simply stated: "The merger in the present case was neither vertical nor horizontal, but conglomerate. The second Commission has characterized it as product extension." Under Section 7, the Court continued,

> It is necessary to determine whether there is a reasonable probability that the merger may result in a substantial lessening of competition. Amended Section 7 was intended to arrest anticompetitive tendencies in their incipiency. A mere possibility is not enough. (Citations omitted.)

P & G, according to the Court, "merely stepped into the shoes of Clorox" and whether it could do better than Clorox remained to be seen.

> The Nielsen tables . . . for a period of five years prior to the merger and four years after, do not reveal any significant change in the rate of growth of Clorox.
> . . . Subsequent to the merger, competitors of Clorox sold substantially more bleach for more money than prior thereto. This evidence certainly does not prove anticompetitive effects of the merger. The Commission gave it no consideration.

The Sixth Circuit held the Commission in error in ruling that postmerger evidence was admissible only in unusual cases. Since a Section 7 proceeding involves the "drastic remedy of divestiture," said the justices, "any relevant evidence must be considered." The extent of the inquiry into postmerger conditions and the weight to be attached to the evidence may well depend on the circumstances of the case, they wrote, but where, as here, the evidence has been obtained, it should not be ignored. As for the contention that P & G's postmerger behavior may have been influenced by the pending litigation, this again, said the Court, was "pure conjecture." If, in the future, Procter engaged in predatory practices, the Federal Trade Commission had ample powers to deal with it.

13. The Court noted that this issue had not been raised until after all the evidence was in and the appeal taken to the second Commission.

Finally, the Court observed, Clorox wanted to sell its assets. A small company could not qualify; it "had to sell to a larger company or not sell at all."

SUPREME COURT [14]

The Federal Trade Commission appealed the Sixth Circuit's ruling and with Justice Douglas delivering the opinion (dated April 11, 1967), the Supreme Court in a 7 to 0 decision reversed the judgment of the Court of Appeals and remanded with instructions to affirm and enforce the Commission's order.[15]

In essence the Court said "Amen" to the Federal Trade Commission's exhaustive opinion. It adopted the Commission's product-extension merger characterization.[16] The Court agreed it did not "aid analysis to talk of this merger in conventional terms, namely, horizontal or vertical or conglomerate"; and it repeated the Commission's statement that "all mergers are within the reach of § 7, and all must be tested by the same standard, whether they are classified as horizontal, vertical, conglomerate, or other."

The majority opinion declared: "The anticompetitive effects with which this product-extension merger is fraught can easily be seen: (1) the substitution of the powerful acquiring firm for the smaller, but already dominant, firm may substantially reduce the competitive structure of the industry by raising entry barriers and by dissuading the smaller firms from aggressively competing; (2) the acquisition eliminates the potential competition of the acquiring firm." The pre-merger liquid bleach industry, Justice Douglas wrote, was already oligopolistic. Clorox held a dominant position nationally and in certain localities its position approached monopoly proportions. Thus, with P & G replacing Clorox, it was probable that Procter would become the price leader, causing the oligopoly to become more rigid, making smaller firms more cautious in competing with P & G.

Additionally, the merger may have the tendency of raising the entry barriers, for Procter's tremendous advertising budget would enable it to divert monies to meet the short-term threat of a newcomer. And the substantial advertising discounts which Procter enjoyed might put off potential competitors. Regarding this latter point, the opinion flatly stated: "Possible economies cannot be used as a defense to illegality."

14. 35 LW 4329.
15. Justice Stewart and Justice Fortas did not participate in the decision. Justice Harlan wrote a concurring opinion.
16. The opinion noted: "Since the products of the acquired company are complementary to those of the acquiring company and may be produced with similar facilities marketed through the same channels and in the same manner, and advertised by the same media, the Commission aptly called the acquisition a 'product-extension merger.'"

In reversing the judgment of the Court of Appeals, the Court agreed with the FTC—the merger eliminated competitor P & G.

> The evidence . . . clearly shows that Procter was the most likely entrant. . . . Procter was engaged in a vigorous program of diversifying into product lines closely related to its basic products. Liquid bleach was a natural avenue of diversification since it is complementary to Procter's products, is sold to the same customers through the same channels, and is advertised and merchandised in the same manner.

In its reliance upon postmerger evidence, Justice Douglas wrote, the Court of Appeals misapprehended the standards applicable in a Section 7 proceeding.

> Section 7 . . . was intended to arrest the anticompetitive effects of market power in their incipiency. The core question is whether a merger may substantially lessen competition, and necessarily requires a prediction of the merger's impact on competition, present and future. The section can deal only with probabilities, not certainties. And there is certainly no requirement that the anticompetitive power manifest itself in anticompetitive action before § 7 can be called into play. (Citations omitted.)

OPINION OF JUSTICE HARLAN

While agreeing that the Federal Trade Commission's order should be sustained, Justice Harlan took issue with the majority opinion because it made no effort to formulate standards for the application of Section 7 to mergers "which are neither horizontal nor vertical and which previously have not been considered in depth by this Court."

> It is regrettable to see this Court as it enters this comparatively new field of economic adjudication starting off with what has almost become a kind of *res ipsa loquitur* approach to antitrust cases.

The majority opinion "leaves the Commission, lawyers, and businessmen at a loss as to what is to be expected of them in future cases of this kind." While the Court declares that all mergers (no matter what they are called) must be tested by the same standard, it is equally important, Justice Harlan wrote, "to recognize that different sets of circumstances may call for fundamentally different tests of substantial anticompetitive effect."

The Justice agreed with the Commission's finding that the postmerger evidence was irrelevant and that in conglomerate or product-extension merger cases inquiry "should be directed toward reasonably probable changes in market structure," for "only by focusing on market structure can we begin to formulate standards which will allow the responsible agencies to give proper consideration to such mergers and allow businessmen to plan their actions with a fair degree of certainty."

Justice Harlan gave the following summation for determining the legality of conglomerate or product-extension mergers:

> First, the decision can rest on analysis of market structure without resort to evidence of postmerger anticompetitive behavior.
>
> Second, the operation of the premerger market must be understood as the foundation of successful analysis. The responsible agency may presume that the market operates in accord with generally accepted principles of economic theory, but the presumption must be open to challenge of alternative operational formulations.
>
> Third, if it is reasonably probable that there will be a change in market structure which will allow the exercise of substantially greater market power, then a prima facie case has been made out under § 7.
>
> Fourth, where the case against the merger rests on the probability of increased market power, the merging companies may attempt to prove that there are countervailing economies reasonably probable which should be weighted against the adverse effects.

And he found the Commission's opinion to conform to this analysis.

While agreeing that the Commission was justified in giving no weight to P & G's efficiency defense (because discounts on large advertising outlays are not "true efficiencies"), Justice Harlan felt that the Commission's view on advertising economies was overstated and oversimplified.

> Undeniably advertising may sometimes be used to create irrational brand preferences and mislead consumers as to the actual differences between products, but it is very difficult to discover at what point advertising ceases to be an aspect of healthy competition. It is not the Commission's function to decide which lawful elements of the product offered the consumer should be considered useful and which should be considered the symptoms of industrial sickness. It is the consumer who must make that selection through the exercise of his purchasing power.

ADDENDUM

In February, 1967, nearly two months before the Supreme Court handed down its ruling on the Clorox merger, the Federal Trade Commission split 3 to 2 in accepting a consent settlement,[17] by which

17. Under the Commission's rules, a party against whom the FTC had decided to issue a complaint is served with notice of the Commission's intention and receives a copy of the intended complaint and order. The party served may file a reply indicating willingness to have the proceeding disposed of by entry of an agreement containing a consent order. When such a reply is received, the party served, its counsel, and members of the Commission's Division of Consent Orders participate in the preparation and execution of an agreement containing a consent order. If the Commission subsequently determines that the proposed agreement should be accepted, it issues its complaint and simultaneously enters its decision and order.

Procter & Gamble (in exchange for being allowed to keep Folger coffee company which it had purchased in 1963 [18]) promised not to buy any domestic grocery products companies in the next seven years without prior FTC approval and promised further not to engage in any additional coffee mergers for the next ten years. P & G also agreed that during the next ten years it would report all incipient mergers involving any kind of domestic product to the Commission.

The consent settlement further provided that P & G would not accept any media discounts or rate reductions on coffee advertising during the next five years when such discounts or reductions are based on advertising of other Procter products, and that it would not conduct any coffee promotion in conjunction with its other products during the same period.

The majority, which included Commissioner Philip Elman who had written the Commission's ruling against the Clorox merger, did not give any explanation for its acceptance of the settlement. But Commissioner Mary Gardiner Jones, who dissented on the grounds that regulation was inadequate and the FTC should have sought divestiture, said: "Instead of seeking divestiture, the order seeks to regulate, in a quite direct manner and for a five-year period, certain aspects of P & G's conduct of joint promotions involving coffee and its other products and P & G's ability to exact reductions in media rates because of the magnitude of its several expenditures on advertising." [19]

The text of the FTC's complaint, which released publicly with the announcement of the consent settlement, contended that the merger between P & G and Folger, the nation's second largest non-retailer of regular coffee and fourth in soluble coffee, might substantially lessen competition in the coffee business. Like Clorox, Folger was a single-product company, and, as in the Clorox situation, P & G was entering a new product field with its purchase of Folger.

The Commission had notified P & G in June of 1966 that it intended to challenge the Folger purchase and to seek divestiture, and its complaint stressed P & G's advertising and promotional strength and its ability to achieve significant cost reductions in: the buying of green coffee; the procuring of financing; the buying and placement of advertising; the conducting of consumer and sales promotions; the buying of containers and packaging materials; and the procuring of warehousing and transportation. [20]

18. In a ten-year period, P & G had acquired five grocery product companies: W. T. Young Foods Inc. (peanut butter and peanut products), 1955; prepared mix division of Nebraska Consolidated Mills (cake mixes), 1956; Charmin Paper Mills (paper tissues and related products), 1957; Clorox, 1957; and J. A. Folger & Co. (coffee), 1963.
19. *Advertising Age* (February 27, 1967), p. 36.
20. *Ibid.*

APPENDIX A

Under the Administrative Procedure Act and the Federal Trade Commission's rules, the initial decision of a hearing examiner becomes the decision of the Commission 30 days after it has been served upon the parties to the proceeding unless prior thereto (1) an appeal is made to the Commission; (2) the Commission by order stays the effective date of the decision; or (3) the Commission issues an order placing the case on its own docket for review. In rendering its decision on appeal or review, the Commission may adopt, modify, or set aside the findings, conclusions, and order of the initial decision.

A final decision by the Commission results in a dismissal or a cease and desist order. If the Commission issues a dismissal, the proceedings are at an end, for counsel supporting the complaint may not petition the courts for review. If the Commission issues a cease and desist order, this order may be appealed to a United States Court of Appeals which may affirm, enforce, modify, or set aside the order. The judgment and decree of a Court of Appeals is subject to review by the United States Supreme Court upon certiorari.

A Businessman's View of
Some Antitrust Problems

It is a pleasure for me to be with you this morning and to have this opportunity to join in your discussion. Your chairman first suggested that my remarks might be entitled "A Businessman's View of the Sherman Act." But he was kind enough to add that I would be free to discuss any aspect of the broad antitrust field that I might choose. As my title indicates, I have taken advantage of this latitude, and will limit my remarks to some specific questions.

I am aware, of course, that a great deal is being spoken and written these days on these particular subjects, and it is difficult to advance any ideas regarding them which have not been stated recently by many others. Furthermore, not being a lawyer, I would not pretend to give you a legal treatment of these matters in any case. I speak only as a businessman who has been intimately concerned with antitrust matters in the conduct of his business for some forty years. I am not sure that enough businessmen have spoken out on these subjects. From that viewpoint, therefore, I would like to discuss with you four main thoughts:

1. When one looks at the more recent applications of the antitrust laws, especially in the field of mergers and acquisitions, it seems that, although the laws themselves are aimed against presumed cases of monopoly and suppression of competition, they are often being directed against a quite different target—namely, bigness.

2. Underlying this situation seems to be the acceptance of a number of legal and economic concepts which do not sufficiently reflect the economic realities of the modern business world.

3. The result is that some antitrust decisions may actually operate to diminish competition; hamper the dynamic growth of

By M. J. Rathbone, director and former chairman of the board of Standard Oil Company (New Jersey). This speech dealing particularly with mergers, acquisitions, and corporate size is reprinted with the permission of the author and the American Bar Association from the proceedings of the Section of Antitrust Law, *American Bar Association, Spring Meeting*, Washington, D. C., April 8–9, 1965.

our economy; and hurt the interests of consumers, employees, and business—small as well as large.

4. To correct this tendency and assure the continued strength, competitiveness, productivity, and vigorous growth of the American economy, this nation urgently needs a new look at the impact of the administration of our antitrust laws on bigness, mergers, and acquisitions.

I shall present to you, as well as I can in the brief scope of this talk, the facts and reasoning which have led me to these four conclusions. But before doing so, let me make two points crystal clear, lest my position be misunderstood.

First: In my opinion, every true businessman in this country must believe in and support our competitive free enterprise system—and I stress the word competitive. For virtually all American business, large as well as small, competition is the main force working to keep each company on its toes and thus assure the best possible product or service to the consumer.

There can be no justification for predatory business practices which undermine the competitive system. Nor can restrictive agreements among competitors be justified. Such agreements, in my opinion, are the resort of the lazy, the ineffective, or the shortsighted.

Second: Small business, in my opinion, has an important and permanent place in the American economy. I do not for a moment believe that there is, or should be, any irreversible trend toward bigness that will sweep before it all our hundreds of thousands of small and medium-size enterprises. In fact, in our diverse economy large and small businesses are closely interdependent. My company, and most other large companies, depend on small businessmen not only as customers but as suppliers of countless products and services which they can provide efficiently and expertly, and often at lower cost.

The reasons why small business is so prominent in our economy are not only economic; there are also human reasons. Any enterprising individual with a little capital and a lot of ideas and some business ability is potentially a small businessman. If he is good he may become a big businessman—but there will be other individuals coming along as small businessmen to take his place. I want to stand up and be counted as a strong believer in the importance of small business to our society and our personal incentive system; and I believe, also, that small firms should be shielded by the law against predatory practices of others, whether large or small.

These beliefs, I know, are widely shared among business firms of all sizes. I do not think there are many in the business community who would question the need for antitrust laws or for the vigorous enforcement of them against practices which would injure our competitive system. In this broad area, our antitrust authorities and the business community are in fundamental accord, I am sure.

Unfortunately, in the very important area which is my main subject today—namely, the developing antitrust doctrines concerning bigness and mergers—no such accord exists. On the contrary, many businessmen—and lawyers and scholars too—who study these matters are asking more and more insistently such questions as these:

> Are we approaching a point where bigness in business, in and of itself, is bad and should be curbed by the antitrust laws? Is mere bigness—especially where a merger or acquisition is involved—becoming an offense even when competition remains vigorous and may actually be stimulated, and the public benefited in the final analysis?

These are far from being academic questions. The direction in which our antitrust law seems to be moving in this area can profoundly affect our national life in the years to come.

I can best illustrate this problem by referring to one or two recent decisions in antitrust cases. First, the United States District Court in Rhode Island, in its decision in December, 1964, in the case of *United States* v. *Grinnell Corp.*,[1] made the following rather striking statement:

> To this Court it appears that the day has come for it, and more important for counsel, to proceed on the acknowledged principle that once the government has borne the burden of proving what is the relevant market and how predominant a share of that market defendant has, it follows that there are rebuttable presumptions that defendant has monopoly power and has monopolized in violation § 2 [of the Sherman Act].[2]

Then the Court went on to list what the government need *not* prove as follows:

> . . . defendant's predatory tactics, if any, or defendant's pricing, or production, or selling, or leasing, or marketing, or financial policies while in this predominant role.[3]

Finally, the Court explicitly declared that the defendant company, in order to clear itself of the presumption of having monopolized illegally, must maintain the burden of showing that its eminence is traceable to such highly respectable causes as superiority in means and methods which are 'honestly industrial.'[4]

There are two troublesome points in this statement. First, it appears to justify a dangerous shortcut in proving violations. The case against a defendant company would seem to be already one short step away from completion as soon as that company is held to have

1. 1964 Trade Cas. 80242 (D.R.I. Nov. 27, 1964).
2. *Ibid.* at 80246.
3. *Ibid.*
4. *Ibid.*

achieved a "predominant share" of a "relevant market"—even though the definition of "relevant market" by itself is enough to tax the wisdom of Solomon. No evidence of any improper conduct by the defendant need be produced; the arithmetic alone is sufficient. This comes very close to saying that a certain degree of relative bigness in a certain market—and in each case we don't know in advance what degree, or which market—is illegal per se.

Secondly, the only way for the defendant to prevent that last short step is to assume the burden of proving that he got where he is without doing anything wrong. One of the most basic principles of our law is the presumption of innocence; and in civil cases the corollary is that the burden of proof lies on the one who brings the charge. It would seem to be quite a new departure to deny the protection of these principles to large business firms as much as to anybody else.

A very similar presumptive approach can be found in other cases. For instance, the Supreme Court last June, in deciding that Continental Can had violated Section 7 of the Clayton Act by its merger with Hazel-Atlas Glass, said as follows:

> Where a merger is of such size as to be inherently suspect, elaborate proof of market structure, market behavior, and probable anticompetitive effects may be dispensed with in view of Section 7's design to prevent undue concentration.[5]

I will come back to the matter of "undue concentration" later. My point here is simply that by this decision a merged company's size alone, measured against that rather elusive thing called "relevant market," becomes the major test of legality under the antitrust laws. Whether the words used are "rebuttable presumption" or "inherently suspect," the effect is the same. A presumption of illegality is built upon what may be a rather superficial or oversimplified analysis of the facts regarding a company's market position; and from there on the defendant company must bear the burden of clearing itself of that presumption.

Naturally, such an approach can greatly simplify the administration of the antitrust laws. It seems to provide an attractive shortcut by which one may hope to avoid the rough terrain of economic facts and keep to the relatively smooth ground of simple theory and simple arithmetic. But I believe the attraction is deceptive. You don't simplify rough country merely by drawing a simple map. This is the kind of shortcut that often results in getting lost.

I believe, in fact, that behind these simplified rules there lies a number of erroneous ideas about the realities of modern business life in this country. Some of these ideas relate to the problem of bigness, or "concentration," in American industry. Others relate specifically to

5. *United States* v. *Continental Can Co.,* 378 U.S. 441, 458 (1964).

the economic effects of mergers and acquisitions. Let me now discuss briefly some of these key ideas.

To begin with, what are the facts on industrial concentration? It is widely stated in connection with the consideration of antitrust matters that concentration in American industry has been steadily increasing, so that more and more of the market is shared by fewer and fewer companies. Let's see how well founded this picture really is.

If you have followed the proceedings of the Senate Anti-Monopoly Subcommittee beginning last year, you will have noticed that economists have the greatest difficulty in agreeing on whether concentration has been increasing or not, and even on how it is to be measured. Some figures were presented suggesting an overall increase in concentration in manufacturing generally. Such figures are subject to many questions. But even if we accepted them at face value, they would not be too relevant to the question of competition, which must be judged primarily on an industry-by-industry basis.

Even when you study one industry at a time, there is no really satisfactory yardstick for the measurement of concentration. One basic reason for this, as everybody knows who has attempted such an analysis, is that you cannot define the extent of a particular industry, or of a market within which all producers are in competition with each other, without making some pretty arbitrary assumptions which very much oversimplify the actual workings of the market.

However, certain rough indications can be made. One of the most authoritative of these is a recent analysis of Census of Manufacturers' data made by the United States Census Bureau. This study covered the period 1947 to 1958. For each industry studied, the Census Bureau calculated what percent of the value of all shipments in that industry were made by the four leading firms. Out of 139 industries that were measured in this way, concentration rose between 1947 and 1958 in 61 industries, was unchanged in 12, and declined in 66. Certainly this shows no strong trend toward concentration.

But even figures such as these can overstate the so-called "rising tide" of concentration. For one thing, the "big four" in any industry do not necessarily remain the same. In fact, the Census Bureau reported that 80 percent of the industries it had studied showed a change in the list of the top four companies over the eleven-year period.

From such data as these, inadequate though they may be, it should also be clear that there is nothing irreversible about an increase in concentration in any industry. I think the record would show that most of the decreases in concentration took place not as a result of antitrust action but as a result of changes within the industry and the market—such as new products, new merchandising ideas, new technology, new investments, the entrance of new firms into the industry, and changes in management of older firms. Even a single highly successful firm cannot be sure of sewing up the market against smaller competitors—as a leading auto manufacturer discovered when its market position fell from well over 50 percent in the early 1920's to a much smaller share ever since.

Now I want to turn to a different question. Whether or not bigness has been growing or diminishing, absolutely or relatively in our economy, what are its effects where it does exist? Does it necessarily produce the bad results that are often charged against it? Does it suppress competition? Does it put the consumer and the small businessman at an unfair disadvantage? Let's consider these questions briefly.

We often hear it said, for instance, that the resources of big business give it the power of economic life and death over smaller competitors—and that this power is actually used to crush competition or inhibit its growth.

I would like to comment on this first from experience in the oil industry, with which I am most familiar. In our industry this notion does not square with the facts.

In the production of crude oil and gas, for example, the smaller, so-called independent producer has long been a major factor—and remains so today. For at least the last fifty years he has lived side by side with very large companies and has prospered. In the *Honolulu Oil* case the court said:

> There are in excess of 10,000 crude oil and gas producers, and the latest U. S. Census indicates their number is increasing. Since entry of new firms is relatively easy, there is reason to assume that this trend toward more producers will continue.[6]

We find a similar picture in the marketing end of the business. The so-called private branders have innovated in the location, design, and type of service stations, and in many new merchandising methods. As a result, in the last fifteen years private branders as a group have substantially increased their share of the market. They now sell about 23 percent of the gasoline marketed in the United States, and they have achieved this position in the face of competition from the "big, powerful companies."

If we look overseas, where the most rapid oil industry growth has been taking place, we find a similar picture. At least 75 American companies have entered oil producing outside the United States and Canada since the early 1950's. They account for nearly a tenth of all the crude oil produced in this huge area. Many of them are active in refining and marketing as well, and they are continuing to grow in the keenest competition.

6. *United States* v. *Standard Oil Co.* (*Indiana*), 1964 Trade Cas. 79841; at 79844 (N.D. Cal. July 28, 1964).

Mind you, all this has taken place in an industry which numbers among its members some of the largest companies in the world. And some of it has taken place in countries that have little or nothing in the way of antitrust laws.

Of course the oil industry is not in any sense exceptional in this respect. It is a common fact of experience, over the whole range of American industry, that smaller businesses manage to stay very much alive and prosperous—and indeed new ones are established every day—in the presence of larger competitors. One may argue that it can't be done because of the so-called "power of life and death of big business"—just as experts in aerodynamics are said to have proved that a bee cannot fly. The bee flies all the same, and the small businessman prospers, in spite of theories to the contrary.

There is also the idea that small business constitutes an "economic way of life" that is somehow inherently better than that in large firms, and hence should be preserved even at the cost of less efficiency. As Mr. Justice Harlan said in his dissenting opinion in the *Lexington Bank* case, this amounts to "a presumption that in the antitrust field good things come usually, if not always, in small packages."[7]

I have already stated my own belief that there is an enduring place in our economy and our society for small business as well as big. To me, it seems a mistake to oversimplify the world by supposing that good things come always in small packages, large packages, or any size package.

However, in view of what appears to be the present emphasis in antitrust circles, it might be helpful if I list some of the positive economic and social values that go with bigness.

1. Big manufacturing plants, up to a point, enjoy certain economies of scale which can mean lower unit costs, and lower prices to the consumer.
2. Large firms, because of the size of their financial, personnel, and physical resources, are able to engage in ventures beyond the reach of smaller firms. This was dramatically shown in many instances during World War II.
3. Because of their greater resources, large firms are often better able to withstand short-term adversity. They thus exert a stabilizing effect on both the economy and the society.
4. Large firms which are integrated vertically have the advantage of a steady, reliable flow at each stage between raw materials and retailing. This enables them to plan their expansion with greater assurance, and thus makes them a more efficient source of expansion for the whole economy.

7. *United States* v. *First Nat'l Bank & Trust Co. of Lexington*, 376 U.S. 665, 673–74 (1964).

5. Because of their greater capability to do independent research, large firms are a major source of technological progress which directly benefits the consumer in price, quality, and range of choice.

These are purely economic values. To them I think it is fair to add certain social values which, if less tangible, are no less important. Business firms, as they become more prominent and serve wider markets, abroad as well as at home, tend to become more keenly sensitive to their human environment and to their responsibilities not only to shareholders and customers but to employees, government, and the public. Regarding employees, much has been said about the supposedly colorless and automatic "organization man"—but I sincerely believe the scope for useful and highly creative effort which large firms offer to talented individuals is not exceeded in any other walk of life. Regarding the general public, I think it could be demonstrated that many large firms make purely voluntary contributions to public causes such as education, community service, health, the arts, and attention to the physical environment, which are at least proportionate to their place in the total economy.

These, then, are some of the concrete social and economic merits of large business firms. There are other merits, such as their vital importance to national security, which I do not need to belabor. It is thus no idle or empty generalization to say that large business firms in modern America are vital to the health and life of the nation. America cannot go forward unless its big businesses go forward also.

I have dwelt on this matter of bigness because I believe that only against this background can we realistically gauge the true economic and social meaning of that area which has recently been at the center of the antitrust stage—namely, mergers and acquisitions involving large firms. Such mergers are widely asserted to be harmful to the economy in a number of ways, and I would like to comment on these assertions.

First, it is said that a merger between two competitors reduces the consumer's range of choice. This is not necessarily so.

It obviously reduces the number of competitors but the range of products and services which the merged firm offers the consumer may be—and often is—wider than those of the two preceding firms. Moreover, the merged firms can often serve a wider geographic market area, thus extending consumer choice in another way.

Second, it is said that growth by merger adds nothing to the economy in the way of new investment ,whereas so-called "grass-roots" growth does add in this way. This, too, is not necessarily so. In many cases, a company has the available capital and several other ingredients of success for a new venture, but can only get some missing ingredient—such as qualified technical manpower—by acquiring another company. In such a case the merging of two companies means a new investment which would not have taken place by the "grass-roots" method.

Such a situation often leads to a so-called "conglomerate merger," in which a company diversifies by acquiring a firm in a new line of business. My lawyer friends tell me that the law on this subject has not developed far enough to show any clear trend. But some economic assumptions have appeared in writings on this subject, and in Congressional testimony, which are quite disturbing.

For instance, it is asserted that a diversified company will use profits from one line of endeavor to subsidize its new venture, and thereby undersell and drive out of business its smaller competitors. This assertion shows a poor knowledge of business methods. If a businessman sells below cost for an extended period of time, he will simply lose money—and he will get little consolation from having driven some other firm from the field. If, on the other hand, after putting his competitors out of business he raises prices and sits back to enjoy his monopoly, new competitors will very quickly come into the market under the "umbrella" of his high prices.

Such tactics, therefore, are self-defeating. A good businessman will not diversify into a new field, by merger or otherwise, until careful studies have shown him that he can compete profitably with already established companies in that field. He may provide some financial assistance for a period while the new endeavor is getting on its feet, but he will certainly not plan to run a subsidized operation on a continuing basis. If his new venture doesn't begin to pay out after a reasonable time, he should and probably will get rid of it.

Actually, corporate diversification in the past has served to enhance competition—and I am sure will continue to do so. No company today can confidently look upon today's established competitors as being its only competitors in the future. Tomorrow their ranks may be joined by others now in wholly unrelated industries. If new competitors do enter, by acquisition or otherwise, it will be only because they think in the long run they can market a better product, or sell at a lower price—and make a profit by doing so. Our nation's economic growth ought not to be deprived of these benefits, as they are vital to a dynamic economy.

We should remember, too, still another way in which mergers stimulate economic growth. Quite often a small businessman will start a new venture in the expectation that if it flourishes, and for some reason he does not choose to stay in that business, he can sell out at a profit. If he sees this ultimate "right of exit" endangered by anti-merger decisions, he is likely to become a good deal less venturesome.

So much for the arguments against mergers from the standpoint of the consumer and of the growth of the economy. Now what about the argument that mergers—at least those involving large firms—are inherently harmful to competition?

Obviously, in a so-called "horizontal" merger some competition is lost—namely, that between the merged firms. But competition is not such a simple matter. As I have already mentioned, what is lost in this respect may be more than made up by the enhanced ability of the merged firm to compete with a larger rival or in a larger market area. When we consider the steady tendencies of market areas to widen with the advance of transportation, communications, automatic data processing, and consequent management control, this point is a most material one.

Such are some of the realities which I fear have not been given their due weight in the recent consideration of mergers under the anti-trust laws. Indeed, so narrow a legal test for mergers has evolved that no sizable company can safely hope to grow by the merger route if this is likely to cause any but the most insignificant increase, horizontally or vertically, in that company's position in the industry. This is true regardless of any benefits which the contemplated merger might bring to our economy or our society.

Before I conclude, let me look at this whole subject for a moment in a longer historical perspective.

When the Sherman Act became law 75 years ago, there was genuine alarm in this country because of rapidly growing concentrations of industrial and financial power such as had never been seen before in history. This new power was virtually unhampered by legal restraints. There was no corporate or personal income tax, no regulation of the stock market, no publication of annual reports, no strong labor movement, little legal protection for employees, and only the early beginning of any sort of governmental regulation of any industry. One of the main fears across the nation was not just that monopolies would charge high prices, but that they would become new centers of unfettered political power—big enough, perhaps, to overshadow the government itself.

Even today, in some minds, this kind of fear seems to linger. But the reality behind it disappeared generations ago. The bigness of American industry today is hemmed about by big government and big labor; by taxes, regulation, legislation, judicial decrees, and unremitting publicity. Its size is no more than proportionate to the growth in size of all our national institutions—and of our national responsibilities abroad. Far from being a threat to freedom, bigness is one of the practical conditions of freedom in the modern world.

It seems to me thoroughly unrealistic to look at our nation, our population, the size of our government, the increase in consumer buying power, the forward sweep of our technology, the size and complexity of all our national and international problems, and not expect to see our business corporations—which are as vital to our American society and economy and national strength as any other factor—also growing and expanding greatly.

At the outset of these remarks I suggested that, to bring the law into harmony with modern business realities, especially in the field of mergers and acquisitions, this whole segment of our antitrust laws needs a new look. The perspective of history, I believe, supports this idea. During these same 75 years, many of our American concepts in other matters of great consequence, such as social welfare and civil rights, have changed and developed. What was progressive yesterday may today become an obstacle to progress. May this not be equally true in the field of antitrust law?

If such a new look were to take place, I have no preconceived notion what action would result, nor would I presume to advise a group of distinguished antitrust lawyers in this respect. Specifically, I have no present view as to whether there ought to be changes in the law, or only in the way in which the present laws are interpreted and applied.

To be sure, when we compare some voluminous antitrust decisions with the very brief and general language of the statutes from which they are derived, it might seem wise to have more—and more realistic—statutory guidance for the executive branch and the courts. Just as one example, did Congress really intend that a merger which creates a certain arithmetical share of the market, in a certain category of products or services, in a certain geographic area, should be regarded almost automatically as being tantamount to a forbidden monopoly? Where the intention of Congress was not completely clear, it has been necessary to make assumptions. The situation is a little like Mark Twain's description of the prehistoric skeleton in the museum: "Three bones and two tons of plaster." Perhaps we could get along with less plaster if Congress saw fit to supply more bones.

I am not, however, going so far as to join the advocates of new legislation, because I realize the perils of legislating in this highly complex area. We could well find ourselves worse off than before—and by "we" I mean the entire country. But if those who are qualified in this field of law were to conclude that new legislation is the only way to cure the present situation, I for one would be willing to run the risk.

Whatever the means adopted, the end we seek is of vital importance to the whole nation. It is no less than the adaptation of our national antitrust policy to the realities of the modern world, and to America's aspirations for future growth and future greatness. You, as antitrust lawyers, can render a most important service by applying your influence and your knowledge to that end.

United Brands Company

Ron: Do you remember when I was telling you about that aircraft company which paid a million and a half dollars to some government official in Africa just to sell three planes? You said that kind of money was not believable.

Bob: Yeah. What about it?

Ron: Well, here's a news article which states United Brands Company is willing to pay out two and a half million dollars to a Honduras government official just to keep the tax on bananas down.

Bob: I saw that; there is nothing illegal about that part. United Brands just failed to tell the owners, the stockholders. Did your aircraft company report their payoff? I'll bet they didn't.

Ron: As far as I know, they didn't; but they went about it in a different way. They have agents in Africa, and they paid the agents the necessary funds under various headings—including unusual business expense. The agents then gave a dash or a bribe to the right party, and suddenly the sales agreement was signed. Since the agents are independent entities, the aircraft company has to report only its transactions with them.

Bob: So, that makes it all right?

Ron: Well, it's not illegal; they've met the SEC requirements. Look, if you want to do business with these developing countries you have to give the dash. If you don't, some other company will get the business. In the case of the aircraft company, a foreign competitor was in there trying to get the sale. In the aircraft business, it's very important to get in on the ground floor to get repeat sales. And don't forget that a large chunk of our foreign credits come from the sale of aircraft, aircraft parts, and aircraft technical assistance. Besides, the dash is included in the price, so it doesn't cost the stockholders a penny.

Bob: I understand what you are saying, Ron, but I am having trouble with the concept that it is not illegal. Then I wonder if this way of doing business is not going to backfire. And finally I wonder if it is morally right.

Ron: Okay, let's look at this from the standpoint of morals. We must not try to impose our moral standards on another culture. What may be considered immoral to us may be very acceptable behavior in some other country. For instance, custom officials in some of the Asian countries feel payments made directly to them is part of their take-home pay.

Bob: I don't agree with you, Ron. I must admit, however, the practice of the pay-off is rather widespread. I also understand that there is often some coercion involved. Dorsey of Gulf Oil Company allegedly testified before the Securities and Exchange Commission that if the company had not paid a demanded $200,000 that their $150 million investment would have been in jeopardy. And then there is the Ashland Oil Company which was supposed to have made payments to win oil concessions. That was not coercion, however, just an attempt to get a concession which would not be given to them without the payment. Where is all this leading?

Ron: One thing seems to be quite clear. The system of bribes, pay-offs, consultants' fees, the dash or whatever you want to call it was working very well until the SEC disclosures.

Bob: Let me make one more remark, and then I'll quit. You can say this is necessary—it's the way of doing business; we shouldn't impose our moral standards on others—and yet in the final analysis, the pay-off is neither coming out of the pocket of the corporation nor of the foreign government; it's coming out of the pocket of the peasant, the little guy. The one and a half million dollars added to the price of the aircraft could have been used for roads, schools, or hospitals. The seven million dollar reduction in export revenue in Honduras is a loss to the Hondurian peasant. In that way, it's immoral.

Ron: Okay, Bob, I agree with you. That is not the way to do business. However, as a stockholder of this aircraft company, I would approve of the pay-off. If my company didn't make the pay-off, a competitor would. And United Brands was spending two and a half million dollars to get a seven million dollar reduction in export tax. If you want to do business with these countries, you have to make the pay-off.

J. C. Penney Company (A)

James Cash Penney opened his first retail dry goods store in Kemmerer, Colorado, in 1902, under the banner of the Golden Rule Store. Penney believed the golden rule principles should govern not only man's personal relationships with others but also the conduct of business.[1] Kemmerer was a mining town, and by previous practice the miners made most purchases on credit; thus they were continuously in debt to the company store. James Penney, contrary to advice, established a policy of cash-and-carry and no credit. On this basis he grossed $29,000 the first year.

Company policies were adopted that interpreted the golden rule in terms of the Penney Company's operation:

1. to serve the public, as nearly as we can, to its entire satisfaction;
2. to expect for the service we render a fair remuneration and not all the profit the traffic will bear;
3. to do all in our power to pack the customer's dollar full of quality, value and satisfaction;
4. to continue to train ourselves and our associates so that the service we give will be more and more intelligently performed;
5. to constantly improve the human factor in our business;
6. to reward the men and women of our organization through participation in what the business produces; and
7. to test our every policy, method, and act in this wise: Does it square with what is right and just? [2]

In the next 55 years, the original one-man Golden Rule Store expanded under the name of J. C. Penney Company into a chain of 1,694 stores and 35,000 employees. In 1957 Penney's was ranked number five in the retail chains with sales of $1.3 billion. (See Exhibit 1.) All through this growth period, the cash-and-carry policy remained in effect.

However, in 1957, a decision was made to experiment with consumer credit. The president of Penney was quoted as saying when

1. *Annual Report*, 1956.
2. *Ibid.*

asked why the switchover: "It's not at all like the days when my family couldn't get credit because they couldn't pay. Today credit is a mark of character." [3] Actually there was no intention of an immediate and major switchover to credit; the switchover would be one of experimentation. One of the Penney executives remarked on the general feeling within the company: "Someday we may want to get into the banking business. But until we do, it is nice to know that we can be just retailers and stand on our own two feet at that." [4]

As a result of the favorable credit experience in the pilot run, the J. C. Penney Company in 1959 reversed its long-standing cash-and-carry policy and decided to have all stores extend credit by 1963. The installation was accelerated so that by March of 1962, the total company-wide credit system was completed, and by the year's end there were over four million active accounts.

CREDIT CORPORATION

In April of 1964, the J. C. Penney Credit Corporation was formed as a wholly owned subsidiary with an initial capital investment of $50 million. The objective of the corporation was to finance the credit sales of the J. C. Penney Company. It did this by buying customer receivables from the parent company.

In July of 1964, the corporation sold $50 million of 4½ percent, 20-year debentures to the public. These proceeds were used to buy additional receivables from the Penney Company and also to reduce the short-term borrowing. From April through the end of the fiscal year, the Credit Corporation purchased receivables worth $614,039,-023 from the parent organization. Earnings after taxes of $1,185,000 amounted to $1,193,053. These net earnings were included in the reported earnings of the Company.

In 1965 the total receivables purchased rose to $775,852,543, followed in 1966 by a jump to $987,536,909. In 1967 the total receivables purchased went over the $1 billion mark.

Credit Corporation
Net Earnings

1964	$1,193,053
1965	2,824,736
1966	5,723,143
1967	6,500,000

3. *Forbes*, September 15, 1957.
4. *Ibid.*, November 1, 1958.

The income source of the Credit Corporation was from monthly charges to J. C. Penney Company to cover fixed charges, mainly interest on borrowings. In July, 1967, the equity of the Penney Company in the Credit Corporation was $81 million. This included retained earnings.

The 1967 *Annual Report* made the following statement about the Credit Corporation:

> The earnings of the Credit Corporation bear no relationship to the net cost of credit operations of the Penney Company. The parent bears its own cost of administering its retail credit program. Also, the parent, rather than the subsidiary, receives the service charges paid on customer accounts. Credit operations of the parent have not reached the break-even point.

Exhibit 2 shows the increase in credit sales as a percent of total sales from 1958 through 1967.

CONGRESSIONAL HEARINGS

In 1960 Senator Paul Douglas headed a committee that conducted hearings concerning the truth in lending in business. Part of the hearings were devoted to the rates and advertising practices used in connection with revolving credit accounts. After Senator Paul Douglas was defeated in his reelection bid, Senator Proxmire headed the committee and continued the investigation.

In January, 1967, the chairman of the board of J. C. Penney Company, William Batten, requested to testify before this committee concerning the advertising of the interest rates of the revolving credit accounts. The following is part of the testimony as quoted in the *Congressional Record:*

From *Congressional Record* of January 31, 1967
STATEMENT OF WILLIAM M. BATTEN,
CHAIRMAN OF THE BOARD,
J. C. PENNEY COMPANY

Senator Proxmire: Our next witness is Mr. William Batten, chairman of the board of one of the greatest merchandising institutions of the nation, and certainly one of the most important elements in the state of Wisconsin.

Mr. Batten: Thank you, Senator Proxmire.

Senator Proxmire: I have no account, strictly a cash customer.

Mr. Batten: That shows you how poor we are.

> At the outset, I wish to make it clear that I am not here today as a representative of retailing as a whole. I represent solely the J. C. Penney Company, and my statement will be based entirely upon Penney credit policies and practices.

> The Penney Company has asked for this opportunity to appear because we feel that there are particular aspects of our credit program which should be called to the attention of the committee, and which should be useful in your deliberations.

As you may know, the Penney Company is a relative newcomer in the field of consumer credit. We sold merchandise on a strictly cash basis from 1902 until our first credit card was issued in 1958. We were literally forced into the credit business by consumers who made it clear that they wanted the convenience of in-store credit and that if we didn't provide it for them, they would shop elsewhere.

When we made the move, therefore, we naturally sought to install the type of credit that we felt would be attractive to customers who wanted to buy on credit—and at the same time would be fair to all our customers. With no credit traditions or inheritances, we were in a position to study the various types of credit plans and choose what we believed would best serve the needs of our customers and also be consistent with the policies which built our company.

After considerable study, we installed as our basic credit plan what we call our regular charge account. This is a revolving account with option terms which is designed for our customers' normal recurring purchasing.

There was another consideration in our choice of revolving credit —the computer. Naturally, we wanted the customer's credit card to be honored in all 1,700 Penney stores. Looking ahead, we could see considerable difficulties involved in servicing such a nationwide network of charge accounts. We found that revolving credit is ideally suited to a high volume, electronically processed system.

We are now processing over 12 million of these regular charge accounts—more than American Express, Diner's Club, and Carte Blanche combined—in 11 computer locations.

Perhaps it is this adaptability to automation which causes some observers to regard revolving credit as the fastest growing type of consumer credit and, certainly, the credit plan most likely to be used in the future. Obviously, that is our own prediction as well. Subsequently, when we installed a time-payment account for the purchase of major appliances, furniture, and similar items, this account was also put on a revolving basis. This account extends payments over a longer period of time and thus provides lower monthly payments for this type of merchandise.

We have 260,000 of these accounts with total balance of about $40 million, compared to $400 million in regular charge account balances.

In addition, we offer a specialized plan for the purchase of motor bikes and scooters in order to meet requirements of certain state laws. This plan is inconsequential in number of accounts and total balances.

My remarks are going to deal with our regular charge account, because it is our most important form of customer credit. So let me explain how this account works.

With her Penney credit card, a customer can charge purchases in any of the 1,700 Penney stores across the United States or from our catalog. Each month she receives a consolidated statement of her account from the regional credit office nearest her home.

When she receives her statement each month, our customer makes a choice as to how she wishes to pay her account. She can use the account as a 30-day account by paying the balance in full. In this event, she does not pay any service charge.

If the customer wishes, she can spread the payment over two or more months by making a partial payment on the account. She can pay whatever amount she chooses, provided it is at least equal to the minimum payment (which is approximately 10 percent of the balance due, but not less than $10). In the event she chooses these "option terms," a service charge is added to her next billing. This flexibility in choosing her method of payment is one of the important reasons for the widespread acceptance of the regular charge account by our customers.

In addition, the terms are simple and easy to understand. The customer makes her own choice as to the method of payment that best suits her family's budget—and she makes that choice each time she receives a statement.

Furthermore, no special arrangement or paper work is required to select or change the terms of payment—this is accomplished automatically by the amount of her payment.

Now this flexibility in selecting the method of payment makes it impossible to predict how any given customer will pay her account. Because this prediction cannot be made, it is impossible to know in advance the amount of service charge the customer will pay—or even if she will pay any service charge.

(In practice, we collect about 20 percent of our total outstanding balances each month.)

Because a customer can choose how she wishes to pay, we find that the actual service charges paid by customers range from zero percent to slightly less than 18 percent expressed as an annual rate. Thus it is impossible to advise our customers in advance what the true—or even approximate—annual rate of their service charges will be. This is the first point I wish to make.

Now there is another feature of our revolving credit plan that I want to make sure you understand. This concerns the method of calculating the service charge.

There are two methods in general use for making these calculations in revolving credit plans. One is the "beginning balance" method, whereby the service charge is computed on the beginning balance. The second is the "adjusted balance" method, whereby the service charge is computed on the beginning balance less all payments and credits during the period. The Penney regular charge account uses the adjusted balance method.

These two methods produce a different amount of service charge for a given account. Thus, the cost of credit will be different—both in total dollars and expressed as an annual percentage rate—between a revolving account using the opening balance and one using the adjusted balance method.

I would emphasize that these calculations cannot be made or approximated in advance—they can only be made after the fact. In all cases, however, use of the adjusted balance method will produce a lower charge to the customer.

This leads me to my second point—that any method for disclosing the cost of credit must permit the customer to understand that there is a difference in cost to her in choosing between a revolving account using the beginning balance method and one using the adjusted balance method.

Now let me illustrate this point with an example. If you will turn to the next page of my testimony, you will find a table showing the transactions in an actual Penney regular charge account during a 3-month period. This statement is representative of millions of our accounts and, we believe, fairly illustrates how service charges are applied. (See Table 1.)

On the left-hand side of the table is indicated the date of each transaction. In the first column—column A—are listed the purchases made by this customer.

On November 29, for example, you will note that she charged a purchase of $5.46. On December 4 she made a purchase of $17.45, and later in December and January she made several more purchases.

The next column—column B—lists the payments made by this customer. As you can see, she paid $10 on her account on November 9, another $10 on December 11, and a similar payment on January 26. Each of these payments was in accordance with the terms of her agreement with us. On December 30, you will note a credit of $8.98 for merchandise returned by the customer.

Column C contains the beginning balance of the account at the start of each billing period. On November 2, her statement showed an amount of $28.91—which was the balance carried forward from the previous month. The balances carried forward in subsequent months are shown below this in column C.

Column D shows the "adjusted balance" on which service charges were calculated. For the month of November, this adjusted balance of $18.91 was calculated by taking the opening balance on November 2 of $28.91 and subtracting the payment on November 9 of $10.

In column E is shown the service charge of $0.28 which was computed by multiplying the adjusted balance of $18.91 by the monthly rate of 1½ percent.

At the bottom of column E is shown the total service charges to the account during the 3-month period: $0.88.

Underneath that figure are indicated the effective annual percentage rates—which could only be calculated after the fact.

For November, the effective rate was 15.6 percent; for December, 2.9 percent; for January, 11.5 percent; and for the 3-month period, 9.5 percent.

The next two columns, columns F and G, show how service charges would be applied to this account under the "beginning balance" method.

The difference is that the service charge is calculated on the balance which opens each billing period, as shown in column F. No credit is given for payments and returned merchandise before the service charge is applied.

At the bottom of column G is the total of the service charges: $1.47. The effective annual percentage rates—again computed after the fact—are November, 24 percent; December, 12 percent; January, 15 percent; and for the 3 months, 15.7 percent.

Table 1

A representative Penney charge account showing a comparison of service charges computed by the adjusted balance and beginning balance methods

Date	Purchases (A)	Payments (B)	Adjusted balance method			Beginning balance method	
			Beginning balance (C)	Adjusted balance (D)	Service charge * (E)	Beginning Balance (F)	Service charge (G)
Nov. 2			$28.91			$28.91	
Nov. 9		$10.00					
Nov. 29	$ 5.46			$18.91	$ .28		$ .43
Dec. 2			24.65			24.80	
Dec. 4	17.45	10.00					
Dec. 11		10.00					
Dec. 22	4.00						
Dec. 28	2.98						
Dec. 30	13.90	**8.98		5.67	.09	44.52	.37
Jan. 2			44.09				
Jan. 12	15.53						
Jan. 26		10.00		34.09	.51		.67
Total service charges					.88		1.47
Effective annual percentage rate:							
November					15.6		24.0
December					2.9		12.0
January					11.5		15.0
For the 3-month period					9.5		15.7

* Service charge computed at a monthly rate of 1½ percent.
** Credit for returned merchandise.
Source: Penny Account No. 010–002–541–02, November 1965—January 1966.

In this example, the difference in total service charges between the adjusted balance and the beginning balance methods is $.59, and the difference in effective annual percentage rates for the 3-month period is 6.2 percent. Thus it is clear that the "adjusted balance" method costs the customer less than the "beginning balance" method.

The first state law which requires a statement of the annual rate of revolving credit charges is the Massachusetts statute, the provisions of which I know are under study by this committee.

Now, the account which we have just been examining belongs to one of our Massachusetts customers. Under the statute in that state she must be told that she is being charged 18 percent on her account.

If she had a similar account someplace else where the beginning balance method were used, she would also be told that she was being charged 18 percent on that account.

This account—which is representative of millions of other similar accounts—illustrates the two points which I have previously made:

First, that it is impossible to advise our customers in advance what the true, or even approximate, annual rate of their service charges will be on revolving accounts. As you have seen from the example, the actual charge under that customer's Penney plan was 9.5 percent. But Massachusetts law requires us, as would S. 5 as presently drafted, to tell her that her rate is 18 percent.

Second, that any method for disclosing the cost of credit must permit the customer to understand that there is a difference in cost to her in choosing between a revolving account using the beginning balance method and one using the adjusted balance method.

As shown in the example, the dollar cost and the actual annual rate are considerably different under the two plans. Yet the Massachusetts law requires, as would S. 5 as presently drafted, that both the adjusted balance account and the beginning balance account be disclosed as costing 18 percent annually.

Because the Massachusetts law prevents us from stating the truth to our customers, we decided to examine some of our Massachusetts accounts to see just how much of an untruth we are being forced to tell.

Although it was laborious, we took a random sampling of our active Massachusetts accounts and, going back over a year's time, computed the actual annual rates charged on these accounts.

Based on our use of the adjusted balance method, we knew in advance that none of our Massachusetts customers was paying 18 percent. Also, we knew that some customers were paying no service charge because they paid off their balances completely before any service charge was levied.

But, of those who did pay service charges, the annual rates calculated in this study ranged between a low of .8 percent and a high of 17.1 percent, and the average was 10.5 percent.

We have a report from Peat, Marwick, Livingston & Co., Boston, the statistical affiliate of our public accounting firm, attesting to the validity of these figures.

Once we had verified that we were required to mislead our customers to such a great extent, we decided that it was time to tell them the truth. We prepared an ad, to be run in Massachusetts papers, which would explain to our customers our full credit philosophy and tell them they were not paying 18 percent, even though the law required us to say so. A copy of this ad is attached to your copy of my remarks, and I shall read it to you.

The heading says:

ONE HUNDRED PERCENT DOWN AND NOTHING
A MONTH FOR THE REST OF YOUR LIFE

Try to beat those credit terms.

For many years, there was no other way to buy things at Penney's. Cash is Mr. James Cash Penney's middle name. It is the way he and his partners built the business.

But as business grew, things changed. The economy changed. People's needs changed—and their wants. And Penney's changed to meet them.

When our customers wanted us to build stores in their suburban shopping centers, we built them. When they wanted us to sell more different kinds of goods, we sold them. And when they asked us for credit, we gave them credit.

Our credit policy. Credit is a convenience. It costs money. Who should pay for it? The Penney way is to charge only the people who use it.

We believe that's the fair way—fair to our cash customers, fair to our charge customers, and fair to our 52,000 stockholders, the owners of Penney's.

(Right now, we have to tell our owners that we are losing slightly on our credit operation. We are working to solve this problem, by increasing our efficiency. Our objective is to break even.)

Our credit rates. To cover (almost) the cost of credit, we must make a monthly service charge of 1.5 percent. What does this amount to annually? An often-published figure is 18 percent a year, obtained by multiplying the monthly rate by twelve. This rate seems as high to us as it must to you.

Fortunately, when we studied Penney charge accounts, we found not one of our charge customers paying an annual rate that high. We were encouraged to find that our average charge account customer is paying 10.5 percent per year, which is considerably lower than 18 percent. Many of our customers, by making larger monthly payments, pay around 6 percent, which is better. Some pay nothing, which is better yet.

How to pay no service charge. If you can possibly pay the complete balance of your Penney charge account within the initial 30-day billing period, you pay no service charge, none at all. We know, of course, this isn't always easy. But it certainly is the most economical.

There is a way we save you money that very few people realize. We compute the service charge after you make your payment instead of before. For example, if you receive a bill for $100 and you make a payment of $10, your next bill will call for 1.5 percent of $90 instead of the full $100. This is not everybody's way, but it is the Penney way.

On your Penney charge account, the faster you pay off your balance, the less you pay. (Our Time Payment Account, a different type of credit plan allowing up to three years to pay for major purchases, is computed the conventional way, on the beginning balance. But any month you pay your balance in full within 30 days, you pay no service charge for that month.)

Our business is today. We confess we think a bit nostalgically about "the good old days" when life was a little simpler, perhaps, and everyone paid cash for the things they bought at Penney's. We'd certainly have fewer corporate headaches if they still did today.

But living in the past is the certain way to suicide in retailing. Stores that fail to keep up with the times end up in bankruptcy court. Our business is today.

We recognize that the proper use of credit plays an important part in today's economy. It has helped make our standard of living the envy of the world. It allows people to enjoy a better, more satisfying life much earlier than if first they had to save for it.

Some people find it very difficult to save. For them, credit can provide a form of systematic savings. Other people use credit simply to avoid carrying cash. They pay their bills within 30 days and the service costs them nothing.

Our advice to customers who ask us is the same advice we give our own families. Go into credit carefully, with eyes wide open to what it costs. Don't take more time to pay than you really need. And, above all, keep it in perspective. Credit is a convenience and a service. It should be used to help solve problems, not create them. Thank you.

Our attorneys have advised us that we cannot run this ad in Massachusetts. It would violate the Truth in Lending Act, which prohibits any statement in advertising other than the one prescribed by the law. In other words, the law requires us to lie to our customers and then prevents us from telling them that we cannot tell them the truth.

To us, this entire situation is intolerable, and we are, therefore, challenging the law in the Massachusetts courts. At the conclusion of this statement, I shall supply the committee with copies of our bill of complaint initiaiting this action.

Let me recapitulate for you. We in the Penney Company are convinced that revolving credit is the credit system of the present and the future because of widespread customer preference and operating efficiency. We strongly urge that this committee recognize that revolving credit charges cannot be annualized—they simply do not lend themselves to such a treatment.[5]

5. The *Congressional Record* (January 31, 1967).

Exhibit 1

J. C. Penney Company
Financial Review 1948–1957
Before the Introduction of Credit Sales

Year	1957	1956	1955	1954	1953
Sales	$1,312,278,407	1,291,867,267	1,220,085,325	1,107,156,633	1,109,507,674
Credit Sales % Total Sales	—	—	—	—	—
Net Income	49,410,891	46,780,721	46,139,608	43,616,938	38,472,932
Per Share Results					
Net Income	2.00	1.89	1.85	1.80	1.56
Dividends	1.42	1.42	1.32	1.17	1.17
Customer Receivables					
J. C. Penney Credit Corporation	—	—	—	—	—
J. C. Penney Company	—	—	—	—	—
Number of Stores					
Stores	1,694	1,687	1,666	1,644	1,634
Catalog sales centers	—	—	—	—	—

Year	1952	1951	1950	1949	1948
Sales	1,079,256,505	1,035,201,519	949,711,735	880,200,216	885,195,136
Credit Sales % Total Sales	—	—	—	—	—
Net Income	37,170,071	33,465,139	44,930,816	41,792,675	47,753,929
Per Share Results					
Net Income	1.51	1.36	1.82	1.69	1.93
Dividends	1.17	1.08	1.17	1.00	0.83
Customer Receivables					
J. C. Penney Credit Corporation	—	—	—	—	—
J. C. Penney Company	—	—	—	—	—
Number of Stores					
Stores	1,632	1,621	1,612	1,607	1,601
Catalog sales centers	—	—	—	—	—

DECISIONS INVOLVING PUBLIC RESPONSIBILITY

Exhibit 2
J. C. Penney Company
Financial Review 1958–1967
After the Introduction of Credit Sales

Year*	1967	1966	1965	1964	1963
Sales	$2,745,997,581	2,549,361,688	2,289,209,426	2,079,425,668	1,834,317,527
Credit Sales % Total Sales	37.6	35.1	33.1	30.3	27.6
Net Income	89,549,746	79,059,029	78,898,254	68,271,402	55,292,198
Per Share Results**					
Net Income	3.59	3.17	3.16***	2.74	2.22
Dividends	1.80	1.72½	1.72½	1.50	1.50
Customer Receivables (net)					
J. C. Penney Credit Corporation	483,244,496	439,941,357	298,672,486	187,998,214	—
J. C. Penney Company	13,508,663	12,439,346	62,961,474	101,080,971	224,789,049
Number of Stores					
Stores	1,664	1,661	1,669	1,676	1,680
Catalog sales centers	637	565	458	405	146

Exhibit 2

(con)

Year*	1962	1961	1960	1959	1958
Sales	1,701,332,645	1,553,505,660	1,468,917,982	1,437,489,357	1,409,972,649
Credit Sales % Total Sales	24.7	17.1	8.5	2.8	.3
Net Income	54,804,070	51,738,552	44,994,095	51,523,734	46,876,831
Per Share Results**					
Net Income	2.20	2.10	1.82	2.09	1.90
Dividends	1.50	1.50	1.50	1.35	1.42
Customer Receivables (net)					
J. C. Penney Credit Corporation . . .	—	—	—	—	—
J. C. Penney Company	168,659,516	97,722,383	52,208,936	19,393,451	2,658,177
Number of Stores					
Stores	1,685	1,636	1,695	1,683	1,687
Catalog sales centers	21	—	—	—	—

* Years 1965 through 1967 are 52-week periods ended on the last Saturday in January of the subsequent year; 1959 through 1964 are fiscal years ended January 31 of the subsequent year; and 1958 is the 13-month period ended January 31, 1959.

** Income before federal taxes for 1965 excludes gain on sale of headquarters building. This net gain of $2,840,865 (11 cents per share) is included in net income.

*** Prior years adjusted for 3 for 1 split in May, 1960.

DECISIONS INVOLVING PUBLIC RESPONSIBILITY

J. C. Penney Company (B)

The following is a continuation of the testimony of William M. Batten, chairman of the board of J. C. Penney Company, before the Congressional hearings on Truth in Lending—January 31, 1967:

Senator Proxmire: Let me also say at this point that Ken McLean has prepared, and I have edited and gone over it, an analysis of your revolving account that you presented us with this morning and an analysis of each one of the examples you gave. I think Ken shows very effectively that they are 18 percent, 18 percent, 18 percent in every single case. The reason is a difference in assumptions. The whole case, it seems to me, revolves around whose assumptions are the most reasonable, the most practical, and the most appropriate.

Your assumption is that you should count the entire free ride. In other words, if a customer comes in and buys on the first of the month, you bill him at the end of the month and it is not due until 30 days after he is billed, if it is a 30-day month. You calculate the interest from the point of purchase. I would do so from the day the revolving charge runs against the customer.

Now let me ask you this: You do have, I presume, thousands and thousands of customers throughout the country. Perhaps 50, perhaps 30, perhaps 60 percent, but a large proportion of your customers take advantage of this and pay in full before the time expires, before the bill is due, that is before the end of the month, so they incur no service charge at all. Is that correct?

Mr. Batten: That is right.

Senator Proxmire: Obviously you are carrying these customers along. They are getting credit for nothing. In other words, you have to tie up your money, you have to bill them, you have to go through various cost activities that you wouldn't have to incur if they simply paid cash. So that there is a credit cost involved here, isn't this correct?

Mr. Batten: That is right. It costs money, Senator Proxmire, if you mean to put their name on the books and process their account, yes.

Senator Proxmire: Much of the same cost, although not quite as much, as you would have if they took advantage of the revolving credit. For these credit customers who pay before the end of the time and therefore incur no charge, how is this cost charged?

This is charged, as I understand it, to the cost of your goods. But your prices are not necessarily higher because you are able to sell more goods because you have this. You have greater volume. You have a profit

335

against which you can charge the additional credit costs which you have. It is good business.

Mr. Batten: The charge for carrying those accounts goes in as a part of our total charge for credit.

Senator Proxmire: Up to this point you have a situation in which, if everybody paid on time, and you had nobody who exceeded the time, you would have a situation in which you were promoting free credit, charge accounts, with no revolving credit. The situation is that everybody paid on time.

At this point we get into the revolving account problem. The customer who decides that he will take advantage of your revolving account and pay a minimum, as I understand it, of $10, or 10 percent, whichever is the less, can then take advantage of the revolving account and be extended further credit. On this he must pay 1½ percent per year.

Mr. Batten: A month.

Senator Proxmire: I beg your pardon. One and a half percent per month. And if we calculate what his particular problem is, that is, calculate the difference between taking advantage of this free ride on the one hand and then borrowing money or taking money out of this savings account, or going along with the Penney revolving credit, it would seem that the fair comparison would be whether or not he can get money at less than 18 percent a year. Is this not correct?

Mr. Batten: Senator Proxmire, I think you put your finger on the difference in the viewpoints at the beginning, because it starts from the assumptions that we make. Our view is, you mentioned, we live in the world of reality and we do. We can't live in our business in a world of theory. We live in this hard world of reality.

Senator Proxmire: What is unreal about the question I asked?

Mr. Batten: What I am trying to say is that the first decision point the customer makes, if I could go just through the transaction, is when she decides to buy the merchandise. At that point the salesperson will typically ask is this a charge sale or cash sale. We have all been through that. At that point if it is something that she wants to charge, then it becomes at that point a charge sale. This is no longer a cash sale.

In other words, we have either the money at the time, making it a cash sale, or it is a charge sale at that point.

Senator Proxmire: It is a charge sale but not a credit sale.

Mr. Batten: It is a credit sale at that point.

Senator Proxmire: It is not a credit sale in the sense that any service charge is involved. I repeat no service charge is involved, none, unless he fails to pay at the end of the billing period.

Mr. Batten: It is a sale under our plan which has options as far as the customer is concerned about what she is going to do. At that point we don't know and maybe she may not even know to what extent she is going to exercise the option. At that point we have made a sale under our regular charge account and it is going to go in her account.

In other words, we are extending her credit from the point that she makes the purchase.

As I understand your concept, and perhaps I don't understand it, you are willing to fragment our plan into two parts. The first part is sort of a cash sale, and then the credit sale only starts at the point where she has an option.

Senator Proxmire: I don't want to fragment it at all. I want it exactly the way you do, which is that there is no interest charge, there is no service charge invoked, provided they pay within 30 days of the billing period.

Mr. Batten: The fact that she has these options—and I think they are rather well understood and I won't repeat them—the very fact that she has those options in our view reduces to her the cost of credit when and as she does exercise the option.

Senator Proxmire: If it does, it means she has no cost of credit at all until she exceeds the one month 30-day period during which her bill is due. After that she incurs 18 percent. After that, and at that point, she can decide whether she wants, as I say, to take it out of the savings account or borrow it elsewhere. This is the kind of information that is most meaningful to her certainly.

And furthermore you have control, or do you not have control?

Mr. Batten: In what way?

Senator Proxmire: Of the billing period. You can provide, if you wish to do so, No. 1, that the charge should run from the purchase period, or—this would be unusual but you could do this; this is optional, open to merchants if they wish to do this—you could provide that it run from the first of the month following the purchase, but you have instead decided, because it increases your sales, not to make the charge until the end of the month following the period of purchase.

You have the control. She has the option. And it would be more meaningful to her, it would seem to me, if she could decide at the point when she incurs the service charge whether she wants to borrow or use the Penney service charge.

Mr. Batten: In our case, if she knows what the balance is, and she does, and she knows what the service charge will be. We are disclosing. If the attempt here is to disclose the credit cost, that is being covered.

Senator Proxmire: That is exactly right. You see what this bill tries to do—and what the Massachusetts law tries to do, as I understand it—is to provide that you will have a meaningful, comparative rate. You don't have a meaningful comparison without the annual rate. If you have a monthly rate, there is no way she can compare this with her savings. She might be earning a 4½ percent annual rate in her savings and loan account. Obviously, it might be a good idea under these circumstances to draw money from her savings and loan account, pay it off, and not incur the 18 percent service charge.

On the other hand, maybe she hasn't got a savings and loan account and can't borrow at less than 18 percent. In that case it could be wise to borrow from revolving credit.

Mr. Batten: The point I would make again, and I will try not to make it any more, is that the customer is being extended credit from the time of purchase under this regular plan. She has certain options regarding the amount she will pay, when she will pay it, and the days when there will be no service charge.

The fact that those options are in there, in this total plan, this is one plan; the fact that they are in there reduces the net cost of credit to this customer under our plan. The very fact that those options are in there. And she can take advantage of them.

Senator Proxmire: You see, there are thousands and thousands of other customers who will never pay a nickel of service charge and get free credit. To put her on a comparable basis so that she can make up her mind whether or not to take advantage of the service charge, the only meaningful information would be to provide what the rate is once she goes over the end of the month following the period of purchase. At that point is the only point when she has a relevant choice. Up to that point it is obviously smarter not to borrow money because she is getting her money for nothing. You can't beat that anywhere.

Mr. Batten: I would point out, as I am sure most of you realize, that she has this option every month, not just the first time. This is a continuing option.

Senator Proxmire: I understand. And I think your adjusted system is an improvement. You deserve commendation for your adjusted balance system. I think it is excellent. It makes it much clearer to me. But for those who don't use this system, it simply means they use the beginning balance; they have a shorter free-ride period. You are giving them a longer free-ride period. I think that is fine.

Mr. Batten: Senator Proxmire, we have submitted actual facts here on our situation in Massachusetts. And the figures we think are correct. And we find it impossible, as I have indicated, in our view, to predict in advance and to tell the customer what her annual rate would be under the revolving credit.

I realize that you are taking one set of assumptions, and I am sorry, Senator, I cannot accept that set of assumptions probably any more than you can accept mine. But I think the rationale follows from the set of assumptions we start with.

Senator Proxmire: Isn't it true that you are already charging into your costs the free-ride credit that you give all customers who don't take advantage of the revolving credit?

Mr. Batten: Oh, yes.

Senator Proxmire: Then, aren't you charging it again if you compute from the point of purchase the finance rate which the customer is paying who takes advantage of your revolving credit rather than from the point at which she decides whether or not to take advantage of it?

Mr. Batten: We have charged in the costs when we put your name on the books, Senator Proxmire, that you say you want to buy from us on credit and you buy for $100; the cost of doing that is in our credit operation. Is that the answer to your question?

If you take advantage of the plan, and so forth, the options, and you pay over two or more months, then of course we have the additional cost incurred in connection with your account of billing, keeping it up to date, mailing, all the costs that are involved in that.

Senator Proxmire: I think that your very interesting three short paragraphs under "Our Credit Policy" in your advertising tells the story pretty interestingly to me. You say "Credit is a convenience. It costs money. Who should pay for it? The Penney way is to charge only the people who use it."

You don't charge the people who use it who pay within 60 days. They get credit for nothing. Then you go down to say that right now you are losing slightly on your credit operation. It must mean that you are making a substantial amount of money on the people who incur the revolving credit charge because you are able to charge all the free riders against that revolving credit and still only lose slightly.

Mr. Batten: I would like to make this comment in connection with that statement if I may.

We have 11 credit data centers around the country. While we don't disclose this information publicly, for obviously competitive reasons, we would invite your committee, or some part of your committee, or some part of your staff, to visit one of our data centers where our credit is operated, and we would be very happy to make available to your committee on a confidential basis the actual cost figures.

Senator Proxmire: I am not charging that you are gouging anybody.

Mr. Batten: The statement that you have just made can be verified.

Senator Proxmire: All that I am saying is that if, I think perhaps half, maybe not half but a large number of your so-called credit customers, incur no service charge, and are able to take advantage of this system and get 30 days, 45 days, up to 60 days free credit, obviously this costs you and costs you substantially. And this is part of your credit charge. We know about it. You have made that point very emphatically.

If you are only losing a little bit of money on the whole operation, those who take advantage of the revolving credit must be paying very substantially.

Whether this is true or not—I don't mean once again to cast any aspersion on Penney—whether this is true or not, it would seem very, very clear to me that from the standpoint of the customer who is buying the information that she needs to have is what is the annual rate once this service charge begins to run. And this is what the Massachusetts law and the Douglas bill and the Proxmire bill would tell her.

Mr. Batten: We have submitted facts on our operation in Massachusetts, and we have indicated the rates, based on those buying and paying patterns. And I cannot agree that we can be telling the truth to our customers— and that is what we want to do. We are just as anxious to tell the truth as anybody else because as has been brought out by everybody here, it is good business to tell the truth—we just don't want to be forced to tell an untruth. And we feel in Massachusetts, or we would not have initiated this litigation, that we are being forced to tell an untruth, and we object to that.

Senator Proxmire: The very able and responsible banking commissioner, Mr. Clair, indicated that by and large the retail stores have learned to live with this, and have not indicated opposition. You have the only suit that has been brought to my knowledge, as indicated by the first witness, that while you are one of the biggest national merchandisers, Massachusetts isn't your biggest state by any means and there are other retailers bigger than you in Massachusetts, and many others using revolving credit.

Why is it that others haven't taken this position? Why haven't they complained? How can they live with it and you can't?

Mr. Batten: Senator Proxmire, I can't speak for other retailers.

Senator Proxmire: Doesn't their silence speak pretty loudly?

Mr. Batten: Not necessarily.

Senator Proxmire: I have never found businessmen to be tongue-tied or unwilling to protest if they find they are being put upon by government. They are among the most outspoken and most effective representatives of business that I have seen and I have been in a state legislature, and for 10 years in the Senate.

Mr. Batten: I cannot speak to that subject. You are much better qualified than I am. I can only speak to the subject that here are the facts. To us there is a principle involved here. I don't think it can be affected by the amount of business we do in Massachusetts, or anything else. It is the principle involved. And if it is only one person, one of the great things about our country is that if one individual feels he has a case against the state, he has a right to bring it.

Senator Proxmire: Right. And I think if you feel strongly, I don't blame you.

Mr. Batten: I don't think it is a matter of size or anything else. It is a matter of principle. Because we believe in truth in lending. And we don't see how we can have truth in lending and tell our customers the truth in the state of Massachusetts about our credit plan, and that is why we have initiated the action.

Senator Proxmire: Thank you for an excellent testimony. Senator Bennett?

Senator Bennett: Mr. Batten, I have followed the testimony, having had it in advance, and studied it carefully. It seems to me to lead back to questions to which both Dr. Willett and Mr. Clair answered in the affirmative, that if you set up a supposition or set up a hypothesis, you never know whether it is right until you go back after it has been applied and figure out what that hypothesis produced. It seems to me this is the key to understanding the hypothesis that Senator Proxmire proposes. If you went back on your accounts and discovered that they all figured out to be 18 percent, then he would be right.

Mr. Batten: Right.

Senator Bennett: But you go back on your accounts and discover two things: First, that the rate actually earned by those accounts differs between the two methods that you indicated and another thing that I think is very important and maybe the committee missed, the highest rate you discovered was 17.1. At no point did your particular method reach 18 percent.

I hope, Senator Proxmire, you noticed that on the beginning balance method the first month's rate was 24 percent. This is in evidence that you go over the 18 as well as under the 18.

Mr. Batten: That is right.

Senator Proxmire: Would the Senator yield?

Senator Bennett: Yes:

Senator Proxmire: The analysis we have in the record goes into great detail and shows it is 18 percent in all cases, beginning balance or adjusted balance.

The hour is late and I don't want to detain the Senator.

Senator Bennett: The analysis assumes away some of the time the credit is outstanding. In practice, in terms of the credit the consumer pays for the money he enjoys, it never is actually 18 percent. We had a lot of fun about my statement of 540 percent. This wouldn't happen very often. But if you are going to be technical, that kind of credit rate could be earned. So I think the committee is faced with the basic decision.

Do we assume that Penney's has no right to give x weeks free time as a means of reducing the cost of credit? Or must we assume that even though they do make available to a customer x weeks of free time, the credit has to be calculated as though they had no free time? Out of this is developing another interesting idea, that the smart man goes up to the last day of his free time and then he looks at the situation and decides that he is going to go somewhere, if he hasn't got the money readily available—if he had the money he would pay the bill—go somewhere and borrow enough to pay that off. This is an interesting attempt to give the best of two possible worlds. And it has many problems.

Can you tell me where a man can go and borrow $5.46 in order to pay the account that shows up first in your schedule? I checked the credit unions. They won't lend you $5.46. You have to borrow $25. And you have to go to the credit union, which takes time. And you have to sign a note. And then you have to take the money and you still have to pay the cost of getting it up to Penney's.

Senator Proxmire: Would the Senator yield?

Senator Bennett: Yes.

Senator Proxmire: This is a disclosure bill. The consumer can make up his own mind. I agree in many cases where the amount involved is small, the annual rate would not persuade him to go some place to borrow the money. Of course he would take advantage of the revolving credit. I don't argue that this would even diminish revolving credit necessarily. It is only in the larger purchases where there is substantial enough money involved to concern the customer that he would use his option. But now he would use the option. He has his information. He can make up his own mind.

Senator Bennett: This is a disclosure bill. Mr. Clair admitted that in Massachusetts it is truth by definition. They write the regulation to represent what you must disclose, whether it is the truth or not. And this is the thing that has bothered me about this business all along.

The matter of fact is you have here two completely different ways of providing credit. One, the declining balance method, in which you borrow the amount you are going to pen [sic] and then pay it off afterward. And this newer revolving account method, in which the customer has many more options and you don't start your credit with the total balance that you are going to consider.

I am not at all adverse to disclosing the cost of credit under a revolving charge. But I am and always have been opposed to a requirement or a condition that makes it possible for some officer of the state to set an arbitrary figure and say this is the cost of revolving credit, even though checking after the fact shows in every case that the actual cost is less or more. That, I think, represents the basis of the argument inside the committee and I think you, Mr. Batten, have given us excellent material to demonstrate that in practice, not in theory, but in practice, what the customer actually pays for credit under the Penney plan is, A, less than under the beginning balance plan, and in no case as much as 18 percent. And you have to distort the situation pretty drastically with assumptions to ever arrive at 18 percent.

I appreciate the chance to respond to the information you have given us.

Senator Proxmire: Did you want to speak further, Mr. Batten?

Mr. Batten: No, sir.

Senator Proxmire: You have been an excellent witness and very helpful. Senator Bennett is absolutely right; this did help define the most troublesome parts of this bill. Your testimony has been most useful to us for that reason. I think we have come closer to an understanding of the problem because you brought in these specific examples and because you have given us the benefit of your experience and your very understandable viewpoint.

Consolidated Edison
Company of New York

"The United States," wrote Richard Hofstader, "was born in the country and has moved to the city." The simple, rural, individualistic society which once characterized America has been replaced by one that is complex, urban, industrial, and interdependent—and with this profound transformation has come the defacement of a once fair land. Highways choke with an appalling collection of billboards, junkyards, and drive-ins; rivers, lakes, and the air itself reek of pollution; urban decay erodes the quality of life in the city, and too often relentless bureaucrats and their bulldozers provide cures worse than the disease. Indeed, in the years since World War II, blight has spread virtually uncontrolled through the city and countryside, almost as though the American people had tacitly agreed to make their environment as ugly as possible. In the inevitable clash between esthetics and economic interests, or esthetics and bureaucratic determinations, esthetic considerations usually finished a poor second, and few Americans appeared to lament this fact.

Recently, however, more and more Americans have become acutely aware of what one English magazine described as "the mess that is man-made America." In particular, determined and zealous conservationists have attempted to shake the American people from their apathy, and have not hesitated to engage in lengthy and costly controversies over seemingly lost causes. One such battle was waged over the proposal of the nation's largest gas and electric utility, Consolidated Edison Company of New York, to build a pumped storage hydroelectric project at Storm King Mountain on the west side of the Hudson River, about forty miles north of New York City.

The case not only illustrated the increasing popularity of conservation as a political cause, but also emphasized the growing social and economic conflict between private interests and the public interest over the utilization of America's most limited basic resource—land. The demands for environmental excellence clashed headlong with technical and economic problems, and issues which appeared simple at first glance often acquired exceedingly complex hues upon further examination.

343

THE STORM KING CONTROVERSY

Con Edison, in need of additional electric generating capacity to meet the increasing demands of its densely populated electric service territory (nine million people living within an area of 600 square miles),[1] applied to the Federal Power Commission in January, 1963, for a license to build and operate a two million kilowatt capacity pumped storage hydroelectric plant at Storm King Mountain. The plant, scheduled for completion in 1967, was to provide a means of storing energy to meet Con Edison's daily peak loads, and was also to provide a source of emergency back-up power.[2]

The area surrounding Storm King Mountain is steeped in the history of the colonial period and of the American Revolution, and it is celebrated in American literature. But, with the passage of time, much of the beautiful valley had been ravaged by blight and neglect, and the majestic Hudson choked on waste and debris. Rescuing and refurbishing the Hudson River Valley had, in recent years, become an important project to many individuals and groups, and Con Edison's contemplated hydroelectric plant at Storm King thus encountered a variety of opposition including conservationists, nature lovers, fishermen, historians, and Hudson Highland residents who banded together as the Scenic Hudson Preservation Conference. They objected to the project on the grounds that it would cut a huge gash in the mountainside, lessen the natural beauty of the area, possibly damage marine life in the Hudson River, and scar the countryside with overhead transmission lines.

After extensive hearings on the matter, the Federal Power Commission issued a license to Con Edison in March, 1965. In its decision the FPC held that the company definitely needed the additional generating capacity; that the impact of the project upon scenic resources would be minimal; and that the project's advantages for power supply purposes far outweighed any negative considerations. The demands of conservationists for more underground transmission lines were rejected on the grounds that the FPC did not see why Con Edison "should be required to absorb the extravagant additional costs for more underground cable."[3]

In July, 1965, the conservationists carried their fight to court and filed a petition for review of the FPC's decision in the United States

---

1. New York City and Westchester County.
2. Con Edison's peak loads are reached during daylight hours on weekdays and usually coincide with the working day.
3. *The Wall Street Journal*, March 10, 1965. During the FPC hearings, in a bow to conservationists, Con Edison had agreed to place transmission lines under rather than over the Hudson and to keep them underground as far as a switching station three quarters of a mile inland from the east bank.

Court of Appeals for the Second Circuit.[4] That court, in December, 1965, set aside the FPC's order. Said the court:

> This court cannot and should not attempt to substitute its judgment for that of the commission. But we must decide whether the commission has correctly discharged its duties, including the proper fulfillment of its planning function, in deciding that the licensing of the project would be in the overall public interest. The commission must see to it that the record is complete. The commission has an affirmative duty to inquire into and consider all relevant facts.[5]

Taking the Federal Power Commission to task for its failure to do just that and to properly represent the public interest in the controversy, the court remanded the case to the commission with the instruction that

> the commission's renewed proceedings must include as a basic concern the preservation of natural beauty and of national historical shrines, keeping in mind that, in our affluent society, the cost of a project is only one of several factors to be considered. The record as it comes to us fails markedly to make out a case for the Storm King project on, among other matters, costs, public convenience and necessity, and absence of reasonable alternatives.[6]

The court directed the FPC to consider additional evidence concerning other generating and supply possibilities available to Con Edison.

In March, 1966, Con Edison petitioned the United States Supreme Court seeking a review of the decision of the Court of Appeals. The company contended that the Court of Appeals had substituted its judgment for technical factual determinations of the FPC; but, in May, 1966, the Supreme Court declined to review the ruling of the Court of Appeals. The Federal Power Commission then scheduled new hearings on the matter to begin November 14, 1966.

THE COMPANY YOU LOVE TO HATE

Nobody loves a giant utility, but New Yorkers particularly loved to hate Con Edison—at least according to a 1966 *Fortune* article.[7]

---

4. Decisions of the Federal Power Commission and other federal regulatory agencies may be appealed to the U. S. Court of Appeals. As a general rule, the reviewing court accepts the commission's findings of fact in a case (if based upon substantial evidence) and limits itself to reviewing and interpreting questions of law.

5. *Scenic Hudson Preservation Conference* v. *Federal Power Commission,* 354 F. 2d 608, 620 (1965).

6. *Ibid.,* 624.

7. Thomas O'Hanlon, "Con Edison: The Company You Love to Hate," *Fortune* (March, 1966).

Con Ed's aging management, long and busily engaged in political battles against the threat of public power, had been unable to overcome the antagonism which its customers felt toward the utility.[8] While consumers had been subjected to a series of power failures and five rate increases in a six-year period, Con Edison had fallen behind other utilities in growth and earnings. Despite a substantial construction program in the past decade, much of the company's plant was outdated, inefficient, costly to maintain, and contributed heavily to New York City's air pollution problems. And although the utility looked to the installation of nuclear plants within New York City as a solution to many of its problems, it did not count upon public approval for such plants until the mid-1970s.[9]

The *Fortune* article, though liberally sprinkled with unkind cuts, did recognize that the company faced certain problems which were peculiar to the nature of its operation. Serving nine million residents of New York City and Westchester County, Con Edison's customer density was unique—more than 300 times the industry average—and its peak power loads were enormous. To maintain its complex and concentrated system which serviced high-rise commercial and apartment buildings, public agencies, and slums, the company was required to spend large amounts of cash. A high proportion of Con Edison's electric transmission and distribution facilities was underground, and the cost of installing such facilities was five to twelve times that of an overhead system. Con Edison had in fact the most extensive underground electric system in the world; and, in 1965, at a cost of $220 million, completed construction of an 80-mile, 345,000-volt underground backbone transmission system linking twelve generating stations. *Fortune* reported that for every $1 of plant, the utility had to spend $2 for transmission and distribution—25 percent above the national average at that time. Furthermore, to keep its underground system operable, Con Edison made about 40,000 excavations each year. Such endless digging did little to endear the utility to the hearts of inconvenienced New Yorkers.

Additionally, according to *Fortune*, Con Edison faced the mighty job of making itself more attractive to the investing public.

> Despite capital expenditures of over $2 billion in the past decade, which increased the investment in plant by 8.5 percent annually,

8. The chairman of the board, Harlan Forbes, who had been with Con Edison for 41 years, reached the mandatory retirement age of 68 in February, 1966. Charles Eble, president since 1957, succeeded Forbes. Elbe, a fifty-year veteran with Con Edison (he began his career as a messenger), was 65 at the time of his election. Sixty-four-year-old John Cleary, who had been with the company for 41 years, became president.

9. In 1962, Con Edison had to abandon plans to build a nuclear plant in Queens, as neither the public nor the Atomic Energy Commission was ready to accept a nuclear plant within New York City.

revenues lagged at a disappointing 4.5 percent. . . . Rising costs, particularly local taxes that now eat up 16 percent of revenues, have reduced the benefits that should have resulted from new plant. At a scant 5.4 percent for electric operations, Con Ed's return on its rate base has run 1 to 2 percentage points behind most of the industry, a depressing record to one of the company's most important constituents, the financial community.[10]

Finally, as if existing criticism of the company for its weak financial performance, erratic service, and inability to obtain public goodwill were not enough, Con Edison was then confronted with significant opposition prompted by its proposal to build the hydroelectric plant at Storm King Mountain.

The Storm King project, as was originally approved by the Federal Power Commission, consisted of a storage reservoir, a powerhouse, and transmission lines. The reservoir, located 1,000 feet above the powerhouse, was to be connected to the powerhouse (located on the riverfront) by a tunnel 40 feet in diameter. The powerhouse, serving both as a pumping and generating station, was to be 800 feet long and contain eight pump generators. Transmission lines were to run under the Hudson to the east bank and then underground for 1.6 miles to a switching station to be built in the town of Philipstown. Thereafter, overhead transmission lines would be placed on towers 100 to 150 feet high, and these would require a path up to 125 feet wide through Westchester and Putnam Counties for a distance of some 25 miles until they reached the company's main connection with New York City.[11]

Functionally, the project was to serve as a huge storage battery to cope with the public's uneven demands for electric power. The greatest demands for electricity occurred during the working day; at night, the demand fell below Con Edison's generating capacity. Yet the utility had to have enough generating capacity to meet maximum demand at any given instant, plus adequate reserve for emergency purposes. Thus, Con Edison planned to use its most efficient excess capacity to pump water uphill into the reservoir at Storm King during slack periods of demand for power. During peak periods, the procedure would be reversed, and the stored water would be released to flow back down to the powerhouse to generate electricity. This ability of the Storm King facilities to store energy enabled Con Edison to avoid the daily use of its older and less efficient generating capacity during peak load times. Additionally, and equally important, the company maintained that hydroelectric generating equipment such as

10. *Fortune* (March, 1966), p. 125.
11. This description of the project has been taken from the opinion of the United States Court of Appeals for the Second Circuit.

that proposed for Storm King represented the ultimate in reliability, and in the ability to pick up power loads quickly in an emergency.[12] According to Con Edison, the Storm King project thus would serve two important functions: it would provide economical peaking capacity and rapid response emergency reserve capacity.

THE CONTROVERSY CONTINUED

While the precedent-setting decision of the Court of Appeals represented a stunning conservation victory to many, to Con Edison President John Cleary, in the wake of Black Tuesday (the paralyzing November 9, 1965, Northeast power failure), it was "almost incomprehensible that the company's ability to provide such an important added measure of reliability to New York's power supply should continue to be postponed." One of the basic reasons for proposing the Storm King project in the first instance had been to provide insurance against just such an eventuality as Black Tuesday, and the delay of the project, Cleary also warned, had forced the company to proceed with building a less economical 500,000 kilowatt addition to a Staten Island coal burning plant, and to postpone planned retirement of 750,000 kilowatts of old coal burning capacity in Manhattan, thus adding to New York City's burdensome air pollution problems. Con Edison had argued that the successful completion of the Storm King project would provide necessary additional electric generating capacity in the most economical and practical way, increase reliability of service, and cut down air pollution by enabling the shutdown of several old fuel burning plants.

Pitted against the company's position had been a growing number of private groups whose increasing concern about the condition of the Hudson Valley had been matched by their willingness to campaign aggressively for corrective and protective measures. In addition to their efforts to rescue the banks of the Hudson from blight and neglect, and to rid the river itself of the vast quantity of waste and debris dumped by cities and factories, they had sought to protect the area from future destructive encroachments. The New York State Commission on the Hudson River Valley framed the issue this way:

> . . . Growth pressures are mounting. The state's population will reach 30 million by the end of the century, and the great bulk of this expansion will take place in the valley.
>
> There will be many more industrial plants, new highways, new substations—indeed whole new towns. This growth is vital. The question is whether it can be shaped to enhance the beauty of this great valley, rather than destroy it.[13]

12. Consolidated Edison Annual Report 1965, p. 12.
13. *The New York Times*, February 1, 1966.

At a news conference on January 31, 1966, Governor Nelson Rockefeller invited the state of New Jersey and the federal government to join with New York in a compact to save the Hudson River Valley from ruin. Up to that point, the Governor had publicly supported the Storm King project, but the year before he had appointed his brother Laurance to head a commission which undertook a study of the Valley. The commission's report, which was released on January 31, proposed that the state acquire Storm King Mountain as a park and that a search be instituted for another site for Con Edison's project. The report agreed with the Court of Appeals that an exhaustive investigation should be made of other energy sources. And, referring to Con Edison's project, Laurance Rockefeller added: "We hope they will not have to build this monster." But Harlan Forbes, then chairman of Con Edison, said that the company saw no satisfactory alternative to the Storm King site. Calling a news conference on February 2, Forbes asserted that if the company did not build the project at Storm King, it would have to build more coal burning plants in New York City. This, of course meant continued polluting of the air. He added that only the water storage project could "move up to full production in seconds," while steam plants take a few minutes, which "in some circumstances . . . is too long." [14]

The New York Times editorially applauded both the decision of the Court of Appeals and the report of the Hudson River Valley Commission and argued that the plant should not be built if a feasible alternative could be found. Previously the paper, commenting on the initial decision of the Federal Power Commission to grant the license, had gone so far as to say:

> The many shortcomings of the FPC in failing to give proper consideration to various aspects of the public interest, mainly because they could not be readily measured in dollars and cents, demand remedy. Congress might do well to make FPC decisions affecting sites of natural beauty subject to review by an official or agency less blind than the FPC has shown itself to be. [15]

On May 19, the *Times* again interjected itself into the fray when it editorially deplored the unwarranted concession made by New York Mayor John Lindsay and his task force on air pollution. Two days previously Lindsay had announced a "memorandum of understanding" against air pollution with Con Edison, under which the utility promised to submit a plan within six months for shutting down three plants in New York City and older units at a fourth plant. In exchange, the city promised to support the Storm King project—

14. *Ibid.*, February 3, 1966.
15. *The New York Times*, January 3, 1966.

provided the company met objections on protecting natural beauty and fish life.[16]

Then, on May 31, 1966, in a major concession to its opponents, Con Edison filed an amended application with the Federal Power Commission in which it submitted a proposal for placing the hydroelectric plant underground. Board Chairman Eble noted that "additional geological investigation at the Cornwall site had made possible this further contribution to the preservation of the scenic values of the Hudson River Valley." [17] The project would cost about $167.8 million, compared with the original $162 million, but almost none of the increase was due to the underground installation of the plant. The additional cost of carving a chamber out of Storm King Mountain rock would just about be covered by savings resulting from not needing a building at all. The boost would cover three new transformers needed along the route specified by the FPC for transmission lines.

Replying to this new development, the executive director of the Scenic Hudson Preservation Conference declared that, while it was good to hear that Con Edison was growing more respectful of scenic beauty, his group would continue to fight the granting of a license on the ground that it would set a precedent for other utilities to build plants in the area. He added that Con Edison's plan did not resolve such problems as the protection of fish, undergrounding of transmission lines, and, most importantly, alternative means of generating power.[18]

On June 12, the *Times* reported that the Bureau of Outdoor Recreation of the Department of Interior had submitted a report to Secretary Stewart Udall strongly criticizing the failure of state and local governments to protect the Hudson over the years and recommending the establishment of a three-member Hudson River Valley Commission, with one member each representing the federal government and the states of New York and New Jersey. The commission, the report held, would have the authority to ban all public and private construction that was not in accord with its master plan for development and preservation of the area. The report also said that Con Edison's Storm King plant should not be built "if suitable alternate sources of power can be found." In the event the plant was licensed, the transmission lines should be put underground.

On September 7, 1966, Con Edison filed with the FPC additional testimony in support of its amended application for a license. The company described the Storm King project as "the most economic and practical way to provide that reliability of service which is so particularly vital to New York City without impairing the scenic values of

16. *Ibid.*, May 18, 1966.
17. *Ibid.*, June 1, 1966.
18. *Ibid.*

DECISIONS INVOLVING PUBLIC RESPONSIBILITY

the Hudson River Valley." In his testimony, Con Edison's president stated: "Economic development is probably the major social need in the New York area, and the cost of electric power, along with many other factors, is important." The Storm King project was "the most technically and economically practicable source of reliable, low-cost power available." The company had evaluated six alternatives, but none could respond to such large, sudden load demands.

Con Edison estimated the total capital cost of the project at $183,598,500. Cost of the powerhouse, reservoir, and related facilities, including allowances for proposed recreational and scenic resources, company overhead, and interest during construction was estimated at $151,800,000. Transmission cost to connect the plant to the company's primary transmission was estimated at $31,798,500.

On the basis of studies conducted by General Electric Company and Con Edison of the Storm King project and six alternatives, comparable annual costs of each were developed for a 20-year period, starting in 1972, the expected first full year of operation of Storm King. The annual cost for the most economic alternative, which was 1,000 megawatts of nuclear capacity, plus 1,000 megawatts of kerosene-fueled gas turbines, totaled $78,692,000 more than the Storm King project. Two thousand megawatts of gas-fueled gas turbines were the most expensive alternative, with aggregate annual costs over the twenty-year period totaling $362,886,000 more than Storm King.

The Storm King project would, the company stated, make a significant contribution to the reduction of air pollution in New York City and its environs by enabling Con Edison to cut down the amount of coal and oil it would otherwise burn. Once the plant was built, Con Edison planned to shut down some 1,500,000 kilowatts of fossil-fueled generating units then used for meeting peak load demands. Storm King would also permit other fossil-fueled plants to be operated in a manner which would reduce air pollution by reducing their role during rapid increases and decreases in power loads and by avoiding nightly shutdowns and start-ups the following morning.

As an indication of its concern for the protection of fish life in the Hudson, the company pointed out that it was then spending $175,000 to finance a joint study of the Hudson River Fishery with the New York State Conservation Department and the U. S. Department of Interior. Furthermore, if there was any indication that the operation was adversely affecting the striped bass fishery, Con Edison was prepared to restock and thus replace any lost fish.

Concerning transmission lines, the company had stated that the present underground portion, which increased costs by $8 million was a justified expenditure since the Hudson River Valley in that area was a public area of unique beauty. Underground transmission beyond this, however, was esthetically and economically unjustified.

The only new right-of-way required consisted of an overhead stretch of 12 miles and involved only 68 property owners. If the stretch were placed underground, the additional initial cost would be at least $44,500,000. That meant the company would have to invest an additional $650,000 per landowner. The company would incur direct annual costs of $4,600,000, or approximately $68,000 per landowner affected. "We feel that the facts in the present case are such that any extension of underground cable . . . would amount to saddling nine million people in New York and Westchester with the expense of satisfying the aesthetic sensibilities of a few fortunate owners of country estates."

Con Edison said it planned to invest $5,850,000 in landscaping, scenic overlooks, picnic areas, visitors' facilities, relocating hiking trails, and the riverfront park. Thus, if approved, the Storm King project would produce beneficial by-products in the form of a park and recreational facilities and would restore to scenic beauty an extensive, slighted stretch of Hudson River frontage.

As to alternative sites for the proposed project, the utility declared that there were possible sites underneath Palisades Interstate Park or underneath the West Point Military Reservation, but their feasibility was subject to study following detailed geologic examination. "We have not made such examination because we felt that the importance of expediting the project was so great that we should proceed with the original site, where we already had more complete geologic data."

POSTSCRIPT

The United States Senate, on September 13, 1966, gave final Congressional approval to a bill which directed all federal agencies to consult with the Secretary of Interior for the next three years and allow him 90 days of review before any approval was granted for a federally licensed project affecting the conservation and development of the Hudson River Valley. Eventually, the Secretary turned over responsibility to a federal-interstate compact with enforcement powers. The bill did not affect Con Edison's Storm King project as it exempted projects for which applications were made before July 1, 1966.

The bill cautioned federal agencies that the "sense of Congress" was to forestall any sweeping plans affecting the valley before an interstate compact could be formed, but an FPC representative denied the bill had been a factor in the commission's decision regarding the Storm King project.[19]

19. *The New York Times*, September 18, 1966.

APPENDIX

The Revenue Dollar—1965

We received from

Sales to our customers:		Percent
Electricity	$694,000,000	82.6
Gas	104,000,000	12.4
Steam	38,000,000	4.5
Other—principally rentals	4,000,000	0.5
Total	$840,000,000	100.0

Our costs were

Taxes—federal, state and local	$181,000,000	21.6
Wages—operating payrolls and pensions	171,000,000	20.4
Fuel—coal, oil, natural gas, and nuclear materials	118,000,000	14.0
Materials—supplies, outside services and other charges	78,000,000	9.3
Depreciation—provision for depreciation of plant and equipment	84,000,000	10.0
Purchased energy—electric power and natural gas purchased for resale to customers	36,000,000	4.3
Interest—interest on indebtedness and other charges (net)	60,000,000	7.1
Total	$728,000,000	
Net income	112,000,000	10.9
Dividends—preferred and common	89,000,000	2.7
Retained in the business	$ 23,000,000	100.0

INCOME   OUTGO

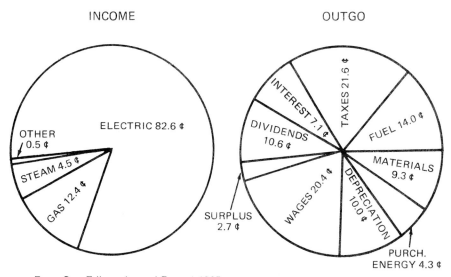

From Con Edison Annual Report 1965.

CONSOLIDATED EDISON COMPANY OF NEW YORK

Exhibit 1

Consolidated Edison Company of New York, Inc
Income Statement

	1965	1964
Operating Revenues		
Electric	$693,591,000	$645,044,847
Gas	104,291,577	103,550,074
Steam	38,424,671	36,934,445
Other	3,933,026	3,761,849
	$840,240,274	$789,291,215
Operating Revenue Deductions		
Operations	$328,411,568	$310,548,865
Maintenance	78,866,385	76,573,395
Depreciation	83,560,592	76,835,338
Taxes, other than federal income	160,102,186	151,676,243
Federal income tax	17,700,000	20,200,000
	$668,640,731	$635,833,841
Operating income	$171,599,543	$153,457,374
Income Deductions		
Interest on long-term debt	$ 62,704,768	$ 57,929,136
Other interest and miscellaneous deductions, net	4,113,409	3,360,196
Amount equivalent to increase in federal income tax resulting from amortization under necessity certificates	(900,000)	(900,000)
Interest charged to construction	(6,096,129)	(7,889,279)
	$ 59,822,048	$ 52,500,053
Net income	$111,777,495	$100,957,321

Exhibit 2

Consolidated Edison Company of New York, Inc.
Balance Sheet

Assets	Dec. 31, 1965	Dec. 31, 1964
Utility Plant, at original cost		
Electric	$3,425,451,709	$3,243,142,627
Gas	227,250,546	219,800,412
Steam	109,020,577	105,527,260
General	113,871,211	109,815,576
Total utility plant	$3,875,594,043	$3,678,285,875
Less—Reserve for depreciation	706,056,472	655,843,634
	$3,169,537,571	$3,022,442,241
Investments, special deposits, and other physical property, at cost or less	6,297,226	7,768,307
Current Assets		
Cash	23,601,613	27,235,646
Accounts receivable, less allowance for uncollectible accounts	85,754,560	77,074,056
Materials and supplies, including construction materials, at average cost .	62,583,444	60,752,460
Prepayments and other current assets .	6,489,631	9,348,536
	$ 178,429,248	$ 174,410,698
Deferred Charges		
Net unrecovered costs relating to gas plant retirements and natural gas conversion costs, being amortized through 1967	6,643,536	11,090,625
Nuclear research and development costs, being amortized through 1977.	8,437,088	9,155,138
Unamortized debt discount and expense	3,250,500	3,382,640
Other deferred charges	4,382,214	5,121,783
	$ 22,713,338	$ 28,750,186
Capital Stock Expense	10,029,117	8,730,114
	$3,387,006,500	$3,242,101,546

Exhibit 2

(con)

Consolidated Edison Company of New York, Inc.
Balance Sheet

Liabilities	Dec. 31, 1965	Dec. 31, 1964
Capitalization		
Long-term debt	$1,610,972,500	$1,610,972,500
Notes payable to banks	100,000,000	—
Capital stock and surplus:		
Capital stock		
Preferred stock	444,999,927	369,999,927
Common stock	750,469,455	750,469,455
Earned surplus	321,662,209	298,871,936
	$1,517,131,591	$1,419,341,318
Total capitalization	$3,228,104,091	$3,030,313,818
Credit equivalent to reduction in federal income tax resulting from amortization under necessity certificates	17,303,627	18,203,627
Current Liabilities		
Notes payable to banks..............	10,000,000	57,000,000
Accounts payable	38,418,801	49,888,433
Accrued taxes	27,377,139	28,428,097
Accrued interest, wages, and other current liabilities	19,987,028	18,861,923
Customers' deposits	28,454,849	25,769,316
Dividends payable	5,810,399	4,938,524
	$ 130,048,216	$ 184,886,293
Deferred Credits		
Unamortized debt premium...........	4,122,038	4,344,801
Other deferred credits	4,452,116	1,386,449
	$ 8,574,154	$ 5,731,250
Reserve for Injuries and Damages	2,976,412	2,966,558
	$3,387,006,500	$3,242,101,546

Exhibit 3

Statistics

Sales and Revenues—1965

Electric	Kilowatt-hours	% Increase or (Decrease) from 1964	Revenues	% Increase from 1964
Residential	5,620,920,793	5.7	$219,767,904	7.6
Commercial- industrial	13,747,161,910	4.7	374,893,947	7.5
Railroads and railways	2,627,152,141	(0.6)	37,793,710	0.9
Public authorities ...	2,312,140,251	4.9	54,220,610	8.0
Other electric utilities	950,879,820	73.0	6,914,829	55.2
Total sales	25,258,254,915	5.9	$693,591,000	7.5

Residential—Sales directly to residential customers and to religious institutions.
Commercial-Industrial—Sales directly to all types of general customers, also to customers who include residential or commercial tenant-use in the rent and to customers who resell energy to commercial and industrial tenants.
Railroads and Railways—Sales to the four electrified railroads running into New York, the New York City Transit Authority, the Staten Island Rapid Transit and Port Authority Trans-Hudson Corporation.
Public Authorities—Sales to municipal and other governmental authorities, including public street and highway lighting.
Other Electric Utilities—Principally delivery over tie lines interconnecting with other New York State utilities.

Gas	Cubic Feet	% Increase or (Decrease) from 1964	Revenues	% Increase or (Decrease) from 1964)
Residential	7,651,233,000	(2.8)	$ 29,750,057	0.9
Residential heating ..	23,154,098,300	5.1	35,572,750	(0.1)
General	19,839,613,600	3.2	37,101,111	1.4
Public authorities ...	1,249,513,100	9.1	1,867,659	(0.3)
Total sales	51,894,458,000	3.2	$104,291,577	0.7

Residential—Sales directly to residential customers and to religious institutions except those customers using gas for space heating.
Residential Heating—Sales for heating residences and religious institutions, including gas consumed for other purposes by these customers, and for heating multiple dwellings.
General—Sales to all general-use customers for use in their operations including heating.
Public Authorities—Sales to municipal and other governmental authorities.

Exhibit 3

(con)

Statistics

Steam	Thousands of Pounds	% Increase from 1964	Revenues	% Increase from 1964
General	1,614,519	1.5	$ 3,772,252	1.1
Annual power	18,965,935	3.6	25,889,976	4.5
Apartment house ...	5,222,808	3.3	7,595,210	2.9
Public authorities ...	839,909	11.4	1,167,233	10.5
Total sales	26,642,271	3.6	$ 38,424,671	4.0

General—Sales to all customers with low load factor use.
Annual Power—Sales for power, or power and heat use.
Apartment House—Sales to apartment houses and hotels.
Public Authorities—Sales to the city of New York.

Operating Revenues

	Electric	Gas	Steam	Other	Total
1965	$693,591,000	$104,291,577	$38,424,671	$3,933,026	$840,240,274
1964	645,044,847	103,550,074	36,934,445	3,761,849	789,291,215
1963	605,188,849	104,981,908	35,259,303	3,524,565	748,954,625
1962	583,667,363	103,618,248	34,177,953	3,689,756	725,153,320
1961	561,922,704	100,312,810	33,464,037	3,377,908	699,077,459
1960	526,505,748	95,267,523	30,740,328	3,299,227	655,812,826
1959	489,968,753	92,556,050	29,545,718	2,837,745	614,908,266
1958	454,537,559	89,530,000	30,164,721	2,867,189	577,099,469
1957	441,849,718	81,521,654	26,356,641	2,940,949	552,668,962
1956	414,421,477	79,578,513	25,584,741	2,946,040	522,530,771

Sales	Electric Kilowatt-hours	Gas Cubic Feet	Steam Thousands of Pounds	Electric	Gas	Steam
				Number at December 31		
1965....	25,258,254,915	51,894,458,000	26,642,271	3,042,138	1,320,427	4,455
1964....	23,847,676,404	50,281,888,200	25,709,663	3,025,282	1,322,937	4,431
1963....	22,185,557,993	49,234,821,000	23,963,739	2,994,773	1,322,574	4,334
1962....	20,833,860,879	47,810,171,200	22,140,657	2,949,389	1,321,169	4,190
1961....	20,204,268,412	46,049,037,300	21,689,834	2,922,732	1,325,140	4,086
1960....	18,899,690,544	43,140,040,000	19,712,184	2,904,624	1,333,007	4,100
1959....	17,653,913,344	42,285,632,200	18,775,282	2,886,299	1,343,634	4,148
1958....	15,961,464,897	40,775,963,800	18,333,839	2,872,695	1,353,448	4,114
1957....	15,395,350,690	38,000,101,500	16,773,249	2,861,341	1,361,935	4,123
1956....	14,505,654,475	37,171,032,800	16,901,594	2,853,805	1,367,728	4,117

Population served, 1965—8,800,000.   *Service area—660 square miles.*

Exhibit 3

(con)

Statistics

Employees Payroll

	Operating	Construction (and other accounts)	Total	*Employees* Average Pay of Weekly Employees	*Employees* Number at December 31
1965...	$149,651,520	$50,597,950	$200,249,470	$146.95	23,863
1964...	147,025,189	46,884,802	193,909,991	139.72	24,417
1963...	143,301,719	45,735,988	189,037,707	134.92	24,621
1962...	141,410,164	44,561,264	185,971,428	133.81	24,962
1961...	137,620,638	43,320,769	180,941,407	131.15	24,545
1960...	136,725,188	42,014,611	178,739,799	126.60	24,866
1959...	129,826,611	35,254,254	165,080,865	116.35	25,792
1958...	121,666,945	34,342,702	156,009,647	110.45	25,153
1957...	117,948,934	29,159,339	147,108,273	103.34	25,342
1956...	114,000,645	36,262,520	150,263,165	104.19	25,725

Payroll figures include overtime and premium payments but exclude pension payments.

Taxes

	Local	State	Federal	Total
1965........	$136,998,774	$23,841,324	$24,322,098	$185,162,196
1964........	128,393,498	21,505,268	22,222,073	172,120,839
1963........	116,019,841	20,798,204	25,470,563	162,288,608
1962........	106,799,254	20,172,902	33,324,952	160,297,108
1961........	102,498,101	20,336,804	41,537,147	164,372,052
1960........	98,076,636	17,658,275	43,436,559	159,171,470
1959........	86,841,002	16,377,769	46,211,619	149,430,390
1958........	77,043,110	15,176,509	45,264,063	137,483,682
1957........	72,362,794	14,556,217	42,350,657	129,269,668
1956........	68,609,304	13,680,406	41,674,790	123,964,500

Electric System

	Generating Capacity December 31 Kilowatts	System Peak* Date	System Peak* Kilowatts	Heat Rate Btu per Kwhr	Residential Kwhr per Customer	Residential Revenuc per Kwhr
1965....	7,595,000	June 23	5,710,000	11,751	2,277	3.9¢
1964....	6,607,000	July 1	5,505,000	11,505	2,161	3.8
1963....	6,663,000	July 29	5,105,000	11,372	2,050	3.9
1962....	5,885,000	June 19	4,852,000	12,149	1,939	4.0
1961....	5,301,000	Sept. 13	4,744,000	12,378	1,937	4.0
1960....	4,883,000	Aug. 30	4,352,000	12,461	1,780	4.1
1959....	4,894,000	Sept. 9	4,245,000	12,746	1,787	4.0
1958....	4,076,000	Dec. 11	3,517,000	12,846	1,676	4.0
1957....	3,717,000	June 26	3,460,000	12,993	1,621	4.0
1956....	3,696,000	Dec. 14	3,241,000	12,828	1,536	4.0

* One hour net maximum load distributed locally.

Exhibit 3

(con)

Statistics

Stockholder Statistics

	Number of Stockholders December 31			Shares Outstanding December 31		Common Stock Record	
						Earn-ings** per Share	Divi-dends** per Share
	Preferred Stock	Common Stock	Total	Common	Preferred		
1965...	24,313	199,635	223,948	4,615,319	37,257,292	$2.42	$1.80
1964...	24,115	178,458	202,573	3,865,319	37,257,292	2.21	1.65
1963...	61,642*	173,435	235,077	4,178,349*	34,977,952	2.09	1.6125
1962...	67,993*	170,032	238,025	4,209,833*	32,188,088	2.20	1.50
1961...	24,991	169,497	194,488	3,265,319	32,178,038	1.89	1.50
1960...	25,014	166,023	191,037	2,425,319	31,035,446	1.94	1.50
1959...	23,935	161,594	185,529	1,915,319	30,182,726	1.96	1.40
1958...	23,350	156,474	179,824	1,915,319	29,802,246	1.87	1.35
1957...	23,848	148,146	171,994	1,915,319	27,433,376	1.72	1.20
1956...	23,849	142,623	166,472	1,915,319	27,409,294	1.60	1.20

* Including Preference Stock called Sept. 11, 1964.
** Restated to reflect two-for-one stock split effective Feb. 5, 1965.

The Dirty Ohio

PITTSBURGH—The sanitary engineers who assess the water of the Ohio River for drinking purposes use a vivid jargon. Sometimes they describe the water's taste and odor as "cucumber." Sometimes it's "medicinal." And all too often it's "pigpen."

That the Ohio River should sometimes smell like a pigpen discourages conservationists laboring to clean up America's polluted rivers. During the past 20 years, the Ohio has been the target of the broadest cleanup effort ever directed at a U. S. river—an effort many experts regard as a model for attacking pollution on other major streams. It has involved eight states, the federal government, hundreds of municipalities, and thousands of private concerns. The cost to date has been close to $1 billion.

The effort has achieved some success. Most experts agree that the Ohio is indeed cleaner today than at any time since the 1930's. But the amount of filth that still pours into the 981-mile-long Ohio—once known to French explorers as *La Belle Riviere*—appalls pollution fighters.

BLUISH-BLACK GOO

For example: At Midland, Pennsylvania, pipes from a Crucible Steel Company titanium plant spew a bright green, poisonous waste fluid into the river. At Steubenville, Ohio, iron oxide from steel company blast furnaces stains the river a reddish brown. Just below Wheeling, West Virginia, an Ashland Oil and Refining Company plant pours a bluish-black goo down a bank into the water. Upstream at Aliquippa, Pennsylvania, oil discharges from a Jones & Laughlin Steel Corporation plant leave iridescent splotches that flash green and blue as they float lazily away with the current.

Private industry is by no means the only offender. In some spots along the Ohio, a powerful stench of raw sewage wafts across the

By Michael K. Drapkin and Thomas L. Ehrich, staff reporters of *The Wall Street Journal*. Reproduced by permission of *The Wall Street Journal*, March 17, 1969.

water, the product of communities that dump their untreated sewage in the river. Three hundred communities on the Ohio and its tributaries have no sewage plants.

Even larger cities that have sewage treatment plants often don't process their sewage adequately. At Pittsburgh, a $100 million plant built in the late 1950's removes lumps of raw sewage, tin cans, and other debris from the area's sewer water before it reaches the river. But the 150 million gallons of water that pass through the plant and into the Ohio daily still carry a heavy load of acid, chemicals, oil, grease, and brine.

One reason the cleanup of the Ohio is taking so long is that it was an enormous technical task to begin with. Industrialization—and pollution—of the Ohio have been under way for nearly 200 years. The Ohio River Basin, draining an area larger than Germany and the Netherlands combined, is rich with raw materials for the making of iron, steel, and chemicals. Three fourths of known U. S. coal reserves underlie the basin, and its forests provide a quarter of the nation's hardwood. The broad, placid river itself provides water, transportation, and a means of waste removal for industry and cities. Today the 10-state basin has a population of 24 million, supported by 38,000 industrial plants.

FROM PITTSBURGH TO CAIRO

The Ohio is formed at the juncture of the Allegheny and Monongahela Rivers at Pittsburgh. It flows in wide loops through the hills of western Pennsylvania, down the border between Ohio and West Virginia, along the Kentucky-Indiana line and past the southern tip of Illinois to empty into the Mississippi at Cairo, Illinois. Into the Ohio flow a dozen major rivers, several of which are themselves centers of industrialization—including the Allegheny, Monongahela, and Beaver in Pennsylvania; the Kanawha in West Virginia; the Miami, Scioto, and Muskingum in Ohio; the Big Sandy in Kentucky; and the Wabash in Indiana.

Over the years, private industry and government alike have tended to regard the Ohio and its tributaries not as something to conserve but as something to use—and a major use is waste disposal. In fact, the main function of most early sewage systems in the basin was to "get the waste into the rivers as fast as possible," says Richard A. Vanderhoof, Cincinnati-based regional director of the Interior Department's Water Pollution Control Agency.

By the end of World War II, the Ohio was almost a dead stream, so laden with pollutants that its waters were unfit for swimming, recreational boating, or even many industrial uses. Fish life was practically wiped out. Though many communities continued to use Ohio

River water for municipal water systems, extensive purification treatment was required.

FORMIDABLE POLITICAL OBSTACLES

Yet the technical problems of cleaning up the river weren't insurmountable. The most formidable obstacles were political and economic—and it is these problems that largely remain unsolved today. The difficulties they have posed for those trying to clean up the Ohio are much like those facing conservationists trying to clean up any interstate river.

The effort to clean up the Ohio was organized in 1948 under the Ohio River Valley Water Sanitation Commission (ORSANCO), formed by a compact among eight of the ten basin states. ORSANCO's job was to draw up antipollution standards and then to encourage government and industry throughout the basin to implement them.

ORSANCO's technical skill has been widely acknowledged. It pioneered in analysis of pollutants and their effects. In fact, criteria for water quality control drawn up by ORSANCO were incorporated into the Federal Water Quality Control Act of 1965.

But ORSANCO lacks enforcement strength. Until the federal antipollution law was passed, ORSANCO had to rely on state laws to control offenders. Even now, it is reluctant to demand legal action because it depends heavily on the political support of state governments—which, in turn, often are more interested in encouraging industry than in regulating it. As a result, some critics say, ORSANCO has sometimes failed to point a finger at offenders and use its influence to see that they are whipped into line.

"You can't clean up the Ohio River by putting out slick paper brochures or using engaging semantics," says Murray Stein, enforcement chief of the Federal Water Pollution Control Agency, "The people of the Ohio Basin have done a lot of talking, but if you want a clean river, you have to have a rigid timetable" for improvement.

ORSANCO officials contend, however, that enforcement isn't their job. They argue that their role is to educate polluters, as well as the public, with the hope that pressures for cleanup efforts will result. ORSANCO has persuaded most industries and communities along the Ohio to take at least some steps toward complying with the commission's standards. But in the absence of stern enforcement measures, most haven't come close to meeting them.

Even with the new enforcement powers of the federal law, authorities are finding it hard to curb polluters. Current federal and state requirements call for polluters to make specific improvements by 1972 or 1973, but some skeptics doubt that the schedule will be met. Federal officials calculate the remaining cost of cleaning up the Ohio Basin at $2 billion—a staggering outlay over a relatively brief period.

A major obstacle is the insistence by many of the polluters that the federal government bear the lion's share of the cost. While the government has become increasingly involved in antipollution work, the Vietnam war and other problems have left little federal money for pollution control.

CORPORATE RELUCTANCE

Industrial concerns, noting that municipalities usually get at least some federal help with pollution control, are reluctant to shoulder the entire burden themselves. As a result, many companies take only those steps that are forced upon them. "We installed a lot of (pollution) abatement equipment at our Aliquippa plant, but we didn't do it until the federal and state people raised their standards," admits Earl Young, manager of technical services for Jones & Laughlin Steel.

One company that has won praise from pollution fighters for its voluntary efforts is National Steel Corporation. When it added a giant new steel-making shop to its plant at Weirton, West Virginia, in 1967, National installed extensive water pollution control equipment that is said to make its waste water cleaner than that of most cities. After the equipment was installed, a huge sludge mass—two inches thick and 2,500 feet long—slowly disappeared from alongside the plant. The sludge had built up from oil discharged by the plant before the new equipment was installed.

But National complains about paying its own way. George Angevine, vice-president, says that the government has paid about 21 percent of the cost of municipal sewage treatment facilities during the past twenty years. "It hasn't paid for any of industry's efforts," he says. "We should get tax credits for pollution control."

Steel men figure that roughly 10 percent of the cost of a modern $1 billion steel-making facility goes for water pollution control—not to mention the cost of equipment for controlling air pollution. Moreover, it costs as much as 35 percent more to equip an old plant with water pollution control gear than it does to build the equipment into a new plant.

Many companies say they would rather close some old plants than meet the high cost of pollution control. "If I know I'm going to phase out a plant in three years, I've got to think twice about putting millions into controlling pollution," says a steel company executive.

PPG Industries, Incorporated, says meeting the state of Ohio's limits on discharge of calcium chloride into the Tuscarawas River, an Ohio River tributary, would force PPG to close its Barberton, Ohio, soda ash plant. This is the second largest chemical plant in the state.

A PPG spokesman says the company has the technical means to solve the pollution problem, but to do so would mean either spending too much money or reducing soda ash output to a level below the break-even point. Some 2,600 workers would be laid off if the plant, built in 1899, should close.

Some companies, of course, may be bluffing when they threaten to close plants rather than meet pollution control standards. But government officials are reluctant to push them too hard. "It's easy to say, 'Clean up, Mac,' but we're not in the business of putting people out of work," says the Interior Department's Mr. Vanderhoof.

SCARING COMPANIES AWAY

In some instances, antipollution rules are said to have scared away companies planning to build plants in the Ohio Basin. A few years ago Union Carbide Corporation decided against building a second chemical plant at South Charleston, West Virginia, where it already had one facility, and built instead in Louisiana. Ed Henry, chief of the West Virginia Water Resources Department, says antipollution requirements were the reason. The company doesn't deny that the requirements were considered, but it contends that other factors, such as access to raw materials, played a larger role in the decision.

State governments are keenly aware of the economic importance of industry in the Ohio Basin, and they have been notably reluctant to enforce antipollution measures that would discourage companies. "Every state has a Department of Commerce that is striving for all the industry it can get, and each state also has a Department of Health that worries about such things as pollution," says Mr. Vanderhoof. "It depends on which is the strongest—and so far the Health Departments haven't been strong enough."

Federal authorities tick off a list of companies that, for whatever reason, continue to be major polluters of the Ohio or its tributaries. The list includes Wheeling-Pittsburgh Steel Corporation, Allied Chemical Company, Koppers Company, U. S. Steel Corporation, Copperweld Steel Company, Textron Inc., American Chain & Cable Company, and Union Carbide.

The companies acknowledge that they are contributing to pollution, but some contend the pollution levels aren't as high as federal authorities say. Moreover, the companies all say they are working, often on state-approved timetables, to clean it up. American Chain & Cable says its pollution problem already has improved substantially with the closing of one operation at its plant on the Monongahela River and adds that it is now setting out to clean up remaining "minor" problems. "We used to be a gross violator," a spokesman says.

Much of the waste dumped into the rivers consists of such highly visible compounds as oil or colored chemicals, but pollution fighters say much pollution is invisible. For instance, Union Carbide dumps phenol, a caustic and poisonous—but invisible—chemical, into the water at its Riverside, Ohio, plant. The Federal Water Pollution Control Agency says the concentration of phenol downstream from the plant is "about 40 times" the acceptable level. (A company spokesman says, however, that Ohio state standards permit the plant to continue dumping phenol until 1975).

One of the most troublesome types of industrial pollution is acid drainage from coal mines. Sulphuric acid is formed when air and water act chemically upon rock in mines. The acid is carried by water drainage to streams that eventually flow into the Ohio or its tributaries. It leaves a dark yellow or brown stain on river banks and rocks, kills fish, and often forces industrial plants to treat their water with softeners and chlorine before they can use it in manufacturing. The acid also corrodes barges and water intake equipment of both industrial and municipal water systems.

While coal companies are credited generally with doing a good job of controlling drainage from active mines, they are criticized by pollution fighters for having failed to find practical ways to stop acid drainage from the thousands of abandoned mines in the Ohio basin. Often the cost of removing acid from an abandoned mine's drainage is more than the mine was worth when it was active. An official of Pennsylvania's Sanitary Water Board estimates the cost of cleaning up acid drainage in western Pennsylvania alone at about $400 million over the next decade.

The effects of acid pollution are most evident in the Monongahela River, which flows through the coalfields of West Virginia before emptying into the Ohio. Mr. Vanderhoof calls the Monongahela an "open cesspool." At Pittsburgh, where the Allegheny and the Ohio are often ice-covered in midwinter, the Monongahela remains completely free of ice, largely because of the acid.

COMMUNITIES' MONEY TROUBLES

Cleaning up municipal sewage is no easy task either. Though most cities installed basic, or primary, treatment facilities like Pittsburgh's during the 1950's, few have the secondary treatment plants that pollution fighters say are now necessary for a thorough job of pollutant removal. Cincinnati, Louisville, Evansville, Indianapolis, Dayton, and Charleston all discharge sewage into the Ohio or its tributaries— and all lack secondary plants. "A large city with only primary treatment is worse than many small towns with no treatment at all," complains one federal official.

But communities are faced with rising costs and voter resistance to tax hikes or bond issues. Thus, they are reluctant to move without federal help.

The jockeying for federal funds has delayed some facilities for years. Several years ago, Wellsburg, West Virginia, a town of 5,000, was offered a federal grant of $346,650, then about 30 percent of the cost of a sewage treatment plant. But town fathers rejected the offer, saying they needed a 50 percent grant. Since then the estimated cost of a plant has risen to $1.8 million from $1.2 million, and Wellsburg now wants at least $900,000 from the government. The $346,650 offer is still open—and Wellsburg, lacking even a primary treatment plant, continues to dump raw sewage into the Ohio.

Some communities resist efforts to get them to build facilities. Pittsburgh's Allegheny County Sanitation Authority has stubbornly resisted demands that it build a secondary sewage treatment plant. The Pennsylvania Sanitary Water Board ordered it in 1965 to build such a facility, but the authority has stalled while trying to get federal help. Despite the present plant's failure to remove many pollutants, the authority's executive director, Leon Wald, contends that a secondary plant is an unnecessary luxury whose need has been "greatly exaggerated."

Part Five

Decisions Involving Organized Labor

Quality Brass
and Tube Company

In June, Will Kettinger, president of the Quality Brass and Tube Company of Bridgeport, Connecticut, was reflecting upon an overture from the City Council of New Center, Rhode Island, to consider relocating to that city. The proposition seemed attractive from a number of points of view:

1. New Center had lost its railroad business and was in the throes of trying to attract new industry. The correspondence from the Chamber of Commerce suggested that the labor population was so anxious to reestablish permanent industries in the town that labor peace was virtually assured, and at rates far lower than the going rates in Bridgeport.
2. The town was willing to give tax concessions and had negotiated with the county and state to develop similar concessions.
3. Considerable assistance in finding plant sites, in negotiating local financing, and in making applications to the Small Business Administration were promised.
4. Such mundane aspects as finding both temporary and permanent housing for relocated employees, together with a promise to assist with liberal financing arrangements for individuals, were part of the plan.

Will Kettinger was considering this in the face of several factors which had been of serious concern to him for some time. Although the company was probably in little danger of going out of business, he was presiding over a company which he considered to be operating at a little better than break-even. His estimate of the company position was that it had found its niche in the brass industry and that future growth would depend on growth of the industry as a whole, not because QBT grew faster than the industry. This observation led him to believe that improved profits would have to come from cost reductions rather than increased volume. He was particularly concerned at this moment because in the months of May and June losses had been generated (see Exhibit 1). He was fearful that this might be a foreshadowing of a general downturn in the economy as a whole which, of course, could mean difficult times for QBT.

Exhibit 1

Quality Brass and Tube Company
Statement of Profit and Loss

	January	February	March	April	May	June	Six Months
Sales	$ 95,000	$ 98,000	$100,000	$105,000	$ 86,000	$ 80,000	$564,000
Cost of Sales	69,000	70,600	71,800	72,000	66,500	63,700	413,600
Gross Profit	$ 26,000	$ 27,400	$ 28,200	$ 33,000	$ 19,500	$ 16,300	$150,400
Expenses:							
Administrative	$ 9,000	$ 9,000	$ 9,000	$ 9,000	$ 9,000	$ 9,000	$ 54,000
Selling	7,000	7,000	7,000	7,000	7,000	7,000	42,000
Supplies and Rent	5,000	5,000	5,000	5,500	4,500	4,200	29,200
Other Expenses	2,000	2,000	2,000	2,000	2,000	2,000	12,000
Total Expenses	$ 23,000	$ 23,000	$ 23,000	$ 23,500	$ 22,500	$ 22,200	$137,200
Profit (Loss) before Taxes ..	3,000	4,400	5,200	9,500	(3,000)	(5,900)	13,200
Taxes	1,000	1,500	1,700	3,200	(1,000)	(2,000)	4,400
Net Profit (Loss) after Taxes .	$ 2,000	$ 2,900	$ 3,500	$ 6,300	$ (2,000)	$ (3,900)	$ 8,800

DECISIONS INVOLVING ORGANIZED LABOR

The New Center offer seemed to be a way out of the dilemma. So, together with selected members of his management team, he embarked upon a rather detailed evaluation of it.

BACKGROUND

The Quality Brass and Tube Company had been in existence since 1962. At that time Will Kettinger and Sam Pelser left the employ of Breckenridge Foundry to start their own business. Will had been a production supervisor for Breckenridge, while Sam had been an outside sales representative. Both men used personal savings plus solicited investment from business associates. The resulting ownership structure was that Kettinger and Pelser each owned about 40 percent of the outstanding stock, while the remaining 20 percent was held among some 50 stockholders. In addition, the two principals had a written agreement that neither would sell his interest without the specific permission of the other.

The invested capital went primarily into two secondhand drawbenches, some inventory, and remodeling work necessary to get a portion of a rented mill into production shape. Will supervised the setting up of the production facilities, organized the systems and procedures that would be used in the operation, and set up bookkeeping records as they became necessary. Sam went out on the road to line up orders for the new company.

The decision to go into business was not entirely a unilateral decision on the part of the principals. The management of Breckenridge had actually encouraged the venture, seeing the desirability of having a small business through which to channel specialty orders for tube sizes and quantities not easily handled by their facilities. Thus, while QBT would be in competition with Breckenridge in some instances, Breckenridge actually welcomed the company to take its "spillage" (and therefore keep favored customers happy by recommending QBT rather than Chase or Bridgeport Brass, major competitors that might take prime business away). While Quality Brass and Tube was not tied to Breckenridge by any legal device, at least in the beginning, theirs was a paternal relationship. (In fact, the location of QBT in relation to Breckenridge was one of being across the street.) There was, however, no financial tie to Breckenridge in any way.

The business in which QBT engaged could best be described as that of a secondary redraw mill for copper and brass tubing. The process was a relatively simple one in concept, but the technology was not simple. There was only one raw material class—1" O.D. copper or brass tubing—even though there were several different alloys of brass or copper that might be used for different jobs. These tubes were fed into drawbenches to effect both a reduction in the outer dimension of the tube and in the gauge of the wall.[1] Several draws might be required depending on the end product. In addition, the drawing technology had to consider the hardness desired, which could be very critical in many applications. Following the drawing operation (and sometimes between operations), pickling (essentially a cleaning exercise) and annealing would take place. From there the tube would go to the cutting room for cutting and polishing. The final step would be packing (sometimes critical in the case of polished brass and long lengths which might be bent) and shipping.

The production operation was not complicated but required technically trained managers to control the drawing operations and production supervision skilled in drawing copper to proper tempers and hardness. All of the QBT managers had worked their way through various brass mills in and around Bridgeport and were skilled in their trade.

In addition to the technology of drawing copper, the success of the business was completely tied into the copper market. A volatile market was a constant source of concern to the management of the company. During a three-year period, copper prices had fluctuated from 25 cents per pound to as high as 55 cents per pound, although the lower price was much more normal. Because of the erratic market, it was necessary to watch inventory levels very carefully lest the company be caught with high stocks at the time of a price cut.[2]

Products

QBT, a secondary redraw mill, specialized in copper and brass tubing items involving relatively short runs and small sizes of tubing. In most cases the products were in semifinished form and would constitute an input for some manufacturers or assemblers. Typical of the products were radio antennas (prior to plating), lipstick cases, lengths of tubing to be used as handles on various devices (e.g., the handle of a razor which would be knurled and plated by the manufacturer), and various components of assemblies going into refrigerator equipment and major appliances. There were very few problems with most runs, although metallurgical quality problems were of major concern. As a matter of specification, the customer

1. The tube was drawn through a collar of a given diameter (but smaller). The result was to make the outside diameter of the tube smaller. A round rod (called a mandril) was inserted inside the tube so that the inside diameter could be controlled during the drawing. The diameter of the mandril and the collar determined the gauge or wall thickness of the tube.

2. An investigation was made into the industry pricing policy. The government claimed that the copper and brass industry in this Bridgeport-Westbury area was guilty of price-fixing. Those in the know claimed that QBT was certainly getting price information from Breckenridge.

usually required certain characteristics of hardness, temper, and, in some cases, ductility if the pieces were to be reshaped.

Management Team

The management team consisted of the president, the vice-president in charge of sales, the production superintendent, the chief engineer and metallurgist, and the chief accountant and office manager. Additionally, there were two supervisors for the mill on each of two shifts as well as a first-shift supervisor in the Finishing and Shipping Department and a manager in these areas on the second shift. (Although one of the two mill supervisors controlled the shift, the manager was in charge of the area.)

President—Will Kettinger. Will was in his late forties and had spent his first 15 years with Breckenridge in the production area. He could best be described as a loner who gave the impression to the casual observer that he was a person given to a great deal of introspection. He felt that he was a person with a purpose. His reputation among his peers was that of a clever executive. To the employees, he was somewhat distant, but he occasionally would surprise a new person by taking over a job when not well done—and Will would usually do it much better. (That was always quite a sight because Will would be on a drawbench with a suit and tie on!) The employees would kid among themselves about it, but it was a respectful type of kidding. Among Will's many accomplishments was the fact that for about ten years he had succeeded in negotiating a sweetheart contract with the union, a UAW division.

Vice-President—Sam Pelser. Sam, slightly older than Will, was in his early fifties. He was a more pleasant person than Will, and everyone agreed that Will and Sam complemented one another very well. Sam was the one with whom one felt immediately comfortable. He had had great success in cultivating contacts throughout the company, and he was thought to be as important to the success of the company as was Will who had the technical competence. Sam spent most of his time on the road traveling from the East to the West Coast, which sometimes resulted in widely disbursed customers. Sam was, among other things, a person of independent wealth and was very proud of the $85,000 house recently built on the outskirts of Bridgeport.

Production Superintendent—Fred Weston. Fred was in his late thirties, married, and had five children. He was the fifth production supervisor in the ten-year history of the company. In fact, he was the third superintendent in the past five years. Many of Fred's predecessors had found that working for Will Kettinger was difficult since Will was as demanding of the superintendent as he was of himself. After being on the job for about a year, Fred was beginning to feel the pressures that the rest had felt. In general, he was thought to be a highly qualified person technically, but he vacillated between being either very tough or very permissive with the subordinates. He had come up through the ranks of the company, and some of the older people in the company thought his promotions were due to unusually friendly relations with Kettinger. Will, however, was not altogether satisfied with him as a superintendent.

Chief Engineer and Metallurgist—Cedric Kappel. Cedric was not really an employee of the company. He was 77 and had retired from a brass mill ten years earlier and was receiving Social Security. A special provision of the Social Security Act allowed Cedric to earn additional money as a consultant without jeopardizing his Social Security benefits. As a result, Will Kettinger had Cedric on a consulting basis, and Kettinger engaged in the subterfuge of paying him as though he were an outside contractor, when in fact he worked a full week each week for QBT. Cedric was liked and respected by everyone in the company. In spite of the fact that he was the senior citizen of the company, he had energy and could keep up with younger people. As the metallurgist, his contribution was very high as were his talents in manufacturing engineering. He seemed to have a way of fitting an exact solution to a given engineering problem. He was from the "old school" of strict disciplinarian rules on the job.

Chief Accountant and Office Manager—Brad Carpenter. Brad entered the company five months ago. The youngest member, age 29, of the management team, his experience in the copper industry was very limited. Prior to joining QBT, Brad had been an employee in a division of Western Electric which made wire and cable products; therefore, he knew nothing about the tube industry. He had participated in a business training course at Western Electric, a three-year program from which he had recently graduated. Will had confided to Brad that he would have an excellent chance of being president of the company one day. Will intended to train him in all phases of the business. Brad's duties were those normally associated with the office management function—bookkeeping, payroll, purchasing (of everything but the copper which the president did), inventory preparation, financial statement preparation, taxes, and many other of the mundane aspects of keeping the records of a business. Brad was married, had four young children, and lived in a town about 20 miles from Bridgeport.

Personality Conflicts

Over the years, the relationship between Will and Sam had deteriorated. To the outside world they seemed to complement each other; face to face there was almost always a clash of some kind. Will felt Sam was not directing enough of the sales effort to the bread and butter accounts. He thought Sam was much too casual in his approach to things; therefore, he was not getting the most out of the sales effort. Sam, on the other hand, felt Will did not have the vision to see the market potentials that he (Sam) was trying to cultivate.

It seemed surprising that a breakup had not taken place earlier. However, there was a recognition that each needed the other, and, of course, the ownership of the enterprise was in their hands on an equal basis (with a 20 percent minority interest). However, this clash was sufficiently transparent that others in the organization found it increasingly difficult to be loyal to both, and there soon developed two major factions—those loyal to Will and those who sided with Sam. There was not an open breach of loyalty to the other party in most cases, rather a leaning to the favored party. Fred Weston, although reporting to Will, tended to favor Sam. Cedric was a Will Kettinger person right down the line. The supervisors, for the most part, were very loyal to Will, but even at that level they were quite aware of the conflict. Brad was too new to have chosen sides yet, but he was leaning toward Sam. Nevertheless, he felt Will might be the more competent of the two.

In addition, Fred professed to think that Cedric was often wrong and felt he became involved in the production effort too often. Fred and Brad seemed to get along reasonably well, but Brad's position with Will seemed to be of concern to Fred since he spent a good deal of time joking with Brad about the latter's "buddy" (meaning Will). Brad and Cedric had very little in common, either professionally or in other areas. This lack of rapport was attributed in part to their great disparity in age. Brad had nothing but respect for Cedric, but it seemed doubtful Cedric even knew of Brad's existence for several months after he was hired.

Financial Structure

In spite of the fact that QBT had been in business for about ten years, it had not experienced the startling growth that many companies had enjoyed during this same decade. The Quality Brass and Tube Company was still a small company, but it had a yearly, million-dollar operation (see Exhibit 1). The principal costs included were those in cost of sales, and of this, material costs were typically 40 to 50 percent of selling price, with labor and applied overhead averaging 20 to 25 percent.

The cost of sales, on occasion, was nearly 75 percent of selling price, a level which Will Kettinger thought was much too high and somewhat out of line with what he thought he knew about his competitors' costs. He felt that labor costs should have been much lower, because with the type of equipment he had, supervision and set-up effort were the primary needs. The most critical element in financial planning was the proper handling of cash requirements (see Exhibit 2). On occasion, cash would get very low for two reasons. First of all, the price of copper during this period was very volatile. Will had some good sources of price information and would know about an impending price raise a day or two prior to its coming into effect. When he learned of such an increase, QBT would load up on copper tubing to the limit of the capacity of the plant. Secondly, because QBT was small and exercised very little leverage among its customers, it had to tolerate late paying situations more than larger companies and was less willing to screen out customers because of a bad Dun and Bradstreet rating than it might have been had business been better. This meant that both inventories and receivables would become extremely large once in a while and put a severe strain on the cash position. Fortunately, such conditions were temporary and Will had established fine relations with a local Bridgeport bank, where the company would borrow as much as $40,000 for short periods of time to see it through a payroll or a period when high inventory was being converted.

As indicated above, the credit risks that QBT was willing to take were high but often yielded plus business. On at least one occasion, however, QBT lost nearly $7,500 on one of these risks. Sam had sold an inventor and manufacturer of a new farm spray device $10,000 of finished tubing on faith. The customer had very little financial backing and some lack of skill in marketing the product. Because of an engineering failure, this customer tried to market a sprayer in the fall when the demand for such equipment was in the spring. Brad had to become involved in a creditors' committee and made at least one trip to Omaha to try to salvage some of the investment.[3]

Labor

While the skills required at the management level were high as far as technology was concerned, the employees operating the draw-benches and the finishing operations could be trained in their jobs in a two-to-three month period without too much difficulty. This, of course, presupposed that the supervisors had the basic skills to do the training. As a result, much of the labor was, at best, semiskilled, was often from a minority group (Puerto Rican or black), and had no particular loyalty to QBT. Many of the employees were not well off financially (as witnessed by the number of garnishments they suffered), and turnover was high.

3. Much later it was learned that the decision to carry this account until the next marketing season was a good one, because a large international company bought the idea of the pump and became a key customer of the pump maker, as well as of QBT.

Exhibit 2

Quality Brass and Tube Company
Balance Sheet

Cash	$150,000	
Accounts Receivable	90,000	
Inventory	200,000	
Current Assets		$440,000
Fixed Assets Less Depreciation		400,000
Total Assets		$840,000
Accounts Payable—Trade	$225,000	
Short-Term Loans	40,000	
Current Liabilities		$265,000
Stockholders' Equity		575,000
Total Liabilities and Net Worth		$840,000

The plant was organized under a branch of the union UAW, which until very recently had not been pressing in their demands. Will had convinced them, for the most part, that any decision to push for elaborate wage increases or fringe benefits would result in QBT's going out of business. It was rumored that Will Kettinger was "paying off" the union business manager, but there was no firm evidence. A turnover in union business managers in the spring had altered this somewhat. Will found that the contract negotiations (the contract expired in the fall) in which he engaged were becoming a little tighter than usual, and the demands were increasing to the point where he was convinced the honeymoon was over. Will continued to feel that any marked increase in wages could put QBT out of business or necessitate a work force reduction which might take its toll on quality.

Will had usually conducted the union negotiations behind locked doors and had rarely involved anyone else in the organization, although, on occasion, he had called upon the production superintendent for facts and figures. This time he decided he would involve both Brad and Fred in the basic conferences. Both had felt their presences were somewhat more of a show of strength by weight of numbers than an actual contribution to the whole affair.

THE PROPOSED MOVE

That summer the Quality Brass and Tube Company, with Will Kettinger as the prime mover, did some serious evaluation of the proposal to move to New Center, Rhode Island. As suggested earlier,

Will realized that further growth of the company would come from industry growth. He also realized that in order to remain profitable, he was going to have to reduce costs in some manner. Better than 70 percent of costs were in sales figures. The cost of materials was high, but Will knew that he could exercise little control here due to the company's size and the control over prices which was effected by the price leaders in the industry. There was a fixity to the overhead content of cost of sales—at least if the company remained in its current location. Further, the overhead element was relatively minor. Remaining was the cost of labor. Will felt that under the existing arrangement, this was becoming less and less controllable and was getting progressively more damaging to the profit picture. He looked to the proposal to relocate to New Center as a possible solution to the high labor cost problem.

After arriving at the decision to go to New Center, a number of events were to transpire, some of them quite orderly and more or less planned and some quite by accident.

First, Will made a trip to New Center to talk to the city planners to learn to what extent their original proposal would be translated into action. He returned from this trip ready to pack his bag and head for New Center. Much of the subsequent work that was performed had a serious bias, for Will had obviously made the decision to move to New Center at the time he returned.

However, Will did realize there were several problems which had to be solved before making final arrangements. Among the more serious—and perhaps in order of importance—were the following problems to be met:

1. To convince Sam Pelser of the wisdom of the move, or failing to do this, convince the minority interest (the majority of the 20 percent anyway) that the move was appropriate.
2. To solve the labor problems in the new community, including convincing some of the key managers and supervisors to move to New Center. Failing to do this, he would find his problems in starting the new plant similar to his efforts of ten years earlier—something he hoped he would not have to duplicate.
3. To be sure that the company could weather the financial burden of the move and bear the costs of building a new plant. He was hopeful, from talking to the people in New Center, that he could negotiate a very favorable SBA (Small Business Administration) loan and have sizable savings in labor costs and taxes with which to carry the new construction over the life of the payback of the SBA loan.
4. To make some arrangements with the union in Bridgeport concerning transfer of employees to New Center, or arrange for some suitable severance-pay arrangement. He assumed that the latter would be the choice of most and, in fact, would be the only alternative offered to other than key skilled labor. He also

hoped that he would arrive in New Center with a plant that was "unorganized" and that he would be able to retrench in wages and benefits until it did become organized, but at a lower base. (This type of thinking was encouraged by the Chamber of Commerce people in New Center.)

5. To make an orderly withdrawal from Bridgeport. This involved planning some public relations work, since Bridgeport was already suffering from an unemployment problem and the laying off of about one hundred people was not going to be very well received. The fact that one is leaving behind an angry community may hurt as much in the new community as in the old. And, in this case, the old community was also housing the businesses which would continue to be the sources of supply for raw material and much business information. Will Kettinger was convinced that the Bridgeport business community must be left impressed with the necessity for the move.

Will began his moves. Sam Pelser was as much opposed to the move as Will was for it. Sam had strong roots in the Bridgeport community, including family, friends, and some other business interests. His defense of his adamancy was on the grounds that the company was not affluent enough for such a move and that many of the proposed gains were not real at all (for example, he did not believe that the company could escape the union as easily as Will thought). In spite of this apparent difference of opinion, Will proceeded with the plan in an orderly way. He campaigned among the minority stockholders and became convinced that when, and if, a showdown became necessary, he would be able to vote at least 51 percent of the stock.

However, Will did not do much better in convincing the subordinates to move. Cedric had very few roots and would go willingly. Fred felt that he would be much more vulnerable to arbitrary action on the part of Will if he were located in the noncopper town of New Center than he was in Bridgeport, where he was reasonably convinced that he could hire himself out with little difficulty. It appeared that he would be a holdout unless Will came through with some pretty good guarantees (such as some stock options, so Fred could gain an interest in the business, and a sizable increase in salary). Brad was somewhat taken aback by the prospect but was not arbitrary in his refusal to go. (Brad was the most easily replaced of the team, so Will could not offer many incentives.) At least one of the supervisors agreed to go, and a second agreed to go for three to six months to help get the place set up. It appeared that, with some effort, Will could go to New Center with a nucleus of a technical work force, but he had really wished that Fred would go along. (Fred was evidently correct in his evaluation of the situation, because Will said privately to Brad that he would not expect Fred to be with the company very long. This suggested that Will was, in fact, going to use Fred to get the place started and then let him go.)

Brad and Will examined the financial picture together. Even though it was hoped a new plant with increased capacity and a more efficient operation would add to product value for the customer and be translated into additional sales, Will and Brad thought it best not to count on this—at least among themselves. The estimate of the cost of moving was reduced to the following:

1. Brad reviewed the financial figures for a period of six months (Will agreed that these were typical months) and calculated a shutdown cost figure at about $40,000 per month.
2. A review of seniority records indicated that the company would probably have to expect to pay out $150,000 in severance pay, but this figure was subject to review by the union and could be higher.
3. The new plant and some new pieces of equipment (most would be moved from the old location) would cost $500,000 including interest. Cedric had done some negotiating with architects in New Center and had preliminary estimates, which Brad and Will inflated by 10 percent and felt this would give a conservative figure.
4. The factory could be moved by private truck for about $10,000. This was a firm figure given by the trucker, a QBT supervisor who would be moving with the company. It was far below union rates.

The next step was very critical. Both Will and Brad agreed that the raw figures that could be presented in the SBA would never get them a loan. Will decided that the pro forma statements submitted to the SBA must in some way establish that the cash to pay back the loan would be generated on a timely basis. He decided that it would not be unreasonable for them to forecast increased sales levels—a reasonable expectation, but hardly a conservative presentation. As a result, he estimated that within three years sales would be up to $1,250,000 per year, which would generate about $72,000 a year in cash. To support this, a profit graph was constructed showing break-even at about $90,000 in sales per month and fixed costs at about $40,000. In April, a sales volume of about $105,000 yielded a profit of $6,300, which, if annualized, would tend to support the estimated profit at the forecasted volume.

The Small Business Administration was most liberal in its acceptance of these projections. A loan for a twenty-year period (actually two back-to-back ten-year arrangements) in which the repayment would be out of profits at an increasing rate in the later portions of the loan was needed. This device was apparently common to allow new, small companies a chance to get moving without the burden of an evenly distributed share of the loan in the early portions of the payback period. Will and Brad were satisfied that, even with the more conservative figures they had calculated, the pressure to pay back the

loan during its early years would not be a strain if any of the anticipated savings were realized. The future would tell about the heavier
later payments.

Based on an estimated shutdown period of three months, the total
additional financing needed was about $800,000. The president esti-
mated that the company could probably finance $100,000 of it with
careful control of inventories, conversion of receivables, and rent
savings. This left a need for about $700,000 in long-term financing.
The Small Business Administration agreed to such a loan arrangement, and a tentative provision was made to have a series of long-
term notes drawn up (still contingent upon acceptance of the whole
arrangement by the QBT stockholders—a tender balance at the time
of the negotiations). Will felt that he had passed the financial hurdle.

Will first approached the union business manager in early August.
The timing of the approach was not particularly fortuitous since both
the union and management had been talking about the new contract
since late spring. Many of the sticky points had been ironed out during
this time, and the proposal to relocate certainly seemed like a very
transparent scheme to escape the effects of the new contract. The
business manager was furious, and upon hearing it, just got up and
stormed out of Will's office. It was clear there was not going to be any
easy solution to this portion of the efforts. At this point, Will decided
that he had best determine, once and for all, whether he had the votes
to go through with the move. He called a meeting of the board of
directors for the middle of August to vote on the issue of relocating.
Although such meetings were held each month, they were no more
than social affairs in comparison. Sam Pelser agreed to be in town
on the day of the board meeting, but before that date, Sam had a heart
attack while on a selling trip in Texas. Though the attack was not
fatal, it was sufficiently incapacitating to keep him from work for
about six months. Sam evidently realized he would be unable to fight
the move, and therefore he made no effort to oppose it. As a result
of Sam's illness, Will obtained complete control. He appointed a long-
time sales representative as acting sales manager and accepted Sam's
resignation as sales manager and vice-president shortly thereafter.
However, Sam retained his financial interest in the company and
remained on the board of directors.

Will now felt that he could go back to the union and finish that
which he had started. At the next meeting, he was no longer solicitous.
Rather, he took the approach that he was leaving town and made a
very low offer of severance pay for the workers to be laid off. The
business manager sensed the futility of the position and made a
counteroffer which was very close to the original $150,000 figure
planned. The business manager promised, however, that Will had
not heard the end of it.

Plans to build the new plant, visits by Brad to New Center to work out the tax problems, and work on problems of arranging housing facilities for the people involved in the move progressed. The dye was cast.

Will had one last mission. He wanted to salvage some measure of goodwill in Bridgeport, although he felt the union would not allow him much room. Will managed to get a piece in the newspaper telling how QBT had found its market was moving away and that it could better serve its trade if it were closer to the geographical center of it—which strangely enough was somewhere near the middle of Rhode Island. The union retaliated with a news release that QBT was just running from the union. The hoped-for favorable impression was no longer possible. Will felt the best course of action at this point was to accelerate the relocation program as much as he could and leave the rapidly deteriorating situation in Bridgeport. He did make some last-minute personal contacts among his business acquaintances and believed that he convinced them that unless he could get a more favorable labor climate he would have to close shop—a result not unlike leaving town as far as Bridgeport was concerned. He hoped he had been convincing.

By the time of the move (November), at least three other events had occurred which had a bearing on the situation:

> 1. The union had kept its promise that "Will had not heard the end of it." Through the offices of the international union, a contact was established between the local Bridgeport and a likely successor local counterpart in New Center.
>
> Word soon leaked that Will planned to let one of his supervisors, who owned a truck adequate for the purpose, do the moving of the plant on an outside contract basis. This truck and driver were strictly extra-union, and the cost would be much lower.
>
> The union said that that was the last straw. Steps were taken by the Bridgeport union to convince the New Center local that QBT was strictly an antilabor company and had no intention of having a union in New Center. In order to make this point, they cited QBT's activity in getting the plant moved by nonunion personnel. The New Center local union was mobilized (much to the unhappiness of the local Chamber of Commerce) and set up pickets at the new plant protesting the use of nonunion trucking to move the plant. In order to move into the new plant, then, the supervisor-contractor had to have the crew cross a picket line. (It later developed that not one day's work was done in the new plant without a union, although there were only small gains in initial wage rates due to pressure by the Chamber of Commerce.)
>
> 2. Fred Weston did not make the move to New Center. Will would not offer him the interest in the company he demanded, and Fred could not be persuaded he would be acting wisely to go.

3. Brad Carpenter also decided not to go. Having been with the company a scant five months, he did not feel the risks of being with this company were commensurate with the long-run opportunities he felt he might enjoy. He realized he had no ownership interest in the company; probably would find it difficult to acquire one; and he might end up spending the next 15 years of his life chasing the end of the rainbow.

Will had one last meeting with Brad Carpenter prior to the latter's departure. Will had asked Brad to lunch to talk things over. According to Brad, Will was not really giving a very hard sell, except perhaps to himself. He told Brad he thought the future of QBT was wide open, and he really believed that they were about to cross the threshold into the big time with the decision to relocate to New Center and build the new plant.

Krandall Furniture Company

Starting with the first shift on Monday, July 17, and extending through Friday, July 21, an unauthorized work stoppage (wildcat strike) took place at the Krandall Furniture Company. Officially the union did not support the strike and, in fact, all union officers and stewards were allowed to go through the picket line. After the unauthorized strike was ended, the company discharged eight employees and suspended 11 others for 30 days without pay.

The union objected strongly to this disciplinary measure, and in accordance with the terms of the labor contract, the company action was appealed through the regular grievance procedure. When the company remained adamant on the penalties, the union requested the case be submitted to an arbitrator for a final decision.

The president of Krandall, Gregory Bartlett, called a meeting to discuss and review the case that was to be presented to the arbitrator. Attending this meeting were Burt Cutwell, the works manager; Alice Smathers, director of industrial relations; and Sol Zimmerman, sales manager. Greg Bartlett opened the meeting by stating that the purpose was to look at this case from all angles to be sure nothing was overlooked. He continued . . .

Greg: Alice, I have read over the material you are planning to submit to the arbitrator (see Appendix 1), and I think you have done a fine job of presenting the facts. However, before we send this off to arbitration, I would like us to ask ourselves the questions: Is it in our best interests to go to arbitration? If we win the decision, and it appears we have a good chance, what will this do to our labor relations? On the other hand, if we lose then what kind of a bind will we be in? Basically I am asking, Should we forgive and forget? What is your thinking on this, Alice?

Alice: Greg, I think I have expressed my views on this before. We did forgive and forget three years ago, and I don't see that we have come out ahead. We have a solid case, and we should take it to arbitration. After we win we can reconsider the forgive and forget.

Greg: And if we don't win?

Alice: Not a chance. The arbitrator has no choice.

Greg: Burt, what do you think?

Burt: First, I think we did gain something three years ago. We have had three years of relative good labor relations; but Alice may be right, this might be the time to crack down. We can't stand too many wildcat strikes.

Sol: Once a company gets a reputation for slow deliveries because of labor trouble, it makes our job much tougher. But on the other hand, those companies handling government contracts want to be sure we are clean.

Greg: What do you mean by that?

Sol: I mean we can't be cited for discriminatory practices and be a sub-contractor on a federal contract. We have to show we are treating the blacks the same as the whites.

Alice: Sol is referring to the fact that of the eight discharged, six are black.

Greg: Maybe Sol has a point.

Alice: When you consider that 80 percent of our work force is black, it's not unreasonable to discharge six blacks out of eight, which is about 75 percent.

Sol: I hope you're right. How about those suspended?

Alice: All except Atlas and Pepper are black. But again this is in the right percentage.

Burt: I think Alice is right. This is not going to be a problem. The major issue to me is concerned with the work stoppages. As I said, we have had pretty good relations for the past three years, and I would be happy if the next three were as good.

Sol: You fellows fought tooth and nail to get Article V into the contract, and now I see you backing away from it. Why?

Burt: We are not backing away. It has served its purpose. Do we have to hit the union over the head to get them to see things our way?

Sol: Read their letter requesting arbitration, and see if you have won your point. (See Appendix 2.)

Alice: The union always talks tough when they put something down on paper. Unofficially they see things our way.

Sol: I wish I could believe that.

Greg: What are the alternatives in this situation? Let me see if I can set them up.
1. Go to arbitration and if we win—make no changes in penalties.
2. Go to arbitration and if a positive decision—reduce the penalties.
3. Do not go to arbitration but negotiate reduced penalties with the union now—say 30-day layoffs for discharged and 15-day layoffs for those with 30-day layoffs.
4. Do not go to arbitration, but instead just have no penalties and forgive and forget.

Are there other alternatives?

Alice: There is a fifth one. Go to arbitration, and if you win, then implement the forgive and forget aspect.

Burt: You need to answer one question in any of the alternatives where penalties are to be reduced. These fellows have served out their penalties, so any reduction is meaningless unless we give them pay for the time they were laid off.

Sol: And if you do that, you are giving the culprits a paid vacation. I think it's a little late for reduced penalties.

Greg: I don't think we have to worry about paid vacations, but we should be concerned about good labor relations; and there is much to be said about a forgive and forget approach. Let me read over that presentation to the arbitrator again, and then I will make a decision.

APPENDIX 1

Company's Hearing Memorandum—Statement of Issue

On Monday, July 17,—despite the clear and unambiguous language in the No Strike provision of the labor agreement between the parties that there shall not be "any slowdown, stoppage, or other interference with production on the part of the employees"—approximately 271 of the 495 employees on the first shift in the company's plant in Jackson, Mississippi, failed and refused to report for work. As second- and third-shift employees were driving to work, they were intercepted by pickets lined along Krandall Lane—the only road leading to the company's plant. The pickets crowded onto the road, narrowing the two-lane highway to one lane for both directions, and exhorted the approaching automobiles to "turn back." Only 28 of the 252 employees on the second shift, and 15 of the 91 employees on the third shift reported for work on July 17.

For three days (July 17 through 19) a small, hard core of pickets lined and spilled onto Krandall Lane, confronting approaching traffic for each shift with demands to "turn back." During this time, the plant's operations virtually stood still, as only a handful of employees reported for work. Thousands of dollars in production time were lost, as rebellion was nurtured by pickets deliberately interfering with the right of other employees to work and to meet their contractual obligations and responsibilities.

On July 20—in the evening of the fourth day of the unlawful and improper work stoppage—company and union representatives met, and the company agreed to a proposal for hearing complaints thus ending the unlawful work stoppage. The background and details of this meeting will be developed later, but it is well to point out at this time that the union and the employees already had a contractual basis for the hearing of complaints—which the employees and the union bypassed, ignored, and failed to follow. On Friday, July 21, part of the work force reported for work, and the remainder reported the following Monday.

After gathering all available facts on the unlawful work stoppage —and in accordance with the union's request to delay taking disciplinary action—the company, by letter dated August 27, notified the union that it was discharging eight employees and suspending 11 employees for 30 days, without pay. These employees—whose names appear below—were also individually notified of the company's action.

In the light of the provisions contained in Article V—the No Strike–No Lockout clauses of the agreement between the parties—which forbids "any slowdown, stoppage, or other interference with production," and provides that, should the union protest and appeal to arbitration the propriety of the company's disciplinary action, "the only issue before the arbitrator shall be limited to the employee's participation in such unauthorized activity." Therefore, the issue before the arbitrator is: Did the company violate the labor agreement, dated September 18, by discharging or suspending from work for thirty days, without pay, the following employees:

Discharged		Suspended
C. R. Bronson	Dept. 135	C. L. Atlas
J. G. Dickson	Dept. 112	K. A. Benton
P. J. Grover	Dept. 132	M. Brown
L. C. Lovelace	Dept. 105	B. G. Campbell
T. A. Lovelace	Dept. 112	F. W. Cecil
A. B. Randall	Dept. 114	A. R. Downs
L. L. Underwood	Dept. 127	P. C. Fairview
C. G. Ventner	Dept. 132	J. J. Manly
		T. F. Munson
		P. J. Pepper
		R .W. Smith

The company will show that the discharged or suspended employees failed and refused to report for work, as scheduled and required, during the unlawful work stoppage; that they did not offer any excuse, which the company could accept as valid, for failing and refusing to report for work; that—contrary to the obligations, duties, and responsibilities required of them under the labor agreement and in their jobs—they participated in an improper and unlawful work stoppage.

The company contends that its action in discharging or suspending these employees was proper and did not violate the labor agreement; and that therefore the arbitrator must deny every grievance in this case.

Background Facts Reported by Company

1. On July 14 there were indications that something was in the offing: when the company tried to find out what was going on, the union's officers pleaded ignorance. The chain of events started when more than one half of the first-shift hourly employees gathered together in the plant parking lot during the noon hour. The shop stewards and Sid Wilson, the union's business agent, also were present in the parking lot, but appeared to be merely observing what was taking place. At 12:25 p.m., the crowd dispersed and returned to

work. Later in the afternoon, at a scheduled grievance meeting, the company's personnel manager, Green, drew Wilson aside and asked him why the crowd had gathered in the parking lot. The business agent said he had been "run off," and could not learn what the meeting had been about.

2. Apparently, as a result of the noon-hour gathering in the company's parking lot, a meeting was held in the City Parking Lot in Jackson, in the evening, Saturday, July 15. Based on the events that began on July 17, the employees at this meeting evidently decided to "wildcat," and to persuade, through picketing, all the other employees to join them in a work stoppage in flagrant violation of their obligations under the labor agreement. The work stoppage which was to take place was a deliberate, premeditated violation of the No Strike provision in the labor agreement.

The employees knew that mere participation in a work stoppage was under the express provisions of the agreement ground for discharge. This bargain had been hammered out at the negotiations in exchange for a No Strike savings clause. The arbitrator was specifically prohibited from delving into the area of penalty. As a practical matter, unless the union, or the employees themselves, come forward to point out the guilty—which they did not do—the company has to act according to its best information. By the terms of the agreement, when disciplinary action, including discharge, arises out of a violation of the No Strike provisions, the arbitrator cannot substitute a personal judgment, or the union's judgment for management's judgment.

3. On Monday morning, July 17, just prior to the start of the first shift at 7:00 a.m., a sizable group of employees congregated in the plant parking lot and milled around. At 6:45 a.m., employees started through the gates. That morning more than one half of the first-shift employees failed to report for work. On the other hand, the union's officers and shop stewards who were employed at the plant adhered to the pattern of assiduously reporting to work throughout the duration of the unlawful work stoppage. At each shift, the pickets eased the union's shop stewards through the gauntlet on Krandall Lane. The shop steward's badge proved an "entrc." Apparently, the employees felt that the union's treasury had to be protected at all costs, even to the extent of affecting their continued employment with the company.

4. In an effort to halt the spread of the unlawful work stoppage, the following letter was distributed to each shift as they left the plant:

July 17, 19—

Dear Krandall Employee:

As you know, a number of our fellow employees did not report for work at the start of the shift this morning. As nearly as we can tell, many employees planned to come to work, but were kept from doing so by a small minority of people. This is a very unfortunate situation and one which, I am sure, you deplore as much as I do.

In the meantime, officials of the local union as well as representatives of the international union are meeting with people in an attempt to straighten things out. As soon as all people have returned to work, the company will sit down and settle whatever problem is involved. I have been assured that things will return to normal tomorrow and that all employees will report for work at the regular time.

Sincerely,

/s/ B. A. Cutwell
Works Manager

The company's plea went unheeded.

5. The second-shift employees—starting at 3:30 p.m. or 3:00 p.m. for continuous operations—were met by a human roadblock at the Track Side Bulk Plant site on Krandall Lane, east of Route 11. The picketing employees moved onto the road from both sides, converting the two lanes to one for both directions. Approaching traffic was forced to run the gauntlet and face the angry shouts and the threatening gestures. Local and state police were summoned to restore order and remove the congestion of pickets obstructing the only street access to the plant. Automobiles that had passed through the picket line turned around in the company's parking lot and went back. Only 28 of the 252 second-shift employees, including 15 shop stewards, reported for work.

6. At 10:00 p.m. on July 17, pickets again formed on Krandall Lane near the Track Side Bulk Plant, to intercept third-shift employees reporting at 11:00 p.m. Again, they exhorted the approaching automobiles to turn around and go back. At times, cars were forced to slow down by the pickets walking onto the road or to stop completely until the pickets were dispersed by the police. As the union's shop stewards approached, flashing their badges, the shouting and threatening gestures stopped, and the road cleared. Of the 91 employees on the third shift, only 15 reported for work.

For three days employees picketed at the start of each shift.

7. Faced with a near total work stoppage, sparked by employees determined to turn the clock back to the middle ages of industrial life, the company sent the following telegram to the employees who did not report for work:

The company-union agreement provides that any employee who participates in a wildcat strike is subject to discharge.

Krandall Furniture Company

The cold fact that the company considered discharge as the penalty appropriate for employees participating in an unlawful work stoppage was ignored. The grieving employees were forewarned of the consequences by the express provisions of the No Strike clause in the agreement; by the company's telegram; and by their union officers through announcements sent over the radio. All to no avail. At noon on July 18, the employees held a strike strategy meeting at the City Parking Lot in Jackson. Those of the international representatives and local union officers who were present remained on the fringe of the crowd and made no effort to talk some sense into the crowd or to persuade them to go back to work.

8. At other times throughout the week of the unlawful work stoppage, the union's officers did advise the striking employees that their course of action was improper, and that the consequences were extreme:

(a) On July 17, the union had radio station WCKQ repeat the following announcement 10 times between 8:49 a.m. and 3:03 p.m.:

> There is a strike at Krandall. The strike is unauthorized and illegal, and the people are urged to come back to work.

(b) On July 19, Sid Wilson, the union's business agent, made the following announcement over WCKQ:

> This is S. L. Wilson, business agent and retiring president of Local Union #2318, United Brotherhood of Carpenters and Joiners of America.
>
> I wish to direct these remarks to all members of Local Union #2318 who are employed by the Krandall Furniture Company and who are not reporting to their jobs. I want to remind each member that the Local Union #2318 has a valid and binding agreement with Krandall Furniture Company which provides a grievance procedure for the settlement of all complaints. This agreement also provides that there will be no work stoppage and that all grievances will be handled through the grievance procedure.
>
> The current work stoppage is neither sanctioned nor approved by Local Union #2318, or any of its officers or agents; and, therefore, each member is urged to return to work immediately in conformity with our obligation to the contract.

(c) And on July 20, WCKQ carried the following announcement by George Offenberg, president of the union:

> This is George Offenberg, president of Local Union #2318. I would like to advise all members of the Local #2318 who are employees of the Krandall Furniture Company that the current work stoppage is not authorized, sanctioned, or approved by Local #2318 or any of its officers or agents.
>
> We have a contract with Krandall Furniture Company which imposes a moral and legal obligation not to participate in any work stoppage or slowdown during the term of our agreement. I want each member to understand that the current work stoppage is in violation of our agreement, also in derogation of our responsibilities under this agreement.
>
> Therefore, as your president, I urge members to return to their jobs immediately in conformity with our obligation and responsibility.

9. On July 18, the company petitioned the Jackson County Court for a temporary injunction to halt the picketing activity on Krandall Lane, the only street access to the plant. Named as defendants in the petition were 18 union officers and employees.

At a hearing of the petition on July 20, the union's plea that it and its officers be dropped as defendants, on the ground that they did not authorize the work stoppage, was denied. Judge Alexander advised the three parties—the union, the picketers and strikers, and the company—to get together within 24 hours to settle their dispute, or he would rule on the petition for the injunction. Immediately, the attorneys for the union and defendant employees met with the company's representatives to arrange for a meeting.

10. On the evening of July 20, the three parties in the injunction petition met, as they had been instructed to by Judge Alexander. The international officers of the union pleaded with the company not to discharge any of the employees. They asked the company to agree to take up all complaints immediately and to waive the right to discharge any of the employees. The company refused to forego the right to discharge the participating employees, as afforded it under the labor agreement. This right to impose discipline, including discharge, for violation of the No Strike provision was the only tool, the only deterrent that the union had given the company. To waive this right would be tantamount to wiping out the only instrument of guaranteeing uninterrupted production. The union forced the company to look solely to the employees for redress, by avoiding financial responsibility and the exercise of leadership through a clause in the agreement.

The meeting concluded with the company representative agreeing to the following proposal:

> Upon the return of a greater majority of the employees Friday and the resumption of normal plant operation by Monday, the officials of Krandall Furniture Company guarantee to conduct an investigation of the complaints to rectify those which are found to be meritorious, waiving the several steps of the grievance process. All grievances which are connected with this work stoppage must be submitted by the union within 10 days to be considered.

Actually what the employees had received in the foregoing proposal was always available to them through the Grievance Procedure contained in the labor agreement. In fact, the provisions of the Grievance Procedure specifically encourage employees to use this forum to air and settle their grievances. A reading of paragraph 6 of the agreement which is part of the Grievance Procedure bears this out:

> No employee covered by this agreement shall be discriminated against or intimidated by the company for seeking resolution of grievances or for serving the union as an officer or as a member of the Grievance Committee in representing the union in any grievance, and any dispute in this connection shall be regarded as a grievance

KRANDALL FURNITURE COMPANY

and shall be settled through the grievance and arbitration procedure, as provided for herein.

11. The company points out that nowhere does the proposal of July 20 mention any modification of the company's contractual right to exercise its complete discretion in setting the penalty for an unlawful work stoppage. At subsequent meetings—after normal operations had resumed—the union again pleaded with the company not to discharge any employees, since they felt that it would spark another unlawful work stoppage. The company again made it clear that this prohibited activity was the "cardinal sin" in the relations of a company with its employees and the union, and that the means to deal with it were not to be diluted in the grievance or arbitration process.

12. Article V, the No Strike–No Lockout provision of the labor agreement, provides that employees will not engage in "any slowdown, stoppage, or other interference with production"—and further provides that:

> This company retains the right to discipline, including discharge, employees who engage in such unauthorized activity, except, however, that the union shall have the right, through the grievance procedure, to protest and appeal the propriety of any such discipline. The only issue before the arbitrator shall be limited to the employee's participation in such unauthorized activity (Para. 21 of Agreement).

In accordance with the foregoing, the company discharged or suspended from work for 30 days, without pay, the 19 employees described below. They did not report for work during the week of the work stoppage; and they did not offer any excuse, which the company could accept as valid, for their absence.

    (a) C. R. Bronson did not report for work July 17th through the 21st. Bronson was discharged.

    (b) J. G. Dickson did not report for work July 17th through the 21st. Dickson was discharged.

    (c) P. J. Grover did not report for work July 17th through the 21st. Grover was discharged.

    (d) L. C. Lovelace did not report for work July 17th through the 20th. Lovelace was discharged.

    (e) T. A. Lovelace did not report for work July 17th through the 21st. Lovelace was discharged.

    (f) A. B. Randall did not report for work July 17th through the 21st. Randall was discharged.

    (g) L. L. Underwood did not report for work July 17th through the 21st. Underwood was discharged.

    (h) C. G. Ventner did not report for work July 17th through the 20th. Ventner was discharged.

    (i) C. L. Atlas did not report for work July 17th through the 20th. Atlas was suspended.

(j) K. A. Benton did not report for work July 17th through the 21st. Benton was suspended.

(k) M. Brown did not report for work July 17th through the 21st. Brown was suspended.

(l) B. G. Campbell did not report for work July 17th through the 21st. Campbell was suspended.

(m) F. W. Cecil did not report for work July 17th through the 21st. Cecil was suspended.

(n) A. R. Downs did not report for work July 17th through the 20th. Downs was suspended.

(o) P. C. Fairview did not report for work July 17th through the 21st. Fairview was suspended.

(p) J. J. Manly did not report for work July 17th through July 21st. Manly was suspended.

(q) T. F. Munson did not report for work July 17th through July 20th. Munson was suspended.

(r) P. J. Pepper did not report for work July 17th through the 21st. Pepper was suspended.

(s) R. W. Smith did not report for work July 17th through the 20th. Smith was suspended.

13. Under the clear and unambiguous language of the labor agreement as intended by the parties in light of the last contract negotiations, the company had the right to discipline, including discharge, employees participating in an unlawful work stoppage. Further, having established the fact of participation, namely, that there was an unlawful work stoppage and the employee failed to report for work without a reasonable excuse—the parties intended that the question of the penalty was within the company's sole and complete discretion. The company's judgment in this area is not subject to review. The contract specifically provides for one reviewable fact, namely, that "The only issue before the arbitrator shall be limited to the employee's participation in such unauthorized activity." The intention of the parties is clearly expressed. Words must be taken to mean what they plainly say. The history of the last contract negotiation leaves no doubt that strikes during the contract term were not to be regarded as a protected activity.

Comments on Negotiations Leading to Current Agreement Between Parties

14. The current labor agreement contains, as Article V, the following No Strike—No Lockout provisions:

19. The union agrees that neither it nor its agents will initiate, sanction, aid, or lend any assistance to any slowdown, stoppage, or other interference with production on the part of the employees, except in case of the company's failure to abide

by an arbitration award, in which case, the union shall submit its contention of failure on the part of the company to abide by such award to an arbitrator for a decision. If the second arbitrator affirms the union's contentions and the company continues its failure to abide by the first arbitration award, then the union is not bound by the provisions of this article. The company agrees that neither it nor its agents will lock out employees during the term of this agreement.

20. Should an unauthorized slowdown, stoppage of work, or interference of production occur, the union shall be absolved of any financial liability if it, upon notice by the company, through its authorized representative, immediately renounces such action to the employees involved and to the company and endeavors to bring about cessation of such activity. The union agrees that it will not negate the provisions of this section by its seclusions or by any other means which would circumvent their responsibilities under this section.

21. The company retains the right to discipline, including discharge, employees who engage in such unauthorized activity, except however that the union shall have the right, through the grievance procedure, to protest and appeal the propriety of any such discipline. The only issue before the arbitrator shall be limited to the employee's participation in such unauthorized activity.

22. The company retains the right to recover such damages as they may incur by reason of a breach of this provision (Article V) under the arbitration provision of this agreement.

15. The part of the No Strike provisions that concerns us in this case is the third paragraph—paragraph No. 21. This provision was not present in the preceding agreement which expired on July 31. The No Strike clause in the expired agreement provided as follows:

The union agrees that it will not initiate any strike action or work stoppage in the plant until all the legal requirements have been complied with. Where unauthorized strikes occur that are beyond the control of the union, the union shall endeavor to require their membership to return to work and adjust their grievances in accordance with the grievance procedure in this agreement, but the union shall not be held responsible for any financial loss incurred by the company through each unauthorized strike or work stoppage.

16. Under the new provision, the parties clearly intended that an employee participating in an unlawful work stoppage was without recourse in the area of the penalty. The only area subject to review was whether the employee participated in the unlawful work stoppage. The new provision was a *quid pro quo* for the saving clause that the union had demanded and received. The company had agreed to absolve the union of financial responsibility, if certain conditions were

met. In exchange, the union agreed that the company had the right to decide the degree of penalty, whether discipline or discharge, and that the company's judgment was not subject to review in arbitration. This was the deal that was made. This was the bargain that was agreed to.

17. Shortly before the old agreement terminated, a decertification drive was launched by the United Mine Workers. The dissidents in the collective bargaining unit were numerous and strong enough to muster the necessary number of cards to force a decertification election. The incumbent union won the election, but the United Mine Workers had polled more than 150 votes. The company was faced with a considerable number of unmollified and disgruntled employees who were dissatisfied and at odds with their collective bargaining agent.

18. This situation was ripe with the possibility of incidents of internal union conflict, whose by-products are often work stoppages and slowdowns. A company without adequate means to stabilize its own relations with the employees and the union would be whipsawed between the two contesting factions. The old No Strike clause lacked the necessary tools to enforce uninterrupted production. The company was at sea without a lifeboat. An antidote for irresponsible union and employee action was necessary.

19. At the renewal contract negotiations, the company demanded a union guarantee that the company would not be faced with any interference with production during the contract term; that the union back up this guarantee with its treasury. The company argued that if they violated the agreement, they were financially responsible to make good the loss to the employee. By the same standard, if the union of an employee violated the contract, resulting in loss to the company, the union should make good that loss.

The union balked and would not agree to accept financial responsibility for any violation of the No Strike provisions; they argued that they could not control the dissident employees who had voted for the United Mine Workers. In the union's view, the company could discharge all employees who participated in a work stoppage. This is an economic absurdity. The company cannot destroy its work force and put itself out of business, although that very same work force properly should be discharged.

The compromise which would satisfy the needs of both parties were "selective punishment" and no limitation on the company's right to impose whatever discipline it deemed appropriate under the circumstances, with a "savings" clause for the union. In return, the union agreed that the company would have the unfettered and absolute right to set the punishment for employees who violated the No Strike provisions of the agreement and that the arbitrator would not have the authority to review the penalty.

KRANDALL FURNITURE COMPANY

Arbitrator's Authority
Under Collective Bargaining Agreement

20. Article VII, Section 2, of the labor agreement provides for arbitration of unresolved grievances. The arbitrator's authority is defined in paragraph 78 as follows:

> The arbitrator shall not have the authority to add to, subtract from, modify, change, or alter any of the provisions of this agreement nor to extend its duration.

In the arbitration of grievances arising from the No Strike provisions, the arbitrator's authority is further delimited, in clear and unambiguous language, to a specific inquiry—that is: "The only issue before the arbitrator shall be limited to the employee's participation in such unauthorized activity." The activity is defined in the agreement as "any slowdown, stoppage, or other interference with production." The arbitrator must confine the inquiry and exercise the authority in accordance with the limitations set forth in the agreement. If delving into the question of penalty, the arbitrator would be usurping a right that the parties gave to the company and would be exceeding the authority invested.

21. Ordinarily, the arbitrator has two standards to apply in the discipline or discharge case. The first standard is: Did the employee commit the offense with which he is charged?; and the second standard: Is the punishment imposed appropriate to the offense? However, under the contract between the parties in this case, the second standard has been removed from the arbitrator's consideration and the arbitrator's area of review is limited solely to whether the offense was committed.

This limitation on the arbitrator's authority must be applied. When a contract limits the arbitrator's authority area, the parties must have intended that that limitation be scrupulously observed.

22. In a recent case between the same parties involved here, Arbitrator, you ruled that the particular language of a clause in the agreement permitted an employee to bump upward on a layoff—although this is contrary to standards of contract administration.

The case arose under the now expired contract of 1964. The pertinent part of the clause read as follows:

> In the event work becomes slack and it is necessary to reduce forces, the employees in any given department seniority group shall be laid off according to seniority, provided there are employees left in that seniority group who can perform the jobs required.

Three employees on three different jobs were involved. The most senior employee's job rate was, as an example, $2.45; the second senior employee's and the junior employee's job rates were $2.35. The second senior employee was scheduled for layoff, and was able to perform the most senior employee's job, not the junior employee's job. The most senior employee could perform the junior employee's job.

Under these facts, Arbitrator, you ruled that the second senior employee could bump upward into the most senior employee's job, and the most senior employee move down into the junior employee's job. The junior employee was laid off.

The operation of the clause in the above manner is, of course, a fluke. Yet the arbitrator thought to be bound by the general language of a clause, even as applied to the unforeseen event of permitting an upward bump or layoff. The contract language in this case applies specifically to a foreseen event that was fully negotiated and expressly provided for. If the arbitrator thinks to be bound by general language, certainly there is no doubt as to what must be done when presented with specific language to cover a specific situation.

23. The written employee grievances filed by the union do not deny that these employees participated in the unlawful work stoppage. The employees claim only that the company's action is "unjust." Do they mean that the company did not render justice, namely, that the company's action in their case violated the labor agreement? This claim cannot be reconciled with the uncontroverted fact that they participated in the unlawful work stoppage. Justice was rendered when the company properly applied the agreement in the manner in which both intended and provided.

Do the employees then mean that it is "unjust" only to discharge or suspend them, and not all the other employees who participated? To follow this to its logical conclusion, the company would be forced to divest itself of the ability to operate, by discharging or suspending almost all of the employees in the bargaining unit. This possibility was anticipated in negotiating the limitation on the arbitrator's authority to review the penalty. It is entirely possible that those employees who were suspended would not have jobs to come back to. Consider also the effect on the company's financial position, shareholders, customers, and numerous other obligations. The company successfully resisted the employees' efforts to bring it to its knees. The company does not intend to do violence to itself by finishing the job that the employees started.

Can the employees mean that unless all who participated are discharged or suspended, no one can be discharged or suspended, and therefore the company's action is "unjust"? What better way is there to promote rebellion than by giving employees the right to participate in an unlawful work stoppage with impunity? What better way is there to encourage industrial strife and make a mockery for our national labor policy?

No matter how the claim is dissected, the answer remains the same. Without the expectation of uninterrupted production, the labor agreement is an empty gesture, a one-sided bargain completely weighted in favor of the union. This was never intended; this is not what the agreement expresses. The company must have some means, however imperfect, to reasonably insure uninterrupted production. The union has agreed that the company should have those means, and this was expressed in the agreement. The arbitrator must enforce the agreement, not dilute it.

24. The parties have agreed that:

> The arbitrator shall not have the authority to add to, subtract from, modify, change, or alter, any of the provisions of this agreement nor to extend its duration.

The parties have also resolved, in Article VII, Section 1, paragraph 67, that the "arbitration procedure cannot be used by either party to deny or affect the rights" expressed in the labor agreement, or be used "to circumvent the intent or the spirit of the terms and conditions of the contract." These guideposts must be given their due.

25. Arbitrator, these employees resorted to the tactics of the industrial jungle with full knowledge and without regard to the fact that such action was cause for discharge and termination of their employment with the company. These employees meted out their own punishment. The company did not discharge or suspend them. They discharged or suspended themselves!

Conclusion

In light of the facts presented in this case showing:

1. That during the week beginning July 17, there was a work stoppage at the company's plant in Jackson, Mississippi, in violation of the labor agreement between the parties;

2. That the employees who were discharged or suspended participated in the unlawful work stoppage by failing and refusing to report for work, without an excuse which the company could accept as valid;

3. That the agreement provides that employees participating in an unlawful work stoppage shall be subject to discipline, including discharge;

4. That the agreement further provides that "the only issue before the arbitrator shall be limited to the employee's participation in such unauthorized activity;

5. And that, by reason of the foregoing contract limitation, the arbitrator does not have the authority to review the appropriateness of the penalties.

Therefore, the company demands that the arbitrator deny the union's grievances and award that the company's action did not violate the labor agreement.

Respectfully submitted,
KRANDALL FURNITURE COMPANY

Memorandum on Discharged and Suspended Employees

C. R. Bronson was hired on May 31, 1962. Prior to his discharge, he was employed as a wet lay-up operator on the first shift.

The company introduced into evidence a photograph (Company Exhibit No. 19 [1]), taken on July 17, 1967, around 10:30 p.m., showing Bronson picketing on Krandall Lane, on the side of the road opposite the Sentinel Discount Corporation parking lot. J. Williams, a company supervisor, testified that the employee was standing at the edge of the paved surface of the road, shouting to automobiles bringing employees in for the third shift to "go on in, turn around (in the plant parking lot), and come back." Williams did not know this employee at the time, but because Bronson stood out from the others, Williams asked another supervisor to identify him. Bronson testified that he learned of the walkout at 6:45 a.m. on July 17 just prior to his shift. This employee who lives in Ardmore, some 25 or 30 miles from Jackson, came back to Krandall Lane in the evening of that same day not to see what was going on as he claimed, but to participate in the picketing activities. This employee, by his own admission, already knew what was going on before he made the trip back to Jackson on the evening of July 17.

2. On July 18, at 12 noon, in the City Parking Lot in Jackson, Bronson participated in an employee's strike strategy meeting. He mounted a truck bed serving as a speakers' platform, and took part in the decisions that were made (Company Exhibits Nos. 12, 30, and 31). P. J. Grover, one of the participants in the unlawful work stoppage, testified that Bronson, from his position on the truck bed, spoke to the employees gathered at this meeting. Bronson's statement at the hearing that he did not say or do anything more than any other employee not only begs the question, but is also patently false.

3. This employee did not report for work from July 17 through July 21. When he should have been working, he was instead busily participating in the unlawful work stoppage.

4. In 1964, this employee, as part of a group of 24 employees, was discharged for engaging in an unlawful work stoppage. This

---

1. All company exhibits mentioned refer to photographs of striking workers taken by a company photographer.

1. On July 18, at 12 noon, in the City Parking Lot in Jackson, Randall stationed herself on the truck bed, which served as the speakers' platform for the meeting that was held and, together with Grover, Bronson, and Fairview, spoke to the group (Company Exhibits Nos. 12, 30, 31, 32, and 33). Randall was one of the moving forces behind the decisions made at that meeting to continue the unlawful work stoppage. She was named by Grover as a member of a committee representing the striking employees.

2. In 1964, this employee was discharged for participating in a wildcat strike. This incident was developed above in connection with Dickson and Bronson.

L. L. Underwood was hired on April 13, 1962. Prior to his discharge, he was employed as a cut-off saw operator and crater on the first shift. Underwood did not contest the facts brought out by the company at the hearing.

1. Green introduced reports of company supervisors that the grievant picketed at almost every shift change until his activities were interrupted, when he was named as one of the defendants in the company's petition, in Jackson County Court, for a temporary injunction. Williams testified that on July 17, between 10 p.m. and 11 p.m., Underwood walked back and forth along Krandall Lane, talking to groups of employees and shouting "come back" to passing cars.

2. Bentley, a superintendent, testified that at 6 a.m. on July 18, on Krandall Lane, this grievant shouted, "Whoa" or "Whoa, where are you going?" at automobiles; or yelled, "Come back here, Joe"; or, as a car turned around and went back, cheered, "You're looking good."

3. Underwood, together with the grievant Grover, submitted the radio release to station WCKQ calling for the striking employees to stick together.

C. G. Ventner was hired on May 5, 1959. Prior to her discharge, she was employed as a filament winder operator on the first shift. Ventner did not testify.

1. The company's supervisor reported that on July 17, at 2:30 p.m., at the Track Side Bulk Plant on Krandall Lane, this employee moved among the clusters of striking employees talking loudly and angrily about complaints against the company, and ignored a supervisor's advice that there was a proper way to settle complaints. Worthington testified to this grievant's threat that if he put names in the notebook he was carrying, "they would walk out again." Worthington did not know Ventner at that time, but because of her menacing attitude, he asked another supervisor to identify the grievant.

2. Between 10 p.m. and 11 p.m. on July 17, and between 6 a.m. and 7 a.m. on July 18, this employee again picketed along Krandall Lane (Company Exhibits Nos. 15 and 22).

Suspended Employees

Of the 11 suspended employees, only three—P. C. Fairview T. F. Munson, and P. J. Pepper—testified in their own behalf. Fairview was honest enough to shoulder his responsibility for participating in the unlawful work stoppage, although he refused to acknowledge an established fact, which he knew, that all the grievants on the truck bed during the July 18 meeting in the City Parking Lot were there to speak, and actually did speak, to the meeting. Pepper could not seem to remember anything, except when it suited his evasive purposes. Munson denied everything except that he was there. The other eight grievants did not controvert the facts which the company introduced and which established their participation in the unlawful work stoppage.

C. L. Atlas was hired on June 10, 1953. She is employed as a filament winder operator on the third shift.

1. Williams and Bentley both testified that on July 17, between 10 p.m. and 11 p.m., Atlas placed two blinking red lights on Krandall Lane, a foot or two in from the edge of the road, near the intersection of this road with Route 11, to halt traffic coming into Krandall Lane. She grudgingly removed the lanterns after the police told her three different times to do so. Thereafter, feeling left out, she joined the other pickets and shouted to automobiles entering to "turn around and come back."

2. Although Atlas, in the grievance meetings, claimed that she was on the picket line Monday night only, Grover testified that she was also there at 2:30 p.m. of the same day.

K. A. Benton was hired on February 17, 1966. He is employed as a prime sprayer on the third shift.

Benton picketed on Krandall Lane on July 17, between 10 p.m. and 11 p.m., interfering with traffic (Company Exhibits Nos. 14, 17, and 18).

M. Brown was hired January 26, 1959. She is employed as an assembler "B" on the first shift.

Green testified that on July 17 at 2:30 p.m., Brown picketed on Krandall Lane, shouting to passing cars to turn around and go back.

B. G. Campbell was hired April 18, 1964. She is employed as a sander and assembler on the third shift.

On July 17, between 10 p.m. and 11 p.m., Campbell picketed on Krandall Lane, interfering with traffic (Company Exhibits Nos. 14 and 17), and again on July 18 between 6 p.m. and 7 p.m. (Company Exhibit No. 22).

F. W. Cecil was hired October 17, 1963. She is employed as a trimmer operator on the first shift.

Cecil picketed on Krandall Lane on July 17 and 18, interfering with traffic (Company Exhibits Nos. 14 and 17).

A. R. Downs was hired May 22, 1965. At the time he was suspended, Downs was employed as a winder operator on the third shift.

This employee picketed on Krandall Lane on July 17, between 10 p.m. and 11 p.m., interfering with traffic (Company Exhibits Nos. 14, 17, and 21).

P. C. Fairview was hired June 18, 1962. He is employed as an assembler "A" on the first shift.

The company entered into evidence photographs of Fairview (Company Exhibit No. 28) sitting in the cab of a truck, holding a paper in his hand. This photograph was taken on July 18, around noon, at the City Parking Lot in Jackson, at the time the striking employees were holding a meeting. Fairview testified that this paper contained a list of alleged complaints against the company and that he read the complaints at the meeting. By his own admission, Fairview participated in the strike activities during the week of July 17. This grievant also was a member of the committee appointed by the striking employees to meet with the company (Company Exhibit 13).

F. F. Manly was hired May 22, 1963. She is employed as a laminator on the first shift.

On July 18, between 6 a.m. and 7 a.m., Manly picketed on Krandall Lane (Company Exhibit No. 27). Later that day she was at the meeting on the City Parking Lot in Jackson on or near the speakers' platform, taking an active part in the meeting (Company Exhibit No. 30). Manly also was a member of the committee appointed to meet with the company (Company Exhibit 13).

T. F. Munson was hired June 22, 1965. At the time of his suspension, he was employed as an erection machinist on the third shift.

Company supervisors testified that Munson picketed on Krandall Lane Monday night, July 17, and Tuesday morning, July 18. Williams and Worthington testified that on Monday night, Munson led employees onto the paved surface, waving at automobiles and shouting for them to "come back." On Tuesday morning, July 18, he stayed close to the edge of the road and called to the automobiles to "come back." During these times, Munson also helped clear the road for shop stewards by calling to other employees to let through cars carrying shop stewards. Company Exhibits Nos. 27 and 30 also show Munson picketing on Krandall Lane.

P. F. Pepper was hired April 24, 1958. He is employed as a loader and bracer on the first shift.

> Pepper was on the speakers' platform at the July 18 meeting in the City Parking Lot in Jackson, taking a leading part in the deliberations (Company Exhibits Nos. 28, 30, and 31.)

R. W. Smith was hired April 10, 1964. She is employed as a winder operator on the third shift.

> On July 17, between 10 p.m. and 11 p.m., Smith picketed on Krandall Lane, interfering with traffic (Company Exhibits Nos. 17 and 19).

APPENDIX 2

Alice Smathers
Director
Industrial Relations
Krandall Furniture Co.
Krandall Lane

Dear Ms. Smathers:

This letter is to notify you that we do not accept the decision reached in the fourth step of the grievance system and that we now are placing the grievance before the arbitrator.

As we have stated throughout, this strike was not authorized by the union or by any of the union officials. However, in spite of this lack of official sanction, you must admit that the sentiments of most of the employees were involved as witnessed by the fact that only the union officials crossed the picket lines. It must also be noted that the strike would have ended sooner had the company agreed to reinstate all employees without prejudice. Certainly the threat of discharge extended the strike all out of proportion to the initial issues.

The important question in this case is: If punitive measures are to be taken, which individuals shall be penalized? Paragraph 21, Article V, of the contract states, "The company retains the right to discipline, including discharge, employees who engage in such unauthorized activity." Inasmuch as all but 15 or 25 employees participated in the strike, all participating employees should be given the same penalty. We would like to emphasize that the same penalty should be meted to all employees who did not come to work, that is, the striking employees. We do not agree that one employee can strike more than another. All striking employees are equally guilty.

We see, in the selective punishments, settlements of old grievances. We would bring to your attention, for instance, the company statements that Bronson and Dickson were participants in an unlawful work stoppage in 1964. Certainly there is nothing in Article V that states that historical incidents should determine the penalties for today's grievances. Precedence has been established that would disallow incidents of three years back to be a factor in setting penalties.

It is our contention that the company is using this unauthorized work stoppage to free themselves of strong union supporters and others with whom they have old scores to settle. The company should be uniform in its punishment and should not allow personalities to dictate severity. There is a discriminatory undercurrent in these tactics which needs to be examined more closely. The union intends to pursue this line of investigation to determine the extent of these biases and to determine the legal recourses.

The union states that the company is not authorized to impose unequal punishments and that since the company is unwilling to negotiate in this area, arbitration is the only step available to correct these injustices.

Sincerely,

S. L. Wilson
Business Agent
United Brotherhood of Carpenters
and Joiners

Able Fasteners, Incorporated

"Your worker, Joe Spellini, is over here in the picket line in front of our plant with your shoes on. What do you intend to do about it?" This was the opening statement and question by Red Simmons to Wilma Wakely.

Red Simmons was the personnel director of the Evanston Screw Machine Company and Wilma Wakely was vice-president in charge of industrial relations for Able Fasteners, Incorporated. Wakely was somewhat puzzled by Simmons' comment since Joe Spellini was a machine operator on Able's third shift.

Wakely: Red, what are you talking about?

Simmons: Just as I said, Spellini is picketing our plant.

Wakely: What do you want me to do about it? What our employees do on their off hours is really not our business. I didn't know that you had a strike. What's going on over there? Why would Joe be in the picket line? He's not even a union member. We don't have a union over here.

Simmons: The hell he's not a union member, and he's a vociferous one at that! He works for you the third shift, but he works for us the first shift, and he's a member of the union.

Wakely: I knew Joe had another job, but I didn't know it was with our chief competitor. But, Red, why do you want me to do something about it?

Simmons: Look, Wilma, I don't mind Spellini telling everyone that Able is a better place to work, and I don't mind his saying that you don't need a union at Able to protect the workers, but you know what he did yesterday? He came on the picket line with your safety shoes on and told everyone that Able gives its employees safety shoes free. Now that's going too far!

Wakely: I see. Well, okay, Red. I'll talk with Joe. But what do you want me to do?

Simmons: I don't know, Wilma, but I wish you would talk to him.

After hanging up the phone, Wilma Wakely sat back in her chair to think about this. She smiled to herself as she thought about a tentative memo stating employees may not wear Able's safety shoes when picketing other people's plants. She knew Simmons would not think it funny. The Evanston Screw Machine Company had a reputation for labor problems, and she figured Simmons was grasping at straws to get relief.

Wakely was proud of the fact that Able Fasteners was not unionized. Attempts had been made by international unions to become the bargaining agent, but each time the employees had voted against the unions. Wakely did not want anything to disturb that relationship.

Joe Spellini, however, was not a troublemaker at Able. Spellini had been hired five years ago, and his job was to work on special orders and newly designed fasteners. He was a whiz of a worker, always on the move, always working, and never sitting down. (The plant physician said that this was probably due to an overactive thyroid.) Spellini, 41 years old, was a tall, good-looking person who had a high school education. He had been married and then divorced. Wakely classified Spellini as an individualist who liked the "good things in life," including cigars, an active weekend, night life, good cars, and well-tailored clothes. However, Spellini was not living beyond his means, especially since he had two jobs.

Wakely had known Spellini had a second job, but since he was never late or absent and was a productive worker, she could find no reason to tell him he could not work a second job. Wakely did wonder, though, about his being a union member at the Evanston plant. She also began to think about his working for both companies, since the Evanston Screw Machine Company was very competitive in some of the fastener lines. Was there any reason why Spellini could not work for both companies? He had access to some of the newly designed fasteners and presumably could take samples over to the Evanston Company if he so wished. However, Spellini had been straightforward in his dealing with Able and at no time had tried to hide the fact he had a second job.

As indicated, Spellini was an above-average machinist but he did have ambitions to become a sales representative. Wakely had stalled him on one excuse or another because he seemed to lack the qualifications and aptitudes necessary for a sales job. She decided to discuss the situation with the plant superintendent, John Bellman.

Neither Wakely nor Bellman thought this was a serious situation, although Bellman was surprised that Spellini was a union member. They were, though, concerned about the fact that he was working for a competitor. Their feeling was that, had Spellini been working for anyone else, they would not take any action. As it was, they decided that he should make a choice for which company he wanted to work.

The following day the manager, Sid Jergens, called Joe Spellini into his office.

Jergens: Joe, I understand you are working days over at Evanston Screw Machine. How do you like it?

Spellini: Fine, Mr. Jergens, although there's a strike on now.

Jergens: What do you do there, Joe?

Spellini: I'm in the service department—customer service. It's a sort of a training program. Later they have promised to let me work in sales, but first I have to work in the service department.

Jergens: Joe, the reason I called you in is to talk to you about this other job. Actually, the company has no official policy on this, and we don't do anything about it unless it interferes with the job here at Able.

Spellini: This job doesn't affect my work here, Mr. Jergens. I'm here every day.

Jergens: I know you are, Joe, and you do good work, too. This is something else. This is concerned with conflict of interests.

Spellini: I'm not with you, Mr. Jergens. What do you mean?

Jergens: Joe, as you know, we are competitors with the Evanston Screw Machine Company. Now you are working for both companies, and we feel that this is not a healthy situation. We don't want you to be put in any embarrassing situations. It would, therefore, seem that the best thing for you to do is to think over this whole job problem and then make a choice, that is, decide whether you want to work for Able or for the Evanston Screw Machine Company. I have checked this decision over with Bellman and Wakely, and they are both agreed that, if you had been working for some other company other than a competitor, this problem would not have arisen. Now I want to impress upon you that your work here has been very satisfactory, and we hope you will choose to remain with us.

Georgetown Post Office

Georgetown, a midwestern, suburban community of 70,000 is served by the United States Postal Service which maintains a facility employing over 250 people. Its business and residential mail volume is such that it requires the office to operate around-the-clock, save for 18 hours on the weekend—the only time that the office completely closes.

The clerical employees fall into two basic categories—window and distribution. As the name implies, the window clerks' primary function is the retailing of postage to the public. Along with a handful of accounting clerks and secretaries, their daily work schedules conform to standard business hours. Distribution clerks sort all types of incoming mail into either pidgeonhole cases or parcel sacks. To do so requires knowledge of the city scheme, a plan which organizes by city block all of the town's addresses into areas which can be delivered by one letter carrier daily. Subsequent sortings include a breakdown of mail for box holders and certain firms which call for their mail at the dock.

To accommodate the steady flow of incoming mail, the distribution clerks are organized into three shifts called tours. Tour 1 operates from midnight until 8:30 a.m. Since most first class mail is received during this time, their primary responsibility is to complete its sorting to insure delivery that morning. Tour 2 begins at 4:00 a.m. to bolster the Tour 1 force at this critical time. Tour 3 punches in at 1:30 p.m. and handles the incoming and outgoing mail until 10:00 p.m.[1] The average daily complements per tour are respectively 25, 13, and 25.

Due to the highly routinized type of work performed at the Georgetown Post Office, management represents only 5 percent of the total work force. It is not uncommon for a first-line supervisor to be responsible for 35 to 40 workers. And with the exception of the postmaster, all line and staff personnel had risen from the ranks of the Georgetown installation. (The postmaster began his career as a clerk in a

---

1. The superintendent of collection and delivery goes on duty with the bulk of Tour 3 at 1:30 p.m. Along with three to four clerks, Tour 3 managers begin work at 3:00 p.m. The latter are then on duty during the period of 10 to 12 p.m.

neighboring state.) The other employees involved are: Bob Summers, clerk, Tour 1; Jim Grabow, clerk, union steward, Tour 1; Rich Randall, clerk, Tour 1; Martha Andrews, clerk, Tour 2; and Gene O'Riely, clerk, union president, Tour 3.

Tuesday, August 12, 2:30 p.m., office of the postmaster
(Bob Summers, Lawrence Elby)

Elby: So tell me, Bob, why you want to come back with us.

Summers: Well, Lawrence, as you know I worked here for seven and a half years before I left three months ago. I thought when I left I was doing the right thing. However, I just wasn't happy with my new job.

Elby: Trapp and I have reviewed your old file, and everything seems to be in order. We couldn't find any records of adverse action taken against you in the past. The only thing that bothers me is the amount of sick leave you had retained when you left. It's pretty low.

Summers: There were a couple of instances in the last couple of years when I had to use up a lot of sick leave at a time. I presented documentation both times, though.

Elby: If we were to take you back, I would expect your attendance to improve. Speaking of attendance, you realize you will probably be assigned to midnights. I hope that won't present any problems.

Summers: I guess I expected to be assigned to Tour I. I'm prepared for it. I knew that, once I left, I would be losing my seniority. But to show you how sincere I am, I've been looking over my old scheme at home, and I realize that there have been some changes. I should become qualified in a couple of days. As you know, the new person takes a couple of months to learn it, if then.

Elby: I can appreciate that. We've been having some trouble lately getting the new people to learn it. (Pause) Your supervisor would be Harold Levinson.

(Summers smirks, half tossing his hands in the air.)

Elby: Please explain your reaction.

Summers: I'm sorry. I didn't mean to react that way. It's just that when Harold was a clerk, he didn't have a reputation for being the best worker.

Elby: We've had to have patience with Harold. He's made some mistakes, but he's an intelligent fellow, and he's learning. In time I expect him to become a topnotch supervisor. If I were to take you back, I'd expect your fullest cooperation.

Summers: I'm prepared. I promise you won't be making a mistake.

Elby: Okay. Go in and see Don Houseman, the personnel officer. He'll fill out the required forms. You start a week from this Saturday, the 23d.

Summers made the transition, working the midnight shift that Saturday. He found his job situation to be an abrupt change from that which he knew three months ago. Without the seniority he had previously enjoyed, he was assigned mundane tasks which every new clerk at the Georgetown installation performed. He unloaded sacks of mail from trailers, emptied these same sacks, and occasionally sorted parcel post.

As he had promised, Summers studied the scheme on his free time. At the end of his first week, he attained proficiency. He took a preliminary examination with test cards which simulated actual letter sorting, and passed with 99 percent correct. Due to the high attrition rate among new employees (most quit because of the hours), he was back to sorting letters on a full time basis within four weeks.

Saturday, October 4, 7:45 a.m., distribution section
(Rich Randall and Bob Summers are sorting letters into adjacent cases.)
Randall: Look at Levinson. It looks like it's going to be close this morning. Already he's running up and down the line. He's giving trays (of mail) to people who haven't finished what they've got yet. He got spoiled, coming on the tour during the summer. In the summer the mail's always light.
Summers: He sure doesn't keep his cool very long. No wonder people don't like to do what he says.
Randall: Yeah. You know, he used to work Tour 2 before they made him supervisor. Sure was a horse of a different color then. The carriers used to stop at his case and go through the mail. I swear each one gave him back half of what he had thrown to them. All misthrows.
(Both laugh.)
Summers: If we don't get this mail up by 8:30, Trapp isn't going to be very happy. Anything we don't get to the carriers before they leave at 8:30 will just sit until Monday.
Randall: Maybe then he'd get on Levinson. God, I wish somebody would! You know what else Harold used to do? He used to tell people to slow down so there'd be overtime. How do you like that?
Summers: Incredible! And to think they made him a supervisor.
Randall: I don't think Elby had any choice. He offered the opening to Gene O'Riely, but he turned it down. Harold was the next in line. I guess he got a pretty good score on the supervisor's test that the Post Office gave last year. But, anyway, if Elby had not offered it to him, I think Levinson would have gone to the district office to complain.
Summers: I know what you mean. What I gather from talking to O'Riely last week, Elby is very cautious. He doesn't want anything going to district, unless he knows he's dead right.

The first class mail was completely sorted by 8:20 that morning. It was the longest time it had taken the clerks in nearly three months. At the previous time, seven had been on vacation (four from Tour 1, three from Tour 2), and three had called in sick. This morning, there were no calls. One was missing due to a scheduled National Guard meeting that day. None were on vacation.

The following Monday and Tuesday, not all the first class mail had been sorted by 8:30. On Monday, volunteers were allowed to work two hours overtime. Half of Tour 1 stayed.

By Tuesday, a large backlog of third class mail had developed, combined with the amount of first class present at 8:00 a.m. The superintendent of mails, George Trapp, ordered all employees to work two hours of mandatory overtime, an alternative to be used only in emergency situations.[2] There were some grumblings, especially among those who normally turned down overtime.

Tuesday, October 6, 8:45 a.m., office of the postmaster
(Lawrence Elby, George Trapp)

Elby: I see you called for two hours of mandatory overtime this morning, George. This overtime is hurting our budget. What happened?

Trapp: Levinson's tour really got hit last night. Adding all of Tour 1 to Tour 2, the first class won't be up for probably another 15 minutes. The third class mail hasn't been touched in almost 24 hours. There's enough of it alone out there to absorb 250 hours of manual sorting.

Elby: Looking over last week's figures, I see that Harold's production figures are about average. But I've called him in this morning to see if he's having any unusual problems. Ah, here he is now. Come in, Harold.

Levinson: Good morning, Lawrence, George.

Trapp: How's the first class going?

Levinson: It should be up in a few more minutes. Dan Nagle is having the third class moved over to the cases now.

Elby: Sit down. Harold, although your production figures show otherwise, I've got a gut feeling that things aren't going quite right. Am I wrong?

Levinson: We're moving the mail, but I'm having my problems. When I reassign people, they move, but reluctantly. There's a lot of talking going on. I don't mind that so much, but they don't throw as much mail then. When I tell them to throw mail, they do. But I know they're talking about me behind my back when I leave.

Elby: Well, Harold, like I told you a few weeks ago, you've got to be firm with your people. That's the only way you'll get them to respect you.

Levinson: And another thing. Small groups are making regular trips to the coffee machine. I've tried to stop that, but the union steward, Jim Grabow, always seems to have some sort of answer for me.

Trapp: I knew Grabow would be doing that. We let him supervise that tour for a month. But I personally didn't like his methods. He was too liberal with his people. True, he got the job done, but we were losing control of the situation. I'd give him specific instructions on things to do and how I wanted them done. At times he just wouldn't listen.

Elby: And now instead of being a supervisor, he's the steward. And he'll grieve the pickiest little things. He's mad at us, and he'll do everything in his power to get back at us. Harold, it's time to make a stand. If anybody is giving you trouble, write them up. If we dish out a few suspensions, maybe they'll get the word we won't tolerate any more nonsense. But when you do write them up, make the case iron-clad.

2. An emergency situation is defined as a nonreoccurring event which management could not reasonably foresee.

If they win a major grievance, the situation could get out of hand, and I might have to resort in a change of supervisors.

For the remainder of the week, varying amounts of first class mail were left after 8:30, but never more than the double shift could work up before 9:00 a.m. One hour of mandatory overtime was declared each day.

The closest the two tours came to the 8:30 mark was Thursday, when the deadline was missed by ten minutes. Then a replacement supervisor was in charge of Tour 1, since it was Levinson's regularly scheduled day off. Two local newspaper issues were received on this day, absorbing approximaely 20 hours for distribution.

Saturday, October 11, 8:00 a.m., distribution section
(Bob Summers, Jim Grabow, and Martha Andrews are on the line together, sorting letters.)

Summers: Boy, Jim, I'm telling you! Before I left, I worked Tour 3, and I never saw things messed up like they are here and now. Hans had an entirely different approach. He wasn't on you every five minutes like this guy. He told you what to do, and that was it. He took a personal interest in his people. He would talk with you about any problems. In the year I was steward on that tour, I didn't have one formal grievance against him. And another thing, he didn't have to pad his volume like this guy does.

Grabow: That's the way I ran things on this tour when I was acting supervisor. But Trapp didn't like that. He likes to call all the shots. Elby told me that I was doing a good job, but they stiffed me anyway. (He laughs sarcastically.)

Summers: They were lucky O'Riely didn't accept the position. Levinson, one of the biggest clowns around here, fits right in. Uh oh, speaking of the devil. . . .

(Levinson walks down the aisle of letter cases, stopping at each clerk.)

Levinson: Jim, one hour, mandatory. Bob. . . .

Summers: I know, one hour, mandatory!

(Levinson finishes the series of personal announcements, and he returns to the head of the aisle, his usual position at this time.)

Summers: They can't do that! This makes five days in a row. I hate working overtime on this shift. As if you aren't burned out enough at 8:30! Mandatory overtime is supposed to be reserved for December and emergency situations. They should have known this would happen. It's Jewish New Year. Half this first class is New Year's cards. They could have had people working their days off. Enough would have done it. They didn't have to stiff the ones who don't want it.

Andrews: Yes, but I was talking to Dan Nagle yesterday, and he says they're worried about the budget. All that overtime makes them look bad to the district headquarters. If they think they can save a few hours pay this way, you know they'll try it.

Summers: But it's obvious that they guessed wrong! All they succeeded in doing was aggravating a lot of people. I'm so teed off, it makes me sick. And that's just what I'm going to tell Levinson. I'm sick. I can't work overtime this morning.

At 8:15 Summers reported to Levinson he was sick and that he was going home at 8:30. When he left to punch out at 8:30, he was followed by six others from Tour 1. Levinson was waiting by the time-clock as the file approached. Summers passed him without a word. As the other clerks followed, Levinson said to each, "I suppose you're sick, too." Each nodded.

As Summers punched his timecard and turned to leave, he noticed the supervisor of the carrier section, John Leitner, walking hurriedly into the front office. He dismissed it as meaningless and left the building.

One week later, all seven received envelopes from Harold Levinson. Six contained formal letters of reprimand for insubordination. Summers' contained notice of his termination, effective in three weeks. The charge cited accused him of "subversion of the Postal Service in leading a walkout in refusal of mandatory overtime." (All seven letters bore the postmaster's signature.)

Upon initial entrance or reentry into the postal service, the employee has no representation rights by the union for 90 days. If he sees fit, the local postmaster may terminate such employees without having to face a formal grievance. Knowing this, Summers still decided to fight the decision. As part of his plan, he recruited the support of the local clerk's union. He also individually approached all the clerks who were in his vicinity at the time of the alleged incident.

Wednesday, October 23, 12:30 p.m., at the home of Gene O'Riely
(Gene O'Riely, Bob Summers)

O'Riely: You know, I went into the postmaster's office to speak on your behalf. Leitner was in there. I almost got tossed out on my ear, and technically he could have done it, but he agreed to listen anyway. I spoke of your good record, how you kept your nose clean for over seven years. But then Leitner jumps in with, 'C'mon Gene! He's guilty as hell. My desk is right by where the clerks were throwing mail. Summers was ranting and raving about having to work that overtime.' He claims a total of three supervisors witnessed it all, himself included.

Summers: I don't care what he claims. I'm not guilty of any subversion. Everyone was shocked when they heard about my letter. And I've got witnesses of my own. I've approached every clerk who was in my vicinity of the workroom floor at that time, including the ones that walked out. They all think this subversion stuff is a lot of baloney, and they're willing to testify to that fact. I'll take this to the Supreme Court if I have to. But, come hell or high water, I'm going to be exonerated. You know damn well I wouldn't do what they say I did. And I've got the people behind me to prove it!

GEORGETOWN POST OFFICE   **417**

Exhibit 1

Managerial Organization
Georgetown Post Office

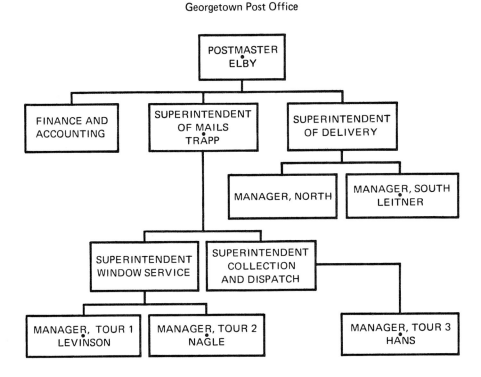

DECISIONS INVOLVING ORGANIZED LABOR

Part Six

Decisions Involving Planning, Strategy, and Policy Formulation

Bolton Screw Company

Julian Mack, the vigorous, 75-year-old president of Bolton Screw Company, wanted to diversify and to increase the liquidity of his investment in the corporation. He had successfully directed the company since its founding in the early 1900s and was the major stockholder with 62 percent of the outstanding shares. Recently, Mack and members of his management team had been giving thought to the possible ways by which he could achieve his objectives. Major stockholders in similar situations generally could look to several alternative courses of action, such as the sale of shares to other stockholders or to the public, the sale of the company, or the sale of the assets of the company. However, when Mack gave serious consideration to matters of valuation, continuity of the organization, and to federal tax liability, his choices appeared to narrow.

A large corporation in another industry had extended an offer for the purchase of Bolton Screw Company, and the offer price was based on a conventional valuation approach of eight times recent earnings —less working capital the buyer would need to furnish—to a price of $2.2 million. Acceptance of this offer required approval by the 50 stockholders of Bolton Screw Company and surrender of their shares for cash or stock in the buying company.

An influential Bolton director and close friend of Mack was Neil Cuplet. Cuplet was considered by Mack to be an outstanding investment banker. The two had met at a social gathering a few years earlier, and their friendship and business relationship had advanced rapidly. At 46, Cuplet was a member of the management of Anderson, O'Neil, and Bell, a company seeking a solution to Mack's ownership change. At Cuplet's suggestion, the group had obtained expert opinions on legal and tax matters pertaining to closely held companies. He also had been able to obtain information relative to the possibilities of marketing shares of common stock to the public and of the possible placement of debt issues.

The management group looked upon the formation of a new corporation as offering attractive tax-position advantages for Mack and proceeded to draw up the necessary information for a prospectus. This group, which held about 14 percent of the outstanding stock of Bolton, also could see certain merits to be achieved by the organization through the use of the new corporation.

BACKGROUND INFORMATION

Bolton's business originally consisted of the manufacture of standard varieties of steel wood screws. Subsequently, various other types of screws and related products were added to the line, including machine screws, sheet metal screws, drive screws, washer assembly screws, stove bolts, tapped rivets, and washers. Products included a wide range of screws and other fasteners, of both standard and special design, in a great variety of materials and finishes. Substantially all of such screws and other fasteners were less than three eighths of an inch in diameter. Screws and other fasteners and related items produced accounted for 90 percent of sales. The balance of the business was the design and production of metal-cutting and other tools, principally ground-thread taps, which were used by other manufacturers in the production of a wide variety of industrial and consumer goods.

For many years, and with increasing emphasis, the design and production of special rather than standard fasteners had been stressed by Bolton to meet more efficiently the needs of industrial customers. Inasmuch as the cost of assembling products was of vital concern to companies in mass-production industries, such companies welcomed the development of fasteners that would cut assembly cost. The company had a substantial number of employees, headed by four graduate engineers, who carried on extensive research in the solution of fastener problems and worked closely with consumer industries to develop improved fasteners and stimulate sales. Such emphasis was believed to have strengthened the company's relations with customers. Bolton's volume of business in special items represented over half of its total sales.

At such time the Bolton Screw Company's plant was one of the most highly integrated in the industry producing screws and screw-type fasteners, and its production equipment was in excellent condition. Facilities were maintained for the drawing of wire from rods, principally of steel, brass, bronze, and aluminum, which were purchased on the open market, each from suppliers. Wire-drawing capacity permitted the prompt production of wire to specifications and reduced wire inventory requirements to expedite delivery.

Substantially all of the screw and fastener products were formed by a cold forging process on machines called headers. After heading or forming, many of the items were processed further on various machines that performed such operations as tapping, drilling, grooving, electroplating, and dip-plating. At that time the finishing facilities one or more finishing processes, such as hardening, anneling, polishing, electoplating, and dip-plating. At that time the finishing facilities were among the most complete of any in the screw industry in the United States.

Sales of standard screws were made primarily by Bolton sales representatives and independent sales agents to hardware wholesalers and industrial supply houses, which in turn, sold to retail stores, small manufacturers, traders, repair shops, and do-it-yourself users. Sales of special fasteners were made primarily by Bolton sales representatives, sales engineers, and independent sales agents directly to large industrial users. Bolton's representatives and sales engineers solicited business through most of the United States, except for certain territories that were canvassed by sales agents.

In consecutive five-year periods, sales had been made to approximately 2,700 customers which represented a wide diversity of industries. During that period, the automobile industry, directly and indirectly, had accounted for an average of 34 percent of dollar sales. No other industry had accounted for more than 15 percent of sales. Military consumption was believed not to have exceeded 10 percent.

Screws and fasteners of the type produced by Bolton were manufactured and sold by over 100 producers in the United States. Only a minority of these competitors, however, had the engineering and manufacturing facilities to turn out products that would meet the increasingly exacting demands required. Bolton was believed to be one of the five largest manufacturers in its size range. (The screws were not over three-eighths of an inch in diameter.) The only products subjected to significant foreign competition were standard wood screws—about 25 percent domestic requirements were imported.

Bolton had developed a considerable number of improvements in its products and processes, which had been patented and were owned exclusively. Bolton also held nonexclusive patent licenses generally extended for the life of the patents and included improvements so that such additional patent protection as the licensors might obtain constituted a continuing protection. Many patents had expired but others would be in force from 1 to 15 years.

Bolton produced Nylok screws and fasteners under a nonexclusive license from the patent holder and was a major producer of the fastener. The Nylok invention used an insert of solid nylon in the threaded area of the fastener to hold the fastener securely in place by expansion of the nylon after assembly. In the belief that this invention represented an advance in fastener techniques, Bolton developed special machinery to produce Nylok fasteners economically.

NEW CORPORATION PLAN

The members of management obtained a charter for the new corporation in August and contributed a total of $10,000 for the initial capital. Since management did not have personal resources sufficient to acquire the business, their attention was centered upon a possible public offering of stock. Cuplet estimated that about $3.8 million could be raised, of which $2.3 million might be obtained through common stock financing and about $1.5 million through a private placement of mortgage bonds. Management desired the stock to be widely distributed.

Common Stock New Company

Common stock, $1 par value, was the only class of stock that the new company was authorized to issue. Holders of common stock had one vote per share, had no preemptive or similar rights, and were entitled on liquidation to share pro rata in assets available for distribution. Stockholders were not liable for any further calls or assessments except for the statutory liability for money due to operatives for services rendered within six months before demand made on the new company and its neglect or refusal to make such payment.

First Mortgage Bonds and Warrants

Contemporaneously with the issue and sale of the common stock offered hereby, the new company would issue and sell at private sale, against the payment to it of $1,500,000 in cash, $1,500,000 principal amount of its first-mortgage, 6 percent bonds due in 15 years, together with warrants exercisable at any time prior to maturity date for the purchase of 22,500 shares of common stock of the new company at a base price of $10 per share.

The first mortgage bond offering was to be secured by a first mortgage on the facilities of the new corporation and also on certain machinery and other personal property located at the plant. The bonds would bear interest at the rate of 6 percent per annum and would be entitled to an annual sinking fund of $100,000 beginning the second year. They would be redeemable for sinking-fund purposes at their principal amount and subject to voluntary redemption at an initial premium of 6 percent through the third year, declining thereafter at the rate of ½ percent per annum, so that the bonds would become redeemable without premium a year before maturity, in all cases plus accrued interest to the redemption date. Redemption was not permitted out of funds borrowed by the company at an interest rate of less than 6 percent per annum.

In the indenture relating to the bonds, the new company agreed not to declare or to pay any dividends (other than in its stock) nor to purchase, redeem, or otherwise retire any shares of its stock if after giving effect thereto the sum of all such distributions exceeding 70 percent of consolidated net earnings (as defined) subsequent to October of that year. Notwithstanding the foregoing, the new company would be allowed to pay a dividend for its first quarter not exceeding $52,200, being at the annual rate of 80 cents per share on the 261,000 shares of common stock to be outstanding.

The indenture required the new company to maintain its consolidated current assets in an amount not less than $1,800,000 in excess of its consolidated current liabilities. The indenture prohibited additional funded debt (as defined) except certain indebtedness under purchase money mortgages, and it prohibited liabilities for money borrowed maturing within one year in excess of $750,000. In addition, the indenture contained restrictions with respect to sales and leasebacks and investments and provisions for the release of mortgaged property.

The common stock purchase warrants contained appropriate provisions protecting them against dilution as a result of subsequent issues of common stock at less than the base price therein or by reason of stock dividends or similar transactions.

Under the management plan, the acquisition of the assets of the Bolton Screw Company would be effected as indicated.

PROPOSED PURCHASE AGREEMENT

The proposed purchase agreement between the new Bolton Screw Corporation and Bolton Screw Company provided for the purchase of the operating assets and business of the old company, including inventories, land and buildings, machinery, factory equipment, office equipment, automobiles and other fixed assets, unexpired insurance, trademarks, trade names, patents, patent applications and goodwill, and all the capital stock of a subsidiary that held certain patents and trademarks, but not including cash, government securities, accounts, notes and interest receivable, life insurance on the lives of officers of the old company, or other minor assets.

The basic purchase price of $3 million was based upon the amount of capital that could be raised by the new corporation in light of the assets to be acquired and their estimated earning power and the new corporation's cash requirements, all as determined by negotiations between officers of the old company and representatives of the underwriters. These officers of the old company were to be officers and directors of the new corporation so that the new corporation was not to be independently represented in these negotiations. If the purchase had been consummated at August 10, the purchase price would have been $3 million and would have been allocated as follows: (1) $28,892 to unexpired insurance; (2) $1,498,512 to property, plant and equipment, which is cost less depreciation and less $368,733 excess of emergency facilities amortization over ordinary depreciation; and (3) $1,472,596 to inventories, which was the balance of the total basic purchase price. The basic purchase price of $3 million was to be adjusted for any difference between the total net book value of the assets to be acquired at the date of the sale and the total net book value of the assets on August 10.

Old Company Plans

The reason for the proposed purchase was that Mack, in connection with the planning of his estate, wished to diversify and increase the liquidity of his investments. The stockholders of the old company were to vote to change its business after the sale to that of an investing company. The old company would not compete with the new corporation. It was contemplated that for the time being, the present officers and directors of the old company, which included substantially all of the officers and directors of the new corporation, would be continued as officers and directors of the old company.

Of the 123,546 shares of common stock of the old company outstanding as of November 1 (excluding treasury shares), the following numbers of shares were held respectively by officers and directors of the new company and their associates: Mack, 76,287; and the seven other officers and directors of the new corporation as a group, 17,639. Mack and his associates intended to retain their shares in the old company, but it was expected that most of the other stockholders would sell their shares to the old company.

Underwriting

Mack and Anderson, O'Neil, and Bell had taken the initiative in organizing and planning the financing of the new corporation and for the sale of the assets of the old company to the new corporation. Mack and his associates were majority stockholders of the old company. Mack would become moderator of the board of directors of the new corporation. Except as a stockholder of the old company, Mack would not receive directly or indirectly any consideration in connection with the transaction. Anderson, O'Neil, and Bell, in addition to its participation in the underwriting discount applicable to the sale of common stock, would receive also a fee of $15,000 in connection with the placement of the first mortgage 6 percent bonds of the new company. Neil Cuplet, of Anderson, O'Neil, and Bell, was also to be a director of both the old company and the new corporation.

Each of the following underwriters expected to make a firm commitment (subject to certain conditions, including consummation of the transactions described) to purchase from the new corporation the number of shares of common stock offered hereby set forth after its name at the top of the next page.

Name of Underwriter	Number of Shares
Anderson, O'Neil, and Bell	100,000
Blough and Bingham	65,000
Harvey and Company	60,000
Jackson, Fuller, and Smith	15,000
Carol and Crotch	10,000
Simpler and Williams	10,000
Total	260,000

None of the underwriters was to be affiliated with the new company except Neil Cuplet of Anderson, O'Neil, and Bell.

The underwriters would offer the common stock to the public at $10 and to certain dealers at this price less a concession not in excess of 60 cents per share. The underwriters could allow, and such dealers could reallow, a discount not in excess of 25 cents per share on sales to other dealers who were members of the National Association of Securities Dealers, Inc. After the initial public offering, the public offering price and concessions and discounts to dealers could then be changed by Anderson, O'Neil, and Bell as the representative of the underwriters.

The common stock was to be offered when, as, and if issued to and accepted by the underwriters and subject to their right to withdraw, cancel, or modify such offer without notice and to reject orders in whole or in part.

Other Considerations

Value in a situation with no prevailing market according to Cuplet should be based upon a consideration of all the evidence affecting the full market value. The value of stocks of corporations engaged in the same or a similar line of business should be taken into consideration along with all other factors. Determination of a capitalization rate to apply to average earnings represented one of the difficult problems in the valuation.

Gain realized by a corporation from the sale of all or a part of the assets is taxable. If a corporation adopts a plan of liquidation and liquidates within 12 months, a sale of the assets does not result in a tax at the corporate level, whether or not the sale is made by the corporation.

Minority Stockholder

One of the minority stockholders sent a letter to Mack with a carbon to O'Neil questioning the advantages to be gained by the formation of the new company.

Dear Mr. Mack:

The formation of a new company may be to your advantage, but can you tell me why I should be in favor of it? Why don't you, for instance, sell stock in the present company rather than go to the expense of starting a new company?

I am not a tax lawyer, but I suspect that you have not considered what this change will do to my income tax. How will it affect it?

In other words, you are spending a lot of company money and executive time on this manipulation and I don't see how I benefit. As you know, I only own a small interest in Bolton, but I would like to know how these changes will affect me.

Sincerely yours,
J. B. Frazer

Exhibit 1

Bolton Screw Company
Balance Sheet
December 31
(000 omitted and figures rounded)

ASSETS

Current assets:

Cash (demand deposits)		$1,603
U. S. government securities at cost, which is approximately market value		700
Accounts receivable, less $74,609 reserve for doubtful accounts		943
Note receivable from officer		9
Inventories at standard costs, which are less than market (Note A)		
Raw materials	$ 618	
Work in progress	283	
Finished goods	1,381	2,282
Unexpired insurance		30
Total current assets		$5,567
Cash surrender value of life insurance		233
Other assets		45
Property, plant and equipment, at cost (Note B)		
Land	$ 34	
Buildings	542	
Machinery	2,044	
Factory equipment	332	
Office equipment	168	
Automobiles and trucks	85	
	$3,205	
Less allowance for depreciation	1,339	$1,866
Total assets		$7,711

Exhibit 1

(continued)

Assets to be sold to the new company

Inventories	$2,282
Unexpired insurance	30
Property, plant and equipment, less allowances for depreciation	1,866
	$4,178

LIABILITIES

Current liabilities:

Accounts payable (trade)		$ 119
Accrued payroll and commissions		79
Provision for federal income tax		378
Other accrued taxes		98
Other accrued liabilities		18
Total current liabilities		$ 692
Provision for deferred federal income tax (Note B)		192

CAPITAL

Common stock—129,180 shares of $10 par value authorized and issued	$1,292	
Earned surplus	5,666	
	$6,958	
Less 5,634 shares common stock in treasury at cost	131	$6,827
Total liabilities and capital		$7,711

Statements of Profit and Loss and Earned Surplus
(000 omitted and figures rounded)

	Year Ending December 31			32 weeks Ending August 10
	1	2	3	4
Net sales	$7,919	$10,262	$9,791	$6,116
Cost of goods sold (Note A) ...	5,640	7,472	6,890	4,183
	$2,279	$2,790	$2,901	$1,933
Selling, general, and administrative expenses	1,593	1,922	1,922	1,225
Income from operations	$ 686	$ 868	$ 979	$ 708
Interest earned	14	13	14	12
Net cost of insurance on officers' lives	(15)	(14)	(12)	(11)
Other income (charges) net	(12)	(13)	40	8
Net income before provision for income tax	$ 673	$ 854	$1,021	$ 717
Provision for federal income tax	296	397	516	374
Provision for deferred federal income tax	44	44	9	(5)
Net income	$ 333	$ 413	$ 496	$ 348

BOLTON SCREW COMPANY

Exhibit 1

(continued)

	Year Ending December 31			32 Weeks Ending August 10
	1	2	3	4
Earned surplus at beginning of period	$4,486	$4,661	$4,946	$5,378
	$4,819	$5,074	$5,442	$5,726
Cash dividends:				
Common stock	(97)	(128)	(64)	(60)
Excess of cost over par value of preferred stock retired	(61)			
Earned surplus at end of period	$4,661	$4,946	$5,378	$5,666

The increase in net income in Year 2 over Year 1 resulted principally from the substantial improvement in control over the costs of manufacturing and a reduction in overtime hours and trainee employees required by the unusual automotive activity in Year 1. The increase in net sales and net income for the 32 weeks ended August 10, Year 4, resulted principally from Bolton's increasing emphasis on higher priced special fasteners as well as a general improvement in the volume of business.

Note A—*Inventories*

Inventories are carried at standard costs, adjusted at the end of the year to approximately the lower of prevailing costs or market. At August 10, the standard costs were not materially different from current costs.

Note B—*Depreciation and Amortization Policy*

It is the practice of the companies to provide allowances for depreciation and amortization through periodic charges to expense accounts, principally on the straight line method, at rates permitted by the Bureau of Internal Revenue that are generally adequate to cover the cost of properties by the end of their estimated useful lives. During the three years and 32 weeks ended August 10, Year 4, the principal rates were as follows:

Buildings	2–3%
Machinery	7½ %
Equipment	5–10%
Automobiles and trucks	20–25%

For income tax purposes and in the books of account, buildings and machinery under certificates of necessity are being amortized at the rate of 20 percent. In the accompanying financial statements such buildings and machinery are being depreciated at the usual rates for those classes of property. Income has been charged with a provision equal to the tax benefit resulting from the use of accelerated amortization for tax purposes.

The companies have adopted the policy of applying accelerated methods of depreciation to certain buildings and automobiles as permitted by the Internal Revenue Code. The application of these methods has not had a material effect upon depreciation provisions.

Upon the sale or retirement of depreciable fixed assets, the cost and related accumulated depreciation are removed from the accounts and the resulting gain or loss is reflected in other income. Fully depreciated assets are removed from the accounts; the companies estimate the cost of such assets still in use exceeds $1,000,000.

Exhibit 1

(concluded)

The cost of research, tool and process development, supplies, patterns, and dyes is charged to expense as incurred.

Maintenance, repairs, and minor improvements and renewals are charged to expense. Cost of new facilities and major improvements are capitalized.

Exhibit 2

Bolton Screw Corporation (new)
Pro Forma Balance Sheet Giving Effect to Financing and to Purchase of Assets of Bolton Screw Company as Though Those Transactions Had Been Consummated at August 10

ASSETS

Current assets:		
Cash		$ 850
Inventories (Note A Exhibit 1)		1,472
Unexpired insurance		28
Total current assets		$2,350
Property, plant and equipment:		
Land	$ 35	
Buildings	270	
Machinery	920	
Factory equipment	130	
Office Equipment	95	
Automobiles and trucks	45	1,495
Deferred debt and organization expenses (estimated)		40
		$3,885

LIABILITIES AND CAPITAL

Current liabilities: accrued debt and organization expenses	$ 40
First mortgage 6 percent bonds due	1,500
Common stock of $1 par value, 350,000 shares authorized, 1,000 shares outstanding at September 23; 261,000 shares to be outstanding after new financing	261
Paid-in surplus	2,084
	$3,885

Exhibit 3

Bolton Screw Company
Proposed Purchase of Assets
(000 omitted and figures rounded)

Old Company				New Corporation	
Current assets					
Cash	$1,600	To Be Sold		Cash	$ 850
U. S. Govt.					
securities .	700				
Receivable .	950	Inventory ..	$2,280		
Inventory ..	2,280	Unexp. ins.	30	Inventory ..	1,470
Unexp. ins. .	30	Property,		Unexp. ins.	30
		plant, etc.	1,850		
	$5,560		$4,160		$2,350
Property, plant,					
and equipment					
Land	$ 35			Land	$ 35
Building ...	540			Building ...	270
Machinery .	2,040			Machinery .	920
Factory				Factory	
equipment	330			equipment	130
Office				Office	
equipment	165			equipment	95
				Automo-	
Automobiles	80			biles	45
	$3,190				$1,495
Less allow.				Organ. exp.	40
for deprec. ..	1,340				
	$1,850				
Total assets ..	$7,410			Total assets	$3,885

Exhibit 4

Bolton Screw Company

| | | | | | | | Per Share | | |
	Sales	Net Income	Plant & Equip.	Depr.	Earn.	Div.	Tang. Assets	W/C	Price Range
American Screw Company									
	(000)	(000)	(000)	(000)					
1973	$12,829	$ 681			$5.78	$3.40			47½ — 39
1974	11,600	498			4.22	3.40			55 — 45½
1975	10,707	(164)	$ 6,416	$ 2,886	(1.40)	3.40	$ 83	$52	50 — 34

Manufactures recessed head and alotted head machine screws, stove bolts, tapping screws, wood screws, thread-cutting screws, lockwashers, and special aircraft fasteners.

	Sales	Net Income	Plant & Equip.	Depr.	Earn.	Div.	Tang. Assets	W/C	Price Range
Atlas Tack Company									
1973	$ 4,958	$ 261			$2.79				15⅜ — 11¼
1974	5,338	143			1.54				12½ — 11¼
1975	5,123	122	$ 3,201	$ 2,377	1.31	$0.25	$ 17	$24	5½ — 5½

Manufactures wire products, cut and wire tacks, nails, soft steel rivets.

	Sales	Net Income	Plant & Equip.	Depr.	Earn.	Div.	Tang. Assets	W/C	Price Range
Pittsburgh Screw and Bolt Company									
1973	$33,873	$1,049			$0.71	$0.20			8¾ — 6⅞
1974	36,758	1,666			1.05	0.45			8⅞ — 6⅞
1975	33,639	1,889	$23,850	$11,958	1.09	0.50	$ 10	$ 5	8½ — 6½

Manufactures wide variety of screws, bolts, nuts, etc.

	Sales	Net Income	Plant & Equip.	Depr.	Earn.	Div.	Tang. Assets	W/C	Price Range
St. Louis Screw & Bolt									
1973	$ 2,223	$ 140			$4.25	$2.00			20 — 18
1974	2,788	244			7.74	2.00			20½ — 18
1975	2,856	257	$ 938	$ 517	8.16	3.00	$ 55	$45	26 — 20

Manufactures bolts, nuts, screw machine products.

	Sales	Net Income	Plant & Equip.	Depr.	Earn.	Div.	Tang. Assets	W/C	Price Range
Standard Screw Company									
1973	$46,352	$2,501			$8.73	$4.00			75 — 62½
1974	49,903	1,635			5.71	4.00			70 — 63½
1975	52,491	1,521	$37,153	$14,868	5.31	4.00	$107	$48	68 — 50

Manufactures special screw machine products, screw threaded fasteners, diesel fuel pumps, and automotive tappet as valve trim parts.

	Sales	Net Income	Plant & Equip.	Depr.	Earn.	Div.	Tang. Assets	W/C	Price Range
United-Carr Fastener Company									
1973	$50,603	$4,134			$6.37	$2.50			57¾ — 34¼
1974	50,195	2,919			4.50	2.25			62 — 41½
1975	52,515	3,088	$13,869	$ 4,052	4.76	2.50	$ 35	$19	46¾ — 38

Manufactures a wide variety of fasteners, snap fasteners, lock nuts, etc.

Exhibit 5

Bolton Screw Company
Table for Computation of Federal Gross Estate Tax*

Taxable Estate (000 omitted)	Tax (000 omitted)	Rate of Tax in Excess of Lower Amount of Bracket
60– 100	9	28%
100– 250	20	30
250– 500	65	32
500– 750	145	35
750– 1,000	233	37
1,000– 1,250	325	39
1,250– 1,500	423	42
1,500– 2,000	528	45
2,000– 2,500	753	49
2,500– 3,000	998	53
3,000– 3,500	1,263	56
3,500– 4,000	1,543	59
4,000– 5,000	1,838	63
5,000– 6,000	2,468	67
6,000– 7,000	3,138	70
7,000– 8,000	3,838	73
8,000–10,000	4,568	76
10,000–	6,088	77

* Subject to certain credits and deductions.

General Bancshares
Corporation

General Bancshares Corporation, a bank holding company that adopted its name at the end of 1958, divested itself of certain non-banking assets in order to comply with the Bank Holding Company Act of 1956. In October, 1961, it owned all or a major interest in eight banks. The Bank of St. Louis, fourth largest in that city, was the largest bank of the group. The three other St. Louis banks were neighborhood institutions. Three subsidiaries in Illinois were the largest in their respective communities. The single subsidiary in Tennessee, with its two branches, was one of the smaller banks of Memphis. (See Exhibit 1 for the comparative size of these banks.)

As a part of its growth program, General Bancshares, in October, 1961, proposed to acquire two new suburban banks in the St. Louis area. Under the Bank Holding Company Act, it was limited to additional banks in its home state of Missouri, and then only upon the approval of the Board of Governors of the Federal Reserve System.[1] This action, the first major move since reorganization in 1958, involved a complex of problems: valuation, merger terms, propriety of corporate dealings with officers and directors, and methods of achieving growth.

PROXY SOLICITATION

On October 16, 1961, General Bancshares Corporation sent a proxy statement to its stockholders. The company announced a special meeting to be held on October 31 to vote on an amendment to the Articles of Incorporation which would authorize the issuance of 500,000 shares of preferred stock with a par value of $10 per share. Such stock would be issued in series, from time to time, at the discretion of the board of directors, with such preferences, priorities, rights, and other characteristics as the board would fix for each series.

1. Branch banking is not permitted either in Missouri (except for certain detached drive-in facilities) or in Illinois. Tennessee permits limited branch banking.

This power meant the right to determine dividend rates, voting rights, preemptive rights, conversion privileges, and redemption and sinking fund provisions. The board would have the power to determine the purposes and consideration for such issues, except that new stock would not be sold for cash for less than its par value.

The proxy statement proposed the corporation to acquire all the stock, save for directors' qualifying shares, of two state chartered banks located in the northwestern part of St. Louis County, Missouri. The stock of one of these banks, the Commercial Bank of St. Louis County, was acquired for cash and that of the other, the Lindbergh Bank, in exchange for an issue of $10 par cumulative preferred stock, 4½ percent convertible series. This preferred would have one vote per share, but no preemptive rights. The conversion privilege would permit the holder to exchange $11.81 of par amount of the preferred for one share of common stock. A sinking fund was provided amounting to 5 percent of original shares at par value to begin eight years after issue. The preferred was callable, in whole or in part, at $10.40 during the first year after issue and at a figure of 5 cents per share less each succeeding year until the end of eight years, after which the redemption price would be par. In the event of dissolution, the preferred would have a priority in an amount up to par value plus accumulated unpaid dividends.

Although it was unnecessary for the cash acquisition of bank stock to be approved by the shareholders, General Bancshares stated the acquisitions would not be made (even if approved by the Federal Reserve Board) unless a majority of the shares voted to authorize the creation of the new preferred stock, part of which would be used for the acquisition of the Lindbergh Bank. Failure of the shareholders to authorize the new preferred would therefore block acquisition of both banks.

The proxy statement contained statements on management's interest in the two banks and its recommendation as follows.

Interest of Company Officers and Directors

Preston Estep, chairman of the board and a director of the company, and certain other directors of the company, were stockholders of the Lindbergh Bank and of the other bank sought to be acquired, the Commercial Bank of St. Louis County. (None of the other directors of the company had any interest in the proposed transactions.)

Estep took no part in the deliberations of the company's senior officers whose deliberations resulted in the decision to recommend to the board of directors that the two banks be acquired and on the bases herein described. He and the other directors interested in the two banks, as described above, abstained from voting when the board

Name	Office held	Bank shares owned	Percent of shares owned	Amount invested	Received in exchange or sale
Lindbergh Bank					
Preston Estep	Chairman of the Board	5,580	55.8	$279,000	38,356.36 (pref. shares)
Leo A. Fisher	Director	500	5	25,000	3,436.95 (pref. shares)
James H. Meredith	Director	500	5	25,000	3,436.95 (pref. shares)
Commercial Bank of St. Louis County					
Preston Estep	Chairman of the Board	2,250	22.5	$113,500	$139,835.02
James H. Meredith	Director	900	9	45,000	55,934.01
Richard A. Meyer	Director	180	1.8	9,000	11,186.80

of directors considered and approved the acquisition of the two banks on the proposed bases.

Management Recommendation

The management of the company recommended the acquisition of the two banks to the stockholders since owning them gave management an opportunity to participate in the growth of a rapidly developing residential, commercial, and industrial area.

PROPOSED ACQUISITION OF LINDBERGH BANK

The Lindbergh Bank had 10,000 shares of $20 par value, all of which, except 275 shares of directors' qualifying stock, were to be acquired. The value figure for which an equal par value of General Bancshares preferred was to be exchanged was to be its book value (capital, surplus, and undivided profits) on the last day of the month preceding the month of exchange plus $200,000. This purchase price was computed by the corporation's senior officers (excluding Estep). They considered the following factors: The Commercial Bank of St. Louis County was available at a $100,000 premium for cash, which was considered a fair price. Management considered the growth and earnings prospects of the Lindbergh Bank to be superior. They also considered the advantage of being able to pay in preferred stock rather than cash, particularly in view of the 4½ percent dividend rate, a sinking fund deferred for eight years, and a relatively high conversion rate. (It was not considered feasible to increase the corporation's debt to handle both acquisitions with borrowed cash.)

The 66,848 shares of the proposed preferred stock to be issued in this exchange on the basis of the June 30, 1961, balance sheet would permit its holders to acquire by conversion 56,603 shares of General Bancshares' common stock worth $8.75 per share on June 30, 1961, and $9.25 per share on October 9, 1961, on the basis of the closing prices on the New York Stock Exchange on those dates. The Lindbergh Bank was chartered (perpetual) December 3, 1958, approved for insurance by the Federal Deposit Insurance Corporation March 24, 1960, and opened for business March 24, 1961, in a new building in the town of Hazelwood, a suburb of the city of St. Louis. The monthly rental of quarters of 5,000 square feet of space amounted to $850.

As is usual for a new bank, operating losses were experienced at first, and for this bank totaled $28,560 to June 30, 1961. Financial statements appear in Exhibits 2 and 3. While no assurance was given that the bank would operate profitably at any future time, it was estimated that it would begin to operate profitably sometime in 1962.

PROPOSED ACQUISITION OF COMMERCIAL BANK

The Commercial Bank of St. Louis County was chartered (perpetual) on August 1, 1958, approved by the Federal Deposit Insurance Corporation for insurance May 27, 1959, and opened for business in rented quarters in the town of Olivette on June 1, 1959. Its 2,400 square feet of rented space cost $200 per month. Initially it operated at a loss, but had shown a monthly operating profit since November, 1960. The proxy statements pointed out that no assurance would be given that the bank would operate profitably in the future.

The proposed purchase price for the stock of this bank was to be based upon the book value on the last day of the month prior to purchase plus a $100,000 premium. Thus, had the 9,825 shares (10,000 less 175 directors' qualifying shares) been purchased on the basis of the $521,489 book value at the end of June 30, 1961, plus a $100,000 premium, the cash purchase price would have been $610,613. The directors considered this purchase price to be fair and equitable and comparable with that which would be paid if the stock were owned by persons unaffiliated with the corporation. The premium was considered reasonable by the management in view of the bank's location and prospects. The entire purchase price was to be borrowed on favorable terms, and it was expected that the loan would be repayable over a period of 20 years. The earnings of the bank were expected to be sufficient to retire such borrowing.

Financial statements for General Bancshares on a consolidated and parent-company basis are presented in Exhibits 5 to 8. Data on prices, earnings, and dividends per share appear in Exhibit 9.

Because ownership of small banks was usually closely held, price quotations and information on earnings and dividends were seldom available. Exhibit 10 presents both selected data for three of General Bancshares' St. Louis subsidiaries for which price quotations were available and comparable information for six of the smallest banks in the St. Louis area on which information was published.

Exhibit 1

General Bancshares Corporation
Majority-owned Subsidiary Banks

	Total deposits * at December 31		Capital surplus and undivided profits at December 31	
	1960	1959	1960	1959
Bank of St. Louis .	$120,316,451	$117,923,667	$ 9,624,807	$ 9,172,871
Commerical and Industrial Bank, Memphis	19,781,487	18,912,509	1,928,112	1,587,866
Illinois State Bank of Quincy	23,335,148	23,928,615	2,183,971	2,049,656
Northwestern Bank and Trust Company, St. Louis	21,752,306	21,490,733	1,887,244	1,793,658
Baden Bank of St. Louis	23,477,058	22,722,815	1,777,336	1,630,339
Jefferson-Gravois Bank of St. Louis	33,511,473	33,758,185	2,590,079	2,469,476
Bank of Benton, Benton, Illinois .	10,718,614	10,286,969	878,363	807,749
Bank of Ziegler, Ziegler, Illinois .	11,235,117	10,909,626	852,711	766,766
	$264,127,654	$259,933,119	$21,722,623	$20,278,381

* Includes intragroup deposits.

Exhibit 2

General Bancshares Corporation
Balance Sheets of Banks to Be Acquired, June 30, 1961
(Based on report submitted by bank to
Federal Deposit Insurance Corporation

	Lindbergh Bank	Commercial Bank
Assets		
Cash, balances with other banks, including reserve balances, and cash items in process of collection	$ 270,670	$ 404,316
United States government obligations	295,130	1,483,880
Obligations of states and political subdivisions	–0–	–0–
Other bonds, stocks, notes, and debentures	100,026	–0–
Loans and discounts less reserve for losses	567,733	930,927
Bank premises, furniture, and fixtures	102,795	56,010
Customers' liability to this bank on acceptances outstanding	–0–	5,000
Other assets	19,494	18,937
Total assets	$1,355,848	$2,899,070
Liabilities		
Demand deposits of individuals, partnerships, and corporations	$ 520,611	$1,553,070
Time and savings deposits of individuals, partnerships, and corporations	166,791	370,172
Deposits of United States government (including postal savings)	15,245	128,836
Deposits of states and political subdivisions	137,061	168,816
Deposits of banks	–0–	105,618
Certified and officers' checks, etc.	4,257	33,428
Total deposits	$ 843,965	$2,359,940
Acceptances executed by or for this bank and outstanding	–0–	5,000
Other liabilities	24,492	12,641
Total liabilities	$ 868,457	$2,377,581
Capital shares and surplus:		
Common stock	$ 200,000	$ 200,000
Surplus	200,000	200,000
Undivided profits	87,391	120,981
Surplus reserves	–0–	508
Total capital accounts	$ 487,391	$ 521,489
Total liabilities and capital accounts	$1,355,848	$2,899,070

Exhibit 3

General Bancshares Corporation
Lindbergh Bank, Hazelwood, Missouri
Statement of Income and Expense
January 1, 1961, to June 30, 1961 *

Current operating earnings:
Interest on securities	$ 3,163
Interest and discount on loans	4,797
Service charges, commissions, fees, and collection and exchange charges	4,186
Other current earnings	362
Total current operating earnings	$ 12,508

Current operating expenses:
Salaries—officers and employees	$ 11,379
Interest on savings and time deposits	700
Depreciation on banking house furniture and fixtures	2,875
Advertising	3,812
Rent—bank premises	2,406
Rent—equipment	2,436
Stationery and supplies	4,108
Other current operating expenses	9,022
Total current operating expenses	$ 36,738
Net current operating earnings (loss)	$(24,230)
Losses and charge-offs—all other	1,745
Income (loss) before provision for income taxes	$(25,975)
Provision for federal income taxes	$ 2,585
Net income (loss)	$(28,560)

* Bank actually commenced business on March 24, 1961; however, charter as a state bank was obtained December 3, 1958, and some income was earned and expenses incurred prior to opening.

Exhibit 4

General Bancshares Corporation
Commercial Bank of St. Louis County, Olivette, Missouri
Statement of Income and Expense
January 1, 1959, to June 30, 1961*

	January 1 to December 31, 1959	Year ended December 31, 1960	January 1 to June 30, 1961
Current operating earnings:			
Interest on securities	$ 32,590	$ 53,630	$24,084
Interest and discount on			
loans	10,212	48,156	27,351
Service charges, commissions, fees, and collection and exchange charges ..	2,627	10,303	6,488
Other current earnings	551	983	685
Total current operating earnings	$ 45,980	$113,072	$58,608
Current operating expenses:			
Salaries—officers	$ 17,075	$ 23,590	$11,250
Salaries—employees	10,590	24,097	13,420
Interest on savings and time deposits	1,143	4,575	4,707
Interest and discount on borrowed money	22	296	27
Taxes, other than on net income	2,640	2,260	1,791
Depreciation on banking house furniture and fixtures	5,347	11,617	5,490
Advertising	2,531	3,500	951
Rent—bank premises ...	1,600	4,800	2,400
Stationery and supplies ..	7,105	8,262	2,617
Other current operating expenses	8,268	15,489	7,923
Total current operating expenses	$ 56,321	$ 98,486	$50,576
Net current operating earnings (loss)	$(10,341)	$ 14,586	$ 8,032
Recoveries and profits:			
Profit on sales of securities	$ –0–	$ 9,551	$ 2,657
Losses and charge-offs:			
Provision for possible future loan losses	72	70	100
All other	16	188	256

Exhibit 4

(con)

Total losses and charge-offs	$ 88	$ 258	$ 356
Income (loss) before provision for income taxes ..	$(10,429)	$ 23,879	$10,333
Provision for income taxes:			
Federal	$ 88	$ 3,701	$ 2,956
State	14	1,445	716
Total taxes on net income	$ 102	$ 5,146	$ 3,672
Net income before transfer from securities valuation reserve	$(10,531)	$ 18,733	$ 6,661
Transfer from (to) securities valuation reserve	(613)	(3,518)	267
Net income (loss)	$(11,144)	$ 15,215	$ 6,928

* Bank actually commenced business on June 1, 1959; however, charter as a state bank was obtained August 1, 1958, and some income was earned and expenses incurred prior to opening.

Exhibit 5

General Bancshares Corporation
Balance Sheets (Parent company only)

	December 31	
	1960	1959
Assets		
Cash in banks	$ 310,681	$ 552,551
Miscellaneous receivables and other assets	535	23,949
Other security investments at cost	63,350	58,350
Investment in constituent banks— at		
net asset value	21,014,852	19,606,438
Total assets	$21,389,418	$20,241,288
Liabilities and capital		
Accounts payable	$ 3,400	$ 4,827
Reserves for taxes, interest, etc.*	18,192	51,724
Notes payable **	3,060,160	3,200,000
Capital:		
Common stock—$2 par value, authorized		
3 million shares, issued 2,342,544³⁄₁₀		
shares	4,685,089	4,655,089
Capital surplus	3,470,491	3,372,991
Earned surplus	350,048	373,344
Surplus from equity in affiliates	9,802,038	8,583,313
Total capital	$18,307,666	$16,984,737
Total liabilities and capital	$21,389,418	$20,241,288

* General Bancshares Corporation and its constituent banks and affiliate will file a consolidated federal income tax return for 1960. The amount of tax which would be payable by each subsidiary on a separate return basis will be paid to General Bancshares Corporation, which will pay the tax liability determined to be due on a consolidated basis.

** Note payable bears interest plus ½ percent per annum, but at a rate not less than 4½ percent per annum. The loan is unsecured, but has a negative asset pledge provision, and is payable on a fifteen-year monthly amortized basis, for five years. On January 2, 1965, the entire unpaid balance is due.

Exhibit 6

General Bancshares Corporation
Statements of Income and Expense (Parent company only)

	Year ended December 31	
	1960	1959
Income:		
Dividends from constituent banks	$1,029,655	$1,020,588
Other dividends and interest	–0–	40
Fees from constituent banks	92,972	90,589
Other income	40,181	33,566
	$1,162,808	$1,144,783
Expenses:		
Interest expense	$ 167,023	$ 159,255
Fees paid constituent bank	23,450	23,450
Taxes, other than income	3,883	3,918
Other expenses	52,151	59,143
	$ 246,507	$ 245,766
Net income before provision for income taxes	$ 916,301	$ 899,017
Provision for federal income taxes *	5,579	17,420
Net income	$ 910,722	$ 881,597

* See first footnote, Exhibit 5.

Exhibit 7

General Bancshares Corporation
Constituent Banks and Affiliate
Consolidated Balance Sheets

	December 31	
	1960	1959
Assets		
Cash and due from banks	$ 30,542,618	$ 32,086,344
United States government securities	44,937,687	46,849,675
State and municipal securities	64,962,753	68,437,710
Other bonds and securities	2,371,379	3,328,186
Loans and discounts	142,077,477	128,941,168
Bank premises and equipment	5,178,255	4,793,635
Accrued income receivable	1,036,812	1,068,061
Other assets	274,554	309,003
Total assets	$291,381,535	$285,813,782
Liabilities and Capital		
Deposits:		
Demand	$114,413,046	$113,427,824
Time	142,180,464	138,700,769
Total deposits	$256,593,510	$252,128,593
Other liabilities:		
Notes payable	3,060,160	3,400,000
Mortgage payable	1,430,017	1,516,643
Reserves for taxes, interest, etc.	1,353,717	1,348,364
Other liabilities	3,245,205	3,098,989
Unearned discounts	5,238,471	5,320,698
Reserves for possible future loan losses	1,446,102	1,337,171
Minority interests in constituent banks	706,687	678,587
Total other liabilities	$ 16,480,359	$ 16,700,452
Capital:		
Common stock—$2 par value, author-		
ized 3 million shares, issued		
2,342,544³⁄₁₀ shares	$ 4,685,089	$ 4,655,089
Surplus (see Exhibit VIII)	13,622,577	12,329,648
Total capital	$ 18,307,666	$ 16,984,737
Total liabilities and capital	$291,381,535	$285,813,782

Exhibit 8

General Bancshares Corporation
Constituent Banks and Affiliate
Consolidated Statements of Income and Expense

	Year ended December 31	
	1960	1959
Operating income	$13,686,793	$12,816,655
Operating expenses	10,543,728	9,689,418
Net operating income	$ 3,143,065	$ 3,127,237
Recoveries and profits	27,068	85,377
Losses and charge-offs	247,656	185,795
Net income before provision for income taxes	$ 2,922,477	$ 3,026,819
Provision for income taxes	714,134	762,457
Net income before minority interest and transfer to securities valuation reserve ..	2,208,343	2,264,362
Minority interest	88,335	91,974
Transfer to securities valuation reserve (portion applicable to General Banschares Corporation)	(5,587)	96,766
Consolidated net income	$ 2,125,595	$ 2,075,622
Consolidated statements of surplus		
Balance at beginning of year	$12,329,648	$11,185,198
Net income from statement of income and expense	$ 2,125,595	$ 2,075,622
Surplus paid in	97,500	–0–
Increase due to acquisition of stocks of constituent banks	3,852	(155)
	$14,556,595	$13,260,665
Deduct: cash dividends on common stock ..	934,018	931,017
Balance at end of year	$13,622,577	$12,329,648

Exhibit 9

General Bancshares Corporation
Selected Data per Share

	1959		1960		1961	
Earnings	$ .93		$ .90			
Dividends	.40		.40			
Book value	7.30		7.82			
Market price	High	Low	High	Low	High	Low
	10⅜	7⅝	9⅛	7⅝		
January					8⅜	7⅞
February					9	7⅞
March					8¾	8¼
April					8¾	8¼
May					9⅝	8½
June					9⅜	8⅝
July					8⅞	8⅝
August					9¼	8¾
September					9⅜	8¾

Exhibit 10

General Bancshares Corporation
Selected Data on St. Louis Banks
(All data for year ending December 31, 1960)

	Total deposits (thousands)	Price Sept. 29, 1961		Per share		
		Bid	Asked	Book value	Earn-ings	Divi-dends
General Banschares subsidiaries:						
Baden Bank (88.06%)	$23,476	45	—	$44.42	$5.67	$2.00
Jefferson-Gravois (97.36%)	33,511	40	—	41.12	4.23	2.40
Northwestern Bank & Trust (93.96%)	21,752	50	—	46.92	5.33	3.20
Independent banks:						
Big Bend Bank ...	6,101	49	—	45.04	6.42	1.50
Bremen Bank & Trust Co.	15,269	65	—	78.39	5.52	2.80
Hampton Bank	20,271	23½	—	23.26	2.46	.60
Southern Commer-cial & Savings Bank	17,787	54	—	48.96	5.47	3.00
Mound City Trust Co.	25,744	21¾	22¾	15.64	2.29	1.50
North St. Louis Trust Co.	16,063	78	—	97.36	7.75	2.65

( ) indicate percent of stock owned by General Bancshares.

Galvor Company* (A)

INTRODUCTION

"In 1936, I borrowed a little money from a friend, made 25 tube checkers working at home, and went out on the road and sold them; that's how Galvor began," commented M. Georges Latour, president and owner of France's Galvor Company. "Today in 1962, Galvor is still here in Bordeaux where it started, but now we make a broad line of electric and electronic measuring and test instruments, and we operate in this large, modern plant. We have just had a record year in every respect: net sales were over 12,000,000 New Francs (NF), profits after taxes were about 1,000,000 NF, and our net worth today is approaching 6,000,000 NF. Twenty-six years ago the firm consisted of my wife and me; today we have about 430 employees and a strong management team to direct our constantly growing affairs. (An organization chart for Galvor is found in Table 1 on page 451.) It has certainly been an exciting and rewarding experience to build the company."

THE FOUNDING OF GALVOR

M. Latour continued, "You might find the detailed story of how the business started rather an interesting one. In 1935, my wife and I had just had our first child, so it was necessary for me to earn a good living. I went to work for a radio manufacturer, selling his radios to retailers. During the summer of '35, as is traditional in France, most people were away on vacation, so business wasn't too good. In an effort to help my customers and earn their good will, as I made my rounds I would try to fix any broken radios which might have been sent in to the retailers. In those days there wasn't the vast network of radio-repair shops which exists today and so if a radio required complicated repairs, it had to be sent back to the factory. The retailers usually didn't have much technical knowledge about radios —they just sold them. But when making my rounds I would carry

---

* Fictitious name.

Table 1

The Galvor Organization, February 1962

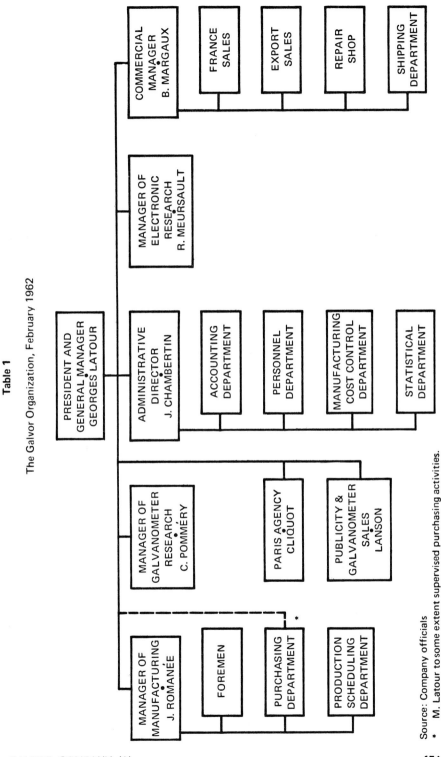

PRESIDENT AND GENERAL MANAGER GEORGES LATOUR•

COMMERCIAL MANAGER B. MARGAUX•
- FRANCE SALES
- EXPORT SALES
- REPAIR SHOP
- SHIPPING DEPARTMENT

MANAGER OF ELECTRONIC RESEARCH R. MEURSAULT•

ADMINISTRATIVE DIRECTOR J. CHAMBERTIN•
- ACCOUNTING DEPARTMENT
- PERSONNEL DEPARTMENT
- MANUFACTURING COST CONTROL DEPARTMENT
- STATISTICAL DEPARTMENT

MANAGER OF GALVANOMETER RESEARCH C. POMMÉRY•
- PARIS AGENCY CLIQUOT•
- PUBLICITY & GALVANOMETER SALES LANSON•

MANAGER OF MANUFACTURING J. ROMANÉE•
- FOREMEN
- PURCHASING DEPARTMENT *
- PRODUCTION SCHEDULING DEPARTMENT

Source: Company officials

•   Company officials

*   M. Latour to some extent supervised purchasing activities.

GALVOR COMPANY (A)   451 along a stock of extra tubes, and so when a retailer gave me a broken radio to look at, I would first replace the radio's tubes with good ones from my stock. Since most radio failures are due to faulty tubes, this method usually fixed the radio. If that didn't work, I could then inspect the wiring to see if that was O.K., and I could check the resistors and condensers to make sure that they were not obviously defective. But if none of these methods fixed the radio, then it had to be sent back to the factory; it was, however, usually an easy matter for me to fix a radio.

"One day that summer, a customer gave me a broken radio. I quickly located the defective tube, but when I substituted one of my tubes, the radio still didn't work. I checked the wiring and the other parts carefully, but I could see no reason why the radio shouldn't work. I regretfully admitted that I couldn't fix it and suggested that it be sent to the factory. I thought no more about the incident until, a little later, another customer gave me a broken radio to fix. This radio, I discovered, also had the same type of defective tube as the first one, and when I substituted my own tube, again the radio didn't work. Again a check of the chassis showed that there was apparently nothing else wrong, but still I couldn't fix it. After a while, and quite by accident, I decided to substitute for the defective tube again from my own stock, but this time I used a different, although identical, tube from my selection. Immediately the radio worked. I was horrified; how was I supposed to do a good repair job if I couldn't be sure that my own stock of tubes, which was brand new and supposed to be perfect, contained some defective tubes?

"I had been educated as an engineer, and it quickly occurred to me that I could easily construct a simple device which would test a tube. You have to understand that, in those days, there were only a few tube testers on the market, and all of them were vastly too complicated and expensive for the average radio retailer. About all the retailer could do was to check tubes by substituting new ones (if he had any); if this didn't work, he could not do much else.

"Well, during the fall I constructed a tube checker at home, and when it was finished I started taking it on my customer calls. This little instrument was very simple: it had only a tube socket and a simple meter, and it only checked the tube's emission.[1] If the meter indicated over 30, the tube was all right, less than 20 the tube was defective, and from 20 to 30 it was questionable. My customers were delighted by this little instrument, because it was simple. They could easily use it themselves to check their customers' radios, and so I got many requests for copies of it.

1. Emission is only one of the characteristics of a vacuum tube; a modern tube tester checks many other tube characteristics as well. Checking emission is rather like determining whether an automobile's fuel pump is feeding gasoline into the engine; after such a check, one still does not know whether the engine is running well and efficiently.

"It occurred to me that somebody ought to make a simple tube checker for the radio retailer to use. I had no interest in doing so, because my sales had started to increase greatly during the fall of '35, so I was making a good living as a salesman. My customers appreciated the repair service I gave them, especially since I did not charge for this service. So, by December, I decided to talk to the president of my company; I hoped to persuade him to make the tube checker himself. When I came to the home office in December, there was a fine commission check waiting for me, and a message that the president of the company wanted to see me. That was fine, because I also wanted to see him.

"As soon as I got to his office, he started explaining to me that I was making too much money; I was even earning more than he was! 'When your contract expires next June,' he said, 'we will have to rewrite it to lower your commission rate.' I said nothing to this and proceeded to show him my tube checker. I guaranteed that it would be an instant sales success and that he could easily manufacture it. He would hardly discuss it at all. I was very disappointed when I left his office.

"In the spring of 1936, my sales and commissions continued to be high, and radio retailers continued to ask me to get them duplicates of my tube checker. Finally, I made my decision. My contract expired on June 1st, and so when I got to the head office late in May, I handed the president my resignation. This upset him considerably, because I was one of his most successful salesmen. He admitted that it was possible to make a mistake, and he offered to keep my commission rate at the old level, but my mind was made up. I told him I was going into business for myself to make the tube checker, and I resigned. His parting words were that, within a year, I'd be bankrupt. The very next day, I started Galvor. (I met the president many years later; by then his company had gone bankrupt.)

"In order to start the business, I had borrowed what would today amount to 6000 NF from a friend in Lyon, and with this I immediately ordered enough parts to make 25 tube checkers. Those first days as my own boss were wonderful; maybe they were the happiest days of my life. My wife and I worked long into the evenings assembling those first 25 checkers; when they were finished, I took them out and sold them almost immediately to radio retailers, except for one that I kept as a demonstrator. With the proceeds from this first batch, I was able to make about 40 more checkers, which I sold just as quickly, and I was on my way. We branched out after that into another, more complicated type of tube checker, and subsequently into related types of test equipment. Within a year I was an employer: I hired an assistant, and Galvor grew from there.

"You know, life is dependent to a great degree on luck, and especially on seizing a piece of good luck when it occurs. If I hadn't one day seen the need for a simple, reliable, cheap tube checker, if I hadn't had the technical skill to design one, if it hadn't been so enthusiastically accepted, and of course if my boss hadn't refused to manufacture it, well, without any doubt, I wouldn't be sitting in this office today.

"My basic business philosophy is this: first, you should find out what people need; then, if someone isn't meeting this need as well as you can, you have an opportunity. Second, if you can build a better product and sell it cheaper than your competitors, you will be successful. Our company has grown by capitalizing on these two facts."

Galvor in 1962

Galvor had grown greatly, since its early days, but in 1962 the firm retained many of the features it had had twenty-six years before. M. Latour still owned 97% of the company, and the basic operation was still one of buying parts and assembling them into electric and electronic measuring and test equipment. During its growth, Galvor had broadened its product line considerably, but the company still concentrated on electric and electronic measuring instruments. In general, the company's products had become increasingly sophisticated technically; this trend was typical of the electronic industry's development throughout the world. In 1962, however, most of the firm's products were still of only moderate technological complexity, and most sales came from products in the price range of 50 to 1000 NF. In comparison, more sophisticated branches of the industry, such as those dealing with electronic computers, often manufactured products of extraordinary complexity which sold for millions of new francs. In its own sector of the industry (measuring instruments), Galvor was one of the major French firms, but there were many firms in other sectors of the industry which were vastly larger than Galvor.

The Galvor Series

Galvor (A) is designed to give the reader a basic familiarity with the company and the way in which various aspects of the firm's operations developed. To this end, the case discusses the development of the product line, manufacturing operations, marketing, research and development activities, and the financial and management control of Galvor. Subsequent cases in the series develop in greater detail certain aspects of Galvor's operations in 1962 and its plans for the future.

THE GROWTH OF THE GALVOR PRODUCT LINE

After the favorable reception of his first tube checker, M. Latour expanded Galvor's product line by the addition of a tube analyzer in

1937. Then in 1937–1938, Galvor produced its first generators and multimeters. In 1941–1943, the company further broadened its operations; during this period, impedance bridges, galvanometers, vacuum-tube voltmeters, and more types of generators were introduced.

After the War, the first order of business was to modernize and upgrade the existing products. When M. Latour felt that his established products were sufficiently improved to meet the demands of the post-war market, he was again ready to expand Galvor's product line. Recalling this period, he said: "In 1946, as soon as it was possible to get a booking, I flew to the United States in order to study the development of electronics there. During the War, we had become very impressed with the high level of U. S. technology; jeeps and bombers were good illustrations, to us, of this level. So I thought I had better go over to see how much progress had been made in measuring instruments. I was very happy to observe that, despite my fears, the design and performance of Galvor's products appeared to be at least as good as that of the comparable U. S. products. This realization encouraged me to continue Galvor after the War and to succeed."

In 1946–1947, after the basic products had been satisfactorily improved, Galvor branched out into several new types of multimeters; the company also introduced its first VHF generator, in anticipation of television's requirements. Then, in 1952–1953, as television became more and more important, additional TV test equipment was added: wobulators, and marker- and pattern-generators. Throughout the post-war period, Galvor's products were steadily improved in terms of performance, reliability, durability, and price. In the late 1950's, as FM radio broadcasting became increasingly important, Galvor introduced its first FM generators. The emergence of transistors at this time also spurred the company to develop a transistor checker. Further development of VHF generators continued as television became increasingly common in France. In 1958, 15 years after Galvor had first started manufacturing galvanometers for use in its own equipment, it began to sell these meters to other instrument manufacturers.

Galvor had traditionally engaged in three different kinds of product development. First, as outlined above, there was the continuous process of adding distinctly new types of products to the catalogue. Second, and of equal importance, each basic product was being updated and improved almost constantly. Thus the original tube checker and tube analyzer were still important Galvor products, but each of these instruments was, in 1962, a vastly more sophisticated and useful device than its ancestor of twenty-odd years before. Third, many of Galvor's basic product types had been gradually expanded into a line of similar instruments for varying applications and requirements. For example, the original multimeter of 1938 had, by 1962, grown to a line of about 15 different multimeters.

In addition to its basic line of measuring and test instruments, Galvor had developed a number of other products of lesser importance. These products could be classified in three groups. First, many Galvor instruments could be made more versatile by the addition of accessories, and so the company manufactured (or bought outside for resale) a considerable number of such accessories. Second, starting around 1950, Galvor had begun to manufacture certain products which were essentially unrelated to its traditional product line. One such product was an instrument which, when attached to an oil burner, would shut off the burner when there was a danger of explosion. Third, in late 1957 the company introduced a small line of instruments under the trade name of TRONEX. This line contained some of the high-volume products in the Galvor line, but TRONEX products were considerably lower, in both price and quality, than the equivalent Galvor products.

In commenting on Galvor's product line and the philosophy which had created it, M. Latour remarked, "You already know why I built our first product, the tube checker. From there, it was a logical step to make a more complicated instrument, with an analogous function, and with similar but more advanced technology: the tube analyzer. Until the War these tube checkers and analyzers were our most important products. But as we gained more technical experience, it was logical to branch out into other types of electronic measuring instruments.

"We entered the electric instrument business with our multimeter for one simple reason: the multimeter is the basic measuring instrument in both electrical and electronic applications and so, when we wanted to expand our product line, we naturally chose the easiest things to sell, which were multimeters. During the War, multimeters, generators, and tube checkers and analyzers were our chief products.

"My basic product philosophy has been this. First, to find a product with which we have some technical familiarity and background, because without this technical basis we cannot really compete. Second, having found such a product, to determine whether we can sell it in profitable quantities. This means finding out (a) if the total market is large enough to justify our entry, and (b) how much competition there is for this market. Our introduction of the impedance bridge is a good illustration of this philosophy. We knew in 1941 that we had the technical ability to make this bridge. We decided to design and manufacture it because, although the total market for bridges was not very large at the time, there was almost no competition for this market, so we thought we could get most of the market for ourselves, which would justify making the bridge. Most of the products which we introduced after the War were in response to the new demands for television and FM radio equipment, two fields which we had the technical ability to enter.

"I think I should also say something about my philosophy of quality. I am proud to be able to say today that Galvor instruments are sold primarily on the basis of their outstanding quality,[2] but this has not been an easy thing to achieve. From the very beginning, and after the War especially, we have constantly aimed to raise quality and lower prices. This has been a basic philosophy of mine and one which, I should say, has contributed greatly to our success.

"In the '50's, as our Galvor products gradually became higher and higher in quality, we found that we were shutting ourselves out of the considerable market for low-price instruments of average quality. The typical radio repairman, for example, doesn't look very far ahead in purchasing his basic test instruments; he wants the cheapest product, no matter what the quality. I decided that we could profitably bring out a line of low-price instruments of good, but not Galvor, quality, to help meet this demand. We did so with our TRONEX product line.

"As for the few products we make which have little relation to our basic product line, such as the oil-burner instruments, we have gone into these when (1) the product in question is essentially a measuring instrument, and thus related in theory to our other products, and (2) when there already exists a good design for such a product, a design on which we can improve. In these cases, we have never developed the fund of technical knowledge which we have in our own area; we have contented ourselves with merely refining somebody else's design so as to get market acceptance. The trouble with this policy is, of course, that since we are not expert in the technology of such products we cannot lead in the market, but must follow others, and so when design changes in some fundamental respect, we lose our market. We have had some success with certain of these products, but they have not been an important factor in our business.

"Finally, I might say that today we are not particularly looking for new fields to enter. We have found that there are plenty of challenges and opportunities remaining in our own specialty of measuring instruments."

Galvor's basic product line was divided into two categories: electric and electronic instruments. The distinction was generally based on whether the instrument contained electronic tubes and/or transistors. Table 2 shows the main groupings in Galvor's product line and gives certain statistics about each group.

MANUFACTURING OPERATIONS AT GALVOR

Physical Facilities

By 1962, Galvor's manufacturing processes bore little superficial resemblance to those of twenty-six years before, when M. and Mme.

2. The U. S. Bureau of Standards, in Washington, D. C., used a number of Galvor instruments as reference sources.

Latour had worked long evenings to assemble the first products. As shown in Table 3, Galvor's total floor space had increased considerably since 1936.

Galvor had acquired a considerable stock of machine tools in the course of its growth, despite the fact that the company's primary activity was still one of assembling purchased parts into instruments. Late in 1961, company officials estimated the real value of all machine tools as approximately 466,000 NF, and the real value of scientific instruments used in testing and research as 208,000 NF. (No value was assigned to the many Galvor instruments which were used in the laboratories and testing departments). Although these machine tools and instruments were estimated to have a true value of about 675,000 NF, they were carried on the company's books at about 168,000 NF.

Table 2

The Galvor Product Line—1961

Product Group	Number of Models	Price Range (NF)	1961 Sales * (NF 000s)	Percentage of Total 1961 Sales
ELECTRIC PRODUCTS:	—	—	—	—
Multimeters	15	100– 550	5,188	36.2%
Galvanometers	over 100	60– 150	1,412	9.8%
Milliameters	2	200– 230	105	0.7%
Special Products	—	—	275	1.9%
Accessories and Spare Parts	—	—	795	5.5%
TOTAL ELECTRIC:			7,775	54.1%
ELECTRONIC PRODUCTS:	—	—	—	—
Tube- and Transistor Checkers and Analyzers	5	250–2340	881	6.1%
Generators:	—	—	—	—
Wobulator	2	700–1800	67	
Pattern gen'tor	1	1100	153	
Audio "	1	680	156	
Service	1	670	191	⟶15.7%
HF	2	1850–2250	1,073	
VHF	2	1665	127	
UHF	1	n.a.	227	
AM and FM	3	1200–2000	245	
Marker	2	800–2000	11	

Table 2
(continued)

Total Generators:	—	—	—	—
Wobuloscopes	2	1320–2050	986	6.9%
Oscilloscopes	3	1115–2200	321	2.3%
VT VM's **	3	365–1300	781	5.4%
Impedance Bridges	3	n.a.	417	2.9%
Vacuum Tube				
Bridge	1	3800	126	0.9%
Accessories and				
Spare Parts	—	—	344	2.4%
Equipment Racks	—	—	11	nil
TOTAL ELECTRONIC:	—	—	6,117	42.6%
SALES TO TRONEX:	—	—	192	1.3%
EQUIPMENT				
REPAIRS:	—	—	281	2.0%
TOTAL:	—	—	14,365	100.0%

Source: Company officials.
  * Including all taxes.
 ** Vacuum-tube Voltmeters.
 n.a.—not available

Table 3

Development of Galvor Floor Space

Year	Location	Total Floor Area
1936	Rue de l'Arbre, Bordeaux *	80 sq. meters
1937	Rue Kafka, Bordeaux	120 " "
1941	Avenue de Camus, Bordeaux	400 " "
1948	New Factory (Rue Costello, Bordeaux)	1850 " "
1953	Factory elongated	2100 " "
1956	Factory partially raised	2600 " "
1958	Wing added to factory	5252 " "
1962	Wing extended	8917 " "

Source: Company records.
 * M. Latour's home.

Commenting on the company's machine tools, M. Jacques Romanée (Manager of Manufacturing), remarked, "In my opinion we should be constantly looking for new machines to replace the ones we have, in order to make our operations more and more efficient.

But M. Latour thinks that Galvor already has all the necessary machine tools, and that no new ones should be bought until all the present tools are being used 100%. I am not sure that our management is sufficiently production-oriented."

M. Latour, in commenting on this question, said, "We have all the machines we need for our present operations. Most of our machine tools are used for producing molds, tools, and special jigs and fixtures. However, the trend in the industry is towards equipment of higher frequencies. Such instruments involve much more mechanical work than lower-frequency products, and so we will have to manufacture more and more of the components ourselves if we are to make the maximum profit from these products. Obviously, this will require that we considerably expand our machine tool capacity." M. Chambertin, (Administration Director), was substantially in agreement with M. Romanée, thinking that Galvor could profitably increase its investment in production equipment.

The Workforce

In commenting on Galvor's workers, M. Romanée said, "On the whole I would say that they are rather highly skilled. We have trained all of our workers ourselves, out of necessity, because they have to do precision work of very high quality. In general, by Bordeaux standards we pay our people well, near the top of the range. We would pay men and women the same wages for the same work, but this issue does not arise, because they never do the same jobs. We pay no incentives, only a straight hourly wage. About half of our workers are women, many of them working in the Galvanometer Department." Galvor workers were ranked in five categories, according to their skills. Category I consisted of unskilled workers, category V included the highly-skilled toolmakers. Table 4 gives pertinent information on the classification of the male workforce early in 1962.

Table 4

Data on the Galvor Male Workforce—1962

Skill Category	Approx. Number of Workers in Category	Pay Rate of Category NF Per Hour		
		Minimum	Average	Maximum
I	31	1.90	2.20	2.90
II	57	2.20	2.75	3.30
III	35	2.75	3.05	4.00
IV	12	3.15	3.35	3.65
V	11	3.50	3.80	4.00

Source: Company records.

Galvor's foremen were paid between 1100 and 1500 NF per month, rates which M. Romanée considered extremely high in comparison with other Bordeaux firms. The average male worker at Galvor had been employed by the company for over 7 years, M. Romanée estimated, and the average woman at least five years. He pointed out that these figures would have been considerably higher, except that the company was expanding so rapidly that many of the workers had been hired only recently. Table 5 shows the growth of Galvor's workforce in recent years, according to the categories used by the company in differentiating among employee groups.

Table 5

Galvor: Average Number Employed by Years

Year	Direct Labor	Indirect Labor	Research	Adminis- trative & Clerical	Total
1953	na	na	na	na	115
1954	80	26	11	10	127
1955	92	26	24	10	152
1956	108	33	20	11	172
1957	133	50	24	13	220
1958	144	58	22	25	249
1959	162	63	30	37	292
1960	195	68	26	42	331
1961 (end)	242	80	33	68	423

Source: Company records.
na: Not available.

Organization of the Department

Table 6 shows the structure of Galvor's Manufacturing Department in early 1962. M. Romanée, in commenting on this organization chart, said, "Unfortunately, since I have no line assistant below me, all of the foremen report directly to me, and as a result I have to give them much more authority, and much better pay, than they really should receive. I'd like to find a good assistant, but I haven't the time to train him; besides, you can't teach a man everything I've learned about this business in thirty years."

The Manufacturing Process

Starting from its early days as a pure assembly operation, Galvor had gradually begun to manufacture an increasing number of the

Table 6

The Galvor Manufacturing Department — 1962

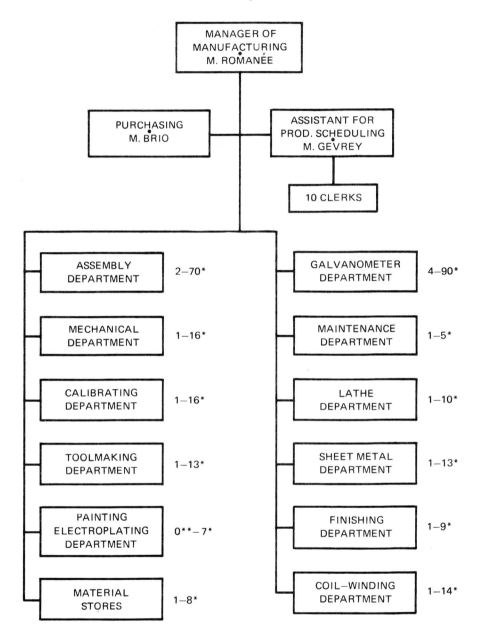

Source: Company officials.
* These pairs of numbers indicate (first) number of foremen in department, and (second) approximate number of workers in department.
** The Chief of this joint department was not officially a foreman, but his pay and responsibility approximated those at the foreman level.

components in its products. M. Romanée remarked, "If we had not done so, we could never have grown to our present size. It was absolutely necessary for us to make more and more of these parts, but even today, most of the pieces in our products are bought from suppliers and assembled here."

For accounting purposes, Galvor divided its direct labor into two categories: assembly labor and manufacturing labor. Manufacturing labor was chiefly used in the fabrication of parts for instruments, but it also included some toolmaking and jigmaking labor. 'Assembly' labor consisted of wages paid to assembly workers. Table 7 shows Galvor's manufacturing cost structure in recent years.

In general terms, Galvor manufactured an instrument's case, the chassis on which it was mounted, the galvanometers used to display the findings of the instrument, the switches and dials used to operate the device, and occasionally certain other important parts as well. As a rule, the electronic components forming the heart of the typical Galvor instruments were purchased from suppliers. These components included: electronic tubes, transistors, resistors, condensers, transformers, coils, potentiometers, and wire. Galvor was, as of early 1962, preparing to enter the so-called "component" industry by manufacturing some of its own resistors.[3] The manufacture of such complicated components as tubes and transistors was a highly sophisticated and specialized operation requiring very large investment and considerable technical background. Since, for example, tube manufacture could only be conducted profitably by mass production, and since Galvor generally required a relatively small number of each of a great variety of tubes, management was not, in 1962, contemplating entry into this field.

"We will make, rather than buy a product," said M. Latour, "under any of these circumstances: (a) when the quantity we require is so small that it is difficult, or very expensive, to subcontract; (b) when we can make a given part ourselves at a substantial saving over purchase price, if we have the capacity; (c) when the part is very crucial to the instrument and we dare not rely on an outside source." Galvor's purchases were of three sorts: (1) wholly-finished components, such as electronic tubes, to be mounted directly in the instruments; (2) partially-finished products which would undergo further manufacturing operations at Galvor; and (3) raw materials, such as sheet metal, where all manufacturing operations were done by the company. In 1961, of Galvor's total purchases from outside suppliers, 8% were raw materials, 87% were partially- and wholly-finished products (mostly components), and 5% were products to be

3. Resistor manufacture was scheduled to begin in the new factory as soon as it was completed.

Table 7

Percentage Breakdown of Galvor Costs in Selected Years
(Sales = 100%)

	1961	1960	1959	1958	1955
PARTS MANUFACTURING:					
Raw Materials [1]	2.8%	3.5%	3.0%	5.2%	8.2%
Direct Labor [2]	2.6	2.9	2.7	3.1	3.0
Subcontracting	.4	.3	.5	.5	1.3
Factory Overhead [3]	4.5	4.7	5.0	9.0	6.2
TOTAL PARTS MFG. COST:	10.3	11.4	11.2	17.8	18.7
PURCHASED PARTS: [1]	29.2	31.7	27.0	24.5	19.7
TOTAL COST OF PARTS:	39.5	43.1	38.2	42.3	38.4
ASSEMBLY EXPENSES:					
Direct Labor [2]	6.7	6.8	6.4	6.3	7.8
Factory Overhead [3]	11.6	11.0	11.7	18.1	16.3
TOTAL MANUFACTURING COST: [4]	57.8	60.9	56.3	66.7	62.5
NET INVENTORY ADJUSTMENT:	1.0	(1.7)	1.6	(4.9)	.2
FINAL MANUFACTURING COST:	58.8	59.2	57.9	61.8	62.7
SALES EXPENSE:	11.8	12.0	12.4	11.7	12.2
RESEARCH EXPENSE: [5]	5.4	5.6	6.6	—	—
ADMINISTRATIVE EXPENSE:	5.4	5.7	5.8	8.4	7.0
OTHER PROFIT AND LOSS: [6]	9.8	9.7	9.5	10.2	7.1
PROFIT AFTER TAXES:	8.8	7.7	7.9	7.8	11.0
TOTAL SALES: [7]	100.0	99.9	100.1	99.9	100.0

Computed from company records by IMEDE staff.

[1] Including purchasing expense.
[2] Including social security charges, etc.
[3] Apportioned between parts manufacturing and assembly in direct proportion to the amount of direct labor used in each department.
[4] Before adjustment for changes in inventory.
[5] Before 1959, Research Expense was not treated as a separate expense item.
[6] This item consisted chiefly of taxes paid on profits; pre-tax profits were taxed at a 50% rate in France.
[7] Sales here are net sales after sales tax is removed from gross sales figures; percentages do not add to exactly 100% in all cases because of rounding off.

resold to Galvor customers, such as leather carrying cases for multimeters. These percentages had not, company officials said, changed very much in recent years.

About 15,000 different parts were used in making the products in the Galvor line. Of this total, about 10,000 were bought in a wholly-or semi-finished state. M. Chambertin remarked that, although it was difficult to generalize, the typical Galvor electric product, such as a multimeter, contained from 2–3 times as much purchase content as direct labor content. The typical electronic product, he added, contained from 3–5 times as much purchase content as direct labor. This was due to the fact that most electronic products contained a considerable number of relatively complicated and expensive components, such as electronic tubes and transistors, while electric products such as multimeters contained few sophisticated components.

Production runs varied considerably in length, depending on the type of product involved. The electric instruments, consisting primarily of multimeters and galvanometers, were assembled in batches of from 1 unit (on a special order) to perhaps 2,000 units. The average figure for runs of these instruments was probably, M. Romanée estimated, between 500 and 1,000 units. The electronic instruments were usually assembled in batches of 25–50 units. In general, the more complicated the instrument, the shorter the run. Company officials cited two reasons for this variation in length of production runs. First, the electric instruments were usually simple devices where substantial cost savings could be realized by long production runs, whereas the cost of electronic instruments was not lowered nearly so much by mass production. Second, unit sales volumes were much higher for galvanometers and multimeters than for the more expensive and specialized electronic products.

There was a considerable amount of special-order production done in the electronic instruments category, most of it at the request of various agencies of the French Military. Company officials estimated that such special orders might average as much as 20% or more of total production of electronic products, but most of these special orders required only minor changes in Galvor's standard products. Little special-type manufacture was done for electric instruments. The Galvanometer Department manufactured to specific customer order, but this department usually produced meters listed in the catalogue, rather than meters designed especially for a customer.

Controlling the Production System

Galvor's production scheduling system was, M. Romanée pointed out, basically a simple one. Every two months, the Statistical Service (under Mme. Bollinger) produced a production schedule for a two-month period beginning eight months hence. This schedule listed the number of units of each Galvor product which were to be produced in each month of the future two-month period. Mme. Bollinger based this schedule on her annual sales forecasts for each product.

When this production schedule was received by M. Gevrey (Assistant to M. Romanée for Production Scheduling), he and his clerks drew up a list of the parts to be purchased outside and the worker-hours called for in each department by the schedule. M. Gevrey was in charge of ensuring that the necessary parts to meet this schedule arrived by the time that it went into effect.

Approximately four months before a given production schedule was to go into effect, Mme. Bollinger again checked that schedule to see if recent developments indicated that it should be changed. There were changes made to every schedule as a result of this reappraisal of sales prospects. These changes were initiated by Mme. Bollinger, who issued an "ordre d'urgence," ("urgent order"), making the appropriate changes in the schedule which was to take effect in four months.

"In general," commented M. Romanée, "the system works pretty well. We have a certain amount of flexibility, because we do have some inventory of most Galvor products on hand, although not very much. We sometimes find that we cannot deliver a product on the planned date, but this problem is usually not severe. Many of our products have, in effect, no direct competition, especially the electronic ones. If a customer wants one of these instruments, he must buy from us; we can make the customer wait for such instruments if necessary. In electrical products there is more direct competition, and so here we are under greater pressure to keep our delivery promises. Accordingly, if we have to postpone making either an electric or electronic instrument, it is usually the electronic instrument which gets delayed." Early in 1962, Galvor's backlog of orders totalled about 1,900,000 NF.

Inventory control at Galvor had recently been a matter of concern to M. Latour. Table 8 gives selected statistics on the company's inventory levels since 1956.

Commenting on current stock levels, M. Latour said, "I am not happy with our present inventories, especially of raw materials and purchased parts. Every time I ask one of my people why we have so large a stock of such-and-such an item, I get a fine explanation. But this fact remains: I would like to have two months' supply of purchases on hand, not what we have now." M. Romanée remarked that in general, he had sufficient stocks on hand to ensure a steady manufacturing operation.

Quality control at Galvor had become increasingly important with the passage of time, as the firm had continually upgraded its product line. M. Romanée described the quality control system as based on "auto-control," i.e. on making the workman responsible for the quality of his own work. There was also a calibrating and test department to make final adjustment and checks on finished products. Galvor had very few problems, said company officials, in maintaining the desired quality levels. "Occasionally," said M. Romanée, "we have troubles in the Galvanometer Department, because the assembly work there is

Table 8

Inventory at Year End as Percentage of Net Sales

Year	Raw Materials and Purchased Parts	Work-in Process	Finished Products	Total All Inventory
1956	13.3%	4.3%	3.4%	21.0%
1957	9.5	3.8	4.1	17.4
1958	12.0	8.5	7.3	27.8
1959	15.4	9.2	4.2	28.8
1960	10.7	9.5	6.6	26.8
1961	11.5	7.5	8.0	27.0

Computed from company records by IMEDE staff.

very repetitive and yet must be done with extreme care. After a girl has mounted, say, several hundred needles in a day, she begins to slack a little bit, and so we have to keep a sharp eye on the department's output."

M. Latour mentioned that the chief foreman of the Galvanometer Department, who had many years' experience with the company, was a fanatic on the subject of precision, and so the department's products were always of higher specifications than designed. "For this foreman," remarked M. Latour, "precision is like an incurable illness. We could cut our labor costs 15% and still put out galvanos of acceptable quality. We were about to transfer this foreman, when suddenly we discovered that we were making the best galvanos in France, so for the time being, I'm not changing anything, but eventually we will cure this over-precision."

M. Romanée commented on his method for controlling manufacturing costs as follows: "M. Chambertin takes care of all our costing, but I generally don't use his figures. I just try to make everything at the lowest possible cost, and I don't really need statistics to tell me how to do this; I can sense what needs to be done." Table 9 shows Galvor's total manufacturing costs as a percentage of sales since 1950.

M. Romanée himself established a standard direct labor cost for each product when the final product design was ready. This cost, plus the cost of material needed to make the product, forced the basis of Galvor's costing and pricing systems.

Galvor Employee Relations

Galvor's executives believed that the workers were generally content with their jobs. M. Latour said, "The workers who have been with

Table 9

Manufacturing Costs as a Percentage of Net Sales

Year	Percent	Year	Percent
1950	71.5%	1956	63.3%
1951	68.5%	1957	62.5%
1952	64.2%	1958	61.8%
1953	58.0%	1959	57.9%
1954	62.5%	1960	59.2%
1955	62.7%	1961	58.8%

Computed from company records by IMEDE staff.

us for many years are generally satisfied, and our pay scale is among the best in Bordeaux. Some of the men we have hired in recent years tend to be a little noisy. Many of them have had bad experiences with other employers and expect the same thing here. Because they are noisy, they tend to be elected as delegates by the workers, and in December (1961) some of them came here to ask me for a pay raise to compensate for increases in the cost of living. I quickly showed them that their recent pay raises had more than covered these increased prices, and so they are silent. I have promised further wage increases based on individual contribution; we're already covering rises in living costs, so now we will pay for human value. We had a meeting on January 15th (1962), and they agreed to this system of raises."

Galvor's workers belonged to a company union unaffiliated with other unions; the chief purpose of this union, remarked M. Romanée, was to "hold conversations with management." Galvor had enjoyed good employee relations throughout its history; there had never been a strike.

In 1962 Bordeaux was still, as for a number of years past, a full-employment area. As a result, Galvor experienced some difficulties in finding workers for its ever-expanding operations. The problem was aggravated because Galvor needed skilled workers, or workers with the aptitude to be trained for precision work; there were many other large firms in Bordeaux requiring such workers, M. Romanée said, and he added that, in an average year, he would expect to lose perhaps 30 workers out of a total of about 300, due to retirement, childbearing, illness, job-changing, and other causes. A typical new Galvor worker had to be trained for 6–12 months before becoming fully productive, so the company was continually operating in-plant training programs. Workers were also encouraged to add to their skills at appropriate institutes in Bordeaux, and Galvor would typically give a worker one day off per week to attend such courses. M. Romanée summed up by saying that, in the past, he had been able to find enough workers to replace those employees who left and to fill the new jobs created by expansion.

Expected Manufacturing Developments

The new addition to the Galvor plant would be ready, it was hoped, near the end of July, 1962. This addition, amounting to some 3700 square meters, would increase Galvor's total floor area by about 70%. It was planned to use the new area to expand all manufacturing operations as a whole, rather than only isolated ones. M. Latour expected, however, that the Galvanometer Department, because of its rapid growth of sales, would require a relatively high proportion of this new area.

Galvor's top management had, after lengthy consideration of the issue, decided that the Manufacturing Service's staff should be expanded by the addition of two groups; first, a Manufacturing Bureau, and subsequently a Methods Analysis Staff. Company executives had generally agreed that a Manufacturing Bureau, by acting as liaison between the Research-and-Development Services and the Manufacturing Service, would speed the process of getting a new design into production. The Methods Analysis Staff, M. Romanée hoped, would enable him to relieve the foremen of their responsibility for methods study. Tentatively, he hoped to have the Manufacturing Bureau by early 1963, the Methods Staff two years later.

"As I said," M. Romanée concluded, "we found in the past that, in order to keep on growing, we had to do more and more manufacturing ourselves, and this trend will continue as we expand further. It is dangerous for us to be too closely tied to our suppliers. This means that my job will become more and more difficult, and that is why these two new staffs are so important: I am overloaded with work all the time; when these staffs are well established, I will have the time to deal with the long-term aspects of manufacturing."

THE GALVOR MARKETING ORGANIZATION

Early in the company's history, M. Latour had adopted the policy of selling Galvor products in France through a network of manufacturers' representatives. M. Latour himself remained in charge of the Commercial Service until 1958, at which time he appointed M. Bernard Margaux the Manager of this service. In 1960, by which time Galvor's sales in the Paris area accounted for over 40% of total sales volume, the company established a wholly-owned sales subsidiary in Paris to cover that region. In early 1962, however, a large part of Galvor's sales volume still came from the traditional manu-facturers' representatives. Table 10 shows the organization of the Commercial Service early in 1962.

In discussing his organization, M. Margaux remarked, "M. Crépy is really only a foreman in charge of our repair shop. At the moment I am taking care of exports myself, but I hope soon to find an assistant to do this for me."

The Paris agency, called Galvor Paris, was moved into new quar-ters in January 1961. M. Cliquot, the head of this agency, was as-sisted by four sales engineers, three of whom prospected in the Parisian region for sales; the fourth remained in the office and as-sisted M. Cliquot. Galvor Paris was not a part of the Commercial Service, but a separate entity reporting directly to M. Latour.

"Galvor Paris was created," M. Latour said, "when our Paris repre-sentative decided to retire. I might add that we were paying this repre-sentative far more in commissions than we are now paying to operate Galvor Paris. But we never would have discharged this agent against his will; he had done fine sales work for us for many years. In 1960, when he retired, we paid him 170,000 NF as a bonus. Eventually, we may have our own agencies in the other major French industrial centers, but at the moment the product line is still too narrow to sup-port the expense of such a network."

Export sales were made directly from Bordeaux to two principal outlets: to COMOR S.A. and to importers outside France. Repairs of exported Galvor instruments were made and billed directly from Bordeaux. COMOR S.A. was a French export company, located in Paris, which had an exclusive license to sell Galvor products in 17 [4] countries. Virtually all of Galvor's other export sales were made through licensed import agencies throughout the world.

Position of Galvor in Industry

Company officials described Galvor as being a producer of high-quality, general-purpose instruments of moderate cost. Certain Galvor competitors sold low-quality measuring instruments; such instru-ments were usually bought by radio and television repairmen for use in applications where high precision was not necessary and were generally cheaper than the equivalent Galvor product. Other com-petitors manufactured ultra-precise instruments for specialized ap-plications; such instruments were usually much more expensive than the equivalent Galvor product. Galvor products generally covered the area between these extremes, in terms of quality and cost. As a result,

4. These countries were: Austria, Belgium, Bulgaria, Czechoslovakia, Den-mark, Finland, Greece, Holland, Hungary, Italy, Norway, Poland, Romania, Spain, Sweden, the U. S. S. R., and Yugoslavia.

Table 10

Organization of the Galvor Commercial Service — 1962

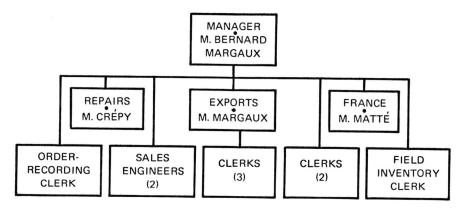

Source: Company officials.

Galvor customers spanned the range from local radio repairmen to highly advanced laboratories. Over 80% of Galvor's sales were made to French customers.

"Our products are sold mainly on the basis of quality," said M. Latour. "Next comes our price, which is usually well below the market for products of equivalent quality, and then our reputation." M. Margaux added that Galvor also won customers by its excellent, low-priced, fast repair service. He said that such good repair service was not always available from Galvor competitors.

Advertising

M. Margaux continued, "Our annual advertising budget of about 50,000 NF is certainly small in comparison with our total sales, but this is typical of our industry. The purpose of our advertising is to keep people aware of our continued existence and, occasionally, to mention some new product. We cannot really sell a product by advertising its specifications. The customer wants to know much more about the product than we can put in an advertisement. As a result, product demonstration and discussion with one of our sales engineers or manufacturers' representatives are very important. Our best publicity is visiting our customers, demonstrating the equipment intelligently, repairing quickly and cheaply, and making a high-quality, low-cost, durable product." Galvor usually allowed its customers 90 days from invoice date in which to pay; this was sometimes extended to 12 months for small customers. The company's bad-debt losses were typically about $\frac{1}{10}\%$.

Galvor's Competition

Most of Galvor's competitors were other French firms which also concentrated in electric and/or electronic measuring instruments. Company officials said that Galvor had 11 significant French competitors, no one of which carried all of Galvor's product types.

There was considerable competition in multimeters and galvanometers, but company officials estimated that Galvor had 80–90% of the total French multimeter market, the rest being shared by about 10 firms. Because of the high quality of its galvanometers, Galvor was, by 1962, a major competitor in this market, and M. Latour hoped that the company would be the leader in galvanos within the near future.

"As for our electronic products," remarked M. Margaux, "competition varies quite a lot. Oscilloscopes are a minor item for us, and we have a small market share. For almost all of our generators, we have only one competitor, and we are not even in direct competition, because he has a different clientele than we have. Our wobulators and wobuloscopes meet little serious competition; we are badly beating our one real competitor in this field. Our impedance bridges are another of our minor products, because the total market is small, and here we have no competition in the same quality range. Our vacuum-tube voltmeters encounter considerable competition, and this is the only Galvor product where we have serious foreign competition in the French market. Our tube checkers and analyzers have no competition in their own class. Our TRONEX products have lots of competition, not only from French firms, but increasingly from Japanese, German, and American imports."

Galvor's Pricing System

In speaking about the way in which prices were set, M. Latour remarked, "I have been using the same pricing system for many years. M. Chambertin thinks that I should adopt a different method, and perhaps in theory he is right, but at the moment I cannot see any good reason to change. I do admit, however, that our prices may not always reflect our real costs." GALVOR (C-2) (GM 73), describes the details of the pricing system.

Possible Marketing Developments

It was M. Margaux's long-term dream, he said, to see Galvor build a network of wholly-owned agencies in the major French industrial centers. He added, however, that until Galvor sales in each area climbed considerably, this was not feasible except in the Paris region.

PRODUCT RESEARCH AND DEVELOPMENT

A Short History

Galvor's Research and Development Staff began in 1937 when M. Latour hired a technician to help him develop Galvor's second product, the tube analyzer. Until late 1940, M. Latour himself supervised the development of the company's products. "When the War came to France," M. Latour continued, "many refugees appeared. In late 1940, I heard about a brilliant refugee engineer named Messer. I managed to find the man but discovered that there were two Messer brothers. Since I couldn't find out which was the brilliant one, I took both of them. When they asked me what I wanted, I said 'I want General Radio quality.[5] Well, the brothers Messer certainly raised the quality and the sophistication of our products. The only complaint ever raised was this: many engineers said that the Messers designed equipment up to the very limits of its capability. All the components in an instrument were pushed very hard. They squeezed the last possible bit out of a given design and the components. But when this was mentioned, the Messers always went into a long, theoretical explanation about how they were actually right. There was one other little problem with the Messers: they were incredibly expensive. They were good, and they charged for their quality.

"By the end of the War, I was paying the better of them about $2200 per month. As you can imagine, I wasn't paying myself any such salary. Well, the brothers decided that they wanted to move back to Paris now that the War was finished. They said they would stay with Galvor only if I moved the factory to Paris, and they gave me 48 hours to make up my mind. I must admit that I spent a bad night, but in the morning I came in and said that Galvor would stay in Bordeaux. They left, and they took a couple of their assistants with them, including Robert Meursault. I had replaced them within a month.

"Within a year or so, we built our research staff back up to the level it achieved under the Messers. Meursault came back in '46. We stopped trying to squeeze the last bit of performance out of a design, and this made our customers happier. I again took charge of our R&D for a year or two after the Messers left, and during this period we mostly expanded on the basic designs they had developed, but by late 1947 things were again in good shape. Beginning around 1950, we made some excursions into fields different from our own, such as

5. The General Radio Company, a U. S. corporation, has for many years manufactured a broad line of high-quality measuring and test instruments.

industrial electronics, but as I said, in these fields we were only improving on somebody else's design, and this didn't work very well. Today we are concentrating in our own specialty. I think that our R&D group now is first-class; Pomméry and Meursault are very effective in creating new products."

The Galvor R&D Organization: 1962

Table 11 shows the organization of Galvor's R&D groups in early 1962.

Describing this organization, M. Pomméry said, "Meursault and I each have our own staff of technicians to develop our respective types of products. We also share the services of the Design and Prototype Services.

"The product development technicians are well-trained, but they are not graduates of the great French technical schools such as Polytechnique. They are not mathematicians and theorists; rather, they are men who can translate ideas into a workable design. These ten men (seven for Meursault and 3 for Pomméry) do most of Galvor's research. We pay them 1000–1600 NF per month. Meursault and I occupy ourselves chiefly with administrative work, and with helping to solve problems which may arise."

The R&D Process

M. Pomméry continued, "The process of product development begins with deciding what products to attempt to design. Generally, market demands indicate what sort of products we will study. We do no pure, or basic, research here; our work is all very much applied research, all designed to produce new Galvor products. Ideas for new products come from our feeling about what people want, or perhaps from seeing what other manufacturers are doing. We try *not* to make *exactly* what other producers are making; we don't want to get into direct competition. Of course, this is easier to do in electronic instruments; in electric instruments, the big differences are in product quality. Most of our research efforts are devoted to products for the Galvor catalogue; however, perhaps 10% of the total research effort in the Galvano Research Service, and about 30% in Electronic Research, is devoted to studying special products for one customer, usually for the French military.

"The decision on whether to do a full-scale study of a product is usually made at the management conference; [6] of course M. Latour

6. This conference, held every week, included Messrs. Latour, Chambertin, Romanée, Pomméry, Meursault, and Margaux.

Table 11

Structure of the Galvor R&D Department — 1962

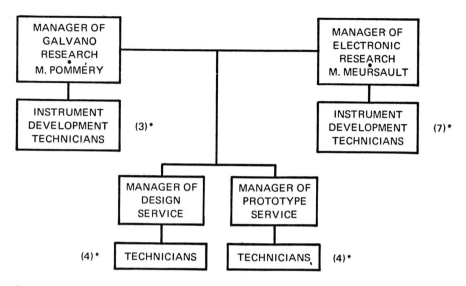

Source: Company officials.
* Indicates number of technicians.

always has the final decision on whether to do a certain piece of research. We have today, as has been true for some years, a backlog of approved research projects to be undertaken when facilities are available. So, whenever we finish a project and have a man free to begin another job, we only have to decide which backlog project he should study.

"The research process itself follows this pattern. First, the instrument development technician will do the basic study required. For my products, mostly multimeters and galvanometers, this stage takes about six months. Meursault's electronic products are more complicated, so that this stage usually requires 1 or 2 years for an electronic product, possibly only six months if the job is not complex. This first stage ends with a mock-up of the new product; this mock-up is a highly finished article in every respect, and it will function as designed, but it has not been constructed with any special consideration towards manufacturing it.

"The second stage begins when this mock-up is given to the Design Service. The Design Service studies our mock-up and then re-designs the product in order to make it more easily manufactured. Blue-prints are drawn up by the Design Service, and then the Prototype Service constructs a prototype which is identical to the final product. The prototype is tested electrically and mechanically, and when we are

GALVOR COMPANY (A)   **475** satisfied, a list of required parts is drawn up, along with the other documents needed to manufacture the product. This second stage takes about 3 months for an electric product, about twice as long for an electronic product.

"Stopping the research process for a given product usually gets done very late, namely, when we have a finished prototype. The usual reason for stopping is that we find that the final price of the product will have to be higher than the market will pay. We haven't found any way around this problem. Our research is always done with the product's final cost in mind, but it is difficult to determine this cost until the process is over.

"In general, I would say that our R&D is quite successful. We do not operate on a tightly fixed budget. If Meursault and I decide that we need an expensive piece of equipment in the lab, we justify it to M. Latour, and then we get it. Our lab is quite well equipped. Of course, if we wanted to try out all the new ideas we have, or even to get rid of the backlog of approved research projects, we'd have to enlarge the research staff. This is gradually being done. We never fully live up to our potential for developing new products, because we have to spend a lot of our time updating the existing products. The Manufacturing Department sometimes requests that we make small modifications in a product's design, and this also takes us away from our main work.

"Another problem is in the process of getting a product from the design stage into manufacture. At the moment, this liaison is being done by the Prototype Service, but when we set up the Manufacturing Bureau, it will be given this responsibility." Table 12 shows Galvor's R&D expense in recent years.

In commenting on the success of Galvor's R&D efforts, M. Latour said. "Maybe, since it is my company, I should say that our R&D is better than that of our competitors, but this simply isn't true. I think

Table 12

Galvor Research and Development Expense, 1958–1969

Year	R&D Expense (000's of NF)	R&D Expense as Percentage of Net Sales
1958	361	5.8%
1959	552	6.6%
1960	561	5.6%
1961	645	5.4%

Computed from company records by IMEDE staff.

that we are very successful, but our competitors are successful too. I think we do as much research work as we need to. You may remember the old fable about the frog and the bull. The frog saw the huge bull and wanted to become as large, so he puffed himself up, but finally he burst. Well, I think that we shouldn't try to expand our activities too rapidly, but to build on a solid foundation, increasing at a steady pace. It may become harder and harder for us to maintain the real competitive advantages which we have today, but it will always be our goal to provide a bit better quality, at a slightly lower price, than the other fellow."

FINANCIAL HISTORY OF GALVOR

The original loan with which Galvor was begun, amounting to about 6000 NF in 1961 purchasing power, had evolved into a net worth of about 6,000,000 NF for the company as of December 31, 1961. At the end of World War II, Galvor was a small business; about fifty people were employed by the firm, and sales and profit were at modest levels. The companys' period of greatest prosperity and growth began around 1950; in early 1962 there was no indication that growth and profitability were decreasing.

Galvor's financial history had largely been shaped by one basic policy of Georges Latour: to maintain complete ownership of the business in his own hands. M. Latour had always believed that only if he had complete ownership of Galvor could he direct its affairs with a free hand. Accordingly, in 1962 he still owned 97% of Galvor's equity: most of the remaining 3% had been given to Jacques Romanée in recognition of his long service to the firm.

Especially after World War II, when Galvors' sales and profits began to grow markedly, M. Latour received a number of offers to buy equity in the company; the offers had been refused. As a result, funds to finance growth had been obtained from three principal sources: retention of earnings, long-term borrowing, and expansion of current liabilities.

With few exceptions, Galvor had experienced considerable difficulty throughout its history in obtaining substantial amounts of long-term bank credit. When the company had been a small one, it had not been a prime credit risk. During the 'fifties, the company became successful and, accordingly, a good credit risk. However, through most of this last decade commercial credit was very tight in France. The Government, in an effort to place this credit where it would provide the greatest impetus to the economy, had discouraged loans to companies which did not absolutely need credit. This policy was easy to enforce, since the ultimate source of all long-term bank credit was the Banque de France; which put into effect the Government's credit policies. Even when 'expanding rapidly during the 'fifties, Galvor had still generated sufficient funds to finance its own expansion, and so its occasional requests for credit to finance new construction had been refused. Galvor could borrow for 2–3 years from its local bank, but for longer term loans the approval of the Banque de France was required.

"In 1948," said M. Latour, "we had our last real financial problem. We were building the new factory, and the price level rose greatly during the course of this construction, so that our initial cost estimates were far too low. I went to the bank for a loan and was, at first, not very encouraged; the bank wanted to buy stock in the company, or for me to raise money by selling stock to others. I was unwilling to do this. Finally, however, I got the loan, and we have had no financial problems since this time. Occasionally we would have liked to borrow to help finance new construction, but lack of long-term credit for such purposes has not affected our plans at all."

M. Chambertin added, "Of course, we could have raised money by selling our own obligations on the open market, and this would not have required very high interest. But M. Latour opposed this idea because he was afraid to let any outsiders get into a position where they might conceivably be able to influence him. Obligations, of course, would not give the bearer as much influence as common stock in Galvor, but M. Latour still preferred not to use this source. Anyway since '48 we have been able to finance everything ourselves."

As Galvor grew and broadened its financial base, one major source of funds was an accompanying expansion of current liabilities, mostly in the form of trade credit, accrued expenses, and unpaid tax liability. However, this source of funds was not by itself sufficient to finance rapid growth, and so retention of earnings had been a firm policy of M. Latour. As of early 1962, the company had never paid a dividend, and none was contemplated for the near future.

Late in 1961, in order to help finance the 1,800,000 NF estimated costs for the new addition to the plant, Galvor had requested a loan of 900,000 NF from the Crédit National. A 3-year loan of 600,000 NF had been granted.

Table 13 shows the evolution of Galvor's capital structure since 1950.

As mentioned, it was after World War II that Galvor began to grow most impressively. Table 14 gives selected statistics which illustrate this growth. Because inflation in France has been considerable since World War II, certain of the figures have been adjusted to constant (1961) NF.

Table 13

Galvor: Development of Capital Structure
(Figures in NF 000's)

End of Year	Equity	Long-Term Debt	Current Liabilities	Equity as a % of (Equity Plus Long-Term Debt)	Equity as a % of Total Assets
1950	252	83	374	75.2%	35.5%
1951	586	70	376	89.3%	56.8%
1952	734	53	483	93.3%	57.8%
1953	1161	40	534	96.7%	66.9%
1954	1453	30	441	98.0%	75.5%
1955	1788	20	737	98.9%	70.3%
1956	2213	10	960	99.6%	69.5%
1957	2714	00	1178	100.0%	69.7%
1958	3202	00	1652	100.0%	66.0%
1959	3908	270 *	2145	93.5%	61.8%
1960	4805	190 *	2546	96.2%	63.7%
1961	5923	147 *	2750	97.6%	67.2%

Computed from company records by IMEDE staff.
* In 1959, 1960 and 1961, Galvor was carrying these amounts under the heading of "Middle-term debt"; this loan had been made in December 1959 and would be fully paid off in December 1962. The loan had been used to help finance the construction of Galvor Paris.

Finally, Table 15 shows Galvor's Profit and Loss Statement for 1961 and the Balance Sheet as of 31st December 1961.

MANAGEMENT CONTROL OF GALVOR

"I am not very happy with our budgetary and accounting control system at the moment," remarked M. Chambertin. "We have our accounting system well organized, and most of the basic data we need are available to us, but we have not gone as far as I should like in the analysis and control of our operations. This is partly because we have grown so fast that, to some extent, it has been difficult to keep tight control over our operations. Perhaps another problem is that responsibility for financial and budgetary control exists only at the highest level of Galvor, namely, in M. Latour's office and in mine.

"We do not have a true budgetary control system. We do not, for example, establish an operating budget for each department at the beginning of the year, and then ask our executives to justify their

Table 14

Development of Galvor Sales and Profits, 1950–1961
(Figures in NF 000's)

Year	Net Sales	Profits after Taxes	Total Assets	Net Sales in 1961 NF	Profits after Taxes in 1961 NF	Profits as a Percentage of Net Sales
1950	1308	71	709	2210 *	120 *	5.4%
1951	1669	126	1032	2203	166	7.5
1952	1568	122	1270	1969	153	7.3
1953	2584	434	1735	3420	574	16.8
1954	2619	297	1924	3530	400	11.3
1955	3205	354	2545	4180	477	11.0
1956	4235	425	3183	5485	550	10.0
1957	5601	520	3892	6835	635	9.3
1958	6197	485	4854	6760	529	7.8
1959	8403	666	6323	8820	699	7.9
1960	10045	776	7541	10200	787	7.7
1961	12030	1062	8820	12030	1062	8.8

Compiled from company records by IMEDE staff.
* The basis used for these price adjustments is the French Price Index computed monthly by the International Monetary Fund and published in the IMF's publication, *International Financial Statistics.*

Table 15

Galvor Financial Statements, 1961
(Figures in 000's)

Income Statement, 1961		
SALES (OF PRODUCTS AND REPAIRS):		14,365
BILLING FOR SERVICES PERFORMED:*		24
TOTAL SALES:		14,389
LESS: Sales Taxes		−2,359
NET SALES:		12,030
LESS: COST OF SALES (FACTORY COST):		−7,074
GROSS MARGIN:		4,956
LESS: OTHER EXPENSES:		
Sales Expense:	1,421	
Administrative Expense:	645	
R&D Expense:	644	
Other Profit and Loss:**	1,184	−3,894
NET PROFIT AFTER TAXES:		1,062

* Charges to TRONEX for services performed by Galvor for TRONEX.
** Mostly comprised of French Corporate Profits Tax, at 50% of pre-tax profits.

Table 15
(continued)

Balance Sheet
31st Dec. 1961

ASSETS			LIABILITIES		
Current Assets:			Current Liabilities:		
Cash:	274		Payables:	1,110	
Securities:	1		Other:	1,640	
Receivables:	2,796				
Inventories:	3,248		TOTAL CURRENT:		2,750
Other Current:	222				
			Depreciation:		
			Buildings:	430	
TOTAL CURRENT:		6,541	Equipment:	978	
			Other:	57	
Fixed Assets:					
Land:	265		TOTAL DEPRECIATION		1,465
Buildings:	1,849		MID-TERM DEBT:		147
Eqpt.:	1,438				
Other:	192		Net Worth:		
			Capital Stock:	2,500	
TOTAL FIXED:		3,744	Surplus, Rsves:	3,423	
			TOTAL NET WORTH:		5,923
TOTAL ASSETS:		10,285	TOTAL LIABILITIES:		10,285

Compiled from company records by IMEDE staff.

departmental expenses. When we have to expand a department, say by hiring a new man, we simply add that man's salary to the expected administrative costs for the coming year.

"Moreover, we do not analyze elaborately the economics of our major investments. When we decided, for example, to make this latest addition to the plant, it was simply a case of deciding that we needed more space, that we could finance this addition, and that we could soon sell the output of this additional capacity. We do not make elaborate analyses in determining whether to buy a new machine; either the idea looks good or it doesn't.

"Perhaps my biggest worry is our cost-price structure. We really do not know what each of our products costs. Until recently, most of our products sold in a relatively narrow price range, say 100–1500 NF. As long as this was so, it was not too incorrect to say that most products should bear about the same proportion of overhead charges; admittedly, there were differences in the true overhead attributable to different products, but these differences were not too significant with this narrow spread. Now, however, the price range is much greater: we are about to make a product selling for 30,000 NF. The complex electronic products contain far more R&D expense, proportionate to their price, than a multimeter, but our pricing structure does not allow for this."

In commenting on the way in which he controlled Galvor, M. Latour said, "At the month's end, M. Chambertin sends me the following figures for the month: net sales, total purchases, direct and indirect labor, R&D expenses, manufacturing overhead, inventory levels, gross profits, commissions, sales taxes, my personal account, and net profit. I check these figures against previous levels in order to determine whether we are up to standard or should take some corrective measures. Finally, I check our balance sheet, total overhead as a percent of sales, and our sales to each country. Of all these figures, I am most interested in the net profit figure. Since I sign all our important checks, this gives me another way of keeping an eye on our purchasing."

"I hope," said M. Chambertin, "to push our financial and accounting analyses much further along during 1962; it is the major job I have set for myself. I especially want to learn more about our product costs."

The Statistical Service

The basic statistical analyses looked at by Messrs. Latour and Chambertin were compiled by the Statistical Service under Mme. Bollinger. These analyses, consisting of tables and graphs, were contained in four books. In general, these books contained two main types of data: sales and expenses. Sales data alone occupied approximately 70% of the pages in these books. It was possible to find out, for example, exactly how many units of each product type had been sold in each month of every year since 1952, in which countries these units had been sold, and in the case of France, who had sold them. Galvor's expenses were broken down into minute detail for each department of the firm, and these expenses were available on a monthly basis for recent years.

Finally, these books contained a certain number of tables and graphs which were not strictly connected with sales and expenses: the growth of the unfilled-orders backlog, growth of the workforce, total hours worked and wages paid, etc. M. Chambertin also had available, although not contained in these books, standard cost sheets for each product. These sheets were used mainly for pricing purposes.

In addition to supervising the design and compilation of these statistical reports, Mme. Bollinger also produced an annual sales forecast. "I must admit," she said, "that the accuracy of this forecast is much better than the technique used. I make a monthly forecast of unit sales of each product for the next year; this is usually done every January. The main basis for the forecast is historical sales data. These data will usually show clearly any seasonal pattern in the product's sales, plus the overall trend. I am able to project from this historical information with considerable accuracy. Of course, we have no sales history for a new product, and so it is almost impossible to make a good forecast for such an item. When I have finished my initial forecasts, M. Margaux and I talk them over, because he often has special information of opinions which can improve these forecasts considerably. The final revised forecasts become the basis for the production schedule, which I also draw up." No sales forecasts were made for sales of galvanometers, accessories, spare parts, repairs, sales to TRONEX, or special-order products. Thus the sales forecasts made covered only about 70% of Galvor's total sales volume. Table 16 gives a quantitative measure of the accuracy of these forecasts.

SUBSIDIARY ACTIVITIES OF GALVOR

Galvor had two principal subsidiary operations, the TRONEX Corporation and Indica S.A. The company also had a very small subsidiary which owned a number of dwellings, which it rented to Galvor employees.

The TRONEX Corporation

TRONEX was essentially a paper corporation owned entirely by M. Latour; TRONEX's assets and operating results were not consolidated in Galvor's financial statements. Galvor manufactured for TRONEX a small number of low-priced measuring instruments. TRONEX instruments were, M. Chambertin said, of substantially lower quality than the equivalent Galvor products. The TRONEX

Table 16

Accuracy of Galvor Sales Forecasts, 1961

Error of Forecast (Plus or Minus)	Percentage of Forecasted *Sales within Error Class
0 to 5 %	37.4%
6 to 10%	17.3%
11 to 15%	2.6%
16 to 20%	20.4%
21 to 25%	14.7%
26 to 30%	2.7%
over 30%	4.9%
	100.0%

Source: Company records.
* As noted only 70% of total Galvor sales were accounted for by products for which sales were forecast.

product line consisted of a multimeter, a vacuum-tube voltmeter, a tube checker, a high-frequency and a pattern generator, and an oscilloscope. TRONEX had no formal organization of its own; M. Margaux to some extent supervised sales of TRONEX products, and one of the development technicians had designed the TRONEX products. As of early 1962, design of new TRONEX products had been suspended but would be resumed at a later time.

TRONEX products were manufactured by Galvor and priced in a similar, but not identical, manner to that used for the Galvor products. Galvor then sold these products to the TRONEX corporation at 35% off list price. M. Chambertin said that, at this price, TRONEX was paying about 15%–20% over factory cost for the products. TRONEX also paid Galvor a flat sum of about 24,000 NF annually to reimburse Galvor for the overhead incurred by Galvor for TRONEX. TRONEX had begun operations in October 1957; as of early 1962, its products were sold by three special manufacturers' representatives who did not sell Galvor products, by two of Galvor's own representatives, and by Galvor Paris. TRONEX sales had developed as follows:

1957 (3 mos.)	NF 28,074	(without taxes)	
1958	135,453	"	"
1959	197,118	"	"
1960	235,534	"	"
1961	197,524	"	"

TRONEX profits for its fiscal year 1961 (ending 30th Sept.), were approximately 16,500 NF. The corporation's net worth at the same time was approximately 19,000 NF.

Indica S.A.

Indica was a Parisian corporation engaged in manufactured dials and faces for all sorts of measurement and indicating instruments. The company was entirely separate (except in terms of ownership) from Galvor and had its own workforce, plant, and management in Paris. Galvor had bought Indica on April 1st, 1955, at which time the latter had been in bankruptcy; the purchase price was 60,000 NF. Indica's financial figures were in no way consolidated with those of Galvor, except that Galvor carried an asset of 60,000 NF under the heading of 'Investments in subsidiaries.' Galvor bought many of its meter dials from Indica, but 90% of the latter's sales volume came from customers other than Galvor. M. Chambertin characterized Indica's manager as very aggressive and dynamic.

Indica's sales had developed rapidly since 1955, as Table 17 shows.

Table 17

Indica Sales, 1955–1961

Fiscal Year *	Sales (without Taxes)	
1955	NF	388,000
1956		575,000
1957		911,000
1958		1,049,000
1959		1,378,000
1960		1,568,000
1961 (9 mos.)		1,537,000

Source: Company officials.
* Indica's fiscal year ended on March 30th.

M. Chambertin estimated that for the fiscal year 1961, (which would end 30th March 1962), Indica's after-tax profit would be about 130,000 NF. He pointed out that the 60,000 NF at which Galvor carried Indica on its books actually represented a true net worth for Indica of about 30,000 NF (as of March 31st, 1961). "As you can see," added M. Chambertin, "Indica is a highly profitable enterprise, and its profits are not added into the Galvor income statement. Moreover, the Galvor balance sheet considerably understates our true equity in Indica."

*　　*　　*　　*　　*

In commenting on Galvor's success since its founding, M. Latour said, "The most important reason for my success, I honestly believe, has been in finding men with whom I could share my problems, men who could solve these problems when I alone could not. I am very proud of my executives; every one of them is first-class. Without them, I should not have had any such success." Galvor (B) gives further information on M. Latour and the other important executives at Galvor.

A Note on the
French Electronic
Industry

INTRODUCTION

This note describes, mainly in quantitative terms, the situation of the French electronics industry in the early 1960's. Most of the basic statistics used to compile this note have been taken from various reports and bulletins of the Fédération Nationale des Industries Electroniques (FNIE), the French industry syndicate which compiles and distributes comprehensive statistics on the electronics industries of France and other countries.

Little attempt has been made to present qualitative information on each individual sector of the industry; to do so in a thorough manner would, because of the industry's diversity, require a report vastly larger than this note. For such information, the reader is referred to the appropriate notes on narrow areas of the French electronics industry. This note follows the industry structure which has been established by the FNIE. The note contains six sections: a general view of the total industry, sections on each of the four sectors into which the FNIE divides the industry, and a final section which gives some forecasts for the future of the industry.

I: AN OVER-ALL VIEW OF FRENCH ELECTRONICS

Industry Growth

Table 1 gives some measure of the growth of the electronic industry in France since World War II. Because there has been considerable inflation in France during those years, certain of the figures are adjusted to constant francs.

Table 1

Development of the French Electronic Industry, 1948–60

Year	Total Industry Sales (NF 000,000's)	Total Industry Sales in 1960 (NF * 000,000's)	Total Industry Employees	Annual Per Cent Increase in Sales 1960 NF *	Annual Per Cent Increase in Employment
1948 ..	256	520	26,500	. . .	. . .
1949 ..	269	487	28,900	6 decr.	9
1950 ..	333	556	28,800	14	nil
1951 ..	504	655	29,800	18	3
1952 ..	590	732	31,000	27	4
1953 ..	717	932	33,400	27	8
1954 ..	919	1,223	41,500	31	24
1955 ..	1,148	1,527	45,900	25	11
1956 ..	1,424	1,807	51,000	18	11
1957 ..	1,820	2,184	56,400	21	11
1958 ..	2,100	2,245	59,400	3	5
1959 ..	2,601	2,680	60,300	19	2
1960 ..	3,203	3,203	69,200	20	15

* Computed from FNIE statistics by researcher. The price index used to adjust sales to 1960 francs was the general price index for France, computed by the International Monetary Fund and published in its periodical, International Financial Statistics.

Total industry employment in the period 1939–44 ranged from about 25,000 to 30,000, the high point being reached in 1941. It can be seen, thus, that, in terms of creating jobs, the industry was relatively static from 1939 until the early 1950's, at which time a period of steady expansion began. As an illustration of this expansion, total employment in the French electronics industry rose, by 1960, to 262 percent of 1948 levels (Table 1). By contrast, total employment in France rose only 111 percent during this same period.[1]

The Industry's Foreign Trade

Table 2 gives over-all statistics on exports and imports by the French electronic industry in recent years. In 1959, the latest year for which complete figures are available, total foreign exports of France were 18.705 billion NF and her foreign imports 16.567 billion NF. A comparison of these figures with those in Table 2 shows that the French electronic industry provided, in 1959, about 1 percent of French foreign exports and accounted, in the same year, for about 0.75 percent of foreign imports.

1. Source: Statistics published by International Monetary Fund.

Table 2 does not include imports from the Franc Zone, because such imports have been very small; they reached a historical high of 810,000 NF in 1960. The foreign balance, rather than the over-all balance, is shown because exports to the Franc Zone do not earn foreign currencies for France and are, therefore, relatively unimportant from an international balance-of-payments viewpoint. It can be seen that, since 1955, the industry has not been an important earner of foreign currencies and that, in fact, in the first six months of 1961, the industry's imports were higher than its exports (if the Franc Zone is ignored).

The French electronic industry has traditionally been a good customer of the United States. For example, in 1960 about 50 percent of the French electronic industry's total imports came from the United States, and about 30 percent more from West Germany and Holland equally. Of its total 1960 foreign exports, the French electronic industry sent 18 percent to Holland, 10 percent to West Germany, 8 percent to the U.S.S.R., and 7 percent to Belgium and Luxembourg com-

Table 2

Exports and Imports of the French Electronic Industry
(NF 000's)

| Year | Exports | | Foreign Imports | Foreign Balance † |
	Foreign *	Franc Zone		
1948	3,862	16,754	14,519	(10,657)
1949	11,355	25,571	17,467	(6,113)
1950	21,473	20,795	21,991	(519)
1951	43,403	36,647	29,357	14,046
1952	49,267	42,339	33,256	16,011
1953	63,840	33,659	48,338	15,502
1954	109,717	38,695	51,208	58,509
1955	187,818	41,595	67,814	120,004
1956	68,516	51,166	81,795	(13,279)
1957	107,187	77,689	99,874	7,313
1958	130,076	108,668	102,873	27,203
1959	181,425	133,943	128,161	53,264
1960	282,057	141,497	246,550	35,507
1961 ‡	180,714	94,616	203,840	(23,126)

* "Foreign" refers to all imports and exports not involving the so-called "Franc zone"; the latter was comprised of France's overseas territories and now consists chiefly of ex-French colonies.
† This is the net inflow (or outflow) of France's foreign exchange as a result of the balance between imports and exports.
‡ First six months only.
Source: FNIE.

bined. The United States accounted for only about 4 percent of the foreign total.

Table 3 shows, for the first six months of 1961, foreign imports and exports in each sector of the French electronic industry.

Table 3

Foreign Trade of French Electronic Industry during the
First Six Months of 1961
(NF 000's)

Sector of Industry	Foreign Exports	Foreign Imports	Foreign Balance
CONSUMER GOODS:			
Radio & TV sets	9,672	10,916	(1,244)
Home sound system	8,383	13,931	(5,548)
PROFESSIONAL EQUIPMENT	89,686	82,308	7,378
COMPONENTS:			
Tubes & semiconductors	42,295	54,283	(11,988)
Condensers	670	7,820	(7,150)
Other components	30,008	34,581	(4,573)
TOTAL INDUSTRY	180,714	203,840	(23,126)

Source: FNIE.

Composition of the Industry

The FNIE divides the French electronic industry into four sectors: (1) Consumer Goods, (also called Receiving Equipment); (2) Professional Equipment (mostly for business and government); (3) Tubes and Semiconductors; (4) Other Components. Those industry products which do not fit any of these categories are grouped under "Miscellaneous." Table 4 shows the development of each sector since 1948.

Since the industry's final products are those in the first two sectors—Consumer Goods and Professional Equipment—it can be seen that only about two-thirds of the industry's gross sales figure is accounted for by final products. The remaining one-third consists of the components to make these products.

As Table 4 shows, the Professional Equipment Sector became more important than the Consumer Goods Sector in the period 1952–56, after which time consumer goods regained their historical dominance of French electronic production. The growth in sales of consumer goods slowed down in the early 1950's because France lagged in establishing widespread television broadcasting, and sales

Table 4

Development of the French Electronic Industry, 1948–60
(Sales figures in NF 000,000's)

	Sales in Each Sector					
Year	Consumer Goods	Profes-sional Eqpt.	Tubes and Semi-cond's	Other Com-ponents	Miscel-laneous	Industry Total
1948	110	57	48	41	. . .	256
1949	108	84	43	34	. . .	269
1950	132	95	55	51	. . .	333
1951	201	139	79	85	. . .	504
1952	186	230	79	95	. . .	590
1953	215	299	99	104	. . .	717
1954	256	420	96	147	. . .	919
1955	343	490	116	199	. . .	1,148
1956	500	500	143	274	7	1,424
1957	650	590	200	370	10	1,820
1958	758	638	255	404	45	2,100
1959	961	669	344	486	141	2,601
1960	1,186	822	413	609	173	3,203

Source: FNIE.

of radios were made during this same period largely to a replacement market. When French television became widespread in the late 1950's, sales of consumer goods received a powerful impetus.

French production of professional electronic equipment appears, nevertheless, to be gaining on production of consumer goods. In 1938, sales of professional electronic equipment were 22 percent of the sales of consumer goods. This ratio was 52 percent in 1948 and 76 percent in 1960. This trend towards an increasing proportion of capital to consumer production will continue for some time if the experience of other nations, with electronic industries more highly developed than the French industry, proves typical. In the United Kingdom, for example, 1959 sales of capital electronic equipment were 160 percent of sales of consumer goods. One reason for the dominance of capital equipment in the United Kingdom electronic industry is that the British Consumer Goods Sector is producing TV sets largely for a replacement market.[2] Conversely, in France there is not yet widespread

2. Precise statistics show that in 1960 the United Kingdom had 0.22 TV sets per capita compared with 0.04 in France.

DECISIONS INVOLVING PLANNING, STRATEGY, AND POLICY

ownership of TV sets, so the French Consumer Goods Sector has still considerable room for growth in meeting primary demand for TV sets.

Structure of the Industry

Table 5 shows the composition of the French electronic industry, by size of individual firms, in 1960.

Table 5

Structure of the French Electronic Industry, 1960

Size of Firm (Number Employed)	Number of Firms	Total Employees	1960 Sales (NF 000's)	Percent of Industry Sales
Over 1,000	10	29,253	1,098,069	37.38
501–1,000	15	10,763	479,228	16.31
201– 500	29	10,112	496,610	16.90
101– 200	44	6,300	260,396	8.86
51– 100	70	5,138	308,401	10.50
21– 50	99	3,391	178,875	6.09
11– 20	65	997	75,444	2.56
Under 11	322	894	40,888	1.40
Total	654	66,848	2,937,911	100.00

Source: FNIE.

II: CONSUMER GOODS

The French electronic industry has, since its beginnings, been dominated by the production of consumer products.[3] In recent years TV and FM radio broadcasting especially have provided great impetus for this sector. Also, there has been some growth in the number of normal "AM" radio sets. Table 6 shows the structure, in terms of products, of the Consumer Goods Sector in 1959 and 1960. TV sets form the most important branch within the consumer goods area, and the sector's over-all growth rate of 24 percent is due primarily to the rapid sales increase of TV and home sound equipment.

3. As noted, consumer goods took second place to professional equipment in 1952–56, but this appears to have been an aberration in the normal relationship between the two sectors.

Table 6

Consumer Goods Sector—French Electronic Industry, 1959–60

Type of Product	Units Sold 1960 (000's)	1960 Sales	1959 Sales	Percentage Change 1960/1959
		(NF 000,000's)		
Auto radios	88	20	16	25 up
Portable radios	1,564	264	189	39 up
Radio-phonographs	74	31	39	21 down
AM radios	450	76	101	25 down
AM-FM radios	38	14	17	18 down
Total radios	2,214	405	362	11 up
Television sets	655	635	487	30 up
Other products *	...	146	108	35 up
Total consumer goods ..	...	1,186	957	24 up

* "Other products" consists mainly of tape recorders and high-fidelity components for home sound systems. This figure is slightly incomplete but not significantly so.

Source: Compiled from FNIE statistics by IMEDE staff.

The statistics in Table 7 show the size of the firms which make up the Consumer Goods Sector of the industry.

III: PROFESSIONAL EQUIPMENT

There is no easy description possible of the products made by this sector of the industry. The electronics industry manufactures many tens of thousands of different types of products falling in the general area of professional equipment. The FNIE subdivides this sector in the manner shown in Table 8.

In 1960, only 3 percent of the French electronic industry's total production went to French business and industry, whereas 17 percent of United States electronic production went to business and industry in the same year. It appears likely that, in the near future, sales of industrial equipment will be a major growth area for the French electronics industry. Sales to industrial customers rose 32 percent in 1960 over 1959, well ahead of the rise for the sector as a whole.

The Professional Equipment Sector is dominated by a few firms, as Table 9 shows.

Table 7

Structure of the Consumer Goods Sector of the
French Electronic Industry, 1960

Size of Firm (Number Employed)	Number of Firms	Total Employees	1960 Sales (NF 000's)	Percent of Sector Sales
Over 1,000	2	4,439	345,309	29.11
501–1,000	6	4,187	272,708	23.00
201– 500	8	2,532	180,106	15.18
101– 200	8	1,011	104,217	8.78
51– 100	23	1,644	135,072	11.38
21– 50	26	844	70,736	5.95
11– 20	24	367	51,788	4.36
Under 11	..	466	25,968	2.24
Total	97	15,490	1,185,904	100.00

Source: FNIE.

Table 8

Professional Equipment Sector—French Electronic Industry, 1959–60

Customer	1960 Sales (NF 000,000's)	1959 Sales (NF 000,000's)	Percentage Change 1960/1959
Government			
Defense	395	363	9 up
French radio-TV	25	30	17 down
P.T.T.*	6	13	54 down
Other agencies	111	64	74 up
Total government	537	470	14 up
Business (France)	91	69	32 up
Foreign exports	123	80	54 up
Franc-zone exports	55	51	8 up
Miscellaneous	16		
Sector totals	822	670	23 up

* Post, telephone, and telegraph services.
Source: FNIE.

Table 9

Structure of the Professional Equipment Sector of the
French Electronic Industry, 1960

Size of Firm (Number Employed)	Number of Firms	Total Employees	1960 Sales (NF 000's)	Percent of Sector Sales
Over 1,000	5	16,982	514,878	62.80
501–1,000	3	2,149	78,419	9.56
201– 500	6	2,481	110,235	13.45
101– 200	14	1,981	48,869	5.96
51– 100	8	632	30,846	3.76
21– 50	23	804	28,286	3.45
11– 20	8	121	4,960	0.60
Under 11	..	90	3,210	0.42
Total	67	25,240	819,702	100.00

Source: FNIE.

IV: TUBES AND SEMICONDUCTORS

Tubes and semiconductors are vital components in virtually all electronic equipment. These devices are separated from other electronic components by the FNIE because of their special importance to the industry. Tubes and semiconductors, while markedly different from one another in design, size, composition, and other characteristics, are generally quite similar in function: they control electron flows with great precision. The demand for tubes and semiconductors is, of course, derived from the demand for finished electronic products, as is the demand for all electronic components.

The manufacture of tubes and semiconductors is work of high precision and must be carried out in spotlessly clean conditions. Since substantial cost savings can be made through mass-production techniques, the tube and semiconductor industry is dominated by a few large firms which make huge volumes of each of many different types of tubes and semiconductors. Few manufacturers of finished electronic products make their own tubes; they prefer to buy from specialists in this area. Only a few of the largest French electronic firms produce tubes and semiconductors and finished products as well. Table 10 shows the importance of large firms in this sector. Semiconductors (the most famous of which are transistors) were discovered as late as 1950, but since that time they have replaced electronic tubes in many applications, especially where low weight and reliability are critical. Table 11 shows the great growth in sales of semiconductors.

Table 10

Structure of the Tube and Semiconductor Sector of the
French Electronic Industry, 1960

Size of Firm (Number Employed)	Number of Firms	Total Employees	1960 Sales (NF 000's)	Percent of Sector Sales
Over 1,000	5	7,832	237,883	57.61
501–1,000	2	1,408	49,416	11.96
201– 500	3	824	65,053	15.75
101– 200	2	357	8,826	2.13
51– 100	5	352	49,975	12.10
21– 50	1	34	43	0.01
11– 20	2	35	1,092	0.26
Under 11	..	24	613	0.18
Total	20	10,866	412,901	100.00

Source: FNIE.

Table 11

Tube and Semiconductor Sector—French Electronic Industry, 1959–60

Product Type	1960 Sales	1959 Sales	Percentage Change 1960/1959
	(NF 000,000's)		
Receiving tubes	126	115	10 up
Cathode-ray tubes *	107	95	13 up
Broadcasting tubes	44	39	13 up
Other tubes	6	10	40 down
Semiconductors	121	84	44 up
Parts of tubes	8	0.5	44 up
Sector total	412	343.5	20 up

* Mostly consists of picture tubes for TV sets, the test being for oscilloscopes.
Source: FNIE.

V: OTHER COMPONENTS

Tubes and semiconductors can be regarded as the heart of most electronic equipment, but a wide variety of other components are nonetheless essential to almost any electronic circuit. Table 12 shows the diversity of components used in electronics. As might be expected from the diversity of its products, this sector of the industry is made

Table 12

"Other-Components" Sector—French Electronic Industry, 1959–60

Component Type	1960 Sales	1959 Sales	Percentage Change 1960/1959
	(NF 000,000's)		
Condensers	114	97	18 up
Coils	51	45	13 up
Transformers	80	52	54 up
Resistors	63	44	43 up
Mounting parts *	62	na	
Switches	17	na	
Fuses & circuitbreakers	3	na	
Vibrators †	0.5	na	
Wire bundles ‡	18	na	
Antennae	51	na	
Crystals, etc.	46	na	
Microphones	5	na	
Loudspeakers	46	na	
Sound pick-ups §	24	na	
Other components	28	na	
Sector total	608.5	486	25 up

na: not available.
* Mainly tube sockets and printed circuits.
† Used as power supplies.
‡ Used in connecting components within an electronic product.
§ Phonograph cartridges and pick-up heads on tape recorders.
Source: FNIE.

up of many rather small firms. Many of these firms specialize in the production of only one or two types of components, and an even greater degree of specialization is not uncommon. For example, some firms will make only special types of loud-speakers, or resistors, or antennae, etc. Table 13 gives data on the size of individual firms in this sector.

VI: FUTURE DEVELOPMENTS IN THE FRENCH ELECTRONIC INDUSTRY

Only parts of the Fourth French Plan have, as of May, 1962, been published; currently available material on the Fourth Plan does not give a complete forecast for the electronic industry. But one French publication, *L'Usine Nouvelle*, has analyzed the future of French electronics and its relation to the Plan. Parts of this analysis are reproduced on the next page.[4]

4. *L'Usine Nouvelle;* June 1, 1961 and January 18, 1962; Paris.

Table 13

Structure of the French "Other-Components" Sector of the
French Electronic Industry, 1960

Size of Firm (Number Employed)	Number of Firms	Total Employees	1960 Sales (NF 000's)	Percent of Sector Sales
Over 1,000	0	0	0	0
501–1,000	4	3,019	78,684	15.14
201– 500	12	4,275	141,216	27.18
101– 200	20	2,951	98,484	18.96
51– 100	34	2,510	92,507	17.80
21– 50	49	1,709	79,810	15.36
11– 20	31	474	17,605	3.38
Under 11	...	314	11,097	2.18
Total	150	15,252	519,403	100.00

Source: FNIE.

Three main problems [face] the French electronic industry: decentralization, recruiting of technical employees, and financing of research.

Electronics, which until recently was more or less included in the electrical-goods industry, now leads an independent existence. The annual growth in its sales has averaged about 15 percent for some years. This growth has been achieved in the face of a ten years' lag, a lag due to the Second World War. This growth will continue when the present problems have been rationally resolved.

One of the first jobs of the French planners will be to organize the electronic industry's decentralization in an appropriate manner. Industry observers think that this drive towards decentralization is already late in starting.

Some firms have already "emigrated" towards outlying areas, but this industrial dispersion meets obstacles which must be thoroughly understood. [In the first place], the four main sectors of the industry are tightly intertwined; any given sector provides products for use by other sectors, so that real supply problems appear when decentralization is considered. Electronic products are often fragile, and shipping them long distances sometimes is a risky proposition.

Moreover, the industry flourishes when various manufacturers can easily exchange information with each other; this exchange becomes increasingly difficult as decentralization progresses.

For these reasons, industry observers point out that any move toward decentralization must take into account the interdependence of the various sectors.

Recruiting of technicians and skilled workers is another major problem. The industry is, above all, an industry where brain power is important, hence a great dependence on engineers, technicians, and skilled workers. Recruiting such employees is already difficult, and may become more so if decentralization takes most companies away from the major population centers. The electronic employee must have not only an excellent technical background but also a sort of vocation for this relatively new field.

Accordingly, many manufacturers have, on their own initiative, increased the number of training centers in hopes of inducing young people to plan careers in electronics. These efforts have, however, not provided enough technicians to keep up with the rapid growth of electronics.

Thus electronics experts are begging for very close cooperation between the University and the Factory, which is only possible if the Factory is not too far from the University. Moreover, in order to find enough skilled workers, a factory has to be located in an area where there is sufficient population density.

Decentralization must, as a result, take into account not only the interdependence of the industry's sectors but also the problem of finding enough engineers, technicians, and workers.

Another obstacle to expansion is the financing of research. The rapid progress which other electronic industries have made is forcing France to devote enormous sums to pure and applied electronic research, lest France be left behind.

This problem is aggravated by the fact that total French electronic sales are not enormous, so that taking a fixed percentage of these sales for research may not provide enough funds to keep France abreast of other and larger electronic industries. The 1960 sales of the American electronic industry were about 20 times larger than those of the French industry; it is difficult to compete under this size disadvantage.

Industrialists have suggested that the government could contribute significantly by acting as a test market for new products and by contributing money for research into such new products.

The electronic industry's research funds depend on the Consumer Goods Sector of the industry, especially on the sale of TV sets, and at the present time there are some problems in this area. For example, the establishing of a second TV network is still 18 months from completion, and this is slowing down sales of TV sets. The Fourth plan forecasts that, in 1965, the industry will produce 2,100,000 radio sets and 1,470,000 TV sets, but this forecast presupposes that the second TV network be rapidly finished and that France continue to restrict the importing of translstorized Japanese radio and TV sets. [Table 6 shows that in 1960 France produced about 2,200,000 radios and 655,000 TV sets.—Ed.]

Despite all these problems, French electronic industrialists show no tendency to pessimism—quite the contrary. From their viewpoint, decentralization is perfectly feasible, provided that it is carried out under optimal conditions. Paying for research is a more serious preoccupation, but the general feeling in the industry is that, considering the industry's dynamism, all difficulties will be surmounted, no matter what their source.

A Note on the French
Electric and Electronic
Measuring-Instrument
Industry

INTRODUCTION

This note is designed to be used in connection with IMEDE cases on the Galvor Company. The note provides factual background on the measuring-instrument industry in which Galvor competes.

Material for this note has been drawn from three sources: (1) the Syndicate Général de la Construction Electrique (SGCE), which collects data on the French electric-goods industry; (2) the Fédération Nationale des Industries Electroniques (FNIE), which collects data on the electronic industries of France and other nations; and (3) officials of the Galvor Company.

The note contains two sections: (1) a description of what measuring instruments are, what they are used for and by whom, and other characteristics of the instruments themselves; and (2) a description of the industry in France as of early 1962.

MEASURING INSTRUMENTS:
DEFINITION AND DESCRIPTION

There are many types of measuring instruments, such as devices to measure heat, light, sound, and other physical phenomena. For the purposes of this note, the broad term "measuring instruments" refers *only* to devices which measure electric and electronic characteristics. The scope of this note is further limited by excluding a large class of products which are actually electric measuring instruments, namely, electric quantity meters. The most common electric quantity meter is the device, found in the household, which measures the amount of electricity consumed. Almost all French quantity meters are manufactured by one firm, and their design, manufacture, and sale bear little relationship to other electric and electronic measuring instruments. It is for these reasons that consumption meters are not included in this note.

The Purpose of Measuring Instruments

There are two main functions in which measuring instruments are employed: checking, and control.

The *checking* function is generally the more common one; it involves the testing, calibrating, servicing, and measuring of electric and electronic devices of all types. Such checking usually involves the measurement of physical characteristics, the most common of which are voltage, current, resistance, capacity, frequency, inductance, phase, and wave form. Other more specialized characteristics are also measurable by certain instruments.

Measuring instruments are used in their checking function to answer such questions about electric and electronic devices as the following:

1. Is the device working?
2. How well is it working?
3. Should adjustments be made? If so, of what sort?
4. How much voltage, or current, or resistance, etc., exists at a given spot within a circuit?

Measuring instruments used for checking are usually self-contained and portable. Occasionally they may be incorporated as part of an electric or electronic system and permanently mounted in the system, where their function is to give continuous checking on the system's operation.

The *control* function also usually involves the installation of the measuring instrument in a larger system. In this case, the instrument's function is not only to measure one or more physical characteristics, but also to make operating adjustments to the system based on the measurement performed.

The Users of Measuring Instruments

Measuring instruments are used in many different fields and are, indeed, indispensable in the modern technological world. They are chiefly found in the following fields:

1. *Industry,* where they are used for controlling processes, for maintaining equipment, for checking product quality, and for performing research. They are also sometimes incorporated in industrial products for resale.
2. *Government,* for research, for maintenance of equipment, and for control.

3. *Laboratories* of such nonprofit institutions as universities and other schools, hospitals, and foundations, where they are used in research.
4. *Radio and TV* repair shops.
5. *Repair shops* for other electric and electronic goods.
6. The *home* of an electric/electronic amateur of some sort, such as a radio "ham." This use is uncommon, however.

As the foregoing suggests, the demand for measuring instruments is, to a certain extent, derived from the demand for other electric and electronic products. Accordingly, sales of measuring instruments are partially influenced by sales of electronic and electric equipment.

The Content of Measuring Instruments

The process of manufacturing measuring instruments proceeds as follows. The manufacturer uses a few raw materials, mostly metal in various forms, which he manufactures into various components of the final product. He also buys many components from other manufacturers. (He typically makes parts which are relatively simple to construct, such as the sheet-metal chassis found in most measuring instruments.) All French manufacturers buy almost all their requirements of the complex electric and electronic components, such as tubes, condensers, resistors, and coils. Some manufacturers do virtually no manufacturing at all except assembly; they purchase all parts, and their manufacturing operation is purely one of mounting the parts.

As the above description suggests, the typical measuring instrument has a very small proportion of raw materials in its final cost, but it contains many purchased components. Purchases almost always account for the largest percentage of direct cost in a French measuring instrument. Assembly labor always accounts for a substantial proportion of direct cost, and other manufacturing labor may be considerable. Manufacturing labor never, however, exceeds assembly labor.

As for indirect costs, research and development expenses can be important, depending on the complexity and sophistication of the firm's products. Marketing costs depend largely on whether the firm attempts (as a few do) to sell to many small customers, or only to concentrate on the government and major corporations. Since manufacture of measuring instruments is dominated by assembly operations and since these operations are usually simple, the industry's capital investment per unit of sales is relatively low, a characteristic of many other branches of the electronic industry.

"Electric" vs. "Electronic" Measuring Instruments

Measuring instruments are generally classified as either electric or electronic. The distinction is one which has grown up over many years and is not always clearcut. As a rule, instruments containing electronic circuitry are called "electronic," and those lacking such circuitry are called "electric." Exceptions to this rule do, however, exist, as in the case of tube and transistor checkers, which contain no electronic circuits but which are called electronic devices because they are used only to check electronic products. Despite its limitations, this classification is used here because it frequently occurs in statistics on the industry.

The principal types of products which fall in each category are as follows:

Electric Instruments	Electronic Instruments
Galvanometers	Tube checkers
Multimeters	Tube analyzers
	Vacuum-tube bridges
	Transistor checkers
	Impedance bridges
	Vacuum-tube voltmeters
	Generators
	Oscilloscopes

These instruments are the basic ones used in measurement of electric and electronic characteristics. There are many other types of electric and electronic measuring instruments made, but such types are usually highly specialized, manufactured by only a very few firms, and not commonly used.

Electric Measuring Instruments

The *GALVANOMETER* (or "Galvano") is the most common measuring instrument used. It is simply a device which measures the amount of electric current passing through it. A galvano's findings are usually displayed in terms of current (amperes), voltage, or electric power (watts), since power and voltage can be ascertained by determining the current. Galvanometers are simple devices which arc usually inexpensive, costing perhaps $10 to $30; they become more expensive as they are made more precise. As a rule, galvanometers are not used alone but are mounted in other measuring instruments, where they measure and display the findings of such instruments. Galvanos are also sometimes incorporated in electric and electronic systems, where they give continuous indications of the level of important characteristics. They are integral parts of multimeters and of vacuum-tube voltmeters.

The *MULTIMETER* is nothing but a very flexible galvanometer; where a galvanometer can be used only to measure one characteristic in one relatively narrow range (e.g., from 10 to 100 volts), the multimeter can, through elaborate circuitry, measure all the basic electric characteristics (voltage, amperage, resistance, and capacity) within rather broad ranges. Multimeters are technologically simple devices which, like galvanometers, are easily manufactured; they range in price from about $15 to $150. The precision of a multimeter depends primarily on the quality of the components used in its manufacture. As a rule, a multimeter is accurate to within 1–5 percent. This accuracy suffices for most applications. When more accurate measurement is needed, a much more expensive instrument of a different type must be used, such as (for voltage measurement) a vacuum-tube voltmeter. The multimeter is the basic tool of electric and electronic technicians.

Other electric measuring instruments include *FLUXMETERS*, *PHASEMETERS*, and *FREQUENCY METERS*. Such devices are, however, much less widely used than galvanometers and multimeters. Only the latter two are important electric measuring instruments.

Electronic Measuring Instruments

Electronic measuring instruments can be roughly divided into two classes: those which measure components, and those which measure circuits.

Component Measurement. The most common instrument in this class is the *TUBE CHECKER*, sometimes called the TUBE TESTER. This is the basic instrument used in determining whether an electronic tube is operating. The simplest instrument of this sort will check only whether the tube is emitting electrons; more complex varieties measure several characteristics at once. A modern tube checker is generally sufficient to determine whether a tube is operating properly. Tube checkers contain relatively simple circuitry and are among the less costly [1] electronic instruments.

The *TUBE ANALYZER* is a complex and rather expensive instrument which measures with considerable precision certain operating characteristics of an electronic tube. Thus the tube checker will reveal whether a tube is functioning, and the tube analyzer gives further indication of how well the tube is operating.

The *VACUUM-TUBE BRIDGE* is a specialized and complex instrument which is used in connection with a tube analyzer, in order to

---

1. In France, electronic measuring instruments range in cost from about $100 to perhaps $2,000. (Certain very specialized instruments cost well over $2,000.)

measure additional operating characteristics of tubes. It is expensive and is not so widely used as are tube checkers and analyzers.

The *TRANSISTOR CHECKER* performs the same function for transistors that a tube checker performs for electronic tubes. It contains no electronic circuitry but is classified as an electronic product because, like the tube checker, it measures only electronic devices (transistors and other semiconductors). It is a technologically simple device and is inexpensive.

The *IMPEDANCE BRIDGE* is a technically uncomplicated instrument which can be made in varying degrees of precision, depending on the quality of components used in its manufacture. It measures three important electric-electronic characteristics with considerable precision: capacity, resistance, and inductance. It can be used either to check components (condensers, resistors, and inductors) or to measure circuits. The bridge is generally considered an electronic instrument, although it contains no electronic circuits. It is, as a rule, a medium- or low-cost instrument.

Circuit Measurement. The *VACUUM-TUBE VOLTMETER* (VTVM), as its name implies, measures voltages by means of circuitry involving electronic tubes. It measures voltage with much more precision than do galvanometers and multimeters. Depending on its precision, the VTVM is of low or medium cost.

GENERATORS form a family of apparati which have, in general, one chief purpose: to create the electromagnetic waves used in many electronic devices, notably in radio and television equipment. The members of this family are chiefly differentiated from one another by two main characteristics: the shape of the waves [2] generated, and the frequency range over which a given instrument produces these waves.

Exhibit 1

Types of Electromagnetic Waves

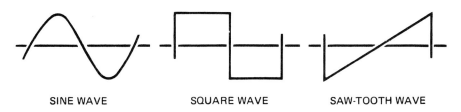

SINE WAVE   SQUARE WAVE   SAW-TOOTH WAVE

The *AUDIO GENERATOR* generates sine waves over a range of frequencies which corresponds approximately to the frequency range audible to the human ear: 50–20,000 cycles per second (cps).

2. There are three principal types of wave forms produced by most generators. They can be graphically represented in the manner shown below:

AM and *FM GENERATORS* produce waves which are used to check the equipment employed in AM and FM radio broadcasting and reception. For AM radio, sine waves in the range 50,000–5,000,000 cps are used. Instruments for FM radio and for television testing usually create sine waves in the range of 5,000,000–250,000,000 cps. The *AM, FM, SERVICE,* and *STANDARD SIGNAL GENERATORS* are all used for *AM* and *FM* radio testing.

VHF (Very High Frequency) and *UHF* (Ultra High Frequency) *GENERATORS* are used in testing TV equipment and also for radar devices, microwave communication equipment, and other electronic products which operate with very—and ultra—high frequencies.

MARKER GENERATORS, PATTERN GENERATORS, WOBU-LATORS, and *WOBULOSCOPES* are special generators used in TV testing exclusively. (The wobuloscope also contains a built-in oscilloscope used in conjunction with the instrument).

All generators contain electronic circuitry, and most of them are fairly expensive instruments. They range in price from perhaps $100 to several thousand dollars, depending on their complexity, precision, versatility, and type.

The *OSCILLOSCOPE* is essentially a type of television set which displays a picture of an electromagnetic wave. This instrument contains fairly complex electronic circuits and ranges from low to high price, depending on its accuracy and flexibility. Like a TV set, its main component is a cathode-ray tube, (the "picture" tube of a TV set).

* * * * *

The foregoing description of the various types of electric and electronic measuring instruments gives only approximate indications of the cost of each type, because this cost can vary markedly within a single type. This variability is due to the fact that oscilloscopes, for example, while all similar in purpose and general design, can differ substantially in precision, sophistication of design, flexibility of measurement, convenience of operation, and elegance of finish.

In fact—and this is a striking characteristic of the French measuring-instrument industry—there is almost no direct competition among manufacturers in the electronic-instrument area. In galvanometers and multimeters, several producers may make some instruments which are essentially similar, but this is not always so. And in electronic instruments, it is rare to find two manufacturers making truly comparable products. Five different companies may produce oscilloscopes, but no two will produce identical ones, and it is unlikely that any two will produce oscilloscopes that are even reasonably similar in all respects. As a result, competition in the industry tends to be somewhat limited.

THE FRENCH MEASURING-INSTRUMENT INDUSTRY

Growth of Sales

The French industry, which consists of only 12 firms of importance, has been growing very rapidly in recent years, but it is still a small one. Its total sales of electric and electronic measuring instruments were only $27.6 million in 1960, compared with sales of $515 [3] million by its U. S. counterpart in 1959. Table 1 shows the growth of the industry since 1956.

Table 1

Sales of the French Measuring-Instrument Industry, 1956–60
(Figures in NF 000,000's)

Year	Sales of Electric Products	Sales of Electronic Products	Total Sales of Measuring Instruments
1956	49.14	19.30	68.44
1957	56.35	26.20	82.55
1958	62.38	37.23	99.61
1959	66.25	39.15	105.40
1960	89.55	48.58	138.13

Source: SGCE.

The industry's total sales had, by 1960, increased 102 percent over 1956 levels (Table 1). Electronic instruments enjoyed a sales increase of 152 percent during this time, and electric instruments an increase of 82 percent. By way of comparison, sales of the French electronic industry as a whole rose 125 percent during 1956–60.

Firms in the Industry

According to Galvor officials, there are twelve firms which are important in the industry. There are a few other French firms which make some measuring instruments, but only in insignificant quantities. The following information on the twelve major firms was obtained from various Galvor executives and represents their opinion on their competitors.

Alpha Corporation [4] employs about 1,000 people. The company makes many types of industrial regulating and control devices, and

3. Source: FNIE.
4. All companies given fictitious names.

it also produces a broad line of galvanometers and multimeters. The firm has recently made tentative efforts to enter the electronic measuring-instrument field. With its beginnings around 1920, ALPHA is one of the oldest and best-known companies in the industry. Its measuring instruments are sold to all types of customers; government, industry, radio and TV repair shops, etc. The company makes instruments of average quality and sells at average prices. It sells through about 10 wholly-owned sales agencies and through a small number of major wholesalers. Its reputation in measuring instruments is somewhat tarnished by its failure to give uniformly good repair service on its products. It is a major competitor in electric measuring instruments.

Beta Corporation is a large French company for which measuring instruments form only one of many product lines. It makes some high-quality and high-cost galvanometers for precision work and other galvanometers of average quality and competitive price. It sells through its large network of wholly-owned sales agencies, chiefly to the government and to large corporations. Its measuring instruments are mostly highly specialized; because of this specialization, BETA is not an important competitor in the industry.

Gamma Corporation is a subsidiary of BETA CORPORATION, employs about 300, and makes only oscilloscopes. Like its parent, it makes high-quality and high-cost instruments which are sold through BETA'S agencies to government and industry.

Delta Corporation, which employs 500, makes galvanometers (and also many devices which are not included in the measuring-instrument industry). It sells almost all of its output, which is of high quality and cost, through its Paris agency to government and industry.

Epsilon Corporation has 400 employees. It makes a rather broad line of electronic measuring instruments and concentrates on oscilloscopes; it also makes TV sets. It is especially well-known in production of TV testing instruments. It sells to all types of customers through a network of fifteen manufacturers' representatives and a Paris agency. Its products are of average quality and price.

Zeta Corporation employs 300 and makes electronic measuring instruments of high quality and price. It sells virtually its entire output through its Paris agency, mostly to the government. It makes a few products other than measuring instruments. It is most importantly a producer of highly specialized instruments manufactured in relatively small series and, as such, does not usually enter into intensive competition with the rest of the industry.

Kappa Corporation employs 200; it is a major manufacturer of galvanometers and also produces some multimeters. All of its products are expensive and well made. It sells almost exclusively to the government and does so through its Paris office. Galvor executives consider KAPPA a serious competitor for them in galvanometers.

Lambda Corporation employs 100 and makes galvanometers and industrial control systems. It sells to industry through wholesalers and is not noted for the quality of its instruments. Galvor executives do not regard the firm as a serious competitor for them.

Mu Corporation makes a wide range of electric and electronic measuring instruments of low quality and price. It sells them to radio and TV repair shops through 8–10 manufacturers' representatives and about 30 wholesalers. It is one of the few firms in the industry which offers one or more items in almost every product type. MU has 50 employees.

Theta Corporation was founded shortly after World War II and now employs 17. The company makes only one type of product: pattern generators for use in TV testing. THETA entered the pattern-generator field at a timely moment and has, as a result, captured virtually the entire market. Its products are of good quality and reasonable price; they are sold through a few manufacturers' representatives and through the sales network of the EPSILON CORPORATION. THETA's principal customers are radio and TV repair shops and manufacturers of TV equipment.

Sigma Corporation, which has about 15 employees, makes a wide range of low-quality, low-cost electric and electronic measuring instruments. The company is able to span most of the industry's product line by confining itself to assembly operations only; no other manufacturing is done. SIGMA's customers are mostly radio and TV repair shops, who buy from about 5 manufacturers' representatives and 30 wholesalers.

The Galvor Company is located in Bordeaux and employs about 450. It sells a very complete line of electric and electronic measuring instruments which are of good quality and reasonable price. GALVOR is especially strong in multimeters, where it has over 80 percent of the French market. It sells through 15 manufacturers' representatives and through its wholly-owned Paris agency; it sells to all of the typical groups of industry customers.

The Industry's Foreign Trade

Table 2 shows the industry's foreign trade in 1960; the figures used include insignificant quantities of products other than measuring instruments.

Table 2

French Exports and Imports of Measuring Instruments, 1960
(Figures in NF 000's)

Electric Instruments		Electronic Instruments	
"Foreign" * exports	10,350	"Foreign" exports	7,450
"Foreign" imports	9,000	"Foreign" imports	24,100
"Foreign" balance	1,350	"Foreign" balance .	(16,650) †
Franc Zone exports	5,170	Franc Zone exports	950
Franc Zone imports	neg. ‡	Franc Zone imports	neg. ‡

* "Foreign" trade figures are those which are due to countries not in the Franc Zone.
† Shows negative trade balance.
‡ Negligible imports of measuring instruments from Franc Zone.
Computed from SGCE statistics by IMEDE staff.

The most striking fact revealed by Table 2 is that the French industry has been unable to meet the demand of French customers for electronic measuring instruments. The industry's 1960 production of electronic instruments was valued at about 48,500,000 NF (Table 1): 8,400,000 NF of this production was exported (Table 2), leaving about 40,100,000 NF for the French market. French customers imported an additional 24,100,000 NF worth of such instruments in the same year. The French industry filled only about 63 percent of domestic demand. Of the 24,100,000 NF of imports, some 17,400,000 NF worth came from the United States alone.

This heavy reliance by French customers on imports, especially from the United States, of electronic measuring instruments is attributed by industry observers to the fact that the United States has a considerable technological lead in electronics over France and other countries. This lead apears to be shrinking as Western Europe rebuilds its industries, but it is still an important factor in the Free World's electronic industry. Galvor officials are confident that the French measuring-instrument industry will, in the near future, be able to supply most demands of French customers for all types of measuring instruments.

Trends in the French Measuring-Instrument Industry

Since World War II, the industry has largely enjoyed a seller's market. There has been sufficient demand to keep the entire industry working at or near its productive capacity. Of equal importance, this high level of demand has enabled manufacturers in many instances to sell equipment at very profitable prices. There has been little price competition in the industry, not only because of the high level of demand, but also because so few of the industry's products enter into direct competition with one another.

This situation could change by 1964–65, for two reasons: first, because it appears that, by this time, the industry will have sufficient capacity, and second, because there is a trend toward increasingly direct competition among manufacturers in the products they offer. More and more frequently, a number of manufacturers will develop a new measuring instrument simultaneously, and their designs for such new products are becoming increasingly similar. For these reasons, there could be a natural tendency for most firms in the industry to compete more aggressively than ever for such new products as are designed.

As a result of these factors, Galvor officials expect to see, within the next few years, a period during which competition will become intense, but it appears likely that the Common Market, by opening a vast new clientele, will compensate for this intensive competition.

There is some possibility that a number of major French electronic corporations could enter the measuring-instrument field. Until recent years, these large corporations have ignored the commercial possibilities of measuring instruments, since total industry sales were rather small (e.g., only 82,550,000 NF in 1957). But, as French sales of measuring instruments have continued their rapid growth, the area has become increasingly attractive to other manufacturers of electronic products.

A final trend in the industry is the increasing complexity and sophistication of its products. This complexity has been necessitated by the tendency toward increasing complexity in electronic products of all kinds. The result of this trend is that research and development are becoming increasingly important, even vital, to the industry. Galvor officials believe that a company's success during the coming period will be largely determined by the extent to which the firm succeeds (a) in outstripping its competitors in research and development of new products and (b) in increasing productivity by means of new manufacturing techniques.

The Galvor Company (B-1)

INTRODUCTION

As of early 1962, six men were mainly responsible for the management of Galvor: M. Georges Latour, president and owner of the company, and his five principal subordinates: Jean Chambertin (Administrative Director), Jacques Romanée (Manager of Manufacturing), Bernard Margaux (Manager of Commercial Service), Robert Meursault (Manager of Electronic Research), and Claude Pommery (Manager of Electric Research). This case (a) gives a brief description of each man, including some of the impressions received about each by IMEDE researchers; (b) quotes some of the sentiments they expressed about one another, and (c) shows how each man viewed his role in the company and the problems associated with this role.

GEORGES LATOUR

In October 1961, when IMEDE first proposed (by letter) to M. Latour the idea of doing case research on his company, he replied: "Since our company is of relatively small importance," he wrote, "and our organization far from perfect, I wonder if . . . our 'case' is worthy of special attention." When assured that these objections were of no consequence, M. Latour immediately agreed to the proposed extensive case research on Galvor. He promised to make all data available and to enlist the whole-hearted support of his executives in this venture. He was as good as his word. By May, 1962, IMEDE researchers had spent about 50 man-days at Galvor; Galvor officials were at all times not only courteous and cooperative, but anxious to be of any possible help to IMEDE in this project. They were almost always available for interviews, even with as little as 24 hours notice.

M. Latour was 53 years old; he was always immaculately dressed and of distinguished appearance and bearing. Researchers were struck by the extent to which his courtesy exceeded the demands of ordinary politeness. "I am always," he remarked, "entirely at your disposal. You have, by your research, contributed significantly to our company; you have asked us questions which we ought to have asked ourselves. Furthermore, you are involved in education, and it is our duty to do what we can to help you." Because M. Latour spoke English fluently, interviews with him were usually held in that language.

In the many hours IMEDE researchers spent with M. Latour, he never raised his voice; he maintained a calm, formal, reserved air at all times. His elegant office, which contained a whimsical ceramic mural of the world on the wall behind his desk, was always uncluttered, and there were few papers on his desk. (Other Galvor executives had somewhat smaller offices which were functional, rather than lavishly decorated. M. Latour remarked that he hoped in the near future to be able to provide better offices for his colleagues.) He was always punctual for appointments with IMEDE staff, and during such interviews was only rarely interrupted by his secretary or by one of his executives. One interruption occurred during a Saturday morning interview, when he answered a telephone call from a customer in Paris. The customer wanted to know why the invoice price of a Galvor instrument was higher than the catalogue price. M. Latour explained politely and patiently that the customer's catalogue was outdated, and that the price used was that in effect on the day of delivery.

M. Latour frequently referred to his top executive group (the five men mentioned in the opening of this case) with pride and with concern for their welfare. He generally called them 'my colleagues' or 'my collaborators' and frequently remarked on the excellence of each man. He spoke often of the 'team' consisting of all Galvor employees, and of the importance of a team concept to him. He once mentioned that, on the occasion of his annual speech to Galvor employees (December 31st), the employees collectively presented either him, or Mme. Latour, with a handsome gift.

M. Latour's hospitality towards IMEDE researchers was very generous. Lunches were always at one of the best restaurants in Bordeaux and always excellent; they generally lasted about two hours. On several occasions, he invited one or more IMEDE researchers to his home, which he had built in 1957–1958. The house, perched on the side of a hill with a panoramic view, was modernistic in design and furnishings; it would have been an appropriate cover illustration for an architectural journal. In summary, IMEDE researchers were uniformly charmed by M. Latour.

*   *   *   *   *

When asked about the satisfactions he received from having built Galvor, M. Latour remarked, "You know, I suppose I could say simply that I have made a lot of money from the company, but it is much more than that. I like to think that we have built a company we can be proud of, one with a good reputation, and one which treats its employees well. I also think that, in a modest way, we have made some real contributions in our field, especially with special instruments for the French and foreign governments; this is a source of great satisfaction to us. This is a much different thing from just selling soap, or something like that. I think we all feel justifiably proud of Galvor.

"You know, in the old days it was an adventure to keep Galvor in business, a dangerous adventure. I used to worry about the fact that any sort of major crisis, particularly an economic crisis, could ruin the company overnight. But when Chambertin came in 1954, one of the things he did was to introduce the idea of routine into many of our operations, and this has profoundly changed the atmosphere of the company. Now things go along more or less according to routine. For example, in the old days there was a real question whether our growth would continue year after year, but now we have been growing at 15%–20% annually for so long that this rate of growth has itself become routine. As this has happened, much of the adventure has gone out of running the business.

"As to how I function as the general manager and owner, let me first point out that this is a 'one-man company' *only* in the financial sense. In every other respect, this is a team effort. I prefer to think of myself not as the owner and the leader, but rather as the chief Galvor employee. I belong in this office only so long as I show that I am the best man to take charge of overall company operations. Of course, I continually check up to see if things are going right in each area, but to me the word 'leadership' implies dictatorship, and I don't want to be thought of as a dictator. I may own the company, but I cannot and do not want to run things all by myself. When we have specialized problems, I go out and find a specialist to take care of these problems.

"One day a close friend of mine, the director of a large British electronics factory, told me that I was running a so-called 'one-man company.' This shocked me greatly, because this is exactly the thing which I have tried to avoid. That is why we have the weekly management conference, where everybody in top management gets a chance to speak. And I listen to what my colleagues say.

"I have not stopped going to school; I continually attend the management seminars which are run by various French institutions, and one of the things I learned sometime ago is what a top manager is: he is a man who keeps on top of his work, and who accordingly has time when he needs it. Every morning I have a certain number of things which I have to do that day, and when I leave at night, these things have been done.

"As the company grows, managing it becomes an increasingly difficult job, and for some time I have needed an assistant. I have just found this man, named Armagnac, and he reported last Monday

(April 2nd, 1962). He will not only have line authority in certain areas, but he will be my personal assistant, and he will relieve me of a lot of the routine work I now have to do. This will leave me free for what I consider is my main job in the years to come; working for the long-term growth and success of Galvor. More specifically, I expect to spend an increasing amount of my time looking at new export markets, and especially at how we will fit into the Common Market. Since my recent trip around the world, I have become convinced that Galvor has the ability to become one of the top four or five firms in measuring instruments in the world, and it is my intention to see that we attain this position. As soon as this new addition to the plant is finished, we will add 200 employees very quickly, and I can see us growing to 1,000 employees within a few more years.

"One of my dreams has been to erect a building to house our administrative and research staffs, five or six stories high, of square form and clad in glass. When we have the necessary capital, probably by 1964, this building will go up beside the plant. One reason I want it is so that I can give my executives nicer offices. I look on this building as being the crowning achievement of my life, but maybe I'll be able to go even further than this.

"Although I have not told any of them about this, I plan eventually to give my main executives stock in the company. This seems to me to be an obligation, because of all they have contributed. Until recently I have not considered such a move too seriously because, after all, my men were well paid, and Chambertin especially so. And I have always stood ready to make interest-free loans to all my employees for good purposes, especially for such things as building a house. My top men can live well; Romanée owns his own house and has a couple of cars, and the others are in equally comfortable circumstances.

"I think the chief reason that my executives enjoy working for Galvor is that they have, I hope, found the same spirit of adventure and enthusiasm that I have in being in this business, and in making a famous product of high quality. I don't think that money is the chief attraction for them, although Chambertin is paid so much more than any of the others that this might be so in his case." (At 4:30 one Saturday afternoon, as M. Latour and several IMEDE people were leaving the plant, they met M. Chambertin, who had been working at the office all day. M. Latour, after saying goodbye to M. Chambertin, remarked: "Chambertin pretends he's just killing time around here trying out a new secretary, and he pretends to grumble about having to do this, but he is just too modest to admit his devotion to his job and to the company.")

"When the company was small, I suppose that I was responsible for almost all of the new ideas which we followed, as was only natural.

But as we have grown, it would have been foolish of me to pretend that only I had good ideas and not to listen to my colleagues.

"Now they provide as many ideas as I do, and I consider not only my own proposals, but those of the others as well." (M. Chambertin once remarked that M. Latour felt a great debt to his colleagues, especially to those who had been with him for many years, and that he was unwilling to impose his ideas on them. On another occasion, M. Meursault said that M. Latour never gave a direct order against his executives' wishes.)

"As to my colleagues' image of me," M. Latour continued, "this is obviously a difficult thing to judge. I hope they like and respect me. They are still with me after many years and they always show their respect in discussions with me, and I am doing all I can to keep Galvor a company of which they can be proud. Regarding their major problems, maybe they want more money, but I do not think this is really important to them. I don't know what problems they may have, if any. I would like to know, so that I could adjust to give them what they want. There is, as I have said, much routine, but there is adventure above that. I think that the company gives my colleagues a chance to live this adventure, and that they consequently commit their goodwill and enthusiasm towards our success. There is no end to this adventure."

JEAN CHAMBERTIN

M. Chambertin was the only one of the main Galvor executives who had not risen through the ranks to his present position. For many years before coming to Galvor, he had been head of the Bordeaux office of Fiduciaire de France, a major firm of public accountants, where he had handled the Galvor account among others. In 1953, M. Latour proposed to M. Chambertin that he come to Galvor; after about a year, M. Chambertin accepted and was made Administrative Director of the company. (M. Chambertin's title of *Director* was equivalent to vice-presidential rank in the firm. The other four main executives had the title of *Manager*, which corresponded to the rank just below Director.)

M. Chambertin was the only Galvor employee besides M. Latour who wore a standard business suit while at the office. All of the other executives wore white smock coats over their street clothes.

IMEDE researchers found that, with the exception of M. Latour, M. Chambertin was the only Galvor executive who would talk about the four Managers. M. Chambertin was always anxious to talk about company problems at great length with members of the IMEDE staff, and he sometimes quoted opinions of IMEDE researchers at the weekly management meetings. As case research progressed, M.

Chambertin devoted more and more time to explaining, in great detail, the workings of the company to IMEDE people, and he often provided IMEDE with highly confidential documents which he had prepared for M. Latour on special problems and issues within the firm.

Although M. Latour referred to M. Chambertin as "the most intelligent of my colleagues, and the one who looks furthest ahead in his work," M. Chambertin himself said that he was probably not as intelligent as his assistant, Mme. Bollinger, a recent graduate of a large French graduate business school. "You know," remarked M. Chambertin, "even though I am ostensibly second-in-comand here, I am fifty-eight years old, and the company badly needs a younger man as the designated successor to M. Latour, I would happily be a subordinate to such a man, even if he were twenty years younger than I, just because it would be for the good of the company."

"I finally came to work for Galvor because in my previous job I had too many accounts to manage, and I was wearing myself out trying to do the job well. I felt that it would be considerably less of a strain to handle the affairs of only one company."

M. Chambertin described his role in the company as follows: "My most important function is taking care of Galvor's external affairs, notably our financial relations. Next in importance comes my responsibility for our accounting and statistical reporting services. I am also responsible for personnel. And finally, I suppose that to some extent I act as adviser to M. Latour, but I should add that, except at critical moments, he usually doesn't solicit my opinion on an issue. It is well to remember that not only has M. Latour 97% ownership of Galvor, but he also has 101% of the responsibility. This responsibility extends all the way down in the organization, at least at some times; M. Latour even hires and fires the janitor. I think it is fair to say that nobody here so much as paints an arrow on the wall without M. Latour's approval. After all, why not? He owns the company."

When asked his opinion as to the most important factors in Galvor's success, M. Chambertin replied, "In the first place, it is important to remember that since the Second World War nobody in our industry has had any difficulty in selling instruments. We have been enjoying a seller's market since 1945. And also very important, the chief [1] has maintained a steady policy of expansion at a reasonable rate. He has made sure that when we make an expansion move we digest the resulting growth before proceeding to the next stage. We have not gone madly ahead in an effort to grow regardless of the consequences. Another reason for our success is certainly the quality of our products, which keeps getting higher, and which we owe largely

1. M. Latour was usually referred to by his employees as *le patron*, which can be translated roughly as 'the boss' or 'the chief.'

to Jacques Romanée. People are well aware of our quality, and so we never have trouble selling our instruments.

"As you know, I have often mentioned areas within the company where I think that we have some real problems, but it is important to keep these problems in perspective. I believe that Galvor today has attained such an eminent position in the industry that our continued success is assured. We may have small problems from time to time, even big ones, but people will always want Galvor products."

JACQUES ROMANÉE

Jacques Romanée, who was about 54, had been with Galvor since 1941 and was accordingly the oldest of the major executives in terms of service to the company. M. Romanée, who had had only a modest amount of formal education, had worked for about ten years in a galvanometer factory before coming to Galvor. While in this previous job he had invented an excellent moving element [2] for galvanometers, and he had further refined this design soon after coming to Galvor. This moving element design was still used in most Galvor multimeters and galvanometers.

Although as a rule M. Romanée confined himself strictly, during interviews with the IMEDE staff, to remarks on manufacturing operations, he often commented on how overburdened he was with work.

M. Latour remarked, "Romanée came here twenty years ago as a worker, a foreman; I hired him especially because of his experience in galvanometers. As the company has grown, and as he has moved up to become Manager of Manufacturing, I have had to bring him along. By this I mean that, every time we have moved up to a new platform in our growth, it has been difficult to get Romanée to accept the responsibilities which he must take on at this new stage. I have found, however, that once I have brought him up to the new level, he then works well within his enlarged sphere of authority.

"But this indicates one real problem which I have had. When Galvor was young and small, it was natural and easy for me to supervise all the operations and to run the company by myself, and in those days I had all of the responsibility and authority. But the company is too big for that now, and I have to get my executives to take responsibility for themselves. Unfortunately, they are so used to the old days, when I *did* want to run everything, that now they find it difficult to change.

2. The moving element of a galvanometer is the most crucial part of the instrument. It consists of a coil of wire very carefully wound around an axis and with a needle (to indicate on the dial) attached. The skill with which the moving element is manufactured largely determines the precision of the galvanometer.

"In the old days, for example, at the end of every day Romanée would come to me with a list of problems which had built up during the day. For him, everything was a crisis: we were short of one little part, and so we were going to have to shut down the plant. He always wanted me to tell him what to do. Well, I managed to cure him of this to some extent; I went to America for a time, and in my absence my wife ran the company. When she was in my office, Romanée would come to her every night, but she would explain that she couldn't help him. The very first evening I was back, Romanée came to my office and told me I'd have to decide what to do with a whole group of problems which had accumulated during my absence. I told him I was no longer willing to do this, and he left. He never came to my office at the end of the day after that. This little story will give you some idea of the difficulty which I have had in getting some of my men to take on more responsibility for themselves. Chambertin is different; I recently noticed that we have a considerable number of new accounting machines in the office. I never heard anything about these machines, much less had anything to say about approving them; Chambertin just ordered them on his own authority, which is what he should have done.

"But when I tell Romanée that he is not to bother me with expenditures of less than X new francs, he just adds up things until they total more than X new francs and then asks for my approval because the amount is too large for him to approve alone. Or else he gets one large purchase, over X new francs, and tacks on a number of smaller machines to the same purchase request. He just doesn't want to decide for himself."

M. Romanée viewed this same problem differently, saying [3] "Galvor's main problem is a simple one: the company is not run with a firm hand. M. Latour gives what one might call 'semi-orders,' where I am never sure what the order is because he is not explicit. I would much rather he would figure out exactly what he wants and then give a definite and clear-cut order. Another problem sometimes is that I receive an order which is impossible; this is a terrible situation, and one which I never create when I give an order. I always make sure before giving an order that it can be carried out.

"The disease of our century, and one which we have at Galvor, is that responsibility is not clearly defined. We have a number of operating groups here in which we have problems, but before we try to fix these problems, we have to know who's in charge. I wish that M. Latour would set up a well-defined organization chart showing the exact responsibility of every executive."

3. This was the one occasion (occurring after five previous interviews) when M. Romanée made any personal comments of significance regarding other Galvor executives.

M. Romanée, it was agreed by all executives, was overloaded with work in early 1962. He was supervising the construction of the new factory and the plans to manufacture resistors. He was also partially responsible for liaison between the manufacturing and research groups, when it came to bringing a newly designed product into mass production. He had considerable methods work to perform and partial responsibility for inventories. And he was also responsible for seeing to it that he had enough workers with the proper skills to perform the manufacturing operations. Finally, he had all the other normal responsibilities associated with being Manager of Manufacturing.

"We know," remarked M. Latour, "that Romanée has far too much to do, and for that reason I have been urging him to hire an assistant to help relieve him of some of the detail work he now has. I have said that he can pay such an assistant as much as is necessary to get a good one. But somehow he never seems to find just the right man."

M. Romanée said, "I've been looking for years for a good assistant, but it's difficult to find the right man, I don't really have time to train him, and besides, you can't teach a man everything I've learned about this business in thirty years."

M. Chambertin said, "Romanée really needs a brilliant young engineer to assist him, because he does not have very strong technical background, especially in the electronic area. But I think that Romanée is afraid that if he hires some bright young man, the new man will show him up, so he does nothing."

BERNARD MARGAUX

M. Margaux, who was about 35, had come to work for Galvor in 1957. M. Latour commented, "A friend of mine in Lyon told me about Margaux, who had been working in production up to that point, and who was looking for another job. So I told him to have Margaux write me a letter stating what sort of things he might be interested in. I hired Margaux and he went out on the road as a field engineer for us, dealing with our representatives and some of our clients. He did a good job, and so soon after we brought him back to Bordeaux, I made him the Manager of our Commercial Service. I have hoped that eventually Margaux would grow sufficiently in stature to become our Commercial Director, that he would be in charge of our Paris agency and galvanometer sales as well as his filling regular role in the Commercial Service. But as time passes, I find two objections to his moving ahead: first, he does not seem to have the important qualifications of being able to keep on top of his job; he never is able to answer his mail the same day, he is always behind. Second, he has no great amount of formal education, and so he really lacks the technical background which is becoming increasingly necessary to handle our products, especially the electronic ones. I think that, in the long run, we need a man with engineering training as our Commercial Director." M. Chambertin also thought that M. Margaux lacked the necessary training and, to some extent, the ability to rise to Commercial Director.

In commenting on his role in the company, M. Margaux said, "My background is primarily technical; I suppose you could say that I am really a technician more than anything else, but at least by previous experience. But now that I am Manager of the Commercial Service, I haven't enough time to deal with the many technical problems which arise in the course of my work. My role is as M. Latour's right-hand man for commercial problems. M. Latour himself is really the Commercial Director of Galvor. I must admit that at the moment I have far too much to do, because I am handling export sales myself, but I am looking for a man to take charge of exports; I must find this man no later than autumn. When I can unburden myself of export problems, I will be able to concentrate on more important things, such as overall marketing problems, and especially the possibility of doing marketing research. I will also have more time to visit our agents and representatives here and in foreign countries.

"Before I came to work at Galvor, I was assistant to the Manufacturing Director of another company, and this man treated men like machinery. Things are completely different here. I enjoy working for Galvor (a) simply because I like the company and am proud to be associated with it, and (b) because I have always had a pleasant relationship with M. Latour, quite unlike the experience in my previous job. M. Latour is courteous, polite, and very friendly, and he is always thinking of his colleagues' well-being. In the six years I've been here, I've never had any quarrel with M. Latour, except for normal disagreements on operating problems. That is why I like working here."

ROBERT MEURSAULT

M. Meursault; who was about 35, had gone to work for Galvor in 1943 as an apprentice. When the Messer brothers left the company in 1945 (as described in *The Galvor Company (A)*), M. Meursault left with them, but he returned to Galvor about a year later and was made Manager of Electronic Research within a few years. M. Meursault's training had been at a type of technical institute, which gave a minimal theoretical background and stressed practical applications of electricity and electronics.

"Meursault," remarked M. Latour, "is a brilliant man, and he has wonderful imagination when it comes to conceiving and designing new electronic products. He is working with very advanced technology, and he keeps abreast of advances in his field, but he is badly overloaded with work. He has too much administrative work to perform and really needs an assistant. But Meursault fears, I think, that if he hires some brilliant young electronic theoretician from Polytechnique, the assistant will outshine him and eventually get his job. I have promised Meursault that he will always be number one in electronic research at Galvor, but he does nothing. I have even told him that, if it is necessary in order to find the right man, he can pay an assistant even twice as much as he himself is earning. I try to give my executives all the support they need to find assistants for themselves, but I don't want to force assistants on them. These men have been with me for many years, and they have contributed greatly to Galvor's growth and success, so I don't want to force them to do anything they don't want to do."

In describing his job, M. Meursault said, "My primary function is to consider future developments in electronic equipment. I have to maintain customer contacts in order to learn what the new instruments should be. I also have to maintain contact with my design engineers, in order to see that they are designing products which will meet future needs of our customers. It takes an engineer, and one intimately familiar with current developments, to be able to sense what kinds of instruments people will be wanting in the future, and this is my most important job.

"In order to give myself more time to do this type of exploration, I hope to bring in two assistants. One will be an administrative assistant to help with the routine work of the department. The other will be technical assistant to be in direct charge of the design men. I will hire one of these men fairly soon and try him out in both jobs; he will eventually take over the area for which he seems better suited.

"At the moment, my time is divided about as follows: 20% on customer contact, 30% on administrative work, 30% on technical work, and 20% lost time shifting from one job to another. Once I have these two assistants, I expect to divide my time in this way: 60% on customer contact, 20% on technical work, 10% on administration, and 10% on lost time."

CLAUDE POMMÉRY

M. Pomméry, who was about 35, was an outstanding graduate of one of the great French scientific universities, and he had spent three years after graduation doing research and teaching at the university in the area of measuring instruments. M. Latour and M. Chambertin both observed that M. Pomméry's greatest difficulty was his inability to say 'no' to anybody. "Pomméry," remarked M. Latour, "is simply too nice. He is anxious to please everybody, with the result that people bring him all sorts of petty problems to solve, and he never puts his foot down. Pomméry is a brilliant man, and he has done some remarkable work in designing new galvanometers and multimeters, but he wastes too much time in petty administrative detail. Now he is hiring an assistant, so I hope this will change somewhat."

M. Pomméry, who was always soft-spoken and formal in manner with IMEDE researchers, described the allocation of his time in this manner: "First of all, I have to do a lot of reading outside of working hours to keep up with the latest innovations in my area. As for time on the job, I ought to analyze it in terms of the demands made on my time. About 50% of my time is theoretically necessary to work on our catalogue, on our commercial displays at trade fairs, and on working on models which we have developed, where it is a question of putting finishing touches on a new model. Another 30% is demanded to supervise my share of the prototype and design services, where Meursault and I are jointly in charge. 20% more is needed to provide answers to small technical problems which arise in my own research group, and I should spend another 20% of my time doing basic research and development on new products. You will notice that this leaves no time for training my design technicians, and no time for free-lance experimenting and engineering, and still the total demand is for 120% of my time. I hope that my new administrative assistant will work on our catalogue (and the instruction books which go with each product), handle commercial inquiries about the possibility of designing a new product for a specific customer, do some of the technical administrative work, and supervise to some extent the prototype and design services."

*   *· *   *   *

When M. Latour had finished reading THE GALVOR COMPANY (B-1) up to this point, he commented to the casewriter, "I am really very unhappy about one aspect of the B-1 case: it makes it appear that I am the 'star' of the company, and that the other men are not nearly so important as I am. This is an entirely false impression, and one which I would not want the reader to get. This is a team effort." Upon the casewriter's assurance that subsequent cases in the series would make it clear that the other Galvor executives were also very important, M. Latour agreed to release the B-1 case.

The Galvor Company (C-1)

DISTRIBUTION POLICY

Galvor's distribution network was designed to handle all types of customers, from the small electrical repair shop purchase of less than 100 francs to large industrial and government orders of several thousand francs. Company officials believed that their present sales network was best suited to their product line and their market. Table 1 shows the various channels through which Galvor products were sold.

Table 1

Galvor Distribution Network, 1961

Distribution Channel	Percent of Total Sales
SALES IN FRANCE: (83.9%)	
Manufacturers' Representatives	32.4%
Galvor Paris	42.3%
Factory Sales	5.9%
Repairs	2.0%
Sales to the TRONEX Corporation	1.3%
EXPORT SALES: (16.1%)	
COMOR S. A.	5.2%
Importing Agents	10.7%
Repairs	.2%
	100.0%

Source: Company records.

Factory sales were made to customers in those areas [1] of France where Galvor maintained no manufacturers' representative: such sales also included certain special order products not included in the

Copyright 1962 by l'Institut pour l'Etude des Méthodes de Direction de l'Enterprise (IMEDE), Lusanne, Switzerland. Reproduced by permission.
1. These areas included 12 of France's 89 Departments.

regular product line. The representatives were given a commission for any sale, whether by them or by the factory, of normal Galvor equipment in their assigned territories.

Although Galvor's products were exported to 43 countries, as can be seen from Table 2, only Europe, the Franc Zone,[2] and the Ameri-

Table 2

Galvor: Export Sales Analysis, 1961

Area	Percent of Total 1961 Sales
EXPORT SALES:	
Europe	7.4
Franc Zone	4.7
The Americas	2.1
Asia	0.7
Africa	0.5
Australia/Oceania	0.5
EXPORT REPAIRS:	0.2
TOTAL:	16.1%

Source: Company records.

cas accounted for significant percentages of sales. (The 1961 percentages given below were, M. Margaux asserted, about the same as those in previous years.)

Galvor's biggest foreign markets were Italy, Spain, Belgium, the U. S., the U. K., and Australia. From 1957 to 1959, Galvor had a U. S. agency, owned equally by Galvor and an American partner. The arrangement had not been satisfactory, however, and as of 1962 Galvor products were sold in the U. S. market through the sales force of a U. S. manufacturer of a related product line.

In early 1962, M. Latour was preparing to enter the German market. A Galvor sales engineer was going to spend six months prospecting the German market. According to M. Latour, "He will make a report on the requirements of the German market. When we can meet those requirements, we will set up our agency in a suitable location to direct a network of representatives just like our French network. We will repeat in Germany factors which made us successful in France, because I think the German market will be our second largest."

M. Latour felt that Galvor's biggest problem in exporting was price. When the company worked through a French exporter and

2. Mostly comprised of former French colonies.

then an importer in the foreign country, (this arrangement accounted for 25% of 1960 export sales), two margins were added to Galvor's prices. The only export markets with which M. Latour was satisfied were Italy and Belgium, where Galvor had exceptional agents.

Galvor grouped its French customers, who accounted for 84% of 1961 sales, into ten categories, which were differentiated as follows:

1) *Grands Administrations* included the large French Government agencies, notably the armed forces; they typically placed very large orders. M. Latour commented, "The Government seldom buys directly from the catalogue. They prefer to deal with a company representative, usually M. Cliquot in Paris. The Government has a technical staff which coordinates the requirements of all Government agencies and then makes contact with the manufacturer. Often we find Government specifications stating 'Galvor or equivalent'. When our salesmen work with Government officials, they try to get these officials to specify Galvor." The Government usually solicited bids for a given item from several manufacturers; the choice was made on the basis of price and on the supplier's reputation and reliability. Galvor had 10 customers in this category.

2) *Administration Locals* comprised French departmental and local Governments, which had their own budgets. "This is one weak spot in our sales effort," commented M. Latour; "our salesmen don't usually call on these purchasers. Such sales as we make in this area are probably due to our good name, which people hear of in schools, in the armed forces, and in other companies." There were about 1,060 Galvor customers in this group.

3) *Industries Electroniques* included makers of electric and electronic products. Such customers, totaling about 450, generally bought Galvor products for (a) use in their laboratories, (b) maintenance of their equipment, or (c) incorporation in their products. M. Latour said, "With most of these firms, we must deal with their purchasing offices. This is a disadvantage when selling products like ours; I feel that if we could talk directly to their technical people, we should have greater success. We ought to visit each of these customers about 4–5 times per year."

4) *Industries Diverses* included all other industrial users of Galvor products. Such customers bought Galvor instruments mostly for their maintenance work, occasionally for laboratory use. Galvor had about 1,950 customers in this category.

5) *Grossistes Electriciens*, or wholesalers of electrical goods, sometimes carried Galvor products in stock or would order such products at their customers' requests.

6) *Grossistes Radios*, radio and TV wholesalers, were important Galvor customers. There were about 700 customers in the wholesaler area, i.e. Groups 5 and 6.

7) *Grandes Ecoles* included the major French institutes and universities; although most of them theoretically belonged in one of the Government categories, these schools were treated separately

because of their importance. Over 700 were Galvor customers. Not only were sales to this group considerable, but even more important, Galvor executives considered it excellent publicity for the firm to have its products used by students.

8) *Utilisateurs Radios* retailed radios and TV sets and used Galvor products in their repair shops. This group contained many individual customers, but the typical customer's account was a very small one. M. Margaux remarked that these customers, while individually unimportant, were very loyal to Galvor.

9) *Utilisateurs Electriciens* included men who installed electrical goods of all sorts, i.e. electricians in general.

10) *Utilisateurs Particiliers* was somewhat of a 'miscellaneous' group, including private 'ham' radio operators, electronic hobbyists, and similar small customers. There were about 13,000 Galvor customers in groups 8, 9 and 10 combined.

The company did not maintain records on sales made to each customer group. Rather, groups 1 and 2 were called the 'Government' sector, groups 5 and 6 the "Wholesaler" sector, and groups 3, 4, 7, 8, 9 and 10 the "Users" sector. An analysis of Galvor's French sales by customer type is found below in Table 3.

Table 3

Galvor Sales in France, 1958–1960

Sector	Percentage of Total French Sales		
	1958	1959	1960
Government:			
Special Products	6.80%	12.67%	5.92%
Catalogue Products	25.46%	24.17%	26.90%
Wholesalers:	16.89%	16.30%	17.55%
Users:	35.15%	31.78%	32.02%
Export:	15.70%	15.08%	17.61%
	100.00%	100.00%	100.00%

Source: Company records.

The Commercial Service maintained an elaborate file on customers and potential customers. (Files on customers in the Paris area were maintained only by Galvor Paris.) M. Margaux described this file of customer cards as the Commercial Service's most important tool. He added, "A customer's card records every letter we have received from him, the number and type of Galvor products he has bought, the number of times this customer has been visited by our representative, and so forth. It is the customer's identity card. We can build up all sorts of useful statistics by using these cards."

THE SALES REPRESENTATIVES

As of early 1962, Galvor had 15 manufacturers' representatives who covered most of France. In 1961, these representatives accounted for 32.4% of Galvor's total sales. Some of these men had been Galvor agents for over twenty years, and M. Latour remarked on the debt which he owed many of them for having helped him to build the company. The typical representative also sold the products of two or more other manufacturers whose products were related to, but not competitive with, those of Galvor. The representative's entire line was, ideally, such that a customer for one of his product lines would be a potential customer for other lines as well. Galvor had used great care in selecting representatives whose product lines were complementary.

Most of these representatives had only a modest amount of technical knowledge; it was hoped that this knowledge would be sufficient to enable them to sell Galvor's products effectively, but as the products became more complex, this aim was increasingly difficult to achieve. Galvor maintained two sales engineers who would help a representative on some of his customer calls, especially by providing expert technical information on Galvor products. The representatives generally appreciated the help, even though limited, which they received from this source.

"Depending upon how many other manufacturers' lines he carries," said M. Margaux, "a Galvor representative should expect to spend from two to six hours per day selling our products. If Galvor is his most important line, his time spent on Galvor should reflect this. Once we hire a representative on a permanent basis, he is protected by the French "Representatives Indemnity Law" which normally requires that he be paid a sum equal to three years' commission if he is fired. Obviously this law makes it very expensive to fire a man, so we give each representative a very careful and lengthy trial before we finally take him on. We have had very good luck with our representatives."

The representatives were paid on a straight commission basis. The rate, which was always paid on the list price before taxes and freight, varied depending upon the product, how much the representative discounted the list price, and the credit terms of the sale. For cash sales, the commission was 9.5% for sales at list price, 7.5% for sales at 10% off list, 5.5% for sales at 15% off list, and 3.75% for sales at 20% off list. For credit sales (always at list price) the commission was always 8.5%, regardless of whether the terms were six, nine or twelve months. Exceptions to the above schedule were spare parts (always sold at list price) on which the commission was 4.75%, and galvanometers (not sold on credit) on which a 7.5% commission was paid regardless of the discount.

In 1961, commissions averaged about 6.3% of a representative's net sales. For the same year, Galvor's commission payments to its agents ranged from 5,900 NF to 54,500 NF. A "typical" representative's commission totaled about 23,000 NF, M. Margaux estimated. The company's sales engineers, both in Bordeaux and Paris, were paid a straight salary.

Galvor had traditionally used manufacturers' representatives, a company document pointed out, because "The sale of measuring apparatus is difficult to accomplish in a single step. Rather, it requires several visits to the customer and perhaps some demonstrations. Thus it is difficult to organize our sales network except by means of manufacturers' representatives, who work from a fixed address in the appropriate region, where their clients can meet them and where operations can be based."

Each representative was given a small inventory of the principal Galvor products. This inventory was controlled by the Field Inventory Clerk of the Commercial Service. "This stock," commented M. Margaux, "serves three purposes. It helps a representative to speed delivery in urgent cases; it can be used for customer demonstrations; and with this inventory available in the field, we can lend a product to a prospective customer."

The performance of the representatives was not formally evaluated until 1960 when M. Margaux developed a measure of performance which he called the "fortune co-efficient." This co-efficient was based on the number of radios, number of TV sets, and the amount of industrial electricity used in France. The arithmetic mean of the percentages of these three factors in each territory was divided into the percentage of the total Galvor sales in France for the territory to obtain the performance co-efficient for the territory. For example, if Brittany had 3% of France's radios, 2% of France's TV's and consumed 1% of France's industrial electricity, then the representative for Brittany needed sales equalling 2%[3] of Galvor's total sales in France to have a fortune co-efficient of 100. M. Margaux discussed the co-efficient in detail with his representative and relied upon it to measure their selling performance. Whenever necessary, he made adjustments in the co-efficient for factors such as how much time the representative could devote to Galvor, and the general economic conditions in an area. M. Margaux considered a co-efficient of 75 as an acceptable average for a good man in a typical territory. 1959 and 1961 sales, commissions, and fortune co-efficients for France by distribution channel are reproduced in Exhibit 1. Data on 1960 sales in France by distribution channel, with each channel ranked according

3. $\dfrac{3\% + 2\% + 1\%}{3} = 2\%$

to net return to Galvor as a percent of list price, are shown in Exhibit 2. Exhibit 3 is an analysis of total 1960 Galvor sales by product category.

As can be seen from Exhibit 1, there was a wide variation in representative performance relative to fortune co-efficient potential. In 1961 the co-efficients ranged from 160 for the representative in Brittany to 43 for the representative in Lille. When a representative's performance was below potential, M. Margaux attempted to get better performance from him. If this did not produce results, he sometimes reduced the representative's territory. On the other hand, when a representative was doing a good job, M. Margaux would sometimes reward him with a larger territory. When making adjustments, M. Margaux's objective was to match the representatives' selling ability with territory potential. The sales territory maps reproduced in Exhibit 4 reflect the territory reallocations during the 1959–1961 period. M. Margaux's brief description of six representatives, selected at random by the researcher, is reproduced in Exhibit 5.

Although M. Margaux felt it would be several years before direct sales offices would be economically feasible outside of the Paris area, he did mention Lyon, Lille, Marseilles, Bordeaux and Strasbourg as cities where it might someday be feasible to open direct sales offices. He gave the following approximate figures as the monthly cost of a direct sales office:

Director's Salary	2,500 NF per month
Rent	500 NF " "
Office Expenses	150 NF " "
Secretary	800 NF " "
Commercial and Travel Costs	2,000 NF " "
Total:	5,950 NF " "

Since the representative received an average commission of 6.3%, M. Margaux reasoned that a direct sales office would have to have sales of more than 1,000,000 NF per year in order to pay expenses. In the long run, M. Margaux thought it would be advantageous to have direct sales offices, because he felt that a Galvor agent with technical training would sell much better than most representatives, who had little technical training.

When asked about the possibility of a direct sales force, M. Latour replied, "Before we can use our own sales force, we need a broader product line. And anyway, we would use such a sales force only in the major industrial centers of France. M. Margaux's dream is to eliminate the representatives and replace them by a direct sales force, but this is a long way away."

Exhibit 1
The Galvor Company (C-1)

1959 and 1961 Galvor Sales, Commissions and Fortune Indexes in France by Distribution Channel*

Distribution Channel	Territory	Total Sales, All Taxes Included NF 1959	Total Sales, All Taxes Included NF 1961	Commissions NF 1959	Commissions NF 1961	Fortune Index 1959	Fortune Index 1961
Representative							
A	Brittany	133,626	226,281	9,436	14,540	143.68	160.25
B	Pyrenée	55,465	124,867	3,568	8,402	37.72	78.76
C	Nice	—	149,776	—	10,199	—	84.92
D	Vendée	162,819	227,755	11,118	14,963	77.90	105.42
E	Dijon	128,783	259,390	9,041	18,208	40.49	85.40
F	Herault	35,383	79,511	2,381	5,903	52.80	126.17
G	Lille	429,863	658,042	28,059	47,214	24.46	43.24
H	Marseilles	379,612	549,972	24,097	36,776	71.54	100.90
I	Normandy	224,037	321,602	14,106	21,400	46.87	63.04
J	Centre	110,920	190,363	6,453	12,468	51.59	62.11
K	Bordeaux	210,433	319,808	12,373	19,836	64.99	90.38
L	Lyon	515,603	793,074	34,362	54,546	63.34	115.12
M	Toulouse	232,877	385,560	13,815	22,973	85.61	120.46
N	Stras-bourg	345,289	554,548	21,313	31,943	36.08	59.06
O	Nice	106,419	—	7,473	—	59.12	—
X		20,136	14,148	1,271	806	—	—
Y		13,367	—	997	—	—	—
TOTAL		3,104,632	4,854,670	199,863**	320,177		
Galvor Paris		4,481,704	6,222,670	72,737	—	201.24	281.54
Factory Sales		580,049	806,434				
Sales Engineer	Z	28,413	14,220	—	—		
GRAND TOTAL		8,194,798	11,897,994	272,600	320,177	—	—

* Not including sales to the Tronex Corporation (1.3% of total 1961 sales).
** In 1959, Paris sales were, for part of the year, made by a sales representative; hence the commission payments in that year.
Source: Company Records.

DECISIONS INVOLVING PLANNING, STRATEGY, AND POLICY

Exhibit 2

The Galvor Company (C-1)

1960 Galvor Sales, Commissions, and Discounts in France by Distribution Channel*
(Representatives Ranked According to Net Return to Galvor as a Percent of List Price)

Distribution Channel	Net Sales After Discounts NF	Commission Paid to Agent NF	Net Return to Galvor after Taxes and Commissions NF	Average Discount on List Price Given %	Average Commission Paid as a Percent of Net Sales %	Net Return to Galvor as a Percent of List Price %
Representative						
A	169,844	11,925	124,176	4.31	7.02	69.82
B	92,793	6,464	67,769	4.42	6.97	69.80
C	109,195	7,370	80,135	5.42	6.75	69.27
D	205,301	12,726	151,514	6.90	6.20	68.71
E	158,574	11,038	115,821	6.11	6.96	68.57
F	75,468	4,433	55,941	7.66	5.87	68.45
G	492,111	34,499	359,218	6.94	7.01	67.92
H	416,919	26,502	307,430	8.52	6.35	67.35
I	236,429	14,636	174,566	8.88	6.19	67.25
J	179,145	11,148	132,209	9.14	6.22	67.03
K	263,332	16,006	194,982	9.43	6.08	66.92
L	738,004	48,482	541,920	9.57	6.57	66.40
M	274,610	15,881	203,807	11.36	5.78	65.79
N	462,053	25,688	349,192	11.81	5.56	65.28
X	52,953	3,135	39,228	12.77	5.92	64.62
Y	66,161	4,012	48,916	13.30	6.07	64.10
TOTAL	3,992,890	253,945	2,946,824			
Galvor Paris	4,825,050	265,869	3,682,572	7.31	5.51	68.85
Factory Sales	729,161	—	583,615	13.95	—	68.82
GRAND TOTAL	9,547,101	519,814	7,213,011			

* Not including sales to the Tronex Corporation.
Source: Company records.

Exhibit 3

The Galvor Company (C-1)

Analysis of Total 1960 Galvor Sales by Distribution Channel and Product Category

Distribution Channel	Electronic Products		Electric Products		Galvanometers		Total		
	Net Sales NF	Average Discount %	Net Sales NF	Average Discount %	Net Sales NF	Average Discount %	Net Sales NF	Average Discount %	% of Total Net Sales
Representative									
A	90,422	2.24	70,837	6.62	8,584	6.08	169,844	4.31	1.454
B	35,388	1.99	53,369	5.82	4,035	6.27	92,793	4.42	0.795
C	36,846	3.59	53,883	7.14	18,464	3.84	109,195	5.42	0.935
D	111,346	2.30	89,769	11.70	4,185	14.20	205,301	6.90	1.757
E	67,342	2.13	75,940	7.27	15,291	15.97	158,574	6.11	1.357
F	32,789	4.44	40,874	10.36	1,804	0.85	75,468	7.66	0.646
G	175,681	4.84	290,887	8.07	25,542	7.99	492,111	6.94	4.212
H	143,881	4.24	229,965	11.10	43,069	8.04	416,917	8.52	3.568
I	80,033	5.59	139,565	11.32	16,831	2.88	236,429	8.88	2.024
J	92,078	7.09	79,651	11.37	7,415	9.47	179,145	9.14	1.533
K	120,398	5.95	129,408	12.08	13,525	13.07	263,332	9.43	2.254
L	287,625	5.94	288,700	9.75	161,678	15.11	738,004	9.57	6.317
M	123,059	9.67	130,325	12.63	21,225	12.97	274,610	11.36	2.350
N	191,497	10.53	255,133	13.09	15,422	5.47	462,053	11.81	3.954
X	21,404	12.61	27,701	12.40	3,848	16.17	52,953	12.77	0.453
Y	27,173	5.39	25,387	10.74	13,599	28.97	66,161	13.30	0.566
Total Representatives:	1,636,962		1,981,394		374,517		3,992,890		34.175
Galvor Paris	2,159,494	5.45	2,038,117	6.23	627,439	16.14	4,825,050	7.31	41.298
Factory Sales	411,964	17.39	319,494	14.90	129,939	24.86	861,397	23.03	7.732
Comer S.A. (French Export Co.)	224,177	19.73	208,434	29.76			432,611	24.90	3.702
Importing Agents									
Franc Zone	240,422	14.02	285,280	15.75	51,328	20	525,702	14.97	4.500
Others	275,870	13.54	436,189	13.97			763,388	14.25	6.534

Sales to the Tronex Corp.

Tronex Sales in France	226,977	18.60	11,812	23.11			238,789	18.84		2.044
Tronex Franc Zone Sales	20,405	25.54	2,945	25.88			23,350	25.58		0.200
Tronex Export Sales	17,482	19.51	3,130	12.16			20,612	18.47		0.175
Grand Total (weighted average discount shown)										
shown	5,213,753	.68	5,286,795	10.61	1,183,223	16.29	11,683,789	10.38		100.00

Source: Company records.

Exhibit 4

1959 Sales Territory Map with Fortune Coefficients

* G.P.= Galvor Paris.

Exhibit 4

1961 Sales Territory Map with Fortune Coefficients

Exhibit 5

The Galvor Company

*M. Margaux's Description of Six Representatives.**

Monsieur N.

	Total Sales	Commissions	Fortune Coefficient
1959	345,289 NF	21,313 NF	36.08
1961	554,548 NF	31,943 NF	59.06
	Territory:	Strasbourg	
	Age:	58 years	
	Years with Galvor:	15	
	Percentage of Galvor products in total sales:	40%	

Annual sales potential (estimated) for his territory if he devoted 100% of his time to Galvor: 1,600,000 NF.

Technical knowledge: None
Qualifications: Personal charm
General remarks: Sells to wholesalers only. Does not try to sell to individuals. This is bad, because he has no direct contact with clients.

Monsieur L.

	Total Sales	Commissions	Fortune Coefficient
1959	515,603 NF	34,362 NF	63.34
1961	793,074 NF	54,546 NF	115.12
	Territory:	Lyon	
	Age:	40 years	
	Years with Galvor:	25	
	Percentage of Galvor products in total sales:	60%	

Annual sales potential (estimated) in his territory if he devoted 100% of his time to Galvor: 1,400,000 NF.

* Selected at random by researcher. Arranged in order of estimated sales potential for their territories.

Exhibit 5

(con)

Technical knowledge: None
Qualifications: A good salesman, knows his area well, dynamic.
General remarks: No technical knowledge. Whenever he gets a technical letter, he just sends a catalogue. Can't give technical advice to customers, we have to do it for him.

Monsieur H.

	Total Sales	Commissions	Fortune Coefficient
1959	379,612	24,079	71.54
1961	549,972	36,776	100.90
	Territory:	Marseilles	
	Age:	34 years	
	Years with Galvor:	12	
	Percentage of Galvor Products in total sales:	50%	

Annual sales potential (estimated) if he devoted 100% of his time to Galvor: 900,000 NF.

Technical knowledge: A little. Can demonstrate.
Qualifications: Good personality, aggressive, dynamic, some technical knowledge.
General remarks: Very good. Tries hard, and is a good Galvor man.

Monsieur M.

	Total Sales	Commissions	Fortune Coefficient
1959	232,877 NF	13,815 NF	85.61
1961	385,560 NF	22,973 NF	120.46
	Territory:	Toulouse	
	Age:	60 years	
	Years with Galvor:	18	
	Percentage of Galvor products in total sales:	50%	

Annual sales potential (estimated) if he devoted 100% of his time to Galvor: 600,000 NF.

Exhibit 5
(con)

Technical knowledge: Electrical engineer
Qualifications: Very dynamic, good technical knowledge, agreeable, well known.
General remarks: Hired an assistant to help him sell. Very good, has the Galvor spirit.

Monsieur E.

	Total Sales	Commissions	Fortune Coefficient
1959	128,783 NF	9,041 NF	40.49
1961	259,390 NF	18,208 NF	85.40
	Territory:	Dijon	
	Age:	50 years	
	Years with Galvor:	3	
	Percentage of Galvor products in sales:	35%	

Annual sales potential (estimated) if he devoted 100% of his time to Galvor: 450,000 NF.

Technical knowledge: None
Qualifications: Hard prospector
General remarks: Tries hard, but doesn't work in depth. In general, however, we are satisfied.

Monsieur C.

	Total Sales	Commissions	Fortune Coefficient
1960	109,195 NF	7,370 NF	NA
1961	149,776 NF	10,199 NF	84.92
	Territory:	Nice	
	Age:	42 years	
	Years with Galvor:	2 (previously 8 years as salesman for the Galvor representative in the Nice area).	

Exhibit 5
(con)

Percentage
of Galvor
Products
in total
sales: 30%

Annual sales potential (estimated) if he devoted 100% of his time to Galvor:
200,000 NF.

Technical knowledge:	Knows what electricity is, and can demonstrate.
Qualifications:	Some technical knowledge. Formerly with electrical wholesaler.
General remarks:	Hard worker, truly digs for business. Has to prospect hard because his area potential is small. In general, we are very satisfied with C.

The Galvor Company (C-2)

PRICING POLICY

Galvor prices were established by decision of the pricing committee, which consisted of M. Latour and M. Margaux (Commercial
Manager). As a basis for the price, the committee used a formula
consisting of three stages. The stages were (1) determination of a
product factory cost; (2) addition of an allowance for profit; and (3)
allowance for direct sales expenses, discounts, and sales taxes. The
price resulting from the above formula was almost always used without adjustment. Occasionally, however, MM. Latour and Margaux
increased or reduced the formula price, depending on the competitive
situation.

Determination of factory cost began by establishing standard
charges for material and direct labor. The cost of purchased materials
was obtained from the Manufacturing Department's bill of materials
for each product. M. Romanée, Manager of Manufacturing, arrived
at the direct labor cost by (a) setting up production techniques and
methods to be used in manufacturing and assembling a product, (b)
determining total standard hours needed to make a product, and (c)
applying the appropriate wage rates to these standard times. Total
factory cost was then arrived at by the following calculation:

> Cost of purchased material
> PLUS: 12% of purchased material cost to cover purchasing ex-
> pense
> PLUS: Direct labor cost
> PLUS: *310% of direct labor* (to cover all overhead)
> Equals: Factory cost.

The 12 percent figure for purchasing costs was an estimate of
actual costs. The 310 percent of direct labor, designed to cover "overhead," was intended to cover factory overhead, depreciation, research
and development costs, administrative expenses, miscellaneous

charges, and indirect selling costs. "I have been using this 310 percent for many years," said M. Latour, "and it seems to work out pretty well, so I see no reason to change it."

The allowance for 20 percent gross profit on factory cost was made simply by multiplying 120 percent times the factory cost previously computed.

The allowance for direct sales expense, discounts, and French sales tax was arrived at by multiplying the amount (120 percent of factory cost) by 1.63, in order to arrive at a final list price. This 1.63, called the "K" factor was arrived at in the following manner. First, the final list price (the catalogue price) was set at 100 percent for purpose of computation. Galvor gave discounts ranging up to 20 percent off list; it was assumed that the maximum (20 percent) discount would always be given. After the assumed discount, the proceeds to the company would be 80 percent of the list price (100 percent—20 percent discount).

Under French law, 20 percent of net sales had to be paid to the government as a sales tax. This meant that, after the assumed 20 percent discount, the sales tax would be an additional 16 percent (20 percent × 80 percent) off the list price. Thus the proceeds to the company after discounts and taxes would be 64 percent (100 percent list—20 percent discount—16 percent sales tax).

The final costs accounted for in the "K" factor were the commissions paid to representatives and the cost of operating Galvor Paris. The representatives were paid commissions which varied inversely with the discount given: the higher the discount, the lower the commission. At the assumed 20 percent discount, sales commissions would be approximately 4 percent. This was the most "expensive" Galvor sale possible. At lower discounts, higher commissions were paid, but not sufficiently high to equal the savings of lower discounts.

Thus the commission assumed was 2.56 percent (4 percent of 64 percent, since commissions were paid on the basis of net sales after discounts and taxes), which left 61.44 percent of list price to cover factory cost and profit on factory cost. This meant that if the amount (120 percent of factory cost) was multiplied by 1.63 (100 percent divided by 61.44 percent), after paying sales taxes, and the maximum discount-commission combination, Galvor would have left a sum exactly large enough to cover its computed factory cost and to provide pretax profits of 20 percent of factory cost. In reality, Galvor gave discounts averaging about 10 percent of list price, and direct sales expense (representatives' commissions plus the total operating cost of Galvor Paris) averaged 6 percent of net sales after discount and sales tax. As a result, Galvor's "K" factor of 1.63 actually contained some allowance for profit. The following table summarizes Galvor's pricing formula:

Purchased material + 12% purchasing
    expense   = A

Direct labor cost   = B

310% (B) to cover all overhead   = C

A + B + C   = (FC) (Factory cost)

FC + 20% (FC) for profit   = D

1.63 (D) to allow for sales taxes, com-
    missions, and discounts   = List price

In commenting on the "hidden profit allowance" in the "K" factor, M. Chambertin said: "It would appear that we are over-pricing our products by leaving in this hidden margin. However, we find that the 310 percent overhead allowance is inadequate to cover our actual overhead, so that the hidden profit allowance tends to compensate for the fact that our true factory costs are higher, on balance, than we compute. We produce over 150 models of 40 basic items, and I suspect that we are losing money on many of the slow-selling models. There are 'hidden costs' in carrying an extensive product line which we do not account for." As an illustration of such hidden costs, M. Chambertin mentioned the cost of maintaining parts inventories to build so many instruments and the increased production difficulties due to more complicated scheduling.

M. Margaux commented on the pricing system as follows: "It is no secret that most of our competitors overcharge for their products. The fact is, we overcharge less than they do, if at all. This is clearly indicated by the fact that nobody offers Galvor quality at our prices. Maybe this pricing method won't work in the future, but Galvor has always operated at capacity; we can sell everything we can produce."

When asked about competitive prices, M. Margaux replied: "We do have perhaps some competitors who sell similar equipment at a similar price, but generally only for a small part of our line. In our industry, especially in measuring instruments, there are almost literally no identical products. There is competition, but mostly in small, overlapping areas. An example of overlapping competition is our No. 462 pocket multimeter which we sell for 170 NF. In 1958, when we introduced this product, we received 133 orders. In 1959, we received 3,068 orders, and in 1960 orders increased to 4,546. The Alpha Corporation,[1] our largest competitor (1,000 employees), tried to move into this market in 1961 by introducing a similar model at exactly the same price as our Model 462. They have not had any success with their model except insofar as they are filling orders we can't supply. Our repair service is better than theirs, and much cheaper."

M. Latour made the following remarks about foreign competition: "The Japanese are starting to enter some markets with products competitive to ours. They produce a good-quality product, but to date they

1. Fictitious name.

have not offered precision as high as ours. Their prices are very low. I bought a Japanese multimeter with precision of 2½ percent and showed it at our management conference. We came up with the following price comparisons:

Item	NF
Galvor's catalogue multimeter (1 % precision)	100
Similar Japanese meter (2½ % precision)	26
Galvor's price (using price formula) for a comparable multimeter of 2½ %) precision	76

This comparison shocked us. We were quite relieved last year when a delegation of Japanese businessmen visited us and asked for rights to sell our products in Japan. I asked them how this would be possible when our products were so much more expensive. They showed me that Japanese products of similar precision and quality to Galvor products were actually priced higher in Japan. In my opinion the Japanese cannot manufacture quality and precision at low cost. Their forte is in mass production; when it comes to high-precision instruments such as our multimeters, their costs go up sharply. We sell precision and reliability. Our production is always small, and therefore we are not susceptible to mass-production competition.

"Production costs in the United States are so high that American companies should not be difficult competitors in the European market, except when they have a unique product. As tariffs go down, Germany will be a stronger competitor in the electronic area. However, we are not worried about German competition. We look at the opening of the Common Market as an opportunity."

ALLOCATION OF RESEARCH AND DEVELOPMENT COST

M. Chambertin had long argued that the simple electric products were being unfairly burdened with R&D (research and development) overhead. Electronic products, he said, should carry more overhead. To support his argument, in mid-1962 M. Chambertin analyzed cost data to determine the actual R&D and factory cost of the two Galvor product categories: electric equipment and electronic equipment. He discovered that the actual cost of R&D and factory overhead for electric products was 177 percent of direct labour. The same figure for electronic products was 245 percent. With these figures, M. Chambertin developed the tentative pricing system shown in Table 1.

The "final" price (not yet the list price) at the bottom of Table 1 is at that point directly comparable with the price of a product priced under the actual Galvor system before the multiplication, in the actual system, by the "K" factor of 1.63 to allow for discounts, sales taxes, and commissions.

Table 1

M. Chambertin's Tentative Pricing System

Electric Products	Electronic Products
Net cost of Purchased Material	Net cost of Purchased Material
Add: 11% of Purchased Material Cost to cover purchasing expense.	Add: 11% of Purchased Material Cost to cover purchasing expense.
Add: Direct Labor Cost (Y).	Add: Direct Labor Cost (Y).
Add: 177% of Y above to cover factory overhead and R&D costs.	Add: 245% of Y above to cover factory overhead and R&D costs.
Equals: Basic Manufacturing cost (BMC).	Equals: Basic Manufacturing Cost (BMC).
Add: 25% of BMC to cover Commercial and Administrative Overhead.	Add: 25% of BMC to cover Commercial and Administrative Overhead.
Equals: Total Product Cost (TPC) (125% BMC).	Equals: Total Product Cost (TPC) (125% BMC).
Add: 14% TPC to cover profit.	Add: 14% TPC to cover profit.
Equals: Final Price *before* allowance for Sales Taxes, commissions, and discounts (114% TPC).	Equals: Final Price *before* allowance for Sales Taxes, commissions, and discounts (114% TPC).

Source: Company officials.

The main difference between M. Chambertin's pricing system and the actual Galvor system was in the handling of overhead costs. Instead of taking 310 percent of direct labor to cover all overhead, M. Chambertin determined R&D and factory overhead for the electric and electronic product categories, and he made a separate allowance for commercial and administrative overhead. Because 12 percent of raw-material costs over-allowed for purchasing expense, he reduced this allowance to 11 percent, the actual cost to Galvor. The 14 percent profit allowance in Table 1 was arrived at empirically by M. Chambertin. He assumed that 1960 had been a normal year in terms of profitability. He then analyzed the 1960 profit and loss statement to find out how much the company earned on its operations excluding windfall losses and gains. The mechanics of what he did were very complex, but the end result was that, had his system been used to price 1960's sales, he believed that Galvor's total revenue and net profit would have been unchanged.

The impact of M. Chambertin's pricing system on several typical electric and electronic products is illustrated in Table 2.

Although M. Chambertin did not advocate an immediate change in Galvor's pricing system, he was convinced that eventually Galvor

Table 2

Galvor: Comparison of Actual with Theoretical Prices

Electric Products

| Catalogue Number | Product Description | Final List Price (in NF) | |
		List Price 1961	With Chambertin's System
400	Transclip	140.00	120.00
410	Electrician's multimeter	89.50	86.00
430	Multirange meter	250.00	234.00
453	Pocket multimeter	129.50	126.00
460	Multimeter	119.50	119.00
462	Pocket multimeter	170.00	142.00

Electronic Products

| Catalogue Number | Product Description | Final List Price (in NF) | |
		List Price 1961	With Chambertin's System
231	Wobuloscope	1,950.00	2,297.00
310	Tube checker	545.00	636.00
626	Precision impedance bridge	1,515.00	2,056.00
661	Vacuum-tube bridge	2,230.00	2,593.00
742	Vacuum-tube voltmeter	350.00	410.00
744	Vacuum-tube voltmeter	735.00	807.00
931	Standard signal generator	1,805.00	2,198.00
936	VHF generator	1,665.00	1,730.00

Source: Company records.

would be forced by competitive pressure to allocate its costs more realistically.

M. Latour, in commenting on M. Chambertin's pricing system said: "I have suspected that our electric products are too high-priced, and our electronic products are too low-priced. So what does this mean? Why should we lower our prices for multimeters and galvanos? At our current prices we can easily sell our entire production of electric products."

The Galvor Company (C-3)

PRODUCT POLICY

One of the major issues at Galvor was the question of catalogue size, or product diversity. As Table 1 shows, the company carried a broad line of measuring instruments, and there was disagreement among company officials as to whether this line was too broad.

M. Margaux summarized the commercial point of view as follows: "Galvor's fame is largely due to the diversity of products it sells. In the six years I've been here, I've noticed that our customers have changed from technicians to high-class engineers. Doors open to us now because of the size and diversity of our catalogue. People come to us because we can meet a broad range of needs. Also, those who are customers for only one of our products at the outset may later need other products that we sell. When this happens, they think of us immediately. There is a big difference, I suppose, in the profitability of our different products. However, we always sell at a profit, because a profit allowance is included in our pricing formula. We almost never make a product at an unprofitable price. When we do so, it is usually to accommodate a Government agency."

M. Chambertin, Administrative Director, disagreed with the proponents of a broad product line, saying, "One of our problems is that we make a number of products which have very small sales volumes. I am fairly certain that many of these products are unprofitable. The real reason we make these products is that M. Latour likes a fat catalogue and will sometimes add a new product to the line for reasons of prestige."

The technical point of view was expressed by M. Meursault, Manager of Electronic Research: "Our R&D effort is too spread out. In an attempt to build a thick catalogue, we have produced a large number of products which have little in common. Instead of specializing in a single product area, we have become so diversified that R&D we do for one type of product has little applicability for other products. For example, the men working on the FM generator are doing work that has no value to the transistor research team. Our effort is so divided that instead of having one company of 450 employees, we have three companies of 150 employees each. This has been all right so far, but what worries me is that in two years, the French measuring instrument industry will have enough capacity to serve all its customers. When that day comes, there will be a shakedown in the industry just like the one we are seeing in the French automobile industry today. Only the best companies will survive and, to be really good, a company must concentrate its effort."

M. Romanée, Manager of Manufacturing, remarked: "In my opinion, we could easily manufacture a broader product line if we could eliminate some problem areas within the company. In the first place, we have no Methods Staff, which loads me and my foremen with methods work. Secondly, liaison between R&D and manufacturing is not working smoothly, which further complicates life. Thirdly, the R&D groups keep modifying products which have been approved for production, and this means that our manufacturing activities are constantly being disrupted and schedules changed. When we can iron out these problems, we can handle a much broader product line, but at the moment even our present line is far too broad for smooth operations."

The most important products in the line in terms of volume were multimeters. As Table 1 shows, 15 multimeters accounted for 36.2% of Galvor's total 1961 sales. Table 2 gives the unit orders received for all types of multimeters which Galvor manufactured between 1954 and 1960, and the list price value of the 1960 orders.

One company official, upon examining Table 2, observed that five models (A, G, H, P, and R) accounted for over 75% of the total list price value of 1960 multimeter orders. (This ignores minor list price values for types I and N, for which data were not available.) He pointed out that by eliminating many of its small volume multimeters Galvor could reallocate its marketing, production, and R&D efforts over its large-volume items. This, he argued, would have three main effects: (a) a concentrated R&D effort would result in better product design for the remaining multimeters; (b) a smaller and better product line would be sold more intensively by the marketing organization, resulting in greater unit sales volumes; and (c) factory costs would be cut by longer and more efficient production runs. He concluded by saying, "I think that by gradually cutting our product line we could continue to increase our sales as much as we have in the past, if not more. The big difference would be in our profitability, which would be much greater due to lower factory costs."

M. Latour replied to this argument as follows: "I know that not all of my colleagues agree with me that we should carry so many multimeters, but I have four arguments in favor of keeping our line as

Table 1

The Galvor Product Line—1961

PRODUCT GROUP	Number of Models	Price Range (NF)	1961 Sales* (NF 000s)	Percentage of Total 1961 Sales
ELECTRIC				
PRODUCTS:	—	—	—	—
Multimeters	15	100–550	5,188	36.2%
Galvanometers	over 100	60–150	1,412	9.8%
Milliammeters	2	200–230	105	0.7%
Special Products	—	—	275	1.9%
Accessories and				
Spare Parts	—	—	795	5.5%
TOTAL ELECTRIC:			7,775	54.1%
ELECTRONIC				
PRODUCTS:	—	—	—	—
Tube- and Transis-				
tor Checkers and				
Analyzers	5	250–2340	881	6.1%
Generators:	—	—	—	—
Wobulator	2	700–1800	67 ⎫	
Pattern gen'tor	1	1100	153 ⎪	
Audio "	1	680	156 ⎪	
Service	1	670	191 ⎪	
HF	2	1850–2250	1,073 ⎬ →	15.7%
VHF	2	1665	127 ⎪	
UHF	1	n.a.	227 ⎪	
AM and FM	3	1200–2000	245 ⎪	
Marker	2	800–2000	11 ⎭	
Total Generators:	15	680–2250	—	—
Wobuloscopes	2	1320–2050	986	6.9%
Oscilloscopes	3	1115–2200	321	2.3%
VTVM's **	3	365–1300	781	5.4%
Impedance Bridges	3	n.a.	417	2.9%
Vacuum Tube Bridge	1	3800	126	0.9%
Accessories and				
Spare Parts	—	—	344	2.4%
Equipment Racks	—	—	11	nil
TOTAL ELECTRONIC:	—	—	6,117	42.6%
SALES TO TRONEX:	—	—	192	1.3%

Table 1
(continued)

EQUIPMENT REPAIRS:	—	—	281	2.0%
TOTAL:	—	—	14,365	100.0%

Source: Company officials.
* Including all taxes.
** Vacuum-tube Voltmeters.

Table 2

Unit Orders Received for Galvor Multimeters, 1954–1960, and
List Price Value of These Orders in 1960

Model	1960 List Price (NF)	Orders Received (Units)							List Price Value of 1960 Order (in NF)
		1954	1955	1956	1957	1958	1959	1960	
A	140	1591	1484	2232	2195	2227	3000	4866	681,240
B	304	—	—	—	—	—	130	434	131,936
C	100	243	647	1071	1347	1530	1813	1565	156,500
D	—	465	147	247	412	2	—	—	—
E	370	200	221	84	335	298	349	402	148,740
F	—	22	1	—	—	—	—	—	—
G	255	988	2036	2871	3347	2851	3056	2887	736,185
H	375	—	—	—	—	2	253	869	325,875
I	na	—	—	—	—	—	30	25	na
J	212	67	57	106	53	135	142	217	46,004
K	220	236	85	369	230	200	267	122	26,840
L	—	—	26	—	120	—	—	—	—
M	273	—	193	310	386	365	377	717	195,741
N	na	—	—	—	125	—	150	386	na
O	136	—	—	—	1	678	985	1384	188,224
P	124	6425	7748	9516	11034	9961	10411	11387	1.411,988
Q	—	—	—	—	—	—	100	—	—
R	170	—	—	—	—	133	3068	4546	772,820
S	250	—	—	—	—	—	1500	—	—
T	na	1144	809	1370	1663	1096	895	762	—
U	535	—	—	—	—	1	146	593	317,225
V	380	—	—	—	—	—	—	68	25,840

Total List Price Value of 1960 Orders:	5,165,158

Source: Company records. na: not available.

broad as it now is. First of all, I want our customers to think of Galvor as the company which can provide *any* type of multimeter, not just the few most common ones. I want engineers and technicians to identify Galvor and measurement as being synonymous. Second, I want our customers to be able to come to Galvor for any multimeter, even if an uncommon type; if one of our customers has to go to a competitor for a special multimeter, maybe he'll try some other products of that competitor, instead of dealing exclusively with us. Third, if we didn't offer every type of multimeter, some of our competitors would be encouraged to try to fill demands we weren't meeting; they would start making these special multimeters, and I don't like to give my competitors such encouragement. And fourth, it doesn't cost us much to do the research on these special types, and they don't require expensive tooling. We indeed do devote our main efforts to the high-volume types; it would be unthinkable to do otherwise. So it doesn't cost us much to make these special types. And remember, since we allocate overhead on the basis of the amount of direct labor used for a given product, we always make a profit. I admit that if we made these special types in larger quantities, we could lower the labor hours on some of them, but since we put overhead right into labor, we always make a profit. When all is said and done, however, I will be interested to hear what students of business have to say about this question."

PRODUCT QUALITY

M. Latour remarked, "Our policy on product quality is very important to us. As I have mentioned, from Galvor's early days we have continually upgraded the quality of our products. Today all Galvor products are of very high quality, and they are very reasonably priced as well. On my recent trip around the world, (which occurred during March, 1962), I visited a number of measuring-instrument plants, especially some of the famous ones in the U. S. I came back from this trip convinced that Galvor is today in a position to aim for being one of the top four or five companies in the world in measuring instruments. This will only be possible if our quality is impeccable, and I have urged all our employees to concentrate on quality above all.

"As you know, in 1957 we set up the TRONEX Corporation to manufacture measuring instruments of modest price and quality. But this decision was in no way inconsistent with our aim to make Galvor first class in quality, quite to the contrary. I set up TRONEX for two main reasons. First, and most important, I wanted to discourage our competitors from trying to undercut our prices for Galvor instruments with their low-price and low-quality equipment. Two of these competitors, the MU and SIGMA [1] Corporations, were at that time especially aggressive in pushing their equipment, and our salesmen were beginning to complain about this. The instruments manufactured by these two firms were of cheap quality, but they were nonetheless taking some sales away from us. I thought that, by starting our own company in their specialty, we might dissuade them from trying to make further inroads into our business. The second reason I started TRONEX was to introduce a line which might, some day, become a major part of our business. I foresaw that we might eventually sell TRONEX products in kit form to reach an even broader market.

"As time passed, we found that MU and SIGMA were not causing us serious problems, so today that reason for TRONEX's existence has disappeared. I am afraid that, at the moment, we all tend to regard TRONEX as a 'poor relation' of Galvor. I am the only one here who thinks it worthwhile to keep TRONEX alive; it would have disappeared long ago if I weren't president of the company. And I must admit that we haven't had the time we need to give TRONEX a real push. But I am maintaining the corporation nonetheless, because some day it may be valuable to us. Perhaps eventually we will give it a complete organization of its own, and set it up in a plant away from Bordeaux, where TRONEX can operate independently of Galvor influence; this is how our INDICA S.A. operation is run in Paris. Besides, with our pricing system, we make money on every TRONEX product we sell, so why not keep it going?"

Selecting New Products

When asked what criteria were used to select new products for manufacture at Galvor, M. Latour replied, "We try to find a product in an area where we have a strong technical background, because without this background we cannot really compete. Secondly, having found such a product, we try to determine whether we can sell it in profitable quantities. This means finding out (a) if the total market is large enough to justify our entry, and (b) how much of the total market we can capture for ourselves. We must, however, also pay attention to customer demands. We may develop products for customers without full confidence in the commercial prospects for these products.

"The future growth and development of the electronic industry will continuously open new product opportunities for us. For example, the complicated and extremely accurate generator which we are building for the Air Force is an entirely new product that was unnecessary before the jet plane came into use.

1. Fictitious names.

"We try to be first with products and features, and we continuously watch competitors to maintain this lead. Trade shows are very useful in this regard. I attend all the important shows (Paris, New York, Hanover etc.) from the minute they start until they end. Our chief engineers attend to find out what other manufacturers are doing, and to look for parts that we might use.

"Generally speaking, the representatives are not a good source of product ideas. Usually, they wait until a competitive product is hurting their sales before they report anything to us. Our sales engineers are far more useful, for they react to changes, demands, and needs faster than the representatives. They have a real technical curiosity to find out what is going on and what is needed. The foreign agents are, for the most part, too far out of touch with overall market consideration to be of much help in product development.

"At the management meetings when **we** are considering a product we discuss what quantities might be sold. Occasionally we have the Paris salesforce conduct a survey. Then we roughly try to determine what we could sell the product for, and what it would cost to make, and how much we might have to invest. After these considerations, we discuss the product until we come to an unanimous decision on whether to adopt it.

"After deciding upon a new product, we develop a prototype model. This prototype will be identical in all respects to the mass-produced instrument. If we have done all of the research needed to develop a finished prototype, it is almost 100% sure that we will go into production of the instrument. After an engineer has spent one or two years developing a product, it is a great blow to him if the product is never put on the market. Occasionally I have to veto production. An example of this was a photoelectric cell we developed. After the prototype was completed, we discovered that it would have to be sold at double the price of comparable models already available in the market. It was clear that we would have to drop our cell.

"We do not make elaborate cost calculations when we are considering a product. We determine costs in the usual manner—by estimating direct labor costs and allocating overhead on this basis and adding in the cost of the necessary purchased materials and parts. The result of this system is that the small, low-priced units sold in volume are over-priced, while the large individual units, which sometimes require years of development work, are underpriced. This system has worked up to now, however, and I am not going to bring in a bevy of accountants until I have to, which will be when the market gets much tougher than it is now. We make no payback or return on investment calculations."

M. Meursault, Manager of Electronic Research, when questioned upon product policy, emphasized the importance of market demands in guiding preliminary research efforts. He remarked, "I try to get to

Paris often enough to visit top-notch engineers in order to find out what kinds of new instruments they would like to have. I ask them about the physical specifications of the instruments, the characteristics they want to measure and how they would like to measure them, and what degrees of precision is required. After gathering this information I estimate the requirements for such an instrument. If it appears that the instrument is of a type for which we are well equipped to do research, and which is suitable to our manufacturing operation, I will make a rough cost and price estimate. I then return to the engineers I first queried and ask them if they would be interested in an instrument with X precision, Y specifications, and costing Z NF. This is the kind of market research which I find most useful, and it can only be done by an engineer who is intimately familiar with current technology. A man doing this job has to be able to distinguish between the usual customer request, which is simply a 'one-shot' application, and the unusual request which indicates a wide-spread new need for an instrument.

"As you know, up to the present time we have tried to sell Galvor products to all customer sectors, from the home electronic hobbyist up to the French Air Force. This has been a very sound policy while we have been building the company, but in recent months I have become convinced that, for the future, we should concentrate all our efforts on a narrower range of customers, rather than attempting to sell to all. More specifically, I think that Galvor's true vocation will be to equip manufacturers of electronic goods with measuring and control equipment. So far, this group of customers has been only one segment of our business, but this sector is going to grow enormously in coming years, and we can become dominant in this sector if we start now. For this reason, in my thinking about new products, I keep in the back of my mind the idea that ultimately we will concentrate on instruments for the electronic industries."

Ideas for new products came to Galvor mainly from two sources. The most frequent source was a specific customer request for a special modification of an existing instrument, or for an entirely new instrument which did not yet exist. Galvor received hundreds of such requests each year, either in writing or in interviews with customers, and there was a considerable problem of sorting out such requests. Most requests were for instruments so specialized that there would be no real market for the product. Company officials were always looking for the less common request, one which signalled a major new demand which Galvor could profitably fulfill. The second source of new product ideas was the Galvor executives themselves, especially the engineers, who in the course of their talks with various people in electronics might hear of some new problem which was as yet unsolved. For example, in the mid-1950's Galvor executives heard from many customers about the problem of defective transistors. Because transistor sales were growing rapidly, company officials began to think about how to develop a transistor checker. In this case, the engineers worked only with an idea of what had to be done, not with a set of specifications submitted by the customer.

A Proposed New Product

"For about three years," remarked M. Latour, "I have been asking my engineers, 'How about making a digital voltmeter?' But they kept putting me off saying it was unfeasible, so I did not press the point. But when I was at the I.R.E.[2] Show in New York last month, (March, 1962), I noticed that in about half of the booths there was a digital voltmeter on display. Everybody is making them, and I am beginning to be a little more concerned about whether we should get into this area; it may be the coming thing."

A digital voltmeter (DVM) was a measuring instrument which, like the conventional vacuum tube voltmeter (VTVM), measured voltages by means of electronic circuitry. But whereas the VTVM was read by observing the position of a moving needle on a dial, the DVM had on its face a panel in which numbers appeared and indicated the size of the voltage being measured. These numbers were typically 2–4 cm. in height. Another significant difference between the two was in precision. A VTVM usually had a precision on the order of plus-or-minus 1%–1.5%. A DVM was accurate to within .01%–.001%, or about 100 to 1,000 times more precise than a VTVM.

As for the comparative advantages of the DVM. M. Meursault mentioned these facts: First, it was much easier to read a DVM than a VTVM. A DVM could be read from a distance of several meters, whereas a VTVM had to be read from a distance of 50 cm. or less. Furthermore, an unskilled person could read a DVM with ease, while some training was required to operate a VTVM. On many DVM's, the decimal point was automatically positioned when the voltage measurement was displayed; on a VTVM, the reader had to have some idea of the size of the voltage being measured, in order to read the actual voltage on the appropriate scale. VTVM's often had seven or more scales on their faces. The next most important advantage of the DVM, M. Meursault asserted, was its extreme precision, which was useful in some applications. He added, however, that precision requirements on the order of .01%–.001% were unusual and that a VTVM's precision sufficed for most applications.

A third advantage of the DVM was its suitability for incorporation in control systems. For example, a machine could be linked to a DVM, and the DVM could then be used to control the machine's operation:

2. The Institute of Radio Engineers (IRE) included a large number of U. S. electronic engineers; the Institute sponsored an annual Trade Show where many electronic manufacturers displayed their new products.

if voltage were from 7.500 volts to 9.500 volts, say, the machine could be speeded up or otherwise given commands. This sort of operating control was impossible, as a rule, with a VTVM. Related to this function was the ability of the DVM to accept or reject within precise error limits. A DVM could be connected to a scale on a conveyor which was carrying, for example, cans of foods. The weight registered by the scale could be expressed in terms of voltage on the DVM, and the DVM could signal when an underweight can was sent through. This was especially valuable in the case of untrained personnel, who could easily read several digits on a DVM, but who might have difficulty (and eyestrain) in trying to make the same readings on a VTVM. M. Meursault added that, in general, the DVM was useful for making rapid readings and decisions based on these readings, especially where people without electronic training were involved.

As for the advantages of the VTVM over the DVM, M. Meursault cited two. Most important, the VTVM was much cheaper. The typical VTVM cost from 500 to 1,000 NF, depending mostly on its precision and flexibility. The DVM cost from about 2,500 to 5,000 NF, again depending on its precision and flexibility. A second major advantage of the VTVM was its 'analogue' feature. The swinging needle of the VTVM exactly traced the speed and range of voltage changes, so that by observing this swing the electronic technician or engineer could make very precise adjustments and gain considerable insight into the workings of the system on which voltage measurement was being performed. The DVM had no analogue feature; it was impossible to observe the rate and degree of change of a continuously varying voltage.

As of early 1962, there were several DVM's available on the French market, but all of them were made by foreign firms or by French subsidiaries of foreign firms; none was made by any of the French measuring instrument companies which Galvor officials thought of as competitors. Galvor had no information available as to the total size of the French market for DVM's but knew there was a very active sale of this product in the United States.

M. Meursault said, "I don't think we ought to make a DVM, mainly because this instrument is useful mostly outside the electronic industry. An electronic engineer or technician will generally prefer to use a VTVM, because of its analogue feature. Since I think we ought to concentrate on the electronic industry in the future, I can't see much future for us in making a DVM. I am also opposed to the DVM because it would not fit into our distribution network very well. Nonetheless, I have made a preliminary estimate of the cost to develop a DVM at Galvor." (M. Meursault's estimate is found in Table 3.) "The 250% of straight salary as an allowance for overhead is just a rough estimate, but I think it gives a fair idea of what our overhead really is. Now, you can see that I estimate about 54,000 NF to develop two prototypes of a DVM, but engineers tend to be a bit optimistic, and I

Table 3

Estimated Development Cost of a Digital Voltmeter

Mockup Development Costs	Cost
6 mos. R&D work by research technician	7,800 NF *
2 mos. work by lab. technicians who would help the research technician to make a preliminary mockup of the DVM.	2,000 NF *
Overhead on the above research time, at 250% of straight salary (2.5 × 9800 NF)	24,500 NF
New laboratory instruments needed for research on this project.	2,000 NF
Purchased DVM made by some other firm, to give an idea of how others do the job.	3,000 NF
TOTAL COST TO DEVELOP MOCKUP	39,300 NF
Prototype Development Costs	
1 month of designer's time (to design a prototype from the mockup)	1,000 NF *
1 month of prototype builder's time	1,000 NF *
1 month of clerk's time (to draw up papers for manufacturing the DVM)	1,000 NF *
Purchased components used to make one mockup and two prototypes	3,750 NF
Overhead on time of designer, prototype builder, and clerk (250% × 3000 NF)	7,500 NF
TOTAL PROTOTYPE DEVELOPMENT COSTS	14,250 NF
TOTAL DEVELOPMENT COST	53,550 NF

* These were the straight salaries paid these men for the period of time indicated.

am probably no exception. Let's say that a more realistic figure might be around 60,000 NF. After spending this money, we would have two finished prototypes and the necessary manufacturing plans to put these prototypes into production. As to the time for this project, my cost estimate shows a total of about 9 months: the first six months for R&D, then three successive months for designing, building, and writing the manufacturing documents for the prototypes. In reality, the R&D would probably not be done in one concentrated six-month period, but spread out over an interval of perhaps a year, and the same slowing down would occur in the prototype stage. Thus it would take us about 1½ to two years to get a prototype, after which it would be another 9 months before the first models would come off the production line. Finally, I estimate that we would sell this instrument for a list price of about 3,000 NF, which would be a fair price for a good instrument such as we would try to design.

"We have the background to do this research project, and the DVM would fit in reasonably well with our other manufacturing operations. I think we could cover our R&D costs of 60,000 NF by selling from 100 to 200 DVM's at 3,000 NF each, and I think we could sell this many. I am nevertheless not very enthusiastic about doing this job. First of all, I don't yet see any strong market for this instrument in France, and merely covering our R&D costs is not worth the effort. We could spend this R&D time better, I think, on another instrument which would have a wide appeal. We don't have many industrial customers outside the electronic industry, and it is [sic] precisely these non-electronic manufacturers who would be the best customers for a DVM. Our sales network is not set up to concentrate on non-electronic manufacturers, nor do I think it should be. We ought to concentrate on electronic manufacturers, so I disagree with M. Latour: we should not develop this instrument, at least at this time."

In commenting on M. Meursault's arguments, M. Latour said, "Well, I don't want to force my engineers to study something which doesn't interest them, and I know that their technical backgrounds are very strong, but I still am not convinced that we shouldn't make a DVM. Judging from what I saw, it's one of the coming things in instrumentation in the U.S."

The Galvor Company (E)

THE GALVOR INVENTORY CONTROL SYSTEM

"I am not happy with our present inventories, especially of raw materials and purchased parts," said M. Latour in commenting on Galvor's current stock levels early in 1962. "Whenever I ask why our stock of a given item is so high, I get a wonderful explanation. But this fact remains: I would like to have two months' supply of purchases on hand, not what we now have. One of these days I am going to fix this inventory problem, and I'll tell you how: I'll hire a strong man, give him a pistol, and set him on our receiving platform. He'll be told how much we have on hand of every item, and when a supplier tries to deliver more than we need (a two months' supply), he'll refuse the excess."

M. Chambertin stated, "I disagree with M. Latour. We don't need a man with a pistol, we need a man with a machine gun, because there are so many different problem areas in our inventory control system."

The Nature of Galvor Inventories

Galvor's purchases were in three major categories: (1) wholly finished components, such as electronic tubes, to be mounted directly in the instruments; (2) partially finished products which would undergo further manufacturing operations at Galvor; and (3) raw materials, such as sheet metal, where all manufacturing operations were done by the company. In 1961, of Galvor's total purchases from outside suppliers, 8% were raw materials, 87% were partially and wholly finished products (mostly components), and 5% were products to be resold directly to Galvor customers, such as leather carrying cases for multimeters. These percentages had not, company officials stated, changed much in recent years.

About 15,000 different parts were used in making the products in the Galvor line; some 10,000 of these were purchased in a partially or wholly finished condition. The typical Galvor electric product, such as a multimeter, contained 2–3 times as much purchase content as direct labor content, while the typical electronic product contained 3–5 times as much purchase content as direct labor. This was due to the fact that most electronic products contained a considerable number of relatively complicated and expensive components, such as electronic tubes and transistors, while electric products generally contained few sophisticated components. In 1961, purchased parts accounted for almost 50% of total manufacturing cost, and raw materials accounted for an additional 5%.[1]

Table I shows the size of Galvor inventories in recent years as a percentage of net sales.

Table 1

Galvor Inventories at Year End as a Percent of Net Sales

Year	Raw Materials and Purchased Parts	Work in Process	Finished Products	Total
1956	13.3%	4.3%	3.4%	21.0%
1957	9.5	3.8	4.1	17.4
1958	12.0	8.5	7.3	27.8
1959	15.4	9.2	4.2	28.8
1960	10.7	9.5	6.6	26.8
1961	11.5	7.5	8.0	27.0

Computed from company records by IMEDE staff.

Table 2 gives the percentage relationship of these same three inventory categories to total assets since 1956.

Pricing of Inventories

Galvor's inventory of purchased materials and parts was priced annually when the physical inventory was taken. (This inventory was taken soon after the close of Galvor's fiscal year on December 31st.) The price of a given item was set by estimating what the recent price of the part had been and what it was likely to be in the near future. The cost of freight was not added into this price. For example, if a given tube had recently been purchased for about 5 NF per piece, and if it appeared that the price would remain there for some time to come, the price was set at 5 NF in valuing the inventory of this tube.

1. Computed from figures in Table 7 of *The Galvor Company* (A).

Table 2

Galvor Inventories at Year End as a Percent of Total Assets

Year	Raw Materials and Purchased Parts	Work in Process	Finished Products	Total
1956	17.6%	5.7%	4.5%	27.8%
1957	13.7	5.5	5.9	25.1
1958	15.3	10.8	9.3	35.4
1959	20.5	12.2	5.6	38.3
1960	14.2	12.6	8.8	35.6
1961	15.8	10.3	11.0	37.1

Computed from company records by IMEDE staff.

The pricing of the work-in-process inventory proceeded by adding together, for a given instrument, the total purchased parts actually installed in the instrument (without purchasing cost), plus an allowance of 7.92 NF per estimated hour of direct labor to cover direct labor cost and overhead charges.

Finished instruments were priced in a similar manner to that for work-in-process, the only difference being that, for a finished product, the exact direct labor hours were known. Thus, a finished product was priced at the cost of the purchases it contained, plus 7.92 NF per hour of direct labor. Purchasing cost was not included in the calculation.

As can be seen from an analysis of Galvor's true product costs, the method of pricing work-in-process and finished goods made insufficient allowance for the total overhead costs applicable to each product. The inventory pricing method allowed 7.92 NF for each hour of direct labor. Since the average hourly direct labor cost was, company officials estimated, about 3 NF, this left about 5 NF per direct labor hour to cover all overhead, or 100% of direct labor cost. Galvor officials estimated that true overhead was something in excess of 310% of direct labor charges.

Inventory Turnover

In 1961 Galvor used, in order to make the products which it sold, about 3,660,000 NF worth of purchased materials and parts. (This figure does not contain purchasing expense.) At the end of that year, the company valued its inventory of such materials at about 1,387,000 NF (again not including purchasing expense). Assuming, as company officials said was correct, that both parts used and the parts valued in inventory were costed on the same bases, it can be seen that in 1961 the company turned over its inventory of purchases approximately 2.64 times (the result of dividing 3,660,000 by 1,387,000). In other terms, the company was maintaining, at the end of 1961, approximately a four-and-one-half months' supply of such materials.

In the same year, the company's total factory cost, or cost of goods sold, was about 7,074,000 NF. The finished goods inventory on hand at the end of the year was valued at 963,000 NF. This inventory was turned over 7.35 times in 1961 (7,074,000 divided by 963,000). It follows that, in 1961, the inventory at year's end represented about 1.6 months' cost of goods sold.

Inventory Control Procedure for Purchased Materials and Parts

Two systems of inventory control were employed by Galvor for purchased materials and parts. If a given item was used for only one product, its inventory was controlled by the 'Program' system. If it was used in more than one product, it was controlled by the 'Mini' system. Of total 1961 purchases, 72% were made under the Program system and 28% under the Mini system.

The *Program System* was based on the production schedule prepared by Madame Bollinger for a two-month period beginning eight months hence. Upon receipt of this schedule by M. Gevrey (Assistant to M. Romanée for Production Scheduling), he and his clerks drew up a list of the parts which would have to be purchased to fulfill the program's requirements. Some of these parts would be needed not only for the planned manufacturing, but also for making repairs and for sale as spare parts. Accordingly, the stock of a given part under the Program system was determined not only by the production schedule's requirements, but also by an estimate made by the appropriate inventory clerk of the extra parts which would be required to cover repairs and sales of spare parts. These latter two needs were determined largely on the basis of past experience.

Under the *Mini System*, the stock of a part was set at a four months' supply. This period was based on an allowance of three months to cover the time from placing an order until delivery, plus a one month safety margin. All parts controlled under this system used the same four months' minimum stock level, except for a very few where lead time was known to be significantly longer than three months; in these few cases, a larger minimum stock was maintained.

The Reorder Point

The two inventory control systems described above determined the reorder points. For those stocks controlled by the Program system, materials and parts were ordered as needed every two months. For parts controlled by the Mini system, pieces were reordered when the supply was down to the minimum four months' level. In practice, according to M. Chambertin, nearly all parts were ordered about every two months, regardless of the system of control used. No formal study had been made of the order frequency for individual parts.

The company's programs did not vary significantly with the value of the item stocked. While lead times for ordering might vary from four weeks to six months, as far as was known there was no relationship between the item's value and the lead time necessary for ordering and receipt. Some complicated and expensive parts, which were manufactured outside to special order, might have higher lead times, on the average, than other parts. Purchases from suppliers were never on a contractual basis, but were made by individual orders. The cost range for various parts ranged from about .001 NF to a realistic maximum of about 20 NF. A few parts might cost as much as 100 NF or so. Cost of the part played no role in its treatment. No data existed on the cost of carrying various items in inventory. In this connection, M. Chambertin stated: "Because we have had for many years plenty of ready cash, with no particularly good alternative use for it, this cost has not seemed important to us. We are usually not borrowing and paying interest, so it's not worth figuring out."

Virtually no parts were individually analyzed, although up-to-date inventory records were kept for every part. M. Chambertin remarked that standardized parts could be much more widely used in Galvor products than was being done. Mme. Bollinger commented, "The two steps we could take which would most cut down our inventory are: increased standardization, and individual minimum stock levels for Mini-controlled items."

M. Romanée remarked that, in general, there were sufficient stocks on hand to insure a steady manufacturing operation. He continued, "As long as we will ultimately be able to use it, it's no terrible handicap or error to keep a part in stock for six months, especially if lack of a certain part can delay finishing a very valuable product for delivery. But our engineers are modifying products so continually, and changing the necessary parts as they go along, that we end up with lots of pieces which we'll never use. The storeroom is full of such pieces—God only knows how many."

Storeroom Facilities and Procedures

Separate storerooms existed for finished instruments and for purchased materials and parts. Both storerooms were kept under lock and key. The man in charge of the parts and raw materials storeroom, a foreman, was, according to M. Chambertin, "Pretty good—he knows all about every product we make and the parts required, but since he has nothing to do with ordering, he has not the responsibility and importance often enjoyed by his counterpart in other firms. He is not brilliant, but he works 65 hours a week, and he knows exactly where every part is and how many of each we have in stock—he'd be a difficult man to replace, almost impossible.

"One problem we have is that sometimes parts are taken out of stock to make repairs or to sell as spare parts, when we have only enough on hand for manufacturing requirements. When this happens we are out of luck; we may not be able to finish our production run of an important product until a new supply comes in. To avoid this eventuality, the ordering clerks load us up on parts to make sure we won't run out, and inventory goes up way too much."

Parts and materials were issued from the storeroom only upon receipt of a ticket, which the appropriate workman and his foreman both initialed. This ticket listed the code number of the piece being requisitioned, the units needed, the purpose of these pieces (i.e., for a given production run, or for repairs, or for sale as spare parts), and the date. The storeroom accumulated throughout the day all of these tickets, and the next morning the tickets were taken to the inventory records rooms and used to adjust the stock cards for the appropriate pieces.

Maintenance of Inventory Records

The inventory records for all purchased parts and materials were kept in files in a special room set aside for the purpose. Each item had its own stock card; the cards were coded in different colors to distinguish between various categories of materials.

The card, when properly used, showed how many units were on hand, how many of these units were necessary for each of the production schedules which had been processed, how many units were on order, how many of the units on hand were available for resale or making repairs, and if appropriate, the reorder point (in number of units) for those items controlled by the Mini system. Every time pieces were put into inventory (through receipt of an order) or taken out (through requisition from the storeroom), the card was updated, so that at all times it theoretically showed the company's exact stock and the availability of this stock for different purposes.

Causes Cited for Excess Inventory

Only recently had Galvor officials become concerned with the problem of inventory control. In commenting on the problem, M. Chambertin stated, "I am not convinced that M. Latour fully understands the dimensions of our inventory problem. He thinks that it is a simple thing, that it has only one cause. The other day I took a walk in the woods, and I came up with 17 reasons why we have too much inventory. When I showed this list to Romanée, he added another cause, and Mme. Bollinger added eight more. I have just prepared a memorandum which discusses the problem and gives these 26 causes." M. Chambertin's memorandum is reproduced below.

MEMORANDUM ON INVENTORIES

I: Introduction

"We must not underestimate the long-term problems which can arise from having our cash tied up in inventories of all types. We can measure the extent of this problem by noting that from Jan. 1, 1960, to Dec. 31, 1961, we had within 10% as much money tied up in inventories as we spent in erecting the new factory addition. This has created some problems in our cash budgeting for 1962, since aside from our investment in the new plant (only 60% of which was covered by outside credit), we have needed funds to pay for an apparently irreversible increase in our inventories.

"The rise in our inventories is almost exactly parallel to our sales increase, and as a result we must note that it would be difficult to increase sales if our inventories did not rise at the same rate. All the same, even if we accept this relationship between sales and stocks, we should be certain that the inventory curve, no matter how exactly it follows sales, does not start from a bad base point— this error, if made, would be difficult to correct. Thus, we ought to do at least a summary analysis of our inventory position.

"Based on our balance sheet as of Dec. 31, 1961, we have on hand a 1.5 months' supply of finished instruments, about 1.5 to 2 months' worth in process, and 4 months' supply of purchased materials. We must remember that these are only overall figures, and that we can easily have, in finished goods, no stock at all of some items and be vastly over-stocked in others. Accordingly, one can easily make a commercial error in holding back deliveries and uselessly tying up for months capital which could be better used in productive investments.

"On this last point, we can make four important observations:
—The growth of the company is the fruit of its investments in physical plant and research.
—Management's most difficult problem is in choosing the proper investments.
—Return on investment ought not to be below 20% (or, at worst, 15%).
—According to most experts, the cost of carrying inventory is 1% per month, or 12% per year.

"Which four observations lead to the conclusion that:
—1,000,000 NF invested in inventories has a value, one year later, of 880,000 NF.

—The same 1,000,000 NF, invested rationally, would grow to 1,200,000 NF within the same year's time.

"The solution of any difficult problem demands an intensive preliminary study. It therefore seems wise to recapitulate the reasons for which our inventories have been rising.

II. Reasons for Increase in Our Inventories

A: Stocks of Purchased Materials and Parts and Stocks of Work in Process.

Increases Due to Our Suppliers:

1: The quantity delivered is larger than ordered. (We even find this happening in the case of our own subsidiary, Indica, S. A.)

2: Delivery ahead of schedule. (We usually take care of this problem by holding back payment.)

Increases Due to Our Purchasing Department:

3: We increase the theoretically necessary quantity if it is too small. (This often occurs when ordering metal bar and tube stock.)

4: We increase the order at the supplier's request.

5: We increase the order to avoid paying a premium for very small orders.

Increases Due to Our Scheduling and Inventory Control Departments:

(under the MINI system):

6: A tendency to round off (upwards) the number to be ordered.

7: The fact that all parts have a minimum stock level of four months' supply, when for many parts much less is needed.
(under the PROGRAM system):

8: The impossibility of finding out how many have been set aside for sale as spare parts, which quantity must be added to the number ordered for production runs, causes the clerk to buy too many in order to avoid running out. This observation is equally true of parts needed for repairs, and also to replace parts wasted during the manufacturing process.

Increases Due to Production Scheduling Procedure:

9: Failure to use parts which have been ordered, when the initial production schedule is changed after orders have been placed on the basis of its requirements. Schedules are changed in this manner when we find that our sales forecast, on which the original production schedule was based, is too optimistic for a given product, so we change the schedule in order to make less of that product.

Increases Due to Manufacturing:

10: We are steadily increasing the number of types of instruments which are in process at a given time; this is probably unavoidable as our company expands.

11: As the number of types in process increases, we find that we have to keep more and more parts on hand in the storeroom.

12: The time during which an instrument is in manufacture some-times is unusually long. This often happens if the manufacturing process is interrupted for some reason.

Increases Due to Our Research Groups:

13: We throw away parts we have ordered. This occurs when the Research Groups modify an instrument after we have bought the parts to make it, and when they label this modification 'Top Priority'. Top Priority means that the change *must be made immediately,* regardless of what parts have already been bought.

14: When we get a 'Second Priority' modification, it allows us to finish production of all series we have started. However, we may have ordered surplus parts for sale as spares and for use in repairs, and this surplus becomes valueless.

15: When we make a modification, it usually involves not just one part, but an entire group of parts which depend on one another. Thus, a minor modification may result in our having to abandon many parts.

16: Since we have no expert on product standardization, diversity of parts is our law.

17: When a new product is insufficiently prepared for manufactur-ing, this product may spend an unusually long time in the manufacturing process. This is the case of Model 404, for example, where the first series has not yet been finished, al-though we have already parts on hand for the second and third series.

Increases Due to Our Commercial Service:

18: We sometimes agree to manufacture for one customer a new product type which has no commercial value except for this customer.

19: Our policy of repairing even our very old models means that we have to stock parts which cannot be used for any other purpose.

20: Our catalogue is steadily expanding. This policy, which we will not discuss here, obviously bears on all the 19 reasons pre-viously cited in this memorandum.

B: Stocks of Finished Instruments and Accessories

1: Our sales of a product may be far below the forecasted level on which the manufacturing program was based.

2: Our Manufacturing Department may request the right to make units of an instrument, in a given production run, than the Com-mercial Service wants; this is done in order to make economic production runs.

3: Delivery of products we are holding in stock may be slowed down through no fault of ours. For example, delivery of an export license may be retarded.

4: Sometimes we keep in stock instruments for special customers, when we could easily sell these instruments elsewhere.

5: Since in large unit orders (especially from the Government), we may have to pay a penalty if we deliver late, we sometimes keep a heavy stock of the item on hand, just in case the production run from which the order should be filled is slowed down.

6: We sometimes set aside, for our sales representatives, excessive quantities of products which are low-volume items.

The Galvor Company (G-1)

INTRODUCTION

Galvor had expanded very rapidly throughout its history, and especially during the 1950's. Company officials remarked that this rapid growth had imposed some strains on the organization. At the outset of IMEDE's research at Galvor, M. Latour pointed out that "our organization is far from perfect"; soon afterwards M. Chambertin observed that IMEDE would probably find that Galvor's most interesting problems were organizational in nature.

This case contains two sections. Section I briefly describes the way in which the Galvor organization evolved from 1936 until the end of 1961. Section II contains (a) an analysis by company officials of the total organizational structure at the end of 1961; (b) similar analyses of each of the company's major departments; and (c) remarks as to the manner in which the company officials hoped to develop the organization in coming years.

I: A SHORT HISTORY OF THE GALVOR ORGANIZATION

During Galvor's early years, M. Latour managed the company with a minimum of formal organization. In 1941, at which time the company had 20 employees, M. Romanée was brought in to take charge of manufacturing and especially to supervise manufacturing of galvanometers. During the Second World War, research and development were under the responsibility of the Messer brothers, but when they left the company in 1945 (as described in *GALVOR (A)*), M. Latour resumed direction of research and development. By 1948, when the company had 50 employees, M. Meursault had taken charge of electronic research, and M. Pomméry was employed in 1951 to oversee electric research, at which time about 100 people were employed in the company. After M. Pomméry arrived, M. Latour concentrated his activities on commercial affairs and on the financial management of Galvor. During all of the company's history, M. Latour always supervised to some extent every department of the company, but as the organization grew he was able to delegate more and more responsibility: first in manufacturing, to M. Romanée, and next in research and development, to Messrs. Meursault and Pomméry.

This process of delegation continued with the addition, in 1954, of M. Chambertin as the Administrative Director. Despite his title, M. Chambertin's primary responsibilities were in finance and accounting. "I brought in Chambertin," M. Latour said, "because our financial problems were becoming very complex, and I needed an expert in this area. Furthermore, I was not very interested in finance; I wanted to concentrate more on the commercial side of the business, and Chambertin's coming really freed me to do so."

M. Latour created more assistance for himself when he promoted M. Margaux to Manager of the Commercial Service in early 1958. Prior to this time M. Latour himself had been in charge of all commercial activities. M. Margaux was added to the Galvor staff in February, 1956, and spent his first two years with the company as a travelling sales engineer, visiting sales representatives and customers. After M. Margaux's promotion in 1958, no important changes occurred in the formal organization through the end of 1961.

In describing the way in which he had built up what he referred to as his 'executive team,' M. Latour said, "As the company grew, it was naturally necessary to find experts to assist me, and I found these men, beginning back in 1941 with Romanée. I cannot stress enough that my success would not have been possible without this team of experts."

II: THE GALVOR ORGANIZATION, DECEMBER 1961

A: The Overall Organization

The following comments on the Galvor organization were made during November–December 1961:

M. Latour: "We certainly have some organization problems, especially insofar as my colleagues are generally over-loaded with work and don't have good assistants to help them. Furthermore, I find some unwillingness, especially in Romanée's case, to take on added responsibilities as the company grows. In general, however, we have a very solid executive team whose members work well together. For myself, I am trying more and more to work on long-range policies of the company, such as the development of our export markets. I am trying to leave more and more of the detail work to my colleagues. I manage to keep on top of my work, which I think is one important sign of a good manager; I finish by night all the jobs that were waiting for me when the day started."

M. Chambertin: "M. Latour makes all our major policy decisions alone; since he is not always in touch with daily operating details, he sometimes creates problems. As for our other executives, I think that they suffer from what seems to me a common administrative problem: all of them have too much to do, because they haven't the assistants they need, so they do the easy jobs first and leave the difficult problems unsolved. As a result, our executives don't always deliver the value for which they are paid: they are supposed to make the important and difficult decisions, but they often just do detail work that any clerk could do.

Our major problems here are probably organizational. We do not have a good organizational structure, and we badly lack depth in our management. This is because the company has grown rapidly; the organization has not kept pace with this growth. The organization which we have today is much too weak: it would have been insufficient at our operating level of two years ago.

The weakest point in our structure appears in the question of a true second-in-command for M. Latour. At the moment, we have nobody who can run the company except M. Latour. I suppose that I am ostensibly the second man here, but I am 58 years old, and I have no technical background at all, so that some of the other executives would not consider me a very good leader. Margaux is probably the best-suited of the other executives to run the company, but he would never be accepted by the others.

We have never had any true forward planning in the company, with the possible exception of our 12-month sales forecasts. We have operated pragmatically, and this policy has clearly worked well, at least judging by our results. We feel that this has been the best policy, because we have had to go where technology has taken us, but in the future we will probably need to do more long range planning."

M. Romanée: "I am afraid that we have some real organizational problems here. In the first place, M. Latour gets involved far too deeply in the trivial operating details of the company. This is probably unavoidable, when you consider that in Galvor's early days he *had* to run all aspects of the business, but it is a real problem nonetheless. Because M. Latour does get involved in such detail work, our responsibilities and chains of command are very unclear. I am not really sure what our true organization chart should look like, but it would certainly show that M. Latour's role extends from the top of the structure to the bottom. If we cannot improve our organization, and do so rapidly, I fear that we shall miss our chance to capitalize on the opportunities for growth and success which are open to us."

M. Margaux: "There are three reasons for Galvor's success. First, we give excellent technical support to our customers in helping them to solve their measuring problems. Second, M. Latour's basic policy has been steady and prudent; we have moved ahead consistently, and he has been willing to alter his policies to meet the demands of special situations, but he keeps a firm and steady hand on the rudder. Third, we have a fine organization whose members work very well together."

Messrs. Meursault and Pomméry never commented on the overall organization of Galvor during interviews with IMEDE researchers. They confined themselves to remarks on the functioning of their own departments.

B: Departmental Organizations

1: The Research Departments, one for electronic research (under M. Meursault) and the other for electric research (under M. Pomméry) suffered from two main organizational problems, according to company executives.

The first problem was that Messrs. Meursault and Pomméry both had too many responsibilities and badly needed assistants. This problem was mentioned not only by Messrs. Latour and Chambertin, but also by Messrs. Meursault and Pomméry themselves. M. Chambertin commented, "I suspect that the real problem here is that, despite the fact that Meursault and Pomméry are well aware that they have too much to do, they enjoy the wide responsibilities which accompany this situation, so they don't want to hire assistants and give up even some petty responsibility for detail work."

"Meursault," remarked M. Latour, "really needs a brilliant young engineer as an assistant, but he is afraid that such an assistant might show him up. Thus, although I have promised to write him a contract guaranteeing that he will always be Manager of Electronic Research, and although I have said that he may pay an assistant as much as necessary, even twice what he himself makes, he does nothing. I don't want to push him into anything, because he has been with me since he was a boy, but if I find a man I think would make a suitable assistant for him, I'll hire the man on the spot and worry later about how to sell him to Meursault."

As described in *GALVOR (B-1)*, Messrs. Meursault and Pomméry were both keenly aware that they needed assistants, and as of late 1961 both claimed that they were searching intensively for such men.

The second problem in the research groups was in their liaison with the Manufacturing Department. Under the system in effect as of late 1961, the Research Services were responsible for carrying new product research to the point of building and testing a prototype of the product. They also had to draw up the necessary documents for putting this product into manufacturing: such documents included, for example, a list of parts to be purchased for assembly work and a list of parts to be manufactured in the factory. The Manufacturing Department entered the process by accepting the prototype (which was supposed to be identical in all ways to the mass-produced product), and the accompanying documents. The Manufacturing Department would then determine how the manufacturing and assembly operations were to be handled in the plant.

Problems arose frequently between manufacturing and research. According to M. Meursault, after the prototype of a new product had been tested, finished, documented, and turned over to Manufacturing, the latter department would request minor modifications in order to simplify certain manufacturing processes. This meant, claimed M. Meursault, that he was constantly being called away from his important duties in order to supervise such minor changes required by Manufacturing.

M. Pomméry added that the Research Departments were often asked to update existing Galvor products; such requests normally came either from M. Latour or from the Commercial Service. "As a result of these demands by the Manufacturing Department and the Commercial Service," said M. Pomméry, "we fall far short of our true potential for developing new products. We have on hand a huge backlog of desirable new products to develop, but we simply have too much updating and modifying to do." During the approximately seven interviews held by IMEDE researchers with M. Meursault and/or M. Pomméry, neither man ever commented on the other except insofar as described in the GALVOR series.

2: **The Manufacturing Department,** under M. Romanée, viewed this liaison problem with the research groups somewhat differently. M. Romanée said, "There certainly is a big problem in getting new products from research into manufacturing. The chief difficulty is that after a design has been 'frozen' for manufacturing, the research people will decide that they have to make some further modifications in order to improve the product. This makes it difficult to plan a smooth work flow in the plant, and it also creates inventory problems: we end up having parts on hand which we'll never use, and then there is a big rush to get the new parts required for the modification. We really need a special service to take charge of transferring new products from design to manufacturing.

"Another problem in our department is that my foremen have far too much responsibility, especially in that they have to devise many of the manufacturing methods and techniques. We have no Methods Department, which we badly need. I fully realize that I need an assistant, because I have far too much to do, but I can't teach such a man everything he would need to know to be truly valuable to me.

"I view my role as that of being a coordinator for the various manufacturing departments, and also for getting new products through the manufacturing process. When problems arise, I look at the trouble and take the necessary steps. The difficulty with the Manufacturing Department's organization is that we have had to expand our operations so rapidly that we have not been able to develop the staffs of specialists, in methods, coordination with research, and other areas, which we need today.

"My other major problem is in factory equipment. M. Latour does not like to buy machinery until every machine we have is being used 100% of the time; this means that we often go on using machinery long after it should be replaced. I have no authority to buy new equipment myself; I have to ask M. Latour for his approval first. This often means a delay of several months before I can get the machine I want."

Speaking on this point, M. Latour said, "I cannot get Romanée to buy machinery on his own authority. He refers virtually all his purchase requests, no matter how small, to me."

3: **The Commercial Service,** under M. Margaux, actually controlled only about 50% of Galvor's total sales. The rest of the company's sales were accounted for by Galvor Paris (42% of 1961 sales) and the Galvanometer Sales Department (10% of 1961 sales), supervised by Messrs. Cliquot and Lanson respectively. Messrs. Margaux, Cliquot and Lanson all reported directly to M. Latour.

"In effect," M. Chambertin said, "M. Latour is really our Commercial Director, although the official post does not exist, because he is in general charge of *all* sales activities. I doubt that M. Margaux has the ability to fill the job of Commercial Director, although I may be wrong."

M. Latour commented that one difficulty of M. Margaux' was that the latter had too many things to do, and that he needed an assistant. M. Latour continued, "Margaux is the only one of my colleagues who has come to me and admitted that he needs an assistant; this pleases me very much, because it shows that he is beginning to understand the responsibilities of a real manager." As of late 1961 M. Margaux was personally supervising the Export Department, since he had not yet found an assistant to supervise this department for him.

"In general," commented M. Margaux, "The Commercial Service is in good shape, and things will be even better when I can find a suitable assistant for exports."

4: **The Administrative Department,** under M. Chambertin, had four main functions: bookkeeping, financial management, personnel, and statistical reporting. M. Chambertin had assistants in charge of Personnel (starting January 1st, 1962), Accounting, and Statistical Services (under Mme. Bollinger). He also created, effective January 1st, 1962, a special group of several men to analyze factory costs, because he hoped to do intensive research into Galvor's direct and indirect cost structure during 1962.

"I have all the help I need," M. Chambertin said. "Mme. Bollinger is a superb assistant, because she is brilliant and well-educated in statistics and other areas of management." (Mme. Bollinger was a recent graduate of INSEAD, a new graduate school of business administration located in Fontainebleau, France.) "I try to make sure that I have a good staff to help me, and as you can see, I have just created two new departments to relieve me of additional detailed work. I myself supervise our financial management, in cooperation with M. Latour, and I also maintain our external financial relations, such as those with our bankers." As far as IMEDE researchers could determine, the Administrative Department had no organizational difficulties.

5: The Weekly Management Conference was, company officials said, an important element in Galvor's organization and operation. This conference, which met starting at 8:30 every Tuesday morning, brought together M. Latour and his five main executives for a general discussion of technical, manufacturing, and commercial problems. The conference had been instituted in 1959; prior to this time M. Latour had discussed such problems only with the specific executive whose area was involved. "Our first conferences," said M. Latour, "dealt only with technical matters, but after a year or so we enlarged the scope of this meeting to include manufacturing and commercial problems as well. It is a very effective way of maintaining our executive team."

M. Chambertin observed, "The only trouble with the conference is that we spend hours discussing details which ought not to concern the upper level of management. The conference seldom lasts less than four hours, and it has on occasion been known to run the whole day. I think that M. Latour involves himself unnecessarily in details, especially in technical matters."

In March, 1962, while M. Latour was on his trip around the world, nonmanagement conferences were held at Galvor, M. Chambertin said, "When the first Tuesday after M. Latour's departure arrived, we suddenly realized that there was no real purpose in holding the conference—we had nothing to talk about, so we abandoned it until his return."

C: Organizational Plans as of December, 1961

"In the long run," said M. Chambertin, "we know how we would like to develop the organization; M. Latour and I have already talked about this at some length. We envision the company as being organized into three main departments, Technical, Commercial and Administrative, with a Director at the head of each. The Administrative Department and its Director already exist, of course. The Commercial Department would unite under one Director the Commercial Service, Galvanometer Sales, and Galvor Paris. The elements of this department already exist, as you know, but the true Director is M. Latour.

The major change would be in grouping both the Research Services *and* the Manufacturing Department under a single Technical Director; this man would have complete responsibility for designing and producing all Galvor products. In my opinion we have nobody in the company who meets the specifications for Technical Director, nor have we a solid candidate for Commercial Director.

This new Technical Director, whoever he is, ought to be (a) a brilliant engineer, with a sound theoretical background; (b) a first-class administrator who can take all of research and manufacturing under his control; (c) about 35 years old. I suggest age 35 because, in my opinion, this is the man we ought to train to be M. Latour's successor."

* * * * *

In speaking of future developments in the Manufacturing Department, M. Romanée said, "We are planning to bring two new staffs into existence: first a Manufacturing Bureau, in about two years, and then a Methods Staff perhaps a year later. The Manufacturing Bureau, which will be under my charge, will be responsible for transferring a new product from research to manufacturing. The Methods Staff will relieve me and my foremen of a lot of the methods work we now have to do. With these two services, I think we can significantly reduce the time now required to move from a finished prototype to a mass-produced instrument. This time lag is now 9–12 months, depending mostly on the instrument's complexity and whether we encounter many modifications and other problems."

M. Chambertin said, "Only in recent months has M. Romanée begun to admit that he and his foreman have too much work to do and badly need to enlarge the Manufacturing Department's staff services."

* * * * *

M. Margaux spoke of his search for an assistant as follows: "I am now looking intensively for a man to take charge of our Export Department, and I must have this man not later than the autumn of 1962. His arrival will free me from a large part of the detail work I now have to do, so that I can concentrate on the two things which seem to me most important: (1) doing more intensive analyses of our marketing procedures, especially determining the feasibility of marketing research in our industry; (2) developing the technical side of our commercial organization, first in France, and afterwards abroad. By this I mean building up our staff of sales engineers and using other means to strengthen the technical support we can give to our sales representatives."

"All in all," said M. Chambertin, "I think that our organizational structure is slowly being developed along desirable lines, but we are far from being where we should be in this area. In my opinion, the other executives badly need assistants, we certainly need a thoroughly accepted second-in-command to M. Latour, and we ought to define our organization more sharply by getting competent Technical and Commercial Directors."

The Galvor Company (G-2)

On January 2nd, 1962, M. Latour announced at the weekly Management Conference that he had just employed a new man, M. Roger Armagnac, to assist him in his work. M. Latour added that M. Armagnac would begin in his position on April 2nd. "For ten years," remarked M. Latour, "I have been looking for a high-level assistant for myself; the need for such a man became especially obvious during the last three months of 1961. I think that M. Armagnac is just the man we need; he ought to work out very well."

* * * * *

In explaining the circumstances which lead to his coming to Galvor, M. Armagnac said, "I was educated by the French Navy as an engineer from 1942 to 1950, at the end of which time I was 23 years old. After finishing my education, I had a contract to serve eight years as a Naval officer, and I expected to spend all my working life in the Navy. By 1961, I was in charge of Electronic Research and Development at the Toulon Naval Base; I had slightly more than 100 engineers and technicians under my command. By this time, however, I began to consider the possibility of leaving the Navy to go into industry. When I was in Paris in April '61, I looked up my old schoolfellow Cliquot, who is the Manager of Galvor Paris. He had also been a Naval officer before going to work for Galvor. Cliquot knew of my interest in industry, and he suggested that I consider Galvor as a place to work. Naturally, everything was very tentative at this time, because I was still in the Navy. I was not sure I could get a discharge on short notice.

"Cliquot suggested that I send my dossier to Galvor, which I did in May. Aside from the usual background information, I also included an explanation of why I was thinking of leaving the Navy." This explanation is reproduced below:

"The following ideas are strictly personal and apply only to one particular case: mine. It is difficult to analyze one's self objectively; I hope I can do so without either boasting or excessive modesty.

I think that a private corporation to which a military engineer is offering his services should ask the following questions:

What are the engineer's motives? Why is he considering abandoning a stable and comfortable career, with a well-defined place in the hierarchy, with almost mathematical rules for promotion, and with many honors and social advantages, for a career which, while offering significant material advantages, must be at the outset, at least, riskier and less well defined?

To understand the answers to these questions, the following must be borne in mind:

The Navy is structurally very compartmentalized in each branch, and the functions within each branch are narrowly and precisely defined. In certain branches, including mine, and especially in electronics, many men reach at an early age the highest post attainable within the branch. I have been at the top for two years, and the rules do not allow me any chance of rising higher.

I think (as do my superiors) that private industry, which is growing and is less compartmentalized than the Government, would permit me to develop more broadly in the future.

"In short," added M. Armagnac, "I had gone about as high as I could for the foreseeable future. That is why I considered a career change. I sent M. Cliquot my dossier, which he forwarded to Bordeaux. I received a reply suggesting a visit to the factory, which took place in November."

M. Latour said, "My preliminary reaction to Armagnac's resumé was favorable, so I thought it would be wise to talk to him here and to show him the plant. During this tour of the plant, he asked many intelligent and penetrating questions about various operations; I was impressed by the perception which these questions revealed. After the visit, I suggested that he write me a letter outlining where and how he saw himself fitting into our organization. Various people who had known Armagnac told me that he was brilliant, an outstanding man in his field. He had earned a fine reputation as an administrator while at Toulon."

M. Armagnac said, "After the visit to the plant, I considered things for a month before I decided to make a written proposal to Galvor. I don't like to make up my mind in a hurry, and I still had to decide whether I would leave the Navy. So I talked things over with my wife. I also found out that I could get a discharge from the Navy, on a so-called 'temporary' basis, to work in industry. If things didn't work out I could return to the Navy.

"After considering all aspects of the decision carefully, I decided to propose myself for a position at Galvor. I wrote to Galvor on December 26th, as follows:

"Dear Monsieur Latour,

I very much appreciated the visit to your factory, for which my warm thanks.

I came away with an excellent impression of your plant.

1:) As a result of this visit and the information given me on the organization structure of the company, it seems to me that Galvor's management could be strengthened by the addition of an engineer as Technical Director; the role of this man would be to oversee the various research teams and especially, for a given manufacturing program, to:

—keep an eye on the jobs being done by the research engineers, give them advice, coordinate their activities and, in time, to improve their relationships;

—organize manufacturing operations, (which would require a complete understanding of potentialities), to keep general control over manufacturing, and to improve the workings of this department if possible;

—to control and coordinate the job of transforming a prototype into a mass-produced instrument;

—to cooperate actively with the other staffs of the company which would not be directly under my command, such as:

—defining the stocks of raw materials and components needed to make a given product;

—issuing a memo giving my opinion on the value of various personnel;

—etc.

In short, the Technical Director would have to be the administrator of the technical side of the business.

2:) The foregoing definition of the job of the Technical Director is clearly not exhaustive. Nevertheless, using it as a general guide, and assuming you should be interested, I would be happy to enter your team in this capacity."

The rest of M. Armagnac's letter dealt with the exact terms of employment and with the formalities which would be required to secure his release from the Navy. M. Latour considered M. Armagnac's application and accepted his proposal. On January 2nd, 1962, M. Latour informed his colleagues that M. Armagnac would be joining the staff around April 1st, as an assistant to himself. He did not at that time discuss M. Armagnac's role and title in the company.

* * * * *

During the negotiations with M. Armagnac, M. Latour discussed M. Armagnac's possible function and role in Galvor only with M. Chambertin. M. Armagnac was to be given the title of Technical Director, but as of January 2nd, 1962, the place of the Technical Director in the organizational structure had not been established.

"Chambertin," commented M. Latour, "looks to the future more than any of the other executives, and the first thing he said at the January 2 meeting was that we must define M. Armagnac's position very carefully. I generally agreed with M. Armagnac's definition of his job in the letter of December 26th, 1961, that is, I agreed that he would have responsibility over research and manufacturing. Chambertin said that if we put Armagnac *only* in charge of R&D and Manufacturing, we might create some human problems, notably in the case of Romanée, who might well not want to be under a much younger man. Chambertin then suggested that Armagnac might conceivably be appointed the executive vice president, or assistant managing director, which would mean being second-in-command of the company. It is typical of Chambertin's selflessness that he was willing to subordinate himself and give up being second man at Galvor. I replied that I did not propose to give Armagnac control over finances, that his excellence was in manufacturing and research—he is not a financial expert, after all."

M. Chambertin said, "On February 7th, 1962, I sent M. Latour a memorandum outlining my thoughts on the way in which M. Armagnac might be fitted into the organization structure. Mme. Bollinger and I did some preliminary research on the subject of organizational structure and the usual responsibilities of Manufacturing and Technical Directors. This research suggested that it would be appropriate to have both a Technical Director and a Manufacturing Director; one would be in charge of conceiving the product, the other of manufacturing it. We did recognize, however, that one problem at Galvor was the poor liasion between research and manufacturing, and that we also had difficulties with purchasing, production scheduling, and methods. We saw that, because of their interdependence, purchasing and production scheduling should be under the control of the same man, and we realized that both of these staffs were inadequate for our current level of operations.

"Recognizing as we did that Romanée already had far too much to do, we questioned whether M. Armagnac might not assume control of scheduling, purchasing, and methods: It was clear that Armagnac would have to be given *formal* authority over these three areas if he was to improve them; he could not do the job as a trespasser on another man's domain.

"We concluded that M. Armagnac must be given explicit responsibility in every area where he expected to make changes. If he were only a staff assistant to M. Latour, without real power, he would be useless. Therefore, if we wanted Armagnac not only to supervise research, but also to attack the problems in some of our services (purchasing, scheduling, and methods), M. Romanée would have to turn over control of these services to M. Armagnac. We suggested that this be done, that Romanée, Armagnac, and I be on the same level, and most important, that Armagnac be given a position with well-defined authorities and responsibilities. It would not work if M. Armagnac were just a high-level trouble shooter for M. Latour."

M. Latour said, "Although it would have been possible, as suggested by this memo, to put Romanée on the same level with Armagnac and Chambertin, I knew that Romanée's technical background was not strong. On my recent trip around the world, I observed that the companies which are world leaders of our industry are very technically oriented. It seemed to me that if we wanted to become one of the industry leaders it might not be appropriate to elevate Romanée to the same rank as Chambertin and Armagnac. So I finally decided that Armagnac should be Technical Director in charge of all manufacturing and research. On April 2nd, when M. Armagnac arrived and was formally introduced to his colleagues, I described very precisely M. Armagnac's position in our company. There were no problems; the whole thing was done and accepted within a minute.

"Our next major organizational development will probably be to find a Commercial Director to run the Commercial Service, Galvanometer Sales, and Galvor Paris. I am in no great hurry to find this man, who must really be superb, because now that Armagnac is here, I can concentrate more and more on the commercial side of the business, especially on exports. This Commercial Director will have to have a very strong technical background, because our product line is becoming steadily more complex, and this probably means that Margaux will not be able to fill the job, but we shall see."

*   *   *   *   *

Until April 2nd, 1962, when M. Armagnac arrived, only two executives besides M. Latour made any comment to the IMEDE researchers on M. Armagnac's probable role in the company: Messrs. Chambertin and Romanée.

On February 13, M. Chambertin said, "As you can see from the memo I wrote, I was worried lest M. Latour use Armagnac merely as an errand boy in solving minor problems. If this were done, Armagnac would be worthless, and he would quit very soon. I was therefore happy to see M. Latour define very carefully what he expected of Armagnac; I just hope things work out as planned."

Late in March, M. Romanée said, "It's no use asking me what M. Armagnac will do when he gets here; we have not discussed it at all, which seems to me a strange state of affairs. I haven't the least idea as to how he will fit into the company; you had better see M. Latour on this subject."

On April 26th, after M. Armagnac had been at Galvor about three weeks, IMEDE researchers asked each executive for his reactions to the way in which M. Armagnac was proceeding in his work. The following replies were received:

M. Margaux: "I think that Armagnac's presence here will be exceptionally valuable. M. Latour can no longer be expected to have the technical knowledge which is becoming increasingly important, and Pomméry and Meursault have far too much to do without providing M. Latour with technical assistance, so M. Armagnac will help to fill this gap. I am also pleased because M. Armagnac will be able to help me with the many technical problems which arrive in the course of my work, whereas Pomméry and Meursault are so busy that they cannot always give me this assistance. If I have a pressing technical problem of importance, now I can take it to the chief's right-hand technical man.

I suspect, although this is only my opinion, that Pomméry and Meursault will be less enthusiastic than I about M. Armagnac's arrival. This is only natural, because now they are no longer directly below the chief, but must work through M. Armagnac. I think, however, that they will find Armagnac relieving them of many of their problems, and their departments will probably produce more high-quality products. I must also admit that there may be some real problems in having M. Romanée under M. Armagnac. M. Romanée is a self-taught man who has learned by experience, and he's been in this industry a long time, so there may be some friction here."

M. Romanée: "My first reaction to M. Armagnac is very favorable. He has started already to analyze some of our difficult problems, especially in the relationship between manufacturing and research. Obviously it is too soon to judge him, but I find him to be a real leader, a man who can and will make decisions on his own responsibility. He will also serve to screen M. Latour from the petty problems which are always appearing. I think he will prove a big help to the company."

M. Chambertin: "I think Armagnac will be a real manager and decision-maker. He and I together have planned a new system of management conferences which M. Latour has approved. Under this system there will be two Management Committees: a Technical Committee and a General Management Committee. The Technical Committee will include Armagnac, Cliquot, Meursault, Pomméry, and Romanée; it will meet around the 9th of each month (except for its first meeting, which began April 25th.) This group will study all manufacturing and research problems which are worth presenting to the General Management Committee, which will meet on the next day. The General Management Committee consists of Messrs. Latour, Armagnac, Chambertin, Cliquot, Meursault, Pomméry, Romanée, Margaux and Mme. Bollinger. This group will consider developments of importance during the previous month, the state of the market for our products, such technical problems as are brought up by the Technical Committee, and administrative problems if any. If at some time we need more than one meeting a month, this will be easy to arrange.

I think that Armagnac will avoid getting involved in detail work; he wants to stay at the policy level, which is certainly a wise decision. He has the important talent of getting the men under him to come to a unanimous decision where before they could not agree. From what Cliquot has said, Armagnac will never have to rush; he is well-organized. The only problem which might arise would occur if he and M. Latour were to disagree on an important issue."

M. Meursault: "It is far too early to judge, but I am already beginning to wonder if M. Armagnac may not get too involved in the detail work of research, rather than staying up top as general coordinator."

M. Pomméry was unavailable at the time of this interview.

M. Latour: "I am very satisfied with the way Armagnac has come in and started to work on our problem areas."

*   *   *   *   *

In speaking of his activities since arriving at Galvor, M. Armagnac said [1], "Although I was educated as an engineer, I have had considerable experience with administrative problems. It appeared to me that the major problems at Galvor were administrative in nature, and so I saw my role primarily as that of an administrator, a sort of orchestra conductor, helping to coordinate production and research activities. My proposal to M. Latour in December was made with this basic idea in mind. I did not want to get into detailed technical matters; I knew that we already had good men in this area, and that my value would be as an administrator.

"The first job I set for myself was to define the boundary between research and manufacturing. As you know, this has been a constant problem at Galvor, and I might add that it seems to be common to many other technically-oriented companies. After I had considered the subject for some time, I felt that I knew where this boundary should be set. I did not want, however, to set it by dictatorial decree, to impose my will on my colleagues. Obviously, if the research and manufacturing people were to work willingly within this boundary definition, they would have to participate in its creation. I therefore made this question the major topic for discussion at our first Technical Committee meeting, which took place during April 25–27.

"In this meeting, my colleagues pointed out to me some details of company operations which I had not known and which affected our decision. I am happy to say that, as a result of this meeting, we were able to agree unanimously on a precise definition of the boundary between research and manufacturing. I also found that, with minor

1. This interview took place on May 7th, 1962.

changes, the definition we arrived at was basically the one which I had initially felt to be the best.

"Our definition is as follows: the research process ends when there are two finished prototypes produced, both of which are *exactly* what we want in the mass-produced instrument. The prototypes will be identical. One will be called the 'reference' prototype; it cannot be taken apart under any circumstances by the manufacturing people. The other prototype may be disassembled for study if desired.

"The Manufacturing Department will have *no* responsibility for, or authority over, the technical functioning of the instrument. This responsibility rests solely with the research groups. The research groups on the other hand have no say in how the instrument is to be manufactured.

"Now in order to smooth out liaison between research and manufacturing, around the end of '62 we will initiate a 'Staff for Preparation for Manufacturing,' which we will call the Manufacturing Bureau. This staff will receive from the research group the two prototypes of a new product. It will then dissect one of these prototypes and decide what tooling requirements will be and what parts are to be purchased. This staff will *not* judge the instrument's performance: it will merely decide how to make it. Obviously we will need experts to serve on this staff, men who know the factory and our production capabilities perfectly.

"At some time in the future we shall add a Methods Staff; this will consist largely of experts in production methods and time study. These men will analyze every factory operation, tell us how to do it most effectively, and how much time it should take. Eventually this staff will analyze the entire production line which is set up to make an instrument.

"Up to now, there has been a wonderful spirit, almost a family feeling, at Galvor, but I think this will have to change in the future. The Methods Staff, for example, will be oriented towards worker efficiency and performance. Unpleasant as these changes may seem at first, I am sure they are necessary if Galvor is to realize its potential for becoming an industry leader.

"My first objective at Galvor is to establish a good working relationship with my colleagues, and especially with Pomméry, Meursault and Romanée. You know, I am a newcomer to the company, and I am just under 35 years old. It seems to me that I will have to walk a narrow line between exercising too much authority and not exercising enough. If I always insist on making decisions myself, my colleagues will resent me. On the other hand, if they don't realize that I can and will make decisions when necessary, then I will be useless here. I don't want to have to use my authority, but I want them to know it exists. My most important task here will be in creating teamwork between manufacturing and research."

*   *   *   *   *

On April 7th, M. Latour summarized his views on M. Armagnac's role within the company, saying, "I long ago saw the need for a highly qualified man to assist me by supervising manufacturing and research. I believe I have found this man in M. Armagnac; my first impression is that he is highly capable, has a solid technical background, has solid administrative ability, and has a strong character.

"His position as Technical Director gives him the responsibility and authority to work on our difficult problem areas. And he will not only coordinate research and manufacturing, but he will also relieve me of much of the detail work I now have to do. The men under him will no longer have to come to me with trivialities: they will discuss them with Armagnac, who will then report to me on significant issues. This is the way in which he will assist me.

"In my opinion, hiring Armagnac means more than merely finding an assistant for myself: it is a basic change in our policy. For the first time, somebody will really be taking overall charge of our research and manufacturing.

"As to my colleagues' reaction to Armagnac's being brought in, I believe that they will not fight him, but will recognize that he can be a great help to them, and that we badly need the type of assistance he can give us. I think that, from a human point of view, Armagnac will work out very well. I have a sixth sense which tells me if problems are arising with my colleagues. We always have free and open discussions, so I will be able to find out what his colleagues think of him and whether he is making any mistakes. I will pass this information on to him so that he can make the necessary adjustments.

"I admit that if Armagnac is not both strong and very competent, the men under him will destroy him, but I am confident that he can handle himself.

"I have already told Armagnac that because he is my assistant he must not fail; his failure would be very bad for morale. I am 53 years old, and I need this man's assistance, so I shall give him my full support. Little by little, as he proves himself here, I shall give up research and manufacturing completely to his control. I must foresee the day when I shall have to give up my whole job to a younger man."

Greenwood Paper
and Products Company

The Greenwood Paper and Products Company of Cleveland, Ohio, was originally only a paper processing company. The processing included putting coatings on paper, impregnating the paper with various chemicals, and/or cutting the paper to specified size and packaging it. When copy machines began to infiltrate business after World War II, a need for photocopy paper arose. In 1952 Greenwood accepted its first contract for coating photocopy paper.

Before the advent of copying machines, industry had used secretarial talent for copying material of various sorts. For instance, if a complaint letter came in from a customer, a secretary would retype it and circulate it to the departments concerned. Sometimes, extra copies were needed for a meeting; and as typists copied it, there were the possibilities of errors and omission of parts.

According to the vice-president of sales of Greenwood the copy machine sold itself. "With a shortage of skilled typists and with office salaries increasing by leaps and bounds, the copy machine is part of the answer to rising office overhead costs. Even the fastest typist on the latest electric typewriters cannot begin to compete with these machines."

Straight page copy by retyping cost a minimum of 20 cents per page. Forty cents per page was closer to actual cost of typing labor, but this did not include cost of paper or carbons or depreciation of typewriters. With the introduction of photocopy equipment, the labor cost per page decreased to seven to ten cents per page and later became as low as three to five cents. In addition, the labor costs saved in reproducing charts and tables were even more dramatic. A chart took eight or nine hours to reproduce without the benefit of copying equipment; yet, with a copying machine, the same job was done in three to four minutes. Such savings made the office copying machine a highly desirable product.

Office copy machines were, for the most part, based on two methods of reproduction. The heat and carbon base system, known as "thermagraphic," was a dry process. In order to make a copy of material, the subject matter, which was subjected to infrared rays, had to contain carbon. Most typewritten and some printed materials did contain carbon and, therefore, could be reproduced by this method. However, the material was reproduced on a tan sheet of paper that was considered unattractive by many customers. The chief advantages of this method were that no chemical in the liquid state was needed for the machine, that the quality of the copy was consistent, and that the price per copy was a relatively low five cents.

The second method was known as the transfer-diffusion process. This procedure involved exposing a negative film and material to be copied to light. The negative coated sheet was then put into a developing fluid after which it was pressed against a sheet of positively coated paper. In the early stages, the operator used a squeegy and sponge to remove excess chemical from the paper. Later, improved machine design resulted in the making of a copy in a two-step operation. In the first step, the operator inserted the original and negative into the machine where it was exposed to light and then returned to the operator. The second step involved putting the exposed negative sheet and a positive sheet into another part of the machine where they passed through a liquid chemical bath. The two sheets emerged from the machine pressed together. When the positive and the negative were separated, the copy of the original material was on the positive sheet. The drawbacks of this type of machine were that the copy came out wet and had to be dried and that the operator had to work with chemicals. The quality of the copy varied as the chemical bath became "old," or as the temperature of the chemicals changed. Also, the cost per copy was eight cents. The advantages were that all materials, whether containing carbon or not, could be reproduced and that the copy was on a white sheet. Color could also be copied and would reproduce in various shades of gray.

ENTRANCE INTO EQUIPMENT FIELD

As the sales of copying equipment boomed, the sales of Greenwood also rose sharply. The management of Greenwood reviewed the whole market area for copying equipment and decided that profits in the business were mainly from the supplies rather than from the sales of the machines. In addition, some of the equipment companies had already started to process their own paper, and Greenwood was concerned about future markets for their paper.

It was decided that Greenwood could best compete by marketing its own machine. The decision of the board of directors was not unanimous. Against the diversification was the fact that the competition was already well entrenched. In the field were such companies as the Minnesota Mining and Manufacturing Company, American

Photocopy Equipment Company, Eastman Kodak Company, and Xerox Corporation. Some of the members of the board of directors of Greenwood feared that their present paper customers would cancel their orders if Greenwood came out with its own copy machine. This latter argument was ruled out since, at that time, there was an industry-wide shortage of coating capacity. In addition, some of the board members pointed out that the main business of Greenwood would remain paper processing, which was Greenwood's forte.

Research

Greenwood purchased a small company that had marketed a photocopy machine and that also had a small research engineering staff working on improvements. All parts specifically manufactured for the machine were purchased from various vendors. All assembly operations were moved to Cleveland when Greenwood assumed ownership of the company. Greenwood management strongly supported the research staff since the history of the photocopy machine had not been all good. A budget equal to 2 percent of sales was set aside for research and development.

As noted, the first machines required an operator to work with a squeegy and sponge. To avoid contact with the chemicals, the operator had to wear rubber gloves. Office personnel soon avoided this "messy" setup and, as a result, it was found that the purchaser had abandoned the copy machine within six to eight months after purchase. This meant that the sale of supplies to the customer ceased. Since income from paper accounted for 65 percent of the profits and 5 percent came from the sale of chemical solutions, this was considered a critical problem and received the greatest attention.

All companies recognized the customer demanded a machine that could be operated easily without any mess, would reproduce copies of any materials, would cost less than five cents per copy (excluding cost of machine), and would produce an attractive copy.

The company, through the Research Department, made some progress toward this goal and produced a highly improved machine. Although it was still a wet transfer-diffusion process, the machine was enthusiastically accepted by the customers. Greenwood's machine sales were so successful that they soon ran out of paper-coating capacity and had to seek other sources as well as to expand their own facilities. As a result of this demand, Greenwood ceased supplying its former paper customers and concentrated its total production on its own requirements.

The Research Department continued to explore other means of reproducing a copy. Certain new electronic devices seemed to offer the best prospects for a dry process. Refinements of the present transfer-diffusion system, however, were not neglected since it was felt this type of reproduction would be the "bread and butter" of the company for some years.

Quality Control

One of the duties of the Research Department was to maintain the quality of the finished product, both of machines and materials. Problems of distance between the research laboratory in Cleveland and the Toledo plants came to a head when some serious paper quality problems arose. When the Toledo plant started a paper run with a given batch of chemical coatings, samples of the coated paper were sent to the Research Department. After running tests, the lab would then send back word that the run was approved or not.

This procedure of quality control did not encourage the improvement of the quality since the testing of the coating took place after the production run rather than prior to it. Since a given run represented an inventory value of from $15,000 to $20,000, the quality control inspector was under a great deal of pressure to approve the runs. Actually, the standard was a somewhat nebulous measurement which involved a great deal of judgment. For this reason, the Research Department could not draw a definite quality specification. Competitors, however, were raising their standards for the coatings to the point where the difference could be distinguished by the customer. This inferior Greenwood quality gave rise to customer dissatisfaction and an increasing number of lost sales. Finally, a crash program to investigate the quality standard was put into action, and the quality was raised by tightening standards and by changing the chemical formulas. However, the image of the company to the customer had already been damaged.

Production

In its expansion of facilities, Greenwood leased two plants in Toledo, Ohio. These plants, designated as Plants No. 1 and 2, contained the coating facilities of a former film manufacturing company. Plant No. 1 contained three coating alleys equipped to coat negative or positive paper, and Plant No. 2 contained two coating alleys that coated positive paper only. All alleys in the two plants operated at speeds of 80 feet per minute. The home plant in Cleveland contained one alley and could coat either positive or negative paper. This alley had the potential operating speed of 300 feet per minute, but the driers were unable to dry the paper at that speed. (See Exhibit 1.) The maximum production speed was 150 feet per minute. New methods of drying were investigated to increase the machine speed.

Exhibit 1

Monthly Plant Capacity * in Square Feet

	Toledo No. 1	Toledo No. 2	Cleveland
Negative	16,600,000		
Positive, Base	7,520,000	9,100,000	
Positive, Top Coat	970,000	9,100,000	6,550,000
Scansheet			10,500,000

* 3 shifts per day, 5-day week.

The coating alley consisted of a series of rollers, drums, driers, and coolers as shown in Exhibit 2. Purchase price of the Cleveland alley was $250,000, and rental of the five Toledo alleys amounted to $12,000 per month including power, heat, and light.

It was necessary to coat the negative paper in darkness with red light as the only source of illumination. Positive paper which required a double coat could also be coated on these same alleys. Found through experience, the festoon dryer in Plant No. 1 in Toledo produced a better quality on the base coat. This was attributed to the fact that these alleys incorporated a coagulator system that "set" the coating immediately after application. The coagulator required an expensive refrigeration system with a brine coolant. (See Exhibit 3.) The equipment was part of original Plant No. 1. No such equipment was available in the other plants. Some consideration had been given to installing coagulators in the other plants, but there was some question as to their use when the machine speeds were increased.

Much of the positive paper with the superior base coat from only Plant No. 1 was shipped to the home plant. Then the Cleveland plant processed the top coat as well as cut and packaged the paper at a lower cost than would be curtailed by Plant No. 1. These differences in costs were the results of obsolete plant and equipment and higher labor costs in Toledo. The workers in the Toledo plants were represented by a union while the Cleveland workers were unorganized.

During the period from 1952 to 1961, sales increased from $2,782,531 to $38,543,791 (see Exhibits 4 and 5). At the same time, the sales force increased from 74 to 576 sales representatives. When again in 1959 the sales increased, the production facilities were unable to keep up with the demand, even though the alleys were operated 24 hours a day, five days a week. Relief was sought by buying both positive and negative coated paper from the Erie Paper Company, which was located in Erie, Pennsylvania. However, the cost of the Erie coated paper was considerably higher than that produced by Greenwood (see Exhibit 6). The gross margin on Erie paper was 50 percent while the average margin on Greenwood's was 72 percent.

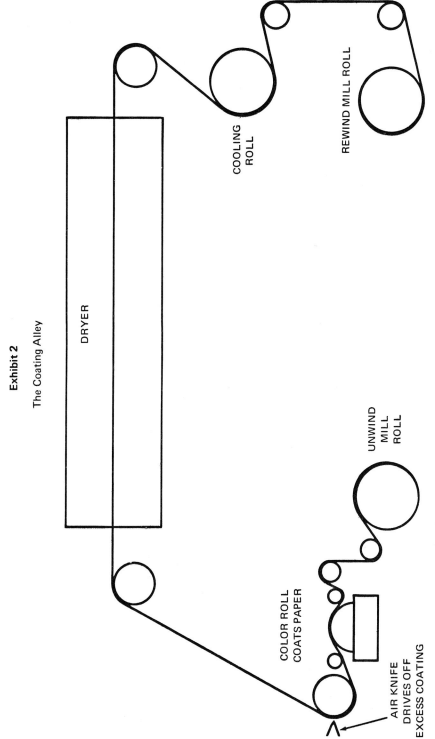

Exhibit 2

The Coating Alley

DRYER

COOLING ROLL

REWIND MILL ROLL

UNWIND MILL ROLL

COLOR ROLL COATS PAPER

AIR KNIFE DRIVES OFF EXCESS COATING

Mill roll in Cleveland plant is 53" wide but can also run rolls from the Toledo plants.

Exhibit 3

Festoon Method of Drying

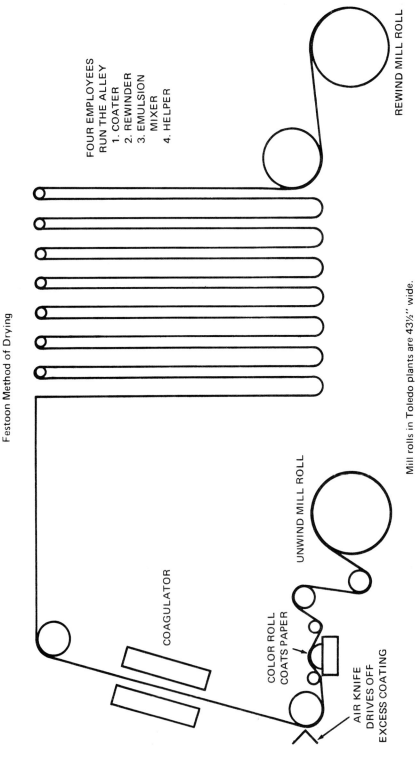

FOUR EMPLOYEES
RUN THE ALLEY
1. COATER
2. REWINDER
3. EMULSION
   MIXER
4. HELPER

REWIND MILL ROLL

UNWIND MILL ROLL

COAGULATOR

COLOR ROLL
COATS PAPER

AIR KNIFE
DRIVES OFF
EXCESS COATING

Mill rolls in Toledo plants are 43½″ wide.

Exhibit 4

10-Year Financial Review
(Year Ended November 30)

	1961	1960	1959	1958	1957	1956	1955	1954	1953	1952
Net sales*	$38,543,791	$32,786,748	$27,287,187	$19,291,501	$16,387,759	$13,384,984	$10,258,962	$7,952,879	$5,842,723	$2,782,531
Net income before taxes	11,142,076	8,862,484	6,925,951	4,493,964	3,586,494	3,030,037	2,046,869	1,986,427	1,123,041	458,761
Provision for taxes on income	5,723,722	4,606,650	3,474,301	2,320,377	1,821,243	1,593,580	1,027,487	1,010,132	590,901	233,200
Net income after taxes	5,418,354	4,255,834	3,451,649	2,173,587	1,765,250	1,436,457	1,019,382	976,295	532,140	225,561
Net income per share**	.66	.52	.42	.27	.22	.19	.14	.13	.07	.03
Dividends per share**	.31	.23	.16	.12	.12	.10	.09	—	—	—

* Coated paper accounted for 65 percent of sales, equipment 30 percent, and chemicals 5 percent.
** Based on shares outstanding each year after adjusting for a three-for-one stock split in 1959 and again in 1961 and on shares outstanding after the merger of predecessor corporations into the company in March, 1957. Dividends of December 1, 1961, 1960, 1959, and 1958 have been included as distributions of the preceding fiscal year to permit comparisons with prior periods.

Exhibit 5

Average Monthly Sales

	Negative	Positive	Scansheet
Square feet	17,187,000	17,187,000	6,000,000
Dollars	$ 798,000	$ 577,000	$ 324,000

Exhibit 6

Cost of Production—Per 1,000 Sheets 8½″ × 11″

	Toledo No. 1	Toledo No. 2	Cleveland	Erie, Pa.
Negative	$10.67			$13.50
Positive	8.54	$7.62	$6.57	10.72
Scansheet			7.05	

New Process Breakthrough

In the meantime, each of the competing companies was pushing forward in its research efforts to meet the criterion of the acceptable copying machine. The Xerox Corporation was one of the first to come out with such a machine. This introduction was followed closely by others, including Greenwood. Greenwood's machine was named the G. W. Copymatic. It required a different type of coated paper since its process was essentially based on an electronic scanning principle. The patent for the basic reproduction principle was owned by another corporation, but it was licensed to Greenwood on a nonexclusive basis. The machine itself, though, was patented by Greenwood. Only one sheet of coated paper called Scansheet was required. The cost per copy to the customer was three and a half cents.

Scansheet paper had to be produced in an explosion-proof building. Among the materials used in the coating of Scansheet was toluene, a highly explosive chemical. Only the Cleveland plant was constructed with explosion-proof facilities, including motors, lights, switches, and other accessories; thus, it was the only plant that could produce Scansheet. The cost of making the other plants explosion proof was considered too high since the basic construction was not fireproof. The Erie vendor also was unable to manufacture Scansheet because of the explosion-proofing problem.

Sales

The sales organization was established on a nationwide basis with sales offices in all of the principal cities. Sales of equipment and supplies, however, were mainly concentrated in three areas: New York and the East Coast (31 percent of sales), Chicago and suburbs (19 percent), and the West Coast (26 percent). Each sales representative had an exclusive territory and reported to a sales supervisor. The representatives had monthly machine quotas assigned to them and were paid a straight commission on the sales of all products generated in their respective sales territories. Each representative was also responsible for seeing that the photocopy machines in the assigned territory were kept in proper operating condition.

A customer purchase of a transfer-diffusion machine did not necessarily insure that this customer would also buy the paper and chemical supplies. Thus, the sales representatives had to be on the alert for loss of sales to competing supplying companies. One such company, the New Buffalo Paper Company, was especially competitive. New Buffalo succeeded in attracting a number of Greenwood's representatives by offering them exclusive agencies. By this technique, New Buffalo was able to make a direct contact with Greenwood's customers through the former representative turned agent. Whereas Greenwood had an established price of eight cents per copy (including both positive and negative sheets), the agents of New Buffalo were able to undersell by pricing at seven and a fourth to seven and a half cents per copy, but in so doing, took a smaller profit. New Buffalo had been only moderately successful in their competitive efforts until Greenwood developed the previously described quality problem during the summer of 1962. The New Buffalo company with its better quality paper was able to make great inroads into Greenwood's sales. These sales losses were estimated to be as high as $2 million. (See Exhibits 7 and 8.)

Typical in the sales promotion of the photocopy machines was the trade-in technique. When a representative found that a customer was balking at purchasing a new machine because the present machine was still functioning, a trade-in value was allowed. The sale of paper was dependent upon the success of the representative getting the customer to switch to a Greenwood machine. This was especially true when the customer traded in a machine that reproduced by a system other than the transfer-diffusion.

As indicated, Greenwood's sale of transfer-diffusion paper was adversely affected by companies such as New Buffalo. Greenwood's sales manager wanted to meet this threat in three ways:

1. a. Cut the per copy price of the transfer-diffusion paper to six and a half or seven cents or even six cents until the competition was forced out of the market.
   b. An alternative that had not received serious support by anyone, including the sales manager, was to set up agencies for the transfer-diffusion process similar to those established by

Exhibit 7

Income Statement

	1962	1961	1960
Net sales	$36,562,035	$38,543,791	$32,786,748
Cost of sales	13,738,824	14,227,433	11,811,756
Gross profit on sales	$22,823,211	$24,316,358	$20,974,992
Selling, general, and administrative expenses ..	13,770,477	13,330,779	12,394,609
Income from operations (after deducting depreciation and amortization of $736,004 in 1962 and $652,791 in 1961)	$ 9,052,734	$10,985,579	$ 8,580,383
Other income, net	452,661	156,497	282,101
Net income before federal income taxes	$ 9,505,395	$11,142,076	$ 8,862,484
Provision for federal income taxes	4,679,400	5,723,722	4,606,650
Net income	$ 4,825,995	$ 5,418,354	$ 4,255,834

Exhibit 8

Assets

	1962	1961
Current Assets		
Cash	$1,488,669	$4,331,993
Marketable securities, at cost ..	948,247	5,233,368
Receivables less reserves of $166,100 in 1962 and $116,600 in 1961 ...	7,298,235	5,897,522
Inventories, at lower of cost (first-in, first-out basis) or market—raw materials and work in process	2,489,170	1,688,733

Exhibit 8

(con)

Finished goods	2,392,227		2,139,239	
Prepaid expenses and deferred charges	465,408		346,945	
Total Current Assets		$15,081,956		$19,637,800
Other Assets, at cost:				
Equipment leased to customers, less reserves for depreciation of $301,636 in 1962 and $284,000 in 1961	$ 501,589		$ 197,464	
Patents, etc., less reserve for amortization of $27,500 in 1962	522,500		920,260	
Investments in nonconsolidated subsidiaries ..	796,425		56,207	
		1,820,514		1,173,931
Property, Plant and Equipment, at cost:				
Land	$ 387,402		$ 387,402	
Buildings and improvements .	2,891,234		2,834,718	
Equipment	3,117,996		2,762,800	
	$6,396,632		$5,984,920	
Less—Reserves for depreciation and amortization	2,216,992		1,734,839	
		4,179,640		4,250,081
Total Assets		$21,082,110		$25,061,812

GREENWOOD PAPER AND PRODUCTS COMPANY

Exhibit 8

(con)

Liabilities

	1962	1961
Current Liabilities:		
Accounts payable	$ 729,500	$ 885,772
Accrued expenses	952,277	1,054,392
Federal income taxes	1,597,261	4,208,363
Provision for settlement of various litigation less related income taxes .	—	3,356,135
Total Current Liabilities ..	$ 3,279,038	$ 9,504,662
Reserve for future federal income taxes and deferred income .	325,542	211,165
Captial Stock and Surplus:		
Common stock, without par value—authorized 11,000,000 shares; issued and outstanding —1962— 8,253,117 shares	$4,823,681	—
1961— 8,248,683 shares	—	$4,767,818
Earned surplus	12,653,849	10,578,167
	17,477,530	15,345,985
Total Liabilities and Capital	$21,082,110	$25,061,812

the New Buffalo plant. This meant that the current sales force would handle only the G. W. Copymatic line.

2. Unload the inventory of transfer-diffusion machines by selling the machines at cost, thus creating a market for additional paper sales.

3. Step up the sales efforts on the G. W. Copymatic. Since Scansheet was a patented product, the customer would have to rely on Greenwood as its source of supply.

Greenwood's president disagreed on the price-cutting approach. He felt that price should be maintained and that, since the quality problem had been corrected, the representatives could recapture the lost market by "some good, hard selling." He did favor increasing the sales effort of the G. W. Copymatic. "The customer is no longer a pushover; there are too many good machines on the market. We are now in that stage where our people can demonstrate whether they are sales representatives or not. This is a buyer's market." The president went on to point out the market was developing some new characteristics. The rent of copying machines was making inroads into the sale of both paper and machines. Some companies were charging one cent a copy as a rental fee, plus the cost of materials, but a minimum number of copies per month was required. The price of machines also was increasing; some of the new electronic machines sold for $2,500 to $3,000. The price of the Greenwood machine was $985, but it could also be rented. Customers doing considerable copy work desired to buy the machines outright, while those whose quantity was near the minimum charge preferred to rent. (See Exhibit 9.)

EXPANSION PLANS

Early in 1961 the production facilities of Greenwood were taxed to the point where consideration was given to additional facilities or additional purchases from the Erie Company. Greenwood had already reduced the amount of paper purchased from Erie by half. Where previously $100,000 worth of coated paper was purchased per month, $50,000 per month was obtained from the vendor in 1961. The company wanted to avoid the higher cost paper due to the profit squeeze, and it also wanted to plan for anticipated sales increase. (See Exhibit 10.)

Several possibilities for increasing the production of paper were considered by the Greenwood officials. One additional high-speed alley was considered.

1. The modernization of the Toledo plants was examined. It was determined that the new high-speed coater could be installed

Exhibit 9

Competing Brands—Dry Process

	Sale Price	Cost per Copy	Leasing per Month	Min. No. Copies	Copies per Minute
Brand A	$2,975	2½ ¢	$65	6,500	14
Brand B	Not Sold	3½ ¢	$25	2,000	7
Brand C	$ 895	3½ ¢	$50 *	No. Min.	6
Brand D	$ 249	5¢	No leasing		3
Greenwood G. W. Copymatic	$ 985	3½ ¢	$35	2,500	8

* Machine can be purchased for an additional $65 at termination of contract. Contract is $90/mo. for 12 months; $50/mo. for 24 months; or $42/mo. for 36 months.

Competing Brands—Wet Process

	Sale Price	Cost per Copy	Copies per Minute
Brand E	$99.50	8½ ¢	3
Brand F	99.00	8	4
Brand G	99.50	8	4
Greenwood Photomatic	99.50	8	4

Exhibit 10

Predicted Monthly Sales

	Positive	Negative	Scansheet
In five years	$290,000	$390,000	$2,000,000
In ten years	100,000	125,000	3,000,000

for $250,000. However, the building and auxiliary equipment would not be explosion proof. It was also determined that depreciation costs would be increased by 20 percent.

2. An addition could be constructed at the Cleveland plant site since 20,000 square feet of land was available. The new alley could be set up in a space of 4,000 square feet. This included the space necessary for the storage of raw and coated materials. If it was decided to build this addition, it was deemed advisable to add 10,000 square feet for additional storage space. Storage was a critical problem since space had to be provided for Scansheet raw materials, uncoated rolls, coated rolls, and packaged Scansheets. This was in addition to the needs for storage of the transfer-diffusion products. Construction costs for the building were $10 per square foot.

3. A third possibility for obtaining additional production facilities was to purchase a 40,000 square-foot vacant plant two blocks from the Cleveland plant. This plant could be easily made explosion proof since its basic construction presented no problem. The sale price of the land and plant was $425,000.
4. A fourth consideration was to build the alley on the West Coast. This consideration had not been examined in detail, but it was thought that some savings could be obtained on shipping costs. A thousand sheets of Scansheet weighed 19½ pounds, while a thousand sheets of either positive or negative paper weighed 14½ pounds. Since the paper would be in the processed state, the shipping rate classification was that of photographic supplies.[1] Raw material rolls of paper were available from several paper companies in Oregon.

The controlling time factor in any of these choices laid in the lead time for ordering the equipment for the alleys. About nine months were required between order and delivery. In this time the new addition would be completed or the alteration to existing structures made. The West Coast choice was not clear-cut since the location had not been thought through, and the committee making the recommendations held the West Coast choice in the background in the event the first three possibilities did not materialize. No conclusions were reached.

1. Trucking costs from Cleveland to San Francisco were $7.50 per hundred pounds (minimum of 20,000 pounds).

Sumiyoshi Corporation

In April, the executive committee of Sumiyoshi Corporation, Osaka, Japan, was considering the extent to which the company should expand its output of transistor radios during the coming year. In prior discussion of this subject, various members of the committee had proposed figures ranging from 75,000 per month to over 100,000 per month. Recent production was over 50,000 per month, and previously the figure had been less than 15,000 per month. Ever since the company's pioneer introduction of transistor radios in early 1956, demand for the Sumiyoshi output of these products had exceeded the company's production capacity. Even at the current rate of production, output was being rationed among ready buyers.

Transistor radios were currently accounting for 50 percent of the company's monthly sales volume of 550 million yen, or $1.53 million (at the rate of 360 yen per dollar). The other major items were tape recorders, 30 percent; transistors (excluding those used in the company's own products), 10 percent; recording tape, 5 percent; and miscellaneous, 5 percent.

The Sumiyoshi plants and offices were located in Higashi-Sumiyoshi-Ku, Osaka, and Nagoya. Employment was 2,123 and sales volume for a six-month period ending in April, was estimated at 3,500 million yen ($9.72 million). The company had experienced three periods of remarkably rapid growth and some members of the management, including the president, Masao Ishikawa, felt that Sumiyoshi might be on the verge of still another wave of rapid expansion. This feeling was based upon the Sumiyoshi position as a pioneer in the commercial application of semiconductors and upon its continuing program of research and development in that field.

To illustrate his concept of the present state of the commercial application of semiconductors, President Ishikawa drew the diagram shown in Exhibit 1.

OFFICERS, DIRECTORS, AND PRINCIPAL STOCKHOLDERS

Nearly all of the officers and directors of Sumiyoshi Corporation in April, had been with the company since its establishment.

Exhibit 1

Growth Curve of Semiconductor Application

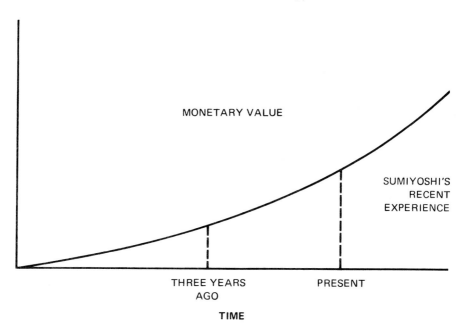

(See organization chart in Exhibit 2.) Juichi Momose (71), chairman of the board of directors, had acted as an advisor to the company since its founding. Until recently the chairman of a large Osaka bank and a past chairman of the National Association of Banks, Momose had devoted much time in his later years to assisting new businesses in becoming established, particularly those types of enterprises which he felt would make a strong contribution to Japan's postwar recovery. Momose's interest in such businesses was in freely offering advice and other types of assistance when asked; the actual conduct of the businesses was the responsibility of others.

Masao Ishikawa (49), president, was perhaps the person most responsible for the initial founding of the company and for the direction of its activities thereafter. A graduate engineer, Ishikawa had been involved in research and manufacturing of devices of recording, measuring, and amplifying sound and light when he had entered a photochemical laboratory. His last association (prior to Sumiyoshi) had been as vice president and director of a measuring instrument manufacturing company. At the end of the war this company was dissolved, and Ishikawa, Hosoi, and a number of other engineers moved to Osaka where they started the research and manufacture of electrical communication equipment.

Arata Miyoshi (40), managing director, also had been a principal in the founding of the company and in its direction since that event.

Exhibit 2

Organization

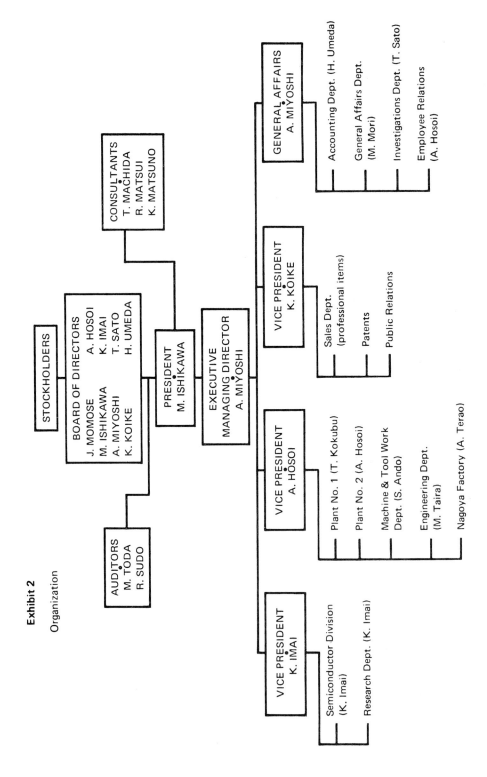

A graduate in the physical sciences, Miyoshi had been a member of the faculty of a university prior to the establishment of Sumiyoshi.

Kiichi Koike (53), vice president and director, was in charge of sales (professional items), patents, and public relations. A graduate in commerce, Koike was one of the few members of top management who had not majored in science or engineering. This difference was more apparent than real, however, for Koike had long been an enthusiastic amateur radio operator and was active in the Japan Amateur Radio League and the Japan Amateur Television Association. Prior to his association with Sumiyoshi, Koike had been an executive in the sales department of a large electrical goods manufacturing firm.

Atsuo Hosoi (46), vice president and executive director, was in charge of all manufacturing except that of semiconductors. Hosoi was a graduate engineer who, prior to joining Sumiyoshi, had been associated with Ishikawa at the measuring instrument company.

Kiyoshi Imai (42), vice president and executive director, was in charge of the Semiconductor Division and the Research Department. A graduate in metallurgy, Imai had been awarded a research assistantship at Osaka Imperial University following his graduation. From the time of his association with Sumiyoshi, Imai had contributed greatly to the company's programs of research and development both as a research scientist and as a supervisor of such activities.

Toru Sato (53), director and manager of the Investigation Department, and Haruo Umeda (59), director and manager of the Accounting Department, had equally impressive backgrounds in their respective areas. Sato had been an auditor of Sumiyoshi prior to becoming a director and comptroller. Umeda had been a Sanji (senior councilor) at the head office of a large metropolitan bank prior to joining Sumiyoshi.

Officers and directors held about 11 percent of the company's stock, with Momose, Ishikawa, and Miyoshi holding 4 percent, 2 percent, and 2 percent respectively. Other large stockholders included Matsuno Co. (15 percent) and the Sase Company (3 percent); a metropolitan bank (4 percent); an insurance company (4 percent); and a photochemical company (4 percent).

The consultants to the president, Taro Machida, Ryoichi Matsui, and Kozaburo Matsuno, had each been associated with the company since its inception. Machida, a former high official in the Ministry of Education, had once served as president of Sumiyoshi. Matsui was president of a photochemical laboratory. K. Matsuno, a prominent business executive in the Kyoto area, had actively interested himself in the company's affairs. Through his holdings in Matsuno Company and Sase Company, K. Matsuno was the largest stockholder in Sumiyoshi Corporation. (It should be noted that the Sumiyoshi Corporation's record of growth was quite remarkable in postwar Japan in that it was one of a very few firms which achieved the status of a large corporation without being affiliated with a *zaibatsu*.[1])

GROWTH AND DEVELOPMENT

The formation of Sumiyoshi had brought together an unusually favorable blend of talents and personalities. Older executives provided business acumen, financial resources, and excellent connections; executives in their middle years, who had already acquired extensive business experience with firms specializing in the application of scientific research to commercial products, became the operating managers; still younger executives who had already demonstrated special promise, usually in a scientific field in which electricity is related to light or sound, brought enthusiasm and scientific talent. Behind these accomplishments stood Masao Ishikawa, the individual who conceived the purpose of the new company, who assembled the resources to bring it into being, and who was to direct its operating activities. This highly purposeful collection of well-qualified personnel began to make its mark very shortly after its founding, as is indicated by the company's record of sales and earnings. (See Exhibits 12 and 13.)

Early Business and Products

The first products of the company were primarily connected with postwar revival of radio broadcasting in Japan and with governmental telephonic and radio communication needs. Among the products were electromagnetic tuning forks, sound oscillators, reluctance type microphones, moving coil type microphones, condensor microphones, and condensor pickups. Sales grew slowly but steadily during this period.

Magnetic Tape and Tape Recorders

At this time Ishikawa became aware of the commercial possibilities in Japan of magnetic tape recorders, and convinced the Sumiyoshi management to "plunge" by mobilizing a special research group to develop designs and manufacturing processes for magnetic tape and tape recorders. A task force of four physicists, five chemists, 20 electrical engineers, and three mechanical engineers was assembled to develop a commercially feasible means of producing the new products, neither of which was yet being manufactured in Japan. Since this group comprised about 80 percent of the company's engineering personnel at the time, the use of the task force idea in the hope of achieving success ahead of competition represented something of a

1. Zaibatsu—vast industrial empires which were under the control and management of a few family dynasties.

gamble on the part of management. Production of magnetic tape in commercial quantities and quality was begun in mid-1950, and of tape recorders later in the same year.

The breakthrough which Sumiyoshi engineers had accomplished was not immediately rewarded with success in the marketplace, however, for the application of tape recorder products was still virtually unknown in Japan. A vigorous campaign was undertaken to gain acceptance by radio broadcasting facilities and by educational institutions. These campaigns were followed by promotion of tape recorders designed especially for use in office work in business and government. Particularly successful was the Sumiyoshi effort to apply tape recorders to audio and audiovisual education. This was followed by a broadening of the market as the professional models of tape recorders were supplemented by lower cost models designed for home use.

As a result of its pioneering efforts, Sumiyoshi was virtually the only domestic producer of magnetic recording tape and of tape recorders for several years. Competition in both fields began, and soon there were three producers of recording tape and 20 producers of tape recorders in Japan. The four largest producers together supplied about 60 percent of the market for recorders. Further information is given in Exhibits 3 and 4.

Sumiyoshi research in the field of magnetic tape application continued and the product line grew to include a stereophonic tape recording system; a synchronous 35 mm. magnetic film recording device; a projector in which film strips or slides run synchronously with recorded materials; and later, such items as a transistorized, portable, battery-operated tape recorder. Developmental work included an audiovideo tape recorder (a substitute for film reproduction of both sight and sound) and a synchronized bookkeeping machine—tape recorder—tape printer which would enable complete bookkeeping records to be maintained on magnetic tape and to be printed selectively.

As a corollary to its work with magnetic tape recording systems, Sumiyoshi developed a patented process for making high quality ferrite cores for magnetic recording heads and other uses. Commercial production of these cores was begun in a factory at Nagoya which had been constructed for this purpose. This location was chosen because of its proximity to a local university in whose laboratories much of the research was undertaken, and because of the availability of low-cost electric power used in the ferrite reduction process.

Transistors and Transistor Radios

Ishikawa, Miyoshi, Imai, and others of the Sumiyoshi management began to give close attention to technical reports on semiconductors and to speculate among themselves on their implications. By that

Exhibit 3

Production of Tape Recorders in Japan
(Units—Sets)

Period	Industry	Company	Percent Total Production
Three Years Ago	20,997	13,231	63
Two Years Ago	49,399	28,706	58
One Year Ago	102,732	50,157	49
January	14,098	5,201	37
February	15,467	4,339	28
March	14,749	3,535	24
April	16,958	3,912	23

Source: Company Estimates

Exhibit 4

Production of Recording Tape in Japan
(Units—Reel)

Period	Industry	Company	Percent Total Production
Three Years Ago	224,943	131,236	58
Two Years Ago	334,394	202,524	61
One Year Ago	509,017	278,522	55
January	72,604	48,093	66
February	70,492	46,676	66
March	70,777	45,010	64
April	75,676	46,056	61

Source: Company Estimates

time, knowledge of the field had progressed to the point where extensive commercial application seemed to depend upon price. At this time transistors still cost $4 per unit in the United States and were used mainly in military applications. About the only commercial application thus far was in hearing aids. There was no Japanese production. Calling upon their experience with magnetic tape, the benefits of which were now beginning to flow into the company, President Ishikawa and his management resolved to initiate another crash program, the end result of which would be a commercially acceptable transistor radio using Sumiyoshi-built transistors. The program employed 40 engineers or about 60 percent of the company's engineering force. The first Sumiyoshi transistors were produced, and the company's first all transistor radio soon followed, only a few months after the first commercial transistor radio had appeared in the United States. In the meantime, the necessary licensing arrangements had been made with the Western Electric Company, and preparations for commercial production had begun. The first Sumiyoshi transistor radio, a five transistor set, went on the market, and Sumiyoshi enjoyed a virtual monopoly of the product in Japan for the next two years. Sales were limited by the cost, however, and no attempt was made to export the product to the United States market until later.

A team of 50 Sumiyoshi scientists and engineers continued to work on improving the quality and size characteristics of the transistor radio. These efforts were rewarded with the company's first all transistor, super heterodyne radio with built-in dynamic speaker. It employed six transistors, measured 1¼″ x 2¾″ x 4½″, and retailed for 13,800 yen or about $38.30. The new set caused a sensation not only in Japan but also in the world markets to which it was introduced later that year. The phenomenal growth of Sumiyoshi was almost wholly attributable to the company's ever increasing output of high quality transistor radios. The Sumiyoshi production of such radios went from 3,000 per month to over 50,000 per month, and the sales value from approximately 20 million yen to over 300 million yen (from about $55,000 per month to over $835,000 per month). At the same time the company's line of transistor radios was greatly broadened and included fifteen production models. Among these was a twelve transistor FM/AM model designed for export, the first commercial model of its kind. It was planned to introduce the new model to the United States market, and the management expected very substantial increases in export orders to result.

Basic to these advances was the company's production of transistors, for all Sumiyoshi radios used Sumiyoshi transistors exclusively. In addition to the production of transistors for its own products, Sumiyoshi produced transistors for sale. Industry and company production of transistors and of transistor radios is given in Exhibit 5. Export of transistor radios is given in Exhibit 6. United States production of transistors and transistor radios is given in Exhibit 7.

Other Products

As already noted, following its breakthrough on magnetic tape and tape recorders, Sumiyoshi Corporation sought to apply the tape recording principle to a wide variety of products, among them a substitute for film in audiovisual recording, a magnetic tape bookkeeping system, and synchronous audiovisual slide projection. After its success with transistors and transistor radios, a similar search for additional applications of these products was pursued. Early results of

Exhibit 5

Industry and Company Production
of Transistors and Transistor Radio Sets

Transistors

Period	Industry	Company	Percent of Total Production
Four Years Ago	N.A.	N.A.	N.A.
Three Years Ago	590,000	398,000	67.5
Two Years Ago	5,803,000	2,631,000	45.3
One Year Ago	26,736,000	4,586,000	17.2
January	4,252,000	681,000	16.0
February	5,229,000	822,000	15.7
March	5,486,000	731,000	13.3
April	5,849,000	638,000	10.9
Fiscal Year (estimate)	80,000,000		

Transistor Radio Sets			
Four Years Ago	7,086	7,086	100.0
Three Years Ago	38,025	38,025	100.0
Two Years Ago	632,000	162,479	25.7
One Year Ago	2,989,806	299,555	10.0
January	380,482	40,964	10.8
February	421,715	50,958	12.1
March	433,933	50,816	11.7
April	482,343	58,189	12.1
Fiscal Year (estimate)	8,000,000		

Notes: N.A.—Not available.
Sources: Electronic Machine Industry Association of Japan.

this effort were the transistorization of much of the company's line of tape recording machines, and the introduction of new portable tape recorders for professional and office use. The Sumiyoshi line of professional broadcasting equipment, especially microphones, also benefited. Farther afield were experimental applications to analogue and digital computers, data sorting machines, electronic memory units, data recording devices, portable television sets, luminescent lighting, and a heat-transfer device used for refrigeration or air-conditioning.

A moderate degree of commercial success had been achieved with the transistorized tape recording units for professional and office use, with microphones, and with the synchronous audiovisual slide projector. None of the other new products were judged to be ready for large-scale commercial exploitation.

Exhibit 6

Industry and Company Exports of
Transistors and Transistor Radios

Transistors
(Exports were negligible.)

Transistor Radio Sets

Period	Industry	Company	Percent of Total Production
Two Years Ago	362,517	66,173	18.3
One Year Ago	1,928,860	148,340	7.7
January	148,388	18,490	12.5
February	276,318	27,739	10.0
March	304,624	37,375	12.3
April	342,617	45,131	13.2

Remarks: Unit is "set" which incorporates more than two transistors.
Source: 1. Electronic Machine Industry Association of Japan.
2. Ministry of International Trade and Industry.

Exhibit 7

United States Production and Imports of
Transistors and Transistor Radios

Period	Transistors		Transistor Radios	
	Production	Imports from Japan	Production	Imports from Japan
Two Years Ago			1,740,000	102,240
One Year Ago	47,050,000	10,000	2,430,000	1,226,318
Present (estimated)	70,000,000	3,220,000	5,000,000	1,800,000

Source: Reports and estimates of the Elecronic Machine Industry Association of Japan and of the Ministry of International Trade and Industry.

Total sales of "other products"—products other than magnetic tape and tape recorders, transistors, and transistor radios—were estimated at 81 million yen ($225,000).

MANUFACTURING FACILITIES AND PROCESSES

The company's Osaka plants and offices were located on 2,500 tsubo of land (one tsubo equals six square feet) of which 260 tsubo were occupied by a two-story office building, 320 tsubo by Plant No. 1, and 350 tsubo by Plant No. 2. Storage buildings, garages, and dormitories occupied an additional 800 tsubo of land. The plants were of eight-story reinforced concrete construction and were designed for light manufacturing. Plant No. 1 had been completed at a cost of 50 million yen ($139,000) and Plant No. 2 three years later, at a cost of 215 million yen ($579,000). Adjacent to the plants were company dormitories housing some 300 young people who were employed in the production of semiconductors and in various assembly operations. Because of the company's rapid growth, the provision of adequate space for manufacturing, engineering, and research had been a continuing problem. The company had two construction projects under way—a 350 million yen, eight-story addition to Plant No. 1 and a 550 million yen eight-story addition to Plant No. 2. The first would add 3,820 tsubo of floor area, and the second 5,000 tsubo. As indicated by the figures, building costs in Osaka (and in Japan generally) had risen drastically over the preceding five years and were expected to continue to rise. Land costs had also risen dramatically.

In addition to the Osaka facilities, the company produced ferrite recording heads and magnetic tape at its 700 tsubo, 100 million yen ($278,000) factory at Nagoya. As noted earlier, this location had been chosen because of its proximity to a local university, with whose research laboratories Sumiyoshi had had a close working arrangement. About 200 persons were employed at the Nagoya location.

The majority of the production operations conducted by Sumiyoshi consisted of simple manual assembly work. Metal and plastic components, vacuum tubes, condensers, resistors, and so forth were purchased in finished form. These were redistributed (or delivered directly) to subcontractors for the preparation of subassemblies for radios and tape recorders. These subassemblies were then tested and incorporated into the final products by Sumiyoshi. A major exception to this pattern was the production of semiconductors which were manufactured from basic materials within Sumiyoshi itself. Approximately 78 percent of manufactured cost was for purchased parts and materials, 12 percent for wages, and 10 percent for other expenses and overhead costs. All manufacturing operations except those involving the production of semiconductors were under the direction of Hosoi, who was also in charge of employee relations and who had been in charge of factory supervision since the founding of the company. The manufacture of semiconductors was under the direction of K. Imai, as was research in the application of semiconductors and of magnetic tape recording systems.

In commenting upon the company's extensive use of subcontractors, Hosoi estimated that the organizations presently supplying Sumiyoshi had in their employ about 2,000 persons who were wholly engaged in the manufacture of Sumiyoshi components and subassemblies. The number of persons so engaged was approximately twice the size of Sumiyoshi's own factory force employed in transistor radio and tape recorder production. Hosoi thought the high cost of land acquisition in Osaka plus the relatively high wages which Sumiyoshi paid its factory employees made it likely that the present scale of subcontracting would continue; i.e., if production were to be expanded 100 percent, the use of subcontractors would expand 100 percent. At the present level of production, however, Hosoi thought it unlikely that the proportion of work allocated to subcontractors would be expanded. The operations which Sumiyoshi now performed in its own plants were those which were considered essential to control over the quality of the finished product.

In the long run, Hosoi desired to increase the proportion of work performed within the Sumiyoshi organization in order to achieve still better control over quality. At the present time, he observed, the "X" condensers were being made by three different small suppliers and the characteristics of the product of each supplier were sufficiently different to create performance variations in the final product. Yet each supplier was producing an acceptable product according to the Sumiyoshi specifications and acceptance tests, and not one of the suppliers was large enough to produce all of Sumiyoshi's requirements of condenser "X." This was an example, he said, of the additional type of production which the company should undertake in its own plants.

About 80 percent of the subcontractors were located within 10 kilometers (one kilometer equals .62 miles) of the Sumiyoshi plants in Osaka; the other 20 percent were all within 40 kilometers. Delivery schedules were carefully coordinated so as to permit uninterrupted production at Sumiyoshi with very low inventories of subassemblies and components. Procurement, inventory control, and production control were all consolidated in one section, where visual records of Sumiyoshi schedules, subcontractors' schedules, and inventory levels were maintained.

The company's production schedules were "frozen" three months in advance of final assembly, i.e., on April 1 orders were released for components for radios scheduled for assembly on July 1. These releases constituted authorization for vendor procurement and for subcontracting as well as for drawing materials, allocating personnel, and performing work within the Sumiyoshi organization.

Most of the subcontractors were small—the average employment was only 50—and their management had very limited technical and administrative competence. Sumiyoshi had already assigned several industrial engineers to assist these suppliers with engineering design, manufacturing processes, and quality control. Financial assistance was also provided where necessary. Hosoi thought that, in the future, even greater technical and administrative assistance would be required. In addition to such temporary measures, Sumiyoshi experts might even be "transferred" to these suppliers on a permanent basis, i.e., they might become permanent employees of the suppliers rather than of Sumiyoshi.

EMPLOYEE RELATIONS

The usual personnel functions of hiring, training, promotion, and transfer; wage and salary administration; health and safety activities; relations with the union; employee recreation and other welfare programs were grouped in the Employee Relations Department. Hosoi, vice-president for manufacturing, was also in charge of this department. Members of the Sumiyoshi top management, and particularly Ishikawa, Miyoshi, and Hosoi, were much concerned about the future of the company's relations with the employees and their union, even though they considered the present state of employee-management affairs to be quite good.

The present labor union at Sumiyoshi had been organized to replace an informal organization which had been representing employee interests up to that time. The formal organization of a union had been led by a group of Sumiyoshi engineers of comparatively long service with the company. This group had discussed its organization plans with the management and had indicated that the basis for their action was a desire to "rationalize" employee-management relations and to affiliate with a national union. Subsequent to its organization, the Sumiyoshi union had affiliated with the National Union of Electrical Workers. The Sumiyoshi management had not opposed the organization drive, and had granted the new union a union shop agreement; i.e., all employees of the company, excepting section chiefs and above, temporary or probationary employees, and employees in sensitive positions such as special members of the accounting and personnel departments and secretaries to executives, were obliged to belong to the union as a condition of employment. Union dues were deducted from wages and salaries by the company and were paid directly to the union. The first president of the Sumiyoshi union and the two subsequent presidents had been graduate engineers. The management felt that the company had never experienced a major dispute with the union representatives, and no strikes or work stoppages had ever occurred.

Ishikawa, Miyoshi, and Hosoi were particularly concerned about three aspects of employee-management relations. The first was the increased difficulty of communication which resulted from the sheer size of the organization. Only a few years earlier, the employees had numbered less than 500; now there were over 2,000. The thought of dealing with another increase of similar magnitude within another three years was not very appealing. To maintain effective communication with even the present size of organization was difficult and time-consuming. Some measure of the importance which they attached to intracompany communication is given by Exhibit 11 which shows the types of regularly scheduled meetings which they or other members of top management attended.

A second problem was the rather flat distribution of ages within the ranks of the company's nearly 1,000 high school and college graduates (Exhibits 8, 9, and 10). Most of this group would expect that the passage of time would bring increased responsibilities with corresponding perquisites of status and income. The college graduates, in particular, would expect to rise from clerk, draftsman, or research assistant to assistant section chief, section chief, assistant department head, department head, and so forth. In older companies such promotion is facilitated by the existence of a fairly wide age distribution within the ranks. The retirement of a department head, for example, might result in four or five promotions along the management ladder. In Sumiyoshi, the average age of the seven top operating executives was only 49 years and the oldest executive was but 59. Moreover, the average age of the employees in office positions was 34 years, and that of the employees in the plants was only 24 years (see Exhibit 10). Opportunities for promotion created by retirement were almost nonexistent at Sumiyoshi, either now or during the next five to ten years. Thus far, the provision of adequate promotional opportunities had not really been a problem at Sumiyoshi because of its rapid and continuous growth. The future might well be a different matter, however, and several members of top management were already aware of some concern among their subordinates in this regard.

A third factor of concern to the president (and the top management generally) pertained to the specialized scientific or engineering personnel who had been brought into the company from time to time to help solve some particularly difficult problems. These people had made key contributions to such things as magnetic tape production, ferrite development, transistor development, and so forth. In many instances they had been induced to leave companies or universities in which they had permanent status. Since their employment, the company's needs had shifted to other areas of research and development, and some of these specialists had either been unable to make, or were uninterested in making, a transition to the new fields of inquiry. The problem of how to motivate these people and how to use them effectively was a vexing one. Yet it was felt that they could not simply be dismissed because their usefulness, in light of the company's new interests, had diminished.

FINANCIAL MANAGEMENT

Sumiyoshi Corporation's rapid growth had required constant attention to financial planning. Earnings, although excellent, were not

Exhibit 8

Personnel Distribution by Amount of Education

Education	Total Percent Three Years Ago	Total Percent Two Years Ago	Total Percent One Year Ago	Total Percent Present
University or College Graduate	83	181	292	364
	(14.7)	(16.2)	(21.0)	(17.2)
High School Graduate	212	339	450	601
	(37.6)	(30.3)	(32.4)	(28.3)
Other Group	269	597	648	1,158
	(47.7)	(53.5)	(46.6)	(54.5)
Total	564	1,117	1,390	2,123

Exhibit 9

Distribution of College and University Graduates
by Major Course

Major Course	Three Years Ago	Two Years Ago	One Year Ago	Present Year
Electricity & Electronics	42	76	109	131
Physics, Chemistry, Metallurgy, & Mechanics	42	83	92	105
Graduates of Other Courses	26	51	97	104
Total	110	210	298	340

sufficient to provide for the expanded working capital requirements or for the necessary additions to plant and facilities.

As already indicated, both J. Momose, moderator of the board of directors, and H. Umeda, director and chief of the Accounting Depart-

Exhibit 10

Personnel Distribution at Osaka

Classification	Office			Plant			Total
	Male	Female	Total	Male	Female	Total	
No. of Employees	157	124	281	612	665	1,277	1,558
Average Pay *	34,035	9,792	23,337	13,490	7,038	10,130	12,512
Average Age	34	25	30	24	18	21	23
Average Duration of Service (Years)	3.9	2.1	3.1	2.3	1.5	1.9	2.1

* Monthly.

ment, had had many years of banking experience. Their understanding of financial management and their wide contacts in financial circles proved to be particularly helpful. The company followed the usual Japanese practice of extending short-term credit to its customers and obtaining short-term credit from its suppliers. In addition, short-term bank loans were used regularly (see Exhibit 14). Rates of interest on short-term loans averaged 7 percent, while rates on long-term loans ranged from 9 to 12 percent. Long-term funds were obtained within the general rule that at least one half the funds should be provided by self-financing (retained earnings and new stock offerings) and the remainder by borrowing the required funds from various financial institutions.

To facilitate financial planning and operating control, a comprehensive budget was prepared annually. The budget was subdivided into semiannual and monthly periods and according to departments and divisions. All department managers and division heads participated in both the budget preparation and the periodic review of operating results for their respective units.

The board of directors reviewed budget proposals and acted as the final approving body. The board received monthly reports of operating results which were compared with the budget and with other measures such as return on sales and return on invested capital.

Profit and loss statements and balance sheets for the fiscal periods are given in Exhibits 12, 13, and 14. It should be noted that public accounting was not well developed in Japan, and a good deal of discretion regarding such matters as depreciation rates and the classification of expenses rested with the officers of a company. Although no taxes are shown as having been levied on profit, the Japanese government did in fact levy a tax of 40 percent on corporate profits. The Sumiyoshi management, in common with the management of other

Exhibit 11

Regular Meeting and Their Attendees

Name of Meeting	Frequency	Moderator, Auditor (2)	President, Managing Director (2)	3 Executive Directors (V.P.s) (3)	Department Heads (8)	Vice-Heads & Section Chiefs (38)	Section Chief-Equivalent (11)	Chief Clerks & Their Equivalent (27)	Average Attendees Total (91)	NOTES (Purpose and Character of the Meetings)
Board meeting	Once a month	X	X	X	two (rotate)	—	—	—	11	Formal (legal requirement)
Meeting of dept. heads	About twice a month	—	X	X	X	X	—	—	13	Communication and coordination
4 man meeting (no official name)	About twice a month	X	X	—	—	—	—	—	4	Top management policy discussions and planning.
Luncheon meeting of dept. heads and above	Every day except Monday & Wednesday	—	X	X	X	X	—	—	11	Communication and discussion of special problems including "brainstorming."

Exhibit 11

(con)

Meeting of dept. heads and sect. chiefs	Monthly, about 2 hrs. from 4:45 p.m.	—	X	X	X	X Spec. Pers.	—	50	Monthly interchange of policies and other information.
Wednesday luncheon meeting	Every Wednesday	X	X	X	X	X	—	20	Similar to Monday meeting, but participation is optional: free personnel attend.
Luncheon meeting of vice heads & sect. chiefs	Every Monday	—	X	X	Spec. Pers. X	Spec. Pers.	—	20	The purpose of this meeting is to promote horizontal communication among heads and chiefs.
Discussion meeting of top-mgt. w middle mgt.	Monday 3–4 hrs. in the evening	—	X	Spec. Pers. X	Spec. Pers. X	X	X	25	This is held at a hotel outside of the company. Every chief clerk is invited to participate twice a year.

Note: X—Present.
Spec. Pers.—Specified personnel.

SUMIYOSHI CORPORATION

Japanese firms, preferred not to make public the amount of corporate tax actually paid. Accordingly, the sum paid as a corporate tax has been included with "cost of sales" (see Exhibit 12).

MARKETING

Domestic sales of Sumiyoshi's consumer products were made through the company's wholly owned subsidiary, Sumiyoshi Shoji, Ltd. This organization had its main office at the company's headquarters in Osaka, and had branch offices in Tokyo, Nagoya, Fukuoka, Sapporo, Hiroshima, and Sendai. Each branch office sold to many regional wholesalers which, in turn, provided a variety of electrical goods to shops in cities, towns, and villages.

The Sales Department was divided into three sections. Section One sold semiconductors and ferrite products directly to radio makers, communication equipment manufacturers, research laboratories, and others. Section Two sold professional models of tape recorders and miscellaneous communication equipment directly to broadcasting companies, motion picture producers, producers of phonograph records, and the Defense Agency. Section Three was responsible for export sales which consisted mainly of tape recorders and transistor radios. Approximately 99 percent of the company's exports were being achieved by overseas shipments of Sumiyoshi transistor radios and most of the remainder by exports of home-use type tape recorders.

Ishikawa also noted that some Japanese manufacturers of transistors and transistor radios had deliberately sought to export parts and components to the United States and to Western Europe rather than to export complete products. In this way, he said, they sought to avoid attracting attention to Japanese imports and to avoid restrictive tariffs. Still other Japanese companies exported complete products for distribution by a domestic corporation under its own trade name, "Kenmore" for example. Such was not the policy of Sumiyoshi, said Ishikawa, although it had had many attractive opportunities to export parts, components, and complete products for sale by others.

Instead, he said, the policy of Sumiyoshi was to create a favorable impression of Sumiyoshi as a producer of high quality electronic products for both consumer and industry, and as a leader in electronics applications. It was anticipated that Sumiyoshi would withdraw from a particular field after it had become popularized to the extent that competition had driven profit margins down to a low level. Ishikawa felt, therefore, that Sumiyoshi would not be adversely affected by tariff legislation. When a company is first in a field, he said, tariffs are not a critical problem.

As a result of these policies, Sumiyoshi had deferred entering the United States market with transistor radios until it was certain that

Exhibit 12

Sumiyoshi Corporation

Profit and Loss Statement (Unit: thousand yen)

(360 yen = $1)

Accounting Period	2	4	6	8	10	12	14	16
	Fourteen Years Ago	Thirteen Years Ago	Twelve Years Ago	Eleven Years Ago	Ten Years Ago	Nine Years Ago	Eight Years Ago	Seven Years Ago
Sales (net)	722	3,535	11,500	17,759	45,841	102,283	173,664	298,824
Cost of Sales	486	2,745	8,864	11,756	32,104	77,355	129,055	204,215
Profit on Sales	236	790	2,636	6,003	13,737	24,928	44,609	94,609
General Admin. & Selling Expense	247	744	2,299	5,208	9,028	16,455	28,445	43,019
Operating Profit	(11)	46	337	795	4,709	8,473	16,164	51,590
Nonoperating Revenue	13	10	13	101	99	856	570	846
Total Profit	2	56	350	896	4,808	9,329	16,734	52,436
Interest	—	—	—	—	38	288	4,287	8,184
Net Profit of This Period	2	56	350	896	4,770	9,041	12,447	44,252

Exhibit 12
(con)

Accounting Period	18	20	22	24	25	26	27
	Six Years Ago	Five Years Ago	Four Years Ago	Three Years Ago	Two Years Ago	One Year Ago	Present Year
Sales (net)	265,376	356,244	677,148	1,773,253	1,672,738	2,527,093	3,353,866
Cost of Sales	179,928	228,283	514,252	1,261,050	1,151,525	1,778,081	2,336,864
Profit on Sales	85,448	127,961	162,896	512,203	521,213	749,012	1,017,002
General Admin. & Selling Expense	57,136	71,423	92,359	267,039	268,476	370,728	544,665
Operating Profit	28,312	56,538	70,537	245,164	252,737	378,284	472,337
Nonoperating Revenue	9,932	2,428	5,170	10,065	8,155	13,442	16,928
Total Profit	38,244	58,966	75,707	255,229	260,892	391,726	489,265
Interest	8,860	13,329	23,154	47,896	62,588	75,247	98,931
Net Profit of This Period	29,384	45,637	52,553	207,333	198,304	316,479	390,334

Note: The customary accounting period is six months. The company's fiscal year runs from November through October.

DECISIONS INVOLVING PLANNING, STRATEGY, AND POLICY

Exhibit 13

Sumiyoshi Corporation
Balance Sheet (Unit: thousand yen)
(360 yen = $1)

Accounting Period	2	4	6	8	10	12	14	16
Closing Date	Fourteen Years Ago	Thirteen Years Ago	Twelve Years Ago	Eleven Years Ago	Ten Years Ago	Nine Years Ago	Eight Years Ago	Seven Years Ago
Current Assets	877	2,131	8,769	24,315	31,284	103,674	136,753	228,107
Quick Assets	303	590	4,460	6,305	15,506	38,939	72,861	137,090
Inventories	574	1,541	4,309	18,010	15,778	64,735	63,892	91,017
Fixed Assets	168	180	1,373	3,497	9,221	30,766	44,957	74,130
Tangible	168	180	1,373	3,497	9,071	23,596	37,271	71,290
Intangible	—	—	—	—	150	120	192	155
Investments	—	—	—	—	—	7,050	7,494	2,685
Deferred Accounts	—	—	—	—	—	—	—	—
TOTAL ASSETS	1,045	2,311	10,142	27,812	40,505	134,440	181,710	302,237
Current Liabilities	443	1,052	4,643	20,860	18,667	90,395	120,896	185,788
Fixed Liabilities	—	—	1,500	2,000	4,000	8,500	13,613	27,879
TOTAL LIABILITIES	443	1,052	6,143	22,860	22,667	98,895	134,509	213,667
Capital	600	1,200	3,600	3,600	10,000	20,000	20,000	20,000
Capital Surplus	—	—	—	—	—	—	1,800	—
Profit Surplus	2	59	399	1,352	7,838	15,545	25,401	68,570
(including net profit of this period)	(2)	(56)	(350)	(896)	(4,770)	(9,041)	(12,447)	(44,252)
TOTAL CAPITAL	602	1,259	3,999	4,952	17,838	35,545	47,201	88,570
TOTAL LIABILITIES & CAPITAL	1,045	2,311	10,142	27,812	40,505	134,440	181,710	302,237

Exhibit 13
(con)

Accounting Period	18	20	22	24	25	26	27
Closing Date	Six Years Ago	Five Years Ago	Four Years Ago	Three Years Ago	Two Years Ago	One Year Ago	Present Year
Current Assets	355,858	527,717	705,894	1,575,762	1,665,779	2,582,590	3,280,421
Quick Assets	149,631	292,264	413,622	1,021,134	995,551	1,805,171	2,485,909
Inventories	206,227	235,453	292,272	554,628	670,228	777,419	794,512
Fixed Assets	185,027	223,258	380,080	658,867	810,462	932,339	1,194,756
Tangible	166,811	187,488	343,392	615,269	758,218	872,655	1,029,191
Intangible	3,027	3,875	3,454	1,687	4,514	5,358	6,130
Investments	15,189	31,895	33,234	41,911	47,730	54,326	159,435
Deferred Accounts	9,336	7,627	3,316	8,079	27,340	26,725	30,126
TOTAL ASSETS	550,221	758,602	1,089,290	2,242,708	2,503,581	3,541,654	4,505,303
Current Liabilities	393,275	514,990	730,085	1,495,757	1,583,336	2,417,761	2,862,455
Fixed Liabilities	18,472	23,372	111,103	210,100	336,936	393,589	495,864
TOTAL LIABILITIES	411,747	538,362	841,188	1,705,857	1,920,272	2,811,350	3,358,319
Capital	50,000	100,000	100,000	200,000	200,000	200,000	400,000
Capital Surplus	3,385	3,394	2,798	2,732	2,625	2,625	2,471
Profit Surplus	85,089	116,846	145,304	334,119	380,684	527,679	744,513
(including net profit of this period)	(29,384)	(45,637)	(52,553)	(207,333)	(198,304)	(316,479)	(390,334)
TOTAL CAPITAL	138,474	220,240	248,102	536,851	583,309	730,304	1,146,984
TOTAL LIABILITIES & CAPITAL	550,221	758,602	1,089,290	2,242,708	2,503,581	3,541,654	4,505,303

DECISIONS INVOLVING PLANNING, STRATEGY, AND POLICY

Exhibit 14

Sumiyoshi Corporation Balance Sheet.
(millions of yen *)

ASSETS		
Cash or equivalent	1,136	
Notes receivable	688	
Accounts receivable	621	
Other quick assets	41	
Quick assets		2,486
Finished goods	183	
Goods in process	306	
Materials	306	
Inventories		795
Current assets		3,281
Land	118	
Building & Structures	384	
Machinery, equipment, tools	349	
Furniture	42	
Construction in process	136	
Tangible assets		1,029
Intangibles (patents, etc.)		6
Investments		159
Deferred accounts		30
TOTAL ASSETS		4,505

LIABILITIES		
Bills & notes payable (to suppliers)	1,679	
Short-term loans payable (to banks)	542	
Accounts payable	137	
Accrued expenses	270	
Advances received	29	
Reserve for price fluctuations	122	
Allowance for doubtful accounts	84	
Current liabilities		2,863
Term debt (to banks)		495
TOTAL LIABILITIES		3,358

NET WORTH		
Capital stock		400
Capital surplus		2
Profit surplus reserves		
Earned surplus reserve	128	
General reserve	149	
Dividend reserve	40	
Employees retirement reserve	38	
Profit this period	390	
		745
NET WORTH		1,147
LIABILITIES & NET WORTH		4,505

* 360 yen equals $1.00

the product would create a favorable impression toward the Sumiyoshi trademark. At that time, it was decided that an effort would be
made to establish a permanent distribution channel for Sumiyoshi
products and to establish the Sumiyoshi trademark through skillful
advertising and sales promotion. To achieve these objectives, the
board of directors decided to give exclusive distribution right in the
United States to a single, well-established firm. Sumiyoshi was well
satisfied with this decision, said Ishikawa, and similar exclusives had
been granted in Canada, Europe, and elsewhere.

PRODUCT ENGINEERING, RESEARCH, AND DEVELOPMENT

In recent fiscal periods approximately 10 percent of sales had
been devoted to product engineering, research, and development. Of
this sum about 35 percent was devoted to the improvement of products already in commercial production, 20 percent was allocated to
the application of magnetic tape to new uses, 30 percent to the application of transistors to new uses, and the remainder (15 percent)
to entirely new products or processing techniques. Classified in another way, 28.8 percent of the budget was applied to wages and
salaries; 61.3 percent to materials, equipment, and space; and 9.9
percent to administrative overhead. In an administrative sense, Hosoi
was responsible for research of recording heads and magnetic recording tape, while Imai was in charge of all other research activities.

In regard to the general objectives of Sumiyoshi's research and
development program, Ishikawa said that the policy was to emphasize research on new products rather than products already on the
Japanese market. On another occasion he said:

> One of the most important things that I learned during my last visit
> to the United States was the research policy of the Du Pont Com-
> pany. Du Pont has a clear-cut policy of always exploiting new prod-
> ucts. . . . For example, when nylon, which the company had devel-
> oped through its research, became popular, the company moved on
> into new fields, receiving patent fees for nylon manufacture. . . .
> Sumiyoshi had advanced by following this policy even before we
> were aware of its successful application by Du Pont. . . . From
> now on we plan to keep this policy and to exploit new technical
> fields. . . . We cannot be merely the keeper of a developed in-
> dustry; we wish to be the pioneer who forever advances. We do
> not wish to become involved in trivial competition, but plan to move
> on to new visions.

Patent Position

As a result of Sumiyoshi's research activities, the company had
been granted more than 250 patents and had more than 450 applications for additional patents pending. Even so, Sumiyoshi's expenses

for patent licenses and for royalties amounted to several times its income from such sources. Thus far the company had experienced no difficulty in obtaining access to any patented manufacturing process which it had desired to use or to any patented product which it wished to manufacture. Royalty fees and licensing fees had in no instance posed formidable bars to any action which the company had wished to take. Sumiyoshi's experience in these respects was probably typical of the radio and electronics industry in Japan and the United States. The patents had been so widely dispersed that the industry had long been forced to adopt extensive cross-licensing arrangements and moderate fees in order to progress.

Perhaps the most publicized recent product of Sumiyoshi's research laboratories was a new type of diode which had been invented by the chief of the semiconductor research section of Sumiyoshi Corporation. The principal benefit was expected to come from the lead which Sumiyoshi would have in the commercial application of the invention. If the lead were as substantial as that which had been enjoyed in respect to magnetic tape and transistor radios, it was expected that the benefits would be substantial.

Production Target for Transistor Radios

For the past several months, President Ishikawa said, the Sumiyoshi top management had been working on the problem of establishing new production goals for the company's line of transistor radios. Current output was coming very close to the previously established target, and production would level off shortly unless a new directive were issued. The tremendous scale of expansion achieved during the past year, from 15,000 per month to over 50,000 per month, had brought extensive changes in the composition of the organization, and all of the directors were concerned about the impact of another large-scale expansion. Said Ishikawa:

> A doubling of transistor radio output now means the addition of almost 1,000 people together with the necessary space and equipment; a doubling of output a year ago meant adding only about one fourth this amount of personnel, space, and equipment. The business is expanding at a geometric rate.

The Sumiyoshi image which most of the directors held was of an engineering research and development organization, and their thinking had been based upon the assumption that the company would progress and grow by moving from one new development or application to another. The tremendous success of the Sumiyoshi transistor radio had, however, involved the company in production of a type and a scale which had already altered the character of the organization by adding a large number of permanent employees whose skills were suitable only for mass production. Another such round of expansion would tie the company to mass production even more firmly. On the other hand, the sales outlook for transistor radios as reported to the executive committee indicated that two to three times the present Sumiyoshi output could be sold at present prices and profit margins. The sellers' market in high quality transistor radios was of uncertain duration, however, and aggressive price competition both at home and abroad might result within another year or two.

1. Appraise the Sumiyoshi management's basic product and market goals and strategies.
2. Recommend production (and marketing) goals for transistor radios for the next few fiscal periods.

Libby, McNeill
& Libby

One of the basic decisions confronting American management in the 1960s was whether or not to initiate or expand foreign operations and, if so, where and on what terms. The inviting growth potential of foreign markets had long been a spur to U. S. corporate interest, and, as a result, aggregate direct private investment abroad jumped from $12 billion in 1950 to almost $50 billion in 1965, and by 1975 reached $140 billion.[1] The average rate of investment grew by more than 6 percent, and in 1965 alone, it grew by 11 percent.[2]

The rapid rise of U. S. business investment overseas did not go unnoticed either at home or abroad. In Washington, the Johnson administration, concerned with the country's persistent balance of payments deficit, attempted to tighten the voluntary restraint program initiated in February, 1965; while abroad, such countries as France, England, Canada, and Mexico, fearful of economic subjugation, sought ways to prevent American domination of local industry.[3]

Despite opposition to additional investment abroad, the American business community's interest in overseas operations had, if anything, increased, not lessened. Evidence of this trend could be found, for example, in the food industry where, *Forbes* pointed out:

> Last year [1966], increasingly, U. S. food companies were telling their stockholders of new affiliations in Spain or Italy, of new

1. Such companies as Standard Oil of New Jersey, Mobil Oil, National Cash Register, Singer, Burroughs, and Colgate-Palmolive derived more than half their income or earnings from foreign sales; while Eastman Kodak, Chas. Pfizer, Caterpillar Tractor, International Harvester, Corn Products, and Minnesota Mining & Manufacturing made from 30 to 50 percent of their sales abroad (*Think*, publication of IBM, November–December, 1966, p. 32).
2. *The New York Times*, December 18, 1966.
3. At that time, President Johnson asked U. S. companies (except those operating in the developing areas of the world) to finance more of their overseas investment by borrowing abroad and by using the earnings of their foreign operations. The business community had argued that restricting private investment abroad jeopardized the competitive position and earning power of existing foreign operations and in the long run sharply cut the inflow of income from these operations which exceeded the outflow of capital from the United States.

products introduced to Britain or West Germany, of new acquisitions in France or Belgium or Holland. When they weren't crossing the ocean, they were crossing the borders to acquire or affiliate in Canada or Mexico. The impetus behind the exodus was profit, of course, and the opportunity for growth.

LIBBY, McNEILL & LIBBY

Toward the end of 1965, Robert Gibson, president of Libby, McNeill & Libby (one of the nation's largest and most diversified food processors), announced that his company was looking very deeply into establishing a canning operation in Mexico.[5]

Libby, a multinational corporation, engaged in the preparation, canning, freezing, packaging, and marketing of canned and frozen foods, had 27 food processing plants in the United States, two in Canada, and one each in Puerto Rico, England, West Germany, Spain, and France. Additionally, the company operated three can-making plants in the United States, two in Canada, and one each in West Germany and Puerto Rico.[6] Libby packaged and sold approximately 68 percent of its products in the United States and derived nearly 74 percent of its sales from canned goods, 20 percent from frozen foods, and 6 percent from other items.[7]

While the company purchased substantially all of its requirements of fruits and vegetables from independent growers, it controlled (leased or owned) 200,000 acres for fruit and vegetable growth in Hawaii, California, Delaware, Florida, Minnesota, and Wisconsin.

In 1963, Libby announced it was 40 percent foreign owned, with Switzerland's Nestle Alimentana holding a 20 percent interest; Fasco (a holding company in Italy's Michele Sindona industrial complex), 10 percent; and Paribas Corporation (a wholly owned subsidiary of the Banque de Paris et des Pays Bas), 10 percent. According to *Business Week*, Libby management "blessed" the Sindona-Paribas investment, but Nestle's increase in holdings from about 5 to 20 percent came as a surprise and was clearly upsetting. As a result of a tender offer, the Sindona and Paribas groups had purchased 900,000 shares; while Nestle, at the same time, had gone onto the open market. Libby's president denied that the tie-up with Sindona-Paribas was the price the company had to pay to gain entry

4. *Forbes*, January 1, 1967, p. 35.
5. *The Wall Street Journal*, November 2, 1965.
6. Libby began can manufacturing in 1960, and by 1966, made over 90 percent of its total can requirements. In addition, Libby, together with Anheuser-Busch, formed Lianco Container Corporation to manufacture cans for Anheuser-Busch.
7. *A. G. Becker Guide to Publicly Held Corporations in the Chicago Area* (1966 ed.), p. 148.

into the Common Market for its Libaron Project,[8] though he stated that the "prestige and importance" of all three interests "should be of assistance to us." [9]

Gibson,[10] who became president in January, 1962, upon the death of Charles S. Bridges, inherited a reorganization program which the company had initiated late in 1960 in an effort to improve its profits and competitive ability.[11] Taking a look at some of the problems which the new president faced, *Business Week* wrote:

> Competitors, customers, and management consultants characterize Libby as a company with a good name, a quality product, and a reputation for aimless wandering. A management consultant says the image that emerged from his study was of a "company that never forgot an idea, and never adopted a new one."

Gibson himself declared that timid and unimaginative marketing had harmed Libby most. "If Libby has done a poor job anywhere, it's in orienting itself to the needs of its customers. We've always had good products, but we've never gone out and sold them." As a production specialist, he said, "It was axiomatic for me to hate sales people. Instead, production should be geared to sales needs." [12]

Striving to become a "more fully customer-oriented" company, during the next few years Libby built new distribution centers, increased expenditures for advertising and marketing activities, intensified and accelerated its program for the development of new products and redesigned almost its entire line of labels. But, while Libby's sales reached an all-time high of $300,655,665 for fiscal 1965, net income dropped to $2,500,870 from the previous year's $7,078,702

8. Noting that "the increasing cost of U.S. production is speeding up the development of local food processing industries abroad," in 1960 Libby began a three-year study of agricultural and marketing conditions in France and Italy. In 1963, the company started construction of a processing plant in southern France. Known as the Libaron Project, this operation was looked upon as Libby's "key" to the Common Market.

9. After meeting with Nestle's managing director, Gibson said he was convinced that Libby was not being "taken in" by a private agreement among the three groups. See *Business Week*, August 10, 1963, and Libby, McNeill & Libby *Annual Report* for the year ended June 29, 1963. Each group had a representative on Libby's eleven-man board of directors.

10. Gibson, who had been with Libby for 22 years, was, at 43, the company's youngest president. Holding a bachelor's degree in food technology from the University of California and a master's degree in industrial management from Massachusetts Institute of Technology, he had been elected a vice-president in 1958, and a director and senior vice-president in 1961.

11. Due to the wide variety of canned and frozen foods it produces, Libby had no single direct competitor. California Packing Corporation, the world's largest canned fruit and vegetable packer (the company does not pack frozen foods), probably came closest to playing this role. Calpak passed Libby in sales in 1958 (*Business Week*, June 30, 1962). For a ten-year comparison of the sales and earnings of the two companies. See Exhibit 1.

12. *Business Week*, June 30, 1962, p. 86.

on sales of $289,685,751. Although noting that earnings were severely penalized by many unfavorable supply and pricing situations, the company said that the most significant factor in the decline was a reversal of profits in Libby's overseas operations.

> Earnings from overseas operations for the year amounted to a loss of $581,000 compared to a gain last year of $932,000 or a drop in earnings of $1,513,000. About one half of this decline in earnings was due to a temporary situation in the United Kingdom and the other half was due to losses sustained in initial operations, principally in France and Spain.[13]

By the end of fiscal 1966, sales reached $317,556,080, and net income was $4,008,068.

In an effort to improve performance, Libby's management structure underwent two major reorganizations within a six-year period. In 1961, the company divided its operations into seven units—an eastern division, western division, frozen foods division, international division, Canadian company, canned meats division, and can manufacturing division. Except for the latter two units (which did not engage in marketing), each division was complete in itself—performing buying, producing, selling, marketing, warehousing, invoicing, and accounting activities. And each was headed by an officer who was charged with responsibility for profits.

Then, in July, 1966, following a study by Booz, Allen & Hamilton, Libby again revamped its management structure and established the following units: *international*, with jurisdiction over all business outside of the United States; *marketing*, with jurisdiction over domestic product management, advertising, and related marketing services; *sales*, with jurisdiction over the domestic selling organization; *operations*, with jurisdiction over all domestic manufacturing, including farming and nonfood manufacturing business; *distribution*, with jurisdiction over all phases of domestic distribution and customer service; and *product procurement*, with responsibility for integrating all outside sources of supply with world market requirements.[14]

In the highly competitive food processing industry, which was always beset by weather problems, a situation of major concern arose in 1965—a shortage of farm labor due to the termination of the federal government's bracero program. It was the government's cutoff of an abundant source of low-cost farm labor which had prompted Gibson to declare that Libby was seriously considering setting up a canning operation in Mexico.

13. Libby, McNeill & Libby *Annual Report* for the year ended July 3, 1965, p. 3. In 1964, Libby set up a Spanish subsidiary, Libby Espana, S. A., which is now both a producing and marketing entity.
14. Libby, McNeill & Libby *Annual Report* for the year ended July 2, 1966, p .7.

TERMINATION OF BRACERO PROGRAM

The bracero program, Labor Secretary Wirtz warned in 1965, was dead. He gave notice to farmers and food processors that they had better learn to live with the ban on the importation of seasonal agricultural workers from Mexico.[15] "I consider getting rid of the bracero program one of the most important social and economic developments we have seen," he bluntly stated.

This was hardly the view of U. S. farmers who had become increasingly dependent on low-cost and highly productive Mexican labor to perform the back-breaking work necessary to the hand harvesting of such crops as tomatoes, cucumbers, strawberries, lettuce, asparagus, and melons. The bracero ban, growers and food processors warned, would only lead to higher costs, an inadequate labor supply, lower work productivity, rotting fruits and vegetables, reduced plantings, and higher prices. And, they predicted, many farming and canning operations would move abroad to avoid the federal government's experiment of holding harvest-time work for unemployed Americans.

Officially, the bracero program had come to an end with the expiration, on December 31, 1964, of Public Law 78. Enacted in 1951 as a means of controlling the movement of Mexican farm workers into the United States, the statute had permitted braceros to enter this country for a period of six to twelve weeks. Once the harvest was in, the workers returned home with their earnings. Congress annually extended the law, but in 1964, for several reasons, allowed it to lapse.

California, the largest agricultural state in the union and the greatest user of Mexican farm labor, had long been a battleground for the controversial bracero system.[16] In their twenty-year struggle to organize domestic farm workers, unions had strongly opposed the importation of Mexican labor and had called for a halt to the program. Then, in 1964, with California's unemployed totaling 6 percent of the state's work force, Congress allowed the bracero law to lapse—the rationale being that the cutoff of foreign labor would help to cut down unemployment.

With the bracero program at an end, federal and state officials set about recruiting harvesters from among California's jobless. But the atmosphere in the state was bitter, and charges and countercharges flew. Growers contended that the workers sent by the state employment office were not only unfit for but were also unwilling to perform the strenuous work required. The unemployed from the cities,

15. In 1964, about 200,000 foreign farm workers entered the U. S. Of this number, approximately 180,000 were from Mexico.

16. In 1964, California contracted for about half of the 180,000 braceros who entered the country. During the peak month of September, 70,000 braceros were employed in the state. *Business Week* (January 16, 1965), p. 32.

they said, thoroughly disliked "stoop labor" (even at the new California minimum wage of $1.40 an hour), and quickly deserted after a day, a week, or two weeks of harvesting.[17] The Labor Department retorted the growers were simply trying to buck the government's program in an effort to bring back the bracero system. After taking a look at the labor camps on California farms, Wirtz described some of the camps he had inspected as "filthy, shameful blots on America," and he warned growers they must compete in the open labor market, along with other industries, by offering decent wages and working conditions; in other words, the Secretary maintained, if the work could not be made more attractive, then the inducements to do the work had to be increased.[18]

Midway through 1965, Wirtz told a Senate subcommittee that terminating the bracero program had not, thus far, resulted in overall labor shortages, crop losses, or higher food prices. According to the Secretary, any unusual price increases were attributable to special weather conditions; only a few isolated instances of crop losses could be identified with labor shortages; and 50,000 to 100,000 more farm jobs would be filled during the year by domestic workers. In addition, at the end of January, 1966, the Department of Labor issued "Year of Transition," a report which stated that, while the use of foreign farm labor had dropped 83 percent in 1965, the market price of fruits and vegetables had declined 3 percent, despite the fact that the price for all foods rose by 3.5 percent. Moreover, some 100,000 Americans who would have been unemployed found jobs in the fields for at least part of the year.[19]

This bright picture of the success of the government's program in recruiting domestic workers differed markedly from the one which growers and food processors saw. Pleading extreme hardship because of an inadequate supply of help, farmers throughout the year appealed to Secretary Wirtz to ease his ban on bracero labor. For tomato growers, the situation was particularly acute.[20] The California Tomato Growers Association asserted that nearly 30 million pounds of ripe tomatoes rotted in fields, and in early August, 1965, Wirtz authorized the importation of 8,000 braceros to help with the crop. The California Department of Labor had previously recommended

17. The federal minimum wage law did not cover farm workers. In 1964, in California, the going rate for domestic farm labor was a dollar an hour. The Labor Department established the $1.40 minimum for those California growers who wanted to remain eligible for foreign help. (The Secretary of Labor also would have to certify an actual need for foreign workers before they could be hired.) In Florida, the Department set the level at $1.15.

18. *Business Week* (April 17, 1965), p. 46.

19. *Newsweek* (February 7, 1966), p. 61.

20. California grew about 60 percent of the nation's canning tomatoes.

that 16,500 braceros be allowed entry, and the tomato growers had asked for 23,000. California's Governor E. G. Brown hurriedly put in a request for additional workers, and by the end of the month, Wirtz's total authorization of braceros had jumped to 18,400.

Underscoring the food packers' antipathy to the federal government's program, Libby's 1965 *Annual Report* declared:

> The harvesting of crops, important to the food processing industry, has been placed in jeopardy following the expiration . . . of Public Law 78. . . .
>
> It has become increasingly evident that the U.S. Department of Labor's program to substitute domestic labor in an effort to reduce unemployment is wholly unworkable. Because of heavy losses due to unharvested crops, consumers will be confronted with rising prices on canned, frozen, and fresh produce. We expect to be able to minimize the adverse effects on the company's production through our geographical diversification and more extensive use of mechanical harvesting equipment.[21]

MECHANICAL HARVESTING

Faced with Wirtz's staunch opposition to any revival of the bracero system, in 1965 growers and food processors began turning more and more to mechanical harvesting as the long-range answer to labor difficulties. While experimental mechanical harvesters had been developed for asparagus, celery, lettuce, and cucumbers, and agricultural engineers perfected harvesters to pick citrus fruits, the initial breakthrough was the development of the tomato harvester.

Back in the forties, the University of California at Davis had grappled with the related problems of designing an effective tomato harvesting machine and of breeding a strain of tomatoes with a uniform ripening time and a sufficiently tough skin so that mechanical pickers could be used. Research efforts were eventually successful; and by 1965, 260 machines harvested more than 20 percent of California's tomato crop (in 1964, only three percent of the crop was mechanically harvested). The machine, using a 20-man crew to sort the picked tomatoes, did the work of 70 to 80 workers. Moreover, in 1965, the yield per acre of tomatoes in California averaged 21 tons, compared with 17 tons in previous years. New plant strains, plus the fact that mechanical harvesting permitted closer planting, contributed to this increase. Although the machines cost about $22,000, *Business Week* reported that farmers were sold on the economics of mechanical harvesting.[22] According to one report, hand harvesting of tomatoes

21. Libby, McNeill & Libby *Annual Report* for the year ended July 3, 1965, pp. 7–8.
22. January 8, 1966, pp. 108–110.

in Yolo, California, cost $17 per ton while machine harvesting was under $10.[23]

And from their annual reports, it was evident that the large food processing companies looked to the increased use of mechanical equipment as the eventual solution to the farm labor problem. In 1965, H. J. Heinz Company reported that it had machine picked 85 percent of its California tomato crop and in 1966 planned to machine harvest 100 percent of the crop. Campbell Soup Company told stockholders that it had mechanically harvested a "substantial portion" of its 1965 California tomato crop; and at the November, 1966, annual meeting, Campbell's president reported that the company was working hard to come up with a tomato which could be harvested mechanically in the East and Midwest in order to offset rising costs of farm labor. On the other hand, California Packing Corporation, while noting its use of mechanical equipment, stressed the fact that Calpak's program in recent years of employing domestic workers on its own farms meant that the company was "affected very little" by the lapse of the bracero law—although independent farmers under contract to Calpak were experiencing difficulty.

But in its 1966 *Annual Report*, Calpak stated:

Decreased supplies and higher cost, largely due to farm labor shortages accentuated by termination of the bracero program, have caused prices of both canned fruits and canned vegetables to increase over the past year.[24]

And the economics of mechanical harvesting still troubled Libby. At the annual meeting on October 19, 1966, Gibson told stockholders that the federal government's curtailment of the use of braceros had raised Libby's costs. According to Libby's president, American "unemployables simply won't do stoop labor and produce enough," and mechanization initially raises production costs.

Tomato growing, where the industry 'has gone into mechanization too rapidly,' costs more than it did before, he said. For one thing, with mechanization all the crop must ripen at once, he explained, because mechanical picking involves cutting plants at one time while hand laborers can continue picking over a longer period.

. . . Mr. Gibson said suspension of the 7 percent tax credit for machinery and equipment purchases will 'have just the opposite

---

23. *Tomato Harvesting Costs by Machine—1966—Yolo County,* Agricultural Extension Service, Woodland, California.

24. In 1966, about 7,000 Mexican farm workers were employed in California, compared with 90,000 in 1964. According to the state's deputy agriculture director, asparagus was the only crop to experience serious losses in 1966 because of a labor shortage—20 percent of the asparagus crop was lost. *San Francisco Chronicle,* December 27, 1966.

effect to what's intended,' because it will discourage acquisitions of new equipment that could help lower costs and prices.[25]

INVESTMENT IN MEXICO

Because of the high cost of production in the United States, Libby was interested in finding a more economical source of supply of tomatoes and pineapples for its eastern U. S. markets. If the company set up an operation in Mexico, it would be following H. J. Heinz and Calpak south, for both firms operated plants in Mexico for several years.[26] In 1960, Calpak organized Productos Del Monte (60 percent owned) to pack tomato and chili products, and by 1966, this company produced more than 50 items for sale in Mexico; additionally, in 1966, Calpak set up two snack-food operations in Mexico. As for Heinz, in 1965, it acquired 80 percent ownership of six Mexican food companies which it operated since 1963 under an interim agreement. Heinz's Mexican subsidiary was a major producer of frozen strawberries and pineapple for domestic sale and for export to the United States and Canada.[27] Mexico's proximity to the U. S., its variety of soils and climates, its expanding middle-class market, and its abundant supply of low-cost labor were strong attractions for American food processors to set up operations there.[28]

Before deciding to invest abroad, any U. S. firm had to take a long, hard look at the monetary, political, and social stability of the country involved. Mexico, which had a rapidly growing economy and a solid currency, and which had had no revolutionary change in government for several decades, offered a climate for investment not matched elsewhere in Latin America. A developing nation, Mexico had been shifting away from farming and mining to manufacturing, and had increased its gross national product by an annual average of six percent. Mexico's Secretary of the Treasury predicted the country "will be approaching the threshold of a fully industrialized state." [29] But, while the nation's wealth had been steadily increasing, it had also tended to concentrate in a few urban areas, and the Republic faced the long-range challenge of achieving a more equal opportunity for all its citizens to participate in the country's economic growth. (In 1962, only 21 percent of Mexico's families had incomes of more than $120 a month.) [30]

25. *The Wall Street Journal*, October 20, 1966.

26. In addition, Campbell Soup; Green Giant; Corn Products; General Foods; Gerber Products; and Anderson, Clayton operated in Mexico.

27. Food and food products accounted for 60 percent of Mexican exports to the United States.

28. *Business Week* (March 19, 1966), p. 104.

29. *The New York Times*, December 25, 1966.

30. Edmund K. Faltermayer, "We're Bullish on Mexico," *Fortune*, (September, 1965), p. 254.

There were two nominal opposition parties, but one-party rule was the order in Mexico. The dominant Institutional Revolutionary Party (the PRI) had elected every president since 1929; and in 1966, every senator and all but six of the 178 members of the Chamber of Deputies belonged to the PRI.[31] The country's political stability had been attributed mainly to the fact that the Institutional Revolutionary Party had tried to represent the Mexican people as a whole without catering to particular factions and interests.

Although Mexico had experienced a remarkable industrial upsurge, about half of its population lived on small and extremely primitive farms. There were in Mexico some farm operations as mechanized and efficient as any to be found in the United States, but "the vast bulk of the rural sector remains mired in deep poverty and antiquated methods of agriculture not removed from the wooden-plough days of 16th-century Spanish rule."[32] President Gustavo Diaz Ordaz, deeply concerned about the poverty of the rural population, promised to give priority to improving the lot of the farmer. The Mexican government had been making a determined effort to help the small farmer through an agricultural credit program which was designed not only to make loans but also to provide technical assistance; and the presence in Mexico of American food processing plants was lending an added impetus to agricultural progress.

Ample availability of cheap unskilled labor served as an initial attraction to potential foreign investors, but there were drawbacks to opening a subsidiary in Mexico. A proud and nationalistic people, especially sensitive to any appearance of domination by their northern neighbor, Mexicans had no wish to see their country overrun by American executives or American capital. In their dealings with the Mexican government, U. S. companies learned that it was expedient to have Mexican executives on their staff, and to share ownership with Mexican partners. Knowledgeable about local temperament, customs, and laws, Mexican employees and partners were better able to guide American executives around the intricacies of doing business in the Republic.

U. S. firms operating in Mexico long complained of bureaucratic red-tape, harassment, and discrimination, and accused the Mexican government of undermining their competitive ability by granting fiscal advantages, higher production quotas, and greater freedom to import raw materials to Mexican-controlled companies. To encourage the development of local industries, the government followed a program of import substitution and protectionism, and favored treatment was accorded local investors who built plants to manufacture goods

31. A Mexican president serves a six-year term and cannot be reelected.
32. *The New York Times*, January 23, 1967.

formerly imported. Mexico adhered to governmental supervision of pricing, with the Minister of Industry and Commerce controlling the price of 48 "basic" commodities—from milk to automobiles.

In 1938, Mexico expropriated the foreign-owned petroleum properties, but expropriation is now considered a minor business risk; it was "Mexicanization" which foreign-controlled companies faced. From time to time, the government put pressure on American companies to Mexicanize; that is, to sell at least a 51 percent interest to local investors. This policy had, in the past, been most aggressively applied to businesses involved in exploiting the country's natural resources. Mexico's Secretary of the Treasury pointed out that while government policy encouraged foreign investment to Mexicanize, this was not compulsory, and the same was true, he added, with regard to reinvestment of profits made in Mexico.[33]

Direct foreign investment in Mexico totaled an estimated $2 billion, with U. S. companies accounting for about 80 percent of this amount. But the strongly nationalistic attitude of President Diaz Ordaz's administration caused some second thoughts among American investors. As *The New York Times* put it, "the atmosphere for foreign private investment in Mexico is beginning to sour." [34] In 1965, American investment totaled $197.6 million, more than double the amount five years before,[35] but the Mexican government showed "little enthusiasm for the foreigner who might want to open a plant here on his own." [36] President Diaz Ordaz gave evidence of this attitude when, late in 1966, he listed the following order of preference for the foreign financing which his country needed for development. Mexico, he said, first preferred loans from governments or international agencies; its second choice was indirect investment through the purchase of local securities; and last on its list was direct foreign investment which was in "minority partnership with national capital." To keep the economy growing, the President called upon the private sector to invest $14.5 billion in new industries by 1970 (almost double the probable outlay of public capital during the same period). [37]

Just how far the government pushed its stepped-up drive for Mexicanization was problematical. As critics pointed out, Mexicanization diverted local private capital from creating new sources of production and employment. Furthermore, there were disturbing political implications. Mexicanization contributed to the emergence of a powerful "financial oligarchy," for there were relatively few Mexicans

33. *The New York Times*, December 25, 1966.
34. *The New York Times*, November 8, 1966.
35. *The New York Times*, December 25, 1966.
36. *The New York Times*, November 8, 1966.
37. *Ibid.*

LIBBY, McNEILL & LIBBY

who had the kind of resources needed to purchase control of American firms. What this development portended for the Institutional Revolutionary Party remained to be seen.[38]

Late in 1966, a New York banker was asked what advice he gave to industrial concerns which were thinking of opening subsidiaries in Mexico.

> I tell them all the economic indicators there are good. I tell them profit margins are satisfactory. Then I warn them to expect pressure to Mexicanize. Most of them go anyway.[39]

When Libby announced at the end of 1965 that it was studying the feasibility of setting up a canning operation in Mexico, the company had just finished an extremely disappointing year. Profits had taken a sharp drop, while costs of operation had risen steadily. One contributing factor to the company's increased costs had been the government's cutoff of bracero labor. It was natural, therefore, that in looking around for a more economical source of supply, Libby's attention focused on Mexico. That country's proximity to the United States, its political and economic stability, and its abundant supply of low-cost labor appeared to offer a climate favorable to foreign investment. At least a number of other American food processing concerns apparently deemed this to be the case, for they had recently initiated or expanded operations in Mexico.

Before reaching a decision as to whether or not it should invest in Mexico, Libby's management had to take into consideration a number of factors: What were its prime objectives in going into Mexico? What was the potential profitability of the proposed investment, including the payout criteria which should be adopted? What was the quality (plus quantity and dependability) of Mexican produce? What influence would federal policies regarding the balance of payments problem have on the company's decision? What impact would the Mexican government's attitude concerning direct foreign investment have on the company's decision? And finally, how would the company go about obtaining the various types of information it needed to make a decision?

38. *Ibid.*
39. *Business Week* (November 26, 1966), p. 118.

Exhibit 1

Ten-Year Review (Stated in thousands of dollars) *

	Libby, McNeill & Libby			California Packing Corporation	
Fiscal Years Ended	Sales	Net Income	Fiscal Years Ended	Sales	Net Income
July 2, 1966	$317,556	$4,008	February 28, 1966	$478,972	$23,458
July 3, 1965	300,656	2,501	February 28, 1965	449,019	19,974
June 27, 1964	289,686	6,079	February 29, 1964	409,813	18,006
June 29, 1963	276,324	2,524	February 28, 1963	385,756	15,913
June 30, 1962	268,456	3,006	February 28, 1962	379,809	17,226
July 1, 1961	252,964	2,608	February 28, 1961	358,165	15,684
July 2, 1960	277,183	4,204	February 29, 1960	352,535	14,530
June 27, 1959	278,496	5,807	February 28, 1959	346,285	11,785
June 28, 1958	278,902	2,701	February 28, 1958	325,452	8,428
June 29, 1957	286,307	3,676	February 28, 1957	287,632	12,602

* Figures taken from Libby, McNeill & Libby's *Annual Report* for the year ended July 2, 1966, and California Packing Corporation's *Annual Report* for the year ended February 28, 1966.